JUSTICE ADMINISTRATION LEGAL SERIES

John C. Klotter, B.A., J.D.
Professor Emeritus and Former Dean
School of Justice Administration
University of Louisville

CRIMINAL LAW

Third Edition

 anderson publishing co.
2035 reading road
cincinnati, ohio 45202
(513) 421-4142

CRIMINAL LAW Third Edition
JUSTICE ADMINISTRATION LEGAL SERIES

Copyright © 1990 by Anderson Publishing Co., Cincinnati, OH

ISBN 0-87084-525-X
Library of Congress Catalog Number 89-86001

Kelly Humble *Managing Editor*   *Project Editor*—Elisabeth Roszmann

PREFACE

This book has been prepared primarily for those who are performing, or preparing to perform, duties related to criminal justice activities; including personnel who are, or intend to be, police, probation and parole officers, corrections officers, prosecutors or judges. The material in the book emphasizes substantive criminal law rather than criminal procedure. While criminal procedure deals with the legal steps through which a criminal case passes, from the initial investigation of the crime to the determination of punishment, this book emphasizes the acts, the mental state and the attendant circumstances that are necessary ingredients to these crimes.

It is difficult to prepare a text in criminal law which will serve in all jurisdictions, as the laws in the various jurisdictions are not consistent. While most states do *not* follow the common law without modifications, reference must be made to that law for background purposes and definitions. Without a study of the common law relating to criminal law, it would be difficult to understand the provisions of the modern statutes and codes. Therefore, where the acts were crimes at common law, the common law elements are defined before examining existing statutes.

The Model Penal Code prepared by the American Law Institute, which was completed in 1962, played a very important part in the revision and codification of the substantive criminal laws of the United States. This Model Code was adopted at the 1962 Annual Meeting of the American Law Institute at Washington, D.C. on May 24, 1962. The three volumes containing Part II of the Model Code, with comments, were published in 1980. In 1985, an official publication of the complete text of the Model Penal Code was released.

The Penal Code has had a profound influence in arriving at some uniformity of the laws of the various states. Between 1962 and 1983, 34 states enacted new criminal codes. These 34 enactments were all influenced by positions taken in the Model Penal Code. The extent to which particular formulations or approaches of the model were adapted varies extensively from state to state. According to the Foreword in the volume entitled Model Penal Code, Complete Statutory Text, copyrighted in 1985 by the American Law Institute, these states have enacted legislation which was influenced, at least in part, by the provisions of the Model Code: Illinois, Minnesota, New Mexico, New York, Georgia, Kansas, Connecticut, Colorado, Oregon,

Delaware, Hawaii, New Hampshire, Pennsylvania, Utah, Montana, Ohio, Texas, Florida, Kentucky, North Dakota, Virginia, Arkansas, Maine, Washington, South Dakota, Indiana, Arizona, Iowa, Missouri, Nebraska, New Jersey, Alabama, Alaska and Wyoming. In addition to these 34 states, draft codes have been prepared in other jurisdictions and some of these are pending in the various legislative bodies.

As the Model Penal Code has had such an influence on state criminal codes, and is likely to have great influence in the future, some provisions of the Model Penal Code are stated and discussed. These are presented with the consent of representatives of the Institute. The copyright acknowledgement is as follows:

Despite the trend toward uniformity in the state criminal laws, there is still a great variance and it is necessary for students of the law to refer to the statutes of the states in which they intend to practice. To make the discussion more comprehensive, selected state statutes are included and discussed. Also, state and federal decisions are included as examples in the text and in the footnotes. However, no effort has been made to use the local law of any particular jurisdiction.

To make the discussion more valuable to criminal justice practitioners who will be enforcing federal laws, some United States Code provisions are included. Emphasis here is on those laws that are of most concern to criminal justice personnel.

Chapter 1, Part I of the book, deals with sources, distinctions and limitations in relation to criminal law and sets the stage for an understanding of the criminal law concepts. In Chapter 2, Part I, the principles of criminal liability, such as the criminal act requirements and the criminal state of mind are promulgated in general terms. In Chapters 3-12, the crimes most frequently encountered are defined and explained. In Chapter 13, some of the possible defenses that can be claimed by defendants charged with crime are enumerated and explored.

In Chapters 3-11, the various offenses are categorized according to social harm, primarily for purposes of organization and discussion. In these chapters, the format for designating, illustrating and explaining the various offenses is:

A. Traditional Definitions and Elements
B. Contemporary Statutes and Codes

1. Model Penal Code
2. Federal Codes
3. Other Statutes and Codes

In Part II of the book, leading decisions of the U.S. Supreme Court, lower federal courts, and state courts have been included to give the reader an understanding of the application of the specific laws. These cases not only interpret the statutes and define terms used in the statutes, but also provide the reader with an understanding of the process used by the courts in reaching decisions. The cases are included in Part II, rather than immediately following the related discussion, as many of them have broader application than the subject matter of any single chapter. The decisions should be studied in conjunction with the respective chapters.

When the book is used as a text, it is strongly recommended that the student be required to brief the cases as well as any additional cases which the instructor feels are of current importance. In addition, students should be required to study the laws of the state or states in which they will practice; especially if these are different from the Model Penal Code. As the criminal law is constantly changing, only by reading and studying the latest pronouncements of the courts and legislative bodies can one keep up to date.

John C. Klotter

TABLE OF CONTENTS

Chapter 12
Preparatory Activity Crimes

Section

Chapter 13
Capacity and Defenses

Section

PART II: JUDICIAL DECISIONS

APPENDICES

INDEX   707

TABLE OF CASES   717

PART I
TEXT

Chapter 1
SOURCES, DISTINCTIONS AND LIMITATIONS

The question "What behavior should be made criminal?" is, therefore, in part answered by rational analysis, common knowledge, empirical investigation, and an evaluation of the consequences of behavior in terms of some definition of the welfare of the state.

Michael and Adler, *Crime, Law and Society* 353 (1933).

§ 1.1 Introduction

While a study of substantive criminal law primarily focuses attention on the various common law and statutory crimes and their elements, this complex body of law cannot be understood without a preliminary discussion of the sources of the law, the distinctions made and the limitations placed upon those who make and enforce such laws. To attempt to understand criminal law without considering the theory and the history of the criminal law concepts as they developed in other countries, and in the United States, is to overlook an opportunity for a comprehensive understanding of that law and the purposes of the law.

In this first chapter the objectives of criminal law are stated and discussed along with alternatives that may be taken to protect society. To set the stage for a later discussion of the specific crimes and their elements, the factors which determine what behavior should be made criminal are reviewed with a view toward developing an understanding of the process followed by the courts and the legislatures in determining what acts should be controlled.

The legislative bodies are not without limitations in enacting and enforcing criminal laws. For example, ex post facto laws are prohibited by the U.S. Constitution. Also, the courts have laid down rules to be followed in the construction of criminal laws. These, too, are considered in this chapter.

As the substantive criminal law in this country developed over a period of many years and had its immediate origin in the laws of England, the common law crimes, as well as statutory crimes, are considered and discussed. Because substantive criminal law is only a part of the total legal process developed to determine rights and duties of individuals, a distinction is made between criminal law, tort law and contract law.

Finally, the responsibilities of the various actors in the criminal law process, such as the prosecutor, the judge and the defense attorney, are explained with emphasis on the "burden of proof" (the responsibility of the prosecution to prove the various elements of the crime).

§ 1.2 Criminal Law Theory

When one causes harm to the person or property of another, not only the victim is concerned, but so are society and the state. Although the harmed individual may take action, himself, to recover civil damages from the person who engaged in the wrongful behavior, there still may be sufficient reasons for imposing criminal sanctions.

Criminal law, then, is that branch or division of law which defines crimes, traits of their nature, and provides for their punishment.[1] In a criminal case, the sovereign is the plaintiff, and the purpose of the prosecution is to preserve the public peace, or redress an injury to the public-at-large.

A definition of "criminal law" would not be meaningful unless accompanied by a definition of "crime." Several attempts are made, in cases and dictionaries, to define the term "crime." Blackstone defines crime as "an act committed or omitted in violation of public law, either forbidding or commanding it."[2] In a broad sense, the word "crime" comprehends every violation of laws including treason, felonies, and misdemeanors.[3] In its narrow sense, it does not include petty offenses as were triable without a jury at common law.[4] Among the many other definitions are these: "A crime may be generally defined as the commission or omission of an act which the law forbids or commands under pain of punishment to be imposed by the state by a proceeding in its own name,"[5] and "a crime is a violation or a neglect of legal duty, of so much public importance that the law, either common or statute, provides punishment for it."[6] Common to these definitions is the fact that there is a violation of a duty established by law and for which a punishment is imposed.[7]

Substantive criminal law is that which declares what acts are crimes and prescribes the punishment for committing them, as distinguished from procedural law which regulates the steps by which one who commits a crime is to be punished.[8]

As the purpose of criminal law is to protect society so that members of that society can be reasonably secure in carrying out their constructive activities, only behavior which is detrimental to the welfare of society should be made criminal. And as criminal law is generally stated in terms of imposing punishment for conduct not socially desirable rather than of granting rewards for good conduct, the emphasis is more on the prevention of the undesirable than on the encouragement of the desirable. To state this differently, criminal law aims to achieve a standard of conduct which society regards as desirable, and to prevent individuals from doing what society considers to be undesirable.

---

[1] 22 C.J.S. *Criminal Law* § 1 (1952).

[2] 4 Blackstone, COMMENTARIES 15.

[3] Schick v. United States, 195 U.S. 65, 49 L.Ed. 99, 24 S. Ct. 826 (1904).

[4] Callan v. Wilson, 127 U.S. 540, 32 L.Ed. 223, 8 S. Ct. 1301 (1888).

[5] Marshall, LAW OF CRIMES § 201 (7th ed. 1967).

[6] Miller, CRIMINAL LAW 16 (1934).

[7] Perkins & Boyce, CRIMINAL LAW (3rd ed. 1982).

[8] 22 C.J.S. *Criminal Law* § 1 (1952).

Criminal law is one weapon which society uses to prevent conduct which harms, or threatens to harm, public interests. In protecting society and the public interests, the criminal law approach is a negative one. As there are more positive approaches, punishment for violation of criminal laws should be a last resort. For example, education as to the type of conduct that society considers good and bad, and education which emphasizes the need to have rules and regulations in any organized society, perhaps would limit the need for so many criminal laws. Also, the establishment of ethical and religious codes with emphasis on distinguishing between good and evil conduct would reduce the need for the enactment and enforcement of criminal laws.

Nevertheless, in modern times, as in Old Testament times, laws have been established with the threat of punishment to those who violate the laws.[9]

In a constitutional form of government, the objective of criminal law is not only to protect society but, in so doing, to protect the rights of the individuals of that society. As a result, there is a continuing attempt to reach the proper balance between these two objectives. If this balance is not maintained, either society will not be sufficiently protected, or the rights of the individual will be in jeopardy.

Specifically, the objectives of criminal law in a free society are to:

(a) make it possible for individuals to coexist in the society,
(b) define the wrongs that are considered necessary to protect the individuals,
(c) define the method of determining guilt or innocence, and
(d) designate the type of punishment or treatment following conviction for violation of the laws of the society.

§ 1.3 Determining Conduct to be Made Criminal

Recognizing that standards of conduct must be established in any society, how do the representatives of that society go about determining what acts (or failure to act) should be made criminal? Who should have the authority in establishing standards? Should all acts which may be considered immoral also be made illegal?

In an article in 1933, the authors Michael and Adler listed three factors which determine what behavior should be made criminal:[10]

---

[9] *Exodus* 20:23.

[10] Michael & Adler, THE LAW AND SOCIETY 353 (1933).

(1) the enforceability of the law,
(2) the effects of the law, and
(3) the existence of other means to protect society against the undesirable behavior.

If the law is unenforceable, then the act probably should not be prohibited. A lesson learned during the Prohibition Era was that enactment of unenforceable laws only breeds contempt for the law.

If enforcement of a law results in more disadvantages than advantages, it is questionable whether the behavior should be prohibited. Empirical investigation will assist in determining whether there are undesirable results. If another society has determined, by empirical investigation, that the positive effects of a law condemning certain conduct outweigh the disadvantages, then it would be more logical to prohibit that conduct in our society.

As society becomes more complex, additional laws (especially of a regulatory nature) are enacted. But, are there other means of protecting society than by making laws in an effort to further regulate conduct? Should, for example, consideration be given to more utilization of tort law as an alternative method of protecting society? In this country, the legislative bodies are given the primary responsibility for determining what conduct is to be made criminal. Too often, laws are enacted to meet some current demand, without giving adequate consideration to the possible negative consequences. Nevertheless, criminal justice personnel are charged with enforcing these laws, and must do so until they are repealed or declared to be unconstitutional.

§ 1.4 Common Law Crimes

Every civilization and every people have devised a system for protecting life and property of the citizens and in so doing mores, codes, laws, rules, and regulations have been established.[11] In some instances, criminal laws are interrelated with religious commandments and some rules are established by a monarch or a dictator. Some codes are the product of the legislative body, and in some instances, the court or the judicial branch of government has established the criminal laws. The system of laws in the United States is especially difficult in that the criminal law is based upon the law that was developed in England over many centuries.

---

[11]   *See generally,* Klotter, CRIMINAL EVIDENCE (4th ed. 1986), for a discussion of the methods followed in determining guilt or innocence in various cultures and civilizations.

Most of the present-day crimes in the various states have their origin in the so-called "common law" of England. This was the law as developed in the early English case decisions. The English courts, having decided that a certain act should be prohibited in that society, established this as a guide for future conduct. In addition to imposing these legal restrictions on human behavior, the courts prescribed penalties for violations of these principles and restrictions. The judges held themselves bound to decide the cases which came before them according to those principles and, as new combinations of circumstances arose, the principles were more and more fully developed and qualified. In England, as the population increased and more problems arose, legislation supplemented the court-made law. As a result, there came to be a body of authoritative material most of which was found not in the statutes, but as a result of judicial decisions. All of this body of English law, except that which was not applicable in the American colonies because of different circumstances and conditions, was brought to our shores by the colonists when they immigrated from England, and it became the starting point for our criminal law.[12]

In referring to "common law," some authorities hold that the common law, strictly speaking, is that court decision law of England as it existed at the time of the American colonies, and does not include changes by the courts of this country. Other authorities are convinced that the common law includes changes brought about by early court decisions in the United States.[13]

Regardless of which approach is more persuasive, the study of the common law is still important. In those states that have not abolished the common law, a few are still enforced. In some states, it is essential to consult the common law in order to define the various crimes which are enumerated in the statute or code, but are not defined. Even in those states which have abolished the common law crimes by statute, a study of the common law still serves a practical useful purpose.

§ 1.5 Statutory Crimes

While most of the present-day crimes in the various states have their origin in the common law of England, it can be safely said that most state law is now statutory law rather than common law. Statutes of many states specifically provide that conduct does not constitute an offense unless it is a crime or violation under the code or another statute of that state. Where such provisions have been adopted, the person's act or omission may go unpunished,

---

[12] Patterson v. Winn, 5 Pet. 233 (1831).

[13] State v. McElhinney, 80 Ohio App. 431, 100 N.E.2d 273 (Ohio Ct. App. 1950).

despite the basic seriousness or undesirability of such act or omission, unless the legislature has specifically decreed certain conduct or omissions to be criminal in nature. In the federal system there are no common law crimes, as the Federal Government has only that power that is delegated to it by way of the Constitution.

When the legislative body (federal or state) determines that certain conduct is undesirable and should be forbidden, a bill is prepared describing which conduct should be prohibited, and this is introduced in the House of Representatives or Senate, and voted upon by the elected members of the legislative body. If both houses of the legislature approve the bill, it then goes to the governor or president for consideration and approval. If the chief executive officer signs the legislation, then it becomes law to be enforced by those involved in the justice process. Even if the chief executive official refuses to sign (vetoes), the bill may become law if enough members of the legislative body approve it.

In drafting criminal laws, the legislature has much freedom, but certainly is not without limitations. There is a fundamental principle of criminal law that the legislation must not be vague and must not be so uncertain as to leave doubt as to its meaning. For example, the Court of Appeals of New York, in the case of *People v. Munoz*, held that:

> They (statutes) must afford some comprehensive guide, rule or information as to what must be done and what must be avoided, to the end that the ordinary member of society may know how to comply with its requirements.[14]

There, the court held that a statute which provided that:

> [i]t shall be unlawful for any person under the age of 21 years to carry on his person or have in his possession, in any public place, street, or park any knife or sharp-pointed or edged instrument which may be used for cutting or puncturing

was unconstitutional and void as too broad in scope and too vague. The court agreed that crimes may be created without intent as a factor other than intent to commit the prohibited act, but that there must be some reasonable relationship between the public safety, health, morals or welfare and the act prohibited.

But a federal statute which proscribes "mailing pistols, revolvers and other firearms capable of being concealed on the person" was not too

---

[14]　9 N.Y.2d 51, 172 N.E.2d 535 (1961).

vague.[15] Here the Supreme Court discussed the "void for vagueness" doctrine but concluded that this statute did not come in that category. The court agreed that the law intelligibly forbids a definite course of conduct: the mailing of concealable firearms. It continued by indicating that the drafting of a law did not have to be foolproof and ended with this paragraph:

> But the more important disagreement we have with this observation of the Court of Appeals is that it seriously misconceives the "void for vagueness" doctrine. The fact that Congress might, without difficulty, have chosen "clearer and more precise language" equally capable of achieving the end which it sought does not mean that the statute which it in fact drafted is unconstitutionally vague.[16]

In drafting criminal legislation the legislative body is also limited by constitutional restrictions. Obviously, if the legislation is contrary to the provisions of either the federal or state constitution, as interpreted by the respective courts, that legislation cannot stand. This is especially true if the First Amendment to the Federal Constitution is in question. If the legislation infringes upon those rights protected by the First Amendment, then the legislation is unconstitutional and unenforceable.[17]

A. State Legislation

The primary police power is in the state, i.e., the respective states have the authority to enact and enforce legislation to protect the health, welfare, morals and safety of the persons of the state. This "police power" is inherent in the government of the state and is a power which the state did not surrender by becoming a member of the Union.[18] The police power of the state, according to the Supreme Court, is one of the most essential powers and always one of the least limitable of the powers of government. Under this power, the states have passed laws defining crimes, regulating traffic and providing for criminal procedural rules.[19]

---

[15] United States v. Powell, 423 U.S. 87, 96 S. Ct. 316, 46 L.Ed.2d 228 (1975). *See* case in Part II.

[16] *See also*, United States v. Petrillo, 332 U.S. 1, 67 S. Ct. 1686, 91 L.Ed. 1877 (1946); Coates v. City of Cincinnati, 402 U.S. 611, 91 S. Ct. 1686, 29 L.Ed.2d 214 (1971).

[17] Miller v. California, 413 U.S. 15, 93 S. Ct. 2607, 37 L.Ed.2d 419 (1973).

[18] Jacobson v. Massachusetts, 197 U.S. 11, 25 S. Ct. 358, 49 L.Ed. 643 (1904).

[19] District of Columbia v. Brook, 214 U.S. 138, 29 S. Ct. 560, 53 L.Ed. 941 (1909).

When the First Congress met, the Tenth Amendment to the Constitution was added to make clear that the powers not delegated to the United States by the Constitution would remain in the states respectively and the people. The wording of that provision is:

> The powers not delegated to the United States by the Constitution, nor prohibited by it to the States, are reserved to the States respectively, or to the people.

But state legislative bodies are not without some limitations when enacting laws. First, the laws must comply with the state's own constitution. Secondly, no laws can be enacted which are in conflict with the Federal Constitution as interpreted by the Supreme Court. However, the state is still primarily responsible for enacting and enforcing criminal laws to protect the health, safety, welfare and morals of the people.

B. Federal Legislation

Strictly speaking, the Federal Government has no inherent police power. However, Congress may exercise a similar power as incident to the powers expressly conferred upon it by the Constitution.[20] The validity of any statute enacted by Congress depends upon whether it directly relates to one of the powers delegated to the Federal Government by way of the Constitution. The enumerated powers granted to the Federal Government to enact and enforce criminal laws are found primarily in Article 1, Section 8 of the Constitution. Although these powers are stated specifically and succinctly in these clauses, their interpretation has been a matter of debate for almost two centuries. In Article 1, Section 8, Congress has been delegated seventeen specific powers and one power of a general nature.[21] These powers have been broadly interpreted. For example, under the power to regulate interstate and foreign commerce, Congress has enacted legislation making it an offense to transport stolen vehicles in interstate commerce, imposing penalties for kidnapping an individual and transporting that person across a state line, and many other criminal laws that are enforced by the Federal Bureau of Investigation and other federal law enforcement agencies. Also, parts of

---

[20] United States v. DeWitt, 76 U.S. 41, 19 L.Ed. 593 (1869).

[21] *See generally*, Klotter & Kanovitz, CONSTITUTIONAL LAW (5th ed. 1985).

the 1964 Civil Rights Act are predicated on the Interstate Commerce Clause.[22]

Although the powers of Congress to enact criminal laws have been broadly interpreted, Congress, too, is not without limitations. As stated in the case of *McCulloch v. Maryland*:[23]

> This government is acknowledged by all to be one of enumerated powers. The principle, that it can exercise only the powers granted to it, would seem too apparent to have required to be enforced by all those arguments which its enlightened friends, while it was depending before the people, found it necessary to urge. That principle is now universally admitted....

Also, the Congress is limited by the provisions of the Constitution and especially by the first ten amendments which were added specifically to limit the power of Congress.[24]

C. Legislation by Political Subdivision

Legislative bodies of political subdivisions including cities, counties, townships and municipal corporations also have limited authority to make and enforce rules and regulations prohibiting acts or penalizing one for failure to act. After the Revolution, the state legislature became the depository for all legislative power and took over the granting of power to political subdivisions. These units of government have been invested by the state legislature with subordinate legislative powers to administer the government and enact legislation which is not in conflict with the constitution or laws of the state. The state may withhold, grant or withdraw powers and privileges as it sees fit. However great or small its sphere of action, the political subdivision remains a creature of the state, exercising and holding powers and privileges subject to the sovereign will of the state.[25]

The preservation of health, safety, welfare and comforts of dwellers in political subdivisions requires the enactment and enforcement of regulations that are often not necessary in the state taken as a whole. Therefore, the

---

[22] Heart of Atlanta Motel, Inc. v. United States, 379 U.S. 241, 85 S. Ct. 348, 13 L.Ed.2d 258 (1964).

[23] 17 U.S. 316 (4 Wheat.), 4 L.Ed. 579 (1819).

[24] Eriksson, AMERICAN CONSTITUTIONAL LAW 220 (1952).

[25] Bissel v. Jeffersonville, 66 U.S. 287, 16 L.Ed. 664 (1861); City of Owensboro v. Commonwealth, 105 Ky. 344, 49 S.W. 320 (1899).

states have delegated certain authority to political subdivision, either specifically, or by way of broad general authority, to enact ordinances to protect the safety and welfare of its inhabitants and the preservation of good order within its limits.[26] Unlike states, however, police powers of political subdivisions are not inherent and the police power of the municipality exists solely by virtue of legislative or constitutional grant of powers.[27]

Municipal ordinances, and other legislation enacted by legislative bodies of political subdivisions, are subject to the same state and Federal Constitution limitations and restrictions as state laws. Specifically, the police power of a municipality, broad as it may be, cannot justify the passage of law or ordinance which runs counter to any of the limitations of the Federal Constitution.[28]

§ 1.6 Ex Post Facto Laws

In addition to other restrictions, the U.S. Constitution, and provisions of the constitutions of the various states, specifically limit the powers of congress, of the state legislature and of municipalities in enacting and enforcing ex post facto laws. The two sections of the federal constitution which relate to ex post facto laws are Section 9, Article 1, which provides that "no bill of attainder or ex post facto law shall be passed," and Section 10 which provides that "No state shall...pass any ex post facto law."[29]

These provisions were added to the Constitution of the United States and similar provisions added to the constitutions of the respective states to prohibit legislative bodies from punishing a person for an act which was not a crime nor punishable when the act was committed, or from increasing the punishment after the fact.

An "ex post facto law," within the meaning of these constitutional provisions, is "one which, in its operation, makes that criminal which was not so at the time the action was performed, or which increases the punishment, or, in short, which in relation to the offense or its consequences, alters the situation of a party, to his disadvantage."[30]

---

[26] Salt Lake City v. Young, 45 Utah 349, 145 P. 1047 (1915).

[27] Akron v. McElligott, 166 Iowa 297, 147 N.W. 773 (1914).

[28] Spann v. Dallas, 111 Tex. 359, 235 S.W. 513 (1921).

[29] U.S. CONST., art I, §§ 9 and 10.

[30] Duncan v. Missouri, 152 U.S. 377, 38 L.Ed. 485, 14 S. Ct. 570 (1894).

In 1977, the U.S. Supreme Court considered the constitutional provisions relating to ex post facto in a death penalty case.[31] There, the majority indicated that the changes in the death penalty statute between the time of the murder and the time of the trial were procedural and, hence, there was no ex post facto violation. In defining ex post facto, the court noted that:

> Any statute which punishes as a crime an act previously committed, which was innocent when done, which makes more burdensome punishment for a crime after its commission, or which deprives one charged with crime of any defense available according to law at time when the act was committed, is prohibited as ex post facto.

In this case, the statute in effect at the time of the offense was declared unconstitutional and the penalty was imposed under a subsequently enacted constitutional statute. This, the court reasoned, did not violate the ex post facto provisions.

The limitation on the power of the states and the federal government reaches every form in which their legislative power may be exerted, whether it be a constitution, a constitutional amendment, an enactment of the legislature, a by-law or ordinance of a municipal corporation.[32] However, provisions are directed against legislative action, and does not reach erroneous or inconsistent decisions by the courts.[33]

It should be noted that the fact that a law is ex post facto, as to one person who committed an act before its enactment, does not affect its validity generally. A legislative body, after considering all of the consequences, may determine that the act of an individual should be made a crime and enact legislation to prohibit such acts in the future. Such legislation would be ex post facto in relation to a person who committed the act prior to the enactment of the legislation, but would not be considered ex post facto, and thereby make the legislation invalid, when applied to persons who commit the same act after the legislation.

The ex post facto provisions of the constitutions apply if legislation relates to substantive criminal law or the rules of evidence. For example, a change in a rule of evidence which would allow a conviction on less evidence

---

[31] Dobbert v. Florida, 432 U.S. 283, 53 L.Ed.2d 344, 97 S. Ct. 2290 (1977); *see also* Illinois v. Coleman, 140 Ill. App. 3d 806, 489 N.E.2d 455 (1986), which held that statutes relating to supervision of a defendant convicted of driving under the influence did not violate ex post facto laws.

[32] Ross v. State of Oregon, 227 U.S. 150, 57 L.Ed. 458, 33 S. Ct. 220 (1913).

[33] Frank v. Mangum, 237 U.S. 309, 59 L.Ed. 969, 35 S. Ct. 582 (1915).

of proof than one previously required is considered an ex post facto law and non-enforceable.[34]

In a 1986 case, the U.S. Court of Appeals for the sixth circuit determined that an amended rule which excluded expert opinions regarding the defendant's ability to conform his behavior to the law did not violate the ex post facto clause even though the rule was not in effect at the time the crime was committed.[35]

§ 1.7 Construction of Criminal Law Statutes

Criminal law statutes are not always clear to those who must interpret them. In fact, many who are charged with violating criminal statutes are set free when their attorney convinces the court the construction given to the statute by the state is not accurate. As indicated in previous sections of this chapter, there is a fundamental principle of criminal law that the legislation must not be vague; must not be so uncertain as to leave doubt as to its meaning. If persons of ordinary intelligence must guess at the meaning of a statute, then that statute is unenforceable.

When the meaning of a statute is doubtful, the court may take into consideration the purpose of its enactment in construing it and give effect to the intention of the legislature.[36] However, if the wording is clear and the statute is clear on its face, it is not permissible to add or vary the provisions of the statute to accomplish a supposed legislative purpose.[37]

Finally, in construing a statute, the intention of the legislature is not to be ascertained from any particular expression or section but from the whole act. All of the words used in the act are to be given force and meaning rather than any one section of the statute.[38]

§ 1.8 Classification of Crimes

Acts may be statutory crimes or common law crimes, but in either case they fall in various categories or grades.

---

[34]   Duncan v. Missouri, 152 U.S. 377, 38 L.Ed. 485, 14 S. Ct. 570 (1894).

[35]   United States v. Prickett, 790 F.2d 35 (1986).

[36]   United States v. Lacher, 134 U.S. 624, 33 L.Ed. 1080, 10 S. Ct. 625 (1890).

[37]   State v. Meyers, 56 Ohio St. 340, 47 N.E. 138 (1897).

[38]   United States v. Standard Brewing Co., 251 U.S. 210, 64 L.Ed. 229, 40 S. Ct. 139 (1920).

A. Classification According to the Nature of the Crime

Crimes have been divided according to their nature into crimes that are *mala in se* and crimes that are *mala prohibita*.

1. Mala in se

These are acts which are immoral or wrong in themselves, or acts that are naturally evil. *Mala in se* crimes are wrongs that are considered wrong in any society, and include the common law crimes such as murder, rape, arson, burglary and larceny.

2. Mala prohibita

These crimes are those which are not naturally evil but are prohibited by statute because they infringe upon the rights of others. This type of act is not wrong in some societies, but is wrong in other societies. They are wrong because they are prohibited by statute.

Generally crimes *mala in se* involve moral turpitude while crimes *mala prohibita* do not.

B. Classification According to Degree

Crimes are all classified as treason, felony and misdemeanors. These classifications become important not only in determining the degree of punishment, but also when determining the authority of justice personnel to take action. For example, in some states, law enforcement officers may make arrests for *felonies* not committed in their presence, while they cannot arrest for *misdemeanors* not committed in their presence.

1. Felonies

According to most authorities, crimes punishable by death or by imprisonment in a state prison or penitentiary are felonies. A crime may be made a felony by reference to the punishment attached or it may be made a felony by a statute which specifically says that it is a felony. When an offense is not designated by statute either as a felony or misdemeanor, but a specific punishment is prescribed, then the grade, or class of such offense is determined by the punishment.[39] Generally, felonies are punishable by at least one year,

---

[39] Eckhardt v. People, 126 Colo. 18, 247 P.2d 673 (1952).

but this is not a requirement if the statute provides that the crime is a felony and sets the punishment at less than a year.

2. Misdemeanors

Crimes or offenses not amounting to felonies are misdemeanors. Another definition is that misdemeanors are offenses for which the punishment is other than death or imprisonment in a state prison, or which have not been designated felonies by statute. A person convicted of a misdemeanor will ordinarily be incarcerated in a local jail or be required to pay a fine but will not ordinarily be sent to a state penitentiary.

Although there is apparent consensus in the technical definition of a felony and a misdemeanor, what may be regarded as a felony in one state may constitute a misdemeanor in another. Except for the most serious crimes, such as murder, robbery and rape, generalizations in the area of what crimes are felonies or misdemeanors are unreliable. Therefore, the legislative designations in the particular jurisdiction must be carefully examined.[40]

3. Treason

Treason is the only crime that is described in the Constitution.[41] Because those who commit treason threaten the very existence of the nation, it is given a higher classification than felonies. According to the Constitution, "Treason against the United States shall consist only in levying war against them, or in adhering to their enemies, giving them aid and comfort." Also, the Constitution provides that no person shall be convicted of treason unless on the testimony of two witnesses to the same overt act, or on confession in open court.

§ 1.9 Distinction Between Crimes and Torts

When one person is wronged by another, he may seek a remedy against the wrongdoer by bringing action in what is known as a "civil action." The state may also initiate criminal action against that person for the same wrongful act. The process by which a person himself initiates action against another is known as the "law of torts." A function of tort law is to compensate someone who is injured for the harm he has suffered. For example, if A is struck by B

---

[40] The Model Penal Code includes the definition of a lesser class of crimes as a "petty misdemeanor." Model Penal Code § 1.04(4) (Proposed Official Draft 1962).

[41] U.S. CONST., art. III, § 3.

causing him bodily injury, A may bring an action in court for recovery of expenses and for compensation for losses incurred. Also, the state may initiate action against B for assault and battery and prosecute the case in criminal court.

With torts, the emphasis is on the adjustment of conflicting interests of individuals to achieve a desirable social result. A crime is a public wrong in that it affects public rights and is an injury to the whole community.[42]

In spite of the differences between tort law and criminal law, there are many ideas and concepts common to both branches of law. For example, some of the defenses that are available to a defendant in a civil case are also available to a defendant in a criminal case.

In distinguishing between tort law and criminal law, it is less difficult to understand the difference if the methods by which the remedy is perceived are compared.

Distinctions between torts and crimes

Torts	_Crimes_
Private wrong	Public wrong
Action initiated by an individual	Action taken by the state
Private attorney represents plaintiff	Prosecutor represents the state
Action for money damages	Punishment by fine or imprisonment
Unanimous verdict of jury not usually required	Unanimous verdict of jury usually required[43]
Proof by preponderance of the evidence	Proof beyond a reasonable doubt

---

[42] Huntington v. Attrill, 145 U.S. 657, 13 S. Ct. 224, 36 L.Ed. 1123 (1892).

[43] _See generally_, Klotter & Kanovitz, CONSTITUTIONAL LAW §10.9 (5th ed. 1985), for a discussion of some of the applicable exceptions.

As criminal justice personnel may be called upon to testify in tort cases as well as in criminal cases, they should be aware of the procedures followed in both types of trials.

§ 1.10 Distinction Between Crimes and Contracts

As indicated in previous paragraphs, a crime is a wrong against the state and the actor looks to statutes and the common law to determine what acts are crimes and the elements of those crimes. In a tort action, the plaintiff seeks compensation for losses incurred. Before one can successfully pursue a tort action, he must demonstrate that the defendant had a duty, that he breached that duty, that there was a causal connection between the breach of duty and the injury, and finally an injury. In determining if there has been a duty or breach of duty, the court looks at statutory law, constitutional law and cases which have been previously decided.

In a third type of action, the instigator seeks to enforce a contract or seeks damages for breach of that contract. In a contract action, the parties look to the terms of the contract to determine the duties, obligations and specifications. As one case explained:

> A contract is a transaction between two or more persons in which each party comes under an obligation to the other, and each reciprocally acquires a right to whatever is promised by the other.[44]

In another case, an early court explained that the parties impose on themselves obligations subject to the paramount law of the country where the contract is made.[45]

The law relating to contracts is voluminous and complicated. Courts have considered the requirements for a legal contract, and have attempted to interpret contracts which were not clear. Thousands of decisions have been rendered concerning breaches of contracts. Here it is sufficient to note that failure to comply with a contract is not a crime, and that in a contract action, courts look to the terms of the contract rather than to criminal laws to determine duties and obligations. A contract action is brought by an individual or corporation against another while criminal action is instigated on behalf of the state, and courts look to the statutes and previous decisions to determine what acts are crimes.

---

[44] Trustees of Dartmouth College v. Woodward, 17 J.W. 518, 17 U.S. 518, 4 L.Ed. 629 (1819).

[45] Ogden v. Sanders, 25 U.S. 213, 12 Wheat. 213, 6 L.Ed. 606 (1827).

§ 1.11 Burden of Proof – Prosecution

In a criminal case, the state has the burden of proving the guilt of the accused beyond a reasonable doubt. That means that the prosecution has the responsibility to prove each of the elements of the crime with which the accused is charged. For example, the common law crime of burglary has six elements:

(1) breaking,
(2) entering,
(3) dwelling,
(4) of another,
(5) at night, and
(6) with intent to commit a felony therein.

These elements must be proved in accordance with the definition of each element as described by the court. If the prosecution fails to prove one element of the crime beyond a reasonable doubt but proves the other elements, the accused may sometimes be found guilty of a lesser crime. But if one element is not proved beyond a reasonable doubt, the person charged cannot be convicted of the crime charged. Failure of those involved in the criminal justice process to gather and introduce sufficient evidence to meet this burden will result in an acquittal or, at least, in the reduction of a more serious crime to a less serious one.

While in a civil case, the degree of proof is the "preponderance of the evidence," in a criminal case, the degree is "beyond a reasonable doubt."[46] In some states, the exact wording of the charge to the jury dealing with the standard of proof is stated by statute. In other states, there is no such requirement and, in fact, the judge does not have to explain the term at all.[47] Where a statute specifically includes the charge that the judge is to read to the jury, this must be read as stated. An example of such a statute is that in California, which provides that:

It is not a mere possible doubt; because everything relating to human affairs, and depending upon moral evidence, is open to some possible or imaginary doubt. It is that state of the case which, after the entire comparison and consideration of all the evidence, leaves the minds of the jurors in that condition that they cannot say that

---

[46] *See generally*, Klotter, CRIMINAL EVIDENCE (4th ed. 1986).
[47] McCormick, EVIDENCE 684 (2d ed. 1972).

they feel an abiding conviction, to a moral certainty, of the truth of the charge.[48]

The standard of proof "beyond a reasonable doubt" is a constitutional requirement. In 1970, the Supreme Court left no doubt about the requirement by emphasizing:

> Lest there remain any doubt about the constitutional stature of the reasonable-doubt standard, we explicitly hold that the Due Process Clause protects the accused against conviction except on proof beyond a reasonable doubt of every fact necessary to constitute the crime with which he is charged.[49]

While the law relating to the burden of proof is most often in the form of case law, legislative bodies may enact legislation modifying the burden of proof where this does not violate constitutional principles. Perhaps the best example is the law relating to the burden of proof where insanity is an issue.

In some states, the matter of a defendant's insanity must be put in issue by the defendant, but the prosecution has the ultimate burden of proving insanity, as he has the burden of proving other elements of the crime. However, in a number of states, the defendant has the burden of proving his legal insanity by the preponderance of evidence. The U.S. Supreme Court in several instances has determined that this placing of the burden on the defendant does not violate the Constitution of the United States.[50]

Shortly after the attempted assassination of President Reagan, Congress considered legislation which would place a greater burden on the defendant in insanity issues. In 1984, as part of the Comprehensive Crime Control Act, Congress enacted legislation entitled "Insanity Defense Reform Act of 1984."[51] In this act, Congress provided that "the defendant has the burden of proving the defense of insanity by clear and convincing evidence." This places the burden on the defendant and establishes a different standard of proof: clear and convincing evidence. This is a higher degree than a mere "preponderance of the evidence;" however, it is less than "beyond a reasonable doubt."

---

[48] Cal. Penal Code, § 1096 (1970).

[49] In re Winship, 397 U.S. 358, 90 S. Ct. 1068, 25 L.Ed.2d 368 (1970). *See* case in Part II.

[50] Henderson v. New York, 432 U.S. 197, 53 L.Ed.2d 281, 97 S. Ct. 2319 (1977).

[51] Pub. L. 98-473, Chap. 4, § 402 amending 18 U.S.C. § 20 (1984).

§ 1.12 Burden of Proof – Defendant

Unlike the prosecution, the defense does not have the burden of producing evidence to prove defenses "beyond a reasonable doubt." If a defendant in a criminal case relies upon distinct substantive matters which exempt him from punishment and absolve him from liability, he has the burden of proving his defense usually by a "preponderance of the evidence." As was indicated in the previous section, however, Congress may, without violating the Constitution, require the defendant to prove defenses such as insanity by "clear and convincing evidence."

Generally, when the state has made out its case and the defendant interposes defenses such as duress, alibi, or self-defense, the defense then has the burden of proving such defense. And where the defendant seeks to escape criminal liability for a violation of statute on the grounds that his act comes within one of the exceptions, it is incumbent upon him to show that he is within the exception.[52]

Although the defendant may be required to go forward with the evidence so that matters of defense may be raised and submitted to the jury, and may be required to introduce evidence to show affirmative defenses by the preponderance of the evidence, it is unconstitutional to shift the burden to the defendant to show that he is innocent. Any instruction that tends to require the defendant to prove his innocence or any instruction which relieves the prosecution of proving an element of the crime, violates the due process requirement.[53]

§ 1.13 Summary

When one causes harm to the person of another or the property of another, not only is that person concerned, but society and the state has an interest. Criminal law then is that branch or division of law which defines crimes, treats of their nature, and provides for their punishment. In a criminal law case, the sovereign is the plaintiff, and the purpose of the prosecution is to preserve the public peace or address an injury to the public-at-large.

Since the beginning of time, various societies have been faced with the problem of determining what standards of conduct must be established in that society. In determining what acts should be made criminal, at least three factors should be given weight:

---

[52] Kuzmics v. Santiago, 389 A.2d 587 (Pa. 1978); *see* Klotter, CRIMINAL EVIDENCE (4th ed. 1986).

[53] Sandstrom v. Montana, 442 U.S. 510, 61 L.Ed.2d 39, 99 S. Ct. 2450 (1979).

(1)   the enforceability of the law,
(2)   the effects of the law, and
(3)   the existence of other means to protect society against the un-
      desirable behavior.

Once the legislative or judicial branch of government decides that certain conduct is prohibited or required, criminal justice personnel are charged with enforcing those laws, and have the responsibility to do so until the laws are repealed or declared to be unconstitutional.

Most of the present-day crimes in the various states had their origin in the so-called common law of England. This was the law as developed in the early English case decisions and modified by the English legislative bodies. All of this body of English law, except that which was not applicable in the American colonies, was brought to our shores by the colonists when they emigrated from England. These became the starting point for our criminal law.

While most of the present-day crimes have their origin in the common law of England, no states currently follow the common law without modification. When the legislative body determines that certain conduct should be prohibited or certain acts required, a bill is prepared (describing which conduct is prohibited or required) and introduced into the legislature. Generally, if both Houses act positively on the bill and it is signed by the chief executive, then it becomes law to be enforced by those involved in the justice process. In drafting criminal laws, the legislature has much freedom, but is limited by the constitutions of the various states and the Constitution of the United States, as interpreted by the courts. Legislation which is contrary to the provisions of either the federal or state constitution, as interpreted, cannot stand.

The Constitution of the United States provides that no state nor the federal government may pass "ex post facto" laws. An ex post facto law within the meaning of this provision is one which, in its operation, makes that criminal which was not so at the time the action was performed or which increases the punishment, or in short, which, in relation to the offense, alters the situation of a party, to his disadvantage. Also, in construing criminal laws, the U.S. Supreme Court has determined that due process requires that the would-be actors be given fair notice of what conduct is prohibited before punishment is allowed.

Crimes are classified according to the nature of the crime, such as *mala in se* and *mala prohibita*. Crimes are also classified as felonies, misdemeanors and treason. According to most authorities, crimes punishable by death or imprisonment in the state prison are felonies, while other crimes not amounting to felonies are classified as misdemeanors. What is regarded as a felony in some states may constitute only a misdemeanor in others, although the more serious crimes such as murder, robbery and rape are classified as felonies in all jurisdictions.

When one person is wronged by another, he may seek a remedy against the wrongdoer by bringing a civil action or a tort action. With torts, the emphasis is on the adjustment of conflicting interests of individuals to achieve a desirable social result, while a crime is a public wrong in that it affects public rights and is an injury to the whole community.

When a crime is committed, attorneys and judges look to the statutes, codes, constitutions and case decisions to determine what conduct has been prohibited by law and for procedures to be followed in proving guilt. In a contract case, the parties look to the provisions of the contract to determine the rights and duties of the parties.

In the system of criminal law in this country, the prosecution has the heavier burden of proof. The prosecution has the responsibility to prove each element of crime with which the accused is charged, beyond a reasonable doubt. If one element is not proved beyond a reasonable doubt, the person charged cannot be convicted of that particular crime. Although it is unconstitutional to shift the burden of proof or guilt, or any element of the crime to the defendant in a criminal case, the defendant may be required to go forward with the evidence to show an affirmative defense, such as alibi or insanity.

Perhaps criminal justice personnel could get by without fully comprehending the theory and distinctions as discussed. However, with this background knowledge, and with a comprehensive understanding of the various crimes and their elements, justice personnel will act with more confidence and perform their duties in a more competent manner.

Chapter 2
PRINCIPLES OF
CRIMINAL LIABILITY

Crime, as a compound concept, generally constituted only from concurrence of an evil-meaning mind, with an evil-doing hand, was congenial to an intense individualism and took deep and early root in American soil.

Morissette v. United States,
342 U.S. 246, 72 S. Ct. 240,
96 L.Ed. 288 (1952).

§ 2.1 Introduction

In later chapters the elements of specific crimes are enumerated and discussed. Before the specific crimes are examined, however, it is necessary to study some general principles regarding criminal responsibility and liability. These principles of criminal liability apply to all violations and set the stage for a consideration of specific laws.

Not only are those persons who actually commit a prohibited act responsible, but others who encourage, assist or hinder apprehension also may be liable under the law. The prosecutor must prove that there was, in fact, a criminal act (*actus reus*) and that persons charged committed the act or participated illegally.

Under modern concepts, even if a party commits a prohibited act or one fails to act when he is obligated to do so, usually there cannot be a successful prosecution unless the "state-of-mind requirements" are present (*mens rea*). Also, the state has the responsibility to show that the defendant's conduct was the proximate cause of that result (causation), and that there was a causal connection between the conduct and the result.

Criminal law, then, is concerned with:

(1)   parties to crimes,
(2)   the criminal act or omission,
(3)   the criminal state of mind; and
(4)   causation.

These and other principles are discussed in this chapter.

§ 2.2 Parties to Crimes

At common law, all participants in felony crimes were either principals or accessories. Principals were either principals of the first degree or principals of the second degree. Accessories were divided into accessories before the fact and accessories after the fact. In misdemeanor situations, all participants were considered principals. In many states, under the statutory law, the common law distinction is eliminated. However, some states still refer to principals in the first degree and principals in the second degree in the statutory definitions. The theory for making the distinction is important in the study of criminal law.

A. Principals

1. Principals in the first degree

One who actually commits the act which causes a crime to occur, or one who is actually or constructively present during the commission of the crime, is a principal in the first degree. If one is present and commits some act which is a part of the offense, he is a principal in the first degree, provided that another principal completes the offense.

One who is constructively present is a principal in the first degree, even if the crime is committed through an innocent agent. The principal can perpetrate the crime by his own act, by acts of an innocent human being or by means of an inanimate agency.

2. Principals in the second degree

One who aids or abets a principal in the first degree as he commits the criminal act, or incites the commission of the crime, and who is actually or constructively present at the time of the commission, is a principal in the second degree. A principal in the second degree differs from a principal in the first degree only in that he does not commit the offense himself or with an innocent agent, but instead aids or encourages the principal party to commit the crime; for example, one who is posted as a look-out or the driver of the getaway car in a robbery situation is a principal in the second degree.

In order for one to be a principal in the second degree, one must be present at the scene of the crime. His presence may be either actual or constructive. A person is constructively present when he assists the principal in the first degree at the very time the offense is committed, but from such distance that he is not actually present.[1]

In the case of *State v. Owens*, the North Carolina Court of Appeals determined that a person who is actually or constructively present when a crime is committed and who aids or abets another in its commission is a principal in the second degree. In this armed robbery case, the defendant was guilty, even though not actually in the area where the armed robbery took place.[2] In a joint trial in Virginia, the husband was found guilty of raping his wife's fifteen-year-old niece, and the wife was found guilty as a principal in the second degree, even though the wife was not actually present. The Supreme Court

---

[1] State v. Sauls, 29 N.C. App. 457, 224 S.E.2d 702 (1976); State v. Wade, 11 N.C. App. 169, 180 S.E.2d 328 (1971).

[2] State v. Owens, 75 N.C. App. 513, 331 S.E.2d 311 (1985).

of Virginia agreed that the wife was guilty of rape as a principal in the second degree since she procured, encouraged, countenanced and approved the husband's having sexual intercourse with the victim against her will by intimidation.[3]

In a 1986 case, a Maryland court reaffirmed the rule that "a principal in the second degree is one who actually or constructively was present when the felony was committed, and who aids or abets in its commission."[4] In this case, the defendant was convicted of two counts of robbery with a deadly weapon, two counts of kidnapping, two counts of the use of a handgun in the commission of a crime of violence, and unauthorized use of an automobile. The Court of Special Appeals agreed that evidence supported the convictions of the defendant as a principal in the second degree even though the defendant did not actively participate in the acts but was present when the acts occurred.[5]

Mere presence at the scene of the crime is sufficient to warrant the conviction of one as a principal in the second degree if the prosecution proves that one aided, abetted, advised, assisted or encouraged the actual perpetration of the crime.

Generally, the prosecution must prove that a crime was committed by the principal and that the defendant aided and abetted him in order to obtain a conviction of one as a principal in the second degree. It makes no difference, however, if the principal in the first degree is found not guilty by another jury so long as the jury which convicts one as an aider or abettor finds as a matter of fact that the principal in the first degree is guilty beyond a reasonable doubt.[6]

B. Accessories

One may be guilty of a criminal offense if one participates as an accessory before or after the fact.

---

[3] Sutton v. Commonwealth of Virginia, 228 Va. 654, 324 S.E.2d 665 (1986). *See* case in Part II of book.

[4] Smith v. State, 66 Md. App. 603, 505 A.2d 564 (1986).

[5] *See also*, Ramsey v. Commonwealth, 2 Va. App. 265, 343 S.E.2d 465 (1986), where the court held that the defendant was a principal in the second degree to forgery and to uttering a forged instrument when present at time of the acts.

[6] Forbes v. State, 513 S.W.2d 72 (Tex. Crim. App. 1974).

1. Accessory before the fact

Accessories before the fact are persons who counsel, procure or command the principal to commit a criminal offense, yet who are themselves too far away to aid in the felonious act. Accessories before the fact are distinguished at common law from an aider and abettor or principal in the second degree by the fact that the latter must be present during the commission of the offense.[7]

To be guilty of an accessory before the fact, the defendant must have acted in some manner as a participant in the scheme of events in preparation for or commission of the offense. Mere knowledge that a crime is to be committed is insufficient to support a guilty verdict, even though defendant might have later concealed the crime. It is immaterial that such participation is to a small degree, so long as it has the effect of inducing the principal to commit the crime.[8]

If, however, the defendant attended meetings during which the planned robbery was discussed, he may be an accessory before the fact. In a North Carolina case, the defendant, Benita Darby, attended meetings held by the robbers during which the robbery was discussed. The robbers agreed to use a real gun and talked about who would drive the getaway car. In addition, a witness at the trial described an attempted earlier robbery of the same store and Darby was described as the driver of the car during the aborted attempt. The reviewing court again held that those who counsel, encourage or abet may be guilty of accessories before the fact. Here, after agreeing to commit the robbery, Darby participated in its preparation and its planning. That she was not present at the commission of the crime does not prevent her participation as an accessory before the fact.[9] In finding the defendant guilty, the court explained that accessories and principals are now treated equally for guilt and sentencing purposes.

An accessory before the fact is guilty of the offense charged just as are the principals of the first and second degree. An accessory before the fact must be indicted, tried and punished as a principal.[10]

---

[7] State v. Mower, 317 A.2d 807 (Me. 1974); Huff v. State, 23 Md. App. 211, 326 A.2d 198 (1974).

[8] State v. Alvarey, 189 Neb. 276, 202 N.W.2d 600 (1972).

[9] State v. Walden, 75 N.C. App. 79, 330 S.E.2d 271 (1985).

[10] Lee v. State, 51 Ala. App. 330, 285 So. 2d 295 (1973), *cert. denied*, 291 Ala. 787, 285 So. 2d 500 (1973).

2. Accessory after the fact

An accessory after the fact is one who receives, comforts or assists another, knowing that the other has committed a felony in order to hinder the perpetrator's arrest, prosecution or conviction.[11] In order to convict a party charged as an accessory after the fact, it is essential to prove that a felony has been committed, that the person knew the felony had been committed, and that the person intended to shield the perpetrator from the law.

If an act of assistance is offered to enable a felon to escape justice after the crime has been committed, the assistance is rendered with the knowledge that the act has been committed, and the person assisted did in fact commit the crime, this constitutes the crime of accessory after the fact. The fact that the person who gave the assistance discontinues the assistance at a later date, and notifies the authorities, does not relieve that person of criminal liability for the acts committed before notification.

C. Classification of Participants Under Modern Statutes

1. The Model Penal Code

§ 2.06 Liability for Conduct of Another; Complicity[12]

(1) A person is guilty of an offense if it is committed by his own conduct or by the conduct of another person for which he is legally accountable, or both.

(2) A person is legally accountable for the conduct of another person when:

    (a) acting with the kind of culpability that is sufficient for the commission of the offense, he causes an innocent or irresponsible person to engage in such conduct; or

    (b) he is made accountable for the conduct of such other person by the Code or by the law defining the offense; or

    (c) he is an accomplice of such other person in the commission of the offense.

---

[11] Whorley v. State, 45 Fla. 123, 33 So. 849 (1903).

[12] Model Penal Code, § 2.06(1), (2) and (3).

(3) A person is an accomplice of another person in the commission of an offense if:

    (a) with the purpose of promoting or facilitating the commission of the offense, he

        (i) solicits such other person to commit it; or

        (ii) aids or agrees or attempts to aid such other person in planning or committing it; or

        (iii) having a legal duty to prevent the commission of the offense, fails to make proper effort so to do; or

    (b) his conduct is expressly declared by law to establish his complicity.

The Model Penal Code provides that a person is guilty of an offense if it is committed by his own conduct or by the conduct of another person for which he is "legally accountable." One is "legally accountable" for the conduct of another if he causes an innocent person to engage in conduct constituting a crime or if he is an accomplice to the conduct of the other person.[13]

An accomplice is one who solicits the commission of an offense, aids in its commission or, having a legal duty to prevent the commission of the offense, fails to make proper effort to prevent it, or his conduct is expressly declared by law to establish his complicity.[14]

Under modern statutory authority, those who incite or abet the commission of a crime are generally guilty of the crime itself. In states that have adopted such statutes, no longer is a distinction drawn among the participants with the exception of an accessory after the fact.[15]

2. Other statutes and codes

Adopting the common law principle, the U.S. Supreme Court explained that a person may be convicted as an aider and abettor despite the earlier acquittal of the principal offender.[16] After tracing the history of the judge-made and statutory rules, the court made reference to 18 U.S.C. Sec. 2 which

---

[13] Model Penal Code, § 2.06(1) (Proposed Official Draft 1980).

[14] Model Penal Code, § 2.06(3) (Proposed Official Draft 1980).

[15] Cal. Penal Code, § 31 (1970).

[16] Standefer v. United States, 447 U.S. 10, 100 S. Ct. 1999, 64 L.Ed.2d 689 (1980).

makes one who "aids, abets, counsels, commands, induces or procures" a "principal." The majority made this comment:

> Read against its common-law background, the provision evinces a clear intent to permit the conviction of accessories to federal criminal offenses despite the prior acquittal of the actual perpetrator of the offense.

An accessory after the fact is different from the other common law parties and is accorded a different treatment in the modern codes. The common law principle that the accessory after the fact was guilty of the original felony and punishable to the same extent as a principal has been discarded by most courts.[17] In most modern statutes, an accessory after the fact is treated as a special misdemeanant.[18] The Model Penal Code which has been adopted by some states is specific in stating that a person commits the offense if he:

    (a) harbors or conceals another,
    (b) provides aid,
    (c) conceals, destroys or tampers with evidence,
    (d) warns of impending discovery or apprehension, or
    (e) volunteers false information to a law enforcement officer.

§ 2.3 Criminal Act Requirements

In the general scheme of the criminal law, courts and legislative bodies have provided a formula which must be followed if one is to be convicted of a completed crime. This formula is:

Criminal Act + Culpability + Concurrence of Act and State of Mind + Causation

If the prosecution is unable to meet the requirements in regard to each of the parts of the formula, there can be no conviction for a completed crime. The Model Penal Code includes this Section describing criminal acts or omissions.

---

[17] White v. Commonwealth, 301 Ky. 228, 191 S.W.2d 244 (Ky. 1945).
[18] Model Penal Code, § 242.3 (Proposed Official Draft 1980).

§ 2.01 Requirement of Voluntary Act; Omission as Basis of Liability; Possession as an Act[19]

(1) A person is not guilty of an offense unless his liability is based on conduct which includes a voluntary act or the omission to perform an act of which he is physically capable.

(2) The following are not voluntary acts within the meaning of this Section:

    (a) a reflex or convulsion;
    (b) a bodily movement during unconsciousness or sleep;
    (c) conduct during hypnosis or resulting from hypnotic suggestion;
    (d) a bodily movement that otherwise is not a product of the effort or determination of the actor, either conscious or habitual.

(3) Liability for the commission of an offense may not be based on an omission unaccompanied by action unless:

    (a) the omission is expressly made sufficient by the law defining the offense; or
    (b) duty to perform the omitted act is otherwise imposed by law.

(4) Possession is an act, within the meaning of this Section, if the possessor knowingly procured or received the thing possessed or was aware of his control thereof for a sufficient period to have been able to terminate his possession.

Before a person may be convicted of a crime, the prosecution must show that that person (whether it be a principal or an accessory or an accomplice) committed a criminal act or a prohibited act, or failed to act where he had a legal obligation to do so. Often this principal is referred to as the "*actus reus.*"

The law does not punish mere criminal thoughts nor punish one for "status." As a rule, legal liability is based upon an affirmative physical act by the person charged but, in some instances, liability can rest upon a total failure to act, if it is determined that a person had a legal obligation to act under

---

[19] Model Penal Code, § 2.01 (Proposed Official Draft 1980).

the circumstances. In this Section, the criminal act requirement is discussed. The omission is analyzed in the following Section.

The authorities are in general agreement that no one should be subjected to criminal punishment except for specifically designated acts or conduct. The act or the conduct may consist of a physical movement of the person, such as pulling the trigger of a gun or breaking into a house to commit theft therein, or it may consist of verbal acts; for example, making slanderous statements about another.

A related doctrine is that acts or conduct may not be treated as criminal unless this act or this conduct has been so defined by statute or case decision as to make the conduct prohibited reasonably clear. When the prohibited act or conduct is made reasonably clear by the appropriate lawmakers and a specific person has acted in violation of such prohibitions, the state is interested and state officials may take action to prosecute.

The criminal law is not concerned with people's thoughts and emotions, or with their personality patterns or character. No legitimate function could be served by subjecting persons to criminal liability solely for harboring an evil intent; but when such evil intent is converted to action and the action violates a specific and ascertainable prohibition, a legitimate function is served by the state in taking action.

Following this reasoning, the courts have determined that defining a crime in terms of *status*, rather than in terms of a particular activity, violates the Eighth Amendment, which prohibits cruel and unusual punishment. For example, certain kinds of status, such as "vagrancy," "being a common drunkard" or being "addicted to the use of narcotics" are not subjects of criminal penalty.

In the case of *Robinson v. California*, the Supreme Court of the United States declared that the state law which provided "no person shall use, or be under the influence of, or be addicted to the use of narcotics..." was unconstitutional as in violation of the Eighth Amendment as applied to the states by way of the Fourteenth Amendment.[20] The Court explained that the part of the statute which makes the "status" of narcotics addiction a criminal offense violates the Constitution. The justices made clear, however, that this interpretation did not prohibit punishment for the use of narcotics, as this use is prohibited conduct. The Court summarized with the paragraph:

> We hold that a state law which imprisons a person thus affected as a criminal, even though he has never touched any narcotics drug within the state or been guilty of any irregular behavior there, in-

---

[20] Robinson v. California, 370 U.S. 660, 82 S. Ct. 1417, 8 L.Ed.2d 758 (1962). *See* case in Part II.

flicts a cruel and unusual punishment in violation of the Fourteenth Amendment.

However, a statute which punishes for being in public while drunk does not fall within the *Robinson* holding.[21] In distinguishing these cases, the Supreme Court explained that the State of Texas in the *Powell* case has not sought to punish a mere "status" as California did in *Robinson*, nor has it attempted to regulate appellant's behavior in the privacy of his own home. Rather, the Court said, it has imposed upon appellant a criminal sanction for public behavior which may create substantial health and safety hazards. This, the Court reminded, is a far cry from convicting one for being an addict, being a chronic alcoholic, or being mentally ill or a leper.

In referring to the criminal act (*actus reus*) requirement, the majority of the *Powell* court concluded:

> We cannot cast aside the centuries-long evolution of the collection of interlocking and overlapping concepts which the common law has utilized to access the accountability of an individual for his antisocial deeds. The doctrines of *actus reus*, *mens rea*, insanity, mistake, justification, and duress have historically provided the tools for a constantly shifting adjustment of the tension between the evolving aims of the criminal law and changing religious, moral, philosophical, and medical views of the nature of man. This process of adjustment was always thought to be the province of the States.

"Possession" offenses sometimes pose problems because it is claimed that, in some instances, the possession of property often involves no affirmative movement to gain control of the contraband item. Although in some of the early cases the court held that mere possession was not a crime because no "act" was involved, modern statutes, which make possession of contraband (such as narcotics or stolen goods) a crime, have been upheld. The rationale is that the "act" requirement is complied with as the defendant either actively procured or received the items, or violated the legally imposed duty to divest oneself of control as soon as possible.[22]

To summarize, to be convicted of a crime, the accused must have committed a criminal act (except as explained in the next Section). The act may involve an actual physical movement, or may consist of verbal acts. One cannot be punished for evil intent alone, nor for violation of a statute which

---

[21] Powell v. State of Texas, 392 U.S. 514, 88 S. Ct. 2145, 20 L.Ed.2d 1254 (1968).

[22] Model Penal Code, § 2.01(4) (Proposed Official Draft 1980).

makes "status" alone a violation. Where the criminal liability is based upon the defendant's affirmative act, usually there must be a showing that he made some conscious movement. However, "possession" crimes have been upheld even if there is no proof of a conscious movement.

§ 2.4 Criminal Omission

Although in the usual case an affirmative act is required to support conviction of a given crime, in some instances liability can rest upon failure to act at all. This is referred to as "criminal omission," "acts of omission" or, in some instances, "failure to act." Obviously, it is easier to show that a person acted in a certain way, or on a given occasion, than it is to prove that he failed to act when he had a duty to act. On the other hand, it would certainly be a miscarriage of justice if there were not some provision for criminal penalties against those who fail to act when there is a legal duty to do so.

There are many statutes which make failure to act a violation of the law; for example, failure to register for the draft or failure to prepare income tax reports. Although the cases concerning failure to act generally arise in homicide cases where the defendant's conviction is predicated on the theory that the defendant failed to take steps to save the victim's life, the rationale also applies in other cases. The rule is that defendant's omission will support a finding of criminal liability where it is shown that he was under legal duty to act and that it would have been possible for him to act.[23] In the *Jones* case the court sustained liability for homicide against one who failed to act, declaring:

> There are at least four situations in which the failure to act may constitute a breach of legal duty. One can be held criminally liable: first, where a statute imposes a duty to care for another; second, where one stands in a certain status relationship to another; third, where one has assumed a contractual duty to care for another; and fourth, where one has voluntarily assumed the care of another, and so secluded the helpless person as to prevent others from rendering aid.

A. Statutory Duty

Where a statutory duty is placed on one to care for another (for example, a duty of one spouse to support and provide the other spouse with necessary food, clothing, shelter and medical care), criminal liability could result if

---

[23] Jones v. United States, 308 F.2d 307 (D.C. Cir. 1962).

the person charged had the opportunity to do the act, the omission of which causes the death. Other examples are the statutory obligations to file tax returns and to report automobile accidents.

B. One Person Stands in a Certain Status or Relationship to Another

At common law, certain affirmative duties were placed upon persons with designated relationships. For example, a parent has a duty to prevent physical harm to his or her children. Where such a duty is made clear and the person has the opportunity to prevent harm, then criminal liability could exist.[24]

C. Duty Arising from Contract

Where one has a contractual duty to protect or care for others and fails to carry out that contractual duty, he may be criminally liable for not performing his duty. For example, in the case of *People v. Montecino*, a nurse was held liable for failure to care for a patient she had been hired to care for.[25] Another example is the failure of a railroad gateman, who was employed to lower the gates to protect the cars and pedestrians from passing trains, with the resulting death of a driver of a car. The gateman was criminally responsible for failure to carry out his contractual obligation.[26]

D. Failure to Care for Another Where One Has Assumed the Responsibility for Such Care

One of the most difficult assignments is determining liability where one who is not otherwise legally obligated to render aid voluntarily undertakes to render such aid but fails to continue to render aid. If a person who has no legal or statutory obligation to render aid assumes this obligation, that person must not put the helpless person in such a position as to prevent others from rendering aid. The rationale is that abandoning one's effort would leave the imperiled person in a worse condition than before. For example, a grandmother who took care of a grandchild violated the duty of reasonable care

---

[24]   Commonwealth v. Breth, 44 Pa. 56 (1915).

[25]   66 Cal. App. 2d 85, 152 P.2d 5 (1944).

[26]   State v. Harrison, 107 N.J.L. 213, 152 A. 867 (1931).

when she got so drunk that she let the child smother. In that case, the court held the grandmother guilty of manslaughter.[27]

Two caveats are in order here. One, before a person can be determined guilty for failure to act, an opportunity to perform the act, or failure to perform the act, must be shown. The majority view is that, although one may be under a legal duty to act, an omission will not render the defendant criminally liable unless he has knowledge of the *facts* creating the duty. For example, a person convicted for failure to stop at a hit-and-run accident in violation of the statute must be aware that the accident had occurred. The responsibility of showing knowledge falls upon the prosecutor.[28]

On the other hand, lack of knowledge of the law does not excuse one. For example, a defendant's claim that he did not know that he had to report an accident as required by law would not be a defense. However, if a statute punished for *wilful* failure to return an income tax report, then knowledge of the law must be proved. The reasoning is there can be no *wilful* violation if there is no knowledge.[29]

The second caveat is especially important to criminal justice investigators. That is, that there can be no criminal prosecution if failure to act is based upon impossibility. There is no criminal act, or criminal failure to act, where the defendant's omission was due to the fact that he lacked the means or ability to perform. Evidence should be introduced to show the defendant did have the ability to take action.[30] On the other hand, failure because of impossibility is not a defense where a person could have gotten help, even if he himself were not able to perform the duty; for example, failure to seek aid for a person who needs medical care.[31]

Before leaving the subject of failure to act, consideration should be given to the philosophy and theories existing in this country as compared to countries in Europe. In 1964, when 28-year-old Catherine Genovese was killed while 37 people who saw the murder didn't call the police, there was no criminal liability on the part of those who refused to help. The newspaper expressed shock that we, in this country, are not interested enough in our fellow man to take action under such circumstances.[32]

---

[27] Cornell v. State, 159 Fla. 687, 32 So. 2d 610 (1947).

[28] People v. Henry, 23 Cal. App. 2d 155, 72 P.2d 915 (1937).

[29] United States v. Murdock, 290 U.S. 389, 54 S. Ct. 223, 78 L.Ed. 381 (1933).

[30] *See* Model Penal Code, § 2.01(1) (Proposed Official Draft 1980).

[31] People v. Beardsley, 150 Mich. 206, 113 N.W. 1128 (1907).

[32] N.Y. Times, Mar. 28, 1964.

In most European countries, some of the people who witnessed the death could have been criminally liable under statutes making it an offense punishable by fine or imprisonment knowingly to fail to give aid to a person in serious danger.[33]

§ 2.5 Criminal State of Mind – *mens rea*

The Model Penal Code includes this Section on Culpability.

§ 2.02 General Requirements of Culpability[34]

(1) Minimum Requirements of Culpability
Except as provided in § 2.05, a person is not guilty of an offense unless he acted purposely, knowingly, recklessly or negligently, as the law may require, with respect to each material element of the offense.

(2) Kinds of Culpability Defined

(a) Purposely
A person acts purposely with respect to a material element of an offense when:

(i)   if the element involves the nature of his conduct or a result thereof, it is his conscious object to engage in conduct of that nature or to cause such a result; and
(ii) if the element involves the attendant circumstances, he is aware of the existence of such circumstances or he believes or hopes that they exist.

(b) Knowingly
A person acts knowingly with respect to a material element of an offense when:

---

[33] *See generally*, *Good and Bad Samaritans*, 14 Am. J. Comp. L. 630 (1966). *See also*, French Penal Code, art. 63.
[34] *See* Model Penal Code, § 2.02 (Proposed Official Draft 1980).

(i)   if the element involves the nature of his conduct or the attendant circumstances, he is aware that his conduct is of that nature or that such circumstances exist; and

(ii) if the element involves a result of his conduct he is aware that it is practically certain that his conduct will cause such a result.

(c) Recklessly

A person acts recklessly with respect to a material element of an offense when he consciously disregards a substantial and unjustifiable risk that the material element exists or will result from his conduct. The risk must be of such a nature and degree that, considering the nature and purpose of the actor's conduct and the circumstances known to him, its disregard involves a gross deviation from the standard of conduct that a law-abiding person would observe in the actor's situation.

(d) Negligently

A person acts negligently with respect to a material element of an offense when he should be aware of a substantial and unjustifiable risk that the material element exists or will result from his conduct. The risk must be of such a nature and degree that the actor's failure to perceive it, considering the nature and purpose of his conduct and the circumstances known to him, involves a gross deviation from the standard of care that a reasonable person would observe in the actor's situation.

As discussed in the previous Sections, to be convicted of a crime, the defendant must have committed a criminal act (*actus reus*), or failed to act when there is a legal duty to do so. However, a crime is not committed if the mind of the person doing the act is innocent. The second requirement, then, to constitute a crime is that the act, except as otherwise provided by statute, must be accompanied by a criminal intent on the part of the accused or by such negligent and reckless conduct as to be regarded by the law as equivalent to criminal intent. This criminal state of mind (*mens rea*) must be combined with the criminal act.

The reasoning is that it is not the policy of the law to hold individuals or groups criminally liable unless their activities clearly show an intention to commit, aid, advise and encourage (willfully and intentionally) a criminal act. To put this differently, the criminal intent or negligence generally must unite with the overt act, or there must be a union or joint operation of the criminal act and intention.[35] The criminal intent need not have existed for any length of time before the act, so long as it existed at the instant of the act.[36]

Over the years, the courts have wrestled with the problem of criminal intent. Part of the problem is that the courts, after first declaring that criminal intent is a prerequisite to guilt, have had some difficulty in finding this criminal intent when the act is committed through recklessness or negligence. Except in strict liability offenses, the *mens rea* requirement for the various crimes traditionally falls into three categories: general intent, specific intent or negligence. In the case of *People v. Hood* the majority of the Supreme Court of California acknowledged that "Specific and general intent have been notoriously difficult terms to define and apply."[37] The Court went on to distinguish between the two, however, especially in cases involving crimes committed by an intoxicated offender. Others, too, have argued that the courts should acknowledge that, for some crimes, intent is not needed, but that recklessness or negligence will suffice. In fact, many statutes have, in effect, done away with the traditional distinction and have substituted "purposely," "knowingly," "recklessly" and "negligently."[38]

As the terms "general intent," "specific intent," and "negligence" often appear when discussing *mens rea*, they are defined here.

1. General intent

General intent is present when one consciously chooses to do a prohibited act. The only state of mind required is an intent to commit the act constituting the crime. The person charged need not have intended to violate the law, nor need he have been aware that the law made the act criminal. If specific intent is not required as an element of the crime, general intent may be inferred from the fact that the defendant engaged in the conduct prohib-

---

[35] United States v. Lester, 363 F.2d 68 (6th Cir. 1967), *cert. denied*, 385 U.S. 1002 (1967).

[36] State v. Morgan, 22 Utah 162, 61 P. 527 (1900).

[37] 1 Cal. 3d 444, 462 P.2d 370 (1969).

[38] *See* Model Penal Code, § 2.02 (Proposed Official Draft 1980). *See also*, Ohio Rev. Code Ann., § 2901.21 (Page 1987) and Ky. Rev. Stat. § 501.00 for other definitions of the required state of mind.

ited. In other words, one who voluntarily commits an act is presumed to have intended that act.[39]

2. Specific intent

Specific intent means that the prosecution must show that the person charged purposely intended to violate the law. If the statute defining a crime includes a specific intent as an ingredient of criminality, such intent must be established as any other element.[40] In such instances, proving general intent is insufficient. In discussing crimes and their elements in future chapters, specific intent will be given further attention where it is an element of the crime.

3. Negligence

In criminal law, negligence is failure to perform a duty owed by the person charged where such conduct is reckless and indifferent to the consequences. It must be more, or of a greater degree, than "ordinary negligence."[41] Criminal negligence is not established simply by the fact that the defendant failed to exercise "due care;" the negligence must involve a higher probability of harm than is necessary for purposes of imposing civil liability. But where a statute adopts degrees of negligence as a basis for fixing criminal responsibility, the court must give effect to them, even though they are not recognized in civil cases.[42]

Where the required mental state is defined in other terms by statute, such as knowingly, wantonly or recklessly, these definitions must be used in proving guilt.[43]

Before concluding the study concerning criminal state of mind, attention is called to the fact that the legislature may make an act criminal without regard to the intent or knowledge of the doer. This is especially true where the offense is *malum prohibitum*. In such cases, the doing of the prohibited act constitutes the crime, and moral turpitude, motive or knowledge of its criminal character, are immaterial circumstances on the question of guilt. Such

---

[39] State v. Carlson, 5 Wis. 2d 595, 93 N.W.2d 354 (1958).

[40] U.S. v. Schneidermann, 106 F.Supp. 906 (Ca. 1952).

[41] Copeland v. State, 154 Tenn. 7, 285 S.W. 565 (1966).

[42] State v. Bolsinger, 221 Minn. 154, 21 N.W.2d 480 (1946).

[43] *See* Model Penal Code, § 2.02 (Proposed Official Draft 1980), for the general requirement of culpability.

legislation is enacted and is upheld on the grounds of necessity and is generally not violative of federal or constitutional prohibitions.[44]

§ 2.6 Causation

This provision is included in the Model Criminal Code.

§ 2.03 Causal Relationship Between Conduct and Result; Divergence Between Result Designed or Contemplated and Actual Result, or Between Probable and Actual Result[45]

(1)   Conduct is the cause of a result when:

    (a)   it is an antecedent but for which the result in question would not have occurred; and

    (b)   the relationship between the conduct and result satisfied any additional causal requirements imposed by the Code or by the law defining the offense.

In order for one to be guilty of a crime, his act or omission must have been the proximate cause thereof. Therefore, the prosecution must not only show that:

(1)   a specific party or parties were involved,

(2)   criminal acts or omissions occurred, and

(3)   the existence of a criminal state of mind in certain instances, but also

(4)   the alleged unlawful act or omission must be so integrated with and related to the offense that it can be said to have approximately caused or contributed to it.

In some instances, there is little difficulty in showing that the conduct was the proximate cause of the crime, or to say this another way, the offense was the direct result of the act. In other instances, this becomes very difficult.[46]

---

[44]   Smith v. California, 361 U.S. 147, 80 S. Ct. 215, 4 L.Ed. 205 (1959).

[45]   Model Penal Code, § 2.03(1) (Proposed Official Draft 1980).

[46]   Mitchell v. State, 43 Ala. App. 427, 191 So. 2d 385 (Ala. Ct. App. 1966).

One whose act or omission results in a criminal offense is guilty of the crime, even though other forces or causes contributed thereto, and even though intervening causes were involved.[47] For example, where the defendant struck the deceased, who was a hemophiliac, once on the jaw with his fist, which resulted in a hemorrhage from which the deceased died ten days later, the defendant was properly convicted of manslaughter.[48] The court explained in the *Frazier* case that it is immaterial that the defendant did not know that the deceased was in a feebled condition, which facilitated the killing, or that he did not reasonably anticipate the result would cause death.

If the act of the accused started a legal chain of causation which led directly to the result, he is guilty of the crime. Where, for example, the defendant struck the victim, knocking him unconscious, and while unconscious, the victim attempted to vomit and choked to death, the defendant's act was the proximate cause of death.[49] The fact that the defendant did not anticipate causing death by choking made no difference, as there were no intervening factors. In the case of *United States v. Hamilton*, the defendant was found guilty of manslaughter, even though the death of the victim was the result of the victim pulling out supporting tubes while he was in a semi-conscious condition after being taken to the hospital as the result of wounds inflicted by the defendant.[50] In this case, the court repeated:

> It is well settled that if a person strikes another and inflicts a blow that may not be mortal in and of itself but thereby starts a chain of causation that leads to death, he is guilty of homicide. This is true even if the deceased contributes to his own death or hastens it by failing to take the proper treatment.

The court concluded that injuries inflicted upon the deceased by the defendant were the cause of death, as the defendant was responsible for putting the victim in the position where he could cause his own death.

On the other hand, if there is a superseding intervening factor, an independent act or occurrence that supersedes the defendant's act as the legally significant causal factor, then the defendant's conduct will not be the legal *cause* of the result. To constitute a supervening cause the independent occurrence must be:

---

[47] United States v. Guillette, 547 F.2d 743 (2d Cir. 1977), *cert. denied*, 434 U.S. 389 (1977). *See* case in Part II.

[48] State v. Frazier, 339 Mo. 966, 98 S.W.2d 707 (1936).

[49] People v. Geiger, 10 Mich. App. 339, 159 N.W.2d 383 (Mich. Ct. App. 1968).

[50] United States v. Hamilton, 182 F.Supp. 548 (DC 1960).

(a) intervening,
(b) unforeseeable, and
(c) the sole direct cause of the result.

For example, if the victim is taken to a hospital after being injured by defendant, and the injury would not normally be serious, but the victim contracts scarlet fever from a doctor and dies of the disease, the proximate cause is the disease rather than the original injury.[51] Here the contracting of scarlet fever is unforeseeable and a superseding factor. However, if surgery is performed after a shooting by the defendant and the victim dies as a result of failure to provide adequate blood transfusions, this is not a superseding factor as the risk of surgery is ordinarily considered foreseeable.

What is the proximate cause of death if a non-fatal wound is inflicted by one person and a fatal wound is inflicted by the second? This was the situation in the case of *Bennett v. Commonwealth*, where one brother fired a shot which entered the front of the victim and another brother fired a shot which entered the back.[52] Joe Bennett, who inflicted the wound in front, which he claimed was not the fatal wound, claimed that the court erred in instructing the jury to find him guilty if he shot Lawson "so as to cause or hasten his death." He claimed that, although he shot Lawson, it was not his, but his brother's shot, which caused the death. The court, in holding that the instruction was correct, made this comment:

> These brothers, according to the testimony, both shot Lawson in the one encounter. The law will not stop, in such a case to measure which wound is the more serious, and to speculate upon which actually caused the death. In many such cases the Commonwealth would be helpless; for each defendant would go free because it could not be proven against him that his wound is the fatal one. Whether one actually inflicts the fatal wound, or contributes or hastens the death in some minor way, he is guilty of the crime.

§ 2.7   Concurrence – Criminal Act and State of Mind

Although this principle is not as well known, and becomes an issue in relatively few cases, it should be commented upon. In some situations, in order to convict a person of an offense, there must be a showing that the mental fault actuates the act or omission. If the crime is one that requires some

---

[51]   Busch v. Commonwealth, 78 Ky. 268 (1880).
[52]   150 Ky. 604, 150 S.W. 806 (1912).

mental fault such as "intention," "knowledge" or "negligence," in addition to the act or omission, the physical act and the state of mind must concur. For example, in some states, the crime of first degree burglary is committed when the person "knowingly enters or remains unlawfully in a dwelling with the intent to commit a crime." Under the principle of concurrence, the intent to steal must be concurrent with the entry or with unlawful remaining in the dwelling.[53] If the intention or the mental fault does not exist at the time of the entry, then that particular crime has not occurred. In criminal law, the intent will not relate back to the entry. Of course, the person might be found guilty of another offense where the mental fault is not in issue.

To state this principle more succinctly, one might have the *mens rea*, but not commit the act, or one might act without intent or mental fault. Unless there is a concurrence between the two, there is no crime.

This does not mean that a person must have (in intent cases) the intent to do a particular harm to a particular person. For example, A's intent to kill B may suffice as to his causing the death of C. This is sometimes referred to as "transferred intent." This is applicable only within the limits of the same crime, however, as for example, A's intent to kill B would not suffice as to causing the burning of C's property. That is, while a defendant can be convicted when he has both the *mens rea* and commits the *actus reus* required for a given offense, he cannot be convicted if the *mens rea* relates to one crime and the *actus reus* to another. The drafters of Model Penal Code in providing for this principle included a provision that the elements of "purposely" or "knowingly" causing a particular result is not established when the actual result is not within the purpose of contemplation of the actor.[54]

§ 2.8 Attendant Circumstances

Before concluding the principles of criminal liability, mention must be made of the fact that, in some crimes, proof must be offered to show that certain circumstances existed at the time of the act in question. For example, the common law crime of burglary requires that the entry be made in the night time, the crime of receiving stolen property requires that the goods received be stolen goods, and bigamy requires proof of a previous marriage. Also, statutory rape requires that the girl be underage and perjury requires that the person be sworn. In these cases, evidence must be offered to prove that the circumstances existed at the time the act occurred. Thus, evidence must be

---

[53] Jackson v. State, 102 Ala. 167, 15 So. 344 (1894).

[54] *See* Model Penal Code, § 2.03 (Proposed Official Draft 1980), and the other included exceptions.

introduced in a statutory rape case to show that the victim was under the statutory age.

In some instances these attendant circumstances are listed as elements of the crime as will be noted in some of the future paragraphs.

§ 2.9　Strict Liability

This provision describing liability is included in the Model Penal Code.

§ 2.05 When Culpability Requirements Are Inapplicable to Violations and to Offenses Defined by Other Statutes; Effect of Absolute Liability in Reducing Grade of Offenses to Violation[55]

(1) The requirements of culpability prescribed by §§ 2.01 and 2.02 do not apply to:

    (a) offenses which constitute violations, unless the requirement involved is included in the definition of the offense or the Court determines that its application is consistent with effective enforcement of the law defining the offense; or

    (b) offenses defined by statutes other than the Code, insofar as a legislative purpose to impose absolute liability for such offenses or with respect to any material element thereof plainly appears.

(2) Notwithstanding any other provision of existing law and unless a subsequent statute otherwise provides:

    (a) when absolute liability is imposed with respect to any material element of an offense defined by a statute other than the Code and a conviction is based upon such liability, the offense constitutes a violation; and

    (b) although absolute liability is imposed by law with respect to one or more of the material elements of an offense defined by a statute other than the Code, the culpable commission of the offense may be charged and proved, in which event negligence with respect to such elements constitutes sufficient culpability

---

[55] *See generally*, Model Penal Code, §§ 2.01, 2.02, 2.05 (Proposed Official Draft 1980).

and the classification of the offense and the sentence
that may be imposed therefor upon conviction are
determined by § 1.04 and Article 6 of the Code.

As indicated in § 2.5, a criminal intent or guilty knowledge is usually
considered an essential element of a crime. On the other hand, the legislature may forbid the doing of (or the failure to do) an act and make the
commission or omission criminal without regard to the intent or knowledge
of the doer. The rationale for such strict liability crimes is that, if the prosecution were required to prove the mental element, convictions would be so
difficult to obtain that the existence of the crime would not provide a deter-
rent to the conduct. The legislature might reason that it is important to reduce the harmful conduct at all cost even at the risk of convicting innocent-
minded persons as a result. Usually, but not always, the statutory crime-
without-fault is a misdemeanor offense, and courts have been more ready to
approve a statute which defines a misdemeanor rather than a felony.

Where such statutory crimes are approved, the doing of the prohibited
act constitutes the crime, and the moral turpitude or purity of the motive by
which it was promoted, and knowledge or innocence of its criminal character,
are immaterial circumstances on the question of guilt.[56]

A specific intent to violate the law is not essential, but only the intention
to do the specific forbidden act. The doer of the prohibited act may be liable
criminally even though he does not know the act is criminal or even know
that the law exists.[57] In the case of *United States v. Park*, a federal court reminded that a previous case (*Dotterweich*) dispensed with the need to prove
"awareness of wrongdoing" but not the need to prove "wrongful action."[58]

Although such liability is usually limited to the so-called "regulatory" or
"public welfare offenses" or to violations that carry only a relatively small
penalty and do not involve moral stigma, the rationale for not requiring
criminal intent has been held to apply in some *mala in se* crimes. The crimes
of bigamy and statutory rape are the classic examples of traditional crimes
that incorporate an element of strict liability. Under the majority rule, one
can be convicted of bigamy even though he reasonably believed that he was
unmarried at the time of the second marriage.[59] And one can be convicted

---

[56] Hargrove v. United States, 67 F.2d 820 (5th Cir. 1933).

[57] Landen v. United States, 299 F. 75 (6th Cir. 1924).

[58] United States v. Park, 499 F.2d 839 (4th Cir. 1974).

[59] People v. Vogel, 46 Cal. 2d 798, 299 P.2d 850 (1956).

of statutory rape even though he reasonably believed the female with whom he had intercourse was above the age of consent.[60]

Generally, when the offense is *malum prohibitum*, the courts find little problem with enforcing the statute where intent and knowledge are not elements of the crime and the statute makes it clear that they are not to be elements. On the other hand, the courts have had some difficulty with the statutory crimes where the penalty was more severe. Where the criminal statutes are empty of words denoting fault, but do not affirmatively provide for liability without fault, the courts have sometimes held that the statute means what it says and imposes criminal liability without regard to fault. Also, in some instances, the courts have read into the statutes some requirements of fault.[61] Making reference to this type of statutes, the Supreme Court reasoned:

> Neither this court nor, so far as we are aware, any other has undertaken to delineate a precise line or set forth comprehensive criteria for distinguishing between crimes that require a mental element and crimes that do not. We attempt no closed definition, for the law on the subject is neither settled nor static.

In reaching a compromise on the issue, the Model Penal Code provides that culpability is an element of all offenses, except in specific classes of crimes.[62] Under the Code, the maximum penalty for violation in strict liability situations is a fine.

For practical purposes, those involved in the criminal justice process, such as police, probation officers and corrections personnel, may generally rely upon the state statutes, which designate the requirements for criminal liability. For example, the Ohio Criminal Code provides:

> When the Section defining an offense does not specify any degree of culpability, and plainly indicates a purpose to impose strict criminal liability for the conduct described in such Sections, then culpability is not required for a person to be guilty of the offense. When the Section neither specifies culpability nor plainly indicates

---

[60] State v. Superior Court, 104 Ariz. 440, 454 P.2d 982 (1969). These crimes will be discussed more fully in later chapters.

[61] Morisette v. United States, 342 U.S. 246, 72 S. Ct. 240, 96 L.Ed. 288 (1952).

[62] *See* Model Penal Code, §§ 2.02(1), 2.05 (Proposed Official Draft 1980), *see also* LaFave & Scott, HANDBOOK ON CRIMINAL LAW 219 (1972).

a purpose to impose strict liability, recklessness is sufficient culpability to commit the offense.[63]

§ 2.10 Liability for the Acts of Others – Vicarious Liability

In previous Sections, it was indicated that, in order for a crime to be committed, there must be a concurrence of *actus reus* and *mens rea*. In the Section discussing the strict liability exception, it was pointed out that, in some instances, a person may be held strictly liable without the *mens rea*, or mental element, requirement. The second exception concerns situations in which liability may be imposed even though the acts were committed by others.

Vicarious liability, then, is liability for crimes committed by another person, imposed simply because of the relationship between the parties. Where the relationship exists, it is unnecessary to show that the defendant acted in any way or participated in the offense; it need only be established that the crime was committed by another person and that the defendant stood in the required relationship as stated by statute.

In most instances, vicarious liability applies where one conducting a business is made liable without personal fault for the conduct of someone else, generally an employee. For example, some criminal statutes specifically impose criminal liability upon the employer if his agent sells articles at short weight. And some statutes provide that persons under 14 shall not be employed at certain jobs.[64] These statutes are generally misdemeanor in character, and are construed to impose vicarious liability upon the employer even though the employer was not aware that his agent acted in violation of the statute.[65]

Statutes imposing criminal liability upon an innocent employer for the illegal conduct of his employee are generally upheld as constitutional.[66] That is, the courts have found that this is not violation of the due process clause. However, if the statute, as interpreted, imposes a jail sentence as well as a fine, there is a good possibility that the courts will find that this is a violation of due process.[67]

Although the vicarious liability concept will not arise in many situations, and generally it can be stated that this concept does not apply in felony situa-

[63]   Ohio Rev. Code Ann., § 2901.21(B) (Page 1987).

[64]   Ky. Rev. Stat., § 339.220.

[65]   In re Marley, 29 Cal. 2d 525, 175 P.2d 832 (Cal. Ct. App. 1946).

[66]   *Id.*

[67]   Pennsylvania v. Koczwara, 397 Pa. 575, A.2d 825 (1959).

tions, it is a concept that criminal justice personnel should be aware of, especially in enforcing minor statutory and regulatory laws.

§ 2.11 Summary

At common law, and by statute in some states, participants in crime are either principals or accessories. Principals are further divided into principals in the first degree and principals in the second degree. A principal in the first degree is one who actually commits the act which causes the crime to occur, while a principal in the second degree does not actually commit the crime himself, but instead aids or encourages the principal party to commit the crime, and is present at the scene.

An accessory also may be guilty of a criminal offense even though he did not actually participate in the crime and was not present when the crime occurred. Accessories are categorized as accessories before the fact and accessories after the fact. An accessory before the fact is one who counsels, procures or commands the principal to commit a criminal act, but who is too far away to aid in the felonious act. An accessory after the fact is one who gives comfort, or assists another, after the crime has occurred, knowing that the other has committed a felony, in order to hinder the perpetrator's apprehension, prosecution or conviction.

Most modern statutes dispense with the distinctions between principals and accessories, and hold persons legally accountable if they commit the act, solicit the commission of offense, aid in commission or fail to take proper efforts to prevent it in some instances. Modern statutes treat the accessory after the fact as a misdemeanant, even though the act itself was a felony.

In order for a person to be convicted of a crime, the prosecution must show that the person charged committed a prohibited act or failed to act where he had the legal obligation to do so. This principle, referred to as *actus reus*, may involve an actual physical movement or may consist of verbal acts. However, one cannot be punished for evil intent without an act, nor for a violation of a statute which makes status alone a violation. Although in the usual case, an affirmative act is required to support a conviction, in some instances, liability can rest upon failure to act where there was a legal responsibility to do so.

The second requirement to constitute a crime is that the act, except as otherwise provided by statute, must be accompanied by criminal intent on the part of the accused, or by such negligence and reckless conduct as to be regarded by the law as equivalent to criminal intent. This criminal state of mind is referred to as *mens rea*. The reasoning for requiring the *mens rea* is that the law is generally interested in punishing only those who are morally wrong.

The third requirement is that the alleged unlawful act or omission must be so integrated with and related to the offense that it can be said to have approximately caused or contributed to it. In other words, the prosecution must show that the conduct was the proximate cause of the crime. This principle is often referred to as *causation*.

In some crimes, it is necessary not only for the prosecution to prove:

(1) that the person acted or refrained from acting when he had a legal duty to do so,
(2) that this was accompanied by a criminal intent (*mens rea*), and
(3) that the act or omission resulted in the criminal offense, but also the prosecution must introduce evidence to show
(4) the physical act and state of mind were in concurrence.

That is, the prosecution must show that the intention or mental fault existed *at the time* the act was perpetrated.

Likewise, in some situations, where the crime involves the existence of certain circumstances, these circumstances must be proved to exist. For example, in a statutory rape case, the prosecution must show that the victim was under the statutory age.

Although in criminal law guilty knowledge is usually considered an essential element of a crime, legislatures have, in some instances, held persons strictly liable for acts. In such instances, the doing of the prohibited act constitutes the crime, and moral turpitude is immaterial on the question of guilt.

Finally, in some situations, liability may be imposed even though the acts were committed by others. In most instances, this "vicarious liability" applies only where one conducting a business is made liable without personal fault for the conduct of someone else, generally an employee. These statutes have been upheld; especially if the penalty is a fine rather than a jail sentence.

Criminal justice personnel must be familiar with these general principles of criminal liability and be prepared to introduce evidence to prove the essential elements of crimes. A knowledge of these principles will be especially helpful in considering the elements of specific crimes, as discussed in future chapters.

Chapter 3
OFFENSES AGAINST PERSONS (EXCLUDING SEX OFFENSES)

In order that one may commit homicide the first requisite is that he be the cause of the death of the deceased; in other words, the deceased must be shown to have been killed by the act or agency of the accused. The form or manner of death and the means or instrument with which it was committed are immaterial.

Miller, *Criminal Law*, § 82 (1934).

§ 3.1 Introduction

For purposes of discussion, crimes are often classified according to social harm caused. Other approaches could be made, but most statutes and most codes have adopted a similar system for classifying crimes, and there is no valid argument for changing. Therefore, in this and future chapters, crimes are placed by categories for discussion purposes only.

Although the terminology is often "offenses against a person" and "offenses against the habitation," what is really meant is that this is an offense against the state in the form of harm to the person as well as an offense against the state in the form of harm to the habitation. In the so-called "offenses against property," the defendant is prosecuted in the interest of the state, and not in the interest of the individual whose property was involved, although, of course, the individual who owns the property is concerned.[1] When searching state statutes for specific laws, criminal justice personnel should bear in mind that these classifications exist, although they are not the same in all statutes. For example, in the Ohio Revised Criminal Code, the crimes are generally categorized as homicide and assault, kidnapping and extortion, sex offenses, arson and related offenses, offenses against the public peace, offenses against family and offenses against justice and public administration.[2]

In this book, the discussion is divided into these segments:

(1) offenses against persons excluding sex crimes,
(2) offenses against the person, sex crimes,
(3) offenses against property, destruction and intrusion offenses,
(4) offenses against property involving theft,
(5) offenses involving property (forgery, counterfeiting and other fraudulent practices)
(6) offenses against the public health and morals,
(7) offenses against the public peace, and
(8) offenses against justice and public administration.

In this chapter, (after first defining and explaining homicide in general) the specific crimes of murder, manslaughter, suicide, assault and battery, kidnapping and related offenses: mayhem, and other crimes against the person are explained. As one must look to the common law for definitions and explanations, and because the laws vary from state to state, the common law is

---

[1] People v. Gilliam, 141 Cal. App. 2d 824, 297 P.2d 468 (Cal. Dist. Ct. App. 1956).
[2] Ohio Rev. Code Ann., § 2903 *et seq.* (Page 1987).

discussed along with some of the crimes included in the Model Penal Code and the statutes which represent the law in some states.

§ 3.2 Homicide

A. Traditional Definitions and Interpretations

The fact that an illegal act has been committed and death occurs as a result of that act does not necessarily mean that a homicide has been committed. Homicide is generally defined as the killing of a human being by another human being.[3] Homicide has also been defined as the killing of a human being under any circumstances, by the act, agency or omission of another.[4] The use of "another" separates homicide from suicide. According to the most modern definitions, suicide is not a homicide, and may or may not be a crime, depending on the statutory provisions of the jurisdiction.

Applying this definition, it is not homicide for a man to kill an animal or for an animal to kill a man.[5] It is a homicide if an animal is used as a means of killing another person. Here, the law attributes the killing of the human to the one who set in motion the means of causing death.

A homicide is not committed unless the death results from an act of another human being. For example, when one dies as a result of an accident where other persons are not involved, the death is not considered a homicide. And when one drowns without fault of any other persons, this is not a homicide.

In defining homicide, the term "killing" is a key word. Traditionally, the end of a life of a person occurs when the cardiac and respiratory functions have ceased. In one case, the court noted that "when the heart stopped beating and the lungs stopped breathing, the individual was dead according to physicians and according to law."[6]

Today, there is some question concerning this definition of death. As medical science is able to maintain cardiorespiratory systems even after the brain is dead, a brain-dead statute has been suggested. Some states have enacted such legislation, however, most cases have rendered decisions based upon the common law definition of death.

The National Conference of Commissioners for Uniform Laws proposed the Uniform Brain Death Act that provides "for legal and medical

---

[3] Kinsey v. State, 49 Ariz. 201, 65 P.2d 1141 (1937).

[4] See Wharton, HOMICIDE, 3d ed., page 1, § 1.

[5] Kinsey v. State, 49 Ariz. 201, 65 P.2d 1141 (1937).

[6] In re Welfare Bowman, 94 N.W.2d 407, 617 P.2d 731 (1980).

purposes an individual who has sustained irreversible cessation of all functioning of the brain, including the brain stem, is dead." This uniform law states that a determination of brain death must be made "in accordance with reasonable medical standards."

Another attempt to define death is included in the proposed Uniform Determination of Death Act.[7] This provides "An individual who has sustained either (1) irreversible cessation of circulatory and respiratory functions, or (2) irreversible cessation of all functions of the entire brain, including the brain stem, is dead. A determination of death must be made in accordance with accepted medical standards."

Even without such statutes, some courts have determined that death has occurred when the victim is brain dead.[8] It is safe to predict that a defendant will find it difficult to avoid conviction for murder by claiming that removing a life-saving device caused death when the victim is brain dead as a result of an act by the defendant.

B. Statutes and Codes

1. Model Penal Code

§ 210.1 Criminal Homicide[9]

(1) A person is guilty of criminal homicide if he purposely, knowingly, recklessly or negligently causes the death of another human being.

(2) Criminal homicide is murder, manslaughter or negligent homicide.

The Model Criminal Code classifies all criminal homicides into the three basic categories of murder, manslaughter and negligent homicide. Under this provision, the three elements of homicide to be proven are:

(a) purposely, knowingly, recklessly or negligently,
(b) causing death,
(c) of another human being.

---

[7] Uniform Determination of Death Act, 12 Uniform Law Ann., 1987 Pocket Part 287.

[8] State v. Fierro, 124 Ariz. 182, 603 P.2d 746 (1979); Commonwealth v. Goldston, 366 N.E.2d 744 (1987).

[9] Model Penal Code, § 210.1 (Proposed Official Draft 1980).

2. Other statutes and codes

Some states have adopted much of the wording of the Model Penal Code, but have retained a distinction between degrees of murder in order to provide a distinction for death penalty purposes.[10] Other states have divided manslaughter into degrees.[11]

C. Distinguishing Elements of Homicide

Although the law of homicide has been changed greatly by statute, one can get an overall concept of the common law relating to homicide if the elements of the various crimes are summarized and distinguished.

Murder -- first degree (aggravated or premeditated)
(a) Unlawful killing
(b) One person by another
(c) With malice aforethought
(d) With deliberation, purpose, design or premeditation

Murder
(a) Unlawful killing
(b) One person by another
(c) With malice aforethought

Voluntary manslaughter
(a) Unlawful killing
(b) One person by another
(c) Intentional killing but with adequate provocation and committed in the heat of passion

Involuntary manslaughter
(a) Unlawful killing
(b) One person by another

---

[10] Examples are Ariz., Ark., Conn., Fla., Ind., Mont., N.H., N.M., N.Y., Pa., Tex., Utah and Wash.

[11] Examples are Conn., Ga., Ill., Ind., Iowa, Kan., Ky., Minn., N.M., N.Y., Or., S.D., Tex. and Wash.

§ 3.3 Murder

A. Traditional Definitions and Elements

1. Common law elements

At common law, and traditionally, in the United States, murder is defined as a homicide committed with malice aforethought. A definition which includes the elements is that murder is the "unlawful killing of a human being by another human being with malice aforethought." As the prosecutor is required to introduce evidence to prove each of the specific elements, each of the elements are discussed.

a. Unlawful killing

In homicide, a killing is unlawful unless it comes in the justifiable or excusable category. Homicide is justifiable if it is either commanded or authorized by law; for example, the killing of an enemy on the field of battle as an act of war and within the rules of war. Another example is the execution of the sentence of death pronounced by a competent tribunal.

Excusable homicide is that committed by one doing a lawful act without intention to hurt, or in self defense. If death occurs by accident while the person causing the death is engaged in a lawful act and performing it with due care, the homicide is excusable.[12] Under the common law rule, a homicide is excusable if the accused kills his adversary as a necessary means of saving his own life even though the death occurs as a result of combat which might have been avoided initially.[13]

The distinction between justifiable and excusable homicide was important under the common law, as excusable homicide resulted in forfeiture of goods, however, the distinction is not as important today, as neither entails any responsibility. Today, the two terms are often used synonymously.[14]

b. A human being

In the absence of a statute, a person cannot be convicted of murder unless the person whose death occurred was born alive. As one court stated,

---

[12] U.S. v. Meacher, 37 F. 875 (1888); People v. Lyons, 110 N.Y. 618, 17 N.E. 391 (1888).

[13] Gill v. State, 134 Tenn. 591, 184 S.W. 864 (1960).

[14] Hammond v. State, 147 Ala. 79, 41 So. 761 (1906).

"there is no murder without homicide, and no homicide without birth alive."[15] However, some states have amended the statute to define murder as the "unlawful killing of a human being or a fetus."[16]

c. By another human being

Proof that the killing was by another human being requires that evidence be produced to show that the person charged committed the act or put into motion the means which resulted in the death.

d. Malice aforethought

To prove malice aforethought is sometimes difficult, as, under the modern interpretation, it is not necessary to prove either malice as it is commonly defined, nor aforethought. Therefore, it is preferable not to rely upon this misleading expression for an understanding of murder.

At early common law, the courts did require at least an attempt to kill, plus an element of hatred, spite or ill will, in order to bring the killing within the malice definition. Also, at first, the judges required that the prosecution prove the defendant actually had a previously thought-out intent to kill, though probably spite was never actually necessary.[17] Gradually, the judges in England came to recognize that a murder may be committed, even though there was no actual intent to kill. The older authorities resorted to an "implied intent" rationale where no intent, in fact, existed. Now the courts speak more factually and say frankly that murder may be committed under some circumstances without intent to kill.[18]

This excerpt from the report of the Royal Commission on Capital Punishment sheds some light on the meaning of malice aforethought:

> The meaning of "malice aforethought," which is the distinguishing criterion of murder, is certainly not beyond the range of controversy. The first thing that must be said about it is that neither of the two words is used in its ordinary sense... It is now only an arbitrary symbol. For the "malice" may have in it nothing really malicious; and need never really be "aforethought" except in the sense

---

[15] Keeler v. Superior Court, 80 Cal. Rptr. 865 (Cal. App. 1969).

[16] Cal. Penal Code, § 187 (1970).

[17] See generally, Moreland, THE LAW OF HOMICIDE (1952); Perkins, The Law of Homicide, 36 J. CRIM. L. & CRIM. 391 (1946).

[18] People v. Hartwell, 341 Ill. 155, 173 N.E. 112 (1930). See also, State v. Russell, 106 Utah 116, 145 P.2d 1003 (1944).

that every desire must necessarily come before -- though perhaps only an instant before -- the act which is desired. The word "aforethought," in the definition, has thus become either false or else superfluous. The word "malice" is neither; but is apt to be misleading, for it is not employed in its original (and its popular) meaning. "Malice aforethought" is simply a comprehensive name for a number of different mental attitudes which have been variously defined at different stages in the development of the law, the presence of any one of which in the accused has been held by the courts to render a homicide particularly heinous and therefore to make it murder...[19]

Malice need not be exhibited toward the person killed. For example, if one has malice toward a person or group of persons but instead kills someone else, this is sufficient to bring the crime within the category of murder.[20] Malice also may be present even though the killing is a "mercy killing."[21] And in a 1977 case, the Arizona Supreme Court agreed with the lower court that malice can be implied when the circumstances show an "abandoned and malignant heart."[22] In this case, the defendant was charged with the murder of his wife. The defendant had consumed a large amount of alcohol, and moved for a directed verdict of acquittal of the charge of first degree murder on the ground that the evidence presented was insufficient as a matter of law for the jury to find the requisite premeditation and malice. The court would not sustain a finding of premeditation, but did sustain a verdict of second degree murder, finding that defendant's conduct showed malice.

In a federal case in 1983, the court explained that malice required for a conviction of first and second degree murder does not require subjective intent to kill, but may be established by evidence of conduct which is reckless, wanton and a gross deviation from reasonable standards of care, of such a nature that the jury is warranted in inferring that the defendant was aware of a serious risk of death or serious bodily harm.[23]

In another homicide case, where death occurred as a result of a fatal stabbing, it was proper to instruct the jury that malice could be inferred from use of a deadly weapon.[24] In the *Vallez* case, the court instructed that malice

---

[19] Report of the Royal Commission on Capital Punishment 26-28 (1953).

[20] Banks v. State, 85 Tex. Crim. 165, 211 S.W. 217 (1919).

[21] Commonwealth v. Noxon, 319 Mass. 495, 66 N.E.2d 814 (1946).

[22] State v. Lacquey, 571 P.2d 1027 (1977).

[23] U.S. v. Shaw, C.A. Miss. 1983, 701 F.2d 367, *rehearing denied*, 714 F.2d 544, *cert. denied*, 104 S. Ct. 1419 (1983).

[24] U.S. v. Vallez, 653 F.2d 403 (1981).

could be inferred where the victim was stabbed six times during the struggle with the defendant and the codefendant, and where one witness saw the defendant stab the victim while the codefendant held him down and another witness saw the defendant wielding a "rock in a sock" while the codefendant wielded a knife.

2. Degrees of murder

In most states, the legislatures decided very early that the crime of murder should be divided into two categories for the purpose of fixing the penalty. In these states, first degree murder encompasses intent to commit murder, accompanied by premeditation and deliberation. In some states, the first degree category of murder includes murder by lying in wait, by poison or by torture.

The distinguishing factors in first degree murder are premeditation and deliberation. Where these terms are used, the prosecution must show not only that there was malice, but, in addition, he must prove premeditation and/or deliberation. It is difficult to define premeditation and deliberation, but not as difficult as it is to define malice. Perhaps the best definition is that it requires a time of reflection. Premeditation means that one did, in fact, reflect, at least for a short period of time, before his act of killing.[25]

In a 1983 case, a federal court explained that, although deliberation and premeditation involves prior design to commit murder, no particular period of time is necessary for such deliberation and premeditation.[26] In a second case, the court held that, in a murder prosecution, it is not a question of how long the defendant may have deliberated before the homicide, since no particular length of time is necessary for deliberation and premeditation which will make a homicide first degree murder.[27] Another example of premeditation was mentioned in the case of *United States v. Blue Thunder*, where the court commented that the jury is generally allowed to infer premeditation from the fact that the defendant brought a deadly weapon to the scene of the murder.[28]

---

[25] State v. Bowser, 214 N.C. 249, 199 S.E. 31 (1938). *See also*, State v. Hutchins, 303 N.C. 321, 279 S.E.2d 788 (1981). In *State v. Hutchins*, the North Carolina Supreme Court reaffirmed that premeditation and deliberation may be inferred from circumstantial evidence. The court also determined that no fixed time is required for these mental processes to occur.

[26] U.S. v. Shaw, 701 F.2d 367 (1983).

[27] Weakley v. U.S., 198 F.2d 940 (1952).

[28] U.S. v. Blue Thunder, 604 F.2d 550, *cert. denied*, 444 U.S. 902, 62 L.Ed.2d 139, 100 S. Ct. 215 (1979).

Second degree murder (in those states that divide the crime) is defined as a killing committed without deliberation or premeditation, but with malice aforethought.

3. Felony-murder

In England, a doctrine gradually developed which came to be known as the felony-murder doctrine. Under the early English law, one who, in the commission or attempted commission of any felony, caused another's death could be found guilty of murder. Under this doctrine, no consideration was given to the dangerous nature of the felony involved, or to the likelihood that death might result from the defendant's manner of committing or attempting the felony.[29] Blackstone's view was that: "If one intends to do another a felony, and undesignedly kills a man, this is also murder."[30] The justification for this rule is that it places upon one committing or attempting a felony the hazard of possible guilt of murder if he creates any substantial risk which could result in the loss of life. According to this reasoning, common experience points to the presence of a substantial human risk from the perpetration of some felonies.

When the felony-murder doctrine was originated, it was included to protect human life, but at that time there were few felonies. Later, as the number of felonies multiplied so as to include a great number of relatively minor offenses, many of which involved no great danger to life or limb, it became necessary, in order to alleviate the harshness of the rule, to limit it to certain felonies. Therefore, in many states the felony-murder rule has been limited in scope by a requirement that the felony attempted or committed by the defendant must be dangerous to life.[31] Other courts have required that the felony be one which was a felony at common law; for example, rape, sodomy, robbery, burglary, arson, mayhem or larceny.[32]

The felony-murder rule can produce some harsh results. For example, a defendant may be found guilty of a felony-murder even though he is not aware that the felony he is about to commit is one included in the statute defining felony-murder. In a New York case, the defendant attempted to snatch the pocketbook of a woman standing on the subway platform and, when the woman resisted, she was pulled between the train and the platform, causing her death. The defendant was convicted of felony-murder and, on appeal, argued that the purse-snatching cannot be anything more than

---

[29] Regina v. Serne, 16 (Cox) CC 311 (1887).

[30] Davis v. State, 246 Ala. 101, 19 So. 2d 358 (1944).

[31] People v. Pavlic, 227 Mich. 562, 199 N.W. 373 (1924).

[32] Idaho Code, § 18-4003 (1979).

larceny, which would not support a conviction for felony-murder. However, the court upheld the conviction, reasoning that a purse-snatching unaccompanied by any resistance on the part of the victim, is generally insufficient to constitute a robbery. However, in this case, there was sufficient evidence to support a jury finding that the victim resisted, by clinging to her purse, and that the overcoming of the resistance made the offense attempted robbery.[33] As the death occurred during the attempted commission of a felony, the murder conviction was proper.

In the *Enmund v. Florida* case, the defendant was convicted, along with his codefendant, of first degree robbery and murder of two elderly persons in their farmhouse, and both were sentenced to death.[34] The defendant claimed that, as he was not present at the killings, but that he was only the driver of the car parked by the side of the road near the farmhouse at the time of the killings, the imposition of the death sentence was inconsistent with the Eighth and Fourteenth Amendments. The Supreme Court of the United States agreed. The majority pointed out that only a small minority of states (nine) allowed the death penalty to be imposed solely because the defendant somehow participated in the robbery in the course of which a murder was committed, but did not take or intend to take life, or intend that lethal force be employed.

The court also indicated that, while robbery is a serious crime deserving serious punishment, it is not a crime so grievous an affront to humanity that the only adequate response may be the penalty of death. The court concluded that putting the defendant to death to avenge two killings that he did not commit or intend to commit or cause would not measurably contribute to the retribution end of insuring that the criminal gets his just deserts.

In the case of *Tison v. Arizona*, in 1987, the Supreme Court affirmed the defendant's conviction for capital murder under the state's felony-murder and accomplice-liability statutes. The defendants had attacked their death sentence in a state post-conviction proceeding alleging that the *Enmund v. Florida* case discussed above required a finding of "intent to kill." They argued that the finding in the *Enmund* case included situations in which the defendant intended, contemplated or anticipated that lethal force would or might be used, or that life would or might be taken in accomplishing the underlying felony. To understand this argument, it is necessary to look at some of the facts of the case.[35]

---

[33] People v. Santiago, 62 A.D.2d 572, 405 N.Y.S.2d 752 (1958). In the case of *State v. Hutchins*, 303 N.C. 321, 279 S.E.2d 788 (1981), the court upheld a felony murder instruction where the underlying felony was the murder of a third person.

[34] Enmund v. Florida, 458 U.S. 782, 73 L.Ed.2d 1140, 102 S. Ct. 3368 (1982).

[35] Tison v. Arizona, 482 U.S. 921, 95 L.Ed.2d 127, 107 S. Ct. 1676 (1987).

The petitioners in the *Tison* case were brothers who, along with other members of the family, planned and effected the escape of their father from prison, where he was serving a life sentence for having killed a guard in a previous escape. The petitioners entered the prison with a chest filled with guns, armed their father and another convicted murderer, and later helped to abduct, detain and rob a family of four, and watched as their father and the other convict murdered the members of that family with shotguns. Although the petitioners stated that they were surprised by the shooting, they made no effort to help the victims, and, in fact, drove away in the victims' car with the rest of the escape party. In their argument to the Supreme Court, they claimed that, as they had no "intent" to kill, as required in the *Enmund* case, they should not be found guilty of first degree murder and sentenced to death.

The majority of the U.S. Supreme Court agreed that the Eighth Amendment does not prohibit the death penalty as disproportionate in the case of a defendant whose participation in a felony that results in murder is major and whose mental state is one of reckless indifference. In explaining their decision, the majority referred to a survey of state felony murder laws and judicial decisions after *Enmund*, which indicate a societal consensus that a combination of factors may justify the death penalty, even without a specific "intent to kill." However, as the Arizona Supreme Court had affirmed, the death sentences upon a finding that the defendants had "intended, contemplated, or anticipated that lethal force would or might be used or that life might be taken," the case was remanded.

In summary, while the felony-murder rule had some restrictions in application, a defendant may be found guilty of murder even if he does not "intend to kill" or participate in the act which results in the killing. He may be found guilty and may receive the death penalty if the court finds a reckless disregard for human life in combination with major participation in the felony resulting in the death.

B. Statutes and Codes

Some states have modified the common law relating to murder, others have adopted the Model Penal Code in substance; while still others have taken parts of the Model Penal Code and retained parts of their previously written statutes. The Model Code relating to murder contains much of the wording of the common law, but provides that murder committed in a perpetration, or an attempt to perpetrate, other crimes will be murder in the first degree only if certain designated crimes are involved.

As the Model Penal Code has had great influence on the revision of the state laws, parts of that code are included, as well as some of the rationale for the changes recommended. Also, some state codes are included to exemplify the modifications. The federal statute, as amended in 1984, defines the law that applies when a person is charged with murder under the federal law.

1. Model Penal Code

§ 210.2 Murder[36]
(1) Except as provided in § 210.3(1)(b), criminal homicide constitutes murder when:

    (a) it is committed purposely or knowingly; or
    (b) it is committed recklessly under circumstances manifesting extreme indifference to the value of human life. Such recklessness and indifference are presumed if the actor is engaged or is an accomplice in the commission of, or an attempt to commit, or flight after committing or attempting to commit robbery, rape or deviate sexual intercourse by force or threat of force, arson, burglary, kidnapping or felonious escape.

(2) Murder is a felony of the first degree [but a person convicted of murder may be sentenced to death, as provided in § 210.6].

The Model Penal Code makes no reference to such terms as "malice aforethought" and "premeditation," but instead substitutes a new grading structure. Under § 210.2(1)(a) a person may be found guilty of murder if the killing was purposely or knowingly done. These terms are defined in § 2.02 as follows:

(1) Minimum Requirements of Culpability. Except as provided in § 2.05, a person is not guilty of an offense unless he acted purposely, knowingly, recklessly or negligently, as the law may require, with respect to each material element of the offense.

---

[36] Model Penal Code, § 210.2.

(2) Kinds of Culpability Defined

    (a) *Purposely*
    A person acts purposely with respect to a material element of an offense when:

        (i)   if the element involves the nature of his conduct or a result thereof, it is his conscious object to engage in conduct of that nature or to cause such a result; and
        (ii) if the element involves the attendant circumstances, he is aware of the existence of such circumstances or he believes or hopes that they exist.

    (b) *Knowingly*
    A person acts knowingly with respect to a material element of an offense when:

        (i)   if the element involves the nature of his conduct or the attendant circumstances, he is aware that his conduct is of that nature or that such circumstances exist; and
        (ii) if the element involves a result of his conduct, he is aware that it is practically certain that his conduct will cause such a result.

Under Subsection (b), criminal homicide constitutes murder when it is "committed recklessly under circumstances manifesting extreme indifference to the value of human life." Recklessness is defined as:

    (c) *Recklessly*
    A person acts recklessly with respect to a material element of an offense when he consciously disregards a substantial and unjustifiable risk that the material element exists or will result from his conduct. The risk must be of such a nature and degree that, considering the nature and purpose of the actor's conduct and the circumstances known to him, its disregard involves a gross deviation from the standard of conduct that a law-abiding person would observe in the actor's situation.

The Model Penal Code does not distinguish between first degree and second degree murder, and provides that murder is a felony of the first degree. The Code leaves open the question regarding the imposition of the death penalty.

2. Federal Code

The U.S. Code provides that:

Murder is the unlawful killing of a human being with malice aforethought. Every murder perpetrated by poison, lying in wait, or any other kind of willful, deliberated, malicious and premeditative killing; or committed in the perpetration of, or attempt to perpetrate, any arson, escape, murder, kidnapping, treason, espionage, sabotage, rape, burglary, or robbery; or perpetrated from a premeditated design unlawfully and maliciously to effect the death of any human other than him who is killed, is murder in the first degree. Any other murder is murder in the second degree.[37]

The federal code retains the common law definition of murder and divides murder into first and second degrees. The felony murder concept is retained, but the person charged may be found guilty of murder in the first degree only if the felony is, in fact, committed, and the crime perpetrated is one designated in the statute. It is noted that those crimes that are designated are the most serious felony crimes and most were felonies at early common law. The 1984 amendment to the statute added these felonies: escape, murder, kidnapping, treason, espionage and sabotage.

3. Other statutes and codes

While some states have adopted language similar to that of the Model Penal Code others retain modified versions of the common law crime and still others have adopted language that is derived from the Model Penal Code but include provisions which retain the felony-murder doctrine.[38]

An example of a revised statute which deviates from the common law, but uses different language from the Model Penal Code, is that of the Commonwealth of Kentucky. This statute provides:

---

[37] 18 U.S.C. § 1111, as amended in 1984.

[38] *See also*, Model Penal Code, § 210.2 (Comments following Section) (Proposed Official Draft 1980).

§ 507.020 -- Murder.
(1) A person is guilty of murder when:
    (a) With intent to cause the death of another person, he causes the death of such person or of a third person; except that in any prosecution a person shall not be guilty under this Subsection if he acted under the influence of extreme emotional disturbance for which there was a reasonable explanation or excuse, the reasonableness of which is to be determined from the viewpoint of a person in the defendant's situation under the circumstances as the defendant believed them to be. However, nothing contained in this Section shall constitute a defense to a prosecution for or preclude a conviction of manslaughter in the first degree or any other crime; or
    (b) Under circumstances manifesting extreme indifference to human life, he wantonly engages in conduct which creates a grave risk to another person and thereby causes the death of another person.[39]

In fixing the penalty, this Code provides that murder is a Class A felony (life imprisonment), except that it is a capital offense where:

    (a) the defendant's act of killing was intentional and was for profit or hire,
    (b) the defendant's act was intentional and occurred during the commission of arson in the first degree, robbery in the first degree, burglary in the first degree, or rape in the first degree,
    (c) the defendant's act of killing was intentional and the defendant was a prisoner and the victim was a prison employee engaged at the time of the act in the performance of his duties,
    (d) the defendant's act of killing was intentional and the death was caused through the use of a destructive device (defined in another Section),

---

[39] Ky. Rev. Stat., § 507.020.

    (e) the defendant's act or acts of killing were intentional and resulted in multiple deaths, or

    (f) the defendant's act of killing was intentional and the victim was a police officer, sheriff or deputy sheriff engaged at the time of the act in the lawful performance of his duties.

The Kentucky Code retains the provisions relating to felony-murder and enumerates the felonies.

An Ohio statute, which was revised in 1974, but retained the felony-murder provision, uses these words:

> No person shall purposely cause the death of another while committing or attempting to commit, or while fleeing immediately after committing or attempting to commit kidnapping, rape, aggravated arson or arson, aggravated robbery or robbery, aggravated burglary or burglary, or escape.[40]

This Section defines the offense of felony-murder and requires that the killing must be purposeful. It expands the offense of felony-murder by listing kidnapping and escape in addition to rape, arson, robbery, and burglary as a felony during which a purposeful killing constitutes aggravated murder. In this Section premeditation is not a necessary element in felony-murder but the killing must be committed in connection with one of the felonies listed.

As is the case with other crimes, the words used must be carefully defined. Some definitions are found in the statutes, others in cases. Some of the more important definitions are included.

§ 3.4   Voluntary Manslaughter

As was noted in a previous Section, two of the elements of manslaughter are exactly the same as those which must be proved for murder:

    (a) an unlawful killing, and
    (b) one person by another.

---

[40]   Ohio Rev. Code Ann. § 2903.01 (Page 1987).

The difference is that while malice is an essential ingredient of murder, manslaughter may be committed without malice as where one kills in sudden passion aroused by lawful provocation.[41]

Some confusion can be avoided by considering homicide in terms of the process of elimination. If there is no "malice aforethought," but there is an *unlawful* killing of a human being by another human being, then the crime is manslaughter. Another approach is to consider first degree murder as the most serious offense with the most severe penalty, second degree murder as the second most serious offense, and manslaughter third in this hierarchy. Manslaughter is a distinct offense, however, not a degree of murder.

Some other definitions from cases will help in defining these terms and distinguishing manslaughter from murder. In the case of *State v. Lillibridge,* the court stated "manslaughter is the unlawful killing of a human being without malice aforethought, either express or implied."[42] In the case of *State v. Cousins,* the court distinguished manslaughter by stating that "manslaughter is the unlawful killing of a human being without malice and without premeditation and deliberation."[43] And in a third case, the New Hampshire Court noted that the distinguishing element between murder and manslaughter is absence of malice; that while the killing may be with design to effect death, the offense is reduced to manslaughter by circumstances of great and sudden provocation.[44]

Traditionally, manslaughter is divided into two categories:

(1) voluntary, where a homicidal act is intentional but passion-induced or occasioned by some provocation, and
(2) involuntary, where death results from the commission of certain unlawful acts not accompanied by any intention to take life.

In this Section, voluntary manslaughter is considered. In the next Section, involuntary manslaughter is discussed in detail and involuntary manslaughter further is distinguished from voluntary manslaughter.

---

[41] State v. Williams, 323 S.W.2d 811 (Mo. 1959).
[42] State v. Lillibridge, 454 A.2d 237 (R.I. 1982).
[43] State v. Cousins, 223 S.E.2d 338 (N.C. 1976).
[44] State v. Nelson, 103 N.H. 478, 175 A.2d 814 (1961).

A. Traditional Definition and Elements

Voluntary manslaughter is the intentional killing of one human being by another without justification or excuse, but committed under the influence of passion induced by great provocation.

In most societies, the law does not condone the killing, even though there is provocation or passion; however, the law does not ignore the weaknesses of human nature. Therefore, if there is absence of malice and the killing is due to the influence of sudden passion, then the crime is reduced from murder to manslaughter. The cases are harmonious in holding that there must be sufficient cause for the provocation and a state of rage or passion, without time to cool, placing the defendant beyond control of his reason and suddenly impelling him to commit the deed.[45] The court, in defining the term manslaughter, used this definition.

> Manslaughter is the killing of another intentionally, but in a sudden heat of passion due to adequate provocation and without malice, and provocation is deemed to be adequate, so as to reduce the offense from murder to manslaughter, whenever it is calculated to excite the passion beyond control and it must be of such a character as would, in the mind of the average and reasonable man, steer resentment likely to cause violence, endangering life, or as would naturally tend to disturb and obscure the reason and lead to action from passion rather than judgment, or to create anger, rage, sudden resentment or terror, rendering the mind incapable of reflection.[46]

In order for a killing which would otherwise be murder to be reduced to manslaughter, these conditions must exist:

(1) there must have been adequate provocation,
(2) the killing must have been in the heat of passion,
(3) it must have been a sudden passion, i.e. the killing must have followed the provocation before there has been a reasonable opportunity for the passion to cool, and
(4) there must have been a causal connection between the provocation, the passion and the fatal act.

---

[45] White v. State, 44 Tex. Crim. 346, 72 S.W. 173 (1901).

[46] State v. Smart, 328 S.W.2d 569 (Mo. 1959). For another definition, see People v. Milhem, 350 Mich. 497, 87 N.W.2d 151 (1957).

1. Degree of passion engendered by provocation

Provocation necessary to reduce the crime from murder to manslaughter must be of such a nature as to be recognized at law as adequate for that purpose. Provocation must be of a nature calculated to inflame the passions of an ordinary reasonable man under the circumstances.

A bare claim of "fear" is not enough provocation to show sudden passion.[47] The courts have indicated that staggering blows to the face of the person, the infliction of pain and bloodshed, or the killing or assaulting of a relative are sufficient provocations to reduce the crime from murder to manslaughter.[48]

Although the courts are not in agreement, even some recent cases have found sufficient provocation where the husband discovered his wife in the act of committing adultery. For example, in a Tennessee case in 1987, the court found that a defendant who fatally shot a man he found engaged in sexual relations with his estranged wife should not be convicted of first degree murder but at most of voluntary manslaughter.[49] In this case, the court recognized that:

> it has long been a well-settled principle that the commission of unlawful sexual intercourse with a female relative is an act obviously calculated to arouse ungovernable passion, and that the killing of the seducer or adulterer under the influence or in the heat of that passion constitutes voluntary manslaughter and not murder, in the absence of actual malice.

The court explained that the necessary elements of malice and premeditation are missing where the defendant discovered his wife *in flagrante delicto* with a man who was a stranger to him, at a time when the defendant was desperately seeking to save his marriage. The court commented:

> In our opinion the passions of any reasonable person would have been inflamed and intensely aroused by this sort of discovery.

Generally, the slayer must discover the deceased in the very act of intercourse or immediately before or after the commission, and the killing must

---

[47] Moore v. State, 694 S.W.2d 529 (Tex. Cr. App. 1985).

[48] Stewart v. State, 75 Ala. 436 (1885); State v. Michael, 74 W.Va. 613, 82 S.E. 611 (1914); Commonwealth v. Paese, 220 Pa. 371, 69 A. 891 (1908).

[49] State v. Thornton, 730 S.W.2d 309 (Tenn. 1987). *See* case in Part II.

have followed immediately on detection and must have been committed under the influence of passion engendered by the discovery.[50]

While the common law rule was that words alone will not be sufficient provocation, there are some exceptions in the state cases. If the words are informational, i.e. convey any information of a fact which constitutes reasonable provocation rather than morally insulting or abusive words, this could be sufficient provocation.

2. The killing must have been in the heat of passion

Not only must there be provocation, but the provocation must have led to "heat of passion" or "hot blood." That is, the emotional state must have actually dominated the slayer at the time of the homicidal act, and it must have been entertained toward the person slain, and not to another person.

It is difficult to separate the provocation from the resulting heat and passion. In determining whether the act which caused the death was impelled by heat of passion, all of the surrounding circumstances and conditions are to be taken into consideration. In order to reduce the crime to manslaughter, the provocation must be such as would naturally and reasonably arouse the passions of an ordinary man beyond his power of control.

The extent or degree of mental disturbance caused by the provocation of the deceased that will constitute passion or heat of blood characteristic of voluntary manslaughter has been defined in various terms by the courts. For example, one court indicated that a passion of the slayer must have been such as to negate deliberation. That is, the degree of mental disturbance must have been such as to deprive him of power to perform a design to kill with a deliberate mind.[51] Another court noted that the passion of the slayer must have been such as to render his mind incapable of cool reflection and to overcome and dominate or suspend the exercise of judgment and self-control.[52]

Manslaughter may also be present if one kills another in the heat of sudden combat, if upon reasonable provocation. Reasonable provocation is the provocation that would inflame a reasonable and law-abiding person to the point where he would be capable of killing another. However, the general rule is that words alone, no matter how abusive or humiliating, cannot provide a reasonable provocation.[53]

---

[50] State v. Young, 52 Or. 227, 96 P. 1067 (1908).

[51] White v. State, 44 Tex. Crim. 346, 72 S.W. 173 (1902).

[52] State v. McLawhorn, 270 N.C. 622, 155 S.E.2d 198 (1967); State v. Coop, 223 Kan. 302, 573 P.2d 1017 (1978).

[53] Commonwealth v. Medeiros, 479 N.E.2d 1371 (Mass. 1985).

But while the courts generally have been consistent in holding that words alone cannot provide a reasonable provocation, some exceptions have been made where the words rather than being abusive or humiliating relate facts which tend to break down the restraint to action. For example, it has been held by some courts that a husband who slays the paramour of his wife in the heat of passion engendered by her confession of adultery, and before the lapse of reasonable cooling-off time, is guilty of manslaughter only.[54]

While assault could be sufficient provocation to reduce the homicide from murder to manslaughter, the law does not recognize circumstances as a legal provocation which, in themselves, do not amount to an actual or threatened assault as the legal provocation must generally be more than words, however abusive.[55] Again reiterating the rule, the Georgia court held that in a prosecution for murder, evidence that the victim, who was a black man, said to black defendants, "niggers, get out of my house," did not constitute sufficient provocation to authorize a charge of voluntary manslaughter.[56] In order to reduce the act from murder to voluntary manslaughter, the killer must be deprived of the mastery of his understanding.[57]

Even with these general definitions, it is difficult to define the line where the degree of passion is sufficient to reduce the crime from murder to manslaughter. For example, what might be heat and passion which would justify a reduction of the crime in one instance will not apply in another. A good example was brought out in the case of *People v. Spurlin* in 1984.[58] In this murder prosecution, arising out of defendant's infliction of hammer blows and strangulation to his wife and nine-year-old son, following a marital argument with his wife, the trial court properly limited instructions on voluntary manslaughter to the wife's killing only. While the defendant's fury at his wife could be said to have ignited a long-smothered resentment leading to her death, the son's killing lacked both elements necessary to warrant a manslaughter instruction based on provocation and heat of passion. Although both killings occurred at about the same time, the defendant confessed and testified that the son's life was taken not as a result of rage, passion, or anger aroused by the son, but as a part of the plan to eliminate the family. The court explained that under the common law principle, such death was not the consequence of passion directed at the son.

As was stated in another case, in order to meet the test of heat of passion "the defendant must have in fact been deprived of his self control under

---

[54] Haley v. State, 123 Miss. 87, 85 So. 129 (1920).

[55] State v. Watson, 287 N.C. 147, 214 S.E.2d 85 (1975).

[56] Hill v. State, 236 Geo. 703, 224 S.E.2d 907 (1976).

[57] State v. King, 37 N.J. 285, 181 A.2d 158 (1962).

[58] People v. Spurlin, 156 Cal. App. 3d 119 (1984).

the stress of such provocation and must have committed the crime while so deprived."[59]

3. The cooling-off time

Even if there was sufficient provocation to reduce the crime from murder to manslaughter, and there were sufficient facts to constitute passion or heat of blood, a manslaughter instruction is not justified if the passion did not continue to exist until the commission of the homicidal act. If, from any circumstances whatever, it appears that the party reflected, deliberated or cooled any period of time before the fatal act, the killing will amount to murder, being attributable to malice or revenge and not to mental disturbance.

What constitutes "cooling-off time" depends upon the nature and circumstances of provocation, the extent to which the passion has been aroused, and the nature of the act causing the provocation. Therefore, no precise time can be laid down as a rule within which the passions must be held to have been subsided and reason to have resumed its control. In some instances, the court is authorized to say, as a matter of law, that the cooling-off time is sufficient if an unreasonable period of time has elapsed between the provocation and the killing,[60] while in other situations this determination becomes a difficult problem and one that must be decided by the jury.

In the case of *State v. Landry*, the defendant, Rodney Landry, appealed from his jury conviction for second degree murder for which he was to serve the remainder of his life at hard labor without benefit of parole, probation or suspension of sentence.[61] In this case, the reviewing court did not find error in the lower court's decision that a manslaughter verdict was not justified. After first deciding that provocation shall not reduce a murder to manslaughter if the jury finds that the offender's blood had actually cooled at the time the offense was committed, the court went on to determine that, according to the evidence, the defendant's blood had actually cooled.

The facts were these. The deceased, Clyde Pounds, and the defendant, argued over money with Pounds grabbing the defendant and dragging him downstairs, where he beat the defendant's head against a car. After the fight broke up, the deceased, along with two other men, returned to the apartment by a fire escape. The defendant went inside the apartment, while the others remained outside on the fire escape. Some time later, the door to the apartment opened and the defendant called out "Clyde" and a shot rang out. The

---

[59] State v. King, 37 N.J. 285, 181 A.2d 158 (1962).
[60] State v. Flory, 40 Wyo. 184, 276 P. 458 (1929).
[61] State v. Landry, 499 So. 2d 1320 (La. App. 4th Cir. 1986).

deceased, Pounds, fell fatally wounded. After the fatal shot, the defendant was heard to remark, "He got what he deserved."

The defendant, on appeal, contended that, because of the fight between the defendant and the victim, the homicide should have been mitigated by "hot blood" or "sudden passion" which would reduce the crime to manslaughter. The reviewing court reasoned that, as the defendant remained inside the apartment for several minutes, and the victim went back to the car in the parking lot to get, and later smoke, a cigarette on the fire escape, this was sufficient cooling-off time. The court indicated:

> The evidence supports the conclusion that a verdict of second degree murder is appropriate as the factfinder could have found that the defendant's blood had actually cooled.

However, in another case, the defendant contended that information given him by his wife as to rape and incest committed upon her by the deceased so aroused his passions and deprived him of self control that his act cannot be held to be murder. While indicating that the report of the incest and rape, if true, could not justify the killing of the deceased, the evidence may be admissible for the purpose of reducing the crime to manslaughter. The state contended that the testimony should not be admissible because ample time (at least a day, and probably longer) had elapsed after the defendant had been informed of the acts of the deceased and that his blood had cooled and he was no longer perturbed.[62] But even though a day had passed between the time the defendant's passion had been aroused and the killing, the court agreed with the defendant's contention that the defendant's mind was still perturbed on the day of the killing. The court explained that the crime of the deceased, if true, was most heinous and was calculated to create a most violent passion in the mind of the defendant, and it hardly can be expected that it would, as a matter of law, subside within so short a time, especially when, as testified, a situation arose by which past facts were clearly recalled. The court then stated:

> Courts are not altogether agreed as to the question of cooling-off time is one of law or for the jury. Some hold it to be a question of law and that 24 hours is sufficient for the mind to cool. We think, however, that the weight of authority is that, in cases like that at bar, the question of cooling-off time depends on the circumstances and is ordinarily one for the jury.

---

[62] State v. Flory, 40 Wyo. 184, 276 P. 458 (1929).

There is no definite time within which the passions when aroused by such a wrong may be said to have so far subsided and reason to have resumed its sway to such an extent as that thereafter the killing may be denounced as in vengeance alone. The question is one of reasonable time and dependent upon all of the facts of the case. While the time may be so long as to exclude all doubt on the subject and exact the exclusion of evidence insofar as offered in extenuation, more frequently it should be submitted to the jury under proper instructions.

4. The causal connection

In order for a homicide to be reduced from murder to manslaughter, the defendant must show that the heat of passion resulted from justifiable provocation and that the heat of passion *caused* the act which resulted in death.[63] If the heat of passion element was in existence prior to the provocation, there can be no justification for reducing the crime to manslaughter. If there was adequate provocation, but the order of provocation and the heat of passion are reversed, i.e. the provocation was not the cause of the heat of passion, there can be no reduction.[64]

To state this differently, there must be a causal link between the provocation, the passion and the act. For example, if one has, for some time, had an intent to kill the victim to get even for mistreatment over a period of years, but immediately before he is about to carry out his intent to kill the victim, he finds the victim in bed with his daughter, it would be difficult to justify a reduction of the crime from murder to manslaughter.

B. *Statutes and Codes*

While few states seek to punish violators under the common law as such, most retain some of the common law distinguishing factors and use common law definitions. The Model Penal Code differs from the common law in regard to voluntary manslaughter, but it retains the concept that reducing the crime from murder to manslaughter is justified where there is sufficient mental or emotional disturbances. The U.S. Code also retains the provision relating to sudden quarrel or heat of passion which reduces the homicide from murder to manslaughter. For a comprehensive understanding of the

---

[63]   Rex v. Thomas, 7 Car. P. 817, 173 Eng.Rep. 356 (1837).

[64]   State v. Speors, 76 Wyo. 82, 300 P.2d 555 (1956).

law relating to voluntary manslaughter, the Model Penal Code, the Federal Code, and some of the state statutes are discussed, before moving to involuntary manslaughter.

1. Model Penal Code

§ 210.3 of the Model Penal Code provides:

(1)   Criminal homicide constitutes manslaughter when:[65]

    (a)   it is committed recklessly; or
    (b)   a homicide which would otherwise be murder is committed under the influence of extreme mental or emotional influence for which there is reasonable explanation or excuse. The reasonableness of such explanation or excuse shall be determined from the viewpoint of the person in the actor's situation under the circumstances as he believes them to be.

(2)   Manslaughter is a felony of the second degree.

The Model Penal Code does not distinguish between voluntary and involuntary manslaughter in § 210.3. The Code differs from common law voluntary manslaughter in that reckless homicide is included as well as intentional homicide.[66] It retains the concept of reducing the crime from murder to manslaughter where there is sufficient mental or emotional disturbances. The Code places more emphasis on the actor's mental state than does the traditional definition as interpreted.

2. Federal Code

Title 18, § 1112 of the U.S. Code provides:

(a)   Manslaughter is the unlawful killing of a human being without malice. It is of two kinds; voluntary -- upon sudden quarrel or heat of passion...

---

[65]   Model Penal Code, § 210.3 on Manslaughter.
[66]   *See* § 2.02(2) for definitions.

(b) ...whoever is guilty of voluntary manslaughter, shall be imprisoned not more than ten years.[67]

In explaining the provision of this Code, one court noted that manslaughter occupies the middle ground between excusable, or justifiable, homicide on the one hand, and murder on the other.[68] Another court pointed out that the crime of manslaughter is, in some sense, "irrational" by definition in that it arises out of a person's passions, but provocations to reduce murder to manslaughter must be such as would arouse reasonable and ordinary persons to kill someone.[69]

3. Other statutes and codes

Some states have adopted the Model Penal Code concepts. Some retain part of the common law distinctions, and some have elements of both.[70]

An example of a statute revised in 1974 which generally follows the Model Penal Code, but has a different provision concerning voluntary manslaughter, is that of Ohio, which provides:

No person while under extreme emotional stress brought on by serious provocation reasonably sufficient to incite him into using deadly force, shall knowingly cause the death of another.

This differs from the traditional offense in that this Section requires that the slaying be committed knowingly while the common law requires that it be intentional. Also under the common law interpretation, voluntary manslaughter contemplated killing done in a *sudden* fit of rage or passion, while this Section includes emotional stress that may be the result of stress built up over a period of time.[71]

It is apparent from this discussion that it is necessary to check the statutes and cases of the states to determine the existing law and the elements to be proved to convict a person of voluntary manslaughter.

---

[67] 18 U.S.C.A. § 1112.

[68] United States v. Hart, 162 F. 192 (1908).

[69] United States v. Collins, C.A.L.A. 1982, 690 F.2d 431, *cert. denied*, 460 U.S. 1046, 75 L.Ed.2d 801, 103 S. Ct. 1447 (1982).

[70] *See* American Law Institute, Model Penal Code and Commentaries, Part II, Comments, § 210.3.

[71] Ohio Rev. Code Ann. § 2903.3 (Page 1987).

§ 3.5 Involuntary Manslaughter

A. Traditional Definition and Elements

Involuntary manslaughter is designated in some Codes as "manslaughter in the second degree." Involuntary manslaughter or second degree manslaughter is often referred to as the "catch all" in the law of homicide. It includes all unlawful homicides that are not covered under one of the other categories. To state this differently, when the loss of life has not been caused intentionally or does not come within any of the murder definitions, it is either manslaughter or excusable or justifiable homicide. If it is not excusable or justifiable homicide and it is not murder or voluntary manslaughter, then it must be involuntary manslaughter. Some definitions will help distinguish involuntary manslaughter from voluntary manslaughter.

Manslaughter in the second degree or "involuntary manslaughter" is the unlawful killing of a human being without malice, either express or implied, and without intent to kill or inflict injury causing death, committed accidentally in the commission of some unlawful act not felonious, or in the improper or negligent performance of an act lawful in itself.[72]

"Manslaughter in the second degree" occurs where it plainly appears that neither death nor great bodily harm was intended but death was accidentally caused by some unlawful act or act strictly lawful in itself but done in unlawful manner and without due caution.[73]

As these cases indicate, the distinguishing factor is that involuntary manslaughter is unintentional. If the act was intended, then it could not come within the involuntary manslaughter category. The definitions also indicate that there are two kinds of involuntary manslaughter when:

(1) the killing occurs in the course of committing an unlawful act, and
(2) death occurs during the negligent commission or omission of an otherwise lawful act.

---

[72] Callahan v. State, Ala. Cr. App. 343 S.2d 551 (1977).

[73] Pitts v. State, 122 S.2d 542 (Ala. App. 1960).

The elements of involuntary manslaughter are:

(1) an unlawful killing, and
(2) one person by another.
The unlawful killing element is common to all lawful illegal homicides. The unlawful killing may occur as:

(a) a result of the act of the defendant while he is engaged in the commission of an unlawful act not amounting to a felon,
(b) as a result of culpable negligence, or
(c) due to failure to perform a legal duty.

If death occurs while one is engaged in certain felonies, the crime could be murder under the felony-murder doctrine. If the unlawful act is not one of the enumerated felonies, but is unlawful and death results, then the crime is involuntary manslaughter.[74]

To constitute involuntary manslaughter, the prosecution must show that there is a "causal connection" between the unlawful act and the death; that is, the unlawful act was the cause of the death.[75]

A killing may also be unlawful to meet this element of involuntary manslaughter if death results from gross, wanton or culpable negligence. A distinction is made between simple or ordinary negligence and culpable negligence. The required degree of negligence associated with involuntary manslaughter is conduct which amounts to a "wanton or reckless disregard of human life."[76]

The third type of unlawful killing under the traditional definition is failure to perform a legal duty. If a person is required by law to do an act, but disregarding that duty, causes the death of another, he can be guilty of involuntary manslaughter.[77]

It is quite clear that if one intends to strike the victim or an intentional unlawful battery was likely to endanger life, the crime is voluntary manslaughter and cannot be classified as involuntary manslaughter. Some cases will make this distinction more clear. In the case of *Commonwealth v. Medeiros*, the defendant was convicted of murder in the second degree and appealed. His claim on appeal was that the court erred in failing to give an involuntary manslaughter instruction. As a result of questioning, the defen-

---

[74] People v. Penny, 44 Cal. 2d 861, 285 P.2d 926 (1955).
[75] People v. Mulchy, 318 Ill. 332, 149 N.E. 266 (1925).
[76] Maryland v. Chapman, 101 F.Supp. 335 (D.C.M.D 1951).
[77] Jones v. United States, 308 F.2d 302 (D.C. 1962).

dant admitted that the victim had made homosexual advances toward him which he warded off by striking the victim. According to the defendant, the victim allegedly hit the defendant as he attempted to leave the apartment and the defendant struck him back, causing the victim to fall onto the bed. The defendant then climbed atop the victim and struck him on the head twice more. At this point, according to the confession, the victim appeared to be unconscious, his face was bloody and he was foaming at the mouth. The defendant then alleged that he put a pillow over the victim's face and loosely looped the end of a rope, which was in the room and used as a fire escape device, around the victim's neck.

On appeal, the defendant claimed that the judge erred in failing to instruct the jury properly on involuntary manslaughter, but the Commonwealth argued that involuntary manslaughter instructions are not warranted by the evidence and, therefore, the deficiency in the instructions could not prejudice the defendant.[78] The reviewing court agreed with the Commonwealth. The court explained its position with this definition of involuntary manslaughter:

> Involuntary manslaughter is an unlawful homicide, unintentionally caused:
>
> > (1) in the commission of an unlawful act, *malum in se*, not amounting to a felony nor likely to endanger life
> >
> > ... or
> >
> > (2) by an act which constitutes such a disregard of probable harmful consequences to another as to constitute wanton or reckless conduct.

The court noted that, even assuming the victim's advances constituted reasonable provocation, and that there was some continuing threat to the defendant's well being, this is insufficient to warrant an involuntary manslaughter instruction. The judge explained that the defendant deliberately and repeatedly struck the victim, even while the victim was subdued and lying on his back, therefore, "the unlawful battery was quite likely to endanger life and hence could not be classified as involuntary manslaughter."

In a California case, the court again pointed out that if a shooting is intentional, an instruction on involuntary manslaughter is not justified. In this case, the defendant, while drinking at a bar, exchanged angry words with the victim and then invited him to "come outside" to fight. Once outside, the defendant shot the victim three times with the gun he carried in his pocket. The

---

[78] Commonwealth v. Medeiros, 479 N.E.2d 1371 (Mass. 1985).

third shot was fired after the defendant was on the ground. The victim was unarmed.[79]

In distinguishing between murder, voluntary manslaughter and involuntary manslaughter the court made these points. Manslaughter, like murder, or, for that matter, any true crime, requires an act and a culpable state of mind or *mens rea*. The *mens rea* of murder is characterized as malice aforethought. Such malice may be expressed or implied. Manslaughter is an unlawful killing without malice. Case law has developed the principle that, where reasonable provocation is coupled with a "sudden quarrel" or "heat of passion," there is no malice and a killing under such circumstances, while still unlawful, is only voluntary manslaughter. Thus, if a killing which would ordinarily amount to murder is mitigated to the extent that malice is found to be absent, the crime amounts to voluntary manslaughter.

The intentional shooting or stabbing of an individual is a "man-endangering" act, whether or not there was the express intent to kill and if unjustified, unexcused, or unmitigated, is murder. It is not involuntary manslaughter for the reason that an intentional shooting or stabbing, with or without an intent to kill, is a felony (voluntary manslaughter).

While an intentional killing will generally not amount to involuntary manslaughter, a charge of involuntary manslaughter is proper where death results from the commission of an unlawful act not amounting to a felony, or some act done in an unlawful or culpable negligent manner.[80] Where the facts indicated that the defendant was driving after drinking and taking drugs, did not stop after hitting a parked Volkswagen, crossed to the left side of the roadway to strike the deceased who was on the proper side of the road as a pedestrian, was driving 30-35 miles per hour on a roadway in an apartment area where speed bumps were located, and did not reduce his speed to avoid colliding with the deceased, he had a thoughtless disregard of the consequences of his acts and indifference to others. Under these facts, there was sufficient evidence to submit the case to the jury on the charge of involuntary manslaughter.

B. Statutes and Codes

1. Model Penal Code

The Model Penal Code has no Section on involuntary manslaughter. It does have a provision regarding negligent homicide which is similar to some

---

[79] People v. Renteria, 235 Cal. Rptr. 807 (Cal. App. 2 Dist. 1987).
[80] State v. Hefler, 310 S.E.2d 310 (N.C. 1984).

of the existing statutes and addresses homicide caused by negligence which was included in common law involuntary manslaughter. A provision of the Code is as follows:

§ 210.4 Negligent Homicide[81]

(1) Criminal homicide constitutes negligent homicide when it is committed negligently.
(2) Negligent homicide is a felony of the third degree.

The standard of negligence required for violations of § 210.4 requires proof of substantial fault and limits penal sanctions to cases where there is a gross deviation from ordinary standards of conduct.[82]

2. Federal Code

The U.S. Code definition of involuntary manslaughter is similar to the traditional definition. It provides:

§ 1112 Manslaughter (Involuntary)
Manslaughter is the unlawful killing of a human being without malice. It is of two kinds:

...

Involuntary. In the commission of an unlawful act not amounting to a felony, or in the commission in an unlawful manner, or without due caution and circumspection, of a lawful act which might produce death.
...

Whoever is guilty of involuntary manslaughter, shall be fined not more than $1,000 or imprisoned not more than 3 years, or both.[83]

The present Federal Code is based on the Code that was drafted in 1940. Some minor changes were made in phraseology, but the law generally remains intact.

---

[81] Model Penal Code, § 210.4 (Proposed Official Draft 1980).
[82] *See* Model Penal Code, § 2.02 (Proposed Official Draft 1980) for a definition of negligence.
[83] 18 U.S.C § 1112.

In interpreting this provision of the federal statute, the federal courts have held that manslaughter may result from an accidental or unintentional act and that neither intent nor malice is a factor in involuntary manslaughter.[84] As to the degree of negligence, a federal judge explained that a charge of manslaughter by negligence is not made out by proof of ordinary simple negligence that would constitute civil liability, but must amount to a gross negligence, to be determined on consideration of all the facts of a particular case and the gross negligence must be shown beyond a reasonable doubt.[85]

3. Other statutes and codes

Some states that have revised Codes have followed the Model Penal Code and use the negligent homicide definition. Other jurisdictions retain the common law involuntary manslaughter rule, at least in part.[86] Still others have added special statutes to meet the needs of a society where many homicides involve automobiles. For example, the Ohio Criminal Code includes the crimes of negligent homicide, aggravated vehicular homicide and vehicular homicide.[87] These are in addition to the crimes of aggravated murder, murder, voluntary manslaughter and involuntary manslaughter. The Ohio Criminal Code provides:

Negligent homicide. No person shall negligently cause the death of another by means of a deadly weapon or dangerous ordnance as defined in § 2923.11 of the Revised Code.[88]

Aggravated vehicular homicide. No person, while operating or participating in the operation of a motor vehicle, motorcycle, snowmobile, locomotive, watercraft, or aircraft, shall recklessly cause the death of another.

Vehicular homicide. No person, while operating or participating in the operation of a motor vehicle, motorcycle, snowmobile, locomo-

---

84 Thomas v. U.S., 419 F.2d 1203 (1969); U.S. v. Pardee, 368 F.2d 368 (1966).

85 Maryland v. Chapman, 101 F.Supp. 335 (1951).

86 Statutory schemes of said legislation may be found in: Alaska Stat. § 11.15.040 (1968); Cal. Criminal Code § 192 (West 1970); D.C. Code Ann. § 22-2405 (1981); Md. Crim. Law Code Ann. § 387 (1975); Mass. Gen. Laws Ann. ch. 265, § 13 (West 1980); Mich. Comp. Laws § 750.321 (1968); Miss. Code Ann. § 97-3-27 (1972); Nev. Rev. Stat. § 200.040 (1973); N.C. Gen. Stat. §§ 14-18 (1983).

87 Ohio Rev. Code Ann. § 2903 *et seq.* (Page 1987).

88 Ohio Rev. Code Ann. § 2923.11 (Page 1987).

tive, watercraft, or aircraft, shall negligently cause the death of another.

Note that the difference between "aggravated vehicular homicide" and "vehicular homicide" is that "recklessly" is used in the former and "negligently" in the latter.

Where the elements of the crime are spelled out by statute and terms are specifically defined, there can be no conviction unless these elements, as defined, are each proved beyond a reasonable doubt. In searching for clarification of definitions, it is often necessary to look at cases that have further interpreted the statutes or, in some instances, to even look for common law rationale.

§ 3.6 Suicide

A. Traditional Definition and Elements

Suicide is defined as intentional self-destruction. Although suicide is not strictly a homicide as there is no killing of one person by *another* person, it is often considered in relation to the law of homicide. Suicide at common law was a felony. At common law this was known as *felo de se* or felon of himself. One who killed himself before he arrived at the age of discretion or while he was *non compos mentis* was not a *felo de se* or suicide.[89] At early common law suicide was punished by ignominious burial and forfeiture of goods and chattels to the king.[90] If two persons mutually agreed to commit suicide, and the means employed to produce death was effective only as to one, the survivor was guilty of murder of the one who died.[91]

While some early courts took the position that suicide was a crime even if no punishment could be inflicted,[92] it is safe to say that suicide is no longer considered a crime.[93] Some states provide for punishment of one who participates in the taking of the life of another.[94] This approach is justified on the theory that it establishes complicity in another's self-murder.

Also, in some jurisdictions, an attempt to commit suicide is or was defined as a misdemeanor.[95]

---

[89] Comm. v. Mink, 123 Mass. 422 (1877).

[90] Grace v. State, 44 Tex. Crim. 193, 69 S.W. 529 (1902).

[91] Burnett v. People, 204 Ill. 208, 68 N.E. 505 (1903).

[92] State v. Carney, 69 N.J.L. 478, 55 A. 44 (1902).

[93] State v. Campbell, 217 Iowa 848, 251 N.W. 917 (1933).

[94] People v. Roberts, 211 Mich. 189, 178 N.W. 690 (1920).

[95] State v. Willis, 255 N.C. 473, 121 S.E.2d 854 (1961).

B. Statutes and Codes

1. Model Penal Code

§ 210.5 Causing or Aiding Suicide[96]

(1) *Causing Suicide as Criminal Homicide.* A person may be convicted of criminal homicide for causing another to commit suicide only if he purposely causes such suicide by force, duress or deception.

(2) *Aiding or Soliciting Suicide as an Independent Offense.* A person who purposely aids or solicits another to commit suicide is guilty of a felony of the second degree if his conduct causes such suicide or an attempted suicide, and otherwise of a misdemeanor.

The Model Penal Code does not recognize suicide, or attempted suicide, as a crime. Section 210.5 provides, however, that a person is guilty of criminal homicide if, with the requisite culpability, he causes the death of another by "causing another to commit suicide." It is only when the person actively participates in inducing the suicide that criminal penalties will result.

The second Subsection of § 210.5 more closely defines an act which was a crime under the common law. This Section creates a separate offense of aiding or soliciting suicide, even where suicide itself is not a crime. To prove a violation here, the prosecutor must introduce evidence to show that the accused "purposely" aided or solicited another to commit suicide. Thus, conduct not seriously intended to aid or persuade another to take his own life may not be punishable under this Section.

The grading of the crimes depends on the conduct of the person who is aided or solicited; the Model Penal Code provides for different degrees of punishment depending on whether the person actually commits suicide or attempts to do so. If the actor's conduct leads to an actual suicide or attempted suicide by the person who is aided or solicited, the crime is punishable as a felony. If the person does not try to kill himself, the offense is a misdemeanor.

2. Federal Code

The U.S. Code has no provision relating to suicide.

---

[96] Model Penal Code, § 210.5 (Proposed Official Draft 1980).

3. Other statutes and codes

While some modern statutes use the terminology of the Model Penal Code, others employ other phrases to describe the conduct that constitutes the offense, and still others have no provisions relating to suicide or aiding or soliciting suicide.

In Arkansas:

(1) A person commits *manslaughter* if:

...

(b) he purposely causes or aids another person to commit suicide.[97]

In some other states, a separate offense is established. For example, the California Code provides:

Every person who deliberately aids, or advises, or encourages another to commit suicide, is guilty of a felony.[98]

Even if there are no specific laws relating to suicide, sanctions provided for other crimes may be applied where one aids or encourages another or even where one attempts suicide and fails.[99] In such cases, all of the elements of the crime (murder, manslaughter, assault, etc.) must be proved.

§ 3.7 Assault and Battery

A. *Traditional definitions and elements*

Assault and battery were two separate common law crimes. In many jurisdictions, and in the Model Penal Code, the crimes are classified under the designation of "assault" without use of the word "battery." However, as the terms are distinguished in some statutes, and a knowledge of the distinction is important in understanding the development of the law, each is defined and discussed.

---

[97] Ark. Stat. Ann. § 41.1504 (1977). *See also* N.Y. Penal Law § 125.15 (McKinney 1975).

[98] Cal. Penal Code § 401 (West 1970).

[99] Stephenson v. State, 205 Ind. 141, 179 N.E. 633 (1933).

1. Assault

An "assault" is any unlawful offer or attempt to injure another, with apparent present ability to effectuate the attempt under circumstances creating a fear of imminent peril.

Various courts have defined the term "assault." Some of these definitions are included here.

An assault is an attempt with unlawful force, to inflict bodily injury upon another, accompanied with apparent present ability to give effect to the attempt if not prevented.[100] Generally, "assault" is a demonstration of unlawful intent by one person to inflict immediate injury on the person of another then present, and even though physical contact is not an essential element, violence, threatened or offered, is essential.[101]

According to these definitions, to constitute an assault, no touching is necessary but there must be an unlawful offer to do bodily harm to another with the apparent present ability to accomplish the deed if not prevented.[102]

In the *Heitman* case, the court agreed with the prosecution that "a person who points a loaded firearm at another to cause injury or induce fear is guilty of an assault." The court went on to explain that intent of one charged with the offense is ordinarily not susceptible of proof by direct evidence, and that intent may be, and usually is, shown by circumstantial evidence.

2. Battery

Battery is the unlawful touching of the person of another by the aggressor or by some substance put in motion by him. A battery has been defined as the "consummation of the assault," and the "unlawful application of force to the person of another."[103] "Battery" is the actual use of force and occurs when the violence is accomplished.[104]

---

[100] State v. Murphy, 7 Wash. App. 505, 500 P.2d 1276 (1972).

[101] State v. Murphy, 128 Vt. 288, 262 A.2d 456 (1970).

[102] State v. Heitman, 618 S.W.2d 902 (Mo. App. 1981).

[103] State v. Hefner, 199 N.C. 778, 155 S.E. 879 (1930).

[104] Commonwealth v. Hill, 237 Pa. Supp. 543, 353 A.2d 870 (1975).

In distinguishing assault and battery, one approach is to look at assault as an attempt to commit a battery and that, in an assault, actual injury is not necessarily inflicted. If touching, either direct or indirect, occurs then the offense is battery.

3. Elements of assault

To constitute an actionable assault, these elements must be proved beyond a reasonable doubt:

(1) an attempt or offer,
(2) with force and violence,
(3) to do some immediate physical injury to the person of another, and
(4) with apparent present or immediate ability.

If any one of the four elements is not proved beyond a reasonable doubt, there can be no conviction for the crime of assault. As each element has a technical meaning, they are discussed separately.

(1) Attempt or offer. The force intended to be applied must be put into motion. Mere preparation does not amount to an assault; there must be some act which could apparently produce injury.

(2) The force or violence offered must be unlawful, but it may be in any degree. For example, where a defendant attempted to apply force to the victim's person and grab money held fast in the victim's hand, this action constituted the necessary force to constitute assault.[105]

(3) The attempt or offer must be directed toward another person. There need not be any touching or striking of the person; there must be an offer to use force to injure another.[106]

It is not necessary that the prosecution prove actual present ability to constitute the offense of assault. All that is necessary is to show "apparent present ability." As one court explained, the prosecution must show that the person is placed in reasonable apprehension of receiving an immediate battery.[107] In another case, the court advised that there must be a showing of

---

[105] People v. LeFlore, 96 Mich. App. 557, 293 N.W.2d 628 (1980).
[106] Albright v. State, 214 S.2d 887 (Fla.App. 1968).
[107] Taylor v. State, 52 Md. App. 500, 450 A.2d 1312 (1982).

force or menace of violence which would be sufficient to put a person of reasonable firmness in fear of immediate bodily harm.[108]

(4) Assault does not occur unless the individual is placed in reasonable fear of imminent bodily harm,[109] but if the victim is placed in reasonable fear of bodily harm, by conduct of the defendant, and the defendant had the *apparent* ability to carry out the threatening nature of his act, it is not necessary that the prosecution show that the defendant had the actual ability to carry out the act. For example, one may be found guilty of assault by pointing an unloaded firearm at another when the person threatened does not know that the gun is not loaded.[110]

4. Elements of battery

While, in assault, it is not necessary that any actual injury be inflicted, in battery, there must be some touching or striking of the person. As one case indicated, an "assault" is an offer to show violence to another without striking him, whereas a "battery" is the carrying of the threat into effect by infliction of the blow; it being without consent of the person on whom the offer of violence was made or who actually received the blow.[111]

The elements of battery are:

(1) unlawful,
(2) application of force, and
(3) to the person of another.

Each element must be proved by the prosecution.

(1) Unlawful
The force applied is unlawful unless it is justified by law. For example, a police officer, in making a physical arrest, commits battery unless his actions are lawful. His actions are made lawful by statute, ordinance or court decisions. Generally speaking, the force applied is unlawful if there is intentional contact with another which

---

[108] State v. Harding, 22 N.C. App. 66, 205 S.E.2d 544 (1974).

[109] Profit v. Ricci, 463 A.2d 514 (1983).

[110] Allen v. Hannaford, 138 Wash. 223, 244 P. 700 (1926).

[111] Ormond v. Crampton, 16 N.C. App. 88, 191 S.E.2d 405 (1972).

is unpermitted.[112] One court decided that choking, kissing and straddling of a female by a male without her consent, intending at the time to use whatever force might be necessary to have sexual intercourse with her, would be battery and would be unlawful.[113] Here, the use of force was unlawful, because the female did not consent.

(2) Application of Force

Force may be applied to another person directly; for example, striking with one's fist, kicking or holding the victim. Force may also be applied indirectly, as by exposing a helpless person to the inclemency of the weather.[114] Any touching, if it is unlawful, may constitute the force necessary for a battery.[115]

(3) To the Person of Another

This third element of those elements necessary to constitute battery is usually not difficult to prove. As indicated in the paragraphs above, any touching of a person without permission which is made unlawfully is all that is necessary. Touching may be directly to the person, as for example, the defendant putting his hand into the victim's pants and upon his penis.[116] But it is not necessary that the victim's body or even his clothing be touched as touching anything connected with his person is sufficient. For example, an intentional snatching of the patron's dinner plate from him by the manager of the hotel's club in a loud and offensive manner was sufficient to constitute battery.[117]

While touching with one's hands may constitute application of force to another person, not every touching is a criminal battery. Generally, the courts have required that the act must be done in a wrongful or intentional angry, resentful, rude or insolent manner to make the act a battery. Also, if the touching is a result of an unavoidable accident in the pursuance of a lawful act, this is a valid defense.[118]

---

[112]   Trougn v. Fruchtman, 58 Wis. 2d 569, 207 N.W.2d 297 (1973).

[113]   State v. Caldwell, 293 N.C. 336, 237 S.E.2d 742 (1977).

[114]   Pallis v. State, 123 Ala. 12, 26 So. 339 (1899).

[115]   Scruggs v. State, 161 Ind. App. 666, 317 N.E.2d 807 (1974).

[116]   Brenneman v. State, 458 S.W.2d 677 (1970).

[117]   Fisher v. Carrousel Motor Hotel, 424 S.W.2d 627 (1967).

[118]   Crabtree v. Dawson, 83 S.W. 557 (Ky. 1904).

B. Statutes and Codes

1. Model Penal Code

§ 211.1 Assault[119]

(1) *Simple Assault*. A person is guilty of assault if he:

    (a) attempts to cause or purposely, knowingly or recklessly causes bodily injury to another; or

    (b) negligently causes bodily injury to another with a deadly weapon; or

    (c) attempts by physical menace to put another in fear of imminent serious bodily harm.

Simple assault is a misdemeanor unless committed in a fight or scuffle entered into by mutual consent, in which case it is a petty misdemeanor.

(2) *Aggravated Assault*. A person is guilty of aggravated assault if he:

    (a) attempts to cause serious bodily injury to another, or causes such injury purposely, knowingly or recklessly under circumstances manifesting extreme indifference to the value of human life; or

    (b) attempts to cause or purposely or knowingly causes bodily injury to another with a deadly weapon.

Aggravated assault under paragraph (a) is a felony of the second degree; aggravated assault under paragraph (b) is a felony of the third degree.

Even before the Model Penal Code was drafted, some states, by statute, included assault and battery in the crime of assault, with graduated degrees and penalties. To provide more serious penalties for assaults that were considered especially troublesome, legislation was passed which designated specific assaults as crimes. One of the most common is assault with a deadly weapon.[120] Others are assault with a caustic chemical,[121] and assault which produces grievous bodily harm.[122] In these statutes, "assault" includes both "assault" and "battery."

---

[119]   Model Penal Code, § 211.1 (Proposed Official Draft 1980).

[120]   S.D. Codified Laws Ann. § 22-18-11 (1970).

[121]   Cal. Penal Code, § 244 (West 1970).

[122]   LaFave & Scott, Criminal Law 602 (1972).

The Model Penal Code eliminates the common law categories and many of the statutory modifications and collects several kinds of misconduct under the generic offense of assault.[123] Offenses are graded according to the gravity of harm intended or caused and the dangerousness of the means used.

Under the Model Penal Code provisions assault is limited to cases involving either the fact or prospect of physical injury. Also, there is no grading of punishment based on the status of the victim, as was and is provided under some statutes.[124]

2. Federal Code

Although the primary responsibility for enforcing the criminal law, including laws relating to assault and battery, is in the states, Congress has enacted specific laws prohibiting the assault on specific classes of persons. The three primary federal laws relating to assault are: Title 18, § 111, "Assaulting, resisting, or impeding certain officers or employees"; Title 18, § 112, "Assaulting certain foreign diplomatic and other official personnel"; and Title 18, § 113, "Assaults within maritime and territorial jurisdiction."

The federal law relating to assault that is most often enforced is Title 18, § 11, which provides:

Whoever forcibly assaults, resists, opposes, impedes, intimidates, or interferes with any person designated in § 111 of this title while engaged in or on account of the performance of his official duties, shall be fined not more than $5,000 or imprisoned not more than 3 years, or both.

Whoever, in the commission of any such acts uses a deadly or dangerous weapon, shall be fined not more than $10,000 or imprisoned not more than 10 years, or both.

The purpose of this federal law is to protect the integrity of federal functions and the safety of federal officers, and to provide a federal forum in which to try alleged offenders. As stated in the case of *United States v. Lopez*, the purpose is to provide a federal offense, triable in a federal forum, by which to interdict attacks upon federal officers, which is a matter central to the efficiency of federal law enforcement activities, and not to entrust the states with sole responsibility for punishment of such attacks.[125] The *Lopez*

---

[123] *See* Model Penal Code, § 211.1 (Proposed Official Draft 1980), and following comment.

[124] N.J. Rev. Stat. § 2C:12-1 (1982).

[125] U.S. v. Lopez, 710 F.2d 1071 (Ct. App. 5th Cir. 1983).

case also makes it clear that, in determining whether the officers are acting in the performance of their "official duties," the decision is made by federal, not by state law.

The federal law relating to assault encompasses both assault and battery as defined under the common law. Therefore, physical contact is not necessary, however, the threat of use of force must be a present one and there must be ability to inflict harm, not merely interference with the performance of duty.[126] According to the interpretation by the federal courts, it is not necessary that the assailant be aware that his victim is a federal officer; all that Section requires is an intent to assault, not an intent to assault a federal officer.[127]

Title 18, § 112 of the U.S. Code provides a penalty for one who assaults, strikes, wounds, imprisons or offers violence to a foreign official, official guest or internationally protected person.[128]

Section 113 provides a penalty for assaults within the maritime and territorial jurisdiction of the United States.[129]

3. Other statutes and codes

Some states have followed the reasoning of the drafters of the Model Penal Code. Others have retained separate provisions relating to assaults on police officers and other designated categories of persons.[130] Still others take a different approach and define degrees of assault, or provide more or less serious penalties according to the offender's degree of guilty mind, the means used to commit the offense, and the actual harm to persons involved.[131] An example of the latter is Ohio, where six categories of assault and menacing deal with offenses formerly characterized as different kinds of assault, battery and menacing threats.[132] The Ohio Code provisions are included here as an example of this approach:

---

[126] U.S. v. Bamberger, 452 F.2d 696 (1971); cert. denied, 405 U.S. 1043, 31 L.Ed.2d 585, 92 S. Ct. 1326 (1971).

[127] U.S. v. Feola, 420 U.S. 671, 43 L.Ed.2d 541, 95 S. Ct. 1255 (1975).

[128] 18 U.S.C.A. § 112.

[129] 18 U.S.C.A. § 113. See appendix for definition of "maritime and territorial jurisdiction of the United States."

[130] N.H. Rev. Stat. Ann. § 631.1 (1974); N.J. Rev. Stat. § 2C:12-1 (1982); Pa. Cons. Stat. 18 § 2701 (1983).

[131] Ky. Rev. Stat. § 508.

[132] Ohio Rev. Code Ann. §§ 2903.11, 2903.12, 2903.13, 2903.14, 2903.21, 2903.22 (Page 1987).

§ 2903.11 Felonious assault

(A) No person shall knowingly:

(1) Cause serious physical harm to another;
(2) Cause or attempt to cause physical harm to another by means of a deadly weapon or dangerous ordnance as defined in § 2923.11 of the Revised Code.

(B) Whoever violates this Section is guilty of felonious assault, a felony of the second degree.

§ 2903.12 Aggravated assault

(A) No person, while under extreme emotional stress brought on by serious provocation reasonably sufficient to incite him into using deadly force, shall knowingly:

(1) Cause serious physical harm to another;
(2) Cause or attempt to cause physical harm to another by means of a deadly weapon or dangerous ordnance as defined in § 2923.11 of the Revised Code.

(B) Whoever violates this Section is guilty of aggravated assault, a felony of the fourth degree.

§ 2903.13 Assault

(A) No person shall knowingly cause or attempt to cause physical harm to another.

(B) No person shall recklessly cause serious physical harm to another.

(C) Whoever violates this Section is guilty of assault, a misdemeanor of the first degree.

§ 2903.14 Negligent assault

(A) No person shall negligently, by means of a deadly weapon or dangerous ordnance as defined in § 2923.11 of the Revised Code, cause physical harm to another.

(B) Whoever violates this Section is guilty of negligent assault, a misdemeanor of the third degree.

§ 2903.21 Aggravated menacing

(A) No person shall knowingly cause another to believe that the offender will cause serious physical harm to the person or property of such other person or member of his immediate family.

(B) Whoever violates this Section is guilty of aggravated menacing, a misdemeanor of the first degree.

§ 2903.22 Menacing

(A) No person shall knowingly cause another to believe that the offender will cause physical harm to the person or property of such other person or member of his immediate family.

(B) Whoever violates this Section is guilty of menacing, a misdemeanor of the fourth degree.

It is not necessary to prove that the assault can be carried out. For example, according to the decision in *State v. Tate*, the State proved beyond a reasonable doubt all the elements of the crime of felonious assault where the record demonstrated that the accused pointed a gun at another person, but it was undisputed that the gun was unloaded, that the accused knew it was unloaded, and that the accused made no attempt to pull the trigger or to use the weapon in any other manner as a deadly weapon.[133]

The Model Penal Code and many state statutes include the crime of "aggravated assault." Where aggravated assault is charged under the statute, evidence must be introduced to show that the defendant committed the acts as defined by statute. For example, where a statute defines aggravated assault as attempted battery, evidence must be introduced to show that there was a substantial step toward committing a battery in order to sustain a conviction. However, it is not necessary to introduce evidence to show without question that the battery could have been completed.

In a Georgia case, the conviction for aggravated assault was affirmed where the reviewing court found that the defendant had gone past preparation and had begun to perpetrate the crime when he procured the gun and set out after the intended victim. It was no defense, the court reasoned, that completion of the crime was made factually impossible when the intended victim ran from the defendant and hid, so that the defendant could not complete the battery.[134]

Where the state statute includes the crime of assault with a dangerous weapon, the prosecution must show that a dangerous weapon was, in fact, involved. In a Michigan case, the defendant was charged and convicted of felonious assault against two small girls.[135] He had no weapon but used his

---

[133] 54 Ohio St. 2d 444, 377 N.E.2d 778 (1978).

[134] Riddle v. State, 145 App. 328, 243 S.E.2d 607 (Ga. Ct. App. 1978). *See* case in Part II.

[135] People v. Van Diver, 80 Mich. App. 352, 263 N.W.2d 370 (Mich. Ct. App. 1978).

hands to hold both victims, with one hand being placed over the lower face of one victim to quiet her as well as to restrain her. On appeal, the defendant contended that he could not be convicted of felonious assault, as he had no dangerous weapon. The state claimed that the pair of hands should be considered as dangerous weapons.

The reviewing court held that the statute is not limited to the dangerous weapons specifically listed, but bare hands cannot be considered as included. The court based its decision to some extent on the fact that another statute defined assault not involving dangerous weapons, reasoning that if bare hands were construed as being "dangerous weapons," the distinction between categories of assault would be meaningless.

While a person's hand is not generally considered a dangerous weapon under a statute which prohibits assault with a deadly instrument, the courts have found that other instruments can be considered dangerous weapons under certain circumstances. For example, an Alabama court found that intentionally putting an automobile in motion and violently and intentionally driving it against a police officer is "an assault with a deadly instrument," in violation of the statute.[136] And the defendant's conduct in coming up to the driver's door of the victim's car, holding a knife to the back of her neck, and telling her to move over constituted an assault. The use of the knife made it "an assault with a deadly weapon."[137] In this case the court made clear that it was not necessary for the defendant to actually begin cutting the victim in order to constitute the crime of assault with a deadly weapon.

In the case of *State v. Torres*, the court of appeals of North Carolina agreed with the lower court that four large metal rings worn by the defendant were properly the basis for a conviction on a charge of assault with a deadly weapon.[138] In this case, the defendant was involved in a fist fight in the parking lot of a Durham County High School. The defendant was wearing four large silver rings ornamented with a skull or pirate head. The victim suffered a broken jaw, and the rings on the hand of the defendant were found to be covered with blood at the time of the arrest. The defendant was charged with using metal, raised-designed rings on his fingers, as deadly weapons to assault and inflict serious injury. The reviewing court refused to find error on the part of the trial court in allowing this as evidence of a deadly weapon under the North Carolina statute.

It is obvious, from the foregoing discussion, that one must carefully study the statutes of the respective states in order to determine the specific elements that must be proved in an assault situation. However, all of the

---

[136] Kelly v. State, 362 S.2d 1292 (1978).

[137] State v. Gordon, 120 Ariz. 182, 584 P.2d 1173 (1978).

[138] State v. Torres, 335 S.E.2d 34 (N.C. App. 1985).

statutory crimes are predicated on the common law crimes of assault and battery and, although the terminology differs from state to state, in the final analysis, there is quite a bit of similarity between the statutes.

In defining degrees of assault, the terms "serious physical injury," "deadly weapon," and "wantonly" are used. Although they may differ from jurisdiction to jurisdiction, these definitions will help in distinguishing degrees of assault.

(a) Serious physical injury. Physical injury which creates a substantial risk of death, or which causes serious and prolonged disfigurement, prolonged impairment of health, or prolonged loss or impairment of the functions of any bodily organ.[139]

(b) Deadly weapon. A weapon (loaded or unloaded) from which a deadly shot can be fired or a switch blade knife, gravity knife, billy club or metal knuckles.[140]

(c) Wantonly. Defendant is aware of substantial unjustified risk that the conduct will cause death and he consciously disregards the risk.[141]

§ 3.8 Kidnapping and Related Offenses

A. Traditional Definitions and Elements

Kidnapping is defined as "forcibly detaining another against his will to unlawfully obtain ransom, or unlawfully restraining another and forcibly moving the person imprisoned to another place."[142]

The gist of kidnapping is the intentional taking of a person and compelling him to be detained against his will. In the opinion of one court, kidnapping may be committed by willfully seizing, confining or inveigling another; with the intent to cause him, without authority of law, to be secretly confined or imprisoned within the state; to be sent out of the state; to be sold as a slave or to be in any way held to service; or to be kept or detained against his will.[143]

---

[139] Ky. Dept. of Just., Ky. Penal Code Notebook, page 111 (1975).

[140] *Id.*, page 109.

[141] *Id.*, page 1172.

[142] Gwooch v. United States, 82 F.2d 534 (10th Cir. 1936).

[143] State v. Croatt, 227 Minn. 185, 34 N.W.2d 716 (1948).

Although the terms used in defining kidnapping vary from jurisdiction to jurisdiction, the final result is generally the same. Some of these definitions will help in understanding the scope of the offense.

To constitute the crime of "kidnapping," the defendant must have falsely imprisoned his victim by acquiring complete dominion and control over him for some appreciable period of time and must have carried him beyond the immediate vicinity of the place of such false imprisonment.[144]

"Kidnap" means to take and carry away any person by unlawful force or fraud and against his will.[145]

At common law, "kidnapping" is defined as the forcible abduction and carrying away of a man, woman or child from his own country into another.[146]

To clarify some of the technical language used by the early courts in defining the elements of kidnapping, all states have modified the common law. Statutory provisions greatly enlarge the scope of kidnapping and, in some instances, add other offenses which are directly related to kidnapping, but do not require that all elements be proved.

Under the definition first stated, the elements of kidnapping are:

(a) detaining another,
(b) by force,
(c) without his consent,
(d) without legal cause, and
(e) moving to another place or to unlawfully obtain ransom.

In enumerating the elements necessary to prove the crime of kidnapping, a Nevada court included this statement:

"Kidnapping" constitutes carrying away of the person for a purpose such as ransom or committing bodily felony; elements of kidnapping are taking or seizure of a human being, asportation or move-

---

144 State v. Roberts, 286 N.C. 265, 210 S.E.2d 396 (1974).
145 State v. Ayers, 198 Kan. 467, 426 P.2d 21 (1967).
146 Tate v. State, 32 Md. App. 613, 363 A.2d 622 (1976).

ment of the seized individual, by means of unlawful force or fraud, and for the purpose of ransom, reward or committing a felony.[147]

The elements of the crime of kidnapping depend upon the wording of the respective statutes. In order to constitute the offense of kidnapping or similar offense, all of the elements to the crime must be present.[148]

Under the common law, and under some statutes, an element of the crime is the taking, leading, carrying away or transportation of the victim. The degree of movement from one place to another depends upon the wording of the statute. If, for example, the statute provides that the person be removed from the state, then the prosecution must show that the person was, in fact, moved from the state. However, if the statute provides that "a person is guilty if he unlawfully removes one from his place of residence or business, or a substantial distance from the vicinity where he is found," then all that is necessary is to show that such unlawful removal took place. In this regard one court upheld a kidnapping conviction where the accused under pretense of being a good faith passenger, forced a taxi driver at gunpoint to drive him to another destination, as against the contention that the taxicab driver was not carried from any "place" because the moving vehicle was not a place.[149]

In the case of *State v. Morris*, a Minnesota Court determined that the removal of a victim the distance of only 150 feet, and detention for five minutes in the process of committing indecent assault, constituted "kidnapping" and it was proper to charge kidnapping as a separate offense.[150] In another case the court determined that the word "kidnapping," as used in the statute of that state which prohibited kidnapping, means the unlawful taking and carrying away of a person by force and against his will. That court agreed that it is the fact, not the distance of forcible removal of the victim that constitutes the kidnapping; any carrying away is sufficient and the distance is immaterial.[151]

The "force" element of kidnapping may be accomplished either by actual physical coercion or force to the body of such a person, or by coercion of the will of such a person by threats, fear, intimidation or other inducement which deprive him of his will to resist.[152]

---

[147] Lovell v. State, 92 Nev. 128, 546 P.2d 1301 (1976).

[148] People v. Landis, 66 Ill. App. 2d 458, 214 N.E.2d 343 (Ill. App. Ct. 1966).

[149] Epperson v. State, 211 Ind. 237, 6 N.E.2d 538 (1937).

[150] State v. Morris, 281 Minn. 119, 160 N.W.2d 715 (1968).

[151] State v. Dix, 14 N.C. App. 328, 188 S.E.2d 737 (1972).

[152] State v. Brown, 181 Kan. 375, 312 P.2d 832 (1957).

A defendant cannot be convicted of kidnapping if the alleged victim consented to the restraint or consented to go with the defendant. However, the initial consent is converted into an unlawful detention if the defendant refuses to allow the person to leave. For example, where hitchhikers consented to be given a ride to their home, but instead, over their objection and under threats of death, they were driven to a far distant place where one was raped, the court found that, even if the original taking was not forcible or fraudulent, the unlawful detention commenced when the defendant refused to drive the hitchhikers home and drove away from the area.[153]

One of the elements of kidnapping under the common law and under some statutes is *unlawfully* restraining, *unlawfully* removing or *unlawfully* confining. One court affirmed that the act of holding the person for a proscribed purpose necessarily implies an unlawful physical and mental restraint where the detention is for an appreciable period, is against the person's will, and is done with a willful intent to confine the victim.[154]

If all of the elements for the crime of kidnapping are not present, a person may be guilty of a lesser crime with a lesser penalty. For example, a person is guilty under some statutes of unlawful imprisonment when he knowingly and unlawfully restrains another under circumstances which expose that person to a risk of serious physical injury. The elements of unlawful imprisonment under this statute are:

(a) knowingly,
(b) unlawfully,
(c) restraining another, and
(d) under circumstances which expose the victim to a risk of physical injury.

A police officer who restrains another is not guilty of kidnapping if he acts in his official capacity and detains a person pursuant to a warrant issued by a court or is otherwise carrying out his official duties. Here, the act is lawful. But if the officer does not act in good faith and the entire transaction indicates an unlawful purpose, the officer could be technically held for kidnapping.[155] This is especially true when a peace officer goes into another state and, without authority, apprehends a person and returns him to the state where the officer has jurisdiction.

---

[153] Matter of Appeal in Maricopa County Juvenile Action, 25 Ariz. App. 377, 543 P.2d 806 (1975).

[154] Chatwin v. United States, 326 U.S. 455, 66 S. Ct. 233, 90 L.Ed. 198 (1946).

[155] People v. Fick, 89 Cal. 144, 26 P. 759 (1891).

B. Statutes and Codes

1. Model Penal Code[156]

§ 212.1 Kidnapping
A person is guilty of kidnapping if he unlawfully removes another from his place of residence or business, or a substantial distance from the vicinity where he is found, or if he unlawfully confines another for a substantial period in a place of isolation, with any of the following purposes:

(a) to hold for ransom or reward, or as a shield or hostage; or

(b) to facilitate commission of any felony or flight thereafter; or

(c) to inflict bodily injury on or to terrorize the victim or another; or

(d) to interfere with the performance of any governmental or political function.

Kidnapping is a felony of the first degree unless the actor voluntarily releases the victim alive and in a safe place prior to trial, in which case it is a felony of the second degree. A removal or confinement is unlawful within the meaning of this Section if it is accomplished by force, threat or deception, or, in the case of a person who is under the age of 14 or incompetent, if it is accomplished without the consent of a parent, guardian or other person responsible for general supervision of his welfare.

The penalty for kidnapping under the Model Penal Code is determined by the treatment of the victim and the circumstances surrounding the kidnapping. It is a felony in the first degree unless the actor voluntarily releases the victim alive and in a safe place prior to trial, in which case it is a felony in the second degree.[157]

The wording of the Model Penal Code is cast in terms of removal of the victim "from" a location, rather than transporting him "to" another place as was used in some pre-Code statutes. Also, to avoid some confusion and technical interpretations the word "vicinity" is used, rather than "place." Also,

---

[156] Model Penal Code, § 212.1 (Proposed Official Draft 1982).

[157] Model Penal Code, § 212.1, and following comments (Proposed Official Draft 1980).

"substantial" removal is required to preclude kidnapping convictions based on trivial change of location having no bearing on the evil at hand.[158]

The Model Penal Code definition includes unlawful confinement of another "for a substantial period in a place of isolation." This eliminates the "asportation" element which was included in the common law definitions, but still leaves questions as to what is "substantial" and what amounts to "a place of isolation."

The proscribed purposes included in the Model Penal Code include many of these defined in existing statutes. A variety of purposes is covered, but the penalty is not as stringent as some of the penalties for certain types of kidnapping under existing statutes.

Ordinary kidnapping is classified as a felony of the second degree; however, the offense is a felony of the first degree if the victim is not voluntarily released alive.

The term "unlawfully," as used in the Model Penal Code, is defined to include not only the usual forms of force, threat and deception, but also provides that removal or confinement of an underage or mentally incompetent person is unlawful "if it is accomplished without the consent of a parent, guardian or other person responsible for general supervision of his welfare." This includes conduct of the defendant who removes a child or incompetent person at his own request. According to the discussion that follows the provision, the reasoning is that the age line (14 years) was drawn just below the point in adolescence when youngsters commonly begin to exercise independent judgment as to choice of companions and freedom of movement.[159]

2. Federal Code

In 1931, Congress and the public became concerned about mounting incidents of professional kidnapping and the apparent inability of state and local authorities to cope with the interstate aspects of the problem. In response to this, bills were introduced in both houses of Congress forbidding the transportation and interstate or foreign commerce of any person kidnapped and held for ransom or reward. Several months after the kidnapping of the Lindbergh baby in March, 1932, Congress enacted the first Federal Kidnapping Act which became known as the "Lindbergh Law."[160] This law

---

[158] *Id.*

[159] *Id.*

[160] U.S. v. Jackson, 390 U.S. 570, 88 S. Ct. 1209, 20 L.Ed.2d 138 (1968).

has since been modified by Congress and interpreted by the courts. The present Federal Kidnapping statute provides:

> Title 18, § 1201. KIDNAPPING
> (a) Whoever unlawfully seizes, confines, inveigles, decoys, kidnaps, abducts, or carries away and holds for ransom or reward or otherwise any person, except in the case of a minor by the parent thereof, when:
>
> (1) the person is willfully transported in interstate or foreign commerce;
> (2) any such act against the person is done within the special maritime and territorial jurisdiction of the United States;
> (3) any such act against the person is done within the special aircraft jurisdiction of the United States as defined in § 101(36) of the Federal Aviation Act of 1958, as amended (49 U.S.C. 1301(36));
> (4) the person is a foreign official, an internationally protected person, or an official guest as those terms are defined in § 1116(b) of this title; or
> (5) the person is among those officers and employees designated in § 1114 of this title and any such act against the person is done while the person is engaged in, or on account of, the performance of official duties, shall be punished by imprisonment for any term of years or for life.[161]

The purpose of the Federal Kidnapping Act is to prevent transportation in interstate or foreign commerce persons who are unlawfully restrained in order that the captors might secure some benefit to themselves. Because of this interstate feature of the act, a defendant may not be found guilty of kidnapping under the federal statute unless the prosecution can establish transportation in interstate commerce of an unconsenting person who was held for ransom or reward.[162]

---

[161] 18 U.S.C. § 1201 as amended in 1971, 1976, 1977, 1978 and 1984.

[162] U.S. v. Crosby, 713 F.2d 1066 (1983), *cert. denied*, 464 U.S. 1001, 78 L.Ed.2d 696, 104 S. Ct. 506 (1983); U.S. v. McGrady, 191 F.2d 829 (1951).

In proving that the transportation is an interstate commerce, the prosecution need only show that the victim was taken across any state line, even for a short time. For example, if the victim was taken across two noncontiguous state lines, the time elapsed after crossing the first line but before crossing of the second line constituted a holding for at least a period of time and the kidnapping statute applied.[163]

The "holds for ransom or reward or otherwise" element was satisfied when the victim was taken away from her home for purposes of silencing her as a potential witness. This came within the "or otherwise" provision of the Section requiring that the kidnapping be "for ransom or reward or otherwise."[164]

In 1967, the Federal Kidnapping Act, as then written, was challenged as being unconstitutional. A U.S. district court held that the act was unconstitutional because it makes "the risk of death" the price for asserting the right for a jury trial and thereby "impairs" free exercise of that constitutional right. The law in effect at the time included a provision that the offense was punishable by death "if the verdict of the jury so recommended."

The U.S. Supreme Court on review determined that the kidnapping act should not be invalidated in its entirety simply because its capital punishment clause violates the Fifth and Sixth amendments.[165]

The U.S. Supreme Court did agree, however, that penalty provision of the Federal Kidnapping Act, is unconstitutional, as it tends to discourage the assertion of the Fifth Amendment right not to plead guilty, and to deter exercise of the Sixth Amendment right to demand a jury trial. Following this case, Congress amended the act so as to make the wording consistent with the holding of the case.

3. Other statutes and codes

While some states follow the various provisions of the Model Penal Code,[166] others add to the list of proscribed purposes and still others take a different approach. An example of a state statute that differs from the Model

---

[163] Hall v. U.S., 410 F.2d 653 (1969), *cert. denied*, 396 U.S. 970, 24 L.Ed.2d 436, 90 S. Ct. 455 (1969).

[164] U.S. v. Satterfield, 743 F.2d 827 (1984), *cert. denied*, 471 U.S. 1117, 86 L.Ed.2d 262, 105 S. Ct. 2363 (1984).

[165] U.S. v. Jackson, 390 U.S. 570, 20 L.Ed.2d 138, 88 S. Ct. 1209 (1968).

[166] Ala., Ariz., Ark., Conn., Fla., Hawaii, Iowa, Kan., Ky., Me., Mo., Mont., Neb., N.Y., N.D., Ohio, Pa., S.D., Tex., Utah and Wash.

Penal Code in various ways is that of New York.[167] In addition to the offenses of "unlawful imprisonment" in the first and second degree, the New York Code provides heavier penalties for offenses such as kidnapping in the second degree and kidnapping in the first degree.[168]

§ 135.05 Unlawful imprisonment in the second degree
A person is guilty of unlawful imprisonment in the second degree when he restrains another person.
Unlawful imprisonment in the second degree is a Class A misdemeanor.

§ 135.10 Unlawful imprisonment in the first degree
A person is guilty of unlawful imprisonment in the first degree when he restrains another person under circumstances which expose the latter to a risk of serious physical injury.
Unlawful imprisonment in the first degree is a Class E felony.

§ 135.20 Kidnapping in the second degree
A person is guilty of kidnapping in the second degree when he abducts another person.
Kidnapping in the second degree is a Class B felony.

§ 135.25 Kidnapping in the first degree
A person is guilty of kidnapping in the first degree when he abducts another person and when:
1.   His intent is to compel a third person to pay or deliver money or property as ransom, or to engage in other particular conduct, or to refrain from engaging in particular conduct; or
2.   He restrains the person abducted for a period of more than twelve hours with intent to:

     (a)   Inflict physical injury upon him or violate or abuse him sexually;
     (b)   Accomplish or advance the commission of a felony; or
     (c)   Terrorize him or a third person; or
     (d)   Interfere with the performance of a governmental or political function; or

---

[167] N.Y. Penal Law, §§ 135.05-135.30 (McKinney 1975).
[168] *Id.*

3. The person abducted dies during the abduction or before he is able to return or to be returned to safety. Such death shall be presumed, in a case where such person was less than sixteen years old or an incompetent person at the time of the abduction, from evidence that his parents, guardians or other lawful custodians did not see or hear from him following the termination of the abduction and prior to trial and received no reliable information during such period persuasively indicating that he was alive. In all other cases, such death shall be presumed from evidence that a person whom the person abducted would have been extremely likely to visit or communicate with during the specific period were he alive and free to do so did not see or hear from him during such period and received no reliable information during such period persuasively indicating that he was alive.

Kidnapping in the first degree is a Class A-I felony.

§ 135.30 Kidnapping; defense
    In any prosecution for kidnapping, it is an affirmative defense that:

(a) the defendant was a relative of the person abducted, and
(b) his sole purpose was to assume control of such person.

"Restrain," as used in the New York law, means to restrict a person's movements intentionally and unlawfully in such manner as to interfere substantially with his liberty by moving him from one place to another, or by confining him either in the place where the restriction commences or in a place to which he has been moved, without consent and with knowledge that the restriction is unlawful. A person is so moved or confined "without consent" when such is accomplished by:

(a) physical force, intimidation or deception, or
(b) any means whatever, including acquiescence of the victim, if he is a child less than sixteen years old or an incompetent person and the parent, guardian or other person or institution having lawful control or custody of him has not acquiesced in the movement or confinement.

"Abduct," as used in §§ 135.20 and 135.25, means to restrain a person with intent to prevent his liberation by either:

(a) secreting or holding him in a place where he is not likely to be found, or

(b) using or threatening to use deadly physical force.

"Relative" in § 135.30 means a parent, ancestor, brother, sister, uncle or aunt.

The Model Penal Code includes the offenses of Felonious Restraint, False Imprisonment, Interference with Custody and Criminal Coercion as offenses related to kidnapping.[169] These and other specifically defined offenses were added in many states, to make it possible for the state to take action when a wrongful act is committed, but the wrong is not serious enough to come within the technical definition of kidnapping. Generally, these less serious offenses, as defined by statute, have a penalty attached which is of a lower degree than the penalty for kidnapping.

As these vary from state to state, each state statute must be studied to determine the elements to be proved and definitions of terms.

§ 3.9 Mayhem

A. Traditional Definition and Elements

1. Definition

At early common law, mayhem was described as maliciously depriving another of the use of such of his members as may render him less able, in fighting, either to defend himself or to annoy his adversary.[170]

Often the term "maim" is used as the equivalent to the word "mayhem." Some examples of the crime of mayhem at common law are to cut off or permanently cripple a man's hands or fingers, or to strike out his eye or to disable his leg.[171] Under the strict definition of mayhem at common law, an injury, such as cutting off an ear or nose, did not constitute mayhem because

---

[169] Model Penal Code, §§ 212.2-212.5 (Proposed Official Draft 1980).

[170] State v. Taylor, 105 W.Va. 298, 143 S.E. 254 (1928).

[171] State v. McDonie, 89 W.Va. 185, 109 S.E. 710 (1921).

it did not result in permanent disablement but merely disfigured the victim.[172]

As the law developed in the United States, the definition was extended to include unlawfully to disfigure as well as to dismember and to disable and in some instances to specific bodily components, such as the eyes, ears, tongue, nose and lips. Some statutes that were adopted before the Uniform Code was written included parts of the common law as expanded by court decisions and statutes. An example is that of Idaho, which includes this definition of mayhem:

Every person who unlawfully and maliciously deprives a human being of a member of his body, or disables, disfigures or renders it useless, or cuts or disables the tongue, puts out an eye, slits the nose, ear or lips, is guilty of mayhem.[173]

2. Elements

The common law elements of mayhem are:

(a) maliciously,
(b) depriving one of use of members of his body,
(c) rendering him less able to fight or defend himself.

As the crime was broadened to include other injuries which merely disfigured, other elements were added or substituted. Also, in some states the intent to disfigure was, and is, made an essential element of the crime.[174]

In determining the elements to be proved, one must look carefully at the statute. For example, where a statute makes it a crime to disfigure another by "means of a knife or other instrument," evidence must be introduced to show the use of an instrument. However, in one case, carbolic acid was held to be an "instrument" within the meaning of the statute.[175] Where "disfigurement" is required, at least one court has held that a conviction for disfigurement is proper where evidence is introduced that the accused threw acid on the face and arms of the victim, which brought about disfigurement

---

[172] Coleman v. Commonwealth, 280 Ky. 410, 133 S.W. 555 (1939).

[173] Idaho Code, § 18-5001 (1942).

[174] State v. Jones, 70 Iowa 505, 30 N.W. 750 (1886); State v. Hair, 37 Minn. 351, 34 N.W. 893 (1887).

[175] Hiller v. State, 116 Neb. 582, 218 N.W. 386 (1928).

and kept the victim under the treatment of a doctor for some time, although the extent of the injury was not shown.[176]

B. Statutes and Codes

1. Model Penal Code

The Model Penal Code has no special provision entitled mayhem or maiming. The wrongs that were included in the common law definition, and in some state statutes, are included in the Model Penal Code assault definition. Section 211.1(2) provides that a person is guilty of aggravated assault if he (a) attempts to cause serious bodily injury or *causes such* injury purposely, knowingly or recklessly under circumstances manifesting extreme indifference to the value of human life.[177]

"Serious bodily injury" is defined in § 210.0(3) as bodily injury which creates a substantial risk of death or which causes serious, permanent disfigurement or protracted loss or impairment of the function of any bodily member or organ.[178]

Even though the Model Penal Code and some statutes do not include specific provisions regarding mayhem, the broad coverage of assault statutes achieves the same result.

2. Federal Code

The U.S. Code contains no provisions concerning the crime of mayhem.

3. Other statues and codes

Most states have revised their penal code since 1970 and, in most states, the crimes of mayhem and maiming have not been included as specific crimes. In these states, the wrongs covered by the common law and previous statutes are included in the various degrees of assault. For example, in Kentucky the statutory provisions for first, second and third degrees of assault

---

[176]   Lee v. State, 66 Tex. Crim. 567, 148 S.W. 567 (1912).

[177]   Model Penal Code, § 211.1(2) (Proposed Official Draft 1980).

[178]   *Id.* § 210.0(3).

replace common law crimes of assault and battery and the statutory provisions relating to maiming.[179]

Those states that follow the Model Penal Code generally use the definitions included therein. However, in some, the definitions differ. For example, in Wisconsin the definition of "great bodily harm" is defined as:

> bodily injury, which creates a high probability of death, or which causes serious permanent disfigurement, or which causes a permanent or protracted loss or impairment of the function of any bodily member or organ or other serious bodily injury.[180]

This definition more closely follows traditional mayhem statutory or case law.

§ 3.10 Other Crimes Against the Person

In addition to the crimes against the person discussed in previous Sections, some states have enacted legislation to further protect the health, welfare and safety of the inhabitants. Some of these are included here as examples:

A. Extortion. In Ohio, no person, with purpose to obtain any valuable thing or valuable benefit, or induce another to do an unlawful act:[181]

     (1) threaten to commit any felony,
     (2) threaten to commit any offense of violence,
     (3) violate § 2903.21 or 2903.22 of the Revised Code.[182]

The offense is designed to include former Sections dealing with blackmail, extortion or other similar provisions.

B. Wanton Endangerment. In Kentucky, a person is guilty of wanton endangerment in the first degree when, under circumstances manifesting extreme indifference to the value of human

---

[179]   Maiming was a crime under Ky. Rev. Stat. § 435.160 (1975), until changed in 1975.

[180]   Wis. Stat. § 939.22(14) (1982).

[181]   Ohio Rev. Code Ann. § 2905.11 (Page 1987).

[182]   Ohio Rev. Code Ann. §§ 2903.21-2903.22 (Page's 1982) refer to the crime of menacing.

life, he wantonly engages in conduct which creates a substantial danger of death or serious physical injury to another person.[183]

Each state statute must be checked to determine what other crimes against the person may be enforced in that state.

§ 3.11 Summary

Crimes that are considered under the heading "Offenses Against Persons" are homicide, suicide, assault and battery, kidnapping and related offenses, mayhem and "other crimes against the person." The most serious of these are in the homicide category. Homicide is defined as the killing of a human being by another human being. Not all homicides are illegal. At the top of the scale of crimes relating to homicide is murder in the first degree. At the other end of the scale are excusable and justifiable homicides, which are not subject to punishment under the law.

The common law crime of murder is defined as "the unlawful killing of a human being by another human being with malice aforethought." At common law, and in some states, there are no degrees of murder. However, in most states, the crime of murder is divided into two categories: first degree and second degree. The distinguishing factor in first degree murder is premeditation and deliberation.

Manslaughter is defined as the unlawful killing of a human being, done without malice, express or implied, either in a sudden quarrel or unintentionally while in the commission of an unlawful act. Manslaughter is usually divided into two categories: voluntary, where the homicidal act is intentional but passion-produced or occasioned by some provocation, and involuntary, where it results from the commission of certain unlawful acts not accompanied by any intention to take life. In order for a killing, which would otherwise be murder, to be reduced to manslaughter, there must be some adequate provocation, the killing must have been in heat of passion, it must have been a sudden passion, and there must have been a causal connection between provocation, the passion and the fatal act.

Suicide is not a homicide, as there is no killing of one person by another person. While some of the early courts took the position that suicide was a crime, even if no punishment could be inflicted, today suicide is not considered a crime. However, a person may be guilty of criminal homicide if, with the requisite culpability, he causes the death of another by causing another to

---

[183] Ky. Rev. Stat. § 508.060 (1975). *See* Ky. Rev. Stat. § 508.070 (1975) for a definition of the crime of wanton endangerment in the second degree.

commit suicide. Also, under some statutes, a person may be guilty of a separate offense of aiding or soliciting suicide even where suicide itself is not a crime.

Although assault and battery are two separate common law crimes, they are often discussed together and, under the modern statutes, are combined into various degrees of assault. The common definition of assault is "an unlawful offer or attempt to injure another, with apparent present ability to effectuate the attempt under circumstances creating a fear of imminent peril." In assault there is no touching of another. Battery is "the unlawful touching of the person of another by the aggressor or by some substance put in motion by him."

Kidnapping is "the forcible detaining of another against his will to unlawfully obtain ransom, or unlawfully restraining another and forcibly moving the person imprisoned to another place." The gist of kidnapping is the intentional taking of a person and compelling him to be detained against his will. Kidnapping is considered a very serious crime and under the Model Penal Code is designated a felony in the first degree, unless the actor voluntarily releases the person alive and in a safe place prior to trial, in which case it is a felony in the second degree.

While mayhem was a crime at common law, many of the modern statutes have no specific provision entitled "mayhem" or "maiming." This offense was described as "maliciously depriving another of the use of such of his members as may render him less able in fighting either to defend himself or to annoy the adversary." Under modern statutes, the act is included under the broad coverage of the assault statutes.

In addition to those crimes discussed, there are other crimes against a person, such as extortion and wanton endangerment. Various state statutes have other specific crimes which relate to injury to the person.

Chapter 4
OFFENSES AGAINST
THE PERSON – SEX RELATED

If any man shall unlawfully have carnal copulation with any woman child under ten years old, he shall be put to death, whether it were with or without the girl's consent. If any man shall forcibly and without consent ravish any maid or woman that is lawfully married or contracted, he shall be put to death.

Quoted in *Comm. v. Burke*,
105 Mass. 376,
7 Am.Rep. 531 (1870).

§ 4.1 Introduction

Although some sex-related offenses are also offenses against the person, they are considered separately for several reasons. First, the motivation of the violator is not the same as that for other offenses. Also, as will be apparent from the discussion, the laws, which reflect public opinion, have changed more dramatically in sex-related cases. No effort is made to recommend investigative techniques. However, criminal justice personnel should be aware that the techniques for investigating sex-related offenses are different in some respects from those used when investigating other types of crimes.

While in earlier societies (not too far in the past) certain acts where sex was involved were considered serious offenses, these are not considered as serious in modern society. For example, adultery and fornication were classified as felonies at common law and by some statutes. Today they are misdemeanors, if any crime at all.[1]

Some sex-related crimes are consensual and are not "offenses against the person." In this chapter, the non-consensual sex crimes are considered and the elements of the crimes discussed. In the chapter entitled "Offenses Against the Public Health and Morals," other sex-related crimes such as adultery, prostitution, incest and the obscenity offenses are included.

The specific offenses defined and explained are rape, sodomy and related crimes, sexual abuse (sexual assault), lewdness (indecent exposure) and seduction.

§ 4.2 Rape

A. Traditional Definitions and Elements

The common law definition of rape is "the act of having unlawful carnal knowledge by a man of a woman, forcibly and against her will."[2]

In reflecting on the common law, as compared to statutory law, one court indicated that common law rape is the act of a man having unlawful carnal knowledge of a female over age of 10 years by force without the consent and against the will of the victim.[3] The courts have used various phraseology to define the crime of rape. Some of the definitions are included here:

---

[1]   State v. Young, 52 Or. 227, 96 P. 1067 (1908).

[2]   State v. Tuttle, 67 Ohio St. 440, 66 N.E. 524 (1903).

[3]   Hazel v. State, 221 Md. 464, 157 A.2d 922 (1960).

"Rape" requires a touching of the body of a female to the extent that, by force and without her consent, a penetration occurs.[4]

"Rape" is a crime of violence involving non-consensual invasion of a woman's body.[5]

"Rape" is the act of sexual intercourse committed by a man with a woman, not his wife, and without her consent, committed when the woman's resistance is overcome by force or fear, or under other prohibitive conditions.[6]

From these definitions, it is clear that the burden is on the prosecution to prove the various elements in order to convict a person of rape. These elements are:

(a) unlawful,
(b) carnal knowledge (or sexual intercourse),
(c) by force or fear, and
(d) without the consent or against the will of the female.

Each of these elements of the crime of rape must be proved beyond a reasonable doubt and each has a technical definition.

(a) Unlawful

Unlawful, as used in this context, is defined as "not authorized by law," and interpreted to be intercourse between those who are not husband and wife.[7] Under the common law, and as defined by most statutes, rape is an act of sexual intercourse with a female, *not the wife of the perpetrator*.[8]

The rationale for the concept that intercourse between husband and wife is lawful is that the matrimonial consent that the wife gives when she assumes a marriage relationship cannot be revoked.[9] A seventeenth-century jurist, Matthew Hale, formulated the concept that by "their mutual matrimonial consent and contract the wife hath given of herself in this kind unto her husband, which she cannot retract."[10] In some states, courts have decided that a

---

[4] Wilson v. State, 268 A.2d 484 (Me. 1970).
[5] State v. Greer, 616 S.W.2d 82 (Mo. App. 1981).
[6] State v. Lora, 213 Kan. 184, 515 P.2d 1086 (1973).
[7] Frazier v. State, 48 Tex. Crim. 142, 86 S.W. 754 (1905).
[8] Adams v. State, 5 Okla. Crim. 347, 114 P. 347 (1911).
[9] Frazier v. State, 48 Tex. Crim. 142, 86 S.W. 754 (1905).
[10] 1 Hale, HISTORY OF THE PLEAS OF THE CROWN 619 (1800).

man can rape his wife if other factors are proved and some states have merely omitted the words "not his wife" from the statute.[11]

The New Jersey Supreme Court, after discussing the changes in the divorce laws and other legal developments, reasoned that a corollary of a spouse's right to make a unilateral decision to end the marriage is that a "wife can refuse sexual intercourse with her husband during the period of separation prior to divorce." The court commented:

> If a wife has the right to refuse intercourse, or deny consent, then a husband's forceful carnal knowledge of his wife clearly includes all elements of the crime of rape. He cannot defend by claiming that there was no lack of consent because he was still legally married to the victim.

(b) Carnal Knowledge (or Sexual Intercourse)

Carnal knowledge is synonymous with sexual intercourse. According to all authorities, there must be some penetration to complete the crime of rape. In the case of *State v. Bono*, the court announced that "carnal knowledge" involves actual sexual penetration of the sexual organ of the female by the sexual organ of the male.[12] In rape, the least penetration is sufficient but the prosecution must prove the fact of penetration beyond a reasonable doubt.[13] Several older cases made it quite clear the slightest penetration of the vulva is sufficient to constitute rape and emission is not necessary.[14] But while the slightest penetration can constitute rape, there may be many penetrations during the act, which, if a continuous process, constitutes but one crime.[15]

Rupture of the hymen is not an ingredient of the carnal knowledge element, as rape is committed if the male organ enters only the labia or vulva and penetrates. An entering of the vagina or rupturing of the hymen is not required.[16]

(c) Force or Fear

The force that is a necessary element in the commission of the common law crime of rape includes actual physical force in compelling submission of

---

[11] People v. Liberta, 474 N.E.2d 567 (N.Y. 1984).

[12] State v. Bono, 128 N.J. Super. 254, 319 A.2d 762 (1974).

[13] Davis v. State, 43 Tex. 189 (1875).

[14] State v. Pollock, 57 Ariz. 414, 114 P.2d 249 (1941); Harton v. State, 74 Ga. App. 723, 41 S.E.2d 278 (1947).

[15] Beasley v. State, 94 Okla. Crim. 353, 236 P.2d 263 (1952).

[16] Rhodes v. State, 462 P.2d 722 (Wyo. 1969).

the female to the sexual connection and also includes threatened force or violence for the purpose of preventing resistance. This element may be met by showing that there was actual force or the force was constructive. *Forcibly* does not necessarily mean *violently*. In one case, the court determined that "the force must be such as may reasonably be supposed adequate to overcome physical resistance of the woman upon whom rape is charged to have been committed, taking into consideration the relative strength of the parties and other circumstances of the case, such as outcries and giving alarm."[17]

The offense is complete even if no actual force is used if it can be shown by the evidence that the woman is made to yield through fear and does not consent voluntarily to the act of sexual intercourse.[18] The force necessary to constitute rape may also be constructive. For example, if the female is mentally unconscious from drink or is asleep, or for other causes is in a state of stupefaction, so that the act of unlawful carnal knowledge on the part of the man is committed without conscious and voluntary permission, force is necessarily involved in the wrongful act itself. The unlawful connection constitutes the necessary force if the man knows that the woman is in a state of unconsciousness.[19]

Without force, actual or constructive, there can be no rape. If, however, the prosecution can show, by convincing evidence, that actual force was used, or he can show the victim submitted as a result of terror or dread of a greater violence caused by threats, actual force or the intimidation which is the equivalent of force, this is sufficient to meet the "force" requirements in proving the crime of rape.

In the case of *People v. Taylor*, the Supreme Court of Illinois explained the "force" requirement:

...Proof of physical force is unnecessary if the prosecuting witness was paralyzed by fear or overcome by superior strength of her attacker; that it is, however, fundamental that in order to prove the charge of forcible rape there must be evidence to show that the act was committed by force and against the will of the female and if she has the use of her faculties and physical powers, the evidence must show such resistance as will demonstrate that the act was against her will.[20]

---

[17] Powell v. Commonwealth, 179 Va. 703, 20 S.E.2d 536 (1942).

[18] Turner v. State, 32 Ala. App. 465, 27 S.2d 239 (1946).

[19] Commonwealth v. Stephens, 143 Pa. Super. 394, 17 A.2d 919 (1941).

[20] People v. Taylor, 48 Ill.2d 91, 268 N.E.2d 865 (1971).

(d) Without Consent or Against the Will

This element, which is sometimes stated in terms such as "without her consent," has been interpreted to mean that the sexual act must be committed against the will of the woman without her voluntary consent. Intercourse accomplished by force is without consent; however, voluntary consent given at any time prior to the penetration deprives the subsequent intercourse of its criminal character, regardless of how reluctantly it may have been given or how much force theretofore had been employed.[21] Whether the consent was voluntary depends upon the facts of each particular case and if the jury, after hearing all of the evidence, finds that there was consent at the time of the intercourse even though there was some persuasion in the initial contact, the court will be hesitant to find this element of the crime.

It is not necessary that the victim physically resist if the evidence indicates she physically feared the defendant and expressed her unwillingness to engage in intercourse.[22] Where the victim is prevented from resisting by the threats of creating bodily harm, accompanied by apparent power of execution, this element of the crime of rape is present.

The general rule is that if the victim consents to sexual intercourse prior to penetration and withdraws the consent following penetration, there is no rape.[23] However, this does not preclude the perpetrator from being found guilty of another crime, such as assault, if warranted by the evidence.

A woman's consent to sexual intercourse is void if it is given by fear of personal violence.[24] Also, there can be no consent if the woman is wholly insensible so as to be incapable of consenting.[25] Therefore, unlawful intercourse with a woman who had fainted was held to be rape in a Georgia case.[26]

Where the consent is obtained by fraud, there is no legal consent. For example, where a doctor had sexual intercourse with a woman under the fraudulent pretense of medical treatment, this was rape as there was no voluntary consent.[27] Nor is consent by a woman to a nude massage consent to intercourse. In *People v. Reed*, the defendant was convicted of rape and three

---

[21] Reynolds v. State, 27 Neb. 90, 42 N.W. 903 (1889); Whittaker v. State, 50 Wis. 518, 7 N.W. 431 (1880).

[22] State v. Greer, 616 S.W.2d 82 (Mo. App. 1981).

[23] People v. Burroughs, 19 Cal. Rptr. 344, 200 Cal. App. 2d 629 (1962); People v. Vela, 218 Cal. Rptr. 161, 172 Cal. App. 3d 237 (1985). *See* case in Part II.

[24] State v. Schuster, 282 S.W.2d 553 (Mo. 1955); Spaulding v. State, 373 N.E.2d 165 (Ill. 1978).

[25] Commonwealth v. Burke, 105 Mass. 376, 7 Am.Rep. 531 (1870).

[26] Lancaster v. State, 168 Ga. 470, 148 S.E. 139 (1929).

[27] State v. Ely, 114 Wash. 185, 194 N.W. 988 (1921).

counts of deviant sexual assault.[28] On appeal, he claimed that the complainant consented to the sexual activities and explained that she had consented to a nude massage in order to relieve muscle tension and, by her actions, consented to the sexual intercourse. The reviewing court reasoned that, although complainant's consent to a nude massage with no apprehension of sexual involvement was naive, it might reasonably be explained by the fact that defendant, who was 30 years older than she, introduced himself as an acquaintance of her best friend, and indicated that he was a doctor and psychologist. The court found that, notwithstanding this naivete, this was rape and there was no consent to the sexual intercourse.

A variety of opinions relate to the use of liquor or drugs in obtaining consent. There is no doubt that unlawful sexual intercourse by a man with a woman whom he has reduced to a state of insensibility by intoxicating liquor or drugs is rape.[29] But cases have held that inducing a woman to drink intoxicating beverages or to use drugs to excite her passions leaving her at the same time in the full possession of her mental and physical powers, capable of comprehending the nature of the act, does not amount to rape, as there has been consent.[30]

Sexual intercourse with a female under the age of consent

Before examining the recent statutes and codes, earlier modifications of the common law require mention. Under the early English cases, it was not rape to have sexual intercourse with a female child if she consented.[31] However, later English statutes included Sections which provided that females under 12 years of age were incapable of consent and to have sexual intercourse with a female child under this age was considered rape, even though there was consent.[32] In the United States, the age of consent was fixed by statutes in practically all states; some states set the age at 14, some at 16 and some at 18.[33]

The act of having intercourse with a female under the age of consent became commonly known as "statutory rape." Where the female is under the age of statutory consent, as stated by the respective statutes, it makes no difference if the act was accomplished against her will or with or without her

---

[28] 373 N.E.2d 538 (Ill. 1978).

[29] Milton v. State, 160 Tenn. 273, 23 S.W.2d 662 (1930).

[30] State v. Lung, 21 Nev. 209, 28 P. 235 (1891).

[31] Wilson v. Commonwealth, 290 Ky. 223, 160 S.W.2d 649 (1942).

[32] State v. Westminster I, 3, Edward I, chapter 13; 75 C.J.S. *Rape* § 13 (1952).

[33] 75 C.J.S. *Rape* § 13 (1952).

consent.[34] Also, the fact that the female had previously had sexual intercourse with the defendant at a time when, under a prior statute, she was over the age of consent, is immaterial, and the chastity of the female before the age of consent is immaterial.[35]

B. Statutes and Codes

1. Model Penal Code

§ 213.1 Rape and Related Offenses[36]
    (1)   Rape. A man who has sexual intercourse with a female not his wife is guilty of rape if:

        (a)   he compels her to submit by force or by threat of imminent death, serious bodily injury, extreme pain or kidnapping, to be inflicted on anyone; or
        (b)   he has substantially impaired her power to appraise or control her conduct by administering or employing without her knowledge drugs, intoxicants or other means for the purpose of preventing resistance; or
        (c)   the female is unconscious; or
        (d)   the female is less than 10 years old.

Rape is a felony of the second degree unless
        (i)   in the course thereof the actor inflicts serious bodily injury upon anyone, or
        (ii)   the victim was not a voluntary social companion of the actor upon the occasion of the crime and had not previously permitted him sexual liberties, in which cases the offense is a felony of the first degree.

    (2)   Gross Sexual Imposition. A male who has sexual intercourse with a female not his wife commits a felony of the third degree if:

---

[34] Fields v. State, 203 Ark. 1046, 159 S.W.2d 745 (1942).
[35] State v. Porter, 188 N.C. 804, 125 S.E. 615 (1924).
[36] Model Penal Code, § 213.1 (Proposed Official Draft 1980).

(a) he compels her to submit by any threat that would prevent resistance by a woman of ordinary resolution; or

(b) he knows that she suffers from a mental disease or defect which renders her incapable of appraising the nature of her conduct; or

(c) he knows that she is unaware that a sexual act is being committed upon her or that she submits because she mistakenly supposes that he is her husband.

To clarify the required elements of the crime of rape, and to meaningfully grade the sex offenses, the Model Code takes a fresh approach. Some of the elements are stated in terms that were not used in describing the common law offenses but are probably easier to define. Also the grading differentials have no counterpart in prior law.[37]

In Subsection (1)(a), focus is upon the manifestations of aggression by the male actor. The most serious penalty is attached where the actor inflicts serious bodily injury or "the victim was not a voluntary social companion of the actor upon the occasion of the crime and has not previously permitted him sexual liberties." This implies that if previous sexual liberties were permitted, the actor can be found guilty of rape but the crime cannot be a felony in the first degree.

Subsection (2)(a) is designed to cover situations where force is not used, but where the act is accomplished by threats which "would prevent resistance by a woman of ordinary resolution." In this situation, the offense is reduced to a third degree felony.

Section (2)(b) deals with situations where the woman suffers from a mental disease or defect rendering her incapable of appraising the nature of her conduct, and Section (2)(c) provides a penalty where the woman is unconscious or, for some reason, is unaware of the sexual act, or she submits because she mistakenly supposes the man is her husband.

These provisions encompass many of the acts that were made illegal under the common law and various state statutes and bring them together in a more uniform way.

When drafting the Model Code, the offenses were graded on the premise that these factors should determine the seriousness and the penalty attached:

---

[37] *Id.* § 275.

(1) the culpability and dangerousness manifested by the actor,
(2) the presence of absence of factors verifying these conditions in the actor, and
(3) the degree of harm inflicted upon the victim.[38]

2. Federal Code

United States Code Title 18, § 2031 prescribing penalties for the commissions of rape was repealed in 1986. Also, the code provision which was designated "White Slave Traffic" has been renamed "Transportation for Illegal Sexual Activity and Related Crimes." This act relating to the transportation in interstate or foreign commerce of any woman or girl for the purpose of prostitution or debauchery, etc., was originally passed in 1910. The code was amended in 1948, 1978 and 1986. The 1986 version is as follows:

§ 2421 -- Transportation Generally
Whoever knowingly transports any individual in interstate or foreign commerce or in any Territory or Possession of the United States, with intent that such individual engage in prostitution, or in any sexual activity for which any person can be charged with a criminal offense, shall be fined under this title or imprisoned not more than five years, or both.

This Section, unlike previous Sections, does not restrict application to females, although the initial law, when originally passed, was "to curb white slave traffic in interstate commerce and to eliminate traffic in women by procurers who forced victims to lead a life of debauchery."[39]
A second federal statute proscribes knowingly persuading, inducing, enticing or coercing an individual to travel in interstate or foreign commerce to engage in prostitution or other sexual activities prohibited by law. This Section provides:

§ 2422 -- Coercion and Enticement
Whoever knowingly persuades, induces, entices, or coerces any individual to travel in interstate or foreign commerce, or in any Territory or Possession of the United States, to engage in prostitution, or in any sexual activity for which any person can be charged

---

[38] *Id.* § 280.
[39] United States v. Wheeler, 444 F.2d 385 (1971).

with a criminal offense, shall be fined under this title or imprisoned not more than five years, or both.[40]

In order to constitute an offense under § 2421, the prosecution must prove, among other elements, that the defendant knowingly transported an individual in interstate or foreign commerce. Also, the prosecution must necessarily prove that the defendant transported such individual with intent for that person to engage in prostitution or other sexual activity for which a person can be charged with a criminal offense. While the wording of the Section is different from "Immoral Purposes," as was used in previous statutes, it is apparent that transportation with intent to commit rape is a violation of this statute. In a 1985 case, a Federal Court of Appeals agreed that transporting a female for the purpose of committing rape was an "immoral purpose" within the purview of 18 U.S.C. §§ 2421 and 2422.[41]

In addition to the Federal Statutes, which apply nationally, if the prosecution can show transportation in interstate commerce, the code defines crimes and punishments when the acts occur in the "special maritime and territorial jurisdiction of the United States or in Federal Prison.[42] Title 18, § 2241 provides:[43]

§ 2241 Aggravated sexual abuse

(a) By force or threat. Whoever, in the special *maritime and territorial* jurisdiction of the United States or in a Federal prison, knowingly causes another person to engage in a sexual act--

(1) by using force against that other person; or

(2) by threatening or placing that other person in fear that any person will be subjected to death, serious bodily injury, or kidnapping;

or attempts to do so, shall be fined under this title, imprisoned for any term of years or life, or both.

---

[40]   18 U.S.C. § 2422. Section 2423 has similar provisions relating to transportation of minors in interstate or foreign commerce. The maximum term under this statute is ten years.

[41]   United States v. Mitchell, 778 F.2d 1271 (7th Cir. 1985).

[42]   *See* definitions of "special maritime and territorial jurisdiction" in appendix.

[43]   18 U.S.C. § 2241.

(b) By other means. -- Whoever, in the special maritime and territorial jurisdiction of the United States or in a Federal prison, knowingly--

(1) renders another person unconscious and thereby engages in a sexual act with that other person; or

(2) administers to another person by force or threat of force, or without the knowledge or permission of that person, a drug, intoxicant, or other similar substance and thereby--

(A) substantially impairs the ability of that other person to appraise or control conduct; and

(B) engages in a sexual act with that other person;

or attempts to do so, shall be fined under this title, imprisoned for any term of years or life, or both.

(c) With children. Whoever, in the special maritime and territorial jurisdiction of the United States or in a Federal prison, knowingly engages in a sexual act with another person who has not attained the age of 12 years, or attempts to do so, shall be fined under this title, imprisoned for any term of years or life, or both.

(d) State of mind proof requirement. In a prosecution under Subsection (c) of this Section, the Government need not prove that the defendant knew that the other person engaging in the sexual act had not attained the age of 12 years.

This federal statute which became effective in 1986 includes a penalty of up to life imprisonment if one of the aggravating elements is proved.

In addition to the aggravated sexual abuse statute the Federal Code includes the description of a "sexual abuse" crime with lesser penalties. It provides:[44]

§ 2242. Sexual Abuse

Whoever, in the special maritime and territorial jurisdiction of the United States or in a Federal prison, knowingly--

---

[44] 18 U.S.C. § 2242. *See* 18 U.S.C. § 2245 for definitions of terms used in Federal Statutes.

(1) causes another person to engage in a sexual act by threatening or placing that other person in fear (other than by threatening or placing that other person in fear that any person will be subjected to death, serious bodily injury or kidnapping); or

(2) engages in a sexual act with another person if that other person is--

    (A) incapable of appraising the nature of the conduct; or

    (B) physically incapable of declining participation in, or communicating unwillingness to engage in, that sexual act;

or attempts to do so, shall be fined under this title, imprisoned not more than 20 years, or both.

Unlike the "Transportation" statutes discussed previously, these statutes are applicable only if the acts occur within the territorial jurisdiction of the United States or in a Federal prison. If the acts do occur in the jurisdiction of the United States as defined, the trial is in Federal Court and not state.

Finding that child exploitation has become a multi-million dollar industry infiltrated by elements of organized crime, Congress in 1986 added the federal offense of "Sexual exploitation of children."[45] This comprehensive statute makes it possible for federal agents to work in concert with the state agents in apprehending and prosecuting child exploiters. It was found to be constitutional by a Pennsylvania District Court in 1987.[46]

3. Other statutes and codes

Of those states that have departed from the traditional common law approach to the offense of rape, many have followed the Model Penal Code or have used parts of the Code and modified others. Some states have attempted to state the codes in terms that are not gender-specific so as to make it possible to convict a person of a sex crime regardless of whether that person is a male or female.[47] Under the Michigan statute a person is guilty of criminal sexual conduct in the first degree if she or he engages in sexual penetration with another person and if other circumstances exist. There the

---

[45] 18 U.S.C. § 2251.

[46] United States v. Fenton, 654 F.Supp. 379 (E.D. Pa. 1987).

[47] Mich. Comp. Laws §§ 750.520(a)-750.520(1). *See* Michael v. Superior Court of Sonoma Co., 450 U.S. 464, 67 L.Ed.2d 437, 101 S. Ct. 1200 (1981).

terms "male" and "female" are not used and either may be guilty of criminal sexual conduct.

In states where the statutes have been revised in the last decade and do not follow the Model Code the provisions are often similar to the Michigan Code or the New York statute. In New York four categories of rape are based upon factors of age of the actor and the victim.[48]

Parts of the Kentucky Code are included as an example of a statute that differs from the Model Code.

§ 510.040 -- Rape in the first degree.
(1) A person is guilty of rape in the first degree when:

    (a) he engages in sexual intercourse with another person by forcible compulsion; or
    (b) he engages in sexual intercourse with another person who is incapable of consent because he:

        (i) is physically helpless; or
        (ii) is less than twelve years old.

    (2) Rape in the first degree is a Class B felony unless the victim is under twelve years old or receives a serious physical injury in which case it is a Class A felony. (Enact. Acts 1974, Ch. 406, § 84)

§ 510.050 -- Rape in the second degree.
(1) A person is guilty of rape in the second degree when, being eighteen years old or more, he engages in sexual intercourse with another person less than fourteen years old.
(2) Rape in the second degree is a Class C felony. (Enact. Acts 1974, Ch. 406, § 85)

§ 510.060 -- Rape in the third degree.
(1) A person is guilty of rape in the third degree when:

    (a) he engages in sexual intercourse with another person who is incapable of consent because he is mentally defective or mentally incapacitated; or

---

[48] N.Y. Penal Law §§ 130.00-130.35 (McKinney 1978). Other states that enacted statutes patterned after New York are: Ala. Code §§ 13A-6-60 – 13A-6-70 (1975); Ky. Rev. Stat. §§ 510.000-510.150 (1974); and Or. Rev. Stat. §§ 163.305-163.475 (1971).

(b) being twenty-one years old or more, he engages in sexual intercourse with another person less than sixteen years old.

(2) Rape in the third degree is a Class D felony. (Enact. Acts 1974, Ch. 406, § 86)

The elements of rape in the first degree under this statute are:

(a) sexual intercourse,
(b) by forcible compulsion; *or*

(a) sexual intercourse, and
(b) the victim is incapable of consent when;

    (i) physically helpless, or
    (ii) less than twelve years old.

Many of the terms used are defined in the codes or statutes. Some of the more common are:

(a) Sexual intercourse
Sexual intercourse as used in the Model Penal Code and states that have adopted all or parts of this code occurs upon any penetration, however slight. As at common law, emission is not required.

(b) Compels
This means non-consent. Where the term "compulsion" is used, the term is defined as physical force that overcomes earnest resistance, or any threat, express or implied, that overcomes earnest resistance by placing a person in fear of immediate death or physical injury to himself or another person or in fear that he or another person will be immediately kidnapped.[49] A New York court refused to give an instruction that "to be guilty of rape in the first degree the victim must oppose the perpetrator to the utmost limit of her power by genuine active resistance." The trial judge instead explained that

---

[49] *See* Ky. Rev. Stat. § 510.010 (1988), and a notebook prepared by the Ky. Dept. of Justice, June 1, 1975.

"the degree of force required to place somebody in fear will vary with the person involved."[50]

(c) Unconscious female
This has been interpreted to mean that the female, for any reason, is physically unable to communicate unwillingness to an act. In some codes the term "physically helpless" is used, but the definition is approximately the same.

(d) Not his wife
The Model Code and most state statutes retain the "spousal exclusion" interpreted to mean that a man cannot rape his wife. The wording is:

> A male who has sexual intercourse with a female *not his wife* is guilty of rape if...[51]

Marital Rape Statutes and Decisions

While most states and the Model Penal Code retain the spousal exclusion, in some states the courts have decided that a man can rape his wife if other factors are proved. The common law reasoning that a husband cannot be guilty of rape committed by himself upon his lawful wife was predicated on the rationale that "by their mutual matrimonial consent and contract, the wife hath given of herself in this kind unto you, her husband, which she cannot retract."[52] Although Hale cited no authority for this statement, it was relied on by state legislatures which enacted rape statutes with a marital exemption by courts which established a common law exemption for husbands.

The first American case to recognize the marital exemption was decided in 1857 by the Supreme Judicial Court of Massachusetts, which included a comment that "it would always be a defense to rape to show marriage to the victim."[53] Decisions to the same effect by other courts followed, usually with no rationale or authority cited, other than Hale's implied consent view.[54] In New York, a 1922 decision noted the marital exemption in the penal laws,

---

[50] People v. Yanik, 400 N.Y.S.2d 778, 371 N.E.2d 497 (1977) on remand 404 N.Y.S.2d 633, 63 App. Div. 574 (1978); *see also* State v. Ricks, 34 N.C. App. 734, 239 S.E.2d 602 (N.C. 1977).

[51] Model Penal Code, § 213.1(1) (Proposed Official Draft 1980).

[52] This concept was developed by the 17th century jurist, Sir Matthew Hale, 1 Hale, HISTORY OF THE PLEAS OF THE CROWN 629 (1800).

[53] Commonwealth v. Fogarty, 74 Mass. 489 (1857).

[54] *See* cases cited in People v. Liberta, 474 N.E.2d 567 (N.Y. 1984). *See* case in Part II.

and stated that it existed "on account of the matrimonial consent which the wife has given, and which she cannot retract."[55]   According to comments made in the *People v. Liberta* cited, over 40 states still retain some form of marital exemption for rape.

Notwithstanding the fact that the Model Code and most states retain the spousal exclusion, there is a definite movement to remove this exclusion, either by statute or court decision. For example, a recently enacted statute in New Jersey specifically abandons spousal immunity for all sex offenses by providing that "no actor shall be presumed to be incapable of committing a crime under this chapter because of ... marriage to the victim."[56]   Other statutes suspend the spousal immunity when the parties are somewhere in the process of legal separation or divorce and are living apart.[57]

Not only are statutes drafted to remove the spousal exclusion, decisions by judicial bodies have also moved toward removing this exclusion by judicial decree. In a New Jersey case, the state accused the husband of breaking into the wife's apartment and forcing her to have sexual intercourse.[58]   The trial court granted a motion to dismiss the rape charges because the couple was married. The New Jersey Supreme Court, after discussing the changes in the divorce laws and other legal developments, reasoned that the corollary of a spouse's right to make a unilateral decision to end the marriage is "a wife can refuse sexual intercourse with her husband during the period of separation prior to divorce." The court continued by stating:

> If a wife has a right to refuse intercourse, or deny consent, then a husband's forceful carnal knowledge of his wife clearly includes all three elements of the crime of rape. He cannot defend by asserting that there was no lack of consent because he was still legally married to the victim.

In the case of *People v. Liberta*, the Court of Appeals of New York, after carefully considering the "marital exemption rule," declared the rule to be unconstitutional. The court declared that there is no rational basis for distinguishing between marital rape and nonmarital rape. The court reasoned that:

> The various rationales which have been asserted in defense of the exemption are either based upon archaic notions about the consent

---

[55] People v. Meli, 193 N.Y.S. 365 (1922).

[56] New Jersey Statute, § 2C:14-5(b).

[57] *See* Idaho Statute, § 18-6107.

[58] State v. Smith, 85 N.J. 193, 426 A.2d 38 (1981).

and property rights incident to marriage or are simply unable to withstand even the slightest scrutiny. We, therefore, declare the marital exemption for rape in the New York statute to be unconstitutional.

In justifying the decision, the New York Court indicated that rape is not simply a sexual act to which one party does not consent, but is a degrading, violent act which violates the bodily integrity of the victim and frequently causes severe, long-lasting physical, and psychic harm.[59]

While most recent decisions addressing the marital exemption have been unable to find any present justification for it,[60] other decisions have concluded that there is a rational basis for the spousal exclusion.[61] Nevertheless, it is safe to conclude that the rationale for the exclusion has been dissipating rapidly and that the trend is to abolish the marital exemption either by statute or court decision.

Rape Shield Statutes and Decisions

Prior to 1975, there were few statutes addressing the admissibility of evidence of a rape victim's prior sexual conduct. The law concerning the admissibility of such evidence was developed by the courts. More recently, many states, after carefully considering the desirability of protecting the rape victim, enacted legislation which became known as "Rape Shield Laws."[62] The rationale behind such statutes is that evidence of a rape victim's prior sexual activity is of dubious probative value and relevance, and is highly embarrassing and prejudicial. Those who argued for such statutes assert that the protection offered by the statutes would encourage victims of sexual assault to report the crimes without fear of having their past sexual history exposed to the public.[63]

Although the statutes are worded differently, there is no doubt that the intent is to protect the victims of sexual assaults while, at the same time, protecting the rights of the person accused of the crime. An example of a

---

[59] For discussion of the marital exemption and arguments for abolishing the marital exemption, *see Abolishing the Marital Exemption*, U. ILL. L. REV. 17 (1983), and *Marital Rape Exemption*, 52 N.Y.U. L. REV. 311.

[60] People v. DeStefano, 467 N.Y.S.2d 506 (1983); State v. Smith, 426 A.2d 38 (1981); Weishaup v. Commonwealth, 227 Va. 239, 315 S.E.2d 847 (1984); and State v. Smith, 401 S.2d 1126 (Fla. App. 1981).

[61] People v. Brown, 632 P.2d 1025 (1981).

[62] *See* Berger, *Man's Trial, Woman's Tribulations: Rape Cases in the Court Room*, 77 COLUM. L. REV. 1 (1977); *The Road to Reform*, 4 AM. J. CRIM. L. 1 (1975).

[63] Bell v. Harrison, 670 F.2d 656 (6th Cir. 1982).

statute which refers to the admissibility of evidence of prior sexual conduct is that of Kentucky.[64] It provides:

§ 510.145 Inadmissibility of Evidence of Prior Sexual Conduct or Habits of Complaining Witness; Exception; Procedure for Admission

(1) As used in this Section, "complaining witness" means the alleged victim of the crime charged, the prosecution of which is subject to the provisions of this Section.

(2) In any prosecution under KRS 510.040 through 510.140, or for assault with intent to commit, attempt to commit, or conspiracy to commit a crime defined in any of these Sections, reputation evidence, and evidence of specific instances of the complaining witness' prior sexual conduct or habits is not admissible by the defendant.

(3) Notwithstanding the prohibition contained in Subsection (2) of this Section, evidence of the complaining witness' prior sexual conduct or habits with the defendant or evidence directly pertaining to the act on which the prosecution is based, may be admitted at the trial if the relevancy of such evidence is determined in the following manner:

(a) A written motion shall be filed by the defendant with the court no later than two (2) days prior to the day of trial, or at such later time as the court may for good cause permit, stating that the defendant has an offer of relevant evidence of prior sexual conduct or habits of the complaining witness.

(b) A hearing on the motion shall be held in the judge's chambers. If, following the hearing, the court determines that the offered proof is relevant and that it is material to a fact in issue, and that its probative value outweighs its inflammatory or prejudicial nature, the court shall admit the offered proof, in whole or in part, in accordance with the applicable rules of evidence.

---

[64] Ky. Rev. Stat. 510.145 (1976).

In 1986, the Court of Appeals of Kentucky was called upon to interpret this statute insofar as it relates to admissibility of evidence of prior sexual relationship of the rape victim with the defendant. This case involved two men, Jeff Bixler and Floyd Bean, who were convicted of first degree rape in 1984. On appeal, the defendants argued that the lower court erred in refusing to allow the defendants to introduce evidence that the defendant, Bixler, had a previous sexual relationship with the victim during the summer of 1982.

The single issue was whether the trial court erred as a matter of law in ruling that any evidence of a prior sexual relationship between Bixler and the victim was inadmissible. The issue related not only to the question of consent on the part of the victim but to the whole question of her credibility as a witness. In the trial of the case the victim had said that she had never had sexual intercourse with the defendant. The defendant had offered to introduce evidence to prove that she had had a previous sexual relationship.

The reviewing court agreed with the defendant that, under these circumstances, evidence should have been admitted. The court indicated that "under the clear language of the statute, it is evident to the Court that such evidence should be admissible if its probative value outweighs its inflammatory or prejudicial nature, and if it is material to an issue of fact." In reversing the decision of the lower court, the reviewing court noted that "clearly, the testimony was material and relevant to the question of consent. And, this Court finds that its probative value outweighed any resulting prejudice." As to the interpretation of the statute, the court concluded that:

> KRS 510.145, designated as the Rape Shield Law, was designed to exclude any evidence of a prior sexual relationship between a victim and a *third party* in a rape prosecution. (emphasis added)

The so-called rape shield laws have been challenged as being unconstitutional, because they violate the defendant's right of confrontation. In a Texas case, the defendant appealed his conviction of aggravated rape, claiming that the rape shield law in effect in that state violated his right of confrontation and his due process rights.[65] The rape shield law in Texas provided, in part, that:

> Evidence of specific instances of a victim's sexual conduct, opinion evidence of the victim's sexual conduct, and reputation evidence of the victim's sexual conduct may be admitted ... only if, and only to

---

[65]   Allen v. State, 700 S.W.2d 924 (Tex. Cr. App. 1985).

the extent that, the judge finds that the evidence is material to a fact at issue in the case and that its inflammatory or prejudicial nature does not outweigh its probative value.

The Texas statute establishes procedures for introduction of evidence, provides for an on-camera hearing, and requires the sealing of the record.

The reviewing court, in upholding the constitutionality of the Rape Shield Law, reasoned that the right to confront and to cross-examine is not absolute and may, in appropriate cases, bow to accommodate other legitimate interests in the criminal law process. In applying that reasoning to the Rape Shield Law, the court indicated that although statutory, the rape victim shield law is analogous to judge-made rules of evidence which prevent the admissibility of opinion evidence, hearsay testimony, and convictions of very old standing, where the probative value of the evidence is outweighed by the possibility of jury prejudice. In upholding the constitutionality, the court concluded:

> We conclude that § 21.13 is constitutional on its face and is applied to the appellant in the instant case. We reject his claim that it is violative of the Sixth Amendment and Article 1, § 10, the Texas Constitution. We also reject his claim that the Fifth and Fourteenth Amendments were violated in the instant case. Due process was accorded the appellant for the reasons stated.

The Supreme Court of North Carolina also upheld the constitutionality of the Rape Shield Law.[66] In justifying the law, the North Carolina Court wrote that there is no constitutional right to ask a witness questions that are irrelevant and, secondly, its impact and application is primarily procedural and does not alter any of the defendant's substantive rights. Thirdly, the court said there are valid policy reasons aside from relevant questions which support the statute.

From the review of the cases cited, and other cases, it is apparent that the rape shield laws are generally constitutional. Although the statutes differ and each state statute must be considered separately, they will most likely be upheld as constitutional if proper substantive and procedural safeguards are included in the statute as written.

---

[66] North Carolina v. Fortney, 301 N.C. 31, 269 S.E.2d 110 (1980).

§ 4.3 Sodomy and Related Crimes

A. Traditional Definition and Element

The term sodomy has been defined in many ways and in many jurisdictions over many years. In its broadest terms sodomy is the "carnal copulation by human beings with each other against nature, or with a beast." The broad definition includes bestiality, buggery, cunnilingus, and fellatio.[67] A definition, as included in an early case, is:

> A person who carnally knows in any manner any animal or bird, or carnally knows any male or female person by the anus, or with the mouth, or voluntarily submits to such carnal knowledge, or attempts sexual intercourse with a dead body, is guilty of sodomy.[68]

Other definitions are:

> "Sodomy" is carnal copulation with members of the same sex or with an animal or unnatural carnal copulation with a member of the opposite sex;[69] and

> In its broadest meaning, "sodomy" is the carnal copulation by human beings with each other against nature or with a beast including the crime against nature, bestiality, buggery, cunnilingus, and fellatio; in its narrower sense, sodomy is a carnal copulation between two human beings per anus or by a human being in any manner with a beast.[70]

In England, sodomy, at first, was subject only to punishment by the ecclesiastical authorities. However, early English statutes made sodomy a criminal offense, and it was such an offense under the common law that was used as a basis for the laws in this country.[71]

While the original English enactments proscribed only anal intercourse between males, the coverage was extended so as to punish fellatio and cun-

---

[67]   81 C.J.S. *Sodomy* § 1 (1977).

[68]   State v. Schwartz, 215 Minn. 476, 10 N.W.2d 370 (1943).

[69]   People v. Durham, 74 Cal. Rptr. 262, 449 P.2d 198 (1969).

[70]   Pruitt v. State, 463 S.W.2d 191 (Tex. Cr. App. 1971).

[71]   Johnsen, *Sodomy Statutes – A Need for Change*, 13 S.D.L. REV. 384 (1968).

nilingus as well as anal intercourse and bestiality.[72] In some states, the crime was designated by statute as "crime against nature."[73] In the Model Penal Code, the crime is defined as "deviate sexual intercourse by force or imposition."[74]

From the foregoing, it becomes clear that some sodomy crimes are not offenses against another person but consensual. As the tendency at present is to limit the crime of sodomy or related crimes to non-consensual conduct, the offenses are considered in this chapter even though some are not always against the person of another.

As there are many statutory crimes in the general sodomy category, it is difficult to enumerate elements. Where the statute uses the term "carnal copulation," the prosecution must show that some sexual intercourse took place, including intercourse by way of the mouth.[75] Under many statutes, and at common law, penetration is an essential element of the crime of sodomy. Where penetration is an element, any penetration, however slight, is sufficient to constitute the element. For example, in the case of *People v. Hickock*, the complaining witness had been hypnotized to a point where she was unable to move, but retained consciousness and had her teeth tightly clenched when the accused placed his penis inside her lips.[76] Here, the court said this was a penetration sufficient to allow conviction under the statute providing that "any person participating in the act of copulating the mouth of one person with the sexual organ of another is punishable by imprisonment not exceeding fifteen years."

At least according to some cases, any unnatural corporeal copulation constitutes a violation of the sodomy statute and any penetration makes the crime of sodomy complete.[77] When practiced between members of the human species, the crime of sodomy is complete if there is copulation of the male organ of one with either the mouth or anus of another.[78]

Although there has been some conflict in interpretation, the general rule is that there need not be any emission as an element of the offense. This was made clear by some statutes which specifically provide that emission is not essential and that penetration is sufficient to constitute the crime.[79]

---

[72] Fellatio is defined as oral stimulation of the penis; cunnilingus is oral stimulation of the vulva or clitoris, and bestiality is copulation between human and animal.

[73] Mass. Ann. Laws ch. 272, § 34 (Michie Law Co-op. 7 (1980)).

[74] Model Penal Code, § 213.2 (Proposed Official Draft 1980).

[75] Furstonburg v. State, 148 Tex. Cr. 638, 190 S.W.2d 362 (1945).

[76] 96 Cal. App. 2d 621, 216 P.2d 140 (1950).

[77] State v. Dayton, 535 S.W.2d 469 (Mo. App. 1976).

[78] Estes v. State, 244 Ind. 691, 195 N.E.2d 471 (1964).

[79] State v. Massey, 58 N.M. 115, 266 P.2d 359 (1954).

B. Statutes and Codes

1. Model Penal Code

§ 213.2 Deviate Sexual Intercourse by Force or Imposition

(1) By Force or Its Equivalent. A person who engages in deviate sexual intercourse with another person, or who causes another to engage in deviate sexual intercourse, commits a felony of the second degree if:

    (a) he compels the other person to participate by force or by threat of imminent death, serious bodily injury, extreme pain or kidnapping, to be inflicted on anyone; or

    (b) he has substantially impaired the other person's power to appraise or control his conduct, by administering or employing without the knowledge of the other person drugs, intoxicants or other means for the purpose of preventing resistance; or

    (c) the person is unconscious; or

    (d) the other person is less than 10 years old.

(2) By Other Imposition. A person who engages in deviate sexual intercourse with another person, or who causes another to engage in sexual intercourse, commits a felony of the third degree if:

    (a) he compels the other person to participate by any threat that would prevent resistance by a person of ordinary resolution; or

    (b) he knows that the other person suffers from a mental disease or defect which renders him incapable of appraising the nature of his conduct; or

    (c) he knows that the other person submits because he is unaware that a sexual act is being committed upon him.[80]

---

[80] Model Penal Code, § 213.2 (Proposed Official Draft 1980).

Rather than using the term sodomy, the drafters of the Model Penal Code took a different approach, defining the offense as "deviate sexual intercourse by force or imposition." It is immediately apparent that the words *by force or imposition* change the common law concept and make this a crime against another. The Model Code excepts from criminal sanction deviate sexual intercourse between consenting adults. Under the Code, deviate sexual intercourse is not criminal if both participants consent and each is of sufficient age and mental capacity to render consent and they conduct their relations in private and create no public nuisance. Also, it should be noted that, under the Code, homosexual relations between consenting parties is not a violation of the law.

2. Federal Code

There is no general federal code provision relating to sodomy.

3. Other statutes and codes

While some states have followed the Model Code, and, in fact, one state, Illinois, had similar provisions which preceded the Model Code,[81] most states still provide punishment for consensual sodomy, even though, in many states, it is classified as a misdemeanor rather than a felony.[82]

An example of a statute that provides penalties for forced deviate sexual intercourse and deviate intercourse between consenting adults is that of Kentucky.[83]

§ 510.070 -- Sodomy in the first degree.

(1) A person is guilty of sodomy in the first degree when:

    (a)   he engages in deviate sexual intercourse with another person by forcible compulsion; or

    (b)   he engages in deviate sexual intercourse with another person who is incapable of consent because he:

---

[81] Ill. Rev. Stat. ch. 38, § 11-2 (1988).

[82] Kan. Stat. Ann. § 21-3505 (1974); Ky. Rev. Stat. § 510.110 (1975); Mo. Rev. Stat. § 566.090 (1979); N.Y. Penal Law § 130.38 (McKinney 1975); 18 Pa. Cons. Stat. § 3124 (1973); Texas Penal Code Ann. § 21.06 (Vernon 1974); and Utah Code Ann. § 76-5-403 (1978).

[83] Ky. Rev. Stat. §§ 510.070-100 (1975).

(i)   is physically helpless; or

(ii) is less than twelve years old.

(2) Sodomy in the first degree is a Class B felony unless the victim is under twelve years old or receives a serious physical injury in which case it is a Class A felony. (Enact. Acts 1974, Ch. 406, § 87)

§ 510.080 -- Sodomy in the second degree.

(1) A person is guilty of sodomy in the second degree when, being eighteen years old or more, he engages in deviate sexual intercourse with another person less than fourteen years old.

(2) Sodomy in the second degree is a Class C felony. (Enact. Acts 1974, Ch. 406, § 88)

§ 510.090 -- Sodomy in the third degree.

(1) a person is guilty of sodomy in the third degree when:

(a) he engages in deviate sexual intercourse with another person who is incapable of consent because he is mentally defective or mentally incapacitated; or

(b) being twenty-one years old or more, he engages in deviate sexual intercourse with another person less than sixteen years old.

(2) Sodomy in the third degree is a Class D felony. (Enact. Acts 1974, Ch. 406, § 89)

§ 510.100 -- Sodomy in the fourth degree.

(1) A person is guilty of sodomy in the fourth degree when he engages in deviate sexual intercourse with another person of the same sex.

(2) Notwithstanding the provisions of KRS 510.020, consent of the other person shall not be a defense under this Section, nor shall lack of consent of the other person be an element of this offense.

(3) Sodomy in the fourth degree is a Class A misdemeanor.

Deviate sexual intercourse, as used in the statute, means any act of sexual gratification by persons not married to each other involving the sex organs of one person and the mouth or anus of another.[84]

The Texas statute defines "deviate sexual intercourse" as any contact between any part of the genitals of one person and the mouth or anus of another person. The Texas Court of Appeals interpreted this to require only "any contact," not penetration.[85]

Provisions or definitions which provide penalties where the parties are unmarried but no penalties for married persons have been challenged. For example, the majority of the New York Court of Appeals has determined that a New York statute which makes it a crime for unmarried sexual partners to engage in acts of consensual sodomy, while excluding married parties from this crime, is unconstitutional as in violation of the right of privacy and the equal protection clause of the U.S. Constitution.[86]

The court reminded that the right of privacy emanates from several provisions of the Bill of Rights including the First, Fourth and Ninth Amendments, as well as the Fourteenth Amendment's due process clause. Applying the principle of right of privacy, the court determined that as long as the decisions made by the parties are voluntary and made by adults in a noncommercial, private setting, the government cannot interfere. It then concluded that:

> Penal law § 130.38 on its face discriminates between married and unmarried persons, making criminal when done by the latter what is innocent when done by the former ... the statute then must fall as violative of the right to equal protection enjoyed by persons not married to each other.

In the *Onofre* case, the New York court claims that this is not new ground and makes reference to the Pennsylvania case of *Pennsylvania v. Bonadio*,[87] and to an Iowa case of *State v. Pilcher*,[88] and a New Jersey case.[89] Whether other states will follow this reasoning remains to be seen.

---

[84]　Ky. Penal Code Notebook, Kentucky Department of Justice (1975).

[85]　Donoho v. State, 628 S.W.2d 485 (Tex. App. 1982). *See* case in Part II.

[86]　People v. Onofre, 424 N.Y.S.2d 566, 72 App. Div. 2d 268 (1980).

[87]　490 Pa. 91, 415 A.2d 47 (1980).

[88]　242 N.W.2d 348 (Iowa 1976).

[89]　State v. Fiuffini, 164 N.J. Super. 145, 395 A.2d 904 (1978).

§ 4.4 Sexual Abuse (Sexual Assault)

A. Traditional Definitions and Elements

When one person touches another or subjects another person to sexual contact without the other's consent, he commits an act which does not come within the category of rape, but is an act which the legislatures have determined should not be sanctioned. Although this was not a common law crime, several states enacted statutes designed to provide a penalty for such proscribed conduct. Others provided punishment under the general laws relating to assault and battery,[90] and still others provided special coverage for taking indecent liberties with children.[91]

The various statutes were given titles such as "indecent or immoral practices with another," "sexual abuse" or "sexual assault." An example of the first of these is the Kentucky statute passed in 1962, which provided:

> Any person of the age of seventeen years or over who carnally abuses the body, or indulges in any indecent or immoral practices with the body or organs of any child under the age of 15 years, or who induces, procures or permits a child under the age of 15 years to indulge in immoral, sexual or indecent practices with himself or any person shall be guilty of a felony, punishable on conviction thereof by imprisonment in the penitentiary for not less than one year nor more than ten years.[92]

The elements of the specific crimes depend upon the terminology of the statute. In the Kentucky statute, the prosecution would be required to prove that:

(a)   the person committing the act was seventeen years or over;

(b)   the actor carnally abused or indulged in indecent or immoral practices with the body;

(c)   the child was under the age of 15;

or

---

[90]   Mass. Ann. Laws ch. 265 (Michie Law Co-op. 1980).

[91]   Alaska Stat. § 11.13.134 (1978); Idaho Code § 18-6607 (1979).

[92]   Ky. Rev. Stat. § 435.105 (1975).

(a) the person who commits the act was seventeen years of age, or over;

(b) the actor induced, procured, or permitted a child under the age of 15;

(c) to indulge in immoral sexual or indecent practices with himself or any other person.

Although there are still some states that have similar statutes, in most recently written statutes the terminology is more specific.

B. Statutes and Codes

1. Model Penal Code

§ 213.4 Sexual Assault[93]

A person who has sexual contact with another not his spouse, or causes, such other to have sexual conduct with him, is guilty of sexual assault, a misdemeanor, if:

(1) he knows that the contact is offensive to the other person; or

(2) he knows that the other person suffers from a mental disease or defect which renders him or her incapable of appraising the nature of his or her conduct; or

(3) he knows that the other person is unaware that a sexual act is being committed; or

(4) the other person is less than 10 years old; or

(5) he has substantially impaired the other person's power to appraise or control his or her conduct, by administering or employing without the other's knowledge drugs, intoxicants or other means for the purpose of preventing resistance; or

(6) the other person is less than [16] years old and the actor is at least [four] years older than the other person; or

(7) the other person is less than 21 years old and the actor is his guardian or otherwise responsible for general supervision of his welfare; or

---

[93] Model Penal Code, § 213.4 (Proposed Official Draft 1980).

(8)   the other person is in custody of law or detained in a hospital or other institution and the actor has supervisory or disciplinary authority over him.

Sexual contact is any touching of the sexual or other intimate parts of the person for the purpose of arousing or gratifying sexual desire.

In the Model Code, sexual assault is treated as a sexual offense rather than included under the crime of assault.

"Sexual contact" as used in the Code, is defined to include "any touching of the sexual or other intimate parts of the person for the purpose of arousing or gratifying sexual desire." Under this definition, the prosecution must show that the "purpose" of the touching was to arouse or gratify sexual desire. Also, the prosecution has the responsibility of proving the touching of the sexual or other intimate parts of the person. According to an earlier case, such touching need not involve naked contact between the actor's hands and another's sexual or intimate parts, but may be accomplished through the clothing.[94]

In addition to proving the sexual contact as required by the Code, evidence must be introduced to indicate one of a number of other circumstances. Some of the eight possible circumstances are not difficult to prove, for example, "the other person is less than ten years old." However, some, as number 3, "he knows that the other person is unaware that a sexual act is being committed," places the burden on the prosecution to prove "knowledge."

2. Federal Code

The U.S. Code has no specific statutes on "Sexual Assault."

3. Other statues and codes

Some states have followed the Model Code in establishing only one degree of sexual abuse but grade the offense as a lesser felony.[95] The titles of the Sections differ. Some use the terms "sexual imposition,"[96] or "sexual abuse."[97]

---

[94] State v. Kocher, 112 Mont. 511, 119 P.2d 35 (1941).

[95] Ariz. Rev. Stat. Ann. § 13-1404 (1978); Me. Rev. Stat. Ann. tit. 17A, § 255 (1977).

[96] Ohio Rev. Code Ann. § 2907.06 (Page 1987).

[97] N.Y. Penal Law §§ 130.55-130.60 (McKinney 1975); Ky. Rev. Stat. §§ 510.110-510.130 (1975).

In some statutes, the offenses of sexual assault or sexual abuse are graded according to the degree of force and the age or mental condition of the victim.[98] An example of a statute that graduates the penalty dependent upon the age factor is that of New York. Sections of the New York statute are included here, as an example of a statute that does not follow the Penal Code approach.

§ 130.55 Sexual abuse in the third degree[99]

A person is guilty of sexual abuse in the third degree when he subjects another person to sexual contact without the latter's consent; except that in any prosecution under this Section, it is an affirmative defense that (a) such other person's lack of consent was due solely to incapacity to consent by reason of being less than seventeen years old, and (b) such other person was more than fourteen years old, and (c) the defendant was less than five years older than such other person.

Sexual abuse in the third degree is a Class B misdemeanor.

§ 130.60 Sexual abuse in the second degree

A person is guilty of sexual abuse in the second degree when he subjects another person to sexual contact and when such other person is:

(1) incapable of consent by reason of some factor other than being less than seventeen years old; or

(2) less than fourteen years old.

Sexual abuse in the second degree is a Class A misdemeanor.

"Sexual contact" as used in this Section means "any touching of the sexual or other intimate parts of a person for the purpose of arousing or gratifying sexual desire."

In the Commonwealth of Kentucky, the crime of sexual abuse is divided into first, second and third degrees, with first degree sexual abuse being a Class D felony (one to five years imprisonment). Sexual contact, as used in KRS 510.110 (sexual abuse in the first degree), is defined as "any touching of

---

[98] Colo. Rev. Stat. § 18-3-404 (1973); Mont. Code Ann. § 94-5-502 (1979); N.H. Rev. Stat. Ann. § 632-A:3-4 (1979).

[99] N.Y. Penal Laws § 130.60 (McKinney 1975), and following commentaries.

the sexual or other intimate parts of a person not married to the actor done for the purpose of gratifying the sexual desire of either party."

As the statutes concerning sexual abuse or sexual assault differ from state to state it is necessary that each state statute be examined as well as the cases that have defined the terms used in the statutes or codes.

§ 4.5 Lewdness (Indecent Exposure)

A. Traditional Definitions and Elements

At common law, particular acts and forms of lewdness constituted criminal offenses. The word "lewdness" means open and public indecency. Usually in order to amount to an indictable crime, the offense must have been committed in a public place and seen by persons lawfully in that place.[100] However, the early statutes provided a broader interpretation. Under these statutes it was not necessary to allege or prove that such act be committed in a public place or in the presence of many people.

An example of an early statute was that of Vermont, which provided:

If any man or woman, married or unmarried, shall be guilty of open and gross lewdness or lascivious behaviour, he shall be imprisoned in the common jail not more than two years, or fined not exceeding $300.[101]

In the *Willard* case, the highest court of Vermont, in 1845, could find no particular definition in the statute as to what constitutes lewdness, saying that "the indelicacy of the subject forbids it, and does not require of the court to state what particular conduct will constitute the offense."

In this case, the respondent entered the house of a woman and "exposed his private parts and persistently urged her to have sexual intercourse with him." The court said there was no question that this was "lewdness" within the meaning of the statute and was "open within the meaning of the statute," defining openness to mean "undisguised, not concealed, and opposite to private, concealed, and unseen." In regard to the nuisance requirement the court held that the public exposure of himself to a female, in the manner this respondent did, with a view to excite unchaste feelings and passions in her, and to induce her to yield to his wishes was gross lewdness, calculated to outrage the feelings of the person to whom he thus exposed himself, and to

---

[100] Commonwealth v. Wardell, 128 Mass. 52, 35 Am.Rep. 357 (1880).

[101] State v. Willard, 18 Vt. 574, 46 Am.Dec. 170 (1845); the statute is quoted in the case.

show, that all sense of decency, chastity, or propriety of conduct, was wanting in him.

It is interesting to note that disrobing in a house of ill fame and one isolated act of intercourse therein did not warrant conviction for lewdness in an early case.[102]

Under the common law, and early statutes, the elements that were required to convict a person of lewdness were:

(a) intentionally,
(b) indecently and offensively exposing the sex organs,
(c) in the presence of another,
(d) in an offensive manner.[103]

B. Statutes and Codes

1. Model Penal Code

§ 213.5 Indecent Exposure[104]

A person commits a misdemeanor if, for the purpose of arousing or gratifying sexual desire of himself or of any person other than his spouse, he exposes his genitals under circumstances in which he knows his conduct is likely to cause affront or alarm.

Prior to the drafting of the Model Penal Code, indecent exposure and related crimes were covered under a multitude of statutes and given such titles as "Lewd and Lascivious Behavior," "Public Lewdness" and even "Appearing on the Highway in Bathing Garb."[105] To make the offense more definite and the terms less likely to be misinterpreted, the Penal Code defines indecent exposure more narrowly. It requires, specifically, the exhibition of the genitals (a display of the buttocks or breasts is not covered). Secondly, the Code requires that the actor have a purpose to arouse or gratify the sexual desire of himself or another not his spouse. And thirdly, the offense requires that the actor know that his conduct is likely to affront or alarm another. This would exclude from the scope of the crime the member of a

---

102 State v. Gardner, 174 Iowa 748, 156 N.W. 747 (1916).

103 Commonwealth v. Wardell, 128 Mass. 52, 35 Am.Rep. 357 (1880), for a more comprehensive discussion of the requirements.

104 Model Penal Code, § 213.5 (Proposed Official Draft 1980).

105 Ky. Rev. Stat. § 436.140 (1975).

nudist cult and even the bottomless dancer who performs only for those desiring such entertainment.[106]

2. Federal Code

Title 18 of the U.S. Code does not include a provision on "Indecent Exposure."

3. Other statutes and codes

Some statutes retain the terminology used before the Model Penal Code was written, and prohibit essentially the same conduct. Some use the terminology of the Model Code, but prohibit display of "sex organs" or other specifically named areas of the body.[107]

An example is the Texas statute which provides:

Indecent Exposure
(a) A person commits an offense if he exposes his anus or any part of his genitals with intent to arouse or gratify the sexual desire of any person, and he is reckless about whether another is present who will be offended or alarmed by the act.
(b) An offense under this class is a Class C misdemeanor.[108]

The elements of the offense under the Texas statute are:
(a) Exposure of the anus or any part of genitals. This does not proscribe exposure of the buttocks or the female breasts as these two areas of the anatomy are not traditionally included within the term genitals.[109]
(b) Intent to arouse or gratify the sexual desire of any person.

---

[106] People v. Conrad, 334 N.Y.2d 180, 70 Misc. 2d 408 (1972).
[107] For example, Ariz. Rev. Stat. Ann. § 13-1402 (1978), prohibits exposure of genitals, anus and the areola or nipple of a female breast.
[108] Tex. Penal Code § 21.08 (Vernon 1974).
[109] Pendell v. State, 253 S.W.2d 426 (Tex. 1953).

(c) Recklessness about whether another is present who
     would be offended or alarmed.

The Texas Court of Criminal Appeals determined that it is not necessary
to prove to whom exposure is directed, as the crime is accomplished when
the person exposes his anus or any part of his genitals with intent to arouse
and gratify sexual desire of any person and he is reckless about whether another is present who will be offended or alarmed by the act.[110] Also, this
provision was challenged as being impermissibly vague but was held not to be
so.[111]

Where statutes contain language such as "in a vulgar or indecent manner,"[112] or "with an immoral purpose,"[113] or "indecently,"[114] the prosecution
must offer evidence to prove these elements as defined by the Code or by
cases interpreting the Code.

§ 4.6 Seduction

A. Traditional Definitions and Elements

The generally accepted definition of seduction is "the act of a man inducing a woman to commit unlawful sexual intercourse with him by means of
enticement, persuasions, solicitations, promises, bribes or other means without the employment of force, therefore overcoming her reluctance and her
scruples."[115] It refers to a wrong directed specifically against the female and
implies sexual intercourse between the parties.[116] The verb "seduce," in its
common, as well as its legal acceptance, imports the idea of illicit intercourse
accomplished by arts, promises, or deception.[117]

Although most states have modified older statutes to limit the scope of
the crime, some type of seduction offenses still exist in most states. In some
states, statutory provisions specifically grant a seduced woman a right of a
civil action to recover damages for her own seduction. Also the state has an

---

[110] Wallace v. State, 550 S.W.2d 89 (Crim. App. 1977).

[111] Kew v. Senter, 416 F.Supp. 1101 (N.D. Tex. 1976).

[112] Fla. Stat. § 800.03 (1976).

[113] S.D. Codified Laws § 22-24-1 (1979).

[114] Wis. Stat. § 944.20 (1958).

[115] Mackey v. Commonwealth, 255 Ky. 466, 74 S.W.2d 915 (1934); Spangler v. Commonwealth, 188 Va. 436, 50 S.E.2d 265 (1948).

[116] Borst v. State, 64 Tex. Crim. 464, 144 S.W. 589 (1912).

[117] Carter v. Murphy, 10 Cal.2d 547, 75 P.2d 1072 (1938).

interest and may bring criminal action against the seducer even if civil action has already been instigated. Generally, the definition of seduction is the same in civil and criminal matters.

In some states, neither a criminal nor a civil action will lie unless the woman who was seduced was both unmarried and chaste at the time.[118] Under the provisions of some early statutes, as interpreted, consent of the woman seduced to the intercourse was no defense and, in some jurisdictions, unless so provided by statute, marriage after the seduction to the accused was no defense.[119]

The elements of the offense depend upon the statute as interpreted. The elements of the offense, as defined in the previous Sections, are:

(a) Inducement. This term inducement refers to persuasion which overcomes the female's reluctance and scruples.

(b) Unlawful sexual intercourse. This has been interpreted to mean sexual intercourse outside of marriage.

(c) By means of arts, persuasion, solicitations, promises or bribes. These terms import the use of fraud or deceit in order to accomplish the user's purpose and imply a betrayal of confidence.

In some states, and under some statutes, two more elements are required.

(d) The woman is unmarried. This is interpreted to include a widow or divorcee.

(e) Previous chaste character. Under some statutes, the previous chaste character of the woman at the time of seduction is an essential element. This requirement has been construed to mean actual personal chastity and not reputation. According to one definition, a woman of previous chaste character is one who has not had sexual intercourse unlawfully, out of wedlock, knowingly and voluntarily.[120]

---

[118] Smith v. State, 13 Ala. App. 388, 69 So. 402 (1915).
[119] Blount v. State, 102 Fla. 1100, 138 So. 2d (1931).
[120] State v. Dacke, 59 Wash. 238, 109 P. 1050 (1910).

B. Statutes and Codes

1. Model Penal Code

The Model Penal Code includes seduction as a part of a Section entitled "Corruption of Minors and Seduction." This provides, in part:

(1) Offenses defined. A male who has sexual intercourse with a female not his wife, or any person who engages in deviant sexual intercourse, or causes another to engage in deviant sexual intercourse, is guilty of an offense if:

> ...
>
> (d) The other person is a female who is induced to participate by a promise of marriage the actor does not mean to perform.[121]

The Model Penal Code restricts the coverage of seduction when compared with the earlier statutes. It applies to a male who induces a female to participate in intercourse "by a promise of marriage which the actor does not mean to perform." It does not cover other types of deception that might give rise to liability. Under the provisions of the Code, the prosecution must prove,

(a) either normal or deviant sexual intercourse,
(b) with a female not his wife,
(c) that the promise of marriage was made, and
(d) that the actor did not mean to marry the female with whom he had intercourse.

This statute, unlike some of the prior statutes, does not make marriage a defense to liability for seduction.

2. Federal Code

Title 18 of the U.S. Code does not include a Section on "seduction."

3. Other statutes and codes

Many of the pre-Model Code statutes which included the broad definition of seduction have been repealed.[122] However, many states still have

---

[121] Model Penal Code, § 213.3 (Proposed Official Draft 1980).
[122] Ala. 1978, Tex. 1974, Iowa 1979, Mo. 1979, N.J. 1979.

statutes modeled after the ones indicated in this Section and a few contain provisions which resemble the Model Code.[123]

Examples of traditional statutes which are still in effect are those of Georgia and Mississippi.

§ 26-2005 Seduction

A person commits seduction when he, by persuasion and by false promise of marriage or other false and fraudulent means, induces a virtuous unmarried female to engage in sexual intercourse with him. A person convicted of seduction shall be punished by imprisonment for not less than one nor more than five years.[124]

The elements to be established by the state are:

(a) The defendant indulged in sexual intercourse with the person named.
(b) The prosecuting witness was seduced into such acts by the defendant by means of a false promise of marriage or other false and fraudulent means.
(c) The prosecutrix was unmarried and virtuous at the time of the alleged seduction.

The penalty under Georgia law is one to five years.

The Mississippi statute uses different wording. It provides:

§ 97-29-55. Seduction of female over age of eighteen by promised or pretended marriage.

If any person shall obtain carnal knowledge of any woman, or female child, over the age of eighteen years, of previous chaste character, by virtue of any feigned or pretended marriage or any false or feigned promise of marriage, he shall, upon conviction, be imprisoned in the penitentiary not more than five years; but the testimony of the female seduced, alone, shall not be sufficient to warrant a conviction.[125]

Under the provisions, previous chaste character (actual chastity) is required; not mere reputation for chastity.[126] The statute includes the addi-

---

[123] S.C. Code Ann. § 16.10 (Law. Co-op. 1976).

[124] Ga. Code § 26-2005 (1979).

[125] Miss. Code Ann. § 97-29-55 (1972).

[126] Fooshee v. State, 82 Miss. 509, 34 So. 148 (1963).

tional requirement that the prosecutor must introduce evidence to corroborate the testimony of the female seduced.[127]

§ 4.7 Other Sex-Related Offenses Against the Person

In the previous Sections of this chapter, the more serious crimes designated offenses against the person (sex-related) have been discussed. It should be noted, however, that there are other statutes in various states that relate to sex offenses. Some of these are discussed briefly here.

A. Importuning

In some states, the statute includes a provision prohibiting soliciting of sexual activity. For example, the Ohio Revised Code provides:[128]

(a) No person shall solicit a person under thirteen years of age to engage in sexual activity with the offender, whether or not the offender knows the age of such person.

(b) No person shall solicit a person of the same sex to engage in sexual activity with the offender, when the offender knows such solicitation is offensive to the other person, or is reckless in that regard.

(c) No person shall solicit another, not the spouse of the offender, to engage in sexual conduct with the offender, when the offender is eighteen years of age or older and four or more years older than the other person, and the other person is over twelve but not over fifteen years of age, whether or not the offender knows the age of the other person.

This and similar statutes are designed to prohibit soliciting a person under age 13 to engage in sexual activity or soliciting a person aged 13 to 15 to engage in sexual conduct, when the solicitor is eighteen years or older and four or more years older than the person solicited. The solicitation of homosexual or lesbian activity is also prohibited, when the solicitor knows or has

---

[127] Aldridge v. State, 232 Miss. 368, 99 So. 2d 456 (1958).
[128] Ohio Rev. Code Ann. § 2907.07 (Page 1987).

reasonable cause to believe the solicitation is offensive to the person solicited.

Under the statute quoted, importuning is a misdemeanor in the first degree when it involves solicitation of a person under age 13 or solicitation of homosexual or lesbian conduct, and a misdemeanor in the fourth degree when it involves solicitation of an early adolescent.

B. Voyeurism

The Ohio Revised Code includes a Section providing:[129]

(A) No person, for the purpose of sexually arousing or gratifying himself or herself, shall commit trespass or otherwise surreptitiously invade the privacy of another, to spy or eavesdrop upon another.

(B) Whoever violates this Section is guilty of voyeurism, a misdemeanor of the third degree.

This Section is aimed at curbing "peeping toms." It prohibits not only trespass, but any invasion of privacy, to eavesdrop or spy on another for the purpose of obtaining a vicarious sexual thrill. It relates to the trespassing voyeur and the voyeur who uses binoculars from his own or public property, or who peeps over the transom.[130]

C. Sexual Misconduct

Some statutes are created to provide punishment where sexual intercourse is between a defendant under age 18 and a victim under 16. The Kentucky statute provides:[131]

§ 510.140 -- Sexual misconduct

(1) A person is guilty of sexual misconduct when he engages in sexual intercourse or deviate sexual intercourse with another person without the latter's consent.

---

[129] Ohio Rev. Code Ann. § 2907.08 (Page 1987). *See also*, comments included in Criminal Code Training Manual prepared by the Ohio Peace Officers Training Council (1974).

[130] Comments included in Criminal Code Training Manual prepared by the Ohio Peace Officers Training Council (1974).

[131] Ky. Rev. Stat. § 510.140 (1975).

(2) Sexual misconduct is a Class A misdemeanor.

The offense of sexual misconduct was created to deal with sexual inter-course between a defendant under 18 and a victim under 16 who is incapable of consent due to age.[132]

D. Intercourse With a Person in Custody

The Model Penal Code includes a provision which provides a penalty where one engages in sexual intercourse or deviate sexual relations, or causes another to engage in such relationship, if the person with whom he has sexual intercourse or causes another to have sexual intercourse with is in custody of law or detained in a hospital or other institution and the actor has supervisory or disciplinary authority over him.[133] This provides a penalty for one who engages in intercourse with a person under his supervisory or disciplinary authority, and is designed to deter abuse of custodial authority. Some states have adopted this approach while others have a more narrow coverage and still others provide a more serious penalty than recommended in the Code.[134]

The list of other statutes relating to sex offenses is not intended to be in-clusive.

§ 4.8 Summary

In this chapter, non-consensual sex crimes are considered and the elements of the crimes discussed.

The most serious sex crime is rape. Rape is defined as the act of having unlawful carnal knowledge by a man of a woman, forcibly and against her will. While most courts have admitted evidence concerning the complainant's past sexual activities on the issue as to whether the carnal knowledge was against the will of the female, the modern trend is to limit the use of evidence relating to such sexual activities as in the opinion of most courts, such activity does not, without more evidence, tend to establish that consent was given on the occasion in question.

The Model Code defines the crime of rape in different terms than were used in the common law offenses and takes a different approach to the

---

[132] Ky. Penal Code Notebook, Ky. Dept. of Justice (1974).

[133] Model Penal Code, § 213.3 (Proposed Official Draft 1980).

[134] Fla. Stat. § 794.011(4) (1976); Iowa Code § 709.4(4) (1979); Minn. Stat. §§ 609.341-609.342 (1980).

grading of the offenses. In the Code, the culpability and dangerousness manifested by the actor, the presence or absence of factors verifying these conditions in the actor, and the degree of harm inflicted upon the victim are all considered in determining the seriousness of the offense and the penalty attached. Some recently revised statutes use the terminology as expressed in the Model Penal Code, while others retain some of the provisions of the common law crime.

A second sex crime in the category of offenses against the person is sodomy. Sodomy has been defined as "carnal copulation by human beings with each other against nature or with a beast." Rather than using the term sodomy, the drafters of the Model Penal Code took a different approach, defining the offense as "deviate sexual intercourse by force or imposition." The Model Code excepts from criminal sanction deviate sexual intercourse between consenting adults if both participants consent and each is of sufficient age and mental capacity to render consent and if they conduct their relations in private and create no public nuisance. While some modern Codes have adopted the provisions of the Model Code, most still provide punishment for consensual sodomy even though, in many states, it is classified as a misdemeanor rather than a felony.

The third sex crime considered under the offenses against the person is sexual abuse (sexual assault). Under various headings, states provided penalties for unlawfully subjecting another person to sexual contact without the other's consent. The definition of the crime as well as the label attached differs from state to state, some of the titles being "indecent or immoral practices with another," "sexual abuse" or "sexual assault."

The crime is covered in the Model Penal Code under the term "sexual assault." In the Code, it is defined to include "any touching of the sexual or other intimate parts of the person for the purpose of arousing or gratifying sexual desire." Some states have followed the Model Code in establishing only one degree of sexual abuse but grade the offense as a lesser felony. In other states, the offenses of "sexual assault" or "sexual abuse" are graded according to the degree of force and the age or mental condition of the victim.

At common law, particular acts and forms of lewdness constituted a criminal offense. The word "lewdness" means open and public indecency. Under the Model Criminal Code, a person commits the crime of indecent exposure if, for the purpose of arousing or gratifying sexual desire of himself or any other person other than his spouse, he exposes his genitals under circumstances in which he knows his conduct is likely to cause affront or alarm. Some of the more recently revised statutes use the terms used in the Code, but extend the coverage to exposure of other specifically named areas of the body.

The generally-accepted definition of seduction is the act of a man inducing a woman to commit unlawful sexual intercourse with him by means of enticements, persuasions, solicitations, promises, bribes or other means without the employment of force, thereby overcoming her reluctance and her scruples. The elements of the crime vary from state to state, some requiring that the woman victim be chaste, unmarried or virtuous.

The acts subject to penalty are covered in the Model Penal Code as part of the Section entitled "Corruption of Minors and Seduction." Under the Code provisions, the prosecution must prove either normal or deviate sexual intercourse by a male with a female, not his wife, that the promise of marriage was made, and that the actor did not mean to marry the female with whom he had intercourse. A few of the contemporary statutes contain provisions which resemble the Model Code, but some retain the provisions of the earlier statutes.

Various statutes contain other sex-related crimes against the person. These include "importuning," which prohibits solicitation of sexual activity; "voyeurism," which prohibits the trespass or invasion of privacy of another to spy or eavesdrop for the purpose of sexually arousing or gratifying himself or herself; and "sexual misconduct," an offense created to cover sexual intercourse between a defendant under 18 and a victim under 16 who is incapable of consent due to the age. An example of another offense designed to punish a wrong not covered elsewhere is "intercourse with a person in custody." Under these statutes, one who has supervisory or disciplinary authority over another may be guilty of a crime if he has sexual intercourse or deviate sexual relations with one over whom he has supervision.

As statutes relating to sexual offenses against the person now vary from state to state, these statutes must be consulted to determine the particular statute applicable.

Chapter 5
OFFENSES AGAINST PROPERTY – DESTRUCTION AND INTRUSION OFFENSES

The gravamen of the crime with which the defendant was charged (burglary) is the felonious breaking with the intent to steal, and the mere act without the essential element of intention does not constitute a statutory offense.... But proof of the act creates the inference of criminal intention.

Kidd v. Commonwealth,
273 Ky. 300,
116 S.W.2d 636 (1938).

§ 5.1 Introduction

In studying the history of criminal law and procedure, one recognizes that, in most societies, offenses that interfere with the sanctity of a person's home are considered more serious than other property offenses, and are treated accordingly. This is especially true in those countries that have followed the traditional English law where the concept that *a person's home is his castle* was recognized very early, and honored throughout many generations. Therefore, although certain crimes, such as arson and burglary, are essentially offenses against property, they are considered separately here and elsewhere, not only for convenience in organizing the material, but also to place emphasis on the fact that they have been traditionally given special consideration.

Two of the most serious crimes criminal justice personnel deal with are arson and burglary. Although the statutory definitions have enlarged upon the common law definitions, the elements of these two crimes as defined in early cases as well as modern statutes and cases are carefully considered. In addition, malicious mischief and trespass are included in this chapter. These two offenses are not normally as serious as arson and burglary, but are designed to protect the real property of individuals against destruction and intrusion and complement the more serious crimes.

The process followed in discussing these and other property destruction and intrusion crimes is to first define the traditional crime, and then make reference to statutory and code changes that are in effect in most states.

§ 5.2 Arson

Because of the great danger to human life resulting from the burning of a dwelling house, arson at common law was considered to be a heinous felony punishable by death.[1] The primary purpose of the laws relating to arson was to preserve the security of the habitation, to protect dwellers within the building from injury or death by fire, and to protect the possessory interest in the house. It was considered one of the most serious common law felonies and, according to Sir William Blackstone, was frequently more destructive than murder itself.[2] Blackstone explained his opinion by indicating that murder, atrocious as it is, seldom extends beyond the felonious act designed; whereas fire too frequently involves in the common calamity persons un-

---

[1]   Williams v. State, 100 Fla. 1054, 132 So. 186 (1930).

[2]   1 Blackstone, COMMENTARIES 220-28.

known to the incendiary and not intended to be hurt by him, and friends as well as enemies. Even though the law of arson has been changed by statute, it is still considered a very serious crime and remains a felony today in all American jurisprudence.

As the common law offense of arson is still made reference to in deciding current cases, the common law concepts are discussed first, followed by an explanation of the federal laws, then by a discussion of the modern statutes.

A. Traditional Definitions and Elements

Before examining the elements of the common law offense of arson, definitions handed down by court decisions are noted. These will assist in understanding this offense. Some of these definitions are:

At common law, "arson" was the willful and malicious burning of another's dwelling house or of an outhouse within its curtilage.[3]

Common law "arson" is willful and malicious burning of a dwelling house of another person.[4]

When breaking down the definition of common law arson, four elements are common. Each of these has a legal meaning and each element must be considered separately. The four elements are:

(1) burning,
(2) a dwelling house (or outhouse within its curtilage),
(3) the house must belong to or be occupied by another person, and
(4) the burning must be done or caused maliciously.

Each of these elements has legal definitions.

(1) Burning

In order to constitute the traditional crime of arson, there must be some burning, i.e. there must have been some consuming of the material with which the house is built. It was sufficient for common law arson if any part of the dwelling house itself was burned, no matter how small, no matter how in-

---

[3]   Fox v. State, 179 Ind. App. 267, 384 N.E.2d 1159 (1979).

[4]   State v. White, 291 N.C. 118, 229 S.E.2d 152 (1976).

significant to the structural integrity of the building.[5] For example, a spot on the floor which was charred was held sufficient to constitute this element of the crime of arson.[6] There need not be a blaze and it is immaterial how soon the fire was extinguished or whether it was put out or went out by itself.[7] While it was necessary that there be some "combustion," "ignition" or "charring" to constitute burning, this element was not present if there was only damage caused by smoke.[8]

(2) Dwelling House or Outhouse Used in Connection Therewith

As the gist of the offense at common law was the danger to the lives of persons who dwelt in or occupied the house, or the buildings used in connection therewith, it was necessary that the dwelling be occupied. However, it was not necessary that the house be actually inhabited at the time of the burning, provided it was usually inhabited and the owner only temporarily absent.[9]

At least under some interpretations, a building which was not itself a dwelling house could be the subject of arson if it were within curtilage of a dwelling house. This was defined as the space adjoining a dwelling and habitually used for family purposes.[10] Some examples of buildings that were considered "dwellings" for purposes of the arson law are a barn, a stable, a cow-house, a sheep-house, a dairy-house, and a milk-house, all of which were located within the curtilage of a dwelling house.[11]

As will be explained in subsequent Sections, many statutes have modified the common law to cure some of the problems relating to the common law crime of arson. For example, most state legislatures have changed the definition of property so as to include the dwelling only, but have added other related laws to cover burning of other buildings.

(3) The House Must Belong to or be Occupied by Another

The common law definition requires that the house burned be possessed by another. Accordingly, it was arson for the legal owner of the house to burn his own house which was in possession of another.[12] Conversely, it was not arson at common law for a person to burn his own dwelling which was

---

[5]   Commonwealth v. Van Schaack, 16 Mass. 104 (1819).

[6]   State v. Braathen, 77 N.D. 309, 43 N.W.2d 202 (1950).

[7]   State v. Wyatt, 48 N.C. App. 709, 269 S.E.2d 717 (1980).

[8]   State v. Hall, 93 N.C. 571 (1885); Honey v. State, 112 Tex. Crim. 439, 17 S.W.2d 50 (1929).

[9]   State v. Wyatt, 269 S.E.2d 717 (1980). *See* case in Part II.

[10]   United States v. Potts, 297 F.2d 68 (6th Cir. 1961).

[11]   1 Hawkins, PLEAS OF THE CROWN, 105-06 (1716).

[12]   State v. Tennery, 9 Iowa 436 (1859).

occupied by him.[13] While the person could not be found guilty under the common law for burning his own dwelling house occupied by him, it was arson if one tenant in an apartment house burned his own apartment even if the fire were totally contained within that single apartment unit.[14]

As insurance on the dwelling became common and houses were burned in order to collect insurance, additional statutes were enacted to supplement the common law crime of arson. Under these statutes, it is unlawful to burn insured property with the specific intent to injure, prejudice or defraud the insurer.[15]

(4) The Burning Must be Done Maliciously

Perhaps the most difficult task of a prosecutor in proving the common law crime of arson is to show that the burning was willful or malicious. Mere accident, carelessness or simple negligence is not enough to constitute the common law crime of arson. If the prosecutor introduces evidence to show that the person intentionally started the fire which resulted in the burning, this is a clear-cut case. However, it is more difficult to prove the maliciousness where the acts amounted to a wanton burning without justification or excuse. In the latter situation, the requirements of arson could be met if evidence indicated that the actor performed an intentional act which created a very high risk of the burning of a dwelling house. Also, there is sufficient intent or malice to constitute the crime of arson if there exists general malice or an intent to burn some structure; a particular intent or malice against a particular person or thing is not required.[16]

In an effort to protect property other than dwellings and to provide a penalty for the intentional burning of property that was not within the common law definitions, statutes have been enacted in all states establishing degrees of arson. The degree of severity of punishment is sometimes determined by:

(a) the value of the property,
(b) the use of property, such as a dwelling house, and
(c) whether the place is inhabited.

Also, statutes have been enacted to punish those who attempt to commit the crime of arson but fail.

---

[13] State v. Keena, 63 Conn. 329, 28 A. 522 (1893).
[14] State v. Jones, 296 N.C. 75, 248 S.E.2d 858 (1978).
[15] Edwards v. Commonwealth, 204 Ky. 515, 264 S.W. 1083 (1924).
[16] Colbert v. State, 125 Wis. 423, 104 N.W. 61 (1905).

B. Statutes and Codes

1. Model Penal Code

§ 220.1 Arson and Related Offenses.[17]

(1) Arson. A person is guilty of arson, a felony of the second degree, if he starts a fire or causes an explosion with the purpose of:

   (a) destroying a building or occupied structure of another; or
   (b) destroying or damaging any property, whether his own or another's, to collect insurance for such loss. It shall be an affirmative defense to prosecution under this paragraph that the actor's conduct did not recklessly endanger any building or occupied structure of another or place any other person in danger of death or bodily injury.

(2) Reckless Burning or Exploding. A person commits a felony of the third degree if he purposely starts a fire or causes an explosion, whether on his own property or another's, and thereby recklessly:

   (a) places another person in danger of death or bodily injury; or
   (b) places a building or occupied structure of another in danger of damage or destruction.

(3) Failure to Control or Report Dangerous Fire. A person who knows that a fire is endangering life or a substantial amount of property of another and fails to take reasonable measures to put out or control the fire, when he can do so without substantial risk to himself, or to give a prompt fire alarm, commits a misdemeanor if:

   (a) he knows that he is under an official, contractual, or other legal duty to prevent or combat the fire; or

---

[17] Model Penal Code, § 220.1 (Proposed Official Draft 1980).

(b) the fire was started, albeit lawfully, by him or with his assent, or on property in his custody or control.

Under the Model Penal Code, the crime of arson is graded partly according to the kind of property destroyed or imperiled and partly according to the danger to persons. The concept of arson is enlarged to include exploding as well as burning. According to this provision, a person is guilty of arson, a felony in the second degree (the most serious offense), if he starts a fire or causes an explosion, either to destroy a building or occupied structure of another, or his own or another's property to collect insurance for such loss.

Under the Model Penal Code, the most serious crime is designated as arson. According to this provision, there is a violation only when the fire or explosion (1) is ignited for the purpose of destroying a building or occupied structure of another, or (2) is ignited for the purpose of destroying or damaging any property, whether his own or another's, to collect insurance for such loss.

The other two crimes defined in the Penal Code are "Reckless Burning or Exploding" and "Failure to Control or Report a Dangerous Fire." These have obviously been added to provide a penalty for an act which results in a burning or explosion when some of the technical requirements of the crime of arson are not provable.

2. Federal Code

Title 18, § 81 of the U.S. Code provides a penalty for those who commit arson within the special maritime and territorial jurisdiction of the United States. This Section provides:

Whoever, within a special maritime and territorial jurisdiction of the United States, willfully and maliciously sets fire to or burns, or attempts to set fire to or burn any building, structure or vessel, any machinery or building materials or supplies, military or naval stores, munitions of war, or any structural aids or appliances for navigation or shipping, shall be fined not more than $1,000 or imprisoned for not more than five years, or both.

If the building be a dwelling or if the life of any person be placed in jeopardy, he shall be fined not more than $5,000, or imprisoned not more than 20 years, or both.

The punishment provisions are graduated with regard to the gravity of the offense. Also, under this federal statute, the U.S. courts have jurisdiction only when the crime is committed within the maritime and territorial jurisdiction of the United States.[18]

3. Other statutes and codes

According to an article written in 1986, by 1984 only eight states remained fully committed to the principle set forth in the Model Arson Law.[19] The modern state statutes have expanded not only the coverage of arson and related laws, but have simplified the wording so as to make definition less difficult. As the state statutes differ in some respects, it is essential that the statutes be checked to determine the exact elements of arson and related crimes. For example, some states provide for higher sanctions if the actor engages in the act in conscious disregard of the substantial risk that a person might be inside the building or in proximity thereto.[20]

Other states retain a single arson offense and isolate aggravating factors to distinguish among the various levels of the offense. In some states, the statutes are graded according to the type of property; some according to the criminal state of mind; that is, whether the act was done intentionally, willfully and maliciously, or negligently; and some determine the degree of the offense by combination of two or more of these. An example of a statute which takes into consideration the type of property as well as the state of mind is that of California. It provides:[21]

§ 451. Arson of structure, forest land or property; great bodily injury; inhabited structure or property; owned property; punishment

A person is guilty of arson when he willfully and maliciously sets fire to or burns or causes to be burned or who aids, counsels or procures the burning of, any structure, forest land or property.

(a) Arson that causes great bodily injury is a felony punishable by imprisonment in the state prison for five, seven or nine years.

---

[18] For definitions of "special maritime and territorial jurisdiction of the United States," *see* 18 U.S.C. § 7 reprinted in the appendix.

[19] *See*, Poulous, *The Metamorphosis of the Law of Arson*, 51 MO. L. REV. 295 (1986) for a very thorough discussion of the effect of the Model Penal Code on state statutes and codes.

[20] Me. Rev. Stat. Ann. tit. 718A, § 801 (1979); Mo. Rev. Stat. § 569.040 (1979).

[21] Cal. Penal Code, § 451-452 (West 1980).

(b) Arson that causes an inhabited structure or inhabited property to burn is a felony punishable by imprisonment in the state prison for three, five or seven years.

(c) Arson of a structure or forest land is a felony punishable by imprisonment in the state prison for two, four or six years.

(d) Arson of property is a felony punishable by imprisonment in the state prison for 16 months, two, or three years. For purposes of this paragraph arson of property does not include one burning or causing to be burned his own personal property unless there is an intent to defraud or there is injury to another person or another person's structure, forest land or property.

§ 452. Unlawfully causing a fire of any structure, forest land or property; great bodily injury; inhabited structure or property; punishment

A person is guilty of unlawfully causing a fire when he recklessly sets fire to or burns or causes to be burned, any structure, forest land or property.

(a) Unlawfully causing a fire that causes great bodily injury is a felony punishable by imprisonment in the state prison for two, four or six years, or by imprisonment in the county jail for not more than one year, or by a fine, or by both such imprisonment and fine.

(b) Unlawfully causing a fire that causes an inhabited structure or inhabited property to burn is a felony punishable by imprisonment in the state prison for two, three or four years, or by imprisonment in the county jail for not more than one year, or by a fine, or by both such imprisonment and fine.

(c) Unlawfully causing a fire of a structure or forest land is a felony punishable by imprisonment in the state prison for 16 months, two or three years, or by imprisonment in the county jail for not more than six months, or by a fine, or by both such imprisonment and fine.

(d) Unlawfully causing a fire of property is a misdemeanor. For purposes of this paragraph, unlawfully causing a fire of property does not include one

> burning or causing to be burned his own personal
> property unless there is injury to another person or
> to another person's structure, forest land or prop-
> erty.[22]

As stated in the California Code, the seriousness of the crime and the punishment attached is determined by the mental element (whether the action is willful and malicious, or reckless), the type of property burned and the degree of bodily injury suffered.

An example of a statute that punishes for negligent burning is that of Alaska. There, the law provides that a person commits the crime of criminal negligent burning if, with criminal negligence, he damages property of another by fire or explosion.[23]

In proving the crime of arson or a related crime, criminal justice personnel will be required to gather evidence to prove each of the elements as stated in the statute. For example, in California, to prove arson, evidence must be introduced to show:

    (a) willful and malicious conduct,

    (b) the setting, causing to be set, or the aiding, counseling or procuring the setting of a fire, and

    (c) burning of a structure, forest land or property. If the highest penalty is to be assessed, it is also necessary to prove that the arson caused great bodily injury.

If the statute is worded to require that the damage be "without the consent" of the owner, as in Illinois, the defendant may claim "consent" as an affirmative defense.[24] However, the Illinois court determined that the complaint charging the defendant with arson was not void for failure to allege a want of consent.[25]

Although there is considerable variation among the state statutes, there is a striking similarity in the modern statutory law of arson throughout the United States.[26] The writer of the article referenced in the footnote concluded his study of the law of arson with this comment:

---

[22] Cal. Penal Code § 451-452 (West 1980).

[23] AL&S Rev. Crim. Code § 11.46.430 (1980).

[24] Ill. Rev. Stat. ch. 38 § 201(2) (1977).

[25] People v. White, 22 Ill. App. 2d 206, 317 N.E.2d 273 (1974).

[26] Poulous, *The Metamorphosis of the Law of Arson*, 51 MO. L. REV. 295 (1986).

Though deeply rooted in the common law and heavily influenced by the Model Penal Code, the law in the majority of American states resembles neither today. What we see here is the emergence of a modern statutory common law of arson. A common law made by legislatures not judges. A common law produced not by the adoption of a Model Code, as it was at mid century, but by the labors of individual legislatures throughout the United States . . .

§ 5.3 Malicious Mischief (Criminal Mischief)

A. Traditional Definition and Elements

Although there is some doubt concerning whether malicious mischief was a crime at common law in England, a number of states assert that it was an offense and have enforced it as a common law crime.[27] Legislation in many states expands upon the common law crime of malicious mischief in defining particular types of malicious mischief. While the original crime related only to personal property, some legislation enlarged the definition to include malicious injury or destruction of real property, including trees, mines, coal and even tobacco plants. The legislatures apparently responded to needs as they arose in particular jurisdictions.

The crime commonly known as *malicious mischief* is difficult to define, as the name is applied to acts denounced by a multitude of statutes varying widely as to terms, phraseology and purpose. Generally, it has been defined as the willful and unlawful injury to or destruction of the property of another with the malicious intent to injure the owner.

Malicious mischief is distinguished from larceny in that, in larceny, goods are fraudulently taken against the owner's will with the intention of converting the goods to the taker's use, whereas, in malicious mischief, the property is maliciously injured without being taken and converted to another's use.[28] The grade of the offense of malicious mischief and the amount of punishment are ordinarily prescribed by the statute. These are usually determined on the basis of the amount of injury or damage inflicted, or by the value of the property injured or destroyed.

---

[27] State v. Watts, 48 Ark. 56, 2 S.W. 342 (1886); State v. Manuel, 72 N.C. 201, 21 Am.Rep. 455 (1875).

[28] State v. Hawkins, 8 Port. 461, 33 Am.Dec. 294 (Ala. 1839).

The elements of the crime of malicious mischief vary depending upon the wording of the statute; however, there are some elements that are common.

(1) Malice

Malice is generally held to be an essential ingredient of the offense of malicious mischief.[29] The name itself implies that malice must be proved.

(2) Intent

From the definition included in the paragraphs above, it is apparent that one of the elements is willful or intentional injury. Where such wording is used, the intent must be proved by the prosecution.

(3) Injury or Destruction

At common law, either an injury to or destruction of property suffices so far as the physical act constitutes the offense.[30] Any injury to or destruction of property will ordinarily constitute an offense under most statutes, but some require that the damage be measured in terms of monetary damages.

(4) Property of Another

While in some jurisdictions, malicious mischief may be committed as to personal property only, in others, real, as well as personal property, are subjects of the offense. In any event it is necessary to prove that the property belonged to another person.

Failure to prove any element which is an essential ingredient of the offense constitutes a complete defense.[31]

---

[29] State v. Ward, 127 Minn. 510, 150 N.W. 209 (1914).

[30] State v. Watts, 48 Ark. 56, 2 S.W. 342 (1886).

[31] State v. Minor, 17 N.D. 454, 117 N.W. 528 (1908).

B. Contemporary Statutes and Codes

1. Model Penal Code

§ 220.3 Criminal Mischief[32]

(1) Offense Defined. A person is guilty of criminal mischief if he:

  (a) damages tangible property of another purposely, recklessly, or by negligence in the employment of fire, explosives, or other dangerous means listed in § 220.2(1); or

  (b) purposely or recklessly tampers with tangible property of another so as to endanger person or property; or

  (c) purposely or recklessly causes another to suffer pecuniary loss by deception or threat.

(2) Grading. Criminal mischief is a felony of the third degree if the actor purposely causes pecuniary loss in excess of $5,000, or a substantial interruption or impairment of public communication, transportation, supply of water, gas or power, or other public service. It is a misdemeanor if the actor purposely causes pecuniary loss in excess of $100, or a petty misdemeanor if he purposely or recklessly causes pecuniary loss in excess of $25. Otherwise criminal mischief is a violation.

The Model Penal Code is entitled "Criminal Mischief" rather than "Malicious Mischief." The Code takes the approach of consolidating the form of malicious mischief provisions of the various statutes and even the common law into a single comprehensive offense. Section (1)(a) reaches purposeful or reckless damage to the tangible property of another, as well as negligent damage caused by dangerous instrumentalities listed. Section (1)(b) expands the traditional offense to include tampering with another's property so as to endanger the person or property, and § (1)(c) adds a penalty where one purposely or recklessly damages personal property and causes another to suffer pecuniary loss by deception or threat. As in the traditional offense of malicious mischief, the Code offense differs from the theft, forgery and fraud provisions, in that the focus is not upon the misappropriation of property, but rather upon its destruction.

---

[32] Model Penal Code, § 220.3 (Proposed Official Draft 1980).

2. Federal Code

To protect property of the United States as well as property within the special maritime and territorial jurisdiction of the United States, federal legislation has been enacted. This federal legislation was originally part of Title 18, § 1361 and Title 18, § 1363.

Title 18, § 1361 provides:

> Whoever willfully injures or commits any depredation against any property of the United States, or of any department or agency thereof, or any property which has been or is being manufactured or constructed for the United States, or any department or agency thereof, shall be punished as follows:
>
> > If the damage to such property exceeds $100, by a fine of not more than $10,000 or imprisonment for not more than 10 years, or both; if the damage to such property does not exceed the sum of $100, by a fine of not more than $1,000 or imprisonment for not more than one year, or both.[33]

This Section of the Federal Code requires proof that the act was done willfully as was required under common law, and the government must prove specific intent as an element.[34] In addition, the prosecution must show ownership of the property by the United States and some depredation of the property.

The second malicious mischief statute provides:

> § 1363, Building or Property Within Special Maritime or Territorial Jurisdictions
>
> Whoever, within the special maritime and territorial jurisdiction of the United States, willfully and maliciously destroys or injures or attempts to destroy or injure any building, structure or vessel, any machinery or building materials and supplies, military or naval stores, munitions of war or any structural aids or appliances for navigation or shipping, shall be fined not more than $1,000 or

---

[33] 18 U.S.C. § 1361.

[34] United States v. Jones, 607 F.2d 269 (1979), *cert. denied*, 444 U.S. 1085, 62 L.Ed.2d 771, 100 S. Ct. 1043 (1979).

imprisoned for not more than five years, or both, and if the building be a dwelling, or the life of any persons be placed in jeopardy, shall be fined not more than $5,000 or imprisoned not more than 20 years, or both.[35]

In addition to introducing evidence that the acts occurred within the special maritime and territorial jurisdiction of the United States as defined in U.S.C., Title 18 § 7, the government must prove willful and malicious destruction or injury or attempt to destroy or injure a building, structure, vessel or machinery as defined in the statute. If convicted of this felony crime, the defendant may be imprisoned up to 20 years if the building is a dwelling or the life of any person is placed in jeopardy; otherwise the maximum imprisonment is five years.[36]

3. Other statutes and codes

Some of the recently drafted codes have followed the Model Penal Code approach of consolidating the former malicious mischief provisions into a single comprehensive offense or an integrated series of related offenses.[37] Other codes integrate a series of related offenses into a single crime.[38] Still others retain parts of the old approach to criminal mischief.[39]

An example of a statute that consolidates former malicious mischief and similar crimes into two Sections is that of Missouri.[40]

§ 569.100 Property damage in the first degree
(1) A person commits the crime of property damage in the first degree if:

    (a) he knowingly damages property of another to an extent exceeding five thousand dollars; or

---

[35] 18 U.S.C. § 1363; *see* the Appendix for a definition of "special maritime and territorial jurisdiction of the United States."

[36] For other federal crimes relating to malicious mischief, *see* 18 U.S.C. § 1362 relating to damages to communication lines, stations or systems, and 18 U.S.C. § 1366 relating to destruction of an energy facility.

[37] Ala., Del., Fla., Ind., Minn., Mont., Neb., N.II., N.D., Pa., Tex., Utah and Wis.

[38] Ala., Conn., Hawaii, Iowa, Me., Mo., Or. and Wash.

[39] Ark., Colo., Ga., Ill., Kan., Ky., La., N.M., N.Y., Ohio and S.D.

[40] Mo. Rev. Stat. § 569.110 (1979).

(b) he damages property to an extent exceeding five thousand dollars for the purpose of defrauding an insurer.

(2) Property damage in the first degree is a Class D felony.

§ 569.110 Property damage in the second degree
(1) A person commits the crime of property damage in the second degree if:

(a) he knowingly damages property of another to an extent exceeding five hundred dollars; or
(b) he damages property to an extent exceeding five hundred dollars for the purpose of defrauding an insurer.

(2) Property damage in the second degree is a Class A misdemeanor.

To convict a person for violating § 569.100 of the Missouri statute, the prosecution must prove:

(a) property damage.
  Some damage to real or personal property is required.
(b) damage was knowingly caused.
  This requires the prosecution to show that the person did not accidentally damage the property but had knowledge that his acts would damage the property.
(c) property belonged to another.
  This is defined as property in which any person other than the actor had an interest upon which the actor is not privileged to infringe, regardless of the fact that the actor also had an interest in the property.
(d) damage exceeds $5,000,

  or

(a) property damage,
(b) for the purpose of defrauding an insurer,
(c) damage exceeds $5,000.

The elements of the crime described in § 569.110 are:
- (a) property damage,
- (b) knowingly caused,
- (c) property of another,
- (d) damage exceeds $500,

or

- (a) property damage,
- (b) for purpose of defrauding an insurer,
- (c) damage exceeds $500.

§ 5.4 Burglary

A. *Traditional Definitions and Elements*

One of the most serious crimes in practically every society is the crime designated as burglary. Burglary is considered more serious than such crimes as larceny due to the possible injuries to persons within the dwelling and the fact that the courts and legislative bodies have long looked upon the home as deserving special protection. According to one court, the crime is one against possession and is primarily designed to secure the sanctity of one's home, especially at nighttime when peace, solitude and safety are most desired and expected.[41] From early times burglary was considered a felony and at one time was punishable by death.[42]

The term *burglary* is a combination of the Saxon term "burg," a house, and "laron," theft, and originally signified no more than the robbery of a dwelling.[43] At common law, the ownership of the house was essential to the offense and it was required that it should be the house of another.

As the crime of burglary developed, the definition became very technical, with many elements, all of which had technical definitions. Some definitions will help make this point:

"Burglary" is the breaking into a house in the night season with intent to commit a felony, and if a house is so entered, it is burglary, whether the felony be executed or not, and regardless of the kind of

---

[41] State v. Brooks, 277 S.C. 111, 283 S.E.2d 830 (1981).

[42] State v. Allison, 169 N.C. 375, 85 S.E. 129 (1915).

[43] Anderson v. State, 48 Ala. 665, 17 Am.Rep. 36 (1872).

felony intended or the manner in which the felony may be frustrated, or the value of the property taken, or any other circumstance which is not intrinsic.[44]

The common law crime of "burglary" was an offense against habitation, and the essential elements were an actual breaking, in the nighttime, with intent to commit a felony.[45]

Before discussing the elements of the common law offense of burglary, it is essential to point out that, in all of the states, statutes have been enacted to punish persons for committing acts which did not come within the technical definition of burglary. This was necessary because too many persons were found not guilty due to judicially determined technical requirements. In most states, statutes were passed declaring it to be a burglary for a person to break in other places than the dwelling house, as for instance, warehouses, shops, offices, barns, and stables. Also by statute in a number of states, the necessity for "breaking" was omitted and an entry alone was sufficient if the required intent was also present.[46] In almost all states, statutes were enacted to punish those who committed the act in the daytime, as well as at night, and, in many instances, the intent to commit a felony was not required but intent to commit a misdemeanor was sufficient.[47]

The elements of common law burglary are:

(a) a breaking,
(b) an entry,
(c) a dwelling house,
(d) of another,
(e) in the nighttime,
(f) with intent to commit a felony therein.

Although statutes now in force extend the offense of burglary beyond the common law definition, each of these elements is defined and discussed, as they are still referred to in state statutes and court decisions, even in those states that have recently revised their statutes and codes.

(a) Breaking
In order to meet this element, the prosecution must prove that some breaking of the structure, either actual or constructive, occurred. Breaking

---

[44] Conrad v. State, 75 Ohio St. 52, 78 N.E. 957 (1906).
[45] Stowell v. People, 521 Colo. 255, 90 P.2d 520 (1939).
[46] State v. Petit, 32 Wash. 129, 72 P. 1021 (1903).
[47] People v. Webber, 138 Cal. 145, 70 P. 1089 (1902).

consists in putting aside a part of the house which obstructs the entrance and is closed, or in penetrating by an opening which is as much closed as the nature of the case admits.

The law puts a premium upon a reasonable degree of care in acting to prevent burglaries by closing doors, windows and other openings. Therefore, in the absence of statute, an entry to an open door or window would not complete this element, although there may have been an intent to commit a felony.[48]

To close some of the loopholes, the early courts recognized "constructive breaking." To constitute this element, the breaking could be by an entry effected through fraud or by threat or by intimidation.[49] An example is where the defendant pretended that he had business with the owner of the house and gained entry.[50]

(b) Entry

An entry is also necessary to constitute the crime of burglary. A breaking without entry is not burglary, but an entry, however slight after breaking, is sufficient; for example, where a head, a hand, an arm, a foot or even a finger is thrust within the house.[51] In the case of *People v. Peddinger*, the breaking of a window of a service station by the defendant and insertion of an arm into the building was sufficient "entry" in a burglary prosecution.[52] And in the case of *People v. Davis*, the court held that it is not the size of the hole that is determinative of whether an entry was made, but whether a hand or instrument was actually inserted into the hole for the purpose of committing the felony.[53]

Proving the entry was essential under the common law. Where there was a breaking and an entry and an intent to commit theft, the offense of burglary was complete, notwithstanding an abandonment of the undertaking after the breaking and entry.[54]

---

[48] Adair v. State, 19 Ala. App. 174, 95 So. 827 (1923); State v. Hustead, 615 S.W.2d 556 (1981).

[49] Davis v. Commonwealth, 132 Va. 521, 110 S.E. 356 (1922).

[50] Johnson v. Commonwealth, 85 Pa. 54, 27 Am.Rep. 622 (1877); Nichols v. State, 68 Wis. 416, 32 N.W. 543 (1887).

[51] Penman v. State, 163 Ind. App. 583, 325 N.E.2d 478 (1975).

[52] 94 Cal. App. 297, 271 P. 132 (1928); Commonwealth v. Myers, 223 Pa. Super. 75, 297 A.2d 151 (1972).

[53] People v. Davis, 3 Ill. App. 3d 738, 279 N.E.2d 179 (1972).

[54] Schwartz v. State, 114 S.W. 809 (55 Tex. Cr. 36, 1909).

(c) Dwelling House

At common law, and under many statutes declaratory thereof a breaking and an entering, to be burglarious, must be of a dwelling house. The dwelling house has been defined as any kind of structure used as a place of habitation and occupied by persons other than the defendant. Temporary absence of the occupant will not deprive the dwelling house of its character as such.[55] It is not necessary to prove that the owner or occupant or some member of the family was in the house at the time, but the house, although furnished as a dwelling house, loses its character as such for purposes of burglary if the occupant leaves it without the intention to return.[56]

The word *dwell*, as respects burglary, imports a human habitation and the character of the house is generally immaterial. However, the house must be occupied as a dwelling and not merely be suitable or intended for such purpose.[57] As one court indicated, "any and every settled habitation of a man and his family is his house or his mansion in respect to its burglarious entry."[58]

In the absence of statute, shops, stores and warehouses are not the subject of burglary unless they are occupied in part as a dwelling. However, as indicated, in many instances the statutes are worded so as to include this type of structure and, in some instances, the degree of the crime is different. On the other hand, stables, smokehouses, kitchens, shops, offices or other outhouses, if they are within the curtilage of a dwelling house, are regarded as parts of the dwelling so that it is burglary to break and enter the same with felonious intent, although there may be no entry into the dwelling house itself.[59]

(d) House of another

As in the case of arson, the law is concerned with the protection of habitation rather than the title to property; consequently with occupancy rather than ownership. Therefore, it is not a question of whether a person owns the house that is broken into, but possession constitutes sufficient ownership in burglary cases.[60]

---

[55] Smith v. State, 80 Fla. 315, 85 So. 911 (1920).

[56] Henderson v. State, 80 Fla. 491, 86 So. 439 (1920).

[57] Carrier v. State, 227 Ind. 726, 89 N.E.2d 74 (1949).

[58] Smith v. Birmingham Waterworks Co., 104 Ala. 315, 16 So. 123 (1894).

[59] Henderson v. U.S., 172 F.2d 289 (D.C. Cir. 1949); State v. Gatewood, 169 Kan. 679, 221 P.2d 392 (1950).

[60] Wilson v. State, 247 Ala. 84, 22 So. 2d 601 (1945).

(e) In the nighttime

At common law, breaking and entering a dwelling house in the daytime is not burglary. According to some decisions, nighttime begins when daylight ends, or when the countenance ceases to be reasonably discernible by the light of the sun, and ends at dawn, or as soon as the countenance becomes discernible.[61]

"At night" is defined in the Model Penal Code a "the period thirty minutes past sunset and thirty minutes before sunrise."[62]

Statutes which have defined nighttime for purposes of burglary often define nighttime as the period between sunset and sunrise.[63]

(f)   With intent to commit a felony therein

Burglary is another "specific intent" type crime. General intent to commit a crime is not sufficient but the specific intent may be inferred from the facts.[64] The indictment for burglary must allege the specific intent to commit a particular felony and the prosecution must prove that the intent existed in the mind of the perpetrator at the moment of entry.[65] The intent must be concurrent with the breaking and entering and may be formed at the moment of time the breaking occurs. The early courts determined that if the intent does not exist until after the house was entered, there could be no burglary under the common law definition.[66]

Burglary is generally committed with intent to steal, which is a felony, but the indictment may allege breaking and entering with intent to commit other felonies such as murder or rape. In any event, the prosecution must introduce evidence to show specific intent on the part of the perpetrator to commit a specific felony.[67]

It is obvious, from the discussion of the common law elements of burglary, that many wrongs were not punishable when the technical definitions, as interpreted, were applied. As a result, efforts have been made for many years to modify the common law crime or to write statutes to provide a penalty for such crimes as breaking and entering, or provide a penalty where the intent was to commit a misdemeanor rather than a felony. The Model

---

[61]   Ashford v. State, 36 Neb. 38, 53 N.W. 1036 (1893).

[62]   Model Penal Code, § 221.0 (Proposed Official Draft 1980). This is the same definition that was stated in the Texas Penal Code and quoted in Weathered v. State, 101 Tex. Crim. 520, 276 S.W. 436 (1925).

[63]   State v. Richards, 29 Utah 310, 81 P. 142 (1905).

[64]   State v. Fox, 80 Iowa 312, 45 N.W. 874 (1890).

[65]   People v. Markus, 147 Cal. Rptr. 151, 82 Cal. App. 3d 477 (1978).

[66]   Jackson v. State, 102 Ala. 167, 15 S. 344 (1894).

[67]   State v. Robinson, 441 So.2d 364 (La. Ct. App. 1983). *See* case in Part II.

Penal Code, which is discussed in the next Section, closes many of the legal doors which have been opened to those who have utilized the technical requirements to defeat convictions in a burglary case. Also, all of the states have enacted legislation to provide punishment for an offense, usually with a lesser penalty, when one of the elements of the common law crime of burglary is not provable.

B. *Contemporary Statutes and Codes*

1. Model Penal Code

§ 221.2 Burglary[68]
(1) Burglary Defined. A person is guilty of burglary if he enters a building or occupied structure, or separately secured or occupied portion thereof, with purpose to commit a crime therein, unless the premises are at the time open to the public or the actor is licensed or privileged to enter. It is an affirmative defense to prosecution for burglary that the building or structure was abandoned.
(2) Grading. Burglary is a felony of the second degree if it is perpetrated in the dwelling of another at night, or if, in the course of committing the offense, the actor:

    (a) purposely, knowingly or recklessly inflicts or attempts to inflict bodily injury on anyone; or
    (b) is armed with explosives or a deadly weapon.

Otherwise, burglary is a felony of the third degree. An act shall be deemed "in the course of committing" an offense if it occurs in an attempt to commit the offense or in flight after the attempt or commission.

(3) Multiple Convictions. A person may not be convicted both for burglary and for the offense which it was his purpose to commit after the burglarious entry or for an attempt to commit that offense, unless the additional offense constitutes a felony of the first or second degree.

---

[68] Model Penal Code, § 221.1 (Proposed Official Draft 1980).

The Model Penal Code retains much of the common law concept but simplifies the procedure. In Subsection (1), the elements are:

(a) the entry of a building or occupied structure (or separately secured or occupied portion),
(b) with the purpose to commit a crime therein.

In Subsection (2) the factors that accompany the entry and determine the grade of the offense are considered. The common law reasoning that entry at night is more serious than entry in the daytime is carried over into the Code. The Model Code does not provide an offense for one who surreptitiously remains on the premises, and apparently the common law definition as to what amounts to entry still prevails.

Under the Model Code "occupied structure" is any structure, vehicle or place adapted for overnight accommodation of persons, or for carrying on business therein, whether or not a person is actually present.[69] Therefore, it is not necessary to allege that the building was occupied. However, the final sentence of Subsection (1) provides a defense that would bar prosecution for burglary of abandoned or derelict buildings unsuited and, in fact, unused for human occupancy.

The terminology "purpose to commit a crime therein" differs from that used in common law definitions in that "purpose" is substituted for "intent" and "crime" is substituted for "felony." The word "crime" is defined as *an offense for which a sentence of imprisonment is authorized.*[70]

The grade of the crime of burglary, as defined in the Model Code, is determined by:

(1) the time the crime was perpetrated,
(2) whether or not bodily injury was inflicted or attempted purposely or knowingly, and
(3) whether or not the person who is charged was armed with explosives or a deadly weapon.

Burglary is a third degree felony unless there are aggravating factors as indicated, in which case it is a second degree felony.

Apparently, to forestall any arguments concerning the possibility of double jeopardy, Subsection (3) of the Model Code precludes accumulation of penalties for burglary and for the object offense in all circumstances, except where the offense is itself a felony of the first or second degree. For exam-

---

[69] Model Penal Code, § 221.0 (Proposed Official Draft 1980).
[70] Model Penal Code, § 1.04 (Proposed Official Draft 1980).

ple, consecutive sentences may be given where a person is convicted of burglary and the purpose was to commit rape, and the elements of rape are also
proved by the prosecution.

2. Federal Code

Chapter 103 of the U.S. Code includes the federal offenses relating to
robbery and burglary. This chapter defines the crimes which have general
application, such as bank robbery, as well as those crimes that apply within
the special maritime and territorial jurisdiction of the United States. The
offenses which deal with robbery are discussed thoroughly in the next chapter. However, there are some federal crimes which have elements similar to
those which make up the common law offense of burglary. For example, the
Federal Code relating to the breaking into a federal post office provides:

> Whoever forcibly breaks into or attempts to break into any post of-
> fice, or any building used in whole or in part as a post office, with
> intent to commit in such post office, or building or part thereof, so
> used, any larceny or other deprivation, shall be fined not more than
> $1,000 or imprisoned not more than 5 years, or both.[71]

In the case of *United States v. Gibson*, the circuit court, in discussing the
elements of this offense, indicated that an offense is made out when the government shows forcible entry into some part of the building and an intent to
commit larceny in a part of the building used as a post office.[72] As in the
case of a common law burglary offense, if the prosecution indicates in the indictment there is a breaking, then there must be substantial evidence to show
affirmatively and beyond reasonable doubt that there was, in fact, a breaking
of a building in which a post office is located.[73] A second federal crime
which includes some of the elements of common law burglary provides a
penalty for breaking into railway or steamboat post offices.[74]

A more recently enacted federal statute, part of which relates to destruction and intrusion offenses, deals with robberies and burglaries involving
controlled substances.[75] Section (b) of that statute provides a penalty of im-

---

[71] 18 U.S.C. § 2115.

[72] United States v. Gibson, 444 F.2d 275 (5th Cir. 1971).

[73] Smith v. United States, 413 F.2d 1121 (5th Cir. 1969).

[74] 18 U.S.C. § 2116; *see* U.S. Code Annotated for the wording of this offense and the cases
which interpret the provisions of the statute.

[75] 18 U.S.C. § 2118.

prisonment for not more than 20 years, or a fine of not more than $25,000, or both, if one is found guilty of entering or attempting to enter, without authority, business premises or property of a person registered with the Drug Enforcement Administration, with intent to steal any material or a compound containing any quantity of a controlled substance.

3. Other statutes and codes

Some states have recognized the reasons for the Model Code and have adopted similar language. However, some have taken a different approach; for example, in New York, the statute also provides for a penalty for one who remains unlawfully on the premises.[76] Some states have followed the older statute by providing extensive lists of types of buildings or vehicles included. For example, "building, mobile home, tent, or other structure, or any motor vehicle, aircraft, watercraft, railroad car, or other means of conveyance of person or property."[77]

Also some statutes differ in regard to the crime that is attempted to be committed. As an example, Texas includes "an attempt to commit any felony or theft."[78] Also, the state statutes differ as to the penalty annexed.

Some states have a series of statutes dealing with burglary and related offenses. The State of Ohio has three breaking and entering offenses: aggravated burglary, burglary, and breaking and entering.[79] Parts of the statutes are included and explained.

§ 2911.11 Aggravated Burglary.
(A) No person, by force, stealth, or deception, shall trespass in an occupied structure as defined in § 2909.01 of the Revised Code, or in a separately secured or separately occupied portion thereof, with purpose to commit therein any theft offense as defined in § 2913.01 of the Revised Code, or any felony, when any of the following apply:

---

[76] N.Y. Penal Laws §§ 140.20-.30 (McKinney 1975).

[77] Fla. Stat. § 810.01 (1974); Ill. Rev. Stat. ch. 38, § 19-1 (Smith-Hurd 1977); Kan. Stat. Ann. § 21-3715 (1974); Ohio Rev. Code Ann. § 2909.11 (Page's 1979).

[78] Tex. Penal Code Ann. § 30.02 (1974); Ariz. Rev. Stat. Ann. § 13-1506 (1973); White v. State, 630 S.W.2d 340 (Tex. 1982).

[79] Ohio Rev. Code Ann. §§ 2911.11-.13 (Page 1987).

(1) The offender inflicts, or attempts or threatens to inflict physical harm on another;
(2) The offender has a deadly weapon or dangerous ordnance as defined in § 2923.11 of the Revised Code on or about his person or under his control;
(3) The occupied structure involved is the permanent or temporary habitation of any person, in which at the time any person is present or likely to be present.

(B) Whoever violates this Section is guilty of aggravated burglary, a felony of the first degree.

Section 2911.11 of the Ohio Revised Code defines the most serious of the three breaking and entering offenses. Aggravated burglary is a trespass in an occupied structure, accomplished by force, stealth or deception for the purpose of committing a felony or stealing, when the offender is armed, or attempts or threatens to harm anyone, or the structure involved is someone's home and someone is present or likely to be present.

Section 2911.12 of the Ohio Revised Code uses the exact same language as Section (A), but omits the elements of inflicting or threatening injury, or of being armed, or that the structure involved is a home. Anyone who violates this Section is guilty of burglary, a felony of the second degree.

The third provision relating to burglary is entitled *Breaking and Entering*. It provides:

§ 2911.13 Breaking and Entering.

(A) No person by force, stealth, or deception, shall trespass in an unoccupied structure, with purpose to commit therein any theft offense as defined in § 2913.01 of the Revised Code, or any felony.

(B) No person shall trespass on the land or premises of another, with purpose to commit a felony.

(C) Whoever violates this Section is guilty of breaking and entering, a felony of the fourth degree.

The purpose of this statute is to establish a violation where all of the elements of burglary are not present. An offense identical to burglary is defined, except that the structure involved is unoccupied rather than occupied. This is classified as a felony of the fourth degree; the rationale being that there is comparatively less risk of personal harm.

The Ohio statutes provide a higher penalty if the structure is occupied or if at the time any person is present or likely to be present. Other recently drafted codes include other additional aggravating factors. For example, in Oregon, being armed with a burglar's tool is an aggravating factor.[80] In Puerto Rico, a higher penalty is annexed when force is used to enter.[81] And in South Dakota, unlocking the outer door with a false key or by picking the lock is an aggravating factor.[82]

In investigating the burglary cases, criminal justice personnel must look to the statutes of the state and be prepared to offer evidence to show, beyond a reasonable doubt, every element of the offense as included in the statute. If an aggravating element is not proved, then the crime will be reduced to a less serious offense with a reduced penalty attached.

§ 5.5 Trespass (Criminal Trespass)

A. Traditional Definition and Elements

At common law, trespass designated a form of action for the recovery of damages by the direct application of force. In its broadest sense, it comprehends any misfeasance, transgression, or offense which damages another's person, health, reputation or property.[83] At common law, action of trespass was the proper remedy to recover damages where the injury consisted of damage to personal property or real property. Where the trespass was an intrusion upon the real property of another, the writ was known as "trespass quare clausumfregit."[84]

Generally, action in trespass is a means of recovering damages in a civil action. The gist of trespass to realty lies in the disturbance of possession. And at common law, every man's land was deemed to be enclosed, so that every unwarrantable entry on such land necessarily carried with it some damages for which the trespasser was civilly liable.[85] Civil action in trespass is for money damages, and since, from every unauthorized entry into the land of another the law infers some damages, nominal damages are recoverable even though there is no substantial damage to the property. Where there is actual

---

[80]   Or. Rev. Stat. § 164.225 (1979).

[81]   P.R. Laws Ann. tit. 33, § 4277 (Supp. 1979).

[82]   S.D. Codified Laws Ann. § 22-32-1 (1979).

[83]   Cox v. Strickland, 120 Ga. 104, 47 S.E. 912 (1904).

[84]   3 Street, FOUNDATIONS OF LEGAL LIABILITY 229 et seq. (1980).

[85]   Bailey v. People, 54 Colo. 337, 130 P. 832 (1913); Malerba v. Warren, 438 N.Y.S.2d 936 (1981).

damage to realty from the trespass, damages are awarded in an amount which will constitute just compensation for the injury done.[86]

While, at common law, most of the trespass actions were civil actions, certain acts of trespass were regarded as crimes. However, it seems clear, from a study of the cases, that every trespass which was the subject of civil action was not an indictable offense.[87] Where criminal trespass actions were authorized at common law, the definition of trespass was more precise and the mere invasion of private property without a disturbance of the peace was not considered a crime.[88]

Using the common law concept of criminal trespass as a basis, many statutes were passed making certain acts of trespass punishable as crimes. For example, some statutes make it a penal offense to trespass willfully on the premises of another after being ordered not to do so.[89]

Criminal trespass statutes, being penal in nature, have been construed somewhat strictly. For example, where a statute states that the action will lie only after a person has been ordered to depart, the prosecution must introduce evidence to show that there was such an order.

The statutes in some states still have strict requirements that must be met before a criminal action can be brought against a person for trespass. California prohibits "entering upon uncultivated or unenclosed lands where signs forbidding trespass are displayed."[90] In Illinois, there is no criminal trespass unless it is shown that the person accused was given notice that such entry is forbidden.[91] This statute provides:

§ 21-3. Criminal trespass to real property.
(a) Whoever enters upon the land or a building, other than a residence, or any part thereof of another, after receiving, prior to such entry, notice from the owner or occupant that such entry is forbidden, or remains upon the land or in a building, other than a residence, of another after receiving notice from the owner or occupant to depart, commits a Class C misdemeanor.
(b) A person has received notice from the owner or occupant within the meaning of Subsection (a) if he has been notified personally, either orally or in writing, or if a printed or written notice forbidding such entry has been conspicuously posted or

---

[86]   Irvin v. Nolde, 176 Pa. 594, 35 A. 217 (1896).

[87]   State v. Wheeler, 3 Vt. 344, 23 Am.Dec. 212 (1830).

[88]   Id.

[89]   Commonwealth v. Richardson, 313 Mass. 632, 48 N.E.2d 678 (1943).

[90]   Cal. Penal Code § 602(K) (West Supp. 1980).

[91]   Ill. Crim. Code, ch. 38, § 21-3 as amended eff. Sept. 18, 1986.

exhibited at the main entrance to such land or the forbidden part thereof.

(c) This Section does not apply to any person, whether a migrant worker or otherwise, living on the land with permission of the owner or of his agent having apparent authority to hire workers on such land and assign them living quarters or a place of accommodations for living thereon, nor to anyone living on such land at the request of, or by occupancy, leasing or other agreement or arrangement with the owner or his agent, nor to anyone invited by such migrant worker or other person so living on such land to visit him at the place he is so living upon the land.

(d) A person shall be exempt from prosecution under this Section if he beautifies unoccupied and abandoned residential and industrial properties located within any municipality. For the purpose of this Subsection, "unoccupied and abandoned residential and industrial property" means any real estate (1) in which the taxes have not been paid for a period of at least 2 years; and (2) which has been left unoccupied and abandoned for a period of at least one year; and "beautifies" means to landscape, clean up litter, or to repair dilapidated conditions on or to board up windows and doors.

(e) No person shall be liable in any civil action for money damages to the owner of unoccupied and abandoned residential and industrial property which that person beautifies pursuant to Subsection (d) of this Section.

In interpreting this statute, the reviewing court agreed that the defendants were not deprived of their First Amendment rights where they were convicted of criminal trespass after they refused to leave school property when asked to do so by school authorities.[92]

During the 1960s and early 1970s many trespassing statutes were found to be unconstitutional as in conflict with the First Amendment. While trespass statutes protecting private property were generally not found to be unconstitutional, some statutes which restricted use of certain types of public property were in violation of the First Amendment.[93] However, in the case of *Hudgens v. National Labor Relations Board*, handed down in 1976, the Supreme Court decided that shopping center owners are not constitutionally compelled to allow use of property for demonstrations by members of the

---

[92] People v. Thompson, 56 Ill. App. 3d 557, 372 N.E.2d 117 (1978). *See* case in Part II.

[93] *See* Klotter & Kanovitz, CONSTITUTIONAL LAW (5th ed. 1985).

public.[94] Also, the courts now agree that private property is not constitutionally available for picketing, handbilling, marching and other such activities unless the owner is willing to voluntarily submit to this use.

Entry upon the private property without the consent of the owner remains a trespass if a statute so provides and such statutes do not violate the rights protected by the Constitution.

B. Contemporary Statutes and Codes

1. Model Penal Code

§ 221.2 Criminal Trespass
(1) Buildings and Occupied Structures. A person commits an offense if, knowing that he is not licensed or privileged to do so, he enters or surreptitiously remains in any building or occupied structure, or separately secured or occupied portion thereof. An offense under this Subsection is a misdemeanor if it is committed in a dwelling at night. Otherwise it is a petty misdemeanor.
(2) Defiant Trespasser. A person commits an offense if, knowing that he is not licensed or privileged to do so, he enters or remains in any place as to which notice against trespass is given by:

  (a) actual communication to the actor; or
  (b) posting in a manner prescribed by law or reasonably likely to come to the attention of intruders; or
  (c) fencing or other enclosure manifestly designed to exclude intruders.

An offense under this Subsection constitutes a petty misdemeanor if the offender defies an order to leave personally communicated to him by the owner of the premises or other authorized person. Otherwise it is a violation.

---

[94] 424 U.S. 507, 96 S. Ct. 1029, 47 L.Ed.2d 196 (1976).

(3) Defenses. It is an affirmative defense to prosecution under this Section that:

(a) a building or occupied structure involved in an offense under Subsection (1) was abandoned; or

(b) the premises were at the time open to members of the public and the actor complied with all lawful conditions imposed on access to or remaining in the premises; or

(c) the actor reasonably believed that the owner of the premises, or other person empowered to license access thereto, would have licensed him to enter or remain.[95]

Under the provisions of the Code, the prosecution must first show that the actor *knowingly* intruded into a place where he knows he is not licensed or privileged to be. As indicated in Subsection (1), the trespass is aggravated if committed at night. If at night, it is a misdemeanor, while, at any other time, it is a petty misdemeanor.

Subsection (2) deals with the person who enters or remains on property after some form of notice has been communicated. Communication may be actual or by posting or fencing. This provision carries over some of the provisions of previous statutes.

It is noted too that the grading of the offense is determined partly by whether the surreptitious entry is into an occupied building or "any place as to which notice against trespass is given." Unlike the traditional provisions the Criminal Code § 221.2 also lists affirmative defenses.[96]

2. Federal Code

Under Title 18 of the U.S. Code, the chapters relating to general crimes are listed. There is no mention made of criminal trespass.

3. Other statutes and codes

While some of the more recent statutes and codes follow the Model Code substantially, others are worded differently. For example, the Texas Penal Code provides:

---

[95] Model Penal Code, § 221.2 (Proposed Official Draft 1980).

[96] *Id.*

§ 30.05 Criminal Trespass[97]

(a) A person commits an offense if he enters or remains on property or in a building of another without effective consent and he:

    (1) had notice that the entry was forbidden; or
    (2) received notice to depart but failed to do so.

(b) For purposes of this Section:

    (1) "entry" means the intrusion of the entire body; and
    (2) "notice" means:

        (A) oral or written communication by the owner or someone with apparent authority to act for the owner;
        (B) fencing or other enclosure obviously designed to exclude intruders; or
        (C) signs posted to be reasonably likely to come to the attention of intruders.

(c) An offense under this Section is a Class C misdemeanor unless it is committed in a habitation, in which event it is a Class A misdemeanor.

The Texas Code eliminates the "knowing" requirement. However, a trespass into habitations is treated as a Class A misdemeanor, while other intrusions are treated as Class C misdemeanors.

Where the trespass is on land or into a building, there is no violation unless notice was given that the entry was forbidden and the actor entered without "effective consent." Subsection (b)(2) establishes three methods of giving notice.

Unlike the common law definition of entry, where any part of the body amounts to entry, to constitute entry under this Section, the intrusion must be by the entire body.

According to the statutes common in most states today, the elements of trespass are:

---

[97] Tex. Penal Code Ann. § 30.05 (Vernon 1974); Daniels v. State, 633 S.W.2d 899 (Tex. 1982).

(a)　entering or remaining on property,
(b)　without effective consent,
(c)　some form of notice was given that entry is forbidden.

Actual notice generally is not required when an enclosure manifestly is designed to exclude intruders as, for example, the home. In addition, some states require a fourth element: a specific intent to enter for some unlawful purpose.[98]

§ 5.6　Other Property Destruction and Intrusion Offenses

To provide penalties for wrongs that occur that are not technically within the scope of the offenses previously described, various statutes have been enacted by the respective states. Some of these are discussed here.

A. Vandalism

An example of a vandalism statute is that of Ohio, which provides:

§ 2909.05 Vandalism.
(A)　　　No person shall knowingly cause serious physical harm to an occupied structure or any of its contents.
(B)(1)　No person shall knowingly cause serious physical harm to property that is owned or possessed by another, when either of the following applies:

　　(a)　Such property is used by its owner or possessor in his profession, business, trade, or occupation, and the value of the property or the amount of physical harm involved is $150 or more;
　　(b)　Regardless of the value of the property or the amount of damages done, the property or its equivalent is necessary in order for its owner or possessor to engage in his profession, business, trade, or occupation.[99]

This Section of the Ohio statute contains the usual provisions prohibiting vandalism. This would be the crime charged for breaking windows in the

---

[98]　Ga. Code § 26-1502 (1977).
[99]　Ohio Rev. Code Ann. § 2909.05 (Page 1987).

home, destroying furniture, or causing other damages making it temporarily unusable or requiring a substantial amount of time, effort, or money to make good the damage. This Section also embraces a relatively new concept; that of knowingly causing serious harm to property used in or necessary to the occupation of its owner or possessor. Examples of this type of violation include rifling and scattering case files of an attorney, damaging the samples of a traveling salesman, or destroying a plumber's tools.[100]

B. Criminal Littering

Many states have some form of littering provision either by state law or city ordinance or both. A good example is that of Kentucky which provides:

§ 512.070 Criminal littering.
(1) A person is guilty of criminal littering when he:

   (a) drops or permits to drop on a highway any destructive or injurious material and does not immediately remove it; or
   (b) knowingly places or throws litter on any public or private property or in any public or private water without permission; or
   (c) negligently places or throws glass or other dangerous pointed or edged substances on or adjacent to water to which the public has access for swimming or wading on or within fifty feet of a public highway; or
   (d) discharges sewage, minerals, oil products or litter into any public waters or lakes within the state.

(2) Criminal littering is a Class B misdemeanor.[101]

This comprehensive statute covers many situations. Under Subsection (a), all that is necessary is to prove that the person drops, or permitted to be dropped, injurious material on the highway and did not immediately remove it. However, in Subsection (b) the mental element comes into play and evidence must be introduced to show that the suspect knowingly put litter on public or private property. Then, in Subsection (c), a different degree of cul-

---

[100] See notes, § 2090.05 Ohio Criminal Code Training Manual (1974).
[101] Ky. Rev. Stat. § 512.070 (1975).

pability is required, i.e., negligently placing glass or other material next to swimming water or within 50 feet of a public highway.

Other littering statutes are worded differently, but in each situation the prosecution must prove the elements as specified in the statute.

C. Causing or Risking Catastrophe

Several states have statutes similar to the Model Penal Code statute which provides a penalty for the specific wrong of causing or risking a catastrophe.[102] The purpose of such statutes is to punish those who purposely, knowingly or recklessly bring about a catastrophe.

The Model Penal Code provides:

§ 220.2 Causing or Risking Catastrophe[103]
(1) Causing Catastrophe

A person who causes a catastrophe by explosion, fire, flood, avalanche, collapse of a building, release of poisonous gas, radioactive material, or other harmful force or substance, or by any other means of causing potentially widespread injury or damage, commits a felony of the second degree if he does so purposely or knowingly, or a felony of the third degree if he does so recklessly.

(2) Risking Catastrophe

A person is guilty of a misdemeanor if he recklessly creates a risk of catastrophe in the employment of fire, explosives or other dangerous means listed in Subsection (1).

Under the provisions of Subsection (1) if a person purposely or knowingly causes a catastrophe by one of the specified means or by any other means of causing potentially widespread injury or damage, the penalty is second degree felony. However, if the action is reckless rather than purposeful or knowingly, then the offense is a third degree felony.

To prove a violation of Subsection (1) as provided in this Model Code and similar state statutes, these elements must be proved:

(a) A catastrophe occurred;
(b) The person charged caused the catastrophe;

---

[102] Among the states having statutes of this type are Ark., Me., Mo., N.J., N.D., Pa., Utah, Alaska, Vt. and W.Va.

[103] Model Penal Code, § 220.2 (Proposed Official Draft 1980).

(c) The catastrophe is caused by explosion, fire, or one of the other causes enumerated;

(d) The act was purposely or knowingly done (a felony of the second degree); or the act was recklessly done (a felony of the third degree).

Other state statutes provide penalties for offenses of which property damage is the main thrust. Other examples are damaging public utilities property,[104] and unlawfully posting advertisements.[105] If one studies the respective state statutes carefully, most likely a statute will be located to make it possible to arrest and prosecute persons who have wrongfully destroyed or intruded upon the property of another.

§ 5.7 Summary

One of the most serious property crimes is arson. Because of the great danger to human life resulting from the burning of a dwelling house or other buildings, arson is considered a most serious crime, and those who are convicted are subject to penalties of a high degree. Arson is defined as *the willful and malicious burning of the dwelling house of another.*

Modern statutes retain many of the traditional elements, but statutes have been enacted to provide punishment for burning of structures other than dwellings and to provide a penalty where one burns his own house or property in order to defraud an insurer.

The crime of malicious mischief, sometimes designated "criminal mischief," was added to most state statutes early in the development of criminal law in this country, and is generally defined as *the willful and unlawful injury to or destruction of property of another with malicious intent to injure the owner.* As in the case of many statutory provisions, this was designed to punish a person who was not guilty of larceny because there was no fraudulent taking against the owner's will, but there was malicious injury to the person's property. The more recent codes consolidate many of the former malicious mischief provisions that were enacted to meet the needs of the society at the time, into a single comprehensive offense or an integrated series of related offenses.

Another crime that was and is considered most serious is burglary. At common law, the crime consisted of breaking and entering the dwelling house of another in the nighttime with intent to commit a felony therein. Be-

---

[104]   Ohio Rev. Code Ann. § 2909.04 (Page 1987).

[105]   Ky. Rev. Stat. § 512.080 (1975).

cause of the many elements and the technical definitions of these elements additional statutes were enacted to punish wrongs where, for example, the breaking was not of a dwelling house or did not occur in the nighttime. In most states today, the statutes provide a penalty for breaking and entering structures, including homes and other buildings, where the breaking is in the daytime as well as in the nighttime, and where the intent is to commit misdemeanors as well as felonies. The grade of the crime is determined by such factors as the time the crime was perpetrated (day or night), whether or not bodily injury was inflicted or attempted purposely or knowingly, and whether or not the person was armed or unarmed.

At common law, trespass was the civil remedy to recover damages where the injury consisted of damages to personal property or real property. However, in addition, certain acts of trespass were considered as crimes. Trespass can be defined as an *unlawful intrusion upon the real property of another without the other's consent.* Many states enacted specific trespass statutes to prohibit willful and unlawful entry upon the premises of another for certain purposes. In some statutes, one requirement is that a fence be constructed or that the trespasser be ordered off the property before any action could be taken.

All states presently have some provisions prohibiting the entering or remaining on property without the consent of the owner. Some require that notice be given that entry is forbidden, and some require that a specific intent to enter for some unlawful purpose be proved.

To provide penalties for wrongs that occur that are not technically within the scope of the crimes described, various statutes have been enacted by state lawmaking bodies. Examples of these are statutes prohibiting vandalism, criminal littering, and causing or risking a catastrophe.

While there are still some wrongs that probably are not covered by statute, in most instances a statute or code can be found to make it possible to take action against persons who wrongfully destroy or intrude upon the property of another.

Chapter 6
OFFENSES INVOLVING THEFT

If a person honestly receives the possession of goods, chattels, or money of another upon any trust, express or implied, and, after receiving them, fraudulently converts them to his own use, he may be guilty of the crime of embezzlement, but cannot be of that of larceny.... If the possession of such property is obtained by fraud, and the owner of it intends to part with his titles as well as his possession, the offense is that of obtaining property by false pretenses.... If the possession is fraudulently obtained, with intent on the part of the person obtaining it, at the time he receives it, to convert the same to his own use, and the person parting with it intends to part with his possession merely, and not with the title to the property, the offense is larceny.

> *People v. Miller,*
> 169 N.Y. 339,
> 62 N.E. 418 (1902).

§ 6.1 Introduction

All societies have laws or rules which are designed to protect property against theft. In the United States, offenses involving theft make up the great majority of crimes, and criminal justice personnel devote much of their time investigating crimes that relate to theft. Although statutes have changed the common law, it is essential that the history of theft crimes be studied in order to understand the terminology and the elements that make up the various crimes relating to theft.

At early common law in England, larceny was the only form of theft criminally punishable. Because the offense became more and more narrowly construed, many forms of deception were not commonly regarded as criminal. Citizens relied upon the civil laws to correct wrongs that did not come within the technical definition of larceny. However, as commerce increased, the criminal law was expanded to punish other forms of theft, such as embezzlement, false pretenses and extortion.

Even after adding the new crimes, the technicalities made the application of the laws involving theft very difficult. In recent years, efforts have been made to simplify the laws. Some states have abolished the separate offenses of larceny, embezzlement and related theft crimes, and combined them into a new, comprehensive theft statute. Notwithstanding the changes that have been made, it is necessary that criminal justice personnel understand the complexities of the various statutes and recognize that theft offenses are not the same in all jurisdictions.

In this chapter, robbery is included as an offense involving theft, although it is a crime against a person, as well as a crime involving theft. The common law crimes of larceny, and the early statutory crimes relating to embezzlement, obtaining property by false pretenses, and extortion are considered separately, even though, in some modern statutes, they are joined together in one statute.

Before discussing each of the crimes, attention is called again to the fact that there are other offenses involving theft that are not treated in this chapter.

§ 6.2 Robbery

A. Traditional Definition and Elements

Robbery is a crime against property and an aggravated form of larceny, but it is also a crime against the person. There are valid arguments for treating the crime of robbery as a separate and distinct crime. However, there are also arguments for considering it in the category of "offenses involving theft," because, most often, the primary objective of the actor is to take personal property of another. As many of the elements are the same as those elements of larceny and other theft offenses, the aggravating elements of robbery can be distinguished more easily by considering the crime of robbery along with other theft crimes.[1]

The common law offense of robbery, as defined by many courts, is made up of specific elements, each of which has a technical definition. Some of the definitions, as stated by the various decision-makers, exemplify the complex nature of the offense.

> "Robbery" at common law is the taking with intent to steal, property in the possession of another, from his person, or in his presence, by violence or by putting him in fear. The taking need not be from the owner.

> "Robbery" is an aggravated larceny; the taking of something of value from another by putting him in fear.[2]

> "Robbery" at common law, is an offense against both person and property, being the felonious taking of goods of value from the person of another, or in his presence, by violence or putting him in fear.[3]

Pointing out the importance of making reference to the common law terms, one court, in interpreting a statute regarding robbery, made this comment:

> At common law the term "robbery" or "to rob" has but a single meaning and when used in criminal proceedings or in connection with legal matters such words have a technical meaning and, unless otherwise defined by statute, include within themselves all of the elements of the common law crime of robbery.[4]

Where the common law offense of robbery still exists, and in those states where the term is not defined by statute, robbery consists of eight elements:

---

[1]   Parks v. State, 21 Ala. 177, 106 So. 218 (1925).
[2]   State v. Hackle, 110 W.Va. 485, 158 S.E. 708 (1931).
[3]   Parks v. State, 21 Ala. App. 177, 106 So. 218 (1925).
[4]   State v. Domanski, 57 R.I. 500, 190 A. 854 (1937).

six elements of larceny plus two additional elements that are peculiar to robbery. These eight elements are first listed, then briefly described.

Trespass (from possession and against the will)

Historically, one of the elements of robbery and larceny is that the thief take the property out of the possession of its possessor and against the will of one who has actual or constructive possession of it. However, it is not necessary that the victim of a robbery also be the owner of the goods taken, as robbery is an offense against the person who has either actual or constructive possession of the goods.[5]

Taking (caption)

All of the definitions of robbery include the element of taking. Taking is defined as securing dominion over or absolute control over the property. At common law, this was designated "caption." Before the crime of robbery or larceny is complete, the prosecution must offer evidence to show that the actor had actual physical caption; that is, he had dominion over the property and left no control in the owner or possessor. If the accused has not gained complete control of the property, there can be no caption or taking, even if he thinks he has the property in his possession.[6]

Carrying Away (asportation)

The offense of robbery is not necessarily complete at the moment the stolen property is in the robber's possession, as robbery includes the element of asportation.[7] There must be such a carrying away or asportation as to supersede the possession of the owner for an appreciable time. If the prosecution can show that the person charged with robbery removed the property from the place it originally occupied, even for an instant and even to a small degree, this is sufficient asportation to constitute the offense.[8]

Personal Property

In proving this element, all that is necessary is that it be shown that the property is personal, as compared to real property. Generally, the type and value of the property taken are immaterial, insofar as the offense of robbery is concerned. While the property must have some value, proof of a specific monetary value is not required.[9]

---

[5]   People v. Estes, 147 Cal. App. 3d 23, 194 Cal. Rptr. 909 (1983). *See* case in Part II.

[6]   People v. Maier, 75 Cal. 383, 17 P. 431 (1888).

[7]   People v. Melenderz, 25 Cal. App. 2d, 77 P.2d 870 (1938).

[8]   Neal v. State, 214 Ind. 328, 14 N.E.2d 590 (1938).

[9]   People v. Nolan, 250 Ill. 351, 95 N.E. 140 (1911).

Property of Another

To constitute robbery, evidence must be introduced to show that the ownership or right of possession of the property taken is vested in some person other than the taker. It is not necessary that the ownership of the property taken must have been in the person robbed; it is sufficient if he had exclusive possession of it at the time.[10] For example, robbery was a proper charge where the defendant took money from the person of a filling station attendant, even though he was not the actual owner of the stolen property.[11] This element is present, therefore, if the property is taken from a bailee, an agent, an employee or other representative of the owner.

Intent to Steal

One of the most difficult elements to prove in determining whether the crime is robbery or larceny is intent (*animus furandi*). Unless the statute changes the definition of the offense, robbery and larceny require a specific intent. That is, evidence must be introduced to prove, beyond a reasonable doubt, that the accused intended to appropriate the property to a use inconsistent with rights of the person from whom it was taken. Therefore, where the taking is under an honest, though mistaken, claim of ownership, or claim of a lawful right to possess the property, the crime is not robbery or larceny.[12]

The very definition of robbery includes the requirement that there be an intent to steal the personal property of another. This intent must be to deprive owner, wholly and permanently, of his property.[13] But attempts to define this element have resulted in some very technical distinctions. For example, in Arizona, a charge of robbery failed where the attempt was to collect a bona fide debt.[14] However, this defense is not available to a defendant where the amount he claims is uncertain; that is, the defense cannot be based upon an unliquidated claim. The conviction for robbery will stand, even though the defendant claimed he was seeking return of monies lost in an illegal card game, where the jury could have drawn an inference from the evidence that the defendant did not, in good faith, intend to take only money that he had lost, but additional money.[15]

---

[10] Lanahan v. State, 176 Ark. 104, 2 S.W.2d 55 (1928).

[11] People v. Cabassa, 249 Mich. 543, 229 N.W. 442 (1930).

[12] Moyers v. State, 185 Ga. 446, 197 S.E. 846 (1938).

[13] State v. Reposa, 99 R.I. 147, 206 A.2d 213 (1965).

[14] State v. Lewis, 121 Ariz. 155, 589 P.2d 29 (1978).

[15] People v. Lain, 57 Cal. App. 2d 123, 134 P.2d 284 (1943).

In discussing this element, a distinction has been made between the reclaiming of specific personal property and the taking of money claimed to be owed. Making reference to a previous case, one court used the example that although a debtor may owe $100 and $100 is in the debtor's pocket, it is not the property of the creditor, and the creditor may not take the money even if he intends to apply it to the debt.[16]

Because the *intent* element has been difficlut to prove, resulting in the miscarriage of justice, states have modified the statute. For example, in the State of Florida, the legislature expanded the scope of robbery by eliminating the requirement of a specific intent.[17] The Supreme Court of that state upheld a conviction of robbery, under the statute which defines robbery as the "taking of money or other property from the person or custody of another by force."

From the Person or Presence of Another

One of the elements that distinguishes robbery from larceny and justifies a more severe penalty, is this aggravating element of taking from the person. Robbery requires more than a simple trespassory taking. The taking must be from the person or presence of the victim, as well as from his possession. One court summarized the rule:

> Robbery is larceny from the person or immediate presence of another by violence or intimidation and is basically larceny compounded or aggravated by force used in the taking of property from the person or in the presence of another.[18]

Property is taken from the person if it is taken from his hand, his pocket, his clothing or from a package in his hand. But it is not required that the property be taken directly from the person. The element is complete if the property is taken from his presence which includes the area under the victim's immediate control. "Presence" is not so much a matter of being within the view of the victim as it is a matter of proximity and control. The test is that the property taken in the robbery must be close enough to the victim and sufficiently under his control that, had the latter not been subjected to violence or intimidation by the robber, he could have prevented the taking.[19]

---

16 Edwards v. State, 49 Wis. 2d 105, 181 N.W.2d 383 (1970).

17 Bell v. State, 354 So. 2d 1266 (Fla. Dist. Ct. App. 1978).

18 Young v. State, 259 S.C. 383, 192 S.E.2d 212 (1972).

19 People v. Braverman, 340 Ill. 525, 173 N.E. 55 (1930).

By Violence or Intimidation

The second aggravating element of robbery is that the taking must involve some violence or intimidation. This has been explained in several ways. For example, one court indicated that "the taking must be against the will of the possessor accompanied by means of force or fear."[20] Another court determined that "robbery is the taking with intent to steal personal property of another from his person and in his presence, against his will, by violence or intimidation."[21] The particular means of force, or manner in which fear is impaired, is immaterial in determining this element of robbery.[22]

Violence is present, even if the force is very slight, if it is sufficient to achieve the purpose of the accused, and any struggle to obtain the property or any resistance on the part of the victim, which requires greater counterattack to effect the taking, is ordinarily regarded as sufficient to satisfy this requirement. Even the administration of intoxicants or drugs for the purpose of obtaining money has been held to be an exercise of force sufficient to constitute robbery.[23]

As an alternative to violence, the state may prove intimidation. Intimidation in this context means placing the victim in fear of injury to his person, property or character. As in the case of force, the intimidation may be slight if the transaction is attended with such circumstances of terror as in common experience are likely to create an apprehension of danger and to induce a man to part with his property for the sake of his person.[24]

Although both force and intimidation need not necessary be proven, both may be used together to constitute robbery, if acted upon by the victim and the property is given over to the defendant.

Both State and Federal Courts have been called upon to decide whether "pocket picking," without the knowledge of the victim, is robbery. Generally speaking pocket, picking is not robbery, as the element of violence or intimidation is not present. However, if there is struggle by the owner to maintain possession, this element will be present and the actions could amount to robbery. For example, in a 1978 case, a defendant, attempting to snatch the pocketbook of a woman standing on a subway platform, was met with resistance, resulting in the woman being hit by the train. The court reasoned that, while purse-snatching, when unaccompanied by resistance on the part of the victim, generally is not sufficient to constitute robbery, there was, in this case,

---

[20] In re Massie, 283 P.2d 573 (1955).

[21] Pettus v. Payton, 207 Va. 706, 153 S.E.2d 278 (1967); State v. Ellerbe, 209 S.E.2d 813, 23 N.C. App. 708 (1974).

[22] People v. Cortez, 163 Cal. Rptr. 1 (1980).

[23] State v. Snyder, 41 Nev. 453, 172 P. 364 (1918).

[24] Tones v. State, 48 Tex. Cr. 63, 88 S.W. 217 (1905).

sufficient evidence to support a jury finding that the victim resisted by clinging to her purse, and that the overcoming of this resistance through the use of overwhelming momentum of the train, constituted attempted robbery.[25]

B. Contemporary Statutes and Codes

As a result of the technical requirements of robbery under the common law, and the strict interpretations placed upon some of these elements by the courts, some defendants who were responsible for wrongs against others were set free or found guilty of lesser included offenses. To remedy this inequity, state statutes were added to modify the common law. These made it possible to prosecute persons for crimes where the technical elements, such as asportation, were not provable.

As you will note, the Model Penal Code, as well as the Federal Code and the state statutes, often retain the crime of robbery as one offense, but add other offenses or grade the penalty, depending upon the elements asserted. The recommended Model Penal Code, as well as the federal statutes and other state codes, are included here as examples of some of the modifications.

1. Model Penal Code

§ 222.1 Robbery[26]
(1) Robbery Defined. A person is guilty of robbery if, in the course of committing a theft, he:

    (a) inflicts serious bodily injury upon another; or
    (b) threatens another with or purposely puts him in fear of immediate serious bodily injury; or
    (c) commits or threatens immediately to commit any felony of the first or second degree.

An attempt shall be deemed "in the course of committing a theft" if it occurs in an attempt to commit theft, or in flight, after the attempt or commission.

---

[25] People v. Santiago, 62 App. Div. 2d 572, 405 N.Y.S. 2d 752 (1978).
[26] Model Penal Code, § 222.1 (Proposed Official Draft 1980).

(2) Grading. Robbery is a felony of the second degree, except that it is a felony of the first degree if in the course of committing the theft the actor attempts to kill anyone, or purposely inflicts or attempts to inflict serious bodily injury.

In the Model Code, robbery is considered under a separate heading because of the special elements of danger commonly associated with forcible theft from the person. Although there is only one offense of robbery defined, it includes aggravated behavior occurring in the course of committing a theft. For purposes of punishment, a grading scheme is included in the Model Penal Code. Robbery is a felony of the second degree, except that it is a felony of the first degree if in the course of committing the theft, the actor attempts to kill anyone, or purposely inflicts, or attempts to inflict, serious bodily injury.

As stated in the Model Code, a person is guilty of robbery if, in the course of committing a theft, one of these additional elements are present:

(a) he inflicts serious bodily injury upon another; or

(b) he threatens another with or purposely puts another in fear of immediate serious bodily injury; or

(c) he commits or threatens immediately to commit any felony of the first or second degree.

"In the course of committing a theft" includes an attempt to commit theft or flight after the attempt or commission.

In addition to the infliction or threatened infliction of serious bodily harm, which is the usual statutory provision, the Code provides an alternative. Even if there is no actual threat against the personal safety of the victim, the offender can be found guilty of robbery if, within the course of committing the theft, he commits or threatens to commit any other felony of the first or second degree. In accordance with this provision, threatening a felony such as arson will substitute for threatening another with immediate serious bodily injury.

The traditional requirement of "taking from the person" has not been included in the Model Code § 222.1. Also, the Model Code, following the lead of some of the pre-Code statutory provisions of the various states, has eliminated the "intent" requirement.

2. Federal Code

Chapter 103 of the U.S. Code relates to both robbery and burglary. Some Sections of the Code have application throughout the United States, while others relate to crimes committed within the special maritime or territorial jurisdiction of the United States.

Title 18, § 2112 makes it a federal crime for one to rob another of any kind or description of personal property belonging to the United States.[27] Anyone found guilty of violating this statute shall be imprisoned for not more than 15 years.

To be found guilty under this statute, possession or use of a deadly weapon is not required; all that is required is that the government establish that the taking was by force, or threat of force, and the property taken was personal property belonging to the United States.[28]

In addition to providing a penalty for stealing or robbing another of personal property of the United States, the Code provides a penalty for bank robbery.[29] This very comprehensive bank robbery statute was added to make it possible for federal investigators to assist in protecting the assets of banks, credit unions and savings and loan associations. With the 1986 amendment, part of the statute provides:

(a) Whoever, by force and violence, or by intimidation, takes, or attempts to take, from the person or presence of another, or obtains or attempts to obtain by extortion, any property or money or any other thing of value belonging to, or in the care, custody, control, management, or possession of, any bank, credit union, or any savings and loan association, shall be fined not more than $5,000 or imprisoned not more than 20 years, or both.

This Section of the statute also includes a penalty for entering or attempting to enter a bank, credit union or savings and loan association with intent to commit any felony affecting one of the financial institutions, shall also be fined or imprisoned as indicated by the statute. If, in committing or

---

[27] 18 U.S.C. § 2112.

[28] United States v. Torres, 809 F.2d 429 (7th Cir. 1987).

[29] 18 U.S.C. § 2113.

attempting to commit robbery as defined, the perpetrator puts in jeopardy the life of any person by use of a dangerous weapon or device, then the penalty is increased to a $10,000 fine or imprisonment for not more than 25 years.[30]

This statute does not apply unless the bank is a member of the federal reserve system, is organized or operated under the laws of the United States, or is a bank, the deposits of which are insured by the Federal Deposit Insurance Corporation (FDIC). This wording and the limitations which refer to the savings and loan associations and credit unions, are necessary to avoid a successful constitutional challenge.[31]

Many of the common law elements of robbery are carried over into this federal offense of bank robbery. They include taking, by force and violence or by intimidation, from the person or presence of another, and personal property or money or other things of value. In proving ownership or control of the property as a requirement, the prosecution was allowed, in a 1987 case, to introduce into evidence dye-stained currency, which was removed from a hotel room where an accomplice testified that the money was similar to that left by herself and the defendant in the room.[32]

In addition to these federal crimes discussed, the Federal Code includes a penalty for robberies committed within the special maritime and territorial jurisdiction of the United States.[33]

This statute provides:

> Whoever, within the special maritime and territorial jurisdiction of the United States, by force and violence, or by intimidation, takes from the person or presence of another anything of value, shall be imprisoned not more than 15 years.

As in other "special maritime and territorial jurisdiction" statutes, this only applies where the crime takes place within the territory defined.

---

[30] 18 U.S.C. § 2113(d).

[31] United States v. Mays, 822 F.2d 793 (8th Cir. 1987). This case also considers the admissibility of evidence of other crimes.

[32] *Id.*

[33] 18 U.S.C. § 2111; *see* Appendix for a definition of "special maritime and territorial jurisdiction of the United States."

3. Other statutes and codes

Some of the contemporary statutes are the same as the Model Penal Code, and some have used parts of the wording of the Code.[34] Others retain the traditional wording and distinctions.

An example of a state statute with provisions that differentiate degrees of robbery, based upon the seriousness of the injury that has been caused, is that of Texas. This state, as some other states, retains a separate Section related to aggravated robbery.

§ 29.02 Robbery[35]
(a) A person commits an offense if, in the course of committing theft as defined in Chapter 31 of this Code and with intent to obtain or maintain control of the property, he:

  (1) intentionally, knowingly, or recklessly causes bodily injury to another; or
  (2) intentionally or knowingly threatens or places another in fear of imminent bodily injury or death.

(b) An offense under this Section is a felony of the second degree.

§ 29.03 Aggravated Robbery
(a) A person commits an offense if he commits robbery as defined in § 29.02 of this Code, and he:

  (1) causes serious bodily injury to another; or
  (2) uses or exhibits a deadly weapon.

(b) An offense under this Section is a felony of the first degree.

A person violates the provisions of § 29.02 if he:

(a) intentionally, knowingly, or recklessly causes bodily injury to another, or
(b) intentionally or knowingly threatens to place another in fear of imminent bodily injury or death.

If the bodily injury is "serious," or if a deadly weapon is used, then the offense is aggravated robbery and is graded as a felony in the first degree.

---

[34] Model Penal Code, § 221.1 (Proposed Official Draft 1980), as well as following comments.
[35] Tex. Penal Code Ann. § 29.02-29.03 (Vernon 1979).

In a 1979 case, a Texas court held that a person commits aggravated robbery when he, in the course of committing theft with the intent to obtain or maintain control of property, either intentionally, knowingly or recklessly causes bodily injury, or knowingly or intentionally threatens or places another in fear of imminent bodily injury or death, and either causes serious bodily injury to another or uses or exhibits a deadly weapon.[36]

In Illinois, the statute includes the term "armed robbery" to designate the more serious crime, providing that a person commits armed robbery if the robbery is committed while armed with a dangerous weapon.[37] Armed robbery in Illinois is a Class 1 felony for which the offender may be sentenced to death.

In determining what is a dangerous weapon, an Illinois Appeals Court explained that focus should not be so much upon the firearm or pseudo firearm itself, but upon the intention with which the alleged firearm, or other weapon, was used by the perpetrator and the belief that such use instilled, or reasonably could have been expected to instill, fear in the victim.[38]

Various criteria are considered in grading the offense to determine the punishment affixed. Some states use the terms "armed with a deadly weapon" or "dangerous instrument,"[39] while others use such terminology as "appearing to be armed with a deadly weapon" and "having an accomplice present."[40]

While the state provisions differ in some respects, the basic elements that distinguish robbery from other theft crimes are those that existed under the common law.

§ 6.3 Larceny

A. Traditional Definitions and Elements

When discussing the offense of robbery, it was indicated that robbery is an aggravated form of larceny. The elements which distinguish robbery from larceny are:

---

[36] *Ex parte* County, 577 S.W.2d 260 (Tex. Crim. 1979). *See also* State v. Meek, 53 Ohio St. 2d 35, 372 N.E.2d 341 (1978).

[37] Ill. Ann. Stat. ch. 38, § 18-2 (Smith-Hurd Supp. 1980).

[38] People v. Chapman, 73 Ill. App. 3d 546, 392 N.E.2d 391 (Ill. App. Ct. 1979).

[39] Ky. Rev. Stat. § 515.020 (1974).

[40] Examples are Ariz. and Neb.

(1) taking of the property from the person or presence of the victim, and

(2) the requirement that the taking be accompanied by means of force or putting in fear.

If these two elements cannot be proved or are not in the indictment, but the other elements are present, then the crime is most likely to be larceny. One approach, then, in developing an understanding of the crime of larceny is to view larceny as a lesser included offense of robbery.

Larceny was defined at common law as the felonious taking by trespass and carrying away by any person of the personal goods or things of another from any place, without the latter's consent and with the felonious intent permanently to deprive the owner of his property and to convert it to the taker's own use or to the use of some person other than the owner.[41] Definitions by state courts differ, but the general elements are fairly consistent. Some examples will point out the differences and similarities:

To constitute "larceny," there must be an unlawful acquisition of property with intention to convert it to the taker's use and an appropriation by one who took it.[42]

"Larceny" is the wrongful taking and carrying away of personal property of another from any place, with a felonious intent to convert it to the taker's own use without consent of the owner.[43]

Generally "larceny" is the felonious taking and carrying away of personal property of another with intent on the part of the taker to convert it to his own use or to deprive the owner thereof.[44]

To constitute the crime of larceny, the property taken must be personal, as distinguished from real property, and the property must belong to another. It must be taken by trespass from the possession of another and carried away from the place it occupies. In addition, the taking and removal must be accompanied by intent to deprive the owner of the property.

From the various definitions of larceny, some specific elements can be enumerated. Each of these elements has been meticulously defined by the

---

[41] Fitch v. State, 135 Fla. 361, 185 So. 435 (1938); Reid v. Florida Real Estate Comm'n, 188 So. 2d 846 (Fla. Dist. Ct. App. 1966).

[42] State v. Smith, 2 Wash. 2d 118, 98 P.2d 647 (1939).

[43] State v. Jackson, 251 Iowa 537, 101 N.W.2d 731 (1960).

[44] Webb v. State, 55 Ala. App. 195, 314 S.2d 114 (1975).

various courts and these definitions apply in many jurisdictions even though statutes have modified the common law. Each element is discussed and defined.

Trespass

Larceny is a crime against possession rather than ownership. To constitute larceny there must be a taking of the property against the will of one having actual or constructive possession of it. As one court stated, larceny, as it has been developed in common law, is best defined as taking and removal, by trespass, of personal property, which trespasser knows to belong to another, with felonious intent to deprive him of his ownership therein.[45] In larceny, it is not necessary that the trespass be accompanied by violence if the taker secures physical custody of the property and has it in his power to take it away and appropriate it.

The trespass requirement in larceny is the principal basis for distinction between the crime of larceny and the crime of embezzlement. In embezzlement, no trespass is required, hence, there is no larceny if the owner of the property consents to the defendant taking the property.

Taking (caption)

A taking occurs when the offender secures dominion over the property. There can be no taking (caption) or dominion if the defendant, in an attempt to steal another's property, fails to gain possession of it. In a 1978 case, the North Carolina Supreme Court determined that, to satisfy the taking element in larceny, accused must have the goods in his possession and under his control even if only for an instant.[46] Stated in different terms; to constitute larceny there must be a severance of the possession of the owner and an actual possession by the wrongdoer.[47]

Carrying Away (asportation)

To constitute carrying away or asportation the property must be moved from the place that it was before. The least removal of the thing taken will satisfy this element, even though the distance is slight. In the North Carolina case cited, the defendant had moved an air conditioner in a motel room approximately four inches from its base and toward the door. The reviewing court agreed that this movement was sufficient to establish the asportation as an element of the crime.

---

[45] State v. Grant, 135 Vt. 222, 373 A.2d 847 (1977); State v. Wooten, 18 N.C. App. 62, 197 S.E.2d 614 (1973).

[46] State v. Carswell, 296 N.C. 101, 249 S.E.2d 427 (1978).

[47] Mouldin v. State, 376 So. 2d 788 (Ala. Ct. App. 1979).

If there is a complete severance of the chattel from the possession of the person from whom it was taken, and the goods are actually carried away at least a short distance, this is sufficient to constitute taking and asportation, even if possession of the taker is immediately interrupted.[48]

Personal Property

At common law, and in some states today, larceny is limited to theft of goods and chattels. Under this definition, it is not larceny to carry away real property such as trees, crops, minerals and fixtures which are part of the realty. According to the definitions of larceny, unless the statute modifies the common law, one cannot be found guilty of larceny if such items as stocks, bonds, checks and promissory notes were the subject of the taking.

The statutes in most states today have expanded on the scope of larceny by modifying the definition of property, or by including additional offenses which prohibit the taking of specific items of real property as well as tangibles.

Property of Another

To constitute larceny, the property taken must be property of another person. That is, it must be owned by someone other than the thief, or in possession of someone not the accused, that person having the right to the property as against the thief. It is not essential that the thief know who the owner is; it is sufficient if he knows that the property is not his own and takes it to deprive the true owner of the property. As one court indicated, it is not that the property belong to or is owned by a specific person or entity, but rather that it is property of someone other than the thief.[49] Also, it makes no difference that the property stolen belongs to one person or several persons jointly or to several persons each owning separate parts thereof.[50] All that is necessary is that the prosecution include a description of the property for purposes of identification and to show ownership in a person or persons other than the accused.

With Intent to Steal

In larceny, as in robbery, the *intent* element is one of the most difficult to prove. Unless a statute is modified to omit this element, or to substitute other words, the prosecution must introduce evidence to show that the person who took the property and carried it away intended to permanently deprive the owner of possession of the property. Therefore, if the defense in-

---

[48] Hutchinson v. State, 427 P.2d 112 (Okla. Cr. 1967).

[49] State v. Leicht, 124 N.J. Super. 127, 305 A.2d 78 (1973).

[50] Gaynor v. State, 196 So. 2d 19 (Fla. Dist. Ct. App. 1967).

troduces evidence to show that the property was taken for temporary use only, the jury could find that the suspect lacks the intent to steal as required for the crime of larceny. One court explained that it is the intent to return the property, but not its actual return, which constitutes a defense in larceny.[51]

To constitute larceny, the intent to steal must exist at the time of the taking; that is, the taker must have a conscious purpose to steal that which did not belong to him at the time he took the property and carried it away.[52]

B. Contemporary Statutes and Codes

1. Model Penal Code

§ 223.1 Consolidation of Theft Offenses; Grading; Provisions Applicable to Theft Generally[53]

(1) Consolidation of Theft Offenses. Conduct denominated theft in this Article constitutes a single offense. An accusation of theft may be supported by evidence that it was committed in any manner that would be theft under this Article, notwithstanding the specification of a different manner in the indictment or information, subject only to the power of the Court to ensure fair trial by granting a continuance of other appropriate relief where the conduct of the defense would be prejudiced by lack of fair notice or by surprise.

(2) Grading of Theft Offenses.
    (a) Theft constitutes a felony of the third degree if the amount involved exceeds $500, or if the property stolen is a firearm, automobile, airplane, motorcycle, motorboat, or other motor-propelled vehicle, or in the case of theft by receiving stolen property, if the receiver is in the business of buying or selling stolen property.
    (b) Theft not within the preceding paragraph constitutes a misdemeanor, except that if the property was not taken from the person or by threat, or in breach of a

---

[51] Stanley v. State, 61 Okla. Crim. 382, 69 P.2d 398 (1937).

[52] Reid v. Florida Real Estate Comm'n, 188 So. 2d 846 (Fla. Dist. Ct. App. 1966).

[53] Model Penal Code, § 223.1 (Proposed Official Draft 1980).

fiduciary obligation, and the actor proves by a preponderance of the evidence that the amount involved was less than $50, the offense constitutes a petty misdemeanor.

(c) The amount involved in a threat shall be deemed to be the highest value, by any reasonable standard, of the property or services which the actor stole or attempted to steal. Amounts involved in thefts committed pursuant to one scheme or course of conduct, whether from the same person or several persons, may be aggregated in determining the grade of the offense.

(3) Claim of Right. It is an affirmative defense to prosecution for theft that the actor:

(a) was unaware that the property was that of another; or

(b) acted under an honest claim of right to the property or service involved or that he had a right to acquire or dispose of it as he did; or

(c) took property exposed for sale, intending to purchase and pay for it promptly, or reasonably believing that the owner, if present, would have consented.

(4) Theft from Spouse. It is no defense that theft was from the actor's spouse, except that misappropriation of household and personal effects, or other property normally accessible to both spouses, is theft only if it occurs after the parties have ceased living together.

§ 223.2 Theft by Unlawful Taking or Disposition[54]

(1) Movable Property. A person is guilty of theft if he unlawfully takes, or exercises unlawful control over, movable property of another with purpose to deprive him thereof.

(2) Immovable Property. A person is guilty of theft if he unlawfully transfers immovable property of another or any interest therein with purpose to benefit himself or another not entitled thereto.

---

[54] Model Penal Code § 223.2 (Proposed Official Draft 1980).

In the Model Penal Code, the theft offenses are consolidated into a single offense. The traditional offenses designated as larceny, embezzlement, obtaining by false pretenses, cheating, blackmail, extortion, fraudulent conversion, receiving stolen property, and others are not separated into individual statutory offenses.

Because of this deviation from the traditional approach, general provisions that are applicable to the various theft provisions set forth in other articles are explained in § 223.1. After first explaining that the theft offenses are consolidated, the grading of theft offenses is detailed, affirmative defenses enumerated, and for a purpose that is not sufficiently explained, reference is made to the fact that interspousal immunity is abolished except in narrowly specified circumstances. By using terms not generally used in defining the common law offenses, and by avoiding the technical definitions that have developed over the years, some of the problems encountered under the traditional statutes perhaps can be reduced.

Section 223.2 of the Model Code does not use the term *larceny*, but provides a penalty if a person unlawfully takes, or exercises unlawful control over, movable property of another with purpose to deprive him thereof. Under the provision of this Subsection, the elements are:

(a) unlawful,

(b) taking, or unlawfully exercising control over,

(c) movable property,

(d) of another,

(e) purpose to deprive him thereof.

The words "unlawfully takes" or "exercises unlawful control over" are similar to the common law elements of caption and asportation defined in previous Sections.

"Movable property" is defined in § 223.0 as property, the location of which can be changed, including things growing on, affixed to, or found in land, and documents although the rights represented thereby have no physical location.[55] "Property of another" includes property in which any person other than the actor has an interest which the actor is not privileged to infringe, regardless of the fact that the actor also has an interest in the property, and regardless of the fact that the other person might be precluded from civil recovery because the property was used in an unlawful transaction or was subject to forfeiture as contraband.[56]

---

[55] Model Penal Code § 223.0(4) (Proposed Official Draft 1980).

[56] Model Penal Code § 223.0(7) (Proposed Official Draft 1980).

"Deprive" means:

(a) to withhold property of another permanently or for so extended a period as to appropriate a major portion of its economic value, or with intent to restore only upon payment of reward or other compensation, or

(b) to dispose of the property so as to make it unlikely that the owner will recover it.[57]

With these definitions, it is readily apparent the coverage of this statute is more comprehensive than the coverage of the traditional larceny statute. For example, while the traditional statute applied only to personal property, this Section includes a penalty for taking either personal or real property, including intangible property.

Under Subsection (2), a person is guilty of theft if he:

(a) unlawfully,
(b) transfers,
(c) immovable property,
(d) of another,
(e) with purpose to benefit himself or another not entitled thereto.

"Immovable property," as used in Subsection (2), refers to all property other than that which is designated as movable. In the case of unlawful transfer of "immovable" property, as distinguished from "movable property, a "purpose to benefit himself or another not entitled thereto" is required. Here, the focus is on the benefit to the taker or another not entitled thereto rather than the loss to the owner or the possessor of the property.

2. Federal Code

The U.S. Code provision relating to larceny includes the common law elements of larceny plus the requirement that the offense be committed within the special maritime and territorial jurisdiction of the United States.[58] The first paragraph of the Federal Code states that:

---

[57] Model Penal Code § 223.0(1) (Proposed Official Draft 1980).

[58] 18 U.S.C. § 661.

Whoever, within the special maritime and territorial jurisdiction of the United States, takes and carries away, with intent to steal or purloin any personal property of another shall be punished as follows:...

The Code provides for punishment of five years or $5,000 or both if the value of the property taken exceeds $100 and imprisonment of not more than one year or both if the value does not exceed $100.[59]

In interpreting the provisions of the federal statute, the federal courts have indicated that the purpose of the law is to broaden the common law crime of larceny.[60] Some examples of thefts that come within the purview of this provision include stealing from an officer's club on a U.S. Army post in Virginia and taking and carrying away with intent to steal a coat and purse belonging to another at a Veterans Administration Hospital.[61]

3. Other states and codes

Many states that have enacted statutes recently have comprehensive consolidated provisions which include most of the theft offenses into one statute. That is, what was formerly larceny, embezzlement, false pretenses and in some instances other statutory crimes are consolidated into one comprehensive provision.[62] An example of a statute that consolidates many previous theft crimes is that of Kentucky.

§ 514.030 -- Theft by unlawful taking or disposition.
(1) A person is guilty of theft by unlawful taking or disposition when he unlawfully:

---

[59] *See* the Appendix for a definition of "within the special maritime and territorial jurisdiction of the United States." *See also*, 49 U.S.C. § 1472 for references concerning federal violations where the action occurs aboard an aircraft in flight, and 49 U.S.C. § 1151 for provisions relating to larceny committed in Indian territory.

[60] United States v. Henry, 447 F.2d 283 (3d Cir. 1971).

[61] Clark v. United States, 267 F.2d 99 (4th Cir. 1959); England v. United States, 174 F.2d 466 (5th Cir. 1949).

[62] *See* Model Penal Code § 223.1 (Proposed Official Draft 1980), and following comments.

(a) Takes or exercises control over movable property of another with intent to deprive him thereof; or

(b) Obtains immovable property of another or any interest therein with intent to benefit himself or another not entitled thereto.

(2) Theft by unlawful taking or disposition is a Class A misdemeanor unless the value of the property is $100 or more, in which case it is a Class D felony.[63]

This statute replaces approximately 20 previous statutes which dealt with theft of specific types of property; for example, one of the previous statutes related to theft of cattle, a second to theft of timber, a third to theft of coal, a fourth to theft of tobacco plants and a fifth to the conversion of a motor vehicle.

It is noted that the Kentucky law retains the concept of petit and grand larceny. Under this provision, unlawful taking or disposition of property of the value of $100 or more is a Class D felony, while unlawful taking or disposition of property of less value is a Class A misdemeanor.

Under the provisions of this statute and other similar statutes and codes, the elements are:

(a) taking or exercising control,

(b) movable property of another,

(c) with intent to *deprive* him thereof;

or

(a) obtaining immovable property of another or any interest therein,

(b) with intent to benefit himself or to benefit another not entitled to the property.

The first elements include alternative language. The statute describes an offense against the Commonwealth that can be committed in either of two ways, "by taking property or by *exercising* control over property, each to be accompanied by specific intent."[64]

---

[63] Ky. Rev. Stat. § 514.030 (1975).

[64] Commonwealth v. Day, 599 S.W.2d 166 (Ky. 1980).

"Deprive," as used in the statute, means to "withhold property of another permanently, or for so extended a period as to appropriate a major portion of its economic value or with intent to restore only upon payment of reward or other compensation, or to dispose of the property so as to make it unlikely that the owner will recover it."[65]

§ 750.356 Larceny[66]

Sec. 356. Any person who shall commit the offense of larceny, by stealing, of the property of another, any money, goods or chattels, or any bank note, bank bill, bond, promissory note, due bill, bill of exchange or other bill, draft, order or certificate, or any book of accounts for or concerning money or goods due or to become due, or to be delivered, or any deed or writing containing a conveyance of land, or any other valuable contract in force, or any receipt, release or defeasance, or any writ, process or public record, if the property stolen exceeds the value of $100.00, shall be guilty of a felony, punishable by imprisonment in the state prison not more than 5 years or by fine of not more than $2,500.00. If the property stolen shall be of the value of $100.00 or less, such person shall be guilty of a misdemeanor.

According to case law, the essential elements of larceny in Michigan are:

(a) an actual or constructive taking,
(b) of the goods or property of another,
(c) without the consent and against the will of the owner, and
(d) with felonious intent.[67]

If the theft involves property, the value of which exceeds $100, the crime is a felony, while if the value of the property taken is $100 or less, the crime is a misdemeanor. Accordingly, the value of the property alleged to have been stolen is an essential element of the crime and the prosecution must introduce evidence of value.[68]

Where state statutes defining larceny are narrow in scope, it is necessary to look to other statutes for coverage of specific crimes not covered in the general larceny statute.

---

[65] Ky. Rev. Stat. § 514.010 (1975).

[66] Mich. Comp. Laws § 750.356 (1968).

[67] People v. Goodchild, 68 Mich. App. 226, 242 N.W.2d 465 (1976).

[68] People v. Westman, 53 Mich. App. 662, 220 N.W.2d 169 (1974).

§ 6.4 Embezzlement

To one studying the offenses involving theft, it has no doubt become obvious that the common law offenses are most technical. Before discussing the definition and elements of the offense of embezzlement, a review of the offenses discussed up to this point is in order, as well as a look toward the distinguishing factors in other theft crimes.

It was noted that, in distinguishing the common law offense of robbery from larceny, the two aggravating factors in robbery were that the taking of the property be from the person or presence of another and that the taking be accompanied by means of force or putting in fear. To say this differently, the crime of robbery is an aggravated form of larceny.

At common law, there was no specific crime of embezzlement; therefore, if one of the elements of larceny was not proved, as for example if there were no trespass, but the property came into the possession of the taker lawfully, then the person who committed the wrong would often go unpunished. To fill this void, the English Parliament and the states, by legislative action, have enacted laws creating the crime of embezzlement. The early, as well as the recent, decisions agree that the offense of embezzlement did not exist at common law and is purely a statutory offense.[69]

To make the offenses involving theft a little less difficult to understand, the difference between embezzlement, and obtaining property by false pretenses, is mentioned here, but will be examined more thoroughly in the Sections that follow. The distinction between embezzlement and false pretenses is that, in the former case, the defendant does not have to have title to the property, while in the latter (false pretenses), title is passed.[70] In embezzlement, the perpetrator acquires possession of the property lawfully, but converts it to his own use, while in false pretenses possession of the property is obtained by means of deception.

As the chief distinction between larceny and embezzlement lies in the manner of acquiring possession of the property, emphasis is on this distinction. To reiterate, in embezzlement, the property comes lawfully into the possession of the taker but is fraudulently or unlawfully appropriated by him; while in larceny, there is a trespass in the unlawful acquisition of the property.

---

[69] Fortney v. Commonwealth, 162 S.W.2d 193 (1942).

[70] State v. Serkau, 128 Conn. 153, 20 A.2d 725 (1941).

A. Traditional Definition and Elements

Although there is a wide difference in the scope and wording of the statutes of various states defining embezzlement, both as regard the person liable and the kind of property protected, the statutes, as well as the courts, agree that the wrongful appropriation of conversion is a common element. Some definitions by various courts will help in developing a definition of the offense of embezzlement.

> The crime of "embezzlement" builds on the concept of conversion, but adds two further elements; first, embezzled property must have been in lawful possession of the defendant at the time of its appropriate, and, second, "embezzlement" requires knowledge that the appropriation is contrary to the wishes of the owner of the property.[71]

> "Embezzlement" is the wrongful appropriation or conversion of property where the original taking was lawful or with consent of the owner.[72]

To sustain a conviction of "embezzlement," it must be shown that the accused was the agent or bailee of the prosecuting witness in holding alleged embezzled property, that the property actually belonged to the alleged principal, that it was lawfully in possession of the accused at the time of the alleged embezzlement, that the accused must have been guilty of the conversion which the statute denounces, and, there was intent on the part of the accused to deprive the prosecuting witness against his property unlawfully.[73]

From these and other definitions, it has been determined that there are generally four elements of the offense of embezzlement.

(1) Fraudulent Intent

Generally, the statutes do not apply unless the accused held a relationship of confidence or trust with the owner and the accused appropriated the property unlawfully or with a fraudulent intent.[74] The fraudulent intent required as an element may be found from the acts of the defendant in using or disposing of the property. As an example, where an official of a union had

---

[71] United States v. Stockton, 788 F.2d 210 (4th Cir. 1986).

[72] Jones v. State, 79 So. 2d 273 (1955).

[73] People v. Patrin, 122 Cal. App. 2d 578, 265 P.2d 149 (1954).

[74] People v. Meadows, 199 N.Y. 1, 92 N.E. 128 (1910).

control of the union property, directed the sale of the property and appropriated part of the proceeds to his own use, he was guilty of embezzlement, as the intent was clear from the acts of the official.[75]

(2) Appropriation or Conversion

The gist of the crime of embezzlement is that the wrongdoer has money or other property of another person that comes into his hands legally but is not used as intended by the owner. To constitute wrongful appropriation or conversion, there must be a serious act of interference with the owner's rights. While damage to the property does not amount to conversion or appropriation, selling it, pledging it, giving it away, delivering it to one not entitled thereto, claiming it against the owner, unreasonably withholding possession of it from the owner or spending it (in the case of money) is conversion. To prove this element, the prosecution must establish that the accused converted funds to his own use or to the benefit of another; mere receipt of funds and failure to account therefore is not enough.[76]

(3) By One in Lawful Possession

To constitute embezzlement, there must be an actual and lawful possession or custody of property of another by virtue of some trust, duty, agency or employment of the accused.[77] Therefore, if one secures property illegally, the proper charge is not embezzlement, but one of the other offenses involving theft. The very essence of the crime of embezzlement is that the property was converted by one who has been entrusted with the property or into whose hand it has lawfully come. A common example is conversion by a bank employee who embezzles abstracts, purloins, or willfully misapplies bank funds which have come into his possession through his employment. However, agents, executors and administrators may also be charged with violating the embezzlement statutes, and an attorney may be guilty of embezzling money of his client which comes into his possession during the course of business.[78]

(4) Property of Another

As in the case of larceny, to constitute embezzlement, the property wrongfully disposed of must be "property of another." In order to prove a violation of embezzlement statutes, the prosecution must prove the property was that of one other than the accused. The traditional rule is that a person

---

[75] People v. Swanson, 174 Cal. App. 2d 453, 344 P.2d 832 (1959).

[76] State v. Randecker, 1 Wash. App. 834, 464 P.2d 447 (1970).

[77] Hart v. State, 41 Ala. App. 221, 127 So. 2d 390 (1961).

[78] People v. Converse, 74 Mich. 478, 42 N.W. 70 (1889).

cannot be guilty of converting his or her own property.[79] Therefore, if both possession and title of the property have been passed to the defendant prior to the alleged conversion, the defendant cannot properly be convicted of embezzlement.[80] However, where a defendant was the recipient of food vouchers issued for the sole purpose of enabling her to obtain supplemental food for her children, failure to make the required disposition, but instead selling the food vouchers to a stranger for cash, constituted embezzlement under Pennsylvania law.[81] The court, in upholding the conviction for embezzlement, explained that because the food vouchers were not intended to be used for her own benefit, appellant occupied a position comparable to that of a guardian or trustee. The court went on to say "such a person can be convicted of an embezzlement-type offense if he or she misappropriates funds for a use inconsistent with the purpose for which the funds are held."

B. Statutes and Codes

1. Model Penal Code

In an effort to further clarify the law relating to theft offenses where the actor comes into possession of property with the understanding that he will make certain payments or other disposition of property, but deals with the property as if it were his own, additional Code provisions have been added. Section 223.8 of the Model Penal Code provides:

§ 223.8 Theft by Failure to Make Required Disposition of Funds Received

A person who purposely obtains property upon agreement, or subject to a known legal obligation, to make specified payment or other disposition, whether from such property or its proceeds or from his own property to be reserved in equivalent amount, is guilty of theft if he deals with the property obtained as his own and fails to make the required payment or disposition. The foregoing applies notwithstanding that it may be impossible to identify particular property as belonging to the victim at the time of the actor's failure to make the required payment or disposition. An officer or employee of the government or of a financial institution is presumed:

---

[79] Commonwealth v. Austin, 393 A.2d 36 (1978).

[80] *Id.*

[81] Commonwealth v. Coward, 478 A.2d 1384 (Pa. Super. Ct. 1984).

(i) to know any legal obligation relevant to his criminal liability under this Section, and

(ii) to have dealt with the property as his own if he fails to pay or account upon lawful demand, or if an audit reveals a shortage or falsification of accounts.

According to the comments that follow this article of the Model Penal Code, nine states have modified their statutes so as to include provisions identical to or based on § 223.8 of the Code. Under this Code, the conduct proscribed consists essentially of two elements; [1] the obtaining of property upon an agreement and/or subject to a known legal obligation to make a specified payment or other disposition, and [2] dealing with the property as one's own and failing to make the required payment of disposition.

The Superior Court of Pennsylvania noted that this Section of the Model Penal Code was adopted by that state and replaces the fraudulent conversion and embezzlement Section of the earlier Code. In that case, the majority indicated that, in order to prove a violation of this Section, the prosecution must show the existence of four elements:

(1) obtaining the property of another,

(2) subject to an agreement or known legal obligation to make specified payments or other disposition thereof,

(3) intentional dealing with the property as the defendant's own, and

(4) failure to make the required disposition.[82]

2. Federal Code

The federal statute combines embezzlement and theft and provides:

Whoever embezzles, steals, purloins, or knowingly converts to his own use or the use of another, or without authority, sells, conveys, or disposes of any record, voucher, money, or thing of value of the United States or of any department or agency thereof, or any property made or being made under contract for the United States or any department or agency thereof; or

---

[82] *Id. See* case in Part II.

> Whoever receives, conceals, or retains the same with intent to convert it to his own use or gain, knowing it to have been embezzled, stolen, purloined, or converted --
>
> Shall be fined not more than $10,000 or imprisoned not more than ten years, or both; but if the value of such property does not exceed the sum of $100, he shall be fined not more than $1,000 or imprisoned not more than one year, or both.[83]

In determining the meaning of "thing and value" of the United States or any department or agency thereof, one circuit court decided that clothing which an employee of an Army and Air Force Exchange Service sought to remove from exchange premises without paying for them constituted a "thing of value."[84] Also, checks from an agency receiving funding from federal sources constituted a "thing of value" of the United States or department or agency thereof justifying a conviction of embezzlement under this Section.

The federal statute also includes an offense of "theft, embezzlement, or misapplication by a bank officer or employee."[85] This provides a penalty of $5,000 or five years imprisonment or both if the amount embezzled, abstracted, purloined or misapplied exceeds $100, where an employee of a federal bank or a bank that is a member of the Federal Reserve System embezzles, abstracts, purloins or willfully misapplies any of the monies, funds or credits of such bank. The four essential elements of the offense are:

(1) the accused was an officer or director of the bank,
(2) the bank was connected in some way with a national bank or a federally insured bank,
(3) the accused willfully misapplied the funds of the bank and
(4) the accused acted with intent to defraud the bank.[86]

3. Other statutes and codes

While most of the recently enacted statutes include larceny and embezzlement in the same statute and do not distinguish between lawfully taking and exercising unlawful control over the property, even these statutes differ

---

[83] 18 U.S.C. § 641.

[84] United States v. Sanders, 793 F.2d 107 (5th Cir. 1986).

[85] 18 U.S.C. § 656.

[86] United States v. Tidwell, 559 F.2d 1215 (5th Cir. 1977), *cert. denied*, 435 U.S. 492, 55 L.Ed.2d 538, 98 S. Ct. 1520 (1978).

in some ways. In some statutes, the property that is the subject of theft is limited to personal property. In others "property" includes both real and personal property. And in still others, "property" is defined as personal property and real property that has been "severed."

The definition of "deprived," as used in the various statutes, also differs to some extent. While the definition of "deprived," as used in the Model Code, includes deprivation for an extended period of time, some of the codes require an intent to deprive the owner "permanently" of the property.[87]

Some states still have not consolidated the crimes of embezzlement and larceny. An example of such a statute is that of Michigan, which provides:

§ 750.174 Embezzlement[88]

Sec. 174. Agent, servant, employee, trustee, bailee, custodian. Any person who as the agent, servant or employee of another, or as the trustee, bailee or custodian of the property of another, or of any partnership, voluntary association, public or private corporation, or of this state, or of any county, city, village, township or school district within this state, shall fraudulently dispose of or convert to his own use, or take or secrete with intent to convert to his own use without the consent of his principal, any money or other personal property of his principal which shall have come to his possession or shall be under his charge or control by virtue of his being such agent, servant, employee, trustee, bailee or custodian, as aforesaid, shall be guilty of the crime of embezzlement, and upon conviction thereof, if the money or personal property so embezzled shall be of the value of $100.00 or under, shall be guilty of a misdemeanor; if the money or personal property so embezzled be of the value of more than $100.00, such person shall be guilty of a felony, punishable by imprisonment in the state prison not more than 10 years or by a fine not exceeding $5,000.00.

Prima facie proof of intent. In any prosecution under this Section, the failure, neglect or refusal of such agent, servant, employee, trustee, bailee or custodian to pay, deliver, or refund to his principal such money or property entrusted to his care upon demand shall be *prima facie* proof of intent to embezzle.

---

[87] Wis., Kan., Ill., Mo., Tex. Codes Annot. § 31.01(3) (Vernon 1975). Mo. Ann. Stat. § 570.010(8) (Vernon 1979). Ill. Ann. Stat. ch. 15, § 3 (Smith-Hurd 1961). Kan. Stat. Ann. § 21-3705 (1972). Wis. Stat. Ann. § 943-20(1) (West 1977).

[88] Mich. Comp. Laws § 750.174 (1970).

The elements of embezzlement as provided in the Michigan statute are:

(a) a designated fiduciary relationship,
(b) possession of property of another,
(c) fraudulent disposal or conversion to his own use, or to secrete with intent to so convert the property,
(d) property was in the possession of the person by virtue of the relationship.

As in the case of larceny, the crime of embezzlement is a felony if the amount embezzled is more than $100, a misdemeanor if $100 or less.

The Michigan Supreme Court has determined that an administrator appointed by a probate court was a "trustee" within the meaning of the statutes and was therefore subject to prosecution thereunder.[89] As to the "intent" element, the Michigan Court indicated that evidence relating to the acts of the defendant were admissible to show intent and that the existence of criminal intent was not dependent upon a statement by the defendant as to the precise state of mind at the time of the taking of money.[90]

§ 6.5 Obtaining Property by False Pretenses

A. Traditional Definition and Elements

In previous Sections, larceny was defined as the wrongful taking of property from the *possession of another* who has a superior right to possession. In embezzlement, the gist of the offense is *misappropriation* of property by a person who has legal possession. Neither encompass the situation where the perpetrator obtains title and possession of the property without the wrongful taking or the misappropriation, but by means of deception.

As false pretenses, like embezzlement is a statutory crime, the definition varies among the jurisdictions. The general definition is "knowingly and designedly obtaining the property of another by false pretenses, with intent to defraud."

The gist of the crime of obtaining money or property by false pretenses is that the victim transfer the title to the property to the wrongdoer under the influence of false pretenses.[91] The passing of title constitutes the line of de-

---

89   People v. Heber, 42 Mich. App. 582, 202 N.W.2d 571 (Mich. Ct. App. 1972).

90   People v. Zunno, 384 Mich. 151, 180 N.W.2d 17 (1970). *See also* People v. Henderson, 80 Mich. App. 447, 264 N.W.2d 22 (Mich. Ct. App. 1978).

91   People v. Cravens, 79 Cal. App. 2d 658, 180 P.2d 453 (1947).

marcation between larceny and false pretenses. While larceny is essentially a crime committed against possession and involves a trespass, false pretenses involves obtaining title due to the perpetration of a fraud.[92]

While the courts have reached some consensus in defining the offense of false pretenses, the wording of the definitions as they appear in statutes and cases, still differs. Some examples will point out these differences and similarities.

A "false pretense" may consist in any act, word, symbol, or token calculated and intended to deceive, and it may be made either expressly or by implication.[93]

A "false pretense" may be defined to be the false representation of a subsisting fact, whether by oral or written words or conduct, which is calculated to deceive, intended to deceive, and which does, in fact, deceive, and by means of which one person obtains value from another without compensation.[94]

At common law, to constitute the crime of obtaining property by "false pretenses," it is necessary to allege and prove the false pretenses, that property was obtained thereby, that the false pretenses were made with intent to cheat and defraud, and that money was paid in reliance upon and under inducement of false pretenses.[95]

The elements of false pretenses, or obtaining money or property under false pretenses, differ from state to state. However, generally they are:

(a) obtaining money, goods or things of value,
(b) by false representation,
(c) knowing the same to be false and
(d) with intent thereby to defraud the owner.

(a) Obtaining Money, Goods or Things of Value

Generally, this element is defined in broad terms either by statute or case decisions. In some states, specific articles are enumerated in the statute,

---

[92] Courtney v. State, 174 Miss. 147, 164 So. 227 (1935); State v. Serkau, 128 Conn. 153, 20 A.2d 725 (1941).

[93] Fuller v. State, 221 Miss. 227, 72 So. 2d 454 (1954).

[94] State v. Carlson, 171 N.C. 818, 89 S.E. 30 (1916).

[95] People v. Sloane, 300 N.Y.S. 1032 (1937).

while others use such terms as "valuable thing" or "other property." One approach is to consider property that can be obtained by false pretenses in the same class of property which is the subject of larceny. However, some statutes broadened this to include such things as promissory notes, bills of exchange, checks and other securities.[96]

After discussing the definition of "things of value," one court noted that the crime of false pretenses is committed when a chattel, money or a valuable security is obtained from another by making a false representation with intent to defraud and with knowledge of its falsity.[97] However, where a defendant received $600 from a homeowner for work which could have been done for $25, this was not false pretenses, even though ethically indefensible.[98] The court advised that an essential element of the crime is a fraudulent misrepresentation and, in this case, there was no testimony of any misrepresentation.

(b) By False Representation

The general rule is that the representation must be false as to facts, past or existing. Representation that something will happen in the future or a mere promise to do something is not considered sufficient under many statutes. However, a number of states also permit prosecutions in "false promise" situations.[99]

According to a New Jersey decision, false pretenses or false representations means any conduct tantamount to fraud, and is not limited to false representations as to one's financial condition.[100] A Texas Court explained that there must be intent to cheat or defraud, but that this may be inferred from false representations.[101]

(c) Knowing the Same to be False

The mental element of the crime of false pretenses has two essential phases; it must appear:

(1) that the defendant knew the representations which he made to be untrue, and

(2) that he made them with intent to defraud.

---

[96]   People v. Bertsche, 265 Ill. 272, 106 N.E. 828 (1914).

[97]   Baumgartner v. State, 319 A.2d 592 (1974).

[98]   People v. Marks, 163 N.W.2d 506 (Mich. App. 1968).

[99]   Ill. Ann. Stat. ch. 38, § 15-4 (Smith-Hurd 1977).

[100]   Beneficial Finance Co. v. Norton, 76 N.J. Super. 577, 185 A.2d 218 (1962).

[101]   Cowan v. State, 41 Tex. Cr. 617, 56 S.W. 751 (1900).

The prosecution has the responsibility to prove knowledge on the part of the defendant. It is also essential that the indictment alleged that the defendant made the pretenses with knowledge of their falsity.[102]

(d) With Intent to Defraud the Owner

The intent must exist when the property is obtained, but if such intent does exist at that time, a subsequently reformed intent to return the property will not constitute a defense.[103] On the other hand, the prosecution must introduce evidence to show that defendant knew that his representation was untrue and he made it with intent to defraud.

B. Statutes and Codes

1. Model Penal Code

§ 223.3 Theft by Deception[104]

A person is guilty of theft if he purposely obtains property of another by deception. A person deceives if he purposely:

(1) creates or reinforces a false impression, including false impressions as to law, value, intention or other state of mind; but deception as to a person's intention to perform a promise shall not be inferred from the fact alone that he did not subsequently perform the promise; or

(2) prevents another from acquiring information which would affect his judgment of a transaction; or

(3) fails to correct a false impression which the deceiver previously created or reinforced, or which the deceiver knows to be influencing another to whom he stands in a fiduciary or confidential relationship; or

(4) fails to disclose a known lien, adverse claim or other legal impediment to the enjoyment of property which he transfers or encumbers in consideration for the property obtained, whether such impediment is or is not valid, or is or is not a matter of official record.

---

[102] Horton v. State, 85 Ohio St. 13, 96 N.E. 797 (1911).

[103] State v. Neimeier, 66 Iowa 634, 24 N.W. 247 (1885).

[104] Model Penal Code § 223.3 (Proposed Official Draft 1980).

The term "deceive" does not, however, include falsity as to matters having no pecuniary significance, or puffing by statements unlikely to deceive ordinary persons in the group addressed.

First, it is noted the Model Penal Code does not use the traditional terminology but, rather, designates the crime as "theft by deception." This is consistent with the terminology used in other theft-related crimes.

In the Model Penal Code, the term "deception" is substituted for false pretenses or false representation. Even though the words are different, many of the elements that existed under the traditional statutes continue as requirements in the Model Code. For example, under the Code, the actor must have purpose to obtain the property of another and must have a purpose to deceive. These are substitutes for "knowledge" and "intent" as used in some pre-Code statutes.

The Model Code clarifies some of the questions that existed prior to the time that the Code was adopted. For example, "deception," as used in the Code, includes not only creating a false impression, but reinforcing a false impression that the victim may have entertained prior to the intervention by the actor. The wording avoids court decisions to define the meaning of traditional terms.

In interpreting § 405(2) of the Utah statute, which was modeled after this Section of the Model Penal Code, the Utah court found that this Subsection does not support the contention that pecuniary loss must be an element of the crime of theft by deception.[105] In this Utah case, the Supreme Court of that state upheld a conviction of theft by deception where the defendant made false representations that he would invest the victim's money in gold and would clear title to land used to secure the transaction.

After examining another state law modeled after the Model Penal Code § 223.3, the majority decided that this provision does not require that the defendant's deception take the form of express or affirmative misrepresentation.[106] In this case, the Supreme Court of Nebraska upheld a conviction of the defendant where the evidence indicated that the defendant created an impression that the premiums paid to him personally were payments to the insurance company, but instead of making insurance payments, he deposited the victim's check in his own account.

---

[105] State v. Roberts, 711 P.2d 235 (Utah 1985). The case lists 12 states that have adopted the language of § 223.3 of the Model Penal Code.

[106] State v. Fleming, 223 Neb. 169, 388 N.W.2d 497 (1986).

2. Federal Code

Title 18 § 1341 of the U.S. Code is entitled "Frauds and Swindles."[107] The purpose of this statute is to protect the integrity of the mails by making it a crime to use them to implement fraudulent schemes of any kind, including the use of the mails to implement fraudulent schemes directed at a state agency.[108]

3. Other statutes and codes

While some recently revised state Codes contain most of the provisions of the Model Code, some others contain only part of these provisions and some states still use the traditional terminology and definitions. A few of the Codes restrict the scope of theft by deception to misrepresentation of past or present facts; some others authorize prosecutions in false promise situations.[109]

In some states, the traditional crime of false pretenses is incorporated into the theft statute. For example, in the State of Ohio, theft by deception is a part of § 2913.02. This Section provides:

(A) No person, with purpose to deprive the owner of property or services, shall knowingly obtain or exert control over either:

    (1) without the consent of the owner or the person authorized to give consent;
    (2) beyond the scope of the express or implied consent of the owner or person authorized to give consent;
    (3) by deception;
    (4) by threat.[110]

This includes theft by deception which was formerly the subject of a separate Section entitled Larceny by Trick. Under the provisions of this statute, the elements of the crime are similar to the traditional larceny elements, except control over the property is obtained by deception rather than by taking.

Another approach was taken when the Kentucky General Assembly drafted the Code. This Section provides:

---

[107] 18 U.S.C. § 1341; *see also* 18 U.S.C. § 1342 "Fictitious Name and Address" and 18 U.S.C. § 1343 "Fraud by Wire, Radio or Television."

[108] United States v. Rendini, 738 F.2d 530 (1st Cir. 1984).

[109] Model Penal Code § 223.3 (Proposed Official Draft 1980) and following comments.

[110] Ohio Rev. Code Ann. § 2913.03 (Page 1987).

§ 514.040 -- Theft by deception.[111]

(1) A person is guilty of theft by deception when he obtains property of another by deception with intent to deprive him thereof. A person deceives when he intentionally:

(a) creates or reinforces a false impression, including false impressions as to law, value, intention or other state of mind; or

(b) prevents another from acquiring information which would affect his judgment of a transaction; or

(c) fails to correct a false impression which the deceiver previously created or reinforced or which the deceiver knows to be influencing another to whom he stands in a fiduciary or confidential relationship; or

(d) fails to disclose a known lien, adverse claim or other legal impediment to the enjoyment of property which he transfers or encumbers in consideration for the property obtained, whether such impediment is or is not valid or is or is not a matter of official record; or

(e) issues or passes a check or similar sight order for the payment of money, knowing that it will not be honored by the drawee.

The elements of the crime under this provision are:

(a) obtaining property by the defendant,
(b) ownership of property in another,
(c) obtaining by deception,
(d) with intent to deprive the other of the property.

The key word which distinguishes this crime from others is "deception." Deception, as used in the statute, is broadly defined and specifically includes creating or reinforcing a false impression, preventing another from acquiring information which would affect his judgment of a transaction, failing to correct a false impression, failing to disclose a known lien or other adverse claim, and finally, issuing or passing a check or other order for the payment of money, knowing that it will not be honored by the drawee.

---

[111] Ky. Rev. Stat. § 514.040 (1975).

This last part of the definition of deception is peculiar to the Kentucky Code and is not included in the *theft by deception* provision of the Model Code. It was added to make it clear that the statute applied to obtaining property by issuing a known cold check.

Other statutes and codes differ from the Model Code and from those included here in some respects. Therefore, each must be carefully examined before a suspect is charged under this or the other theft statutes.

§ 6.6 Extortion

A. *Traditional Definition and Elements*

Before stating the definition of extortion, the other property-related crimes discussed to this point are briefly summarized.

There are some elements common to all theft crimes; however, the process in acquiring the possession of property involved differs. In robbery, the possession of the property is acquired from the person or in his presence by threats of immediate bodily harm. In larceny, possession is obtained by physical taking and carrying away (caption and asportation). Embezzlement is distinguished by the fact that the property comes into the possession of the person lawfully, but is unlawfully appropriated or converted. The offense of false pretenses consists of obtaining the property by means of material false representations or deception. The victim may be deprived of his property by another means; by threats or coercion. When this occurs and the other elements are present, the crime is "extortion" or "theft by extortion."

The traditional definition of extortion is the obtaining of money or other things of value by the misuse of official power or position.[112] Modern statutes have expanded the crime of extortion to include what is generally termed "blackmail." The crime of extortion under these statutes may be committed by a public officer under color of his office or by a private individual.

Generally, a person is guilty of extortion (or blackmail) if he obtains property of another by threats or coercion. The statutes vary as to the type of threats that will suffice for the crime. Some examples of the types of threats that have been held to be actionable are threats to:

(a) unlawfully injure the person or property of the individual threatened or someone else,

---

[112]   Kirby v. State, 57 N.J.L. 320, 31 A. 213 (1894).

(b) accuse the individual threatened or someone else of a crime, and

(c) expose any secret affecting the individual threatened or some other person.

To constitute the crime, there must be a causal connection between the threats and the victim surrendering the property. That is, there must be a showing that the threat was the controlling factor in the victim's decision to part with the property.[113]

There is often some confusion between the terms *extortion* and *blackmail*. As noted previously, extortion was originally limited to obtaining money or things of value through misuse of official power while blackmail referred to the obtaining of money or property by a private individual. However, as more comprehensive statutes were written, the term blackmail became equivalent to and synonymous with extortion within the non-technical meaning of the term.[114]

The distinction between *robbery* and *extortion* is that, in robbery, the victim parts with his property without consent, while in extortion, the victim consents to part with his money or property even though the consent is induced by unlawful threats.[115]

Although the elements of the crime of extortion vary with the state statutes, the general elements are:

(1) obtaining of money or property. As in theft, usually the property must be personal property;

(2) by threats or coercion. The threat may be either oral or written, and may even be by innuendo or suggestions, but it must be such as would ordinarily create alarm;

(3) to perform certain enumerated acts. Most statutes enumerate specific acts that must be threatened by the perpetrator. One example of one that is common to most statutes is to injure the person or property of the individual threatened.

---

[113] People v. Williams, 127 Cal. 212, 59 P. 581 (1899).

[114] Hess v. Sparks, 44 Kan. 465, 24 P. 979 (1890).

[115] People v. Barondess, 16 N.Y. 436 (1891) *rev'd on other grounds*, 133 N.Y. 649, 31 N.E. 240 (1892).

B. Statutes and Codes

1. Model Penal Code

§ 223.4 Theft by Extortion[116]

A person is guilty of theft if he purposely obtains property of another by threatening to:

(1) inflict bodily injury on anyone or commit any other criminal offense; or

(2) accuse anyone of a criminal offense; or

(3) expose any secret tending to subject any person to hatred, contempt or ridicule, or to impair his credit or business repute; or

(4) take or withhold action as an official, or cause an official to take or withhold action; or

(5) bring about or continue a strike, boycott or other collective unofficial action, if the property is not demanded or received for the benefit of the group in whose interest the actor purports to act; or

(6) testify or provide information or withhold testimony or information with respect to another's legal claim or defense; or

(7) inflict any other harm which would not benefit the actor.

It is an affirmative defense to prosecution based on paragraphs (2), (3) or (4) that the property obtained by threat of accusation, exposure, lawsuit or other invocation of official action was honestly claimed as restitution or indemnification for harm done in the circumstances to which such accusation, exposure, lawsuit or other official action relates, or as compensation for property or lawful services.

The Model Penal Code provides that a person is guilty of theft if he purposely obtains property of another by threatening to do one of the seven specific acts enumerated. The list of acts in the Model Code is similar to some used in states prior to the time the Code was written. The Code does contain a residual provision (Subsection 7) which was not included in most states and makes the Code more comprehensive in its application.

---

[116] Model Penal Code § 223.4 (Proposed Official Draft 1980).

2. Federal Code

Title 18 of the U.S. Code has seven Sections dealing with extortion and threats.[117] The Section which most closely resembles the traditional extortion law is § 873, entitled "Blackmail." This provides:

> Whoever, under a threat of informing, or as a consideration for not informing, against any violation of any law of the United States, demands or receives any money or other valuable thing, shall be fined not more than $2,000 or imprisoned not more than one year, or both.

The essential elements of this crime are coercion and unlawful consideration.[118]

3. Other statutes and codes

Some of the recently enacted statutes and codes contain comprehensive lists of threatened conduct that subjects the person making the threats to criminal liability. For example, the Missouri statute provides:

§ 570.030 Stealing[119]

1. A person commits the crime of stealing if he appropriates property or services of another with the purpose to deprive him thereof, either without his consent or by means of deceit or coercion...

    ...

    (4)   "Coercion" means a threat, however communicated:

        (a)   to commit any crime; or
        (b)   to inflict physical injury in the future on the person threatened or another; or

---

[117] 18 U.S.C. § 871 "Threats Against the President and Successors to the Presidency;" 18 U.S.C. § 872 "Extortion by Officers or Employees of the United States;" 18 U.S.C. § 873 "Blackmail;" 18 U.S.C. § 874 "Kickbacks from Public Works Employees;" 18 U.S.C. § 875 "Interstate Communications;" 18 U.S.C. § 876 "Mailing Threatening Communications;" and 18 U.S.C. § 877 "Mailing Threatening Communications from Foreign Countries."

[118] United States v. Smith, 228 F.Supp. 345 (1964).

[119] Mo. Ann. Stat. § 570.030 (Vernon 1979).

   (c) to accuse any person of any crime; or

   (d) to expose any person to hatred, contempt or ridicule; or

   (e) to harm the credit or business repute of any person; or

   (f) to take or withhold action as a public servant, or to cause a public servant to take or withhold action; or

   (g) to inflict any other harm which would not benefit the actor.

A threat of accusation, lawsuit or other invocation of official action is not coercion if the property sought to be obtained by virtue of such threat was honestly claimed as restitution or indemnification for harm done in the circumstances to which the accusation, exposure, lawsuit or other official action relates, or as compensation for property or lawful service. The defendant shall have the burden of injecting the issue of justification as to any threat.

Here, the crime of theft by extortion is included in the general statutes entitled "Stealing." The elements of the crime where the property is obtained by means of coercion are:

   (a) appropriation,

   (b) of property or services,

   (c) of another,

   (d) with the purpose to deprive him thereof and

   (e) by coercion.

After listing some of the specific threats that will constitute the crime, a general category (to inflict any other harm which would not benefit the actor) is added.

The last paragraph contains an avenue of defense or justification if the defendant injects the issue that he honestly claimed the property as restitution or indemnification for related harm done or as compensation for property or lawful service.

In New York, the crime of extortion is included as a part of the larceny statute. The part relating to extortion provides:

§ 155.05 Larceny; defined[120]

1. A person steals property and commits larceny when, with intent to deprive another of property or to appropriate the same to himself or to a third person, he wrongfully takes, obtains or withholds such property from an owner thereof.

2. Larceny includes a wrongful taking, obtaining or withholding of another's property, with the intent prescribed in subdivision (1) of this Section, committed in any of the following ways:

    (e) By extortion.

    A person obtains property by extortion when he compels or induces another person to deliver such property to himself or to a third person by means of instilling in him a fear that, if the property is not so delivered, the actor or another will:

    (i) cause physical injury to some person in the future; or

    (ii) cause damage to property; or

    (iii) engage in other conduct constituting a crime; or

    (iv) accuse some person of a crime or cause criminal charges to be instituted against him; or

    (v) expose a secret or publicize an asserted fact, whether true or false, tending to subject some person to hatred, contempt or ridicule; or

    (vi) cause a strike, boycott or other collective labor group action injurious to some person's business; except that such a threat shall not be deemed extortion when the property is demanded or received for the benefit of the group in whose interest the actor purports to act; or

    (vii) testify or provide information or withhold testimony or information with respect to another's legal claim or defense; or

    (viii) use or abuse his position as a public servant by performing some act within or related to his official duties, or by failing or

---

[120] N.Y. Penal Law § 155.05 (McKinney 1975).

refusing to perform an official duty, in such manner as to affect some person adversely; or

(ix) perform any other act which would not in itself materially benefit the actor but which is calculated to harm another person materially with respect to his health, safety, business, calling, career, financial condition, reputation or personal relationships.

According to the provisions of this part of the statute, in addition to the intent element, the prosecution must show that the wrongful taking was by compelling or inducing another to deliver property to the person making the threat or to a third person by means of instilling fear. This last element (instilling fear) limits the application of the statute.

In one New York case, the court held that, in order to find a person guilty of violating the part of the statute relating to threats to expose a secret tending to subject a person to hatred, contempt or ridicule (Subsection (e)(v)) there must be evidence of the nature of the secret or asserted fact which tends to subject the complainant to hatred, contempt or ridicule.[121] In this case, the defendant had threatened to send photographs of complainant to her father's place of employment if the complainant didn't deliver certain property to the defendant. The court declared that it was incumbent upon the grand jury to either view the photographs or to be given a specific description of the contents of the photographs so the jury could determine whether they tended to subject the person to hatred, contempt or ridicule.

§ 6.7 Receiving Stolen Property

A. Traditional Definitions and Elements

Apparently, under the early English laws, there was no separate and distinct offense of receiving stolen property, but the receiver was subject to indictment and punishment as an accessory to the theft itself. However, the English courts and legislative bodies soon recognized the necessity of creating a substantive crime indictable and punishable as an offense separate and distinct from the larceny.[122]

---

[121] People v. Homsey, 90 Misc. 2d 1006, 396 N.Y.S.2d 985 (1977).

[122] Kirby v. United States, 174 U.S. 47, 19 S. Ct. 574, 43 L.Ed. 890 (1894).

In an effort to reduce the theft of property by punishing those who receive the stolen property, the drafters of legislation in this country enacted statutes very early which provide for the prosecution and punishment of those who knowingly aid the takers of property by purchasing the fruits of the crime. Some of the earlier offenses designated the crime of receiving stolen property a misdemeanor, but it was soon recognized that a light penalty was not enough to deter the receiver of stolen property. Later statutes made the crime a felony.[123]

Although the terms of the statutes vary, the general definition is receiving stolen property, knowing it to have been stolen with intent to deprive the owner of it. The gravamen of the offense is the felonious receiving of stolen property belonging to another knowing that it has been stolen.[124]

The elements of the crime of receiving stolen property are:

(a)   receipt of property,
(b)   the property was actually stolen,
(c)   the receiver knew at the time that such property had been stolen and
(d)   felonious intent on the part of the receiver.

(a) Receipt of the Property

This has been interpreted to mean that the person has control over the property; not necessarily manual possession. Taking the property into constructive possession is sufficient; for example, where it was agreed that the property would be put in a place where the receiver would have access to it.[125] Nor is it necessary that the receiver receive the stolen property directly from the thief. If he receives it from an innocent agent of the thief, it is the same as a direct conveyance, and if he knows the goods are stolen he is guilty of receiving.[126]

(b) The Property Must Have Been Stolen

To constitute the crime, the goods must have been stolen and the character of the goods, as stolen goods, must exist at the time they are received. This element is not present if they are, in fact, not stolen goods, even though the receiver may have believed them to be stolen.

---

[123]   4 Blackstone, COMMENTARIES 38.

[124]   Curl v. People, 53 Colo. 578, 127 P. 751 (1912); Yeargain v. State, 57 Okla. Crim. 136, 45 P.2d 1113 (1935).

[125]   Sanderson v. Commonwealth, 12 S.W. 136 (Ky. 1889) II. K.L.R. 341.

[126]   Commonwealth v. White, 123 Mass. 430, 25 Am.Rep. 116 (1877).

(c) The Receiver Must Know That It Was Stolen

One of the most difficult elements to prove is the knowledge of the stolen character of the goods. Knowledge at the time the goods were received, that they have been stolen, is absolutely essential.[127] In proving this element, the jury may infer knowledge from the circumstances.[128]

(d) The Receiver Must Have Felonious Intent

In order to be criminally liable, the prosecution must prove felonious intent. For example, one who receives goods, knowing them to have been stolen, is not guilty, if his purpose is to return them to their owner or merely to detect the thief.[129]

B. Statutes and Codes

1. Model Penal Code

§ 223.6 Receiving Stolen Property[130]

(1) Receiving. A person is guilty of theft if he purposely receives, retains, or disposes of movable property of another knowing that it has been stolen, or believing that it has probably been stolen, unless the property is received, retained, or disposed with purpose to restore it to the owner. "Receiving" means acquiring possession, control of title, or lending on the security of the property.

(2) Presumption of Knowledge. The requisite knowledge or belief is presumed in the case of a dealer who:

    (a) is found in possession or control of property stolen from two or more persons on separate occasions; or

    (b) has received stolen property in another transaction within the year preceding the transaction charged; or

    (c) being a dealer in property of the sort received, acquires it for a consideration which he knows is far below its reasonable value.

---

[127] Tolliver v. State, 25 Tex. Crim. 600, 8 S.W. 806 (Tex. Crim. App. 1888).

[128] Id.

[129] Arcia v. State, 26 Tex. Crim. 193, 9 S.W. 685 (Tex. Crim. App. 1888).

[130] Model Penal Code § 223.6 (Proposed Official Draft 1980).

"Dealer" means a person in the business of buying or selling goods including a pawnbroker.

The Model Penal Code retains the general provisions of the pre-Code statutes. Included in the Code, however, are some exceptions which were the result of case decisions under the previous statutes. For example, the penalty is appropriate "unless the property is received, retained, or disposed of with purpose to restore it to the owner." This wording was not included in most traditional statutes, but the courts, by case decisions, usually applied the same rule. Also, the Model Code includes a definition of the word "receiving" in the Code itself.

In the Model Code, the property that may be received, retained, or disposed of is limited to "movable property." Movable property is defined as property, the location of which can be changed, including things growing on, affixed to, or found in land, and documents, although the rights represented thereof have no physical location.[131]

The Code also includes the words "receives," "retains," or "disposes" rather than the single word "receives" as used in previous statutes. Although "receives" was sometimes interpreted broadly, this Code seems to make clear that the application is intended to be more comprehensive than previously existing statutes.

Subsection (2) of the Model Code differs from other statutes in that it details instances in which the requisite knowledge or belief is presumed to exist. This makes it easier to prove the elements of the crime and is apparently aimed also at making it less difficult to prosecute a fence who receives stolen property.

2. Federal Code

Chapter 113 entitled "Stolen Property" deals with transportation and sale of stolen vehicles, securities, and other personal property.

Criminal justice personnel on the state and local levels more frequently are concerned with Title 18, § 2312 which is entitled "Transportation of Stolen Vehicles."[132] This Section provides that:

Whoever transports in interstate or foreign commerce a motor vehicle or aircraft, knowing the same to have been stolen, shall be fined not more than $5,000 or imprisoned not more than 5 years, or both.

---

[131] Model Penal Code § 223.0(4) (Proposed Official Draft 1980).

[132] 18 U.S.C. § 2312.

The federal law relating to transportation of motor vehicles in interstate commerce was first enacted in 1919 to make it possible for federal officers to assist in reducing the number of auto thefts. The constitutionality of this Section was challenged on several occasions but was found not to be void for vagueness.[133]

In order to convict one of transporting stolen vehicles in interstate commerce, the government must prove that the vehicle was, in fact, stolen, and that the defendant transported the vehicle in interstate commerce.[134]

The federal statute which deals with receiving stolen property when the crime is committed within the special maritime and territorial jurisdiction of the United States is Title 18, § 662.[135] This Section provides:

> Whoever, within the special maritime and territorial jurisdiction of the United States, buys, receives, or conceals any money, goods, bank notes, or other things which may be the subject of larceny, which has been feloniously taken, stolen, or embezzled from any other person, knowing the same to have been so taken, stolen, or embezzled, shall be fined not more than $1,000 or imprisoned not more than 3 years, or both; but if the amount or value of the thing so taken, stolen, or embezzled does not exceed $100, he shall be fined not more than $1,000 or imprisoned not more than one year, or both.

After discussing the question of jurisdiction to try one for receiving stolen property within the special jurisdiction of the United States, a court of appeals agreed that receipt or concealment of the stolen property within the confines of a military reservation was a violation of this Section.[136] As in state receiving cases, in order to convict a person for the crimes of receiving stolen property, it must appear first that the property was stolen by some person other than the defendant, secondly, that the defendant received the property and converted it to his own use, and, thirdly, the defendant knew that the property which he received had been stolen.

It is not necessary that the prosecution prove that the defendant had knowledge that the property was moved in interstate commerce; however, the

---

[133]   United States v. Baker, 429 F.2d 1344 (7th Cir. 1970).

[134]   United States v. Spoone, 741 F.2d 680 (4th Cir. 1984), *cert. denied*, 469 U.S. 1162, 83 L.Ed.2d 929, 105 S. Ct. 917 (1984).

[135]   18 U.S.C. § 662.

[136]   United States v. Townsend, 474 F.2d 209 (5th Cir. 1973).

government must prove that the defendant had knowledge of the fact that the property was stolen.[137]

A second federal statute specifies a penalty where one receives, conceals, stores, barters or sells vehicles which have been moved in interstate commerce if he knew that the vehicle was stolen. This Section provides that:

> Whoever receives, conceals, stores, barters, sells, or disposes of any motor vehicle or aircraft, which has crossed a state or a U.S. boundary after being stolen, knowing the same to have been stolen, shall be fined not more than $5,000 or imprisoned not more than five years, or both.[138]

To convict one of a violation of this Section proscribing receiving or concealing stolen automobiles, the government must demonstrate that the:

(1)　motor vehicle involved was stolen;
(2)　defendant knew that motor vehicle had been stolen;
(3)　defendant concealed, stored, received, bartered, sold or disposed of the motor vehicle; and
(4)　vehicle involved was moved in interstate traffic at the time of the defendant's activities.[139]

3. Other statutes and codes

Although all states have statutory provisions prohibiting the receipt of stolen property and providing a penalty for those who violate the respective Sections of the statute, there are differences in the wording of the various statutes. Some, for example, use the word "receiving," which is the traditional term, while others define the prohibited conduct as "obtaining control over stolen property" or "criminal possession of stolen property."[140] As to culpability, some states require that the receiver "know that the property is stolen;"

---

[137]　United States v. Graves, 669 F.2d 964 (5th Cir. 1982); United States v. Beil, 577 F.2d 1313 (5th Cir. 1978).

[138]　18 U.S.C. § 2313.

[139]　United States v. Thomas, 676 F.2d 239 (7th Cir. 1980), *cert. denied*, 449 U.S. 1091, 101 S. Ct. 887, 66 L.Ed.2d 820 (1980). Other federal statutes dealing with the transportation, receipt or sale of stolen property are 18 U.S.C. § 2314 (Transportation of Stolen Goods, Securities, Monies, Fraudulent State Tax Stamps, Articles Used in Counterfeiting); 18 U.S.C. § 2315 (Sale or Receipt of Stolen Goods, Securities, Monies or Fraudulent State Tax Stamps); 18 U.S.C. § 2316 (Transportation of Livestock); 18 U.S.C. § 2317 (Sale or Receipt of Livestock).

[140]　N.Y. Penal Law §§ 165.040-.150 (McKinney 1975).

some provide that the receiver must "know or believe that the property has probably been stolen"; and others use the phrase "reasonable grounds for believing the property is stolen." An example of a statute which provides that a person commits an offense if he unlawfully appropriates property with the intent to deprive the owner of property is that of Texas.[141]

This comprehensive provision states:

§ 31.03 Theft
(a) A person commits an offense if he unlawfully appropriates property with intent to deprive the owner of property.
(b) Appropriation of property is unlawful if:

    (1) it is without the owner's effective consent; or
    (2) the property is stolen and the actor appropriates the property knowing it was stolen by another.

(c) For purposes of Subsection (b)(2) of this Section:

    (1) evidence that the actor has previously participated in recent transactions other than, but similar to, that which the prosecution is based is admissible for the purpose of showing knowledge or intent and the issues of knowledge or intent are raised by the actor's plea of not guilty;
    (2) the testimony of an accomplice shall be corroborated by proof that tends to connect the actor to the crime, but the actor's knowledge or intent may be established by the uncorroborated testimony of the accomplice;
    (3) an actor engaged in the business of buying and selling used or secondhand personal property, or lending money on the security of personal property deposited with him, is presumed to know upon receipt by the actor of stolen property (other than a motor vehicle subject to Article 6687-1, Vernon's Texas Civil Statutes) that the property has been previously stolen from another if the actor pays for or loans against the property $25 or more (or consideration of equivalent value) and the actor knowingly or recklessly:

---

[141] Tex. Penal Code Ann. § 31.03 (Vernon 1981).

      (i)   fails to record the name, address, and physical description or identification number of the seller or pledgor;

     (ii)   fails to record a complete description of the property, including the serial number, if reasonably available, or other identifying characteristics; or

    (iii)   fails to obtain a signed warranty from the seller or pledgor that the seller or pledgor has the right to possess the property. It is the express intent of this provision that the presumption arises unless the actor complies with each of the numbered requirements.

    (4)   for the purposes of Subparagraph (i) above, "identification number" means driver's license number, military identification number, identification certificate, or other official number capable of identifying an individual.

The elements of the crime are:

(a) unlawfully,
(b) appropriates property,
(c) with intent to deprive the owner of the property. Receiving stolen property is brought into the picture by the definition of unlawful appropriation of property.

This element is present if the prosecution proves that the property is stolen and that the person appropriates the property knowing it was stolen by another. This statute also requires that the prosecution prove knowledge on the part of the actor.

The Texas court, in 1976, pointed out that this is essentially the same as "receiving stolen property" under the Penal Code.[142] Here, the court held that the state must introduce corroborating evidences as to the possessory link between the defendant and the stolen property, but an accomplice's testimony will be sufficient, without corroboration, to establish the element of knowledge.

---

[142]   Cooper v. State, 537 S.W.2d 940 (Tex. Crim. App. 1976).

§ 6.8   Operating a Motor Vehicle Without the Owner's Consent

A. *Traditional Definitions and Elements*

Where one takes a motor vehicle with the intent to permanently deprive the owner of the vehicle, he is guilty of larceny. What if one takes the vehicle for the purpose of "joyriding" without the intent to permanently deprive the owner of the property? As this practice of taking an automobile, especially by a young person, for the purpose of driving the automobile temporarily, became common, the term "joyriding" was coined to refer to the act of the person who indulged in this unpermitted use of another's car.

When the courts determined that one of the elements of larceny was not present, and found that persons taking automobiles for such use were not guilty of larceny or any crime, not only the joyriders, but others who were caught with possession of the automobile, claimed they did not intend to deprive the owner of the property. As a result, statutes were modified or new statutes enacted to punish the act. In some states, the larceny statutes were modified so as to include unlawfully taking, driving or operating a motor vehicle without the knowledge and consent of the owner with the punishment the same as larceny.[143] Other specific statutes were designed to punish a person who temporarily took possession of automobiles and other motor vehicles for the purpose of temporarily depriving the owner of the use of the vehicle.

Due to the prevalence of the crime, when some of the statutes were enacted, the crime became a felony in many jurisdictions.[144] However, some of these were modified to reduce the grade of the offense to a misdemeanor and to include the unauthorized temporary use of any vehicles, including motor vehicles. Today, all states have statutes which make it possible to arrest and charge a person with taking of another's motor vehicle, even if it cannot be proven that the taking is to permanently deprive him of the property.

Although the statutes vary, the general provision is that "a person is guilty of unauthorized use of an automobile or other propelled vehicle when he knowingly operates, exercises the control over or otherwise uses such vehicle without the consent of the owner or person having legal possession thereof.[145]

---

[143]   Ky. Rev. Stat. § 433.220 (1975).

[144]   Iowa Code § 321.76 (1976).

[145]   Stovall v. N.Y. Indemnity Co., 157 Tenn. 301, 8 S.W.2d 473 (1928).

As indicated in the paragraphs above, this crime was added to the statutes in order to provide the punishment for one who operated a motor vehicle, but did not intend to deprive the owner permanently of the property. The elements, therefore, are:

(a) knowingly,
(b) operates, exercises control over, or otherwise uses,
(c) an automobile or other propelled vehicle,
(d) without the owner's consent.

B. Statutes and Codes

1. Model Penal Code

§ 223.9 Unauthorized Use of Automobiles and Other Vehicles[146]
A person commits a misdemeanor if he operates another's automobile, airplane, motorcycle, motorboat, or other motor-propelled vehicle without consent of the owner. It is an affirmative defense to prosecution under this Section that the actor reasonably believed that the owner would have consented to the operation had he known of it.

The coverage of the Model Penal Code is broad enough to include any motor-propelled vehicle. Although the consent of one other than the owner apparently will not justify the operation, the Code does explain that it is an affirmative defense if the actor reasonably believes that the owner would have consented to the operation had he known of it.

2. Federal Code

There is no general federal statute relating to the operation of a motor vehicle without the owner's consent.

---

[146] Model Penal Code § 223.9 (Proposed Official Draft 1980).

3. Other statutes and codes

While each state has a statute or code dealing with "joyriding," they differ in scope and even the penalty attached. Some include any vehicle, while others restrict the coverage to propelled vehicles. Some require that the person charged know that he does not have the consent of the owner,[147] while in other states it is an affirmative defense if the defendant reasonably believes that the owner would have consented.[148] In some states, the crime is still a felony, while in others it is a misdemeanor.[149]

An example of a state statute which is broad enough in scope to include the unauthorized use of any vehicle and also requires that the prosecution show that the person operating the vehicle knew that he did not have consent is that of New York.

This statute provides:

§ 165.05 Unauthorized use of a vehicle[150]
A person is guilty of unauthorized use of a vehicle when:

1. Knowing that he does not have the consent of the owner, he takes, operates, exercises control over, rides in or otherwise uses a vehicle. A person who engages in any such conduct without the consent of the owner is presumed to know that he does not have such consent; or

2. Having custody of a vehicle pursuant to an agreement between himself or another and the owner thereof whereby he or another is to perform for compensation a specific service for the owner involving the maintenance, repair or use of such vehicle, he intentionally uses or operates the same, without the consent of the owner, for his own purposes in a manner constituting a gross deviation from the agreed purpose; or

3. Having custody of a vehicle pursuant to an agreement with the owner thereof whereby such vehicle is to be returned to the owner at a specified time, he inten-

---

147   Ky. Rev. Stat. § 514.110 (1974).
148   Pa., N.J., Mass., W.Va.
149   Model Penal Code § 223.9 (Proposed Official Draft 1980) and following comments.
150   N.Y. Penal Law § 165.05 (1988).

tionally retains or withholds possession thereof, without the consent of the owner, for so lengthy a period beyond the specified time as to render such retention or possession a gross deviation from the agreement.

For purposes of this Section, "a gross deviation from the agreement" shall consist of, but not be limited to, circumstances wherein a person who having had custody of a vehicle for a period of fifteen days or less pursuant to a written agreement retains possession of such vehicle for at least seven days beyond the period specified in the agreement and continues such possession for a period of more than two days after service or refusal of attempted service of a notice in person or by certified mail at an address indicated in the agreement stating:

(i)   the date and time at which the vehicle was to have been returned under the agreement;

(ii)   that the owner does not consent to the continued withholding or retaining of such vehicle and demands its return; and that continued withholding or retaining of the vehicle may constitute a class A misdemeanor punishable by a fine of up to one thousand dollars or by a sentence to a term of imprisonment for a period of up to one year or by both such fine and imprisonment.

Unauthorized use of a vehicle is a class A misdemeanor.

In addition to providing a penalty where a person knowingly takes or operates a vehicle without the consent of the owner, the New York statute includes a provision that subjects short-term car renters to criminal liability for failure to return a rental car on time.

The elements of unauthorized use of a vehicle under paragraph (1) of the New York statute are:

(a) taking, operating, exercising control over, or riding in or otherwise using a vehicle,
(b) without the consent of the owner,
(c) knowledge that the owner has not consented.

Unlike some statutes, this specifically requires that knowledge be proven. In the case of *People v. Morris*, the New York Court confirmed that the knowledge requirement is an element of the crime.[151] On the other hand, where the evidence indicated the defendant personally took and used an automobile for two days, the offense of unauthorized use of the vehicle was committed as well as the offense of criminal possession of stolen property.[152]

In determining whether a police officer has the authority to arrest for violation of Subsection (3) of the New York statute, the court cautioned that officers do not have the authority to arrest a driver of an automobile where the rental agreement has expired eight days earlier until they run a "plate check" to determine whether the lessor had made a demand for the return of the vehicle.[153]

Some statutes are worded differently and some contain aggravating elements. For example, the Ohio statute provides:

§ 2913.03 Unauthorized Use of a Vehicle[154]
(A) No person shall knowingly use or operate an aircraft, motor vehicle, motorcycle, motorboat, or other motor-propelled vehicle without the consent of the owner or person authorized to give consent.
(B) No person shall knowingly use or operate an aircraft, motor vehicle, motorboat, or other motor-propelled vehicle without the consent of the owner or person authorized to give consent, and either remove it from this state, or keep possession of it for more than forty-eight hours.

Although both provisions of this Section define the offense commonly known as joyriding, they also cover joyriding in planes, motorcycles, motor boats and other motor-propelled vehicles. In addition, the offense is more serious if the vehicle is either taken out of the state or is kept by the offender for more than two days. The person who violates Subsection (A) is guilty of

---

[151] 73 App. Div. 2d 695, 423 N.Y.S.2d 224 (1979).
[152] People v. Ludolph, 63 App. Div. 385, 407 N.Y.S.2d 85 (1978).
[153] People v. Wright, 65 App. Div. 132, 410 N.Y.S.2d 619 (1978).
[154] Ohio Rev. Code Ann. § 2913.03 (Page 1987).

a misdemeanor in the first degree. If Subsection (B) is violated the crime is a felony in the fourth degree.

§ 6.9 Other Crimes Involving Theft

Although the contemporary statutes in the various states are more uniform than they were even 15 or 20 years ago, there are still specific acts that are offenses in some states but not in others. In this Section, some of the statutes that have not been discussed previously are included as examples of statutes that may or may not be found in the respective states.

A. Dealing in Stolen Property

Closely related to the crime of receiving stolen property is that entitled "dealing in stolen property." The Florida statute defines the crime in these terms:

§ 812.091 Dealing in Stolen Property[155]
(1) Any person who traffics in, or endeavors to traffic in, property that he knows or should know was stolen, shall be guilty of a felony of the second degree...
(2) Any person who initiates, organizes, plans, finances, directs, manages, or supervises the theft of property and traffics in such stolen property shall be guilty of a felony in the first degree...

It is obvious that this statute was enacted to make it possible to prosecute those involved in fencing and those who encourage others to steal property for the specific purpose of fencing it. The elements of the offense defined in Subsection (1) are:

(a) trafficking in or endeavoring to traffic in,
(b) property that is stolen or one should know was stolen.

Trafficking, as used in this Section, consists of buying and selling property. In interpreting this Section, a Florida Court proclaimed that a defendant can be convicted of endeavoring to traffic in property which was known to be stolen or which he should have known was stolen, even though the

---

[155] Fla. Stat. Ann. § 812.019 (West Supp. 1980).

prosecution did not prove that the goods in question had, in fact, been stolen.[156]

B. Theft of Services

Many states have provisions relating to the theft of designated services such as telephone service, while others have general statutes relating to the theft of services. An example is that of Texas, which provides:

§ 31.04 Theft of Service[157]

(a) A person commits theft of service if, with intent to avoid payment for service that he knows is provided only for compensation:

    (1) he intentionally or knowingly secures performance of the service by deception, threat, or false token;

    (2) having control over the disposition of services of another to which he is not entitled, he intentionally or knowingly diverts the other's services to his own benefit or to the benefit of another not entitled to them; or

    (3) having control of personal property under a written rental agreement, he holds the property beyond the expiration of the rental period without the effective consent of the owner of the property, thereby depriving the owner of the property of its use in further rentals.

(b) For purposes of this Section, intent to avoid payment is presumed if:

    (1) the actor absconded without paying for the service in circumstances where payment is ordinarily made immediately upon rendering of the service, as in hotels, restaurants, and comparable establishments; or

    (2) the actor failed to return the property held under a rental agreement within 10 days after receiving notice demanding return.

---

[156] Padgett v. State, 378 So. 2d 118 (Fla. Dist. Ct. App. 1980).

[157] Tex. Penal Code Ann. § 31.04 (Vernon 1977).

(c)   For purposes of Subsection (b)(2) of this Section, notice shall be notice in writing, sent by registered or certified mail with return receipt requested or by telegram with report of delivery requested, and addressed to the actor at his address shown on the rental agreement.

(d)   If written notice is given in accordance with Subsection (c) of this Section, it is presumed that the notice was received no later than five days after it was sent.

(e)   An offense under this Section is:

     (1)   a Class C misdemeanor if the value of the service stolen is less than $5;

     (2)   a Class B misdemeanor if the value of the service stolen is $5 or more but less than $20;

     (3)   a Class A misdemeanor if the value of the service stolen is $20 or more but less than $200;

     (4)   a felony of the third degree if the value of the service stolen is $200 or more but less than $10,000;

     (5)   a felony of the second degree if the value of the service stolen is $10,000 or more.

Under the provisions of this statute and similar statutes, the elements are:

(a)   receipt of services,

(b)   intent to avoid payment,

(c)   knowledge that services are provided only for compensation,

(d)   by one of the three methods indicated.[158]

C. Theft of Property Lost, Mislaid or Delivered by Mistake

One might argue that keeping property that is found, or that was delivered by mistake, should not be a crime. However, in most jurisdictions, the lawmakers have determined that failure to take reasonable measures to restore lost, mislaid or misdelivered property to the owner with the intent to deprive the owner of the property should be a crime, even though this was not a crime at common law. An example of a statute that punishes for theft

---

[158]   Model Penal Code § 223.7 (Proposed Official Draft 1980). *See* comments for states that have statutes relating to theft of services.

of property lost, mislaid or delivered by mistake is that of Kentucky. It provides:

> § 514.050. Theft of Property Lost, Mislaid, or Delivered by Mistake[159]
> (1) Except as provided in KRS 365.710, a person is guilty of theft of property lost, mislaid, or delivered by mistake when:
>
>> (a) he comes into control of the property of another that he knows to have been lost, mislaid, or delivered under a mistake as to the nature or amount of the property or the identity of the recipient; and
>> (b) with intent to deprive the owner thereof, he fails to take reasonable measures to restore the property to a person entitled to have it.
>
> (2) Theft of property lost, mislaid, or delivered by mistake is a Class A misdemeanor unless the value of the property is $100, in which case it is a Class D felony.

Under the Kentucky statute and like statutes, the elements of the offense are:

(a) control of property by suspect,
(b) property of another,
(c) knowledge that property had been lost, mislaid, or mistakenly delivered,
(d) intent to deprive the owner of the property and
(e) failure to take reasonable measures to restore the property to the person entitled to it.

D. Unauthorized Use of Property

In Ohio, a statute entitled "Unauthorized Use of Property" deals with unauthorized use of property other than a vehicle. It provides:

---

[159] Ky. Rev. Stat. 514.050 (1979). *See* Model Penal Code § 223.5 (Proposed Official Draft 1980) for states that have adopted similar statutes.

§ 2913.04 Unauthorized Use of Property. [160]

(A) No person shall knowingly use or operate the property of another without the consent of the owner or person authorized to give consent.

The statute provides for the same affirmative defenses that are available to one who is charged with unauthorized use of a vehicle.

Under the provisions of this statute, the elements are:

(a) *knowingly,*
(b) uses or operates,
(c) property of another,
(d) without the consent of the owner or person authorized to give consent.

E. Possession of Altered Property

Another example of a specific crime designed for a specific purpose is that of Florida which relates to the possession of altered property. This statute provides:

§ 812.016 Possession of Altered Property[161]

Any dealer in property who knew or should have known the identifying features, such as serial numbers and permanently affixed labels, of property in his possession has been removed or altered without the consent of the manufacturer, shall be guilty of a misdemeanor of the first degree....

The elements of this offense are:

(a) the suspect is a dealer in property,
(b) knowledge or constructive knowledge that identifying features had been removed or altered,
(c) without the consent of the manufacturer.

This list of crimes involving theft is not intended to be exhaustive. There are, in fact, many other crimes involving theft that are included in various federal, state, and local statutes, codes and ordinances.

---

[160] Ohio Rev. Code Ann. § 2913.04 (Page 1987).

[161] Fla. Stat. Ann. § 812.016 (West 1977).

§ 6.10 Summary

In the United States, most crimes are crimes against property, and numerically, the majority of these crimes against property involve theft in one way or another. Criminal justice personnel devote a good part of their time to the prevention and investigation of crimes that involve theft.

Although, in many states today, the specific theft crimes of larceny, embezzlement, extortion and others are combined in a single statute, these and other common law and statutory crimes are important, as many states retain the statutes dealing with each separately.

Robbery is often considered in the category of "Offenses Against the Person"; however, this crime is considered in this chapter as it is closely related to other theft crimes. Robbery is defined as the felonious taking of money or goods of value from the person of another or in his presence against his will, by force or putting him in fear. It was a felony at common law and is a felony today in practically all states. The elements that distinguish it from larceny and other theft crimes are "taking from the person or presence of the other," and "the taking is accompanied by means of force or putting in fear." Because of these aggravating elements, the penalty for the crime of robbery is more severe than that for other theft crimes.

At common law, larceny was the only form of unaggravated theft that was criminally punishable. One definition of larceny is the felonious taking of property of another without his consent and against his will with the intent to convert it to the use of the taker or to another. In addition to the element of trespass, other technical elements are taking, carrying away, of the personal property, of another, with intent to steal. If any of these elements are not present, there can be no larceny.

Although embezzlement was not a crime under early English common law, the English legislative body created a new crime to fill the gaps resulting from the technical definition of the elements of larceny. The chief distinction between larceny and embezzlement lies in the manner of acquiring possession of the property. In embezzlement, the property comes lawfully into the possession of the taker but is fraudulently or unlawfully appropriated by him, while in larceny there is a trespass in the unlawful taking of the property.

Another statutorily-created crime is that of obtaining property by false pretenses. This is distinguished from larceny in that the property comes into the possession of the taker not by a trespass or taking, but as a result of false pretenses with intent to defraud. It differs from embezzlement in that, in embezzlement, the property comes lawfully into the possession of the taker, while in false pretenses crimes, the perpetrator obtains title and possession of the property by means of deception. The key element that distinguishes this crime from others is "deception."

If one obtains property of another by means of threats or by coercion and the other elements are present, then the crime is extortion. Extortion was originally limited to obtaining money or things of value through misuse of official power. However, in most states, a private individual, as well as an official, may be found guilty of this crime.

In an effort to reduce the theft of property by punishing those who receive the property, most states have statutes relating to "receiving stolen property." The general definition is "receiving stolen property knowing it to have been stolen with the intent to deprive the owner of it."

When the early courts determined that one of the elements of larceny was not present where a vehicle was taken for the purpose of "joyriding," statutes were enacted to cover this action. In most states, a person is guilty of unauthorized use of an automobile or other propelled vehicle when he knowingly operates, exercises control over, or otherwise uses such vehicle without the consent of the owner or person having legal possession thereof. Under such a statute, a person may be guilty of a crime even though the prosecution does not prove that the user of the vehicle intended to permanently deprive the owner of the property.

To protect the public against those who would deprive persons of their property, states have enacted various theft crimes. Among these are "dealing in stolen property," "theft of services," "theft of lost, mislaid, or property delivered by mistake" and "possession of altered property."

Various federal, state and local statutes, codes and ordinances include other theft crimes designed to protect the public against those who would, by some means, seek to deprive owners of property.

Chapter 7
FORGERY AND
OTHER FRAUD OFFENSES

While it is true that there is a distinction between fraud and forgery, and forgery contains some elements that are not included in fraud, yet all forgeries are a species of fraud.

47 *Corpus Juris Secundum*,
Forgery, Section 1

§ 7.1 Introduction

For centuries, the legislative bodies and courts have been attempting to determine what acts relating to cheating should be made criminal. In England, various types of cheating were made crimes under the early common law. For example, in 1511, it was a crime to add oil or water to woolcloth or to overstretch cloth.[1] On the other hand, early courts and legislatures were hesitant to make simple dishonesty in business a crime, reasoning that a certain amount of dishonesty in business was expected.[2] In 1541, a statute was enacted in England which made it a crime to counterfeit letters or privy tokens or to receive money or goods in other men's names.[3] One who violated this statute was subject to "such correction and punishment, by imprisonment of his body, setting upon the pillory, or otherwise any corporal pain as shall be upon him or them limited, adjudged or appointed by the person or persons before whom he shall be so convicted of said offenses, or any of them."[4]

As the law developed in England and in the United States, criminal statutes were enacted to make it a crime for various types of cheating and fraud.[5] The extensive use of checks and other commercial paper made it necessary that specific statutes be developed in the various states to punish for making false documents or altering documents with intent to defraud.

In this chapter, the more common of forgery and fraud offenses are discussed in detail with other lesser used crimes defined in less detail. The crime that is best known is forgery. Closely related to this is uttering a forged instrument. In addition to these and related offenses, false advertising, commercial bribery and other business and commercial fraud crimes are designated and distinguished.

§ 7.2 Forgery

One of the most common crimes in our society today is forgery. After some hesitation to enact fraud statutes, lawmakers and merchants recognized that there is a strong social interest in maintaining the genuineness of checks and other commercial paper. If false instruments are prevalent in a community or society, a serious handicap is placed upon the use of genuine documents.

---

[1]   33 Hen. 8, c. 6 (1511).

[2]   L. Salzman, ENGLISH LIFE IN THE MIDDLE AGES (1926).

[3]   33 Hen. 8, c. 1 (1541).

[4]   Id.

[5]   State v. Brewer, 258 N.C. 533, 129 S.E.2d 262 (1963). *See* case in Part II.

A. Traditional Definitions and Elements

One definition of forgery is the "fraudulent making or alteration of a writing to the prejudice of another man's right."[6] Another definition provides: the "false making or materially altering, with intent to defraud, of any writing which, if genuine, might apparently be a legal efficacy or the foundation of a legal liability."[7] This last definition has been criticized for using the term "false making" rather than "false writing" and for using more words than are needed to express the meaning.[8] Statutes in all states have provisions relating to forgery. These statutes, for the most part, include the coverage of the common law, sometimes extend the law to include crimes not heretofore within the scope of the common law offense and often increase the severity of punishment.

Other definitions of the term "forgery" are:

"Forgery" is the false making of an instrument, which purports on the face of it to be good and valid for purposes for which it was created, with a design to defraud any person or persons.[9]

"Forgery" requires the making of a writing which falsely purports to be the writing of another, with intent to defraud, and the crime may exist even though the name is fictitious when the fictitious name is shown to have been used with intent to defraud.[10]

At early common law, forgery belonged to the class of misdemeanors called "cheats," and was regarded as a misdemeanor, not as a felony.[11] Later, it was designated a felony in both English and American statutes. Under the modern statutes, forgery is often divided into categories dependent upon the article forged and the amount involved.

Under the traditional definition, the elements of the crime of forgery are:

---

[6]　Ratcliff v. State, 175 Tenn. 172, 133 S.W.2d 470 (1939).

[7]　4 Blackstone, COMMENTARIES 247, 2 Bish. Cr. Law, § 523.

[8]　Perkins, CRIMINAL LAW ＿＿＿ (1957).

[9]　State v. Goranson, 408 P.2d 7 (Wash. 1965).

[10]　State v. Charles, 341 So. 2d 539 (Fla. 1977).

[11]　State v. Murphy, 17 R.I. 698, 24 A. 473 (1892).

(1) Fraudulent or false writing or alteration. It is an indispensable requirement of forgery that the writing be false. It may have been false in its inception or may be made so by subsequent tampering with what was originally genuine.[12]

(2) Writing or document. The subject of forgery may be a deed, a mortgage, a check, bill of exchange, order for goods or money, receipt, and even a diploma.[13] Statistically most forgery cases that reach the courts concern the forgery of checks or money orders. However, any writing or document may be forged and the subject prosecuted if all of the elements are present. For example, a conviction of forgery of a driver's license and a birth certificate by the defendant where the defendant used these documents to establish an identity he assumed as an alias, was proper where statute defined forgery as the "false making or altering of any writing . . ."[14]

(3) Intent to defraud. Unless there is intent to prejudice another's right, there is no crime of forgery. As one court explained, the intent is the very essence of forgery.[15] However, it is immaterial whether anyone is actually defrauded.[16]

(4) Forgery or alteration is material. While this is not spelled out in the definition itself, the courts have insisted that the forgery or the alteration must be material; that is, it must have prejudicial effect. However, even a slight change in the legal meaning will be material and hence an alteration. In one case, the court agreed that it was not forgery to change the figures on a check to correspond with the sum recited in words (a statute provided that where there is a discrepancy, the sum expressed by the words is that payable), since the alteration did not change the legal effect of the instrument.[17]

---

[12] State v. Young, 46 N.H. 266 (1865).

[13] Hicks v. State, 176 Ga. 727, 168 S.E. 899 (1933); Saucier v. State, 102 Miss. 647, 59 So. 858 (1912).

[14] State v. Fraley, 499 So. 2d 1304 (La. 1986). *See* case in Part II.

[15] Ratliff v. State, 175 Tenn. 172, 133 S.E.2d 470 (1939).

[16] People v. Henderson, 373 N.E.2d 1338 (Ill. 1978) 71 Ill. 2d 53.

[17] People v. Lewinger, 25 Ill. 332, 96 N.E. 837 (1911).

In the case of *State v. Fraley*, the Court of Appeals of Louisiana, Fourth Circuit, after citing other cases, defined the crime of forgery and explained the elements. First defining the elements, the court noted those elements are:

(1) issuing or transferring,
(2) with intent to defraud,
(3) a forged writing,
(4) known by the defendant to be forged.

The court explained that the essence of the crime of forgery is that the writing purports to be the act of another. As to intent, it is not necessary to prove that the offender intended to defraud any particular person; intent may be inferred from the circumstances and transactions in the case.

B. Contemporary Statutes and Codes

1. Model Penal Code

§ 224.1 Forgery.[18]

(1) Definition. A person is guilty of forgery if, with purpose to defraud or injure anyone, or with knowledge that he is facilitating a fraud or injury to be perpetrated by anyone, the actor:

    (a) alters any writing of another without his authority; or
    (b) makes, completes, executes, authenticates, issues or transfers any writing so that it purports to be the act of another who did not authorize that act, or to have been executed at a time or place or in a numbered sequence other than was in fact the case, or to be a copy of an original when no such original existed; or
    (c) utters any writing which he knows to be forged in a manner specified in paragraphs (a) or (b).

"Writing" includes printing or any other method of recording information, money, coins, tokens, stamps, seals, credit cards, badges, trademarks and other symbols of value, right, privilege or identification.

---

[18] Model Penal Code, § 224.1 (Proposed Official Draft 1980).

(2) Grading. Forgery is a felony of the second degree if the writing
is or purports to be part of an issue of money, securities,
postage, or revenue stamps, or other instruments issued by the
government, or part of an issue of stock, bonds, or other instruments representing interests in or claims against any property or enterprise. Forgery is a felony of the third degree if the
writing is or purports to be a will, deed, contract, release,
commercial instrument, or other document evidencing, creating, transferring, altering, terminating, or otherwise affecting
legal relations. Otherwise forgery is a misdemeanor.

Rather than enumerating the various documents that are included within
the crime of forgery, the Model Code uses the term "writing" and defines
writing very comprehensively. Also, the Code provision includes what was
defined under previous provisions as uttering a forged instrument. Instead of
the term "intent to defraud," the Code uses "with purpose to defraud or injure
anyone." Subsection (1) provides that forgery is committed if the defendant
acts "with knowledge that he is facilitating a fraud or injury to be perpetrated
by anyone." This makes it clear that a forger commits an offense even though
he does not defraud the person to whom he sells or passes a forged writing.

2. Federal Codes

Title 18 of the Federal Code does not include a Section on the crime of
forgery.

3. Other statutes and codes

Many of the contemporary statutes use comprehensive language to describe what type of document will be included. Some states retain the traditional wording and rely upon the cases for interpretation. Others are more
specific as to the definitions of what instruments are subject to forgery and
what conduct is prohibited. The Kentucky Statute defines a "written instrument" as "any instrument or article containing written or printed matter or its
equivalent used for the purpose of reciting, embodying, conveying, or
recording information, or constituting a symbol or evidence of value, right,
privilege, or identification, which is capable of being used to the advantage or
disadvantage of some person."[19] The statute goes on to identify a "complete
written instrument" and an "incomplete written instrument."[20] To leave no

---

[19] Ky. Rev. Stat. § 516.010(1) (1975).
[20] Ky. Rev. Stat. §§ 516.010(2)-(3) (1975).

doubt what conduct is prohibited, the statute defines what is meant by "falsely altering," "falsely completing" and "falsely making."[21]

Some state statutes have only one degree of forgery. In Ohio, the statute reads:

§ 2913.31 Forgery.[22]

(A) No person, with purpose to defraud, or knowing that he is facilitating a fraud, shall do any of the following:

(1) Forge any writing of another without his authority;
(2) Forge any writing so that it purports to be genuine when it is actually spurious, or to be the act of another who did not authorize that act, or to have been executed at a time or place or with terms different from what was in fact the case, or to be a copy of an original when no such original existed;
(3) Utter, or possess with purpose to utter, any writing which he knows to have been forged.

The definition of "writing" as used in the Ohio Code, includes not only legal and commercial documents traditionally covered by forgery, but also private non-commercial documents not formerly covered. The subject of forgery under this Section may also include any symbol of value, right, privilege or identification, such as credit cards, I.D. cards, trademarks and others. The definition of "forge" comprehends all forms of falsification purporting to authenticate a writing.

In some statutes, the crime of forgery is graded depending on the instrument forged or altered. An example is the Kentucky statute, which designates money, stamps, securities or other valuable instruments issued by a government agency as those instruments that will subject the maker to forgery in the First Degree. Forgery in the Second Degree is the proper charge when such instruments as deeds, wills, contracts and other commercial instruments are forged. Where other instruments are forged or altered, the offense charged is forgery in the Third Degree.[23]

Where knowledge and intent are indicated as elements, the prosecution must introduce evidence to show both the knowledge and the intent. In a Michigan case, the defendant asked a truck-stop cashier to cash a U.S. Trea-

---

[21] Ky. Rev. Stat. §§ 516.010(4)-(5) (1975).
[22] Ohio Rev. Code Ann. § 2913.31 (Page 1987).
[23] Ky. Rev. Stat. §§ 516.020-516.040 (1975).

sury check.[24] The cashier called the police. It was later determined that the check had been stolen and the payee's name forged. The reviewing court held that there are two requisite elements of the crime of publishing and uttering; namely knowledge of the falsity of the instrument and intent to defraud. The court explained, in this case, that the knowledge of the falsity of the check was proven only by weak evidence and was "clearly not inconsistent with other reasonable hypotheses upon which the defendant's innocence might be maintained." The court concluded that without clear proof of knowledge and intent, a conviction cannot stand.

A similar result was reached in a Texas case where the reviewing court held:

> Thus, a necessary element of forgery is that the accused have the intent to defraud or harm another. In a prosecution for forgery, the burden is on the prosecution to prove every element of the offense charged.[25]

§ 7.3 Uttering a Forged Instrument

A. Traditional Definition and Elements

Uttering a forged instrument is offering as genuine an instrument known to be false with intent to defraud.[26]

To utter a forged instrument is to offer it, directly or indirectly, by words or actions, as good. This, if done with intent to defraud, and with knowledge of the falsity of the instrument, is a violation at common law and is made a violation by statutes in some form in all states. Uttering is a distinct offense and is not the same as forgery, although in some statutes the two are combined in one Section.[27] The forged instrument is "uttered" when there is an attempt to make use of it. It is not necessary that there be anything more than a declaration that the instrument is good; it need not be actually passed and accepted.[28] In the case of *State v. Meeks*, the court declared that one may be guilty of uttering a forged instrument, although he does not succeed in getting anything from the one to whom it was offered.

---

24   People v. Mask, 68 Mich. App. 104, 241 N.W.2d 777 (1976).

25   Stuebgen v. State, 547 S.W.2d 29 (Tex. 1977).

26   Maloney v. State, 91 Ark. 485, 121 S.W. 728 (1909).

27   State v. Williams, 152 Mo. 115, 53 S.W. 424 (1899); People v. Brown, 397 Ill. 92, 72 N.E.2d 859 (1947).

28   State v. Meeks, 245 Iowa 1231, 65 N.W.2d 76 (1954); Finley v. Commonwealth, 259 S.W.2d 32 (Ky. 1953).

The elements of the crime of uttering a forged instrument are:

(1) uttering – published or offered,
(2) a forged instrument,
(3) offered or published as true or genuine,
(4) knowledge on the part of the offerer that, the instrument is false,
(5) with intent to defraud.

Both early cases and more recent cases agree that the mere offer of a false instrument with fraudulent intent constitutes an uttering. Therefore, where a defendant presented two falsely made checks, knowing the same to be false, to two tellers at two bank branches and thereby attempted to obtain money, the crime of uttering was complete.[29] And forwarding a forged check to the clerk's office to be recorded, knowing it to be a forgery, was uttering.[30]

As indicated, one of the elements of uttering a forged instrument is that the prosecution prove that the instrument was, in fact, forged. This element is present when it is demonstrated that the person who signed another's name did so without authority.[31]

Knowledge on the part of the offender is an essential requirement. However, such knowledge may be established by circumstantial evidence. For example, flight by the defendant, when he saw the one to whom the check was offered go to the telephone, was a strong circumstance indicating guilty knowledge.[32] And in another case, where the suspect drove away from a bank window, after a bank teller attempted to stall the defendant as another teller phoned the police, this conduct of the defendant was evidence of knowledge and intent.[33]

B. Contemporary Statutes and Codes

1. Model Penal Code

The traditional crime of uttering a forged instrument is included in § 224.1 of the Model Penal Code relating to forgery. The specific provision of the code which applies to uttering a forged instrument is:

---

[29] State v. Seraphem, 368 S.E.2d 643 (N.C. App. 1988).

[30] Thomas v. State, 144 Tex. 533, 164 S.W.2d 852 (1942).

[31] State v. Phillips, 256 N.C. 445, 124 S.E.2d 146 (1962).

[32] Smith v. State, 291 P.2d 378 (Okla. 1955).

[33] Ramsey v. Commonwealth, 343 S.E.2d 465 (Va. App. 1986).

(1) Definition. A person is guilty of forgery if, with purpose to defraud or injure anyone, or with knowledge that he is facilitating a fraud or injury to be perpetrated by anyone, the actor:

...

(c) utters any writing which he knows to be forged in a manner specified in paragraphs (a) or (b).[34]

The penalty for uttering a forged instrument is the same as that provided for forgery.

2. Other statutes and codes

Some states consolidate forgery and uttering a forged instrument, as does the Model Code, but use different terminology. For example, in Nebraska a person is guilty of forgery if the state proves issuing, authenticating, transferring, selling, transmitting, using, presenting, passing, delivering or causing such uttering.[35]

In other states, the crime of uttering a forged instrument is a separate statute and, in some instances, there are separate degrees of the offense.

§ 7.4 Miscellaneous Forgery-Related Offenses

The drafters of legislation in the various states have determined that the forgery statutes, as written, are not broad enough to cover some acts which should be criminal offenses. Some of those are briefly discussed here. It should be noted, however, that this is not meant to be exhaustive, as there are other designations and descriptions of offenses not herein included.

A. Criminal Simulation

Criminal simulation statutes are designed to prohibit forgery where the subject of the offense is not a writing but an object. For example, the Ohio statute provides:

---

[34]   Model Penal Code § 224.1(1)(c) (Proposed Official Draft 1980).

[35]   Neb. Rev. Stat. § 28-605(9) (1943).

(A) No person, with purpose to defraud, or knowing that he is facilitating a fraud, shall do any of the following:

    (1) Make or alter any object so that it appears to have value because of antiquity, rarity, curiosity, source, or authorship, which it does not in fact possess;

    (2) Practice deception in making, retouching, editing, or reproducing any photograph, movie film, video tape, phonograph record, or recording tape;

    (3) Utter, or possess with purpose to utter, any object which he knows to have been simulated as provided in division (A)(1) or (2) of this Section.[36]

B. Misuse of Credit Cards

As the use of credit cards became common, states were forced to enact statutes which covered the various offenses involving the improper use of such cards. An example is that of Ohio, which provides:

(A) No person shall do any of the following:

    (1) Practice deception for the purpose of procuring the issuance of a credit card, when a credit card is issued in actual reliance thereon;

    (2) Knowingly buy or sell a credit card from or to a person other than the issuer.

(B) No person, with purpose to defraud, shall do any of the following:

    (1) Obtain control over a credit card as security for a debt;

    (2) Obtain property or services by the use of a credit card, in one or more transactions, knowing or having reasonable cause to believe that such card has expired or been revoked, or was obtained, is retained, or is being used in violation of law;

---

[36]   Ohio Rev. Code Ann. § 2913.32 (Page 1987). *See also* Ky. Rev. Stat. § 516.100 (1975) and Model Penal Code § 224.2 (Proposed Official Draft 1980), which includes comments relating to states having similar statutes.

(3) Furnish property or services upon presentation of a
    credit card, knowing that such card is being used in
    violation of law;
(4) Represent or cause to be represented to the issuer of
    a credit card that property or services have been fur-
    nished, knowing that such representation is false.[37]

Among other things, this statute prohibits the use of deception in obtaining a credit card in the first instance, buying or selling a credit card, obtaining property or services with a credit card with knowledge that the credit
card has expired or has been revoked. It also provides a penalty for the business operator who furnishes property or services and charges it to a credit
card knowing that such a card is being used in violation of the law.

In some states, the wording is different than that of Ohio.[38] Some provisions require an intent to defraud; others omit any intent requirements.

C. Possession of a Forgery Device

As the forgery statute does not cover the possession of a forgery device,
some states have enacted special legislation to cover this act. An example is
that of Kentucky which provides:

(1) A person is guilty of possession of a forgery device when he:

    (a) Makes or possesses with knowledge of its character
        any plate, die or other device, apparatus, equipment
        or article specifically designed or adapted for use in
        forging written instruments; or
    (b) Makes or possesses with knowledge of its character
        any device, apparatus, equipment or article capable
        of or adaptable to use in forging written instruments
        with the intent to use it himself or to aid or permit
        another to use it for purposes of forgery.[39]

As used in this statute, a "forgery device" means "a plate for counterfeiting, to reproduce tax stamps, or trading stamps, a hard printing set, or rubber

---

[37] Ohio Rev. Code Ann. § 2913.21 (Page 1987).
[38] Model Penal Code § 224.6 (Proposed Official Draft 1980).
[39] Ky. Rev. Stat. § 516.090 (1975).

stamp equipment."[40] One of the elements of this crime is knowledge; therefore, it is incumbent upon the state to prove the required knowledge element.

D. Other Forgery-Related Offenses

Other offenses that are related to forgery are using slugs,[41] fraudulent destruction, removal or concealment of recordable instruments,[42] and tampering with records.[43]

Some other examples of statutes designed to protect the public against those who would obtain property by false representation are criminal impersonation, impersonating a public servant, and impersonating a peace officer.[44]

§ 7.5   False Advertising

A. Traditional Definition and Elements

Although false advertising, as such, was not a crime at common law, making untrue and fraudulent statements about products became so extensive that both municipal and state governments deemed it necessary for the proper protection of the public to prohibit the practice. As a consequence, numerous statutes and ordinances have been enacted prohibiting false or fraudulent statements in advertising.

The crime of false advertising consists primarily in the publication and circulation of deceptive matter and the offense is completed without regard to whether anyone is deceived or damaged.[45]

The elements of the crime, as stated in most statutes and ordinances, are:

(a) publication,
(b) false or misleading statement or representation,
(c) concerning merchandise or anything of value,

---

[40] Ky. Penal Code Notebook, Ky. Dept. of Justice § 7.1 (1975).

[41] Ky. Rev. Stat. §§ 516.120-516.130 (1975); Ohio Rev. Code Ann. § 2913.33 (Page 1987).

[42] Model Penal Code § 224.3 (Proposed Official Draft 1980).

[43] Model Penal Code § 224.4 (Proposed Official Draft 1980).

[44] Neb. Rev. Stat. §§ 28-608-28-610 (1943).

[45] Annot., 89 ALR 1005 (1919).

(d) with intent to sell, barter, or exchange,

(e) intent to deceive or mislead any other person.

B. Contemporary Statutes and Codes

In today's society, advertising has become a way of life with radio, television and other means of conveying messages to the public. The dangers of false advertising have become more and more apparent. On the other hand, the average citizen has become more aware that advertisers will exaggerate their product and are familiar with the term *caveat emptor* (let the buyer beware). As a result, framers of legislative enactments to control false advertising and other deceptive practices had difficulty in fixing responsibility. Generally, the contemporary statutes and codes are more comprehensive than the traditional statutes and have tended to fix responsibility on those who are in a position to know that the advertising is false or misleading.

1. Model Penal Code

§ 224.7 Deceptive Business Practices[46]

A person commits a misdemeanor if, in the course of business, he:

(1) uses or possesses for use a false weight or measure, or any other device for falsely determining or recording any quality or quantity; or

(2) sells, offers or exposes for sale, or delivers less than the represented quantity of any commodity or service; or

(3) takes or attempts to take more than the represented quantity of any commodity or service when as buyer he furnishes the weight or measure; or

(4) sells, offers or exposes for sale adulterated or mislabeled commodities. "Adulterated" means varying from the standard of composition or quality prescribed by or pursuant to any statute providing criminal penalties for such variance, or set by established commercial usage. "Mislabeled" means varying from the standard of truth or disclosure in labeling prescribed by or pursuant to any statute providing criminal penalties for such variance, or set by established commercial usage; or

(5) makes a false or misleading statement in any advertisement addressed to the public or to a substantial segment thereof for

---

[46] Model Penal Code § 224.7 (Proposed Official Draft 1980).

the purpose of promoting the purchase or sale of property or services; or

(6) makes a false or misleading written statement for the purpose of obtaining property or credit; or

(7) makes a false or misleading written statement for the purpose of promoting the sale of securities, or omits information required by law to be disclosed in written documents relating to securities.

It is an affirmative defense to prosecution under this Section if the defendant proves, by a preponderance of the evidence, that his conduct was not knowingly or recklessly deceptive.

The drafters of the Model Code consolidated several older crimes relating to cheating and deceptive practices into one comprehensive statute. Paragraphs (5), (6), and (7) deal with situations where false or misleading statements are made for specific purposes. Under this provision, the criminality of the conduct is not on making statements, oral or written, but upon making "misleading" statements. The last paragraphs of the Code provide an affirmative defense if the defendant proves, by a preponderance of the evidence, that his conduct was not knowingly or recklessly deceptive.

2. Federal Code

There is no specific provision in the U.S. Code designated "false premises."

3. Other statutes and codes

Recognizing the persuasive arguments for consolidating the crimes relating to false advertising, cheating and other deceptive practices into a single statute, legislatures of some states enacted such comprehensive statutes. However, some states retain separate provisions concerning false advertising. An example is that of Kentucky. It states:

A person is guilty of false advertising when, in connection with the promotion of the sale of or to increase the consumption of property or services, he knowingly makes or causes to be made a false or misleading statement in any advertisement addressed to the public or to a substantial number of persons.[47]

---

[47] Ky. Rev. Stat. § 517.030 (1975).

Under the provisions of this and other similar statutes, the elements are:

(a) knowingly making or causing to be made a false or misleading statement,

(b) for the promotion of the sale or to increase the consumption of property, and

(c) the advertisement is addressed to the public.

In addition to false advertising statutes, some states have specific provisions which explicitly deal with "bait advertising." One statute provides:

A person is guilty of bait advertising when in any manner, including advertising or other means of communication, he offers to the public or a substantial number of persons property or service as part of a scheme or plan with the intent not to sell or provide the advertised property or services:

(a) At the price which he offered them; or

(b) In a quantity sufficient to meet the reasonable expected public demand, unless the quantity is specifically stated in the advertisement; or

(c) At all.[48]

§ 7.6 Commercial Bribery

A. Traditional Definition and Elements

At common law, bribery was a crime but was limited to the offering, giving, receiving or soliciting anything of value with intent to influence the recipient's action as a *public* official.[49] The earlier cases recognized that commercial bribery should be a matter of concern in the criminal law as well as under tort law, and statutes were enacted to control commercial bribery.[50] The purpose of the statutes regarding commercial bribery are to outlaw collusion and kickbacks in commercial and business affairs.

---

[48] Ky. Rev. Stat. § 517.040 (1975).

[49] Bribery of public officials is discussed in a later chapter.

[50] People v. Davis, 160 N.Y.S. 769 (1951); State v. Brewer, 258 N.C. 533, 129 S.E.2d 262 (1963). *See* case in Part II.

1. Definition

The New York statute, which is similar to those of other jurisdictions, provides in part:

> A person who gives, offers or promises to an agent, employee or servant of another, any gift or gratuity whatever, without the knowledge or consent of the principal, employer or master of such agent, employee or servant, with intent to influence such agent's, employee's or servant's action in relation to the principal's, employer's or master's business . . . is guilty of a misdemeanor and shall be punished by fine of not more than $500, or by imprisonment of not more than one year or by both such fine and imprisonment.[51]

The remainder of the comprehensive statute defines other relationships that are covered.[52] This part of the statute encompasses the bribery of general agents and employees. The bribe must be given for the purpose of affecting the employer's business and be undisclosed to the employer.

2. Elements

Under this part of the New York statute and similar statutes, the elements are:

(a) giving, offering or promising,
(b) any gift or gratuity,
(c) to an agent, employee, or servant of another,
(d) without the knowledge and consent of the principal, employer or master of such agent, etc.,
(e) with intent to influence such agent's, employee's or servant's action in relation to the principal's, employer's, or master's business.

Very early, the courts upheld this type of commercial bribery statute against the challenge that it was unconstitutional. In the case of *People v. Davis*, a purchasing agent, R.H. Masey, was indicted for accepting $10 in

---

[51] N.Y. Penal Law § 439 (McKinney 1980).

[52] *See, Control of Nongovernmental Corruption by Criminal Legislation*, 108 U. PA. L. REV. 848 (1960), for an analysis and chart, p. 864, listing states that had enacted legislation relating to bribery at that time.

connection with the purchase of sponges.[53]   The defendant attacked the statute as unconstitutional on the ground that it violated equal protection and freedom of contract, and that the state did not have police power to enact such statutes. The court upheld the statute, finding that the state, under its police power, did have authority to enact such statutes for "without such a statute under the fierce competition of modern life, purchasing agents . . . can be lured all too readily into service of hopelessly conflicting interests." The court also agreed that the statute did not violate the equal protection clause of the Constitution and was not in conflict with the agent's freedom of contract.

B. Contemporary Statutes and Codes

1. Model Penal Code

§ 224.8   Commercial Bribery and Breach of Duty
          to Act Disinterestedly[54]

(1) A person commits a misdemeanor if he solicits, accepts or agrees to accept any benefit as consideration for knowingly violating or agreeing to violate a duty of fidelity to which he is subject as:

   (a) partner, agent, or employee of another;
   (b) trustee, guardian, or other fiduciary;
   (c) lawyer, physician, accountant, appraiser, or other professional adviser or informant;
   (d) officer, director, manager· or other participant in the direction of the affairs of an incorporated or unincorporated association; or
   (e) arbitrator or other purportedly disinterested adjudicator or referee.

(2) A person who holds himself out to the public as being engaged in the business of making disinterested selection, appraisal, or criticism of commodities or services commits a misdemeanor if he solicits, accepts or agrees to accept any benefit to influence his selection, appraisal or criticism.

---

[53] People v. Davis, 33 N.Y. Crim. 460, 160 N.Y.S. 769 (1915).
[54] Model Penal Code § 224.8 (Proposed Official Draft 1980).

(3) A person commits a misdemeanor if he confers, or offers or agrees to confer, any benefit the acceptance of which would be criminal under this Section.

The Model Penal Code provision is entitled Commercial Bribery and Breach of Duty to Act Disinterestedly. This is more comprehensive than the traditional statutes relating to commercial bribery. Under the provisions of the Code, a person who solicits, accepts or agrees to accept a consideration must do so "knowingly violating or agreeing to violate a duty of fidelity" in certain specified relationships. In those states that have used this terminology, the prosecution must introduce evidence to prove the mental element "knowingly." Also, the prosecution must prove the relationship such as partner, agent or employee as specified in the Code existed at the time of the transaction.

2. Federal Code

The U.S. Code has no specific offense on commercial bribery.

3. Other statutes and codes

Some states use terminology similar to that of the Model Code, but add to the list of categories of persons subject to prosecution for accepting a bribe. For example, the Nebraska statute adds:

Duly elected or appointed representative or trustee of a labor organization or employee of a welfare trust fund.[55]

Other statutes take a different approach. The statute of the state of Louisiana includes this Section:

§ 73. Commercial bribery[56]
Commercial bribery is the giving or offering to give, directly or indirectly, anything of apparent present or prospective value to any private agent, employee, or fiduciary, without the knowledge and consent of the principal or employer, with the intent to influence such agent's, employee's, or fiduciary's action in relation to the principal's or employer's affairs.

---

[55]   Neb. Rev. Stat. § 28-613 (1978).

[56]   La. Rev. Stat. Ann. § 14:73 (West 1986).

The agent's, employee's or fiduciary's acceptance of or offer to accept, directly or indirectly, anything of apparent present or prospective value under such circumstances shall also constitute commercial bribery.

The offender under this article who states the facts, under oath, to the district attorney charged with prosecution of the offense, and who gives evidence tending to convict any other offender under this article, may, in the discretion of the district attorney, be granted full immunity from prosecution for commercial bribery, in respect to the particular offense reported.

Whoever commits the crime of commercial bribery shall be fined not more than five hundred dollars, or imprisoned for not more than six months, or both.

To convict a person for violation of this statute, these elements must be proved:

(a) giving or offering to give,
(b) anything of value,
(c) to a private agent, employee or fiduciary,
(d) without the knowledge and consent of the principal or employer,
(e) with intent to influence the fiduciary's action in relation to the principal's or employers' affairs.

This also provides a penalty for "acceptance" of anything of value and specifically authorizes immunity for one who gives information to the prosecution.

The statute was challenged as being unconstitutionally vague. However, reviewing courts indicated that, since it prohibits behavior about which men of common intelligence need not guess, it is not unconstitutionally vague.[57]

Some state statutes contain different wording and use other terms to identify the crime. For example, in Massachusetts, the statute provides a penalty of not less than $25 nor more than $500, or imprisonment in the state prison for not more than three years, for one who corruptly gives, offers, or promises to an agent, employee or servant, any gift or gratuity with intent to influence his action in relation to specific business transactions. This statute is entitled "Illegal Gratuity and Penalty."[58]

---

[57] United States v. Perrin, 580 F.2d 730 (5th Cir. 1978).

[58] Mass. Gen. Laws Ann. ch. 271, § 39 (West 1980).

A Massachusetts court, in considering this statute as applied, made it clear that this Section was designed to punish acts of agents, employers or servants of persons or corporations engaged in private business and was inapplicable to acts of public officers.[59]

§ 7.7 Miscellaneous Business and Commercial Frauds

When the courts determined that specific activities, although fraudulent, were not covered by the statutes in existence, other statutes were enacted. For example, a basketball referee was held to be outside the reach of the commercial bribery statute because basketball is not a business or trade, a New York Court reasoned.[60] Therereafter, a statute was enacted to cover this activity. Some of the miscellaneous statutes that have been enacted by the various states relating to commercial and business-type frauds are included here as examples.

A. Offering or Accepting Bribes in Athletic Contests and Sporting Events

Most states have some type of statute that covers corruption related to sporting events, athletic contests and/or other publicly exhibited contests. An example is the statute of Massachusetts which provides punishment by a fine of not more than $1,000 or by imprisonment for not more than two years, or both, if one gives, promises, or offers to professional or amateur athletes anything of value with intent to influence him to lose or try to lose or cause to be lost, etc., a sport or game.[61] This also provides penalties for fraudulent activities relating to horse racing, and specifically mentions various sports and sporting activities.

In a Nebraska statute, the terminology designating this offense is "Tampering with Publicly-Exhibited Contests."[62] The statute is broader in its application than most. It provides a penalty where one tampers with a publicly-exhibited contest as a participant or an official as well as one who offers a benefit.

In Kentucky, the crime is limited to "sporting events." Here, a person is guilty of sports bribery when he:

59   Commonwealth v. Benoit, 347 Mass. 1, 196 N.E.2d 228 (1964).
60   People v. Levy, 283 App. Div. 383, 128 N.Y.S.2d 275 (1954).
61   Mass. Gen Laws Ann. ch. 271, § 39A (West 1980).
62   Neb. Rev. Stat. § 28-614 (1943).

(a) offers, confers, or agrees to confer any benefit upon a sports participant with intent to influence him not to give his best efforts in a sports contest; or

(b) offers, confers or agrees to confer any benefit upon a sports official with intent to influence him to perform his duties improperly.[63]

This is a Class D felony which carries a penalty of one to five years.

B. *Tampering with Records*

Most states have some type of a statute which prohibits knowingly tampering with records with the purpose to defraud. These have different titles, but the purpose generally is the same. One example is that of Nebraska, which is entitled "False Statement or Book Entry: Destruction or Secretion of Records: Penalty: Organization, Defined." There, a person commits a Class 1 misdemeanor if he:

(a) willfully and knowingly subscribes to, makes or causes to be made any false statement or entry into the books of an organization; or

(b) knowingly subscribes to or exhibits false papers with intent to deceive any person or persons authorized to examine into the affairs of any such organization; or

(c) makes, states, or publishes any false statement of the amount of assets or liabilities of any such organization; or

(d) fails to make true and correct entry in the books and records of such organization of its business and transactions in the -manner and form prescribed by the Department of Banking and Finances; or

(e) mutilates, alters, destroys, secretes, or removes any of the books or records of such organization, without the consent of the Director of Banking and Finance.[64]

---

[63] Ky. Rev. Stat. § 518.040 (1975). *See also* Ky. Rev. Stat. § 518.050 (1975), relating to "receiving Sports Bribe"; Ky. Rev. Stat. § 518.060 (1975), relating to "Tampering with or Rigging Sports Contests"; and Ky. Rev. Stat. § 518.070 (1975), relating to "Ticket Scalping."

[64] Neb. Rev. Stat. § 28-612 (1943). *See also* Ohio Rev. Code Ann. § 2913.42 (Page 1987).

In Ohio, the crime is "Tampering with Records."[65] This Section prohibits tampering with all private, as well as public, records for fraudulent purposes. The rationale is that the substantial harm can, in a given case, result from tampering with a personal letter file, bank statement or other private document, as well as from tampering with the correspondence files or records in a public office.

C. Defrauding Creditors

In order to protect those who are involved in business activities, most states have specific statutes dealing with activities that are designed to defraud creditors. These differ from state to state and must be thoroughly studied to determine the elements of the offenses. One example is that of Ohio, which provides that:

> (A) No person, with purpose to defraud one or more of his creditors, shall do any of the following:
>
>   (1) Remove, conceal, destroy, encumber, convey, or otherwise deal with any of his property;
>
>   (2) Misrepresent or refuse to disclose to a fiduciary appointed to administer or manage his affairs or estate, the existence, amount, or location of any of his property, or any other information regarding such property which he is legally required to furnish to the fiduciary.[66]

Under this Section, it is an offense if a debtor deals, in any way, with his property, with the purpose to defraud one or more of his creditors, or if with the same purpose he fails to be truthful with a fiduciary appointed to manage his affairs or property, concerning the nature, extent, or whereabouts of his property.

D. Other Statutes Relating to Business and Commercial Fraud

In addition to those that have been enumerated and discussed, various states have other statutes that are designed to protect an individual doing

---

[65] Ohio Rev. Code Ann. § 2913.45 (Page 1987).

[66] *Id. See also* Criminal Code Training Manual, Ohio Peace Officers Association (1987).

business with another individual or an organization. Examples are "Fraud in Insolvency," which provides a penalty for destroying, removing or otherwise obstructing the claims of a creditor, knowing that proceedings are to be instituted to appoint a receiver, or knowingly falsifying any writing or record, or knowingly misrepresenting or refusing to disclose the existence and identification of property subject to the proceedings.[67] Another example of this type of statute is that relating to "Receiving Deposits in a Failing Financial Institution."[68] The purpose of this type of statute is to protect those who might unknowingly make deposits in a failing financial institution.

It bears repeating that the offenses discussed here are not the only offenses that are designed to protect persons against fraud. Not only are there already statutes on the books to protect against special frauds, other statutes will be enacted as enterprising persons find other ways to defraud the public.

§ 7.8 Summary

While various types of cheating were made crimes under the early English common law, many of the specific laws relating to forgery and commercial fraud did not develop until made necessary, due to the common use of checks and other commercial paper.

One of the most common crimes in our society is forgery. Forgery is defined as the false making or materially altering, with intent to defraud, of any writing, which if genuine, might apparently be a legal efficacy of the foundation of a legal liability. In an effort to more accurately define what wrongs are prohibited, some modern statutes use different terminology and specifically define what instruments are subject to forgery and what conduct is prohibited.

Many modern statutes include the crime of uttering a forged instrument within the statute defining forgery. Others make this a separate offense. To utter a forged instrument is to offer it, directly or indirectly, by words or actions as good. This, if done with intent to defraud and with knowledge of the falsity of the instrument, is a violation of the law in some form in all states.

Finding that some forgery statutes were not comprehensive enough to cover acts which should be made criminal, legislative bodies have enacted legislation to make other acts criminal. Some examples are criminal simulation, where the subject of the offense is not a writing but an object, misuse of

---

[67] Me. Rev. Stat. Ann. tit. 17A, § 902 (1981); N.H. Rev. Stat. Ann. § 638.9 (1974); Utah Code Ann. § 76-6-511 (1973).

[68] Model Penal Code § 224.12 (Proposed Official Draft 1980).

credit cards, possession of forged devices, fraudulent destruction, removal or concealment of recordable instruments, and tampering with records.

Numerous statutes and ordinances have been enacted which prohibit false or fraudulent statements in advertising. The crime of false advertising consists primarily in the publication and circulation of deceptive matter and the offense is completed without regard to whether anyone is deceived or damaged. In the Model Penal Code, this is covered under the Section entitled "Deceptive Business Practices" which covers several crimes relating to cheating and deceptive practices.

Where, at common law, bribery of public officials was prohibited, commercial bribery was not recognized at early common law. However, statutes were enacted to control commercial bribery. Modern statutes encompass the bribery of general agents and employees of commercial concerns, as well as the bribery of public employees.

When the courts determined that specific activities, although fraudulent, were not covered by the statutes in existence, other statutes relating to commercial and business frauds were enacted. Some examples are offering or accepting bribes in athletic contests and sporting events, tampering with records, defrauding creditors and receiving deposits in failing financial institutions.

The so-called fraud statutes are numerous and varied. These have been enacted to protect the public against special frauds. Additional statutes will be enacted as state legislatures determine that legislation is necessary to protect the public against fraudulent acts.

Chapter 8
OFFENSES INVOLVING MORALITY AND DECENCY

Statutes regulating public morals, including the regulation and punishment of prostitution and related offenses fall within the exercise of the state's police power. The state clearly has a legitimate interest in regulating the commercialization of sex.

State v. Allen,
37 Conn. Sup. 506,
424 A.2d 651 (1980)
and cases cited therein.

Section

§ 8.1 Introduction

To determine what acts should be investigated and punished presents problems for the legislative bodies and for criminal justice personnel. Empirical investigation has demonstrated that even after the legislature has declared certain acts, such as fornication, should be made crimes against the state, the law has not been enforced. This places enforcement personnel in a dilemma; while the police have taken an oath to enforce the law, in practice the laws are not strictly enforced.

Some acts, such as murder, burglary, arson and theft, are so obviously wrong that punishment is provided in practically all societies. Other acts may be undesirable to many members of society or even "sinful," but are not always declared to be crimes. Remaining are those that are so near the borderline that they are designated as crimes in some jurisdictions and not in adjoining jurisdictions. In statutes and commentaries, a group of offenses are categorized as "offenses against the public health, safety, morals,"[1] "offenses against morality and decency,"[2] "offenses against the family"[3] and "morals offenses."[4]

In this chapter, titled "Offenses Involving Morality and Decency," the most well-known offenses in this category are discussed. These include adultery and fornication, prostitution and related offenses, offenses related to obscenity, bigamy and polygamy, incest and abortion.

§ 8.2 Adultery and Fornication

A. Traditional Definitions and Elements

Sexual intercourse out of wedlock was punished by the church as an ecclesiastical offense at early common law. In England, the common law meaning of the word "adultery" was sexual intercourse with another's wife. In 1650, during the second year of the Commonwealth, adultery was made a capital crime in England; but the statute was repealed after the restoration.[5] In this country, the offense was punishable in the common law courts when so provided by statute.[6]

---

[1]　Miller, HANDBOOK ON CRIMINAL LAW xi (1934).

[2]　Perkins, CRIMINAL LAW 328 (1957).

[3]　Ohio Rev. Code Ann. § 2919 *et seq.* (Page 1987).

[4]　Dix, GILBERT'S CRIMINAL LAW SUMMARY 145 (11th ed. 1979).

[5]　4 Blackstone, COMMENTARIES 65.

[6]　United States v. Clapox, 35 F. 575 (D. Or. 1888).

(a) Adultery

Although the definition of adultery varies from state to state, to constitute the crime, one of the parties at least must be lawfully married to another and on prosecution such marriage must be proven.[7] Under the old Roman law, it was essential to the crime of adultery that the woman be married to another. The crime was not committed where a married man had sexual intercourse with a single woman, the gist of the offense being the danger of putting spurious offspring upon a man.[8] Under this reasoning, if the woman were married, however, both parties were guilty.[9] At least until recently, the great majority of jurisdictions held that an unmarried woman who had intercourse with a married man did not commit adultery.[10] Some examples of definitions, as framed by the various courts, are as follows:

"Adultery" is the unlawful voluntary sexual intercourse of a married person with one of the opposite sex whether married or single.[11]

"A single act of unlawful sexual intercourse falls within the definition of "adultery" or "fornication" according as the party is married or not.[12]

"Adultery" includes sexual intercourse by a married person with a person who is not his or her spouse, regardless of whether the person accused of adultery is living with his or her spouse at the time.[13]

As state statutes vary concerning the definition of adultery, all three definitions are stated herein.

(1) Voluntary sexual intercourse between persons, one of whom is lawfully married to another, both parties being guilty.

(2) Intercourse by a married person with one who is not his wife or husband, the married person only being guilty of adultery.

---

[7] People v. Stokes, 71 Cal. 263, 12 P. 71 (1886).

[8] Miller, HANDBOOK ON CRIMINAL LAW § 136 (1934).

[9] State v. Fellows, 50 Wis. 65, 6 N.W. 239 (1880).

[10] Lyman v. People, 198 Ill. 544, 64 N.E. 974 (1902).

[11] *In re* Smith, Okla. 153, 37 P. 1099 (1894).

[12] State v. Brown, 47 Ohio St. 102, 23 N.E. 747 (1890).

[13] Milne v. Milne, 266 Ark. 900, 587 S.W.2d 229 (1979).

(3) Intercourse with a married woman by one not her husband, both parties being guilty.

One element is common; one of the parties at least must be lawfully married to another person.

(b) Fornication

Fornication is voluntary, unlawful sexual intercourse, under circumstances not constituting adultery. While fornication was not a crime at common law, it has been made a crime by statutes in many of the states. These statutes provide the same penalty for fornication as for adultery, and from a practical point of view, in those states, there is no point in making the legal distinction.

(a) Adultery

(1) Voluntary sexual intercourse

Intercourse must be voluntary. If force is used in accomplishing the intercourse, it is a defense to the party who was forced into the act.[14]

To constitute intercourse, all that is necessary is that there be some penetration; emission need not be proven.[15]

(2) Persons not married to each other

(3) Lawful marriage of one party

To constitute the crime of adultery, evidence must show that at least one party was lawfully married. Therefore, unlawful sexual intercourse by a divorced person is not adultery if committed with another who is unmarried, provided the divorce is valid.[16] But copulation with another before the entry of the final decree of divorce is adultery.[17]

(b) Fornication

As the definition of fornication is voluntary sexual intercourse between unmarried persons, the only elements that need to be proved are:

---

[14] State v. Summers, 98 N.C. 702, 4 S.E. 120 (1887).

[15] Commonwealth v. Hussey, 157 Mass. 415, 32 N.E. 362 (1892).

[16] State v. Weatherby, 43 Me. 258, 69 Am.Dec. 59 (1857).

[17] Pratt v. Pratt, 157 Mass. 503, 32 N.E. 747 (1892).

(1)   voluntary sexual intercourse and
(2)   the parties participating were unmarried at the time the sexual intercourse occurred.

Distinguishing between adultery and fornication, an Alabama court explained that adultery and fornication are essentially different offenses. To commit the former, one of the parties at least must be, at the time, a married person.[18] While agreeing that the authorities are not in harmony, the court in the *Buchanan* case commented that the court felt that the better opinion seems to be that, in such cases, the married offender is guilty of adultery and the unmarried one guilty of fornication.

In distinguishing between the various crimes, one early Michigan court explained that:

> If a man who is married is guilty of unlawful sexual intercourse we call it "adultery" to him. When the act is between the parties sustaining relationship to each other with certain degrees of consanguinity or affinity, we call it "incest." Where the female consents to unlawful intercourse through fraudulent acts, including a promise of marriage, we call it "seduction." In each case the essential fact which constitutes the crime is "fornication."[19]

B.   Contemporary Statutes and Codes

1. Model Penal Code

Recognizing that many of the penal statutes against fornication and adultery are unenforced, the Model Penal Code omitted any provisions relating to these offenses. A note on adultery and fornication following the discussion of 213.6 of the Model Penal Code explains the rationale for not including the suggested provisions relating to sexual intercourse with a person of the opposite sex where the persons are unmarried.[20]

2. Federal Code

Although Title 18 of the Federal Code contains no provision which directly prohibits adultery or fornication, Title 18, § 2421 includes a penalty

---

[18]   Buchanan v. State, 55 Ala. 154 (1876).

[19]   People v. Rouse, 2 Mich. 209 (1871).

[20]   Model Penal Code § 213.6 (Proposed Official Draft 1980).

for one who knowingly transports an individual in interstate or foreign commerce with intent that such individual engage in . . . "any sexual activity for which any person can be charged with a criminal offense." This applies to adultery if adultery is a crime under the state law.[21]

3. Other statutes and codes

While some states have repealed the statutes relating to fornication and adultery, or have omitted this offense from the revised drafts of the statutes, others still contain provisions making it a crime to participate; in sexual intercourse out of wedlock. In some of these states, simple adultery, that is, one act of adultery, constitutes a criminal offense, while in others, a relationship that is continuous or "open or notorious" is required. In some states, adultery and fornication are not crimes unless the behavior is "open and notorious."[22]

In those states that require a continuous relationship, one act of sexual intercourse, whether adultery or fornication, does not constitute the crime. An example of a statute of this type is that of Mississippi. It provides:[23]

> § 97-29-1. Adultery and Fornication--Unlawful Cohabitation
> If any man and woman shall unlawfully cohabit, whether in adultery or fornication, they shall be fined in any sum not more than five hundred dollars each, and imprisoned in the county jail not more than six months; and it shall not be necessary, to constitute the offense, that the parties shall dwell together publicly as husband and wife, but it may be proved by circumstances which show habitual sexual intercourse.

The Mississippi court has held that a few acts of intercourse without showing unlawful cohabitation would not constitute a violation of this statute.[24]

In some states, the punishment for adultery is more severe than the punishment for fornication.[25] For example, the Massachusetts statute provides a penalty of up to three years for adultery and a maximum of three

---

[21]   18 U.S.C. § 2421.

[22]   Ill. Ann. Stat. ch. 38, § 11-7 (Smith-Hurd 1971).

[23]   Miss. Code Ann. § 97-29-1 (1972).

[24]   Brown v. State, 8 So. 257 (Miss. 1890). See also, Spike v. State, 98 Miss. 483, 54 So. 1 (1911).

[25]   Commonwealth v. Libby, 358 Mass. 617, 26 N.E.2d 641 (1971).

months for fornication. Sections 14 and 18 of the Massachusetts statute are included here as examples.[26]

§ 14. Adultery

A married person who has sexual intercourse with a person not his spouse or an unmarried person who has sexual intercourse with a married person shall be guilty of adultery and shall be punished by imprisonment in the state prison for not more than three years or in jail for not more than two years or by a fine of not more than five hundred dollars.

§ 18. Fornication

Whoever commits fornication shall be punished by imprisonment for not more than three months or by a fine of not more than thirty dollars.

In 1979, the Florida Supreme Court rendered a decision in which the majority declared the Florida fornication statute unconstitutional as in violation of the equal protection provisions of the Constitution because that statute, when considered along with other Florida statutes, made a gender-based distinction between married women who cannot be punished for illicit sexual activity and married men who can.[27] There, after discussing the rationale for the enactment of adultery and fornication statutes, the court concluded that the state failed to offer any governmental justification for a gender-based distinction. The conclusion of the court on this point was:

Since the gender-based classification created by the fornication statute does not bear a rational relationship to a permissible state objective, then clearly it fails to meet the stricter standards, applicable to such a classification, of an important governmental interest. It violates the fundamental guarantee of equal protection of the laws....We hold that it is void as written and must be cured legislatively.

---

[26] Mass. Ann. Laws ch. 272, §§ 14, 18 (Michie/Law. Co-op. 1978). § 14, as included here, is the redefined crime of adultery in gender-neutral terms. Formerly, this Section prescribed a penalty for an unmarried man who had sexual intercourse with a married woman, but no similar penalty for an unmarried woman who had sexual intercourse with a married man.

[27] Purvis v. State, 377 So. 2d 674 (Fla. 1979).

§ 8.3 Prostitution-Related Offenses

A. *Traditional Definitions and Elements*

At the outset, it is noted that the term "prostitution" is not synonymous with the *offense* of prostitution. The term "prostitution" is defined as the practice of a female offering her body to an indiscriminate intercourse with a man, usually for hire.[28] Prostitution was not a crime at common law and is not a crime in all jurisdictions. It is more appropriate to discuss this matter in terms of "crimes relating to prostitution" rather than using prostitution, the offense, as synonymous with prostitution, the practice.

While the act or practice was not a crime at common law, the courts have recognized that states exercising reasonable police powers may enact restrictive legislation pertaining to prostitution and offenses related thereto.[29] As a result, there are numerous specific statutes relating to prostitution. These include: to engage in prostitution, to aid and abet prostitution, to associate with prostitutes, to keep and operate a place or conveyance for the purpose of prostitution, to receive or offer to receive any person into any place for the purpose of prostitution, etc.[30]

While most authorities agree that it is impossible to wipe out prostitution, most states have statutes which repress commercialized prostitution. The statutes vary greatly in their wording, but are fairly uniform with respect to the specific matters to be controlled. The most common statutes relate to a female offering to engage in prostitution for hire.

Probably the best example of a traditional statute relating to prostitution is that which was the law in Wisconsin. This provided "any female who intentionally does any of the following may be fined not more than $500 or imprisoned not more than one year or both."

(1) Has or offers to have non-marital sexual intercourse for money; or

(2) Commits or offers to commit an act of sexual perversion for money; or

(3) Is an inmate of a place of prostitution.

The Kentucky Revised Statutes, until changed in 1974, provided "It shall be unlawful to engage in prostitution or to aid or abet prostitution or to pro-

---

[28] 73 C.J.S. *Prostitution* § 1 (1951).

[29] Hatcher v. Dallas, 133 S.W. 914 (Tex. 1911); *Ex parte* Cannon, 94 Tex. Crim. 243, 250 S.W. 429 (1923).

[30] 73 C.J.S. *Prostitution* § 4 (1951).

cure or solicit any person for the purpose of prostitution...."[31] In the statute, the term "prostitution" was defined as "to include the giving or receiving of the body for sexual intercourse for hire, and shall also be construed to include the giving or receiving of the body for indiscriminate sexual intercourse without hire." Some additional definitions indicate the similarities and differences as interpreted by the various courts:

> "Prostitution" has persisted since biblical times, and, as such, has acquired traditional meaning of indiscriminate illicit intercourse for hire.[32]

> The definition of "prostitution" comprises two grounds for conviction, i.e., performance of indiscriminate sexual acts for hire and indiscriminate solicitation or agreement to perform sex acts for hire; an essential element of proof common to both grounds is the commercial nature of the sexual transaction.[33]

> Common law "prostitution" is the act or practice of a female in offering her body to indiscriminate intercourse with men; consideration is not essential.[34]

It is noted that the various states had and some still have, related offenses. For example, the state of Wisconsin, in addition to the statute quoted, had statutes relating to Patronizing Prostitutes (§ 944.31), Soliciting Prostitutes (§ 944.32), Pandering (§ 944.33) and Keeping a Place of Prostitution (§ 944.34).

Although the statutes differ as to the required elements, some are common to most statutes.

(a) Female

A man cannot be a prostitute within the terms of the general penal statutes.[35]

(b) Offering of One's Self or One's Body

Generally there must be a direct or indirect offer of intercourse. In one case, the court held that where the prostitution is defined by statutes as the offering, giving, or us-

---

[31]   Ky. Rev. Stat. Ann. § 436.070 (Baldwin 1974).

[32]   Commonwealth v. Potts, 314 Pa. Super. 256, 460 A.2d 1127 (1983).

[33]   Commonwealth v. A Juvenile, 6 Mass. App. 194, 374 N.E.2d 335 (1978).

[34]   State v. Illinois, 218 N.W.2d 921 (Iowa 1974).

[35]   State v. Gardner, 174 Iowa 748, 156 N.W. 747 (1916).

ing of the body for sexual intercourse for hire, the term does not necessarily involve indiscriminate intercourse with more than one man.[36]

(c) For Hire or for Money

Gain has been made an element of the crime by statute in most jurisdictions. To constitute the crime of engaging in prostitution, there must be a showing of an offer for money or some profit.[37]

B. Contemporary Statutes and Codes

1. Model Penal Code[38]

§ 251.2 Prostitution and Related Offenses

(1) Prostitution. A person is guilty of prostitution, a petty misdemeanor, if he or she:

    (a) is an inmate of a house of prostitution or otherwise engages in sexual activity as a business; or

    (b) loiters in or within view of any public place for the purpose of being hired to engage in sexual activity.

> "Sexual activity" includes homosexual and other deviate sexual relations. A "house of prostitution" is a place where prostitution or promotion of prostitution is regularly carried on by one person under the control, management or supervision of another. An "inmate" is a person who engages in prostitution in or through the agency of a house of prostitution. "Public place" means any place to which the public or any substantial group thereof has access.

(2) Promoting Prostitution. A person who knowingly promotes prostitution of another commits a misdemeanor or felony as provided in Subsection (3). The following acts shall, without limitation of the foregoing, constitute promoting prostitution:

---

[36] Commonwealth v. Stingel, 146 Pa. 359, 40 A.2d 140 (1944).

[37] State v. Phillips, 26 N.D. 206, 144 N.W. 94 (1913).

[38] Model Penal Code § 251.2 (Proposed Official Draft 1980).

(a) owning, controlling, managing, supervising or other-wise keeping, alone or in association with others, a house of prostitution or a prostitution business; or

(b) procuring an inmate for a house of prostitution or a place in a house of prostitution for one who would be an inmate; or

(c) encouraging, inducing, or otherwise purposely caus-ing another to become or remain a prostitute; or

(d) soliciting a person to patronize a prostitute; or

(e) procuring a prostitute for a patron; or

(f) transporting a person into or within this state with purpose to promote that person's engaging in pros-titution, or procuring or paying for transportation with that purpose; or

(g) leasing or otherwise permitting a place controlled by the actor, alone or in association with others, to be regularly used for prostitution or the promotion of prostitution, or failure to make reasonable effort to abate such use by ejecting the tenant, notifying law enforcement authorities, or other legally available means; or

(h) soliciting, receiving, or agreeing to receive any benefit for doing or agreeing to do anything forbidden by this Subsection.

(3) Grading of Offenses Under Subsection (2). An offense under Subsection (2) constitutes a felony of the third degree if:

(a) the offense falls within paragraph (a), (b) or (c) of Subsection (2); or

(b) the actor compels another to engage in or promote prostitution; or

(c) the actor promotes prostitution of a child under 16, whether or not he is aware of the child's age; or

(d) the actor promotes prostitution of his wife, child, ward or any person for whose care, protection or support he is responsible.

Otherwise the offense is a misdemeanor.

(4) Presumption from Living Off Prostitutes. A person, other than the prostitute or the prostitute's minor child or other legal de-pendent incapable of self-support, who is supported in whole

or substantial part by the proceeds of prostitution is presumed to be knowingly promoting prostitution in violation of Subsection (2).

(5) Patronizing Prostitutes. A person commits a violation if he hires a prostitute to engage in sexual activity with him, or if he enters or remains in a house of prostitution for the purpose of engaging in sexual activity.

(b) Evidence. On the issue whether a place is a house of prostitution the following shall be admissible evidence: its general repute; the repute of the persons who reside in or frequent the place; the frequency, timing and duration of visits by non-residents. Testimony of a person against his spouse shall be admissible to prove offenses under this Section.

First, it is noted that the Model Penal Code applies to both male and female. The Code emphasizes the repression of commercialized sexual activity including "deviate sexual relations" as well as "sexual intercourse." It also deals with procuring, pandering, transportation and other activities ancillary to the business of prostitution.

The Code includes Sections relating to "living off" of prostitutes and patronizing prostitutes. This makes it more readily possible to prosecute those customers of prostitutes who were rarely punished under previous statutes. It is interesting to note that the offense of prostitution, under the Code, is a petty misdemeanor, while in some instances, promoting prostitution is a felony of the third degree.

2. Federal Code

Several federal statutes relate to prostitution.[39] Title 18, § 1952 entitled "Interstate and Foreign Transportation and Aid of Racketeering Enterprises" includes a provision that:

(a) Whoever travels in interstate or foreign commerce or uses any facility in interstate or foreign commerce, including the mail, with intent to--

---

[39] 18 U.S.C. § 1952.

    (1)   distribute the proceeds of any unlawful activity; or

    (2)   commit any crime of violence to further any unlawful activity; or

    (3)   otherwise promote, manage, establish, carry on, or facilitate the promotion, management, establishment, or carrying on, of any unlawful activity--

shall be fined not more than $10,000 or imprisoned for not more than 5 years, or both.

As used in Title 18, § 1952, "unlawful activity" includes:

prostitution offenses in violation of the laws of the state in which they are committed or of the United States.

Title 18, § 2421, provides that:

Whoever knowingly transports any individual in interstate or foreign commerce, or in any territory or possession of the United States, with intent that such individual engage in prostitution, or in any sexual activity for which any person can be charged with a criminal offense, shall be fined as provided by this title and imprisoned for not more than 5 years, or both.[40]

Title 18, § 2422 includes a similar penalty for one who persuades, induces, entices or coerces an individual to travel in interstate commerce for the purpose of engaging in prostitution. It is not double jeopardy to convict a defendant under both Sections 2421 and 2422, as these are separate and distinct offenses.[41] Also, it is not improper to convict one defendant with two violations for the single act of transporting a minor female and an adult woman across the state line for purposes of prostitution.[42]

In addition to these statutes, Title 18, § 1384, authorizes the secretary of the Army, Navy and Air Force to designate areas within reasonable distance of any military or naval camp, station, or post, where prostitution and other related offenses shall be prohibited, and provides a fine or imprisonment for failure to comply with such directive.[43]

---

[40] 18 U.S.C. § 2421.

[41] United States v. Taitano, 442 F.2d 464, *cert. denied*, 404 U.S. 852, 30 L.Ed.2d 92, 92 S. Ct. 92 (1971).

[42] United States v. Parr, 741 F.2d 878 (5th Cir. 1984).

[43] 18 U.S.C. § 1384.

3. Other statutes and codes

Recently revised codes and statutes include penalties not only for soliciting sexual activity for a fee, but related offenses. There is apparently a trend to reduce the grade of the offense of soliciting prostitution for a fee and emphasizing the prosecution of those who promote prostitution.[44]

An example of a statute that probably represents the approach taken in the majority of the states is that of Connecticut. This Code has provisions providing punishment for prostitution, patronizing a prostitute, promoting prostitution in the first degree, promotion prostitution in the second degree, promoting prostitution in the third degree and permitting prostitution.

Connecticut Criminal Code
§ 53a-82. Prostitution: Class A misdemeanor

(a) A person is guilty of prostitution when such person engages or agrees or offers to engage in sexual conduct with another person in return for a fee.

(b) Prostitution is a Class A misdemeanor.

§ 53a-53. Patronizing a prostitute: Class A misdemeanor

(a) A person is guilty of patronizing a prostitute when:

    (1) pursuant to a prior understanding, he pays a fee to another person as compensation for such person or a third person having engaged in sexual conduct with him; or

    (2) he pays or agrees to pay a fee to another person pursuant to an understanding that in return therefor such person or a third person will engage in sexual conduct with him; or

    (3) he solicits or requests another person to engage in sexual conduct with him in return for a fee.

(b) Patronizing a prostitute is a Class A misdemeanor.

§ 53a-86. Patronizing prostitution in the first degree: Class B felony

(a) A person is guilty of promoting prostitution in the first degree when he knowingly:

---

[44] *See* the Revised Codes for Alabama and Arizona as examples of states that omit any Section relating to engaging in prostitution.

    (1) advances prostitution by compelling a person by force or intimidation to engage in prostitution, or profits from coercive conduct by another; or

    (2) advances or profits from prostitution of a person less than sixteen years old.

(b) Promoting prostitution in the first degree is a Class B felony.

§ 53a-87. Promoting prostitution in the second degree: Class C felony.

(a) A person is guilty of promoting prostitution in the second degree when he knowingly:

    (1) advances or profits from prostitution by managing, supervising, controlling or owning, either alone or in association with others, a house of prostitution or a prostitution business or enterprise involving prostitution activity by two or more prostitutes; or

    (2) advances or profits from prostitution of a person less than eighteen years old.

(b) Promoting prostitution in the second degree is a Class C felony.

§ 53a-88. Promoting prostitution in the third degree: Class D felony.

(a) A person is guilty of promoting prostitution in the third degree when he knowingly advances or profits from prostitution.

(b) Promoting prostitution in the third degree is a Class D felony.

§ 53a-89. Permitting prostitution: Class A misdemeanor

(a) A person is guilty of permitting prostitution when, having possession or control of premises which he knows are being used for prostitution purposes, he fails to make reasonable effort to halt or abate such use.

(b) Permitting prostitution is a Class A misdemeanor.[45]

These Sections of the Code make clear that commercial homosexual, as well as heterosexual, activity is prohibited. A distinction is drawn between the various kinds of related activities, and the penalties are graded accordingly.

These elements of the various crimes are fairly clear. To prove a violation, evidence must be introduced to show:

---

[45] Conn. Gen. Stat. §§ 53a-82 – 89 (1971).

(a) engaging, agreeing or offering to engage,
(b) in sexual conduct with another and
(c) in return for a fee.

In the case of *State v. Allen*, this statute was challenged as being unconstitutionally vague and infringing upon the fundamental right of privacy.[46] In this case, the defendant approached an undercover officers' car, opened the passenger door, and inquired if the officer had $20. Upon hearing an affirmative response, the defendant got into the car. A conversation ensued in which the defendant offered to have sex for $20. The officer then drove to a pre-arranged location near a school where the defendant was arrested by other officers. No sexual activity was ever engaged in nor was there any transfer of money. The defendant contended that the statutory terms "sexual conduct" and "fee" are so inherently uncertain in their meanings that they failed to apprise her that her conduct was proscribed. She claimed that the statute is unconstitutionally vague, that her conviction thereunder violated the rights to due process of law under the Fifth and Fourteenth Amendments to the U.S. Constitution.

While agreeing that the laws must give a person of ordinary intelligence a reasonable opportunity to know what is prohibited so that he may act accordingly, the court found no difficulty with the definition of "sexual conduct" and "fee" as appearing in the statute prohibiting prostitution. It was noted that while certain words may appear unconstitutionally vague when viewed in a vacuum, when viewed in the context of a statute they can provide fair notice of the conduct so to be prohibited. In explaining that the term "sexual conduct" is sufficiently explicit, the court referred to the definition of prostitution as "normally suggesting sexual relations for hire." As to the term "sexual conduct" the opinion was that the language of § 53a-82 is sufficiently precise to give the defendant fair notice that her conduct was prohibited.[47] The court also explained that the term "fee" is not so vague as to make persons of common intelligence guess at its meaning.

In this case, the court set aside the judgment and ordered a new trial, not because of the language of the statutes, but because there was no satisfactory instruction concerning the intent requirement. The judges announced

---

[46] State v. Allen, 37 Conn. Sup. 506, 424 A.2d 651 (1980); *See* case in Part II.

[47] In the case of City of Kansas City v. Connor, 5 Kan. App. 2d 260, 615 P.2d 163 (1980), the Kansas City Court of Appeals reversed a conviction under an ordinance which prohibited engaging in sexual activity as a business. The court interpreted "engaging" as requiring proof of a *completed* sexual act. In this case the women only *agreed* to perform a sexual act for a fee.

that, although the general statute, § 53a-82, does not expressly require a mental element, a general intent to do the proscribed act on one's own volition is an element of the crime of prostitution.

Although the elements of the offenses relating to prostitution differ from state to state, there are similarities. Also, it should be noted that the element of "intent" is not required in all states.

§ 8.4 Offenses Related to Obscenity

A. Traditional Definitions and Elements

Under the early English system, matters relating to lewd or immodest acts, conduct and language were handled by the ecclesiastical authorities. Gradually, the courts and legislative bodies assumed the responsibility for setting standards with regard to specific modes of conduct, pictorial representations of conduct, or written and oral descriptions of conduct.

In attempting to define conduct which is obscene and should be prohibited, the courts have, from the beginning, faced a very difficult task. Not only is it impossible to determine what conduct is obscene in any given society at a particular time, the courts and legislative bodies have had difficulty in determining the language to use in order to comply with the provisions of the First Amendment of the Constitution.

Since 1957, it has been established that obscenity is not within the gambit of constitutionally-protected free speech. However, the Supreme Court spent more than a decade in attempting to determine a legal test of what is obscenity.[48]

Practically all states have laws which prohibit conduct which is labeled obscene. Definitions are hard to come by. In *Corpus Juris Secundum*, this statement is included:

> Thus, obscene material has been authoritatively defined as material which deals with sex in a manner appealing to prurient interest, and it has been held that a thing is obscene if, considered as a whole, its predominant appeal is to prurient interest, i.e., a shameful or morbid interest in nudity, sex, or excretion, and it goes substantially beyond customary limits of candor in description of representation of matters.[49]

---

[48] Roth v. United States, 354 U.S. 476, 77 S. Ct. 1304, 1 L.Ed.2d 1498 (1957).

[49] *See also*, Klotter & Kanovitz, CONSTITUTIONAL LAW § 2.4 (5th ed. 1985).
67 C.J.S. *Obscenity* §§ 1,2 (1978).

In some instances, obscene has been said to be synonymous with indecent and immoral.[50] The courts and legislative bodies have usually agreed that to be obscene, conduct or material must be sexual or erotic, but sex is not obscene under all circumstances. Nudity, alone, does not need to be obscene and acts of sadism and brutality do not, in themselves, constitute obscenity.[51]

Some specific definitions, as framed by the courts, are as follows:

> The words "obscene" and "indecent" are words of common usage and are ordinarily used in the sense of meaning something offensive to the chastity of mind, delicacy and purity of thought, something suggestive of lustfulness, lasciviousness, and sensuality.[52]

> "Nudity" and "obscenity" are not synonymous and a nude performance does not become an obscene one, unless, taken as a whole, it appeals predominantly to the prurient interest, a shameful interest in nudity or sex beyond customary limits, it describes any patently offensive way of sexual conduct specifically proscribed by state law, and, taken as a whole, it lacks serious or artistic value as determined by an average person applying contemporary community standards.[53]

In addition to state statutes, local ordinances deal with the subject of obscenity. Although the courts have been divided on the interpretation and constitutionality of statutes in general, most have been upheld. For example in a statute penalizing the sale and advertisement of "obscene or indecent" books, the quoted words were held not to be unconstitutionally vague and indefinite.[54]

The offense of obscenity, as stated and defined in the various statutes, is a distinct crime involving elements different from those of other crimes. For example, the New York Court has held that "consensual sodomy" and "promoting obscenity" consist of different elements and are two separate and distinct crimes.[55] As obscenity statutes are tailored for the particular group

---

[50]   State v. Jackson, 224 Or. 337, 356 P.2d 495 (1960).

[51]   United States v. One Carton Positive Motion Picture Film Entitled "491," Janos Films Inc., 247 F.Supp. 450 (S.D.N.Y. 1965).

[52]   People v. Friedrich, 385 Ill. 175, 52 N.E.2d 120 (1944).

[53]   Midtown Palace, Inc. v. City of Omaha, 193 Neb. 785, 229 N.W.2d 56 (1975).

[54]   People v. Alberts, 138 Cal. App. 2d 909, 292 P.2d 90 (1955).

[55]   People v. Chang, 86 Misc. 2d 272, 382 N.Y.S.2d 611 (1976).

to which they apply, the elements differ depending upon the statute and the definition of terms either provided in the statute or as interpreted by the various courts. But the requisites and sufficiency of indictments and information charging obscenity offenses depend not only on the state law and statute creating the offense, but also on compliance with the constitutional restrictions applicable to the definitions of obscenity. Therefore, in preparing the case for prosecution, criminal justice personnel must look at the provisions of the statute as well as the court decisions.

Some of the elements common to many statutes are:

(1) the matter in question is obscene, and:
(2) the defendant must have knowledge of its obscenity.

The government's burden of proving *scienter* must be met by showing that the defendant knew or was aware of the nature of the material. But the government is not required to prove that the defendant was aware that the material was legally obscene.[56] In providing knowledge, evidence must be introduced to show that the person who is accused shall have knowledge of the general nature and character of the picture, publication or like matter.[57] In the case of *Commonwealth v. 707 Main Corp.,* the court held that under an obscenity statute, knowledge of the specific contents of the matter depicting explicit hardcore sexual conduct will constitute knowledge of the general character of the matter.[58]

Many state and federal cases have attempted to distinguish between conduct that is obscene and that which is not. It is noted that, while a state may not so define obscenity that the minimum constitutional standards as set forth by the U.S. Supreme Court are not met, it may use a definition which requires a greater protection of constitutional rights.[59]

The *Miller* case, in 1973, established some general guidelines. There, the court held that before a motion picture or literary work can be written out of the First Amendment on the basis of being obscene, three elements must co-exist. Applying contemporary community standards, the work viewed as a whole must:

---

[56] United States v. Groner, 494 F.2d 499 (5th Cir. 1974); United States v. Thevis, 484 F.2d 1149 (5th Cir. 1973).

[57] State v. Smith, 422 S.W.2d 50 (Mo. 1967), *cert. denied*, 393 U.S. 895 (1967).

[58] Commonwealth v. 707 Main Corporation, 371 Mass. 374, 357 N.E.2d 753 (1976).

[59] People v. Ridens, 59 Ill. 2d 362, 321 N.E.2d 264 (1974).

(1)　appeal to the prurient interest of the average person;
(2)　portray, in a patently offensive way, specific types of hardcore sexual conduct previously defined by applicable state law and
(3)　lack any serious literary, artistic, or political or scientific value.[60]

If the statutes require other elements, such as age, time and place, motivation or intent, these must be proved by the state.[61]

B.　Contemporary Statutes and Codes

1.　Model Penal Code[62]

§ 251.4 Obscenity.
(1)　Obscene Defined.　Material is obscene if considered as a whole, its predominant appeal is to prurient interest, that is, a shameful or morbid interest, in nudity, sex or excretion, and if in addition it goes substantially beyond customary limits of candor in describing or representing such matters.　Predominant appeal shall be judged with reference to ordinary adults unless it appears from the character of the material or the circumstances of its dissemination to be designed for children or other specially susceptible audience.　Undeveloped photographs, molds, printing plates and the like, shall be deemed obscene notwithstanding that processing or other acts may be required to make the obscenity patent or to disseminate it.

(2)　Offenses.　Subject to the affirmative defense provided in Subsection (3), a person commits a misdemeanor if he knowingly or recklessly:

(a)　sells, delivers or provides, or offers or agrees to sell, deliver or provide, any obscene writing, picture, record or other representation or embodiment of the obscene; or

---

[60]　Miller v. California, 413 U.S. 15, 93 S. Ct. 2607, 37 L.Ed.2d 419 (1973).
[61]　Blum v. State, 417 S.W.2d 66 (Tex. 1967).
[62]　Model Penal Code § 251.4 (Proposed Official Draft 1980).

(b) presents or directs an obscene play, dance or performance, or participates in that portion thereof which makes it obscene; or

(c) publishes, exhibits or otherwise makes available any obscene material; or

(d) possesses any obscene material for purposes of sale or other commercial dissemination; or

(e) sells, advertises or otherwise commercially disseminates material, whether or not obscene, by representing or suggesting that it is obscene.

A person who disseminates or possesses obscene material in the course of his business is presumed to do so knowingly or recklessly.

(3) Justifiable and Non-Commercial Private Dissemination. It is an affirmative defense to prosecution under this Section that dissemination was restricted to:

(a) institutions or persons having scientific, educational, governmental or other similar justification for possessing obscene material; or

(b) non-commercial dissemination to personal associates of the actor.

(4) Evidence; Adjudication of Obscenity. In any prosecution under this Section evidence shall be admissible to show:

(a) the character of the audience for which the material was designed or to which it was directed;

(b) what the predominant appeal of the material would be for ordinary adults or any special audience to which it was directed, and what effect, if any, it would probably have on conduct of such people;

(c) artistic, literary, scientific, educational or other merits of the material;

(d) the degree of public acceptance of the material in the United States;

(e) appeal to prurient interest, or absence thereof, in advertising or other promotion of the material; and

(f) the good repute of the author, creator, publisher or other person from whom the material originated.

> Expert testimony and testimony of the author, creator, publisher or other person from whom the material originated, relating to factors entering into the determination of the issue of obscenity, shall be admissible. The Court shall dismiss a prosecution for obscenity if it is satisfied that the material is not obscene.

Attempting to come to grips with this difficult subject, the Code first defines "obscene" relying to a great extent upon the definition used in the various cases decided by the Supreme Court. According to the definition, the material is obscene only if its predominant appeal is to prurient interest and it goes substantially beyond customary limits of candor in describing or representing such matters.

After defining obscenity, the Code details five offenses associated with obscenity. The provision requires that the prosecution show that the defendant acted purposely, knowingly or recklessly. However, there is a presumption that one who disseminates or possesses obscene material in the course of his business does so knowingly or recklessly. Subsection (3) of the Code provides an affirmative defense where material is for a scientific or educational purpose or dissemination is only non-commercial and only to personal associates.

Subsection (4) specifies the evidence that is to be admissible in obscenity situations. It concludes with a sentence that is probably not necessary, "the court shall dismiss a prosecution for obscenity if it is satisfied that the material is not obscene."[63]

2. Federal Code

Chapter 71 of Title 18 of the U.S. Code includes five Sections relating to obscenity: Mailing obscene or crime-inciting matter, Importation or transportation of obscene matter, Mailing indecent matter on wrappers or envelopes, Broadcasting obscene language, and Transportation of obscene matters for sale or distribution.[64]

Section 1461, relating to obscene or crime-inciting matter, mandates a fine of not more than $5,000 or imprisonment for not more than 5 years, or both, if one violates this statute. One part of the Code provision prohibits mailing papers, writings, advertisements...that may be used for any indecent or immoral purpose.

---

[63] Model Penal Code § 251.4 (Proposed Official Draft 1980), for comments on obscenity.

[64] 18 U.S.C. §§ 1461, 1462, 1463, 1464 and 1465.

In interpreting this provision of the Code, federal courts follow the Supreme Court definition of "obscene" as approved in the case of *Miller v. California*. In this 1984 case, the Court commented:

> In a typical obscenity case, one of the essential elements to be established is that to the average person, applying contemporary community standards, the dominant theme of the material taken as a whole appeals to the prurient interests; however, material appealing to atypical sexual proclivities may be found "obscene" only when its dominant theme appeals to the prurient interests of members of a clearly defined deviant sexual group.[65]

Title 18, § 1462, provides a penalty of $5,000 or 5 years, or both, for the first offense and $10,000 and 10 years for the second offense where the defendant is convicted of importation or transporting obscene matters as defined.

Section 1463 prohibits the mailing of indecent matters on wrappers or envelopes, and § 1464 provides a penalty for one who utters any obscene, indecent or profane language by means of radio communications. Section 1465 makes it a crime punishable by $5,000 or 5 years, or both, to knowingly transport in interstate or foreign commerce for sale or distribution any obscene, lewd, lascivious, or filthy book, pamphlet, picture, film, paper, letter or writing...of indecent or immoral character.

3. Other statutes and codes

State statutes vary in wording and in the penalty attached for violations. Many recently revised statutes follow the Model Code position but the penalties vary. Also, the elements such as "the work taken as a whole appeals to the prurient interest" vary from state to state. Some states refer to "contemporary community standards" while others refer to "state standards" as the appropriate reference point in determining if the predominant appeal is to prurient interest.

An example of a statute which is similar to the Model Penal Code is that of Illinois. It provides in part:[66]

---

[65] United States v. Petrov, 747 F.2d 824 (1984), *cert. denied*, 85 L.Ed.2d 318, 105 S. Ct. 2037 (1984).

[66] Ill. Ann. Stat. ch. 38, § 11-20 (Smith-Hurd 1973).

§ 11-20. Obscenity

(a) Elements of the Offense.

A person commits obscenity when, with knowledge of the nature or content thereof, or recklessly failing to exercise reasonable inspection which would have disclosed the nature or content thereof, he:

(1) sells, delivers or provides, or offers or agrees to sell, deliver or provide any obscene writing, picture, record or other representation or embodiment of the obscene; or

(2) presents or directs an obscene play, dance or other performance or participates directly in that portion thereof which makes it obscene; or

(3) publishes, exhibits or otherwise makes available anything obscene; or

(4) performs an obscene act or otherwise presents an obscene exhibition of his body for gain; or

(5) creates, buys, procures or possesses obscene matter or material with intent to disseminate it in violation of this Section, or of the penal laws or regulations of any other jurisdiction; or

(6) advertises or otherwise promotes the sale of material represented or held out by him to be obscene, whether or not it is obscene.

(b) Obscene Defined.

A thing is obscene if, considered as a whole, its predominant appeal is to prurient interest, that is, a shameful or morbid interest in nudity, sex or excretion, and if it goes substantially beyond customary limits of candor in description or representation of such matters. A thing is obscene even though the obscenity is latent, as in the case of undeveloped photographs.

(c) Interpretation of Evidence.

Obscenity shall be judged with reference to ordinary adults, except that it shall be judged with reference to children or other specially susceptible audiences if it appears from the character of the material or the circumstances of its dissemination to be specially designed for or directed to such an audience.

Where circumstances of production, presentation, sale, dissemination, distribution, or publicity indicate that material is being commercially exploited for the sake of its prurient appeal, such evidence is probative with respect to the nature of the matter and can justify the conclusion that the matter is utterly without redeeming social importance.

In any prosecution for an offense under this Section evidence shall be admissible to show:

(1) the character of the audience for which the material was designed or to which it was directed;

(2) what the predominant appeal of the material would be for ordinary adults or a special audience, and what effect if any, it would probably have on the behavior of such people;

(3) the artistic, literary, scientific, educational or other merits of the material, or absence thereof;

(4) the degree, if any, of public acceptance of the material in this State;

(5) appeal to prurient interest, or absence thereof, in advertising or other promotion of the material;

(6) purpose of the author, creator, publisher or disseminator.

(d) Sentence.

Obscenity is a Class A misdemeanor. A second or subsequent offense is a Class 4 felony.

In 1978, the appellate court of Illinois was called upon to interpret parts of this statute.[67] Defendants were convicted for sales of magazines in violation of the obscenity statute. According to records of the proceedings, the alleged obscene publications were purchased by police officers who paid fifty cents admission to enter the premises, and an additional $9.50 for the publication. The officer had asked the clerk in the store if he would sell this type of publication to a minor and the clerk had responded that he would not.

---

[67] People v. Rode, 57 Ill. App. 3d 645, 373 N.E.2d 605 (1978). *See* case in Part II.

The record shows that the clerk had been employed by the store for two months prior to the sale. His duties were that of clerk and cashier and he did nothing concerning the selection of the merchandise.

One of the defendants in the case, a clerk, Mears, claimed that the trial court erred in finding him guilty of obscenity because:

> (1) the evidence was insufficient to establish that the defendant had sold a publication with *knowledge* of the nature and contents thereof, or recklessly failed to exercise reasonable inspection thereof, and
>
> (2) that the magazines were not obscene.

As to the obscenity issue, the court indicated that "we are required to make an independent judgment of whether this material is constitutionally protected," but held that, in accordance with the obscenity guidelines stated in *People v. Ward*,[68] decided in 1976, "any reasonable person would immediately classify the entire publication as obscene in accordance with the guidelines set out in *Speer*."

As to the knowledge issue, the court made a determination that knowledge of the seller is, in fact, an essential element of the conviction for obscenity. However, the judges indicated that the facts were sufficient to establish that Mears had full knowledge that in fact the material was obscene. The court explained that, like any other legal material fact, knowledge may be proved by circumstantial evidence. As all the elements of the crime as stated in the statute were proved, the court affirmed the judgment of the lower court. The Illinois Supreme Court observed that it is extremely difficult to define the term *obscenity* with a fine degree of precision, stating that the Illinois statutory definition is sufficiently clear to withstand constitutional objection.

Statutes differ in stating the test for "obscenity." Many use the *Miller* test, either restating the terms as used in the decision or by adopting the definition. Some, however, use different terminology in defining what is obscene, and some list the subjects with respect to which prurient interest must be aroused.

An example of a statute which uses terminology different from the Model Code is that of California. Part of the Code provides:

> (a) every person who knowingly sends or causes to be sent, or brings, or causes to be brought, into this state for sale or distribution, or in this state possesses, prepares, publishes, or

---

[68] People v. Ward, 63 Ill. 2d 437, 349 N.E.2d 47 (1976).

> prints, with intent to distribute or to exhibit to others or who offers to distribute, distributes, or exhibits to others any obscene matter is guilty of a misdemeanor.[69]

Obscene matter is defined as:

> matter taken as a whole, the predominant appeal of which to the average person, applying contemporary standards, is to prurient interest, i.e., a shameful or morbid interest in nudity, sex, or excretion; and is matter which taken as a whole goes substantially beyond customary limits of candor in description or representation of such matters; and is matter which taken as a whole is utterly without redeeming social importance.[70]

This Section of the statute was challenged as being unconstitutionally vague, but the California Court of Appeals determined that the Section defining the crime of possessing obscene material with intent to distribute it to others was not unconstitutional under the provisions of the constitution prohibiting laws in restraint or abridgement of liberty or free speech or press.[71]

As the Illinois court indicated, it is extremely difficult to define the term obscenity with a fine degree of precision. During the past decade, legislatures and courts have wrestled with this problem but now that most are following the guidelines established by the U.S. Supreme Court, it appears that the decisions are reasonably consistent in holding that obscenity can be defined so as to meet the constitutional requirements and that obscenity laws, when carefully drafted, can meet the standards required by the Constitution.

§ 8.5 Bigamy and Polygamy

A. Traditional Definitions and Elements

Bigamy was not a crime at common law, but was considered an offense of ecclesiastical cognizance with punishment in the hands of the ecclesiastical tribunals rather than the common law courts.[72] During the reign of James

---

[69] Cal. Penal Code § 311.2 (West 1977).

[70] *Id.* § 311 (West 1978).

[71] People v. Wiener, 91 Cal. App. 3d 238, 154 Cal. Rptr. 110 (1979).

[72] State v. Sellers, 140 S.C. 66, 134 S.E. 873 (1926).

the First, bigamy was made a felony punishable in the civil courts.[73] The crime of bigamy was included in the early Virginia statute and there has never been a time in any state when polygamy has not been an offense against society cognizable and punishable in the criminal courts in this country.[74]

The commonly understood meaning of the term bigamy is the having of two wives or husbands at the same time. Polygamy has been defined as the offense of having a plurality of husbands or wives. The traditional legal definition of bigamy is willfully and knowingly contracting a second marriage where the contracting party knows that the first marriage is still existing.[75]

In some states, the traditional crime was designated as either bigamy or polygamy. The definitions are very similar. For example, in Arizona bigamy was defined, until the statute was repealed in 1978, as a person who, having a husband or wife, marries any other person.[76] The Louisiana statute defines bigamy as marriage to another person by a person already married and having a husband or wife living.[77] In Utah, the polygamy statute provided a penalty for "every person who has a husband or wife living, who marries another, either married or single."[78] For practical purposes, it makes no difference whether the crime is designated as bigamy or polygamy. In this country, if a person who is married contracts a second marriage, that person is violating the law and is subject to criminal penalty.

Before discussing the essential elements of bigamy or polygamy, some additional definitions by the courts will assist in identifying the elements.

> The essential things for pleading and proof to show to establish "bigamy" are the previously established status of the defendant as a married person and his additional marriage during continuance of that status.[79]

> "Bigamy" is committed when a person, who is already legally married, marries another person during the life of his wife, or her husband.[80]

---

[73] Barber v. State, 50 Md. 161 (1878).

[74] 10 C.J.S. *Bigamy* § 2 (1938).

[75] State v. Martinez, 43 Idaho 180, 250 P. 239 (1926).

[76] Ariz. Rev. Stat. Ann. § 13-271 (1977), as amended by Ariz. Rev. Stat. § 13-3606 (1978).

[77] La. Rev. Stat. Ann. § 14:76 (West 1974).

[78] Utah Code Ann. § 76-53-1 (1973).

[79] People v. Lamarr, 20 Cal. 2d 705, 128 P.2d 345 (1942).

[80] Farewell v. Commonwealth, 167 Va. 475, 189 S.E. 321 (1937).

An indictment charging that the defendant was married, and while married and undivorced, knowingly and unlawfully married one named in the indictment, sufficiently charges the offense of bigamy....And the word "bigamy" as used in the statute denouncing the offense, is used in the universally understood meaning, so that a description of the offense would not express more than the word itself.[81]

There are two essential elements to constitute the crime of bigamy:

(1) a prior marriage,
(2) going through a form of a second marriage before the first marriage is dissolved.

It is noted that the criminal intent is generally not essential to bigamy, nor is good faith a defense.

(a) Prior Marriage Element
In order for one to be convicted of the crime of bigamy, the state must prove a valid marriage entered into by the accused before the alleged bigamist marriage. If the defense can show that the prior marriage was non-valid for one reason or another, then there can be no conviction. However, a false assumption of invalidity of a former marriage will not serve as a defense.[82]

Obviously, if the prior marriage has been dissolved by death, divorce or annulment before the second took place, there is no bigamy. But a divorce obtained by fraud or one that, for some reason, is ineffectual, is not a defense.

(b) Subsequent Marriage
Before one can be convicted of the offense of bigamy, proof must be offered to show that the person went through the form of a subsequent marriage. Such a marriage, of course, is void; nevertheless, evidence must be introduced to show that the marriage ceremony was performed.[83]

---

[81] State v. Hayes, 105 La. 352, 29 So. 937 (1901).

[82] Long v. State, 192 Ind. 524, 137 N.E. 49 (1922).

[83] Betheny v. State, 91 Tex. Crim. 59, 237 S.W. 262 (1922). *See also*, State v. Crosby, 420 P.2d 431 (Mont. 1966). *See* case in Part II.

3. Defenses

A person accused of bigamy may defend by showing the absence of one or more of the elements constituting the offense. If the prior marriage has been dissolved, then there will be no conviction. There is no problem if the marriage has been dissolved by actual death or by a legal divorce; however, there are some circumstances where death is not certain and divorce is in doubt.

The general rule is that a marriage contracted in good faith after the expiration of a designated statutory period is valid. Most state statutes provide that if a person is absent and not heard from for a certain number of years he is presumed to be dead. In some instances the period is designated as seven years.

By some authorities, an honest belief reasonably entertained in the exercise of care that a divorce has been granted is a defense to a prosecution for bigamy.[84] The reasoning is that a person should not be held criminally liable when he has been misled without his own fault or carelessness concerning the facts. But even here it is not sufficient that the second marriage was contracted on the strength of a mere rumor of a divorce. A bona fide effort to ascertain the truth of the rumor is essential.[85]

A person who is contemplating a subsequent marriage cannot rely upon the advice of his attorney. One court held that the advice of counsel that there was no impediment to a second marriage was no defense to prosecution for bigamy.[86]

B. *Contemporary Statutes and Codes*

1. Model Penal Code[87]

§ 230.1 Bigamy and Polygamy

(1) Bigamy. A married person is guilty of bigamy, a misdemeanor, if he contracts or purports to contract another marriage, unless at the time of the subsequent marriage:

    (a) the actor believes that the prior spouse is dead; or

---

[84] Adams v. State, 95 Tex. Crim. 542, 252 S.W. 537 (1923).

[85] White v. State, 157 Tenn. 446, 9 S.W.2d 702 (1928).

[86] State v. Hughes, 58 Iowa 165, 11 N.W. 706 (1882).

[87] Model Penal Code § 230.1 (Proposed Official Draft 1980).

(b) the actor and the prior spouse have been living apart for five consecutive years throughout which the prior spouse was not known by the actor to be alive; or

(c) a Court has entered a judgment purporting to terminate or annul any prior disqualifying marriage, and the actor does not know that judgment to be invalid; or

(d) the actor reasonably believes that he is legally eligible to remarry.

(2) Polygamy. A person is guilty of polygamy, a felony of the third degree, if he marries or cohabits with more than one spouse at a time in purported exercise of the right of plural marriage. The offense is a continuing one until all cohabitation and claim of marriage with more than one spouse terminates. This Section does not apply to parties to a polygamous marriage, lawful in the country of which they are residents or nationals, while they are in transit through or temporarily visiting this State.

(3) Other Party to Bigamous or Polygamous Marriage. A person is guilty of bigamy or polygamy, as the case may be, if he contracts or purports to contract marriage with another knowing that the other is thereby committing bigamy or polygamy.

The Model Penal Code defines three offenses and distinguishes between bigamy and polygamy. Although ordinary adultery is not a crime under the Code, bigamist adultery is a crime. The rationale is that bigamist cohabitation amounts to a public affront, and society demands that this act be punished.

The Model Code departs, to some extent, from prior law by creating a separate offense of polygamy with felony sanctions. Such sanctions are provided for those who make a formal commitment to plural marriage.

The Code also makes it clear that a person is guilty of bigamy or polygamy, although that person was not previously married, if he has knowledge that the other party is thereby committing bigamy or polygamy.

Unlike some of the statutes in existence at the time the Code was prepared, the Code provides specific defenses to the crime. Although many of these defenses are found in the traditional statutes or have been interpreted as defenses by the courts in the various states, the enumeration of the defenses make it less difficult to enforce the statute.

2. Federal Code

Title 18 of the U.S. Code contains no specific provision concerning the offense of bigamy.

3. Other statutes and codes

Many of the recently enacted statutes follow the wording of the Model Code, but some still are strict liability offenses and some require knowledge of the ineligibility to contract the second marriage. Examples of contemporary state statutes are as follows.[88]

The Alabama Code proceeds:

> § 13-8-2. Bigamy and bigamous cohabitation.
>
> If any person, having a former wife or husband living, marries another or continues to cohabit with such second husband or wife in this state, he or she shall, on conviction, be imprisoned in the penitentiary for not less than two nor more than five years.
>
> The provisions of this Section do not apply to any person who, prior to such second marriage, had procured a decree from a court of competent jurisdiction dissolving his or her former marriage and allowing him or her the privilege of marrying again; nor to any person who, at the time of such second marriage, did not know that his or her former husband or wife was living and whose former husband or wife had remained absent from him or her for the last five years preceding such second marriage.

The first paragraph is intended to apply not only to marriages which are officially contracted, but also where either the prior or subsequent marriage, or both, was a common law marriage (a type of marriage which is recognized in Alabama). The second paragraph of the Code provides a defense of reasonable belief that one of the events indicated has occurred. The purpose is to cover legitimate cases of mistake of fact or law regarding eligibility to remarry.

---

[88] Ala. Code, § 13A-13-1 (1977).

The Georgia Code is somewhat different. It provides:[89]

26-2007 Bigamy

A person commits bigamy when he, being married and know-ing that his lawful spouse is living, marries another person or car-ries on a bigamous cohabitation with another person. A person convicted of bigamy shall be punished by imprisonment for not less than one nor more than 10 years.

It shall be an affirmative defense that the prior spouse has been continually absent for a period of seven years during which time the accused did not know the prior spouse to be alive, or that the accused reasonably believed he was eligible to remarry.

(Acts 1968, pp. 1249, 1300.)

26-2008 Marrying a bigamist

An unmarried man or woman commits the offense of marrying a bigamist when he marries a person whom he knows to be the wife or husband of another. A person convicted of marrying a bigamist shall be punished by imprisonment for not less than one nor more than 10 years.

It shall be an affirmative defense that the prior spouse of the bigamist has been continually absent for a period of seven years during which time the accused did not know the prior spouse of the bigamist to be alive, or that the accused reasonably believed the bigamist was eligible to remarry.

(Acts 1968, pp. 1249, 1300.)

The Georgia Code requires *knowledge* on the part of the person who marries the second time that the lawful spouse is living. Under this Code, the prosecution must prove knowledge as an element of the crime.

The Georgia Code also specifically covers the person who is marrying a bigamist with knowledge.

Bigamy and/or polygamy have been criminal offenses, in the United States since the formation of the union and continued to be punishable under the statutes of the states. Although the statutes are consistent in holding that a previous marriage and a contract for a subsequent marriage are elements, they may differ in regard to the *mens rea* and in specifying the defenses. The statutes also differ in establishing the criminal liability of the other party to the bigamist marriage and in grading the offenses as misdemeanors or

---

[89] Ga. Code Ann. §§ 26-2007, 26-2008 (1977).

felonies. It is therefore, necessary that the statutes of the respective states, as well as the decisions interpreting those statutes, be carefully researched.

§ 8.6 Incest

A. Traditional Definition and Elements

Incest was not crime at common law, but it was punishable as an offense in the ecclesiastical courts in England.[90] In the United States, incest is a statutory crime, the object of which is to prohibit sexual intercourse between those related within the prescribed degrees and to promote domestic peace and social purity.[91]

Rape and incest are entirely different crimes. Incest is not a lower degree of the crime and is not included therein. However, in some jurisdictions where the consent of the female is not necessary to constitute crime of incest, the same act may constitute both rape and incest.[92]

Incest is defined as the intermarriage, or sexual relations without marriage, between a man and woman related to each other in any of the degrees of consanguinity or affinity within which marriage is prohibited. Consanguinity is defined as a blood relationship or relation of persons descended from the same stock or common ancestry.[93] Consanguinity is distinguished from affinity, which is the connection existing in consequences of marriage, between each of the married persons and the kindred of the other.[94] The crime of incest is closely tied in with statutes which prohibit marriage of persons who are related to the degree established by the statute. Statutes differ as to the degree of the relationship, however, they are fairly consistent in holding that marriage between father and daughter, mother and son, brother and sister, uncle and niece, and aunt and nephew are prohibited. Some have been held to include first cousins but, under other statutes, prohibition of marriage between first cousins does not make their marriage or cohabitation incest.[95]

As there is a moral difference between the marriage or sexual intercourse of persons related by consanguinity and persons related only by affinity, many statutes distinguish between these two. In one case, the court held

---

[90] Commonwealth v. Ashley, 248 Mass. 259, 142 N.E. 788 (1924).

[91] Signs v. State, 35 Okla. Crim. 340, 250 P. 938 (1926).

[92] State v. Hurd, 101 Iowa 391, 70 N.W. 613 (1897).

[93] Henley v. State, 489 S.W.2d 53 (1972).

[94] Sizemore v. Commonwealth, 210 Ky. 637, 276 S.W. 524 (1925).

[95] State v. Couvillion, 117 La. 935, 42 So. 431 (1906).

that a statutory prohibition expressly relating to degrees of consanguinity will not, by implication, extend to degrees of affinity.[96] Some statutes expressly extend to the relationship by affinity. Under these statutes, sexual intercourse between a step-father and a step-daughter, a step-mother and a step-son, or a brother-in-law and sister-in-law is prohibited.[97] As a general rule, affinity ceases on the divorce or death of the blood relative through whom the relationship was created. Therefore, in the absence of a statutory provision, after such a divorce or death, it is not incest for a man to marry or have unlawful intercourse with his former wife's daughter or sister.[98]

In distinguishing between the crimes of adultery, fornication and incest, one court made this concise statement:

> By "fornication" is meant illicit carnal connection; unlawful sexual intercourse. This unlawful intercourse, unaccompanied by any circumstances which tend to aggravate it, is simply fornication; and when, as the result of such fornication a child is born, it is called bastardy. If a man who is married has unlawful sexual intercourse, we call it "adultery" in him. When the act is between the parties sustaining relationships with each other within certain degrees of consanguinity or affinity, we call it "incest." Where the female consents to unlawful intercourse through fraudulent acts, including a promise of marriage, we call it "seduction." In each case, the essential fact which constitutes the crime is fornication.[99]

In further distinguishing between the various sex crimes, the courts have indicated that the destructive ingredient of the crime of incest is the relationship of the parties or as one court framed it, the essence of incest is not intercourse, but intercourse with a relative within the proscribed line of consanguinity.[100]

The elements of the crime of incest are:

(a) marriage or sexual intercourse,
(b) between persons within the degree of relationship proscribed by statute,

---

[96] Maxey v. Commonwealth, 225 Ky. 663, 9 S.W.2d 1001 (1928).
[97] 42 C.J.S. *Incest* § 3 (1944).
[98] Wilson v. State, 100 Tenn. 596, 46 S.W. 451 (1898).
[99] People v. Rouse, 2 Mich. 209 (1871).
[100] People v. Folsom, 51 N.Y. Supp. 2d 733 (1944).

(c) under some statutes knowledge of the existence of the relationship.

As to the element (c) indicated above, some statutes make the persons guilty even if the knowledge of the relationship is not present; therefore, in these states, knowledge is not an element of the offense. In one case, the justices reasoned that knowledge of the relationship on the part of both parties to the incestuous act is not essential to a conviction of the one who had such knowledge.[101] To constitute "sexual relations" as required by the statute, evidence must be introduced to show that there was an actual penetration, but emission is generally not required.[102]

B. Contemporary Statutes and Codes

1. Model Penal Code[103]

§ 230.2 Incest

A person is guilty of incest, a felony of the third degree, if he knowingly marries or cohabits or has sexual intercourse with an ancestor or descendant, or brother or sister of the whole or half blood [or an uncle, aunt, nephew or niece of the whole blood]. "Cohabit" means to live together under the representation or appearance of being married. The relationships referred to herein include blood relationships without regard to legitimacy, and relationship of parent and child by adoption.

Rather than using traditional terms, the Model Code specifically states the relationships that must exist if the crime of incest is committed. The Code also refers to blood relationships without regard to legitimacy and includes relations of both whole or half blood. It is noted that the crime of incest is limited to blood relatives plus the relationship of parent and child by adoption.

---

[101] Morgan v. State, 11 Ala. 289 (1847).

[102] Signs v. State, 35 Okla. Crim. 340, 250 P. 938 (1926); Svehla v. State, 168 Neb. 553, 96 N.W. 2d 649 (1959).

[103] Model Penal Code § 230.2 (Proposed Official Draft 1980).

2. Federal Code

Title 18 of the U.S. Code contains no specific provision concerning the offense of incest except in reference to offenses committed within Indian territory.[104] This Section provides that the offense of incest shall be defined and punished in accordance with the laws of the state in which such offense was committed and as are in force at the time of such offense.

3. Other statutes and codes

Contemporary state statutes are considerably diverse; some prohibit marriage, sexual intercourse and cohabitation, while others apply only to marriage and sexual intercourse.[105] Some states punish all forms of sexual intercourse and explicitly include deviate sexual intercourse, while a few limit the offense to vaginal sexual intercourse. Most require knowledge as an element of the crime; however, a few do not specifically require this culpability element.

An example of a state statute is that of Alabama.[106]

> § 13-8-3. Incest.
> If any man and woman, being within the degrees of consanguinity or relationship within which marriages are declared by law to be incestuous and void and knowing of such consanguinity or relationship, intermarry or have sexual intercourse together or live together in adultery, each of them shall, on conviction, be imprisoned in the penitentiary for not less than one nor more than seven years.
>
> On conviction for incest for marrying within the prohibited degrees, the court must declare such marriage null and void and may require the parties to enter into recognizance, with sufficient sureties, that they will not thereafter cohabit.

The Alabama law on incest declares sexual intercourse between persons related as indicated to be criminal whether or not the relationship is based on a marriage. The relationships that are forbidden are specifically spelled out and knowledge is an element of the crime.

To convict a person who is indicted for incest, the prosecution must prove:

---

[104] 18 U.S.C. § 1153.

[105] Id.

[106] Ala. Code § 13-8-3 (1977).

(a)   marriage or sexual intercourse,
(b)   knowledge of the specific relationship and
(c)   the existence of one of the relationships specified in the statute.

In the commentary following this Section in the Alabama Criminal Code, the reasons for the offense are enumerated briefly. They are:

(a)   the law against incest may represent a reinforcement of civil sanctions of a religious tenet,
(b)   there is a secular utility in a prohibition against in-breeding that results in defective offspring by reason of the higher probability of unfavorable, recessive genes combining in the children of parents with certain blood relationships,
(c)   a sociological and psychological justification is that the prohibition of incest tends to promote solidarity of the family by preventing sex rivalries and jealousies within the family unit and
(d)   the utility of forbidding the views by heads of households, especially males, of their authority and financial power over younger children, especially females.

The Georgia statute is stated differently. It provides:[107]

§ 26-2006 Incest

A person commits incest when he engages in sexual intercourse with a person to whom he knows he is related, either by blood or by marriage as follows:

(a)   father and daughter or stepdaughter;
(b)   mother and son or stepson;
(c)   brother and sister of the whole blood or of the half blood;
(d)   grandparent and grandchild;
(e)   aunt and nephew; or
(f)   uncle and niece.

A person convicted of incest shall be punished by imprisonment for not less than one nor more than 20 years.

---

[107]   Ga. Code Ann. § 26-2006 (1968).

Although the Georgia statute does not specifically require corroboration, a Georgia court has determined that testimony of the female accomplice must be corroborated in order to warrant conviction.[108] The Georgia court also has determined that, under certain conditions, the crime of incest is included within the crime of rape. Therefore, where a man was convicted of statutory rape and incest following an act of sexual intercourse with his 13-year-old daughter and was sentenced to 20 years for each offense, incest was held to be included within the rape, and the conviction for incest was void.[109]

§ 8.7 Abortion

A. Traditional Definition and Elements

The term abortion does not necessarily imply a criminal act. In medical parlance, the expulsion of the ovum, or embryo, within the first six weeks after conception is technically miscarriage; between that time and the expiration of the sixth month, when the child might possibly live, it is termed abortion; if the delivery is soon after the sixth month, it is termed premature labor.[110]

According to Justice Rehnquist's dissenting opinion in the case of *Roe v. Wade* in 1973, as early as 1821, the first state law dealing directly with abortion was enacted by the Connecticut legislature.[111] Justice Rehnquist, in arguing that the Fourteenth Amendment should not be used as a vehicle for overturning state abortion laws, pointed out that by the time of the adoption of the Fourteenth Amendment in 1868, there were at least 36 laws enacted by state or territorial legislatures limiting abortion. Listing the states in the decision, the Justice noted that, at the time of the decision (1973), the states had amended or updated their laws; however, 21 of the laws on the books in 1868 remained in effect as of 1973.

According to these statutes, purposely and unjustifiably terminating the pregnancy of another other than by a birth was a crime. For example, a Kansas statute provided that "whoever with intent to produce a miscarriage of any pregnant woman or of any woman, unlawfully administers, or causes to be given to her any drug or noxious substance whatever, or unlawfully uses

---

108   Andrews v. State, 144 Ga. App. 243, 240 S.E.2d 744 (Ga. Ct. App. 1977).

109   Ramsey v. State, 145 Ga. App. 60, 243 S.E.2d 555 (Ga. Ct. App. 1978).

110   1 AM. JUR. *Abortion* § 1 (1936).

111   Roe v. Wade, 410 U.S. 113, 35 L.Ed.2d 147, 93 S. Ct. 705 (1973).

any instrument or means whatever, with such intent, shall be guilty of the offense."[112]

The Texas law which was challenged in *Roe v. Wade* made it a crime to procure an abortion as defined therein or to attempt an abortion except on medical advice for the purpose of saving the life of the mother.[113] In that case, the Court noted that similar statutes were in existence in a majority of the states and included in the footnote a list of the statutes with the different wording in those statutes.

The elements of the crime of abortion in the majority of the states prior to *Roe v. Wade* were:

(a) an intent to produce a miscarriage,
(b) unlawful administration of drugs or noxious substances or using an instrument, and
(c) a resulting miscarriage.

In regard to the third element, in many states an actual miscarriage was not a necessary element of the offense as the statute included a punishment provision where one prescribed the medicine or drug or used an instrument with the intent to procure miscarriage.

B. *Contemporary Statutes and Codes*

1. Model Penal Code[114]

§ 230.3 Abortion
(1) *Unjustified Abortion.* A person who purposely and unjustifiably terminates the pregnancy of another otherwise than by a live birth commits a felony of the third degree or, where the pregnancy has continued beyond the twenty-sixth week, a felony of the second degree.

(2) *Justifiable Abortion.* A licensed physician is justified in terminating a pregnancy if he believes there is substantial risk that continuance of the pregnancy would gravely impair the physical or mental health of the mother or that the child would be born with grave physical or mental defect, or that the pregnancy resulted from rape, incest, or other felonious inter-

---

[112] State v. Miller, 90 Kan. 230, 133 P. 878 (1913).

[113] Vernon's Ann. Articles 1191-1194.

[114] Model Penal Code § 230.3 (Proposed Official Draft 1980).

course. All illicit intercourse with a girl below the age of 16 shall be deemed felonious for purposes of this Subsection. Justifiable abortions shall be performed only in a licensed hospital except in case of emergency when hospital facilities are unavailable. [Additional exceptions from the requirement of hospitalization may be incorporated here to take account of situations in sparsely settled areas where hospitals are not generally accessible.]

(3) *Physicians' Certificates; Presumption from Non-Compliance.* No abortion shall be performed unless two physicians, one of whom may be the person performing the abortion, shall have certified in writing the circumstances which they believe to justify the abortion. Such certificate shall be submitted before the abortion to the hospital where it is to be performed and, in the case of abortion following felonious intercourse, to the prosecuting attorney or the police. Failure to comply with any of the requirements of this Subsection gives rise to a presumption that the abortion was unjustified.

(4) *Self-Abortion.* A woman whose pregnancy has continued beyond the twenty-sixth week commits a felony of the third degree if she purposely terminates her own pregnancy otherwise than by a live birth, or if she uses instruments, drugs or violence upon herself for that purpose. Except as justified under Subsection (2), a person who induces or knowingly aids a woman to use instruments, drugs or violence upon herself for the purpose of terminating her pregnancy otherwise than by a live birth commits a felony of the third degree whether or not the pregnancy has continued beyond the twenty-sixth week.

(5) *Pretended Abortion.* A person commits a felony of the third degree if, representing that it is his purpose to perform an abortion, he does an act adapted to cause abortion in a pregnant woman although the woman is in fact not pregnant, or the actor does not believe she is. A person charged with unjustified abortion under Subsection (1) or an attempt to commit that offense may be convicted thereof upon proof of conduct prohibited by this Subsection.

(6) *Distribution of Abortifacients.* A person who sells, offers to sell, possesses with intent to sell, advertises, or displays for sale anything specially designed to terminate a pregnancy, or held out by the actor as useful for that purpose, commits a misdemeanor, unless:

(a) the sale, offer or display is to a physician or druggist or to an intermediary in a chain of distribution to physicians or druggists; or

(b) the sale is made upon prescription or order of a physician; or

(c) the possession is with intent to sell as authorized in paragraphs (a) and (b); or

(d) the advertising is addressed to persons named in paragraph (a) and confined to trade or professional channels not likely to reach the general public.

(7) *Section Inapplicable to Prevention of Pregnancy.* Nothing in this Section shall be deemed applicable to the prescription, administration or distribution of drugs or other substances for avoiding pregnancy, whether by preventing implantation of a fertilized ovum or by any other method that operates before, at or immediately after fertilization.

The Model Penal Code is very complex and takes into consideration a recent Supreme Court decision relating to abortion. Subsection (1) prohibits all unjustified termination of the pregnancy of another. This would require an actual termination of the pregnancy. Subsection (2) defines what constitutes justifiable abortion and exceptions. Subsection (3) requires that two physicians certify in advance their belief as to the circumstances justifying the abortion, but violation of this requirement would not itself make the abortion unlawful. Subsection (4) deals with the self-abortion late in pregnancy. Subsection (5) contains a provision relating to one who represents that he is performing an abortion although he may know or believe that the woman is not pregnant, and Subsection (6) deals with the distribution of anything specifically designed to terminate a pregnancy or held out by the actor as useful for that purpose. Subsection (7) is designed to make it clear that the use of contraception devices or drugs to prevent pregnancy do not come within the ambit of the offense.

2. Federal Code

Title 18 of the U.S. Code contains no provision directly prohibiting abortion; however, there are two Sections which prohibit mailing, importation or transportation of instruments, substances and drugs used for producing abortion.[115] Title 18, § 1461 prohibits mailing of articles or things de-

---

[115] 18 U.S.C. §§ 1461 and 1462.

signed, adapted, or intended to produce an abortion. Title 18, § 1462 prohibits bringing into the United States any drug, medicine, article or thing designed, adapted or intended for producing abortion.

3. Other statutes and codes

When the decision in the case of *Roe v. Wade* was announced, many state abortion statutes became invalid. That case held that the Texas Criminal Abortion Statute prohibiting abortions at any stage of pregnancy except to save the life of the mother are unconstitutional. While agreeing that the state has an interest in regulating abortions, the majority concluded that the right of personal privacy includes the right of a pregnant female to make the decision whether or not to terminate her pregnancy. The Court went on to explain, however, that the woman's right to terminate pregnancy is not absolute.

Finding that the state has a legitimate interest in protecting the pregnant woman's health and the potentiality of human life, each of which interests grows and reaches a "compelling" point at various stages of the woman's approach to term, the majority of the Supreme Court did find that the state may regulate abortions. Drawing some guidelines, the majority held that, prior to approximately the end of the first trimester, the abortion decision and its effectuation must be left to the medical judgment of the pregnant woman's attending physician. However, subsequent to approximately the end of the first trimester, the state may regulate abortion procedures in ways reasonably related to maternal health, and at the stage subsequent to viability the state may regulate and even proscribe abortion except where necessary in appropriate medical judgment for preservation of life or health of the mother.

Following the case of *Roe v. Wade*, state legislatures responded with a variety of new abortion regulations. In 1982, the Commonwealth of Pennsylvania enacted the Abortion Control Act, which regulates the information a woman considers before consenting to an abortion, the procedure a physician follows when performing a late abortion, and the data that are reported to public authorities.[116]

This Section of the statute was challenged in the case of *Thornburgh v. American College of Obstetricians and Gynecologists*.[117] In this case, action was brought challenging the constitutionality of the statute and seeking declaratory and injunctive relief. By the time the statute reached the Supreme Court, the dispute centered on three Sections. One Section lists a set of facts which must be recited to every woman who seeks an abortion.

---

[116] Pa. Stat. Ann. tit. 18, §§ 3201-3220 (Purdon 1983).

[117] 106 S. Ct. 2169 (1986).

Another Section prohibits doctors from performing an abortion after the fetus is viable, except when the procedure is necessary to preserve the mother's health. The law further provides that when a physician decides that such a late abortion is necessary, the Section imposes two duties; first, the physician must try to remove the fetus alive, unless the attempt "would significantly increase the risk to the mother," and, secondly, the physician must call a colleague into the room to take exclusive control and care for the aborted fetus.[118]

The Supreme Court, after considering the jurisdiction question, decided that the requirement that the woman be advised that the medical assistance may be available, and that the father is responsible for financial assistance in supporting the child, is unconstitutional. Also, the requirement that the physician inform the woman of the detrimental physical and psychological effects and of all the particular medical risks was also unconstitutional. The reporting requirements of the statute did not meet the constitutional requirements, nor did the provisions governing the degree of care for post-viability abortions. Finally, the provisions requiring the presence of a second physician, by failing to provide medical emergency exception for the situation where the mother's health is endangered by delay in the second physician's arrival, was unconstitutional.

The Court, after specifically reaffirming *Roe v. Wade*, made this comment:

> The states are not free under the guise of protecting maternal health or potential life, to intimidate women into continuing pregnancies. Appellants claim that the statutory provisions before us today further legitimate compelling interests of the Commonwealth. Close analysis of these provisions, however, shows that they wholly subordinate constitutional privacy interests and concerns with maternal health in an effort to deter a woman from making a decision that, with her physician, is hers to make.

It is noted that the *Thornburgh* decision, which reasserted the fundamental right of women to choose abortion, was a 5-4 decision.

In a 1988 case, the Supreme Court again upheld the mother's constitutional right to abortion by deciding that the natural father's interest in an un-

---

[118]   *See, Right to Abortion Remains Unstable*, 21 SUFFOLK UNIV. LAW REV. 888, for a discussion of the *Thornburgh* case.

born fetus, although legitimate and apparently sincere, did not outweigh the mother's constitutionally protected right to abortion.[119]

In a case which received national attention, the Supreme Court, in 1989, again considered the authority of states to restrict abortions.[120] The Missouri statute at issue:

(1) prohibits public employees from performing or assisting abortions not necessary to save a pregnant woman's life;

(2) prohibits the use of public funds for counseling a woman to have an abortion or the use of public facilities for performing abortions, even if no public funds are involved; and

(3) requires doctors, who believe a woman requesting an abortion may be at least 20 weeks pregnant, to perform tests to determine whether the fetus is viable, or capable of surviving outside the womb.

Also, the preamble to the Missouri statute declares that human life begins at conception.

While five justices upheld the state requirements, the majority took three different approaches and the dissenting justices filed two separate opinions.

Writing for the plurality (Justices Kennedy, White and Rehnquist), Justice Rehnquist found that the provision requiring doctors to determine fetal viability only requires a physician to perform such tests as are necessary in accordance with the exercise of the physician's professional judgment. These judges would reject *Roe's* rigid trimester framework.

Justice O'Connor agreed that the Missouri law is constitutional, in that requiring tests to ascertain fetal viability is consistent with the state's interest in potential human life, but refused to reexamine the trimester framework set forth in *Roe*.

Justice Scalia, also recognizing the constitutionality of the law, criticized the plurality opinion for refusing to repudiate *Roe* outright.

The dissenting justices would reaffirm the *Roe* trimester framework and declare the Missouri law unconstitutional. The majority found little difficulty in dealing with the preamble ("the life of each human begins at conception" and "unborn children have protectable interests in life, health, and well being") as the preamble does not, by its terms, regulate abortions or any other aspect of medical practice.

---

[119] Doe v. Smith, 108 S. Ct. 2136 (1988).

[120] Webster v. Reproductive Health Services, 109 S. Ct. __ (1989). *See* case in Part II.

The decision in the *Webster* case did not overrule *Roe v. Wade*. However, it appears that at least four justices (possibly five) no longer endorse the *Roe* standard that a woman's right to have an abortion outweighs the state's interest in protecting fetuses at least until they can survive outside the womb.[121]

As a result of this case, more state legislatures will again enact restrictive state laws on abortion. Many probably will copy the Missouri law to avoid further constitutional challenge. Personnel who are charged with enforcing state abortion laws will find it necessary not only to check on the state law in their jurisdiction, but to keep abreast of any new state laws and court decisions.

§ 8.8 Other Offenses Involving Morality and Decency

In addition to the major crimes discussed, most statutes include other related offenses. These are often included under offenses against the family, moral offenses or offenses against public health and morals. Some examples are included here. The respective state statute should be consulted, however, for provisions that are applicable in the states where the laws are being enforced.

A. Non-Support of Dependants

An example of a non-support statute is that of Ohio. It provides:

(A) No person shall abandon, or fail to provide adequate support to:

    (1) his or her spouse, as required by law;

    (2) his or her legitimate or illegitimate child under 18, or mentally or physically handicapped child under 21;

    (3) his or her aged or inform parent or adoptive parent, who from lack of ability and means is unable to provide adequately for his or her own support;

    (4) Any person whom, by law or by court order or decree, the offender is legally obliged to support.[122]

---

[121] On the final day of its 1988-89 term, the court granted review in three cases challenging abortion laws in Illinois, Ohio and Minnesota. The court will have another opportunity to modify and narrow *Roe v. Wade*.

[122] Ohio Rev. Code Ann. § 2919.21 (Page 1987).

The Ohio Code includes an affirmative defense to the charge if the actor is unable to provide adequate support, or the parent abandoned or failed to support the actor as required by law while the actor was under the age of 18 or was mentally or physically handicapped and under age 21.[123]

B. Endangering Welfare of a Minor

An example of a statute providing a penalty for endangering the welfare of a minor is that of Kentucky. It provides:

(1) a parent, guardian or other person who is charged with the care or custody of a minor is guilty of endangering the welfare of a minor when he refuses to exercise reasonable diligence in the control of such child to prevent him from becoming a neglected dependent or delinquent child.[124]

C. Interference with Custody

An Ohio statute designed to prevent child stealing and enticing a child away is titled "Interference with Custody." It provides:

(A) No person, knowing he is without privilege to do so or being reckless in that regard, shall entice, take, keep, or harbor any of the following persons from his parent, guardian, or custodian:

(1) A child under the age of 18, or a mentally or physically handicapped child under the age of 21;

(2) A person committed by law to an institution for delinquent, unruly, neglected, abused, or dependent children;

(3) A person committed by law to an institution for the mentally ill or mentally deficient.[125]

---

[123]   Model Penal Code § 230.5 (Proposed Official Draft 1980), and following comments relating to state laws on non-support.

[124]   Ky. Rev. Stat. Ann. § 530.060 (Baldwin 1975). Model Penal Code § 230.4 (Proposed Official Draft 1962), providing the penalty for endangering welfare of child (1962).

[125]   Ohio Rev. Code Ann. § 2919.23 (Page 1987).

The Ohio statute provides a defense for enticing a child away if there is a reasonable belief that it is necessary for the child's protection, and also provides a defense to harboring a child if the actor timely notifies the authorities of the child's whereabouts.

§ 8.9 Summary

Some acts such as murder, burglary, arson and theft are so obviously wrong that punishment is provided in practically all societies. Other acts are borderline and are punishable in some jurisdictions and not in others. Within this category are offenses designated as "offenses against the public health, safety, and morals" or "offenses against morality and decency."

Until recently, most states had statutes which prohibited adultery and fornication. Today, adultery and fornication are punished in some states and not in others. The elements of adultery are voluntary sexual intercourse between parties not lawfully married to each other with at least one of the parties being married to another person. Fornication is voluntary sexual intercourse between unmarried persons.

Prostitution is defined as the practice of a female offering her body to an indiscriminate intercourse with a man, usually for hire. In some jurisdictions, to engage in prostitution is an offense. Also, to aid and abet prostitution, to associate with prostitutes, or to keep and operate a place of prostitution is punishable under the statutes. The modern trend is to place less emphasis on prosecuting the prostitute, but to more aggressively enforce the laws relating to promoting prostitution.

An offense that has given the legislative bodies and courts much difficulty is that related to obscenity. Practically all states have laws which prohibit conduct which is labeled obscene. In order to comply with the U.S. Supreme Court decisions, obscenity is very carefully defined. Some of the elements common to many statutes are:

(1) the matter in question is obscene, and
(2) the defendant must have knowledge of its obscenity.

Part of the definition in the Model Penal Code is "material is obscene if, considered as a whole, its predominant appeal is to prurient interest, that is, a shameful or morbid interest in nudity, sex or excretion, and if, in addition, it goes substantially beyond the customary limits of candor in describing or representing such matters."

Bigamy was not a crime at common law but was considered an offense in the ecclesiastical tribunals. It later became a specific crime and was included in the early statutes of the states in this country. The traditional legal definition of bigamy is willfully and knowingly contracting a second marriage where the contracting party knows that the first marriage is still existing. The statutes are consistent in holding that a previous marriage and a contract for a subsequent marriage are elements, but differ in regard to the knowledge requirements and in grading the offenses.

The offense known as incest was also punishable in the ecclesiastical courts in England. Today, incest is a crime in all states. It is defined as intermarriage, or sexual relations without marriage, between a man and a woman related to each other in any of the degrees of consanguinity or affinity within which marriage is prohibited.

The term abortion does not necessarily imply a criminal act, as there are some abortions permitted by law. The general definition of illegal abortion is "whoever with intent to produce a miscarriage of any pregnant woman unlawfully administers or causes to be given to her, any drug or substance, or unlawfully uses any instrument or means whatever, with such intent, shall be guilty of the offense of abortion."

Due to U.S. Supreme Court decisions and the uncertainty of definitions, the enforceability of abortion laws remains questionable.

There are other offenses involving morality and indecency, including non-support of dependents, endangering the welfare of a minor and interference with custody.

As the crimes relating to morality and decency differ from state to state, and as the definitions of various terminology often become technical, it is essential that criminal justice personnel study the specific statutes as well as cases interpreting the statutes in defining the terms used.

Chapter 9
OFFENSES AGAINST
THE PUBLIC PEACE

We cannot cast aside the centuries-long evolution of the collection of interlocking and overlapping concepts which the common law has utilized to assess the moral accountability of an individual for his antisocial deeds.

Powell v. State of Texas,
392 U.S. 514, 88 S. Ct. 2145,
20 L.Ed.2d 1254 (1968).

Section

§ 9.1 Introduction

Many of the offenses discussed in previous chapters, such as the homicide offenses, assault and battery, rape and robbery are, in fact, offenses against the public peace. There are other offenses, however, some of which are minor in character, which have not received the attention that some of the major crimes have received. These too are necessary if law and order is to be maintained. These are often categorized as "Offenses Against the Public Peace" or "Offenses Against Public Order."

In discussing the offenses against public peace, it is important to note that, in many instances, the U.S. Constitution, as interpreted by the courts, limits the police power of the state not only in enacting legislation, but in enforcing legislation that has been enacted. For example, disorderly conduct statutes have, in many instances, been declared unconstitutional as being either too vague or as infringing on the First Amendment rights.

In this chapter, the offenses of riot, disorderly conduct, vagrancy and loitering, drunkenness, obstructing a highway or public place, eavesdropping and wiretapping and other offenses against the public peace are discussed.

§ 9.2 Riot and Related Offenses

While in most offenses only one person may be involved, generally, in riot and riot-related offenses, the number of participants is more than one. Due to the number involved, the behavior is potentially more dangerous to the public peace and poses special problems for the police. In most instances, at least three or more persons must be involved if the offense is classified as a riot.

Also, it is necessary to point out that riots occur only after some preliminary occurrences. In some of the encyclopedias, riot is discussed along with unlawful assembly and rout, all of which constitute disturbances of the public peace. Before defining the term riot, other related offenses are distinguished. The three crimes of unlawful assembly, rout and riot represent the traditional steps in violent mob action.[1]

---

[1] 46 AM. JUR. *Riots and Unlawful Assembly* § 3 (1945).

A. Traditional Definitions and Elements

1. Unlawful assembly

An unlawful assembly consists of the coming together of three or more persons with a common purpose; either to commit a crime by open force or to carry out their common purpose, lawful or unlawful, in such manner as to cause persons of reasonable firmness and courage to apprehend a breach of the peace.[2]

In defining the term "unlawful assembly" and distinguishing this from the crime of "rout" and "riot," a West Virginia court made this comment:

> To constitute "unlawful assembly" there must be a gathering of three or more persons, to the disturbance of the public peace, with the intention of cooperating in the forcible and violent execution of some unlawful enterprise. If they take steps toward the performance of their purpose, it becomes a "rout"; and if they put their design to actual execution, it is a "riot."[3]

2. Rout

A rout is an unlawful assembly which has made a movement toward the execution of a common purpose of the persons assembled. When an unlawful assembly moves toward the accomplishment of the unlawful purpose, but no acts of violence or disorder have occurred, then a rout has been committed.

3. Riot

A riot is either an actual beginning of the execution of an unlawful common purpose, or the execution of an unlawful purpose by an assembly which was lawful when its members first assembled; in each case, force and violence being used to the terror of the people.

At common law, a "riot" was a tumultuous disturbance of the peace by three persons or more, assembling together of their own authority, with an intent mutually to assist one another against any who shall oppose them in execution of some enterprise of a private nature and afterwards actually exe-

---

[2]   Heard v. Rizzo, 281 F.Supp. 720 (D. Pa. 1968).

[3]   State v. Woolridge, 129 W.Va. 448, 40 S.E.2d 899 (1946).

cuting the same in a violent and turbulent manner, to the terror of the people, whether the act intended was, of itself, lawful or unlawful.[4]

In a prosecution for causing a riot at a federal penitentiary, a federal court defined "riot" as a "tumultuous disturbance of the peace by three persons or more, assembling together of their own authority, with an intent mutually to assist each other against any who shall oppose them, in the execution of some unlawful enterprise of a private nature and afterwards actually executing the same in a violent and turbulent manner."[5]

In *Feinstein v. City of New York*, the court, referring to English law, explained that a "riot" has been said to consist of the following elements:

(1) a number of persons, three at least;
(2) a common purpose;
(3) execution or inception of the common purpose;
(4) an intent to help one another by force if necessary against any person who may oppose them in the execution of their common purpose and
(5) force or violence not merely used in demolishing, but displayed in such a manner as to alarm at least one person of reasonable firmness and courage.[6]

4. Inciting to riot

"Inciting to riot" occurs when one incites or encourages other persons to create or engage in a riot as the term has been defined. In the case of *Kasper v. State*, the Supreme Court of Tennessee, in 1959, affirmed that inciting to riot is a common law offense.[7] In the *Kasper* case, the defendant appeared before the City School Board in an attempt to prevent integrating the first grade in the public schools. In making speeches, he was talking about having dynamite and knowing how to use it and that he or someone had a gun and that there would be bombings, dynamiting and even bloodshed. On one occasion, he told the crowd to follow him to the Buena Vista School. During the disturbance, the janitor's automobile was burned and the school yard was filled with sticks, stones and broken bottles. The court said "we are of the opinion that there is ample evidence, both direct and circumstantial, to support the jury verdict of inciting to riot."

---

[4]   Schoolcraft v. State, 84 Okla. Crim. 20, 178 P.2d 641 (1947).

[5]   United States v. Evans, 542 F.2d 805 (1976).

[6]   Feinstein v. City of New York, 283 N.Y.S. 335 (1935).

[7]   Kasper v. State, 206 Tenn. 434, 326 S.W.2d 664 (1959). *See* case in Part II.

As to the defendant's claim that this was a violation of free speech, the court said:

> There is no doubt in anybody's mind that any citizen has a right to express his opinion about the opinions of the Supreme Court of the United States in integration cases but the right of free speech is limited, just as are all other so-called rights and when one goes beyond a proper expression of opinion and incites to riot, he has gone beyond the area of freedom of speech.

One may be guilty of inciting a riot although he does not participate in the actual riot. "Inciting to riot" is a separate, distinct offense. Therefore, one may incite a riot and not participate in it, or he may be concerned in a riot without having incited it. However, the offense of inciting to riot may become merged with the more serious crime of riot if the actor participates during the inciting stage as well as in the execution phase of carrying out the unlawful purpose.[8]

B. Contemporary Statutes and Codes

1. Model Penal Code[9]

§ 250.1 Riot; Failure to Disperse

(1) *Riot.* A person is guilty of riot, a felony of the third degree, if he participates with [two] or more others in a course of disorderly conduct:

    (a) with purpose to commit or facilitate the commission of a felony or misdemeanor;

    (b) with purpose to prevent or coerce official action; or

    (c) when the actor or any other participant to the knowledge of the actor uses or plans to use a firearm or other deadly weapon.

(2) *Failure of Disorderly Persons to Disperse Upon Official Order.* Where [three] or more persons are participating in a course of disorderly conduct likely to cause substantial harm or serious inconvenience, annoyance or alarm, a peace officer or other public servant engaged in executing or enforcing the law may

---

[8]   Commonwealth v. Apriceno, 131 Pa. Super. 158, 198 A. 515 (1938).

[9]   Model Penal Code § 250.1 (Proposed Official Draft 1980).

order the participants and others in the immediate vicinity to disperse. A person who refuses or knowingly fails to obey such an order commits a misdemeanor.

The Model Penal Code does not carry forward the criminal law crimes of rout and unlawful assembly. Subsection (1) of the Model Code punishes for riot one who, under specific circumstances, participates with two or more persons in a course of disorderly conduct; thus, the Model Code includes the requirement that three persons must be involved. This Subsection spells out in three paragraphs the circumstances under which participants may be guilty of riot.

Paragraph (b) of Subsection (1) applies to disorderly conduct committed with the purpose to prevent or coerce official action. This is intended to reach the case of mob agitation against the lawful workings of government.

Paragraph (c) covers disorderly conduct without regard to the purpose of the participation but places the basis of liability on the actor or other participant who uses or plans to use a firearm or other deadly weapon. In the Model Penal Code, riot is a felony in the third degree.

2. Federal Code

The U.S. Code prescribes penalties for one who travels in interstate commerce to incite a riot.[10] It states in part that:

(a)(1)   Whoever travels in interstate or foreign commerce or uses any facility of interstate or foreign commerce, including, but not limited to, the mail, telegraph, telephone, radio, or television, with intent:

(A) to incite a riot; or
(B) to organize, promote, encourage, participate in, or carry on a riot; or
(C) to commit any act of violence in furtherance of a riot; or
(D) to aid or abet any person in inciting or participating in or carrying on a riot or committing any act of violence in furtherance of the riot;

---

[10] 18 U.S.C. § 2101.

and who either during the course of any such travel or use thereafter performs or attempts to perform any other overt act for any purpose specified in paragraphs (A), (B), (C) or (D) --

shall be fined not more than $10,000 or imprisoned for not more than 5 years or both.

This statute goes on to provide that a judgment of conviction or acquittal on the merits of the laws of any State shall be a bar to any prosecution hereunder for the same act or acts.

Title 18, § 2102 defines the term "riot" as used in the chapter. To assure that the First Amendment provisions are not violated, the definition of the term "to incite a riot" includes a statement that this shall not be deemed to mean the mere oral or written advocacy of ideas or expression of belief, not involving advocacy of any act or acts of violence or assertion of the rightness of, or the right to commit any such act or acts. The Federal Riot Act has been upheld as not in violation of the U.S. Constitution.[11]

3. Other statutes and codes

Some states' statutes and codes that have been recently reenacted follow the wording of the Model Code. Some specify five rather than three as the number of participants.[12] According to the comments following § 250.1 of the Model Penal Code, the critical number in some new codes ranges from two in Illinois to ten in Michigan.[13] The wording also varies from state to state. For example, the New York statutes prohibit "violent and tumultuous conduct" by which the actor "intentionally or recklessly causes or creates a grave risk of causing public alarm."[14]

The Section of the Code that applies to disorderly conduct with a purpose to prevent or coerce official action is not common to most state statutes. Some state statutes reach the same result by including the words

---

[11] United States v. Dellinger, 472 F.2d 340 (1972); *cert. denied*, 410 U.S. 970, 35 L.Ed.2d 706, 93 S. Ct. 1443 (1972).

[12] Colo., Ind., Ky., Mont., N.Y., N.D., Ohio, Mass., Mich.

[13] Model Penal Code § 250.1 (Proposed Official Draft 1980), for comment on riots.

[14] N.Y. Penal Law, § 240.06 (McKinney 1975).

"substantially obstructs law enforcement or other government function."[15] An example is the Kentucky statute which provides:

> Riot means a public disturbance involving an assemblage of five or more persons which by tumultuous and violent conduct creates grave danger of damage or injury to property or persons or substantially obstructs law enforcement or other government functions.[16]

According to that statute, a person is guilty of riot in the first degree when:

(a) he knowingly participates in a riot; and
(b) in the course of and as a result of such a riot a person other than one of the participants suffers physical injury or substantial property damage occurs.

§ 9.3 Disorderly Conduct

At common law there was no offense known as "disorderly conduct," although misconduct which was of such a nature as to constitute a public nuisance was indictable.[17] The term "disorderly conduct" is now commonly used in state statutes or municipal ordinances to designate certain minor offenses. Because many disorderly conduct statutes have been declared unconstitutional, most states have reenacted the disorderly conduct provisions so as to comply with the requirements of the U.S. Supreme Court.

Although the courts have declared disorderly conduct statutes to be a valid exercise of the police power, if the statute is contrary to the state or federal constitution, it cannot be enforced.[18] For example, a statute which prohibited persons to engage in or do anything that is disorderly, either by words or unbecoming conduct, was declared unconstitutional as too vague.[19]

---

[15] Colo., Ky., Ind.

[16] Ky. Rev. Stat. Ann. § 525.010 (Baldwin 1975).

[17] 27 C.J.S. *Disorderly Conduct* § 1 (1959), *In re* Garafone, 193 A.2d 398 (1963).

[18] Thompson v. Louisville, 362 U.S. 199, 80 S. Ct. 624, 4 L.Ed.2d 654 (1960).
See case in Part II.

[19] Griffin v. Smith, 184 Ga. 871, 193 S.E. 777 (1937); State v. Koetting, 616 S.W.2d 822 (1981).

A. Traditional Definitions and Elements

What constitutes disorderly conduct depends on the terms of the statute or ordinance in the jurisdiction defining the offense. However, "it may be said that words and acts which tend to disturb the peace and endanger the morals, safety, or health of the community" are punishable as disorderly conduct under these statutes.[20] In one case, the court explained that conduct is disorderly when it is of such a nature as to affect the peace and quiet of persons who may witness the scene and who may be disturbed or provoked to resentment thereby. But a statute which defines "disorderly conduct" as acts which "annoy, disturb, interfere with or obstruct, or are offensive to others" has been declared too broad in its terms.[21]

Not every threatening or insulting word constitutes disorderly conduct. In order for conduct to constitute disorderly conduct, such conduct must be that which reasonably tends to a breach of the peace.

Because the offense of disorderly conduct embraces many acts and forms of conduct, some examples of court decisions are included to exemplify the differences in application. In one case, the court agreed that the acts by the defendant while attending a stage performance before an audience, namely, going onto the stage, taking over the microphone and making a brief admonishment to the audience in which obscene language was used, constituted a violation of the Miami ordinance making a person guilty of "disorderly conduct," if he "uses obscene or profane language in the presence of another," notwithstanding the fact that the defendant's purpose in so acting was not to create or encourage a disturbance, but to avert one.[22] However, the mere presence at an induction center, absent any conduct which tends to cause or provoke a disturbance, does not constitute disorderly conduct.[23]

Defendants who staged a sit-in demonstration in the waiting room of a real estate firm sharing office space with lawyers and remaining there in protest against certain features of the local housing ordinance, were properly found guilty of "disorderly conduct."[24] On the other hand, defendants who sat next to a sleeping man in a practically deserted subway car and who put their hands into the coat of the sleeping man, were not guilty of disorderly

---

[20] 27 C.J.S. *Disorderly Conduct* § 1 (2) (1959).

[21] People on inf. Steeley v. Ennis, 45 N.Y.S.2d 446 (1943).

[22] City of Miami v. Powers, 247 So. 2d 497 (1971).

[23] State v. Werstein, 60 Wis. 2d 668, 211 N.W.2d 437 (1973).

[24] State v. Petty, 24 Conn. Supp. 337, 190 A.2d 502 (1962).

conduct because there could not be attributed to the defendants an intent to breach the public peace.[25]

As disorderly conduct statutes differ in wording and have been interpreted differently by the courts, it is essential that the statutes be studied and court decisions interpreting these statutes be carefully examined.

B. Contemporary Statutes and Codes

1. Model Penal Code[26]

§ 250.2 Disorderly Conduct

(1) Offense Defined. A person is guilty of disorderly conduct if, with purpose to cause public inconvenience, annoyance or alarm, or recklessly creating a risk thereof, he:

    (a) engages in fighting or threatening, or in violent or tumultuous behavior; or

    (b) makes unreasonable noise or offensive coarse utterance, gesture or display, or addresses abusive language to any person present; or

    (c) creates a hazardous or physically offensive condition by any act which serves no legitimate purpose of the actor.

"Public" means affecting or likely to affect persons in a place to which the public or a substantial group has access; among the places included are highways, transport facilities, schools, prisons, apartment houses, places of business or amusement, or any neighborhood.

(2) Grading. An offense under this Section is a petty misdemeanor if the actor's purpose is to cause substantial harm or serious inconvenience, or if he persists in disorderly conduct after reasonable warning or request to desist. Otherwise disorderly conduct is a violation.

Section 250.2 limits disorderly conduct to specifically designated acts likely to create a public nuisance. An effort was made in drafting the pro-

---

[25] People v. Harrison, 173 N.Y.S.2d 128 (1938).

[26] Model Penal Code § 250.2 (Proposed Official Draft 1980).

posed statute to keep within the limitations imposed by the U.S. Supreme Court. The act requires a level of culpability providing that the actor must not only engage in the prescribed conduct, but must do so with the purpose to cause public inconvenience, annoyance or alarm, or recklessly create a risk thereof. This means that the prosecutor must not only show that the defendant acted but must prove the mental element. As the Code limits the definition of the word "public," police officers would not be authorized to intrude into the home to control private misbehavior simply because the acts therein may be offensive to others in the home. Instead, the offense is limited to persons who act purposely or recklessly with respect to public annoyance or alarm. Even with the definitions included in the Code, some words of the statute will no doubt need interpretation by the courts.[27]

2. Federal Code

Title 18, § 1752 provides a fine not exceeding $500 or imprisonment not exceeding six months or both if any person is found guilty of entering or remaining in any building or grounds designated by the Secretary of the Treasury as a temporary residence of the President or other persons protected by the Secret Service in violation of regulations.[28] This Section also makes it unlawful for any person or persons with intent to impede or disrupt the orderly conduct of government business or official functions, to engage in disorderly or disruptive conduct in, or within such proximity to any building or grounds designated as a temporary residence for the President or other person protected by the Secret Service.[29]

In addition, Title 40, § 101 of the U.S. Code provides a penalty of not more than $500 or imprisonment for not more than six months or both if any person is guilty of disorderly and unlawful conduct in and about public buildings and public grounds belonging to the United States within the District of Columbia.[30]

3. Other statutes and codes

According to the comments following the statement of the disorderly conduct statute in the Model Penal Code, most new codes include provisions similar to the Model Code prohibiting abusive language, but only a few have

---

[27] Klotter & Kanovitz, CONSTITUTIONAL LAW § 2.12 (5th ed. 1985), for discussion of the constitutional limitations relating to disorderly conduct statutes.

[28] 18 U.S.C. § 1752.

[29] See 18 U.S.C. § 1752(f) for a definition of "other persons protected by the Secret Service."

[30] 40 U.S.C. § 101.

followed the Model Code's broad prohibition of "offensive coarse utterances." Most statutes that have been enacted recently contain many of the provisions of the Model Penal Code, but some are more specific in their statement of the conduct that is prohibited. An example is the Ohio statute which provides:

  (A) No person shall recklessly cause inconvenience, annoyance, or alarm to another, by doing any of the following:

     (1) Engaging in fighting, in threatening harm to persons or property, or in violent or turbulent behavior;

     (2) Making unreasonable noise or offensively coarse utterance, gesture, or display, or communicating unwarranted and grossly abusive language to any person;

     (3) Insulting, taunting, or challenging another, under circumstance in which such conduct is likely to provoke a violent response;

     (4) Hindering or preventing the movement of persons on a public street, road, highway, or right-of-way, or to, from, within, or upon public or private property, so as to interfere with the rights of others and by any act which serves no lawful and reasonable purpose of the offender;

     (5) Creating a condition which is physically offensive to persons or which presents a risk of physical harm to persons or property, by any act which serves no lawful and reasonable purpose of the offender.[31]

The Ohio statute and other disorderly conduct statutes prohibit a broad range of specific conduct. These combine elements of former offenses of disturbing the peace and many special statutes specifically forbidding various unrelated minor offenses.

    Disorderly conduct statutes vary from state to state. Some are more inclusive and include various forms of misbehavior while others serve as a catch-all for misconduct that is not dealt with more specifically under some other statute.

---

[31] Ohio Rev. Code Ann. § 2917.11 (Page 1987).

§ 9.4 Vagrancy and Loitering

Many, if not most, of the earlier laws relating to vagrancy and loitering have been declared unconstitutional. This has been mandated that the state legislatures draft statutes that are more narrowly worded so as to protect the constitutional rights of individuals. While recognizing that statutes relating to disorderly conduct, vagrancy and loitering are within the police power of the state, the U.S. Supreme Court as well as other courts have made it quite clear that these statutes must meet constitutional standards. For example, in 1983, the U.S. Supreme Court considered a California law which provided:

> Every person...is guilty of disorderly conduct, a misdemeanor...who loiters or wanders upon the streets or from place to place without apparent business and who refuses to identify himself and to account for his presence when requested by any police officer to do so, if the surrounding circumstances are such to indicate to a reasonable man that the public safety demands such identification.[32]

The Supreme Court found that the statute was unconstitutional as in violation of the due process clause as it vested virtually complete discretion in the hands of the police to determine whether the statute had been violated. Other disorderly conduct, vagrancy and loitering statutes have undergone extensive change in order to enable them to withstand constitutional scrutiny.

For purposes of comparing, the traditional definitions of vagrancy and loitering are included here. It is noted that these broadly-defined crimes are not enforceable at the present time but other statutes which follow, including the Model Penal Code and those enacted more recently, have been found to be constitutional.

A. Traditional Definitions and Elements

From the definitions that appear in the earlier cases, it is apparent that neither the legislative bodies nor the courts could agree on a definition of vagrancy. One court defined vagrancy as follows:

> At common law, a person was deemed a "vagrant" who went from place to place without visible means of support, was idle and, al-

---

[32]   Kolander v. Lawson, 461 U.S. 352, 75 L.Ed.2d 903, 103 S. Ct. 1855 (1983).

though able to work for his maintenance refused to do so and lived without labor or on the charity of others.[33]

Another court defined a "vagrant" as:

One who strolls from place to place, an idle wanderer, specifically, one who has no settled habitation, a vagabond.[34]

Other courts determined that vagrancy was a status rather than being committed by one act. For example, a District of Columbia court indicated that "vagrancy" consists of a continued course of immorality, a pattern of iniquity, rather than a solitary incidence of wrong doing.[35]

B. Contemporary Statutes and Codes

Recognizing that statutes which were too broad as being in violation with the due process clause of the Fourteenth Amendment as well as, in some instances, the First Amendment protections, recent legislation is more definite and contains more limiting language. The Model Penal Code is an example.

1. Model Penal Code[36]

§ 250.6 Loitering or Prowling
A person commits a violation if he loiters or prowls in a place, at a time, or in a manner not usual for law-abiding individuals under circumstances that warrant alarm for the safety of persons or property in the vicinity. Among the circumstances which may be considered in determining whether such alarm is warranted is the fact that the actor takes flight upon appearance of a peace officer, refuses to identify himself, or manifestly endeavors to conceal himself or any object. Unless flight by the actor or other circumstance makes it impracticable, a peace officer shall prior to any arrest for an offense under this Section afford the actor an opportunity to dispel any alarm which would otherwise be warranted, by requesting him to identify himself and explain his presence and conduct. No person

---

[33] People v. Banwer, 22 N.Y.S.2d 566 (1940).

[34] Nearing v. Illinois Central R.R. Co., 383 Ill. 366, 50 N.E.2d 497 (1943).

[35] Cooley v. District of Columbia, 177 A.2d 889 (1962).

[36] Model Penal Code § 250.6 (Proposed Official Draft 1980).

shall be convicted of an offense under this Section if the peace officer did not comply with the preceding sentence, or if it appears at trial that the explanation given by the actor was true and, if believed by the peace officer at the time, would have dispelled the alarm.

Section 250.6 differs from prior legislation in that it is narrowly designed to reach only "alarming" loitering. According to the commentary, typical situations covered would be:

(1) a known professional pick pocket who is seen loitering in a crowded railroad station,
(2) a person not recognized as a local resident is seen lurking in the doorway and furtively looking up and down the street to see if he is being watched,
(3) an unknown man is seen standing for some time in a dark alley where he has no apparent business.[36]

Under this Code, the actor must loiter or prowl in a place, at a time, or in a manner not usual for law abiding individuals and under circumstances that warrant alarm for the safety of persons or property in the vicinity.

Obviously, there is still some vagueness in the wording of the statute as the terms used lack specific definition. However, there are some protective provisions in the statute, especially the last sentence which prohibits conviction if the police procedure required by the statute is not followed.

2. Federal Code

Title 18 of the U.S. Code contains no criminal statute relating to vagrancy or loitering.

3. Other statutes and codes

While some states have enacted provisions patterned closely after the Model Penal Code,[37] others have enacted loitering statutes which are more specific. An example of such a statute is that which was enacted by the Commonwealth of Kentucky legislature and provides:

---

[37] Ark., De., N.H. Or., Utah.

§ 525.090 -- Loitering

(1) A person is guilty of loitering when he:

    (a) loiters or remains in a public place for the purpose of gambling with cards, dice or other gambling paraphernalia, except that the provisions of this Section shall not apply if the person is participating in activity defined by KRS 528.010(10); or

    (b) loiters or remains in a public place for the purpose of engaging or agreeing or offering to engage in prostitution; or

    (c) loiters or remains in a public place for the purpose of unlawfully using a controlled substance; or

    (d) loiters or remains in or about a school, college or university building or grounds, not having any reason or relationship involving custody of or responsibility for a pupil or student or any other specific legitimate reason for being there and not having written permission from anyone authorized to grant the same; or

    (e) loiters or remains in any transportation facility, unless specifically authorized to do so, for the purpose of soliciting or engaging in any business, trade or commercial transactions involving the sale of merchandise or services.

(2) Loitering is a violation.

This statute preserves the traditional objectives of apprehending those who are about to commit specific crimes or whose activities are offensive to the public-at-large while limiting possible abuse of broad police authority by setting forth specific standards for determining what conduct is prohibited.[38]

§ 9.5 Drunkenness

Drunkenness was not an offense under the common law of England, but was punishable in the ecclesiastical courts.[39] Statutes enacted in all states of the United States control the use of intoxicating liquors. These statutes are jus-

---

[38] Ky. Rev. Stat. Ann. § 525.090 (Baldwin 1975), and commentary.

[39] 2 Stephen, HISTORY OF THE CRIMINAL LAW IN ENGLAND 410 (1883).

tified under the police power of the state. According to one court, this power is a society's inherent right to protection and rests upon the right of the state to care for the health, morals and welfare of the people.[40]

The state statutes vary in several respects. This was especially true prior to the drafting of the Model Code which is now followed in some states. In some states, the person could be punished for being under the influence of intoxicants in a private or public place while, in others, the penalty applied only if the person appeared in an intoxicated condition in public.

Some statutes have been challenged as violating the due process clause of the federal Constitution. In the case of *Powell v. Texas*, a self-confessed alcoholic was convicted of being drunk in a public place.[41] On appeal, he contended that he was compelled to drink, and, once drunk, would lose control over his behavior and that it was cruel and unusual punishment to impose criminal sanctions on him for appearing drunk in a public place. He relied on the reasoning in the case of *Robinson v. California*, which held that an individual could not be branded a criminal or subjected to penal sanctions, no matter how slight, simply because he occupied a status or condition that was offensive to the community.[42]

The Supreme Court rejected the defendant's argument explaining that although Powell may have been powerless to control his conduct because he was an alcoholic, a status for which the state of Texas could not punish him, the *Robinson* decision did not establish a constitutional doctrine of diminished criminal responsibility for addicts and others similarly affected. Penalizing one for appearing in public while intoxicated does not violate the Constitution.

A. Traditional Definitions and Elements

Punishment for voluntary drunkenness or being drunk in a public place depends on the wording of the various statutes. Where the law requires that the person appear in a public place, the prosecution must prove that the person did, in fact, appear in a public place under the influence. According to one case, a public place does not mean a place devoted solely to the use of the public but means a place which is in point of fact public, as distinguished from private; a place that is visited by many persons and usually accessible to

---

[40]   Eberle v. Michigan, 232 U.S. 700, 34 S. Ct. 464, 58 L.Ed. 803, (1914).

[41]   Powell v. Texas, 392 U.S. 514, 88 S. Ct. 2145, 20 L.Ed.2d (1968).

[42]   Robinson v. California, 370 U.S. 660, 82 S. Ct. 1417, 8 L.Ed.2d 758 (1962). *See* Klotter & Kanovitz, Constitutional Law § 10.19 (5th ed. 1985).

the neighboring public. This includes not only public roads and streets, but various other places such as school houses and places of worship.[43]

B. Contemporary Statutes and Codes

1. The Model Penal Code[44]

§ 250.5 Public Drunkenness; Drug Incapacitation
A person is guilty of an offense if he appears in any public place manifestly under the influence of alcohol, narcotics or other drug, not therapeutically administered, to the degree that he may endanger himself or other persons or property, or annoy persons in his vicinity. An offense under this Section constitutes a petty misdemeanor if the actor has been convicted hereunder twice before within a period of one year. Otherwise the offense constitutes a violation.

The Model Penal Code provides a penalty for appearing in public under the influence not only of alcohol, but also of narcotics or other drugs. It also requires that the influence be to the degree that the person charged may endanger himself or other persons or property, or annoy persons in his vicinity. The Code differs from some traditional statutes, in that it only provides a punishment for public drunkenness but not private drunkennes.

2. Federal Code

The U.S. Code has no specific provision relating to drunkenness or intoxication but does have a Section regulating transportation of intoxicating liquor into any state, territory or district for sale in that state, territory, or district where the state laws prohibit the sale of intoxicating liquor.[45]

The purpose of this Section is to simplify enforcement by federal agents. It was designed to provide federal protection to dry states against violation directed from outside by providing for determination of the legality of liquor

---

[43] State v. Moriarty, 74 Ind. 103 (1881); Thompson v. State, 153 Miss. 593, 121 So. 275 (1929); January v. State, 66 Tex Crim. 302, 146 S.W. 555 (1912).

[44] Model Penal Code § 250.5 (Proposed Official Draft 1980).

[45] 18 U.S.C. § 1262.

importations at the border where the law by the dry state prohibits all importation or requires permits.[46]

3. Other statutes and codes

Some state statutes enacted subsequent to the Model Code follow the provisions of the Model Code, while others are more broad in their coverage. Some continue to punish for intoxication in private, often with conditions attached. For example, in Ohio, a person may be punished for being intoxicated in a public place or in the presence of two or more persons. Also, if he engages in conduct or creates a condition which presents a risk of harm to himself or the personal property of another.[47] As a part of the disorderly conduct Section, the Ohio statute provides:

> (B) No person, while voluntarily intoxicated shall do either of the following:
>
>> (1) In a public place or in the presence of two or more persons, engage in conduct likely to be offensive or to cause inconvenience, annoyance, or alarm to persons of ordinary sensibilities, which conduct the offender, if he were not intoxicated, should know is likely to have such effect on others;
>>
>> (2) Engage in conduct or create a condition which presents a risk of physical harm to himself or another, or to the property of another.

Under the provisions of this statute, the prosecution must introduce evidence to show:

> (1) voluntary intoxication plus,
> (2) either in a public place or, if in a private place, that the conduct is likely to be offensive, etc.

In the alternative, the prosecution may prove:

> (1) voluntary intoxication plus,

---

46   United States v. Williams, 184 F.2d 663 (10th Cir. 1950).

47   Ohio Rev. Code Ann. § 2917.11 (Page 1987). *See also* Fla. Stat. Ann. § 856.011 (West 1976), and S.C. Code Ann. § 16-17-530 (Law. Co-op. 1976).

(2) the person engaged in conduct or created a condition which presents a risk of physical harm to himself or another or to the property of another.

Where the state statute applies only to being drunk in a public place, there can be no conviction if the person is intoxicated in a private residence or a private place. However, the person may be convicted of other offenses, such as assault or disorderly conduct, even though intoxicated at the time he committed the offense.

§ 9.6 Wiretapping and Eavesdropping

Eavesdropping was a common law crime, the essence of which consisted of listening under walls, windows, or eaves in order to vex or annoy another by spreading slanderous rumors against him.[48] An eavesdropper was that unsavory character who snooped under eaves to satisfy his interest in gossip. From this practice, the term eavesdropping was acquired. Modern technology has provided more dignified and sensitive tools to accomplish overhearing conversations of others, and legislative bodies have attempted to draft legislation to control such activity.

A. Traditional Definitions and Elements

The early eavesdropper listened by the naked ear under the eaves of houses or windows, or beyond their walls, seeking out private discourse.[49] Electricity provided a better vehicle and with the advent of the telegraph, surreptitious interception of messages began. The telephone brought on a new and modern eavesdropper known as the "wiretapper." With wiretapping, the interception is made by a connection with a telephone line. According to the comments in the *Berger* case, as early as 1862, California found it necessary to prohibit the practice of eavesdropping by statute and Illinois outlawed wiretapping by legislation in 1895. In 1905, California extended its telegraphic interception prohibition to the telephone. Most of the existing laws relating to wiretapping and eavesdropping result from decisions and legislation of the last two decades. The most far-reaching legislation was that enacted by Congress in 1968.

---

[48] 4 Blackstone, COMMENTARIES 168.

[49] Berger v. New York, 388 U.S. 41, 18 L.Ed.2d 1040, 87 S. Ct. 1873 (1967).

In an attempt to obtain some uniformity in state codes and statutes, the Model Penal Code was drafted as a recommended statute. The Model Penal Code is included here with some comments. This is followed by some of the provisions of the Federal Code and finally by some more recent legislation.

B. *Contemporary Statutes and Codes*

1. Model Penal Code[50]

§ 250.12 Violation of Privacy

(1) Unlawful Eavesdropping or Surveillance. A person commits a misdemeanor if, except as authorized by law, he:

    (a) trespasses on property with purpose to subject anyone to eavesdropping or other surveillance in a private place; or

    (b) installs in any private place, without the consent of the person or persons entitled to privacy there, any device for observing, photographing, recording, amplifying or broadcasting sounds or events in such place, or uses any such unauthorized installation; or

    (c) installs or uses outside a private place any device for hearing, recording, amplifying or broadcasting sounds originating in such place which would not ordinarily be audible or comprehensible outside, without the consent of the person or persons entitled to privacy there.

"Private place" means a place where one may reasonably expect to be safe from casual or hostile intrusion or surveillance, but does not include a place to which the public or a substantial group thereof has access.

(2) Other Breach of Privacy of Messages. A person commits a misdemeanor if, except as authorized by law, he:

    (a) intercepts without the consent of the sender or receiver a message by telephone, telegraph, letter or other means of communicating privately; but this paragraph does not extend to

---

[50] Model Penal Code § 250.12 (Proposed Official Draft 1980).

(i) overhearing of messages through a regularly installed instrument on a telephone party line or on an extension, or

(ii) interception by the telephone company or subscriber incident to enforcement of regulations limiting use of the facilities or incident to other normal operation and use; or

(b) divulges without the consent of the sender or receiver the existence or contents of any such message if the actor knows that the message was illegally intercepted, or if he learned of the message in the court of employment with an agency engaged in transmitting it.

The Model Penal Code prohibits unlawful eavesdropping or surveillance. Subsection (1) deals with the unauthorized eavesdropping or surveillance in a private place and defines that term. Paragraph (a) provides a penalty for one who trespasses on property for the purpose of eavesdropping or engaging in other surveillance in another private place, but limits liability to persons who trespass with the "conscious object" of eavesdropping or engaging in other surveillance. Paragraph (b) prohibits surveillance by mechanical and electronic devices and is more similar to the provisions of the federal statute. Paragraph (c) is designed to reach one who installs or uses outside a private place, a device for overhearing conversations originating within that private place. Following some of the provisions of the Federal Code, both paragraphs (a) and (b) except from liability surveillance of a private place with the consent of "the person or persons entitled to privacy."

Subsection (2) provides a penalty for other interceptions of messages and for disclosure of unlawful intercepted messages. This contains exceptions similar to those of the federal statute.

2. Federal Code

In 1929 and again in 1931, Congress introduced legislation which made certain kinds of wiretapping illegal. However, it was not until 1934, when the Federal Communications Act was passed that federal legislation became effective.[51] This provided that:

No person not being authorized by the sender shall intercept any communication and divulge or publish the existence, contents, substance, purport, effect, or meaning of such intercepted communication to any person.

In 1968, Congress enacted very comprehensive legislation relating to wiretapping and eavesdropping. This was part of the Omnibus Control and Safe Street Act of 1968.[52] The 1968 Act was amended in 1986 to extend its coverage so as to protect communications that involved modern forms of technology.[53] The 1986 law extends privacy guarantees for conventional telephone to communications involving cellular telephones that operate by high frequency radio waves and messages transmitted and stored in computers. Section 2511 of 119 of Title 18, which is entitled "Wire and Electronic Communications, Interception, and Interception or Oral Communications" provides for a fine of $10,000 or 5 years imprisonment or both for violation. In effect, this Section prohibits interception of any wire, oral or electronic communication other than in compliance with the detailed statutory procedures as well as disclosures of the contents of such communications when it is known these have been illegally obtained.[54] However, the statute has specific provisions authorizing certain types of electronic surveillance. For example, it shall not be unlawful under this act for a person acting under color of law to intercept a wire, oral or electronic communication where such person is a party to the communication or one of the parties to the communication has given prior consent to such interception. This makes it possible for police officers to intercept communications if one party consents. The act also provides for wiretapping and eavesdropping when a court order is properly obtained.

3. Other statutes and codes

Virtually all jurisdictions have some provisions concerning wiretapping, eavesdropping and/or privacy.[55] Some include the broad coverage of the

---

[51] 47 U.S.C. § 151 (1934).

[52] 18 U.S.C. §§ 2510-2520.

[53] Electronic Communications Privacy Act of 1986 - Public Law 99-508 Amending 18 U.S.C. §§ 2510-2520. See Appendix 4.

[54] United States v. McIntyre, 582 F.2d 1221 (9th Cir. 1978). See case in Part II. See Klotter & Kanovitz, CONSTITUTIONAL LAW ch. 5 (5th ed. 1985) for a discussion of the constitutional aspects of wiretapping and eavesdropping.

[55] Model Penal Code § 250.12 (Proposed Official Draft 1980), and comments on privacy.

Model Penal Code, while others are stated differently or limited in scope. An example of a statute which is divided into Sections and has broad coverage is that of Kentucky, titled "Eavesdropping and Related Offenses."[56]

EAVESDROPPING AND RELATED OFFENSES

§ 526.010 -- Definition
   The following definition applies in this chapter, unless the context otherwise requires:
   "Eavesdrop" means to overhear, record, amplify or transmit any part of a wire or oral communication of others without the consent of at least one party thereto by means of any electronic, mechanical or other device.

§ 526.020 -- Eavesdropping
(1)   A person is guilty of eavesdropping when he intentionally uses any device to eavesdrop, whether or not he is present at the time.
(2)   Eavesdropping is a Class D felony.

§ 526.030 -- Installing eavesdropping device
(1)   A person is guilty of installing an eavesdropping device when he intentionally installs or places such a device in any place with the knowledge that it is to be used for eavesdropping.
(2)   Installing an eavesdropping device is a Class D felony.

§ 526.040 -- Possession of eavesdropping device
(1)   A person is guilty of possession of an eavesdropping device when he possesses any electronic, mechanical or other device designed or commonly used for eavesdropping with intent to use that device to eavesdrop or knowing that another intends to use that device to eavesdrop.
(2)   Possession of an eavesdropping device is a Class A misdemeanor.

---

[56]   Ky. Rev. Stat. Ann. § 526.01 *et seq.* (Baldwin 1975).

§ 526.050 -- Tampering with private communications

(1) A person is guilty of tampering with private communications when knowing that he does not have the consent of the sender or receiver, he unlawfully:

    (a) opens or reads a sealed letter or other sealed private communication; or

    (b) obtains in any manner from an employee, officer or representative of a communications common carrier information with respect to the contents or nature of a communication.

(2) The provisions of this Section do not apply to the censoring of sealed letters or sealed communications for security purposes in official detention or penal facilities.

(3) Tampering with private communications is a Class A misdemeanor.

§ 526.060 -- Divulging illegally obtained information

(1) A person is guilty of divulging illegally obtained information when he knowingly uses or divulges information obtained through eavesdropping or tampering with private communications or learned in the course of employment with a communications common carrier engaged in transmitting the message.

(2) Divulging illegally obtained information is a Class A misdemeanor.

§ 526.070 -- Eavesdropping -- exceptions

A person is not guilty under this chapter when he:

(1) inadvertently overhears the communication through a regularly installed telephone party line or on a telephone extension but does not divulge it; or

(2) is an employee of a communications common carrier who, while acting in the course of his employment, intercepts, discloses or uses a communication transmitted through the facilities of his employer for a purpose which is a necessary incident to the rendition of the service or to the protection of the rights or the property of the carrier of such communication, provided however that communications common carriers shall not utilize service observing or random monitoring except for mechanical or service quality control checks.

§ 9.7 Obstructing a Highway or Public Passage

In order to make it possible for citizens to carry on the everyday business and to avoid undue interference, statutes have been written and enforced which regulate the use of highways and other public passages. Although the statutes and ordinances regulating the use of streets and buildings have been upheld, these must comply with safeguards of the U.S. Constitution; especially the First Amendment safeguards. The municipality has ample police power to guarantee the repose of citizens in the sanctuary of their own homes. Therefore, an ordinance prohibiting ringing doorbells of private residences for the purpose of soliciting sales has been upheld as constitutional.[57] And a municipality in the exercise of its police power may regulate the time, place and manner of using public streets for the purpose of holding outdoor parades, speeches or mass assemblies.[58] Because of their special characteristics, areas around hospital districts, jail yards, fire houses and court facilities can be more closely protected than other public facilities.[59]

Although local communities are not devoid of the necessary power to confine first amendment conduct within boundaries compatible with metropolitan living, regulations which unduly limit free speech and assembly, for example, an ordinance which permits an enforcement decision to be based on consideration of the message or speech content runs high risk of judicial invalidation.[60]

Recent ordinances and statutes have attempted to balance the right of the public to use streets and highways for purposes of presenting ideas and the right of the public to use the streets and highways for travel.[61]

1. Model Penal Code[62]

§ 250.7 Obstructing Highways and Other Public Passages
(1) A person, who, having no legal privilege to do so, purposely or recklessly obstructs any highway or other public passage, whether along or with others, commits a violation, or, in case

---

[57] Beard v. Alexandria, 341 U.S. 622, 71 S. Ct. 920, 95 L.Ed. 1233 (1951).

[58] Cox v. New Hampshire, 312 U.S. 569, 61 S. Ct. 762, 85 L.Ed. 1049 (1941).

[59] Adderley v. Florida, 385 U.S. 39, 87 S. Ct. 242, 17 L.Ed.2d 149 (1967), reh'g denied, 385 U.S. 1020, 87 S. Ct. 698, 17 L.Ed.2d 559 (1967).

[60] Cox v. Louisiana, 379 U.S. 536, 85 S. Ct. 453, 13 L.Ed.2d 471 (1965).

[61] For a more thorough discussion, see Klotter & Kanovitz, CONSTITUTIONAL LAW § 2.8 (5th ed. 1985).

[62] Model Penal Code § 250.7 (Proposed Official Draft 1980).

he persists after warning by a law officer, a petty misdemeanor. "Obstructs" means renders impassable without unreasonable inconvenience or hazard. No person shall be deemed guilty of recklessly obstructing in violation of this Subsection solely because of a gathering of persons to hear him speak or otherwise communicate, or solely because of being a member of such a gathering.

(2) A person in a gathering commits a violation if he refuses to obey a reasonable official request or order to move:

    (a) to prevent obstruction of a highway or other public passage; or

    (b) to maintain public safety by dispersing those gathered in dangerous proximity to a fire or other hazard.

An order to move, addressed to a person whose speech or other lawful behavior attracts an obstructing audience, shall not be deemed reasonable if the obstruction can be readily remedied by police control of the size or location of the gathering.

The Model Penal Code, as other codes, has taken into consideration the possibility of constitutional challenge. Therefore, the term "having no legal privilege to do so" is included. Also, the language exempts from liability persons who have obtained permits or secured official permits to block off the streets. According to the comments following the statement, the result is to give the widest possible scope to picketing, protests and other lawful assembly consistent with the need to protect reasonable public access to highways and other public passages.

Subsection (2) proscribes refusal to obey a reasonable official in order to prevent obstruction of a public passage or to disperse persons gathered in dangerous proximity to a fire or other hazard. The term "reasonable" is included so as to limit the authority of the police officer to order a person to move if the situation can be handled without stopping the speaker.

2. Other statutes and codes

Some recently enacted codes and statutes include the provisions of the Model Penal Code. Some statutes describe the prohibited conduct more specifically. Arkansas, for example, defines obstruction as "rendering impassable."[63] In some states, the offense is made a part of the disorderly conduct statute. For example, the Ohio statute provides:

> (A) No person shall recklessly cause inconvenience, annoyance, or
>   alarm to another, by doing any of the following:
>
>   * * *
>
>   (4) Hindering or preventing the movement of persons on
>   a public street, road, highway, or right-of-way, or to,
>   from, within, or upon public or private property, so
>   as to interfere with the rights of others and by any act
>   which serves no lawful and reasonable purpose of the
>   offender.[64]

Although the statute does not specifically exempt from liability a speaker or listener who is legally expressing ideas, it does exempt those who have a "lawful and reasonable purpose."

§ 9.8 Other Offenses Against the Public Peace

In order to diminish disorderliness and individual misbehavior and to make it possible for citizens to live in a reasonable, safe and orderly society, legislative bodies have enacted statutes providing for penalties for failure to follow certain standards of conduct. Many of these laws have been written as the immediate need dictated and the laws differ from state to state. Some of those that are included in many of the most recently enacted statutes are discussed here.

1. Harassment

The harassment statutes cover an area of minor assaultive conduct where the intent is to annoy or alarm a specific individual rather than the

---

[63] Ark. Stat. Ann. § 41-2915 (1977).

[64] Ohio Rev. Code Ann. § 2917.11 (Page 1987).

public.[65] Under these statutes, the accused must act with the intent to harass, annoy or alarm another person.[66]

2. Disruptive meetings

While in some states this conduct is within the scope of the disorderly conduct or breach of the peace statutes, in some states it is a separate offense. The Model Penal Code provides that:

> A person commits a misdemeanor if, with purpose to prevent or disrupt a lawful meeting, procession or gathering, he does any act intending to obstruct or interfere with it physically, or make any utterance, gesture, or display designed to outrage the sensibilities of the group.[67]

Under this statute, two distinct kinds of disruption may be punished: *physical disruption* or *offensive utterances.*

3. Desecration of venerated objects

These statutes prohibit desecration of public monuments or objects, places of worship or burial, the national or state flags, or any other patriotic or religious symbol. These statutes are aimed at special kinds of public or quasi-public property damages which result in an affront to members of the public. The statutes are aimed more at the protection of public sensibilities than the impairment of property interests.

4. Cruelty to animals

These statutes prohibit any cruel mistreatment or neglect of an animal, or any killing or injuring of an animal belonging to another. The purpose is

---

[65] Model Penal Code § 250.4 (Proposed Official Draft 1980), and cases cited therein.
[66] State v. Koetting, 616 S.W.2d 822 (Mo. 1981).
[67] Model Penal Code § 250.8 (Proposed Official Draft 1980).

to penalize a class of behavior which outrages the feelings of substantial groups of the population.[68]

As the various state statutes contain other offenses against the public order, these must be researched by those who are involved in the criminal justice process in order to have a thorough knowledge of the charges that are available.

§ 9.9 Summary

In order to protect the public peace, laws defining offenses, some of which are minor in character, have been enacted. These offenses are often characterized as "Offenses Against the Public Peace" or "Offenses Against Public Order."

One offense which has received attention recently is entitled "Riot." Generally, in order to convict one for a riot, the prosecution must prove at least three elements:

(1) an unlawful assembly,
(2) the intent of at least three persons to resist lawful authority and
(3) acts of violence.

Related to "riot" is "Inciting to Riot." This occurs when one incites or encourages other persons to create or engage in a riot as defined.

A crime that is common to all jurisdictions is "disorderly conduct." What constitutes disorderly conduct depends on the terms of the statute or ordinance; however, it may be said that words and acts which tend to disturb the peace and endanger the morals, safety or health of the community are punishable as disorderly conduct under most statutes.

Vagrancy at common law, was defined as the wandering or going about from place to place by an idle person who has no lawful visible means of support and who exists on charity and does not work for a living, although able to do so. Many of the vagrancy and loitering statutes were declared unconstitutional because they were considered too vague. Modern vagrancy statutes are more specific, and designed to make the person accused of the crime aware of what specific conduct is prohibited.

Although drunkenness was not a crime at common law, most state statutes now prohibit the appearance in any public place of a person who is

---

[68] Model Penal Code § 250.11 (Proposed Official Draft 1980). *See also*, Ky. Rev. Stat. Ann. § 525.130 (Baldwin 1975), and following commentaries.

manifestly under the influence of alcohol, drugs or narcotics, if to the degree that he may endanger himself or other persons or property or annoy persons in his vicinity.

After some uncertainty as to what acts should be covered, the Omnibus Crime Control Act and Safe Streets Act of 1968, as amended in 1986 generally prohibits interception of wire or oral communications and provides a penalty for anyone who violates the Act. The Act does contain some exceptions. States, too, have experimented with laws prohibiting eavesdropping, possession of eavesdropping devices, tampering with private communications or divulging illegally obtained information.

In order to make it possible for citizens to carry on their everyday business and to avoid undue interference, statutes have been written and enforced which regulate the use of highways and other passages. These statutes have been challenged as being unconstitutional, but when written in accordance with constitutional guidelines, they have been upheld as a proper exercise of the police power of the state.

Other offenses against the public peace include harassment, disrupting meetings, desecration of venerated objects and cruelty to animals.

Chapter 10
OFFENSES AGAINST PUBLIC JUSTICE AND ADMINISTRATION

Perjury, by common law, seemeth to be a willful false oath, by one who being lawfully required to depose the truth in any proceeding in a course of justice, swears absolutely in a matter of some consequence to the point in question, whether he be believed or not.

1 Hawk D.C. 318
(6th Ed. by Leach, 1788)

Section

§ 10.1 Introduction

In early societies, especially in rural societies, few laws were necessary to ensure that the justice process was administered without undue interference. The early English courts provided the necessary rules to protect the process from willful interference and included sanctions for failure to comply with these rules. As more and more governmental agencies and functions were established to protect society and to administer the complex governmental affairs, the state legislative bodies enacted laws to protect the governmental process from interference from those outside the specific agency as well as those from within the agency who might take advantage of the authority granted to them.

Some of the common law crimes which developed over the years, primarily through judicial action, to protect the public, have disappeared, while new offenses have been added as new or larger agencies have been created. For example, the common law crime of barratry designed to prevent stirring up of strife and litigation is no longer in existence for practical purposes.[1] While these common law crimes have disappeared, others have been added. An example of a modern statute enacted to ensure that evidence is properly protected for trial, is "tampering with or fabricating physical evidence."

If the justice administration process is to accomplish its purpose, it must be kept free from this undue influence. Recognizing this, both state and federal legislative bodies have enacted legislation to supplement those sanctions that have been traditionally recognized.

In this chapter, the well known offenses relating to public justice administration, such as perjury and bribery are defined and explained. In addition, more recent state and federal legislation relating to justice administration or applied in justice administration situations are included for discussion.

§ 10.2 Perjury and Related Offenses

The necessity of guaranteeing the integrity of a sworn statement in a judicial proceeding was recognized at common law. However, common law perjury was limited to the false oath in a judicial proceeding.[1] As the practice of requiring sworn statements in other matters developed, the offense of perjury, whether by that name or some other title, was extended to cover judicial or quasi-judicial proceedings as to some matter material to the issue or point in question.

---

[1]   Common barratry is the offense of frequently inciting and stirring up suits and quarrels. Commonwealth v. Davis, 28 Mass. (11 Pick. 432) (1831).

In some statutes, an offense of false swearing has been added. Although in common parlance, the terms "false swearing" and "perjury" are used interchangeably, in a strict legal sense, there is a difference between them. At common law, false swearing is a separate and indictable offense, and is distinct from perjury in that the false oath in perjury must be made in a judicial proceeding, whereas in false swearing the act need not be made in such proceeding.[2]

A. Traditional Definitions and Elements

At common law, the offense of perjury was defined as a willful assertion as to a matter of fact, opinion, belief or knowledge made by a witness in a judicial proceeding as a part of his evidence, either upon oath or in any form allowed by law to be substituted for an oath, whether in open court, in an affidavit, or otherwise, such assertion being known to such witness to be false, and being intended by him to mislead the court, jury or person holding the proceedings.[3] Although the wording of various statutory definitions differ, perjury is generally defined as the willful and corrupt false swearing or affirming after an oath has been lawfully administered, in the course of a judicial or quasi-judicial proceeding as to some matter material to the issue or point in question.

Other courts have used different words in defining the offense of perjury. Some examples are:

"Perjury" is a crime committed when a lawful oath is administered, in some judicial proceeding, to a person who swears, willfully, absolutely and falsely, in a manner material to the issue or point in question.[4]

"Perjury" at common law was:

    (1) the willful,
    (2) giving of false testimony,
    (3) on a material point,
    (4) in a judicial proceeding,
    (5) by a person to whom a lawful oath had been administered.[5]

---

[2] Martin v. Miller, 4 Mo. 39 (1835); State v. Dallegeiovanna, 69 Wash. 84, 124 P. 209 (1912).

[3] 2 Wharton, CRIMINAL LAW 1780-81 (12th ed. 1932).

[4] Gatewood v. State, 15 Md. App. 314, 290 A.2d 551 (1972).

[5] Bazarte v. State, 117 So. 2d 227 (Fla. 1959).

"Perjury" is the willful, knowing and corrupt giving, under oath, of false testimony material to the issue or point of inquiry; an essential element is that the defendant must have acted with criminal intent -- he must have believed that what he swore to was false and he must have had intent to deceive.[6]

From these definitions, from appropriate statutes and from other decisions, the essential elements of the crime of perjury can be enumerated. While the courts differ to some extent, the elements that normally must be proved are:

(1) an oath or affirmation,
(2) a false statement,
(3) the statement must be material and
(4) the false statement must be given knowingly and with intent to deceive.

Other definitions of crimes relating to the crime of perjury are subornation of perjury and false swearing. Subornation of perjury is the procuring by one person of another to commit the crime of perjury. This crime has two essential elements:

(1) one person must have willfully procured another to commit perjury and
(2) the second person must have, in fact, committed the offense.

Although the crime of perjury and subornation of perjury may be closely related in point of time and conduct, the offenses are dual; each having in it elements not common to the other. One court explained that there are sufficient inherent differences between the two to warrant the law-making power in separating the act into its component parts, making that of the suborner a new and independent offense, punishable with greater or less severity than that inflicted on the perjurer.[7]

---

6   State v. Laurelli, 187 F.Supp. 30 (D. Pa. 1960).

7   Stone v. State, 118 Ga. 705, 45 S.E. 630 (1903) (a defendant who induced his wife to make a false affidavit was guilty of subornation of perjury); Thomas v. State, 231 S.W. 200 (1921).

Another related offense is that of "false swearing." The offense of false swearing is distinguished from perjury in that to be perjury, statements must be in a judicial proceeding while a person may be guilty of false swearing where the false testimony is made regarding nonjudicial matters.[8] Also in some instances, false swearing is the offense where the testimony does not relate to a matter material to the issue.[9] Under most statutes the punishment for the offense of false swearing is less than that assigned to the offense of perjury.

B. Contemporary Statutes and Codes

1. Model Penal Code[10]

§ 241.1 Perjury

(1) Offense Defined. A person is guilty of perjury, a felony of the third degree, if in any official proceeding he makes a false statement under oath or equivalent affirmation, or swears or affirms the truth of a statement previously made, when the statement is material and he does not believe it to be true.

(2) Materiality. Falsification is material, regardless of the admissibility of the statement under rules of evidence, if it could have affected the course or outcome of the proceeding. It is no defense that the declarant mistakenly believed the falsification to be immaterial. Whether a falsification is material in a given factual situation is a question of law.

(3) Irregularities No Defense. It is not a defense to prosecution under this Section that the oath or affirmation was administered or taken in an irregular manner or that the declarant was not competent to make the statement. A document purporting to be made upon oath or affirmation at any time when the actor presents it as being so verified shall be deemed to have been duly sworn or affirmed.

(4) Retraction. No person shall be guilty of an offense under this Section if he retracted the falsification in the course of the proceeding in which it was made before it became manifest that

---

8   State v. Kowalczyk, 66 A.2d 175 (1949).

9   Plummer v. State, 84 S.E.2d 202 (1954).

10   Model Penal Code, § 241.1 (Proposed Official Draft 1980).

the falsification was or would be exposed and before the falsification substantially affected the proceeding.

(5) Inconsistent Statements. Where the defendant made inconsistent statements under oath or equivalent affirmation, both having been made within the period of the statute of limitations, the prosecution may proceed by setting forth the inconsistent statements in a single count alleging in the alternative that one or the other was false and not believed by the defendant. In such case it shall not be necessary for the prosecution to prove which statement was false but only that one or the other was false and not believed by the defendant to be true.

(6) Corroboration. No person shall be convicted of an offense under this Section where proof of falsity rests solely upon contradiction by testimony of a single person other than the defendant.

The Model Penal Code includes a definition of "statement" and also a definition of "materiality." The definition of materiality does not differ substantially from prior law.

The Code in subsection 3 also makes specific the rule that the manner of administering the oath is not a defense. It provides that a document that purports to be made under oath or affirmation shall be considered as under oath if it subsequently presented as being so verified. To make the offense and definitions more clear, the Code also has subsections relating to retraction, inconsistent statements and corroboration.

While subornation of perjury is not specifically spelled out in the Code as an offense, in the comments following the statement of the provision, a comment is included explaining that this is covered under § 2.06(3)(a) of the Code which provides that a person is the accomplice of another in the commission of an offense if he solicits the other person to commit it.

In addition to the crime of perjury, the Model Penal Code includes a separate offense entitled "false swearing." One subsection of the false swearing provision deals with false statements that would be perjurious but for the lack of materiality of the statement. A second Section deals with falsifications that do not occur in an official proceeding but are intended to mislead a public official in the performance of his official function. Both of these are graded as misdemeanors.

2. Federal Code

Chapter 79 of Title 18 of the U.S. Code defines three perjury related offenses; perjury, subornation of perjury and false declaration before a grand jury or court. The crime of perjury is defined as:

Whoever -

(1) having taken an oath before a competent tribunal, officer, or person, in any case in which a law of the United States authorizes an oath to be administered, that he will testify, declare, depose, or certify truly, or that any written testimony, declaration, deposition, certificate by him subscribed, is true, willfully and contrary to such oaths states or subscribes any material matter which he does not believe to be true; or

(2) in any declaration, certificate, verification, or statement under a penalty of perjury as permitted under Section 1746 of Title 28, U.S. Code, willfully subscribes as true any material matter which he does not believe to be true;

is guilty of perjury and shall, except as otherwise expressly provided by law, be fined not more than $2,000 or imprisoned not more than five years or both.

This section is applicable whether the statement or subscription is made within or without the United States.[11] This federal statute contains provisions that are similar to state statutes and has been found to meet constitutional standards.[12]

The essential elements to prove a violation of this section are:

(1) taking of an oath in a case where a law of the United States authorizes the oath to be administered,
(2) to testify willfully and contrary to such oath,
(3) making a false statement,
(4) as to material fact and
(5) which the defendant did not believe to be true.[13]

---

[11] 18 U.S.C. § 1621.

[12] United States v. Masters, 484 F.2d 1251 (10th Cir. 1973).

[13] United States v. Stone, 429 F.2d 138 (2d Cir. 1970).

In a case which was considered by the Supreme Court, the majority agreed that the essential elements of perjury as defined by this section are an oath authorized by law of the United States, taken before a competent tribunal, officer or other person and a false statement willfully made and material to the hearing.[14]

Section 1622 of the federal statute provides:

> Whoever procures another to commit any perjury is guilty of subornation of perjury, and shall be fined not more than $2,000 or imprisoned not more than five years, or both.[15]

A federal court, in interpreting the subornation provision, found that, in order to constitute the offense of subornation of perjury, the offense of perjury must have been actually committed by another.[16] Another federal court indicated that this statute was correctly applied when an attorney was charged with subornation of perjury of the witness in violation of this section.

The third federal provision relating to perjury provides a penalty of not more than $10,000 or imprisonment of not more than five years, or both when one under oath makes any false material declaration in any proceeding before or ancillary to a court or grand jury of the United States.[17]

3. Other statutes and codes

A number of states have adopted the Model Code in substance. Some statutes define perjury to include instances where making a statement is required or authorized by law or where "an oath or affirmation is or may be required or authorized by law."[18] In addition, some states list the specific types of proceedings to which perjury sanctions may be applied.[19]

An example of a state Code that does not follow the Model Code is that of New York. In that state there are three degrees of perjury:[20]

---

[14] United States v. Hvass, 355 U.S. 570, 2 L.Ed.2d 496, 78 S. Ct. 501 (1958).

[15] 18 U.S.C. § 1622.

[16] United States v. Silverman, 745 F.2d 1386 (11th Cir. 1984).

[17] *See* 18 U.S.C. § 1623 for a more comprehensive statement of this provision of the statute. *See also* United States v. Langella, 776 F.2d 1078 (2d Cir. 1985).

[18] Ala., Ill., Iowa, Minn., S.D., Va.

[19] Wis., N.M.

[20] N.Y. Penal Law §§ 210.00-210.15 (McKinney 1965).

§ 210.05 Perjury in the third degree
A person is guilty of perjury in the third degree when he swears falsely.
Perjury in the third degree is a Class A misdemeanor.

§ 210.10 Perjury in the second degree
A person is guilty of perjury in the second degree when he swears falsely and when his false statement is
  (a) made in a subscribed written instrument for which an oath is required by law, and
  (b) made with intent to mislead a public servant in the performance of his official functions and
  (c) material to the action, proceeding or matter involved.

Perjury in the second degree is a Class E felony.

§ 210.15 Perjury in the first degree
A person is guilty of perjury in the first degree when he swears falsely and when his false statement
  (a) consists of testimony, and
  (b) is material to the action, proceeding or matter in which it is made.

Perjury in the first degree is a Class D felony.

In the New York statute, testimony is defined as:

> an oral statement made under oath in a proceeding before any court, body, agency, public servant, or other person authorized by law to conduct such proceedings and to administer the oath or cause it to be administered.

This covers a broad range of proceedings.
In interpreting § 210.05 of the statutes (perjury in the third degree), the New York court explained that while the section defining third degree perjury does not make materiality an element of the crime, the prosecutor must have some good faith purpose behind questions he puts to a grand jury witness, beyond setting the stage for perjury prosecution.[21]

---

[21] People v. Pomerantz, 407 N.Y.S.2d 723, 63 A.2d 457 (1978).

The court also emphasized that materiality is an essential element of the crime of perjury in the first degree and that the false swearing, to be material, must reflect on a matter under consideration during the action or proceeding in which it is made.[22]

In a case where police officers were charged with perjury in the first degree, the court held that evidence was sufficient to find the defendant guilty on the basis of his false denials before a grand jury investigating police corruption, that he met surreptitiously with other police officers and known gamblers at a gambler's home.[23]

In some states, a separate crime of false swearing is included in the statute. Generally, these statutes use somewhat the same language that is used in perjury but do not require materiality as is required in perjury or in some instances do not require intent to mislead. Where the statute includes the crime of false swearing, it is usually a lower degree offense.

§ 10.3 Bribery and Related Offenses

Although history indicates that among the Romans the giving of rewards and emoluments to public officers, especially judicial officers, was tolerated, later civilizations recognized the danger of the effect of corruptive private influences upon official action. Some early cases indicate that only the bribe-taker, for example the judge, and not the bribe-giver, could be found guilty of an offense.[24]

As a public official in the service of the people, his first duty is to protect and further their interest and he should not be permitted to profit through the performance of his public functions. To prohibit this, the offense of bribery as it relates to public officials -- executive, legislative or judicial -- was created. The essence of the offense is the prostitution of a public trust, the betrayal of public interest or the debauchment of the public conscience.[25]

A. Traditional Definitions and Elements

Blackstone defines bribery as the receiving by a judge or other officer connected with the administration of justice, of "any undue reward to influ-

---

[22] People v. Stanard, 42 N.Y.2d 74, 365 N.E.2d 857, 369 N.Y.S.2d 825 (1977), *cert. denied*, 434 U.S. 986, 98 S. Ct. 615, 54 L.Ed.2d 481 (1977). *See* case in Part II.

[23] *Id.*

[24] Perkins, CRIMINAL LAW 396 (1957).

[25] *Ex parte* Winters, 10 Okla. Crim. 592, 140 P. 164 (1914).

ence his behavior in his office."[26] Decisions and statutes define the offense more broadly; that bribery is the offering, giving, receiving, or soliciting of anything of value with intent to influence the recipient's action as a public official, whether executive, legislative, or judicial.[27]

Various courts have defined bribery as it relates to public officials. Some of these are as follows:

"Bribery" was a common law crime classified as an offense against public justice and defined as occurring when a judge or other person concerned in the administration of justice took an undue reward to influence his behavior in office.[28]

The gist of public "bribery," which is offering, giving, receiving, or soliciting anything of value with intent to influence the recipient's action as a public official is the tendency to corrupt.[29]

Under the more recent common law decisions, both the giver of the bribe and its recipient committed the crime of bribery.[30] The elements of bribery are:

(1)   offering, giving, receiving, or soliciting
(2)   a thing of value,
(3)   intent to influence the recipient's action,
(4)   the recipient is a public official.

(1)   Who may commit the crime

The crime is committed by one who gives a bribe as well as by one who receives it. It is also committed by one who offers a bribe or offers to accept it. One who conveys an offer to bribe, from a third person, is himself guilty, though the money is to be paid by the third person.[31]

---

26   4 Blackstone, COMMENTARIES 139 (1898).

27   Honaker v. Board of Education, 42 W.Va. 170, 24 S.E. 544 (1896); Rudolph v. State, 128 Wis. 122, 107 N.W. 466 (1906).

28   United States v. Forsythe, 429 F.Supp. 715 (D. Pa. 1977).

29   State v. Smith, 252 La. 636, 212 So. 2d 410 (1968); United States v. Sisk, 476 F.Supp. 1061 (D. Tenn. 1979).

30   People v. Ginsberg, 80 Misc.2d 921, 364 N.Y.S.2d 260 (1974).

31   People v. Northey, 77 Cal. 618, 19 P. 865 (1888).

(2) Thing of value

Almost anything may serve as a bribe so long as it is of sufficient value in the eyes of the person bribed to influence his official conduct. It is not necessary that the thing have a value at the time when it is offered or promised.[32] However, a vague offer to turn state's evidence, without anything further, was insufficient to constitute a "benefit" under the New York statute.[33]

(3) Intent

Criminal intent is a necessary element. The intent must be to influence corruptly an official in the discharge of his duty. According to at least one case, a person who accepts a bribe with the intent that it shall influence his official action is guilty of bribery although there is no intention on the part of the giver to bribe him.[34]

(4) Public official

Although at one time the term public official was more limited, the modern tendency is to include any public officer, agent, servant, or employee. As an example, the federal law covers any "officer or employee or person acting for or on behalf of the United States, or any department or agency thereof, in any official function."[35] "Public official" includes police officers, sheriffs and deputy sheriffs under most statutes.[36]

B. Contemporary Statutes and Codes

1. Model Penal Code[37]

§ 240.1 Bribery in Official and Political Matters

A person is guilty of bribery, a felony of the third degree, if he offers, confers or agrees to confer upon another, or solicits, accepts or agrees to accept from another:

(1) any pecuniary benefit as consideration for the recipient's decision, opinion, recommendation, vote or

---

[32] People v. Hockberg, 62 A.D.2d 239, 404 N.Y.S.2d 161 (1978).

[33] People v. Cavan, 84 Misc.2d 510, 376 N.Y.S.2d 65 (1975).

[34] Annot., 116 Am.St.Rep. 39 (Wis. 1906).

[35] 18 U.S.C. § 201 (1962).

[36] Usry v. State, 90 Ga. App. 644, 83 S.E.2d 843 (Ga. Ct. App. 1954).

[37] Model Penal Code § 240.1 (Proposed Official Draft 1980).

other exercise of discretion as a public servant, party
official or voter; or

(2) any benefit as consideration for the recipient's decision, vote, recommendation or other exercise of official discretion in a judicial or administrative proceeding; or

(3) any benefit as consideration for a violation of a
known legal duty as public servant or party official.

It is no defense to prosecution under this section that a person
whom the actor sought to influence was not qualified to act in the
desired way whether because he had not yet assumed office, or
lacked jurisdiction, or for any other reason.

The Model Penal Code follows the more recent traditional statutory
provisions in reaching both the person who offers, gives, or agrees to give a
bribe in an official or political matter and the public servant or other covered
individual who solicits, accepts, or agrees to accept a bribe. It applies to full-
time government employees, plus consultants to government, bribery of vot-
ers and political party officials and bribery of anyone who exercises official
discretion in a judicial or administrative proceeding. This section is very
broad in its scope and uses terminology that is less likely to cause problems
in interpretation.

2. Federal Code

Chapter 11 of Title 18 of the U.S. Code is entitled "Bribery, Graft and
Conflicts of Interest." Within this chapter are laws relating to "bribery of
public officials and witnesses," "bribery in sporting contests," "acceptance or
solicitation to obtain appointment of public office," and "acceptance of loan
or gratuity by bank examiner." It also includes ethical standards of conduct
for government employees.

The section that relates specifically to bribery of public officials and witnesses was amended in 1984 and provides in part:

§ 201. Bribery of Public Officials and Witnesses.[38]

(a) For the purpose of this section --

(1) the term "public official" means Member of
Congress, Delegate, or Resident Commissioner, either before or after such official has qualified or an

---

[38] 18 U.S.C. § 201.

officer or employee or person acting for or on behalf of the United States, or any department, agency or branch of Government thereof, including the District of Columbia, in any official function, under or by authority of any such department, agency, or branch of government, or a juror;

(2) the term "person who has been selected to be a public official" means any person who has been nominated or appointed to be a public official, or has been officially informed that such person will be so nominated or appointed; and

(3) the term "official act" means any decision or action on any question, matter, cause, suit, proceeding or controversy, which may at any time be pending, or which may by law be brought before any public official capacity, or in such official's place of trust or profit.

(b) Whoever --

(1) directly or indirectly, corruptly gives, offers or promises anything of value to any public official or person who has been selected to be a public official, or offers or promises any public official or any person who has been selected to be a public official to give anything of value to any other person or entity, with intent --

(A) to influence any official act; or

(B) to influence such public official or person who has been selected to be a public official to commit or aid in committing, or collude in or allow, any fraud, or make opportunity for the commission of any fraud, on the United States; or

(C) to induce such public official or such person who has been selected to be a public official to do or omit to do any act in violation of the unlawful duty of such official or person;

(2) being a public official or person selected to be a public official, directly or indirectly, corruptly demands, seeks, receives, accepts, or agrees to receive or accept anything of value personally or for any other person or entity, in return for:

(A) being influenced in the performance of any official act;

(B) being influenced to commit or aid in committing, or to collude in, or allow, any fraud, or make opportunity for the commission of any fraud, on the United States; or

(C) being induced to do or omit to do any act in violation of the official duty of such official or person;

(3) directly or indirectly, corruptly gives, offers, or promises anything of value to any person, or offers to promise such person to give anything of value to any other person or entity, with intent to influence the testimony under oath or affirmation of such first-mentioned person as a witness upon a trial, hearing, or other proceeding, before any court, any committee of either House or both Houses of Congress, or any agency, commission, or officer authorized by the laws of the United States to hear evidence or take testimony, or with intent to influence such person to absent himself therefrom;

(4) directly or indirectly, corruptly demands, seeks, receives, accepts, or agrees to receive or accept anything of value personally or for any other person or entity in return for being influenced in testimony under oath or affirmation as a witness upon any such trial, hearing, or other proceeding, or in return for absenting himself therefrom:

shall be fined not more than three times the monetary equivalent of the thing of value, or imprisoned for not more than fifteen years, or both, and may be disqualified from holding any office of honor, trust, or profit under the United States.

(c) Whoever --

(1) otherwise than as provided by law for the proper discharge of official duty --

(A) directly or indirectly gives, offers, or promises anything of value to any public official, former public official, or person selected to be a public official, for or because of any official act performed or to be performed by such public official, former public official, or person selected to be a public official; or

(B) being a public official, former public official, or person selected to be a public official, otherwise than as provided by law for the proper discharge of official duty, directly or indirectly demands, seeks, receives, accepts, or agrees to receive or accept anything of value personally for or because of any official act performed or to be performed by such official or person;

(2) directly or indirectly, gives, offers or promises anything of value to any person, for or because of the testimony under oath or affirmation given or to be given by such person as a witness upon a trial, hearing, or other proceeding, before any court, any committee of either House or both Houses of Congress, or any agency, commission, or officer authorized by the laws of the United States to hear evidence or take testimony, or for or because of such person's absence therefrom;

(3) directly or indirectly demands, seeks, receives, accepts, or agrees to receive or accept anything of value personally for or because of the testimony under oath or affirmation given or to be given by such person as a witness upon any such trial, hearing, or other proceeding, or for or because of such person's absence therefrom;

shall be fined under this title or imprisoned for not more than two years, or both.

(d) Paragraphs (3) and (4) of subsection (b) and paragraphs (2) and (3) of subsection (c) shall not be construed to prohibit the payment or receipt of witness fees provided by law, or the payment by the party upon whose behalf a witness is called and receipt by a witness, of the reasonable cost of travel and subsistence occurred and the reasonable value of time lost in attendance at any such trial, hearing, or proceeding, or in the case of expert witnesses, a reasonable fee for time spent in the preparation of such opinion and in appearing and testifying.

(e) The offenses and penalties prescribed in this section are separate from and in addition to those prescribed in sections 1503, 1504 and 1505 of this Title.

The federal statute is very comprehensive and applies to those who receive or accept anything of value. It also applies not only to proceedings before any court but also to proceedings before committees of either House of Congress or any agency, commission, or officer authorized by the laws of the United States to hear evidence, or give testimony. Cases interpreting the provisions of the statute have held that these provisions are neither unconstitutionally vague or overbroad.[39]

3. Other statutes and codes

Many recently enacted state statutes on bribery include most, if not all, of the language of the Model Code. Some, however, require specific intent.[40] Others can be interpreted to require that the benefit be offered, or solicited upon an agreement or understanding that the official conduct will be influenced.[41] This language indicates that an actual agreement must exist. An example of a state statute that is somewhat different from the Model Code is that of New York.[42] It provides:

§ 200.04 Bribery in the first degree

A person is guilty of bribery in the first degree when he confers, or offers or agrees to confer, any benefit upon a public servant upon an agreement or understanding that such public servant's vote, opinion, judgement, action, decision or exercise of discretion as a public servant will thereby be influenced in the investigation, arrest, detention, prosecution, or incarceration of any person for the commission or alleged commission of a Class A felony defined in article two hundred twenty of the penal law or an attempt to commit any such Class A felony.

Bribery in the first degree is a Class B felony.

A New York court has held that the legislative intent in using the words "as a public servant" in this section was to shield from corruption only those actions of a public servant which are related to or within the scope of his

---

[39] United States v. Brewster, 506 F.2d 62 (D.C. Cir. 1974).

[40] Iowa.

[41] Del., N.Y.

[42] N.Y. Penal Law § 210.00 (McKinney 1975).

functions as a public servant.[43] "Public servant" includes a university security officer.[44]

The elements of § 200.04, bribery in the first degree, are:

(1) to confer, offer, or agree to confer
(2) any benefit,
(3) to a public servant,
(4) an agreement or understanding that such public servant's vote, opinion, judgment, action, decision or exercise of discretion will be influenced and
(5) in the investigation, arrest, detention, prosecution or incarceration of any person for the commission or alleged commission of a felony defined in a specific section of the statute.

It should be noted before leaving bribery that bribery statutes are often divided into sections which relate to bribery in specific situations. For example, in the Commonwealth of Kentucky specific statutes relate to bribing a witness, bribing a juror and jury tampering.[45]

§ 10.4 Obstructing Justice

The courts recognized early that some laws were necessary to protect the integrity of the criminal justice process. At common law offenses were created first by court decision and later by statutes which provided misdemeanor penalties for misdeeds which tended to distort or impede the administration of law. From the very beginning courts and legislative bodies have recognized that justice can be administered fairly and impartially only when persons who have knowledge of the transactions are allowed to come before the court for examination without hindrance from one inside or outside the process.[46] On the other hand, the courts and legislative bodies have also recognized the difficulty in framing legislation which would accomplish the purpose of protecting the criminal justice process yet preserve the rights of individuals.

---

[43] People v. Herskowitz, 80 Misc.2d 693, 364 N.Y.S.2d 350 (1975), aff'd, 41 N.Y.2d 1094, 364 N.E.2d 1127, 396 N.Y.2d 356 (1977).

[44] People v. Woodford, 85 Misc.2d 379, 380 N.Y.S.2d 618 (1975).

[45] Ky. Rev. Stat. Ann. §§ 424.050, 424.060 and 424.090 (Baldwin 1975).

[46] 39 AM. JUR. Obstructing Justice § 2 (1942).

A. Traditional Definitions and Elements

Although the definitions relating to the offense of "Obstruction of Justice" differ, there is a common theme running through these definitions. Some examples will assist in understanding the purpose of the offense.

To "obstruct justice" is to interpose obstacles or impediments, or to hinder, impede, or in any manner interrupt or prevent the administration of justice.[47]

The phrase "obstructing justice" means impeding or obstructing those who seek justice in a court, or those who have duties or powers of administering justice therein.[48]

The state has the inherent power to punish for obstruction of justice if it is found that one acted in such a way as to play a human frailty and to defect and to deter the court from performing its duty.[49] For example, conspiracy to induce or aid one who may be required as a witness in a pending proceeding to leave the jurisdiction, in order to escape service of a subpoena or to evade such service, constitutes obstruction of justice.[50]

Other examples of obstruction of justice are an attorney general's persuading a municipal judge to dispose of various criminal cases without the consent and knowledge of the district attorney,[51] and a defendant's statement that he would kill the deputy sheriff where the threats were knowingly made in an attempt to intimidate or impede the testimony of the sheriff.[52]

On the other hand, something more than mere disagreement or remonstrance with a police officer must be shown to constitute "obstruction of justice."[53] In the *McCook* case, the testimony of the officer was that McCook interfered and interrupted him while he was trying to arrest another person. He further testified that "McCook thought I shouldn't arrest the driver for not having a driver's license." The reviewing court was of the opinion that none of these statements adds up to an obstruction of justice. Citing another case, the court held that mere remonstrance is insufficient unless an argu-

---

[47] Baker v. State, 122 Ga. App. 587, 178 S.E.2d 278 (1970).

[48] Shackelford v. Commonwealth, 185 Ky. 51, 214 S.W. 788 (1919).

[49] State v. Sagumaker, 200 Ind. 623, 157 N.E. 769 (1927).

[50] People v. Hefberd, 162 N.Y.S. 80 (1916).

[51] People v. Martin, 185 Cal. Rptr. 556 (1982).

[52] Polk v. Commonwealth, 4 Va. App. 590, 358 S.E.2d 770 (1987). *See* case in Part II.

[53] McCook v. State, 145 Ga. App. 3, 243 S.E.2d 289 (1978).

ment results and becomes violent so as to amount to something calculated to force the officer to desist.

B. Contemporary Statutes and Codes

1. Model Penal Code[54]

§ 242.1 Obstructing Administration of Law or Other Government Function

A person commits a misdemeanor if he purposely obstructs, impairs or perverts the administration of law or other governmental function by force, violence, physical interference or obstacle, breach of official duty, or any other unlawful act, except that this Section does not apply to flight by a person charged with crime, refusal to submit to arrest, failure to perform a legal duty other than an official duty, or any other means of avoiding compliance with law without affirmative interference with governmental functions.

This section of the Model Penal Code does not include bribery, threat, perjury, or escape. The purpose of the Code was to make it possible to punish those that did not come within the technical definitions of the other offenses. According to the comments following the proposed section of the Code, the drafters felt it desirable to include a residual misdemeanor offense but also recognized the necessity of not making the provision too broad in its coverage.

The offense punishes anyone who "obstructs, impairs, or perverts the administration of law, or other governmental function." It is not limited to the administration of justice, but applies to any other governmental function. In order to bring an offender within the statutory prohibition, the prosecution must show first that the person "purposely" obstructs or perverts the administration of law or other governmental function. The prosecution must also introduce evidence to prove that force, violence, physical interference or obstacle, breach of official duty, or other unlawful act was involved in obstructing the administration of law.

---

[54] Model Penal Code § 242.1 (Proposed Official Draft 1980).

2. Federal Code

Chapter 73 of Title 18 of the U.S. Code has 14 sections relating to the obstruction of justice.[55] The section that has had the most use is § 1503, "Influencing or Injuring Officer or Juror Generally." This section provides that:

> Whoever corruptly, or by threats or force, or by any threatening letter or communication, endeavors to influence, intimidate, or impede any grand or petit jury, or officer in or of any court of the United States, or officer who may be serving at any examination or other proceedings before any U.S. commissioner or other committee magistrate, in the discharge of his duty, or injures any such grand or petit juror in his person or property on account of any verdict or indictment assented to by him, or on account of his being or having been such juror, or injures any such officer, commissioner, or other committee magistrate in his person or property on account of the performance of his official duties, or corruptly or by threats or force, or by any threatening letter or communication, influences, obstructs, or impedes, or endeavors to influence, obstruct, or impede, the due administration of justice, shall be fined not more than $5,000 or imprisoned not more than 5 years, or both.

This section was challenged as being unconstitutionally vague but the courts that have heard arguments agree that the statute does not suffer from unconstitutional vagueness.[56]

Under this chapter defendants have been successfully prosecuted for knowingly, willfully and corruptly attempting to impede the administration of justice in a matter under investigation by intentionally destroying documents,[57] for giving false testimony to a grand jury concerning a third person's presence at a meeting,[58] and for corruptly influencing a grand jury witness to refuse to testify.[59]

---

[55] 18 U.S.C. §§ 1501-1515.

[56] United States v. Mitchell, 397 F.Supp. 166 (D.D.C. 1974), *cert. denied*, 431 U.S. 733, 53 L.Ed. 250, 97 S. Ct. 2641 (1974).

[57] United States v. McKnight, 799 F.2d 443 (8th Cir. 1986).

[58] United States v. Langella, 776 F.2d 1078 (2d Cir. 1985), *cert. denied*, 89 L.Ed.2d 320, 106 S. Ct. 1207 (1985).

[59] United States v. Arnold, 773 F.2d 823 (7th Cir. 1985). For other examples, *see* United States v. Silverman, 745 F.2d 1386 (11th Cir. 1984).

In the *Arnold* case cited, evidence was introduced to show that the defendant promised the grand jury witness that he would take care of his expenses, provide an attorney, forgive a debt and visit him in jail if he were imprisoned for remaining silent, if the witness refused to testify.

Chapter 73 also includes a provision making it a federal offense for two or more persons to conspire or to obstruct the enforcement of the criminal law of the state or political subdivision thereof, with the intent to facilitate an illegal gambling business, and a section making it a crime to obstruct the communication of information to a criminal investigator.[60]

3. Other statutes and codes

In states where the statutes have been revised, many have followed the recommendation of the Model Code and consolidated obstruction of governmental functions into one offense. Some use other terminology such as "willful" obstruction.[61] Others do not require any specific means of obstruction.[62] An example of a Code that differs somewhat from the Model Penal Code is that of Ohio. It provides:

> (A) No person, without privilege to do so and with purpose to prevent, obstruct, or delay the performance by a public official of any authorized act within his official capacity, shall do any act which hampers or impedes a public official in the performance of his lawful duties.[63]

This statute consolidates a large number of separate sections that were included in the former law. Under this section, the means used to commit the offense is unimportant, so long as it is done without privilege and with the purpose of preventing, obstructing, or delaying an official act, and actually has its intended effect. According to an Ohio court's interpretation of the statute, there must be some substantial stoppage of the officer's progress before one can say he was hampered or impeded.[64]

In the *Stephens* case, several police officers observed a vehicle belonging to a person whose name was Hannah, for whom they had several outstanding traffic warrants, parked in front of the defendant's house. The officers walked up to the house and asked if they could speak to Hannah. The defen-

---

[60] 18 U.S.C. §§ 1510 and 1511.

[61] Kan.

[62] Ark., Ohio.

[63] Ohio Rev. Code Ann., § 2921.31 (Page 1987).

[64] State v. Stephens, 57 Ohio App. 2d 229, 387 N.E.2d 252 (1978).

dant told the officers she did not know Hannah and had never seen him before. One of the officers had previously seen the defendant in Hannah's company and knew that she did know him. Another officer looked through a window and observed Hannah hiding in the basement. The officers entered the house and arrested Hannah. The defendant was tried and convicted of hampering a public official in the performance of his duties in violation of the Ohio statute.

On appeal, the conviction was reversed, the court holding that the statute which prohibits "any act which hampers or impedes a public official in the performance of his lawful duties" did not encompass the defendant's conduct. The court indicated that the defendant's word in no way interrupted the officers' progress toward their objective and even though the defendant lied, the act did not in fact hamper or impede the officials.

§ 10.5 Escape

As the offenses relating to escape are of considerable importance to criminal justice personnel, these crimes are given more attention. At common law, escape was distinguished from prison break and the offense of rescue. Prison break was defined as the breaking and going out of a place of confinement by one who is lawfully imprisoned. The crime was not committed unless there was an actual breaking or force was used. If there was no force, then the crime was not escape.[65]

Rescue was defined as the forcible delivery of a prisoner from lawful custody by one who knows that he is in custody. Rescue, at common law, was a felony or misdemeanor according to the crime with which the prisoner was charged.

At common law, the crime of escape included the situation where an officer voluntarily suffers a prisoner to escape. Under this law, the officer could be held criminally liable if he unlawfully permitted the prisoner to escape.[66]

A. Traditional Definitions and Elements

An escape has been broadly defined as the voluntary departure of a person without force from the lawful custody of an officer or from any place

---

[65] State v. King, 114 Iowa 413, 87 N.W. 282 (1901).

[66] Houpt v. State, 100 Ark. 409, 140 S.W. 294 (1911).

where he is lawfully confined.[67] The person cannot make an escape unless he has actually been arrested; neither can an escape occur where the preceding arrest was defeated by successful resistance.[68]

However, one who has been taken into custody of the law by arrest or surrender and remains in legal custody and then departs unlawfully is guilty of escape. The fact that the escape occurs as a result of the negligence of a jailer in leaving a door open is not a defense.[69]

An escape is not justified or excused even if a prisoner is wrongfully held in custody and could possibly be released if the proper legal steps are taken. He is guilty of an escape if he wrongfully freed himself.[70] However, there can be no escape if there was no custody. For example, in a Texas case the conviction was reversed when the reviewing court found that the suspect who was charged with escape was not in custody, having refused to submit to the officer's authority.[71] The court explained that the defendant's arrest was not complete when she fled from the police officer after he ordered her to gather her possessions, lock her vehicle and come with him, since the elements of detention and control were lacking. In this case the officer did not take physical custody nor did the defendant submit to the officer's authority, therefore, the defendant was not in custody.

While it is not escape if the suspect is not in custody, conviction for escape is proper where the defendant voluntarily departed from the city jail while in police custody and handcuffed.[72] This is true even if the departure by a prisoner is from restraints imposed upon him at a halfway house where he was confined and the departure was willful and intentional.[73]

The elements of common law escape are:

(1) the person must be in legal custody, and
(2) departure from the area of confinement.

No intent is required for guilt of escape other than the intent to go beyond permitted limits. Proof that the defendant was in legal custody and voluntarily departed therefrom without having been released is sufficient for a conviction in the absence of some satisfactory explanation.[74]

---

[67] United States v. Zimmerman, 71 F.Supp. 534 (D. Pa. 1947).

[68] Whithead v. Keyes, 85 Mass. (3 Allen) 495 (1862).

[69] State v. Hoffman, 30 Wash. 2d 475, 191 P.2d 865 (1948).

[70] People v. Hinze, 97 Cal. App. 2d 1, 217 P.2d 35 (1950).

[71] Snabb v. State, 683 S.W.2d 850 (Tex. 1984). *See* case in Part II.

[72] State v. Brown, 29 Wash. App. 770, 630 P.2d 1378 (1981).

[73] State v. Brown, 8 Wash. App. 639, 509 P.2d 77 (1973).

[74] Wiggins v. State, 194 Ind. 118, 141 N.E. 56 (1923).

According to a Florida court, the crime of escape consists of two elements: *the act of leaving custody* coupled with *the intent to avoid lawful confinement.* The court said when a state has established this right to custody and a conscious and intentional act of leaving, the offense is *prima facie* established. The only defense, according to the court, would be necessity, involving reasonable grounds to believe that the escapee is faced with real and imminent danger if he does not temporarily leave his place of confinement.[75]

B. *Contemporary Statutes and Codes*

1. Model Penal Code[76]

§ 242.6 Escape

(1) Escape. A person commits an offense if he unlawfully removes himself from official detention or fails to return to official detention following temporary leave granted for a specific purpose or limited period. "Official detention" means arrest, detention in any facility for custody of persons under charge or conviction of crime or alleged or found to be delinquent, detention for extradition or deportation, or any other detention for law enforcement purposes; but "official detention" does not include supervision of probation or parole, or constraint incidental to release on bail.

(2) Permitting or Facilitating Escape. A public servant concerned in detention commits an offense if he knowingly or recklessly permits an escape. Any person who knowingly causes or facilitates an escape commits an offense.

(3) Effect of Legal Irregularity in Detention. Irregularity in bringing about or maintaining detention, or lack of jurisdiction of the committing or detaining authority, shall not be a defense to prosecution under this Section if the escape is from a prison or other custodial facility or from detention pursuant to commitment by official proceedings. In the case of other detentions, irregularity or lack of jurisdiction shall be a defense only if:

---

[75]   Watford v. State, 353 So. 2d 1263 (Fla. Dist. Ct. App. 1978).

[76]   Model Penal Code § 242.6 (Proposed Official Draft 1980).

    (a) the escape involved no substantial risk of harm to the person or property of anyone other than the detainee; or

    (b) the detaining authority did not act in good faith under color of law.

(4) Grading of Offenses. An offense under this Section is a felony of the third degree where:

    (a) the actor was under arrest for or detained on a charge of felony or following conviction of crime; or

    (b) the actor employs force, threat, deadly weapon or other dangerous instrumentality to effect the escape; or

    (c) a public servant concerned in detention of persons convicted of crime purposely facilitates or permits an escape from a detention facility.

Otherwise an offense under this section is a misdemeanor.

The Model Penal Code is written in clear language in order to prevent misinterpretation regarding failure to return following leave granted for a specific purpose. Also "official detention" is clearly defined to include arrest and detention for law enforcement purposes.

The Model Code, in § 2, provides a penalty for a public official who permits or facilitates the escape. This is similar to provisions that existed in early common law.

The punishment assigned to the offense of escape takes into consideration the crime charged and the force used in making the escape.

2. Federal Code

Chapter 35 of Title 18 of the U.S. Code includes a provision relating to the escape of prisoners in custody of an institutional officer, a second provision making it a crime for one to rescue a person who has been lawfully arrested and a third provision making it possible to punish an officer who voluntarily suffers a prisoner to escape.[77]

Section 751 of Title 18 of the U.S. Code provides a fine of not more than $5,000 or imprisonment of not more than five years, or both, if one is convicted of escaping from the custody of a federal institution or from custody of an officer or employee of the United States made pursuant to a lawful arrest. This statutory provision, which was first enacted in 1930 in somewhat different form, was intended to reach anyone who was held by virtue of any proper

---

[77] 18 U.S.C. §§ 751, 752 and 755.

and legal process including those who escaped from penal or correctional institutions or escapees from the custody of an officer or employee of the United States pursuant to a lawful arrest.[78]

According to an interpretation by one court, there are three elements of the federal escape offense:

(1) an escape,
(2) from custody of an institution where the prisoner is confined by direction of the attorney general and
(3) the confinement as pursuant to a judgment of conviction or other process issued under the laws of the United States.[79]

This section has been held to apply where the federal prisoner participating in a prerelease or halfway house program by designation of the attorney general willfully violates the terms of his extended confinement,[80] and to the escape of a federal prisoner contemporarily in the custody of state authorities pursuant to the direction of the attorney general.[81]

In addition to § 751 relating to escape, the Federal Code makes it a crime, punishable by not more than $5,000 or imprisonment for not more than five years, or both, if one is convicted of rescuing or attempting to rescue or aid or abet or assist the escape or attempt to escape any person arrested upon a warrant or other process issued under any law of the United States.[82] In prosecuting one for aiding and assisting escape of a federal prisoner under this section, evidence that the defendant knew that the prisoner's departure from prison was unauthorized was sufficient to have sustained a conviction.[83]

A third provision of the federal statute applies only to those who have custody of a prisoner. Section 755 of Title 18 as amended in 1968 provides:

Whoever, having in his custody any prisoner by virtue of process issued under the law of the United States by any court, judge, or commissioner, voluntarily suffers such prisoner to escape, shall be fined not more than $2,000 or imprisoned not more than two years or both; or if he negligently suffers such person to escape, he shall

---

[78] United States v. McKim, 509 F.2d 769 (5th Cir. 1975).

[79] United States v. Spletzer, 535 F.2d 950 (5th Cir. 1976).

[80] United States v. Jones, 569 F.2d 499 (9th Cir. 1978), *cert. denied*, 436 U.S. 908, 56 L.Ed.2d 407, 98 S. Ct. 2243 (1978).

[81] Coonsel - Inf. OP, 4B Op. 011 719 (1980).

[82] 18 U.S.C. § 752.

[83] United States v. Nordstrom, 730 F.2d 556 (8th Cir. 1984).

be fined not more than $5,000 or imprisoned not more than one year, or both.

As the wording indicates, this section applies only if the person accused has custody of a prisoner and either voluntarily allows the prisoner to escape or negligently permits the prisoner to escape.

3. Other statutes and codes

Statutes and codes in the various states differ in wording and in establishing penalties. Some states, such as Ohio, recognize a single grade of escape with no aggravating or mitigating factors, while other states include distinct grading levels depending upon the use of force, the severity of the escapee's original crime and the escapee's status; that is, whether he has been convicted or merely detained on suspicion.

In the Commonwealth of Kentucky, three degrees of the offense of escape are defined.[84]

The Kentucky statute provides:

§ 520.020 Escape in the First Degree
(1) A person is guilty of escape in the first degree when he escapes from custody or a detention facility by the use of force or threat of force against another person.
(2) Escape in the first degree is a Class C felony (5-10 years).

§ 520.030 Escape in the Second Degree
(1) A person is guilty of escape in the second degree when he escapes from a detention facility or, being charged with or convicted of a felony, he escapes from custody.
(2) Escape in the second degree is a Class D felony (1-5 years).

§ 520.040 Escape in the Third Degree
(1) A person is guilty of escape in the third degree when he escapes from custody.
(2) Escape in the third degree is a Class B misdemeanor (up to 90 days).

---

[84] Ky. Rev. Stat. Ann. §§ 520.020, 520.030, 520.040 (Baldwin 1974).

"Escape" is defined as "departure from custody or the detention facility in which a person is held or detained with knowledge that such
departure is unpermitted, or failure to return to custody or detention following a temporary leave granted for a specific purpose or
for a limited period."[85]

"Custody" means restraint by a public servant pursuant to a lawful
arrest, detention, or an order of a court for law enforcement purposes, but does not include supervision of probation or parole or
constraint incidental to release on bail.

The elements of escape in the first degree under the Kentucky statutes are:

(1) escape as defined,
(2) from custody or a detention facility,
(3) by use of force or threat.

If the element of force or threat is not proved, but escape is from a detention facility or the charge is a felony, then the offense is escape in the second degree. If only the first two elements can be proved, then the offense
charged should be escape in the third degree.

According to the Kentucky Court of Appeals, a defendant may be
charged under the statute with escape in the second degree, a felony, despite
the fact that he had been in jail and charged with misdemeanors rather than a
felony. The court explained that the penalty imposed is most severe on those
who effect an escape by force or threat of force. It is less severe when escape
is effected by a means without force if it is from detention or if a felon escapes from custody (arrest). It is least severe when escape is effected from
custody (arrest) and the person charged is not a felon or not charged with a
felony.[86]

§ 10.6 Resisting Arrest

Some statutes dealing with the general offense "obstructing justice" include
the act of resisting arrest. Other statutes deal specifically with the offense of
resisting arrest. At common law resisting arrest was an offense; however, an

---

[85] Ky. Rev. Stat. Ann. § 520.010 (Baldwin 1974).

[86] Commonwealth v. Johnson, 615 S.W.2d 1 (Ky. 1981).

individual had a right to use reasonable resistance to prevent being arrested illegally.[87]

At common law, if the arrest was legal and there was resistance, the offense of resisting arrest was complete. What amounted to resistance depended on the facts of the situation. There are numerous examples of cases where the court found that resistance existed. The use of any weapon such as a club, pistol, revolver or gun is undoubtedly sufficient to constitute the resistance prohibited. However, resisting arrest does not require an attempt to cause serious bodily injury to the police officer. It is sufficient to prove that the defendant created a substantial risk of bodily injury or that he put up resistance requiring the policeman to use substantial force to overcome it.[88]

In distinguishing between escape and resisting arrest, it has been held that "escape from custody" implies the unlawful freeing of oneself from a completed apprehension while "resisting apprehension" means active opposition to attempts to place one in lawful custody.[89]

If an officer does not disclose his authority and the accused does not know that he is an officer, he has the right to resist with whatever force is necessary.[90]

B. Contemporary Statutes and Codes

1. Model Penal Code[91]

§ 242.2 Resisting Arrest or Other Law Enforcement
A person commits a misdemeanor if, for the purpose of preventing a public servant from effecting a lawful arrest or discharging any other duty, the person creates a substantial risk of bodily injury to the public servant or anyone else, or employs means justifying or requiring substantial force to overcome the resistance.

Section 242.2 of the Model Penal Code supplements § 242.1 which deals with "Obstructing Administration of Law or Other Government Function." Section 242.2 is concerned with the resistance to arrest where there is a substantial risk of bodily injury to a public servant or anyone else or employs means justifying or requiring substantial force to overcome the resistance.

---

[87] Fields v. State, 384 N.E.2d 1127 (Ind. Ct. App. 1979).

[88] Commonwealth v. Williams, 344 Pa. Super. 108, 496 A.2d 31 (1985).

[89] United States v. Chavez, 6 Mil. Jus. 615.

[90] Presley v. State, 75 Fla. 434, 78 So. 532 (1918).

[91] Model Penal Code § 242.2 (Proposed Official Draft 1980).

Exempted from liability is one who non-violently refuses to submit to arrest and such minor forms of resistance as running from a policeman or trying to shake free from his grasp.

Under the Model Penal Code, resisting arrest is a misdemeanor regardless of the charge against the person who resists arrest. In the commentary following the statement of the Model Penal Code, it is explained that continued resistance to the arresting officer after the arrest has been made may constitute attempt to escape in violation of § 242.6. Therefore, if the arrest is for a felony, escape from the custody may be punished as a felony.

Unlike some statutes prior to the Model Code and drafted since the Model Code, the Code does not provide a penalty for one who resists arrest if the arrest is not lawful, unless one of the other provisions of the Code is violated.

2. Federal Code

Title 18, § 111 makes it a felony punishable by a fine of not more than $5,000 or imprisonment of not more than three years, or both, if one is convicted of forcibly assaulting, resisting, imposing, impeding, or intimidating an officer in the performance of his official duties.[92] If deadly force or a dangerous weapon is used, then the fine may be increased to $10,000 and imprisonment increased to ten years, or both. This section withstood a challenge of constitutionality.

A federal court of appeals found that this section against assaulting, resisting, imposing, impeding, intimidating, or interfering with federal officers in the performance of their duties gives a person of ordinary intelligence fair notice of what conduct is proscribed and is not unconstitutionally vague, indefinite, or ambiguous.[93]

The provision prohibiting assault against a federal officer was enacted to protect the federal officers and federal functions and to provide a federal forum in which to try alleged offender.[94] As is the law in many states, federal officers engaged in good faith and colorable performance of their duties may not be forcibly resisted even if the resistor turns out to be correct that the resisted action should not have, in fact, been taken. The statute requires the arrestee to submit peaceably and seek legal redress thereafter.[95]

---

[92] 18 U.S.C. § 211.

[93] United States v. Linn, 438 F.2d 456 (10th Cir. 1971).

[94] United States v. Lopez, 720 F.2d 1071 (5th Cir. 1983).

[95] United States v. Cunningham, 509 F.2d 961 (D.C. Cir. 1973).

3. Other statutes and codes

In drafting legislation, the state legislative bodies have differed especially in regard to the resistance to an unlawful arrest. Some have been persuaded by the argument that the officer should be protected even if the arrest is unlawful and that the remedy to the person who is unlawfully arrested is a civil action against the officer. Examples of the statutes in two states will illustrate this point.

In the state of Ohio a provision is as follows:

> No person, recklessly or by force, shall resist or interfere with a lawful arrest of himself or another.[96]

This covers resistance to or interference with an arrest not only by the person being arrested, but by another as well; it provides that there shall be a penalty only if there is an interference with a "lawful" arrest.

In the Commonwealth of Kentucky, the statute provides:[97]

> (1) a person is guilty of resisting arrest when he intentionally prevents or attempts to prevent a peace officer, recognized to be acting under color of his official authority, from effecting arrest of the actor or another by;
>
> > (a) suing or threatening to use physical force or violence against the peace officer or another; or
> > (b) using any other means creating a substantial risk of causing physical injury to the peace officer or another.

Here, the offense of resisting arrest includes only forcible resistance and excludes other forms of nonsubmission to authority. Neither flight from arrest nor passive resistance are punishable under this section since a peace officer has the available remedy of the use of reasonable force to effect the arrest.

To protect the officer and remove disputes from the street to the courts, some statutes provide that the unlawfulness of an arrest may not be raised as a defense to a prosecution when an arrest is made under the color of official authority and when the person making the arrest is identified or identifiable as a police officer acting in his official capacity.[98]

---

[96] Ohio Rev. Code Ann. § 2921.33 (Page 1987).

[97] Ky. Rev. Stat. Ann. § 520.090 (Baldwin 1974).

[98] Ky. Rev. Stat. Ann. § 503.060 (Baldwin 1974).

In prosecuting one for a violation of the Ohio statute, recklessness or force in addition to resistance or interference with a lawful arrest are necessary elements. Under the Kentucky statute, the required elements are:

(1) intent,
(2) preventing or attempting to prevent a peace officer,
(3) that the peace officer was identifiable as such,
(4) the use or threatened use of physical force or violence against the officer or use of other means creating a substantial risk of physical injury to the officer or another.

As the states differ in regard to the elements, it is essential that each officer be aware of the specific wording of the state statute and the decisions that have been rendered which interpret the statute.

In one state case, the court made it clear that even at common law, an individual had a right to use reasonable resistance to prevent being arrested illegally but the rule is no longer in existence. The court indicated that today a citizen can seek his remedy for a policeman's unwarranted arrest by bringing a civil suit, while the common law right tends to promote violence. Thus, the court held that the defendant had no right to resist arrest.[99]

In the *Fields* case, the defendant was convicted of interfering with the police officer after a dispute which developed when the officers ordered a tow truck to remove the defendant's vehicle from the street. The defendant contended upon appeal that he had a legal right to remove his own vehicle because, although it displayed the wrong kind of license plate, it was not otherwise illegally parked and should have been treated as an abandoned vehicle. The court agreed that the officer had no right to have the car removed. However, the defendant also had no right to resist being arrested. Therefore, the conviction for resisting arrest was proper.

§ 10.7 Other Offenses Against Public Justice and Administration

All state statutes include other provisions which relate to conduct which impairs or obstructs governmental operations or public administration. the primary purpose is to preserve smooth and efficient administration of government and to protect those who are charged with the responsibility of enforcing the laws and ordinances.

---

[99] Fields v. State, 384 N.E.2d 1127 (Ind. Ct. App. 1979).

As these vary from state to state, it is obviously necessary that the state statute, and in some instances local ordinances, be studied to determine what conduct is prohibited and what elements must be proved to obtain a conviction when one is charged with violation of the ordinance or statute. Some of the offenses that are found in various state statutes are discussed here. It should be noted, however, that these are not exclusive.

A. Failure to Aid a Law Enforcement Officer

Many early statutes require that persons come to the aid of a law enforcement officer when requested. In fact, at common law it was a criminal offense for any person willfully to disregard the summons of the sheriff to render assistance in apprehending a felon. Every citizen was bound to assist a known public officer in making an arrest when called upon to do so.[100] By statute, in some states, the failure on the part of the citizen to obey the call of an officer to assist in making an arrest makes the citizen subject to prosecution.[101]

An example of a modern statute that restates the requirement that persons come to the aid of officers is that of Ohio. It provides:

> (A) No person shall negligently fail or refuse to aid a law enforcement officer, when called upon for assistance in preventing or halting the commission of an offense, or in apprehending or detaining an offender, when such aid can be given without a substantial risk of physical harm to the person giving it.[102]

This requires that a person aid the officer in apprehending an offender even though the offender has not been formally charged. It excuses the failure to render aid on the ground that there is a strong possibility the person called upon may be hurt in the process.

---

[100] Grau v. Forge, 183 Ky. 521, 209 S.W. 369 (1919); Firestone v. Rice, 71 Mich. 377, 38 N.W. 885 (1888).

[101] Babington v. Yellow Taxi Corp., 250 N.Y. 14, 164 N.E. 726 (1928); 4 AM. JUR. *Arrest* § 129 (1936).

[102] Ohio Rev. Code Ann. § 2921.23 (Page 1987).

B. False Reports to Law Enforcement Authorities

There is some evidence to the effect that giving false reports to police or other law enforcement agencies is punishable under the common law. In the case of *People v. Stephens*, the Illinois court held that one who falsely reports a crime is guilty of disorderly conduct.[103]

After several attempts to draft legislation that provided a penalty for giving false reports to officers, many states now have statutes that accomplish the desired result. An example is that of Florida which provides:

> Whoever knowingly gives false information to any law enforcement officer concerning the alleged commission of any crime is guilty of a misdemeanor of the first degree.[104]

Other states that have similar statutes are Alaska, Georgia, California and Maryland.

Under the Kentucky statute, a person is guilty of falsely reporting an incident when he knowingly causes a false alarm of fire or other emergency to be transmitted.[105] Also, under this section, a person is guilty if he knowingly reports false information to a law enforcement agency with intent to implicate another or initiates a report of an alleged occurrence of a fire or other emergency under circumstances likely to cause inconvenience or alarm when he knows the information reported, conveyed or circulated is false. The major thrust of this statute is to deter those who impede investigations by furnishing fictitious leads. Such statutes are considered necessary in many jurisdictions to aid law enforcement personnel and to avoid inconvenience to members of the public as well as government agents.

C. Tampering with Witnesses

Most state statutes provide penalties for tampering with those who are to testify in trials. In some states, this is dealt with in those provisions relating to obstruction of justice. The crime is closely related to bribery and subornation of perjury, both of which could be charged if the circumstances justify.

---

[103] 40 Ill. App. 3d 303, 352 N.E.2d 352 (1976).

[104] Fla. Stat. Ann. § 837.05 (West 1975).

[105] Ky. Rev. Stat. Ann. § 519.040 (Baldwin 1974).

The Model Code provisions relating to tampering with witnesses includes tampering with informants. It provides:[106]

§ 241.6   Tampering With Witnesses and Informants;
Retaliation Against Them

(1) Tampering. A person commits an offense if, believing that an official proceeding or investigation is pending or about to be instituted, he attempts to induce or otherwise cause a witness or informant to:

   (a) testify or inform falsely; or
   (b) withhold any testimony, information, document or thing; or
   (c) elude legal process summoning him to testify or supply evidence; or
   (d) absent himself from any proceeding or investigation to which he has been legally summoned.

The offense is a felony of the third degree if the actor employs force, deception, threat or offer of pecuniary benefit. Otherwise it is a misdemeanor.

(2) Retaliation Against Witness or Informant. A person commits a misdemeanor if he harms another by any unlawful act in retaliation for anything lawfully done in the capacity of witness or informant.

(3) Witness or Informant Taking Bribe. A person commits a felony of the third degree if he solicits, accepts or agrees to accept any benefit in consideration of his doing any of the things specified in clauses (a) to (d) of Subsection (1).

This provision defines three different offenses, each of which protects against some threat to the veracity and cooperation of witnesses and informants.

Subsection 1 provides that a person commits an offense if he attempts to induce another to testify or inform falsely or otherwise subvert the process of criminal law. Subsection 2 condemns retaliation against a witness or informant. Subsection 3 imposes a felony penalty for solicitation, acceptance or agreement to accept any benefit in consideration of doing any of the acts enumerated in the first ten subsections.

---

[106] Model Penal Code § 241.6 (Proposed Official Draft).

Many of the recently revised statutes and codes have provisions relating to tampering with witnesses. Some are more restrictive and some less restrictive. These, of course, must be studied in detail before any charges are made.

D. Tampering with Evidence

In order to insure that evidence is preserved for presentation in court, many states have enacted legislation which prohibits tampering with evidence or fabricating physical evidence. The provisions of the statutes apply to those who undertake to impair the integrity or availability of evidence in an official proceeding or investigation, or one who purposely fabricates evidence in order to mislead the investigator. This is relatively new in most jurisdictions, and most jurisdictions do not have this form of legislation.

The suggested legislation as prepared by the drafters of the Model Penal Code provides:[107]

§ 241.7 Tampering With or Fabricating Physical Evidence

A person commits a misdemeanor if, believing that an official proceeding or investigation is pending or about to be instituted, he:

(1) alters, destroys, conceals or removes any record, document or thing with purpose to impair its verity or availability in such proceeding or investigation; or

(2) makes, presents or uses any record, document or thing knowing it to be false and with purpose to mislead a public servant who is or may be engaged in such proceeding or investigation.

The Model Penal Code punishes one who alters, destroys, conceals, or removes evidence and reaches those who "makes, presents, or uses any record, document or thing knowing it to be false with the purpose to mislead" those engaged in investigating crimes.

Some states which have similar legislation are Connecticut, Indiana, Maine, Missouri, Montana, New Hampshire, New Jersey, Ohio, Pennsylvania, Utah, Massachusetts and Vermont. Other states have provisions that require that the accused intend to have the evidence "introduced" in the official proceeding.

---

[107]   Model Penal Code § 241.7 (Proposed Official Draft 1980).

The Ohio statute provides that a person is guilty of a misdemeanor if:

(1) knowing that an official proceeding or investigation is in progress or is likely to be started; he
(2) alters, destroys, conceals, or removes evidence with purpose to impair its value or availability, or makes, presents, or uses evidence knowing it to be false with the purpose to mislead the investigator or corrupt the outcome of the proceeding or investigation.[108]

E. Other Offenses

Statutes of the various states include other offenses which relate to public justice and administration. Some include such offenses as compounding a crime, impersonating a public servant, hindering apprehension of prosecution and bail jumping.

§ 10.8 Summary

As government functions developed, the necessity of protecting them against willful interference became apparent. Legislation has been enacted to protect government agencies from interference by those outside the government and to protect the public against those individuals who might take advantage of the authority granted as a result of government employment.

It was early recognized that the integrity of a sworn statement must be guaranteed to insure the truth of statements made in judicial or quasi-judicial proceedings. To this end, the offense of perjury was created. Perjury is generally defined as the willful and corrupt false swearing or affirming after an oath has been lawfully administered in the cause of judicial or quasi-judicial proceedings as to some matter material to the issue or point in questions. The essential elements are:

(1) an oath or affirmation,
(2) a false statement made knowingly,
(3) the statement is material.

Subornation of perjury is the procuring of one person by another to commit the crime of perjury.

---

[108]   Ohio Rev. Code Ann. § 2921.12 (Page 1987).

A second universally recognized offense which relates to the integrity of government administration is bribery. Bribery is defined as the offering, giving, receiving, or soliciting of anything of value with intent to influence the recipient's action as a public official. The elements of bribery are:

(1) offering, giving, receiving, or soliciting,
(2) a thing of value,
(3) intent to influence the recipient's action and
(4) the recipient is a public official.

Recognizing that justice can be administered fairly and impartially only when all persons having knowledge of the transactions are allowed to come before the court for examination without hindrance by anyone, the early courts and legislative bodies added a crime entitled "Obstruction of Justice." Generally these statutes and cases prohibit interference with a witness, harboring criminals, influencing a jury, suppression or destruction of evidence and other related acts.

An offense that is of considerable importance to criminal justice personnel is escape. Escape has been broadly defined as a voluntary departure of a person without force from the lawful custody of an officer or from any place where he is lawfully confined. The elements of escape are:

(1) the person must be in legal custody and
(2) departure from the area of confinement.

No intent is required for guilt other than the intent to go beyond permitted limits.

Related to escape is the offense of resisting arrest. At common law, if the arrest were legal and there was resistance, the offense of resisting arrest was complete. What amounted to resistance depended upon the fact of the situation. Under the Model Penal Code, resisting arrest is a violation where there is a substantial risk of bodily injury to a public servant or anyone else.

Other offenses against public justice and administration include: failure to aid a law enforcement officer, making false reports to enforcement authorities, tampering with witnesses and tampering with evidence.

As the state statutes differ regarding offenses against justice administration, these statutes should be reviewed by criminal justice personnel and action taken only after the elements have been determined.

Chapter 11
DRUG-RELATED OFFENSES

Domestic drug law enforcement or domestic supply reduction is a key part of the federal drug abuse prevention and control program. The major objectives of drug law enforcement are: (1) to reduce the supply of illegal drugs; (2) to control the supply of illegally manufactured drugs in order to prevent diversion into illegal channels; and (3) to achieve the highest possible level of risk for drug trafficking by investigating major drug trafficking organizations and securing sufficient evidence so that successful prosecution can be brought which will lead to prison terms for the violators and the forfeiture of their assets.

(Strategic Council on Drug Abuse
and Drug Traffic Prevention: 1979)

§ 11.1 Introduction

During this century, drug-related crimes have probably received more attention than any other category of offenses. Despite the efforts by both state and federal agencies and despite the addition of both state and federal laws, the use of illicit drugs in this country has risen. According to the remarks made by Colonel James E. Damos at the 94th Annual Conference of the International Association of Chiefs of Police, it was estimated that five million Americans used cocaine in 1985, a 38 percent increase in a three-year period.[1] According to this article it was also estimated that drug use by people over 12 years of age increased from 4 percent to 34 percent between 1965 and 1985.

As the drug problem increased, the federal government assumed a larger degree of responsibility for regulating and controlling the use of addictive and other harmful drugs. Beginning in 1970 with the Comprehensive Drug Abuse, Prevention and Control Act of that year, comprehensive statutes were enacted by Congress to identify and control substances which are extremely harmful when improperly utilized. In an effort to obtain some uniformity in the enactment and enforcement of state laws, most states have adopted the provisions of the Uniform Controlled Substances Act.[2]

The Uniform Controlled Substances Act is designed to supplant the Uniform Narcotic Drug Act and the Model State Abuse Control Act, relating to depressant, stimulant and hallucinogenic drugs, promulgated in 1966. The Act was drafted to achieve uniformity between laws of the several states and those of the federal government and to complement the federal narcotics and dangerous drug legislation. It provides an interlocking trellis of federal and state laws to enable government agents at all levels to control more effectively the drug abuse problem.

---

[1] *The Police Yearbook, 1988,* The Official Proceeding of the 94th IACP Annual Conference.

[2] *See* the Appendix for a list of the states that adopted either the Uniform Controlled Substances Act or Uniform Narcotics Act and the statutory citations.

The state and federal laws relating to the control of narcotics and dangerous drugs are comprehensive and somewhat complicated. However, due to cooperation between the federal and state enforcement agencies and federal and state lawmakers, there is more uniformity in these laws than in most others.

As the majority of the states have adopted the provisions of the Uniform Act with some modifications, little effort will be made to examine individual state laws except to use them as examples of the state laws that follow the Uniform Controlled Substances Act. Also, as both the state and federal laws are extensive and detailed, only those that are of more concern to criminal justice personnel are examined closely with references made to cases interpreting them.

In the following sections of this chapter, the specific Sections of the Uniform Controlled Substances Act provisions will be first examined, followed by an explanation of some of the provisions of the federal acts.

§ 11.2 Authority of the State to Regulate the Use of Narcotic Drugs

A state, under its police power, may regulate the administration, sale, prescription, possession and use of narcotic drugs.[3] The constitutional rights of individuals are not violated by legislation making it unlawful to possess paraphernalia adapted for the use of narcotic drugs or to classify marijuana as a narcotic.[4] In 1978 in the case of *People v. Fillhart*, the reviewing court agreed that the Marijuana Reform Act of 1977, which prohibits the growing, possession and use of marijuana (with some exceptions), is constitutional as the manufacturer and use and possession of any controlled substance which affects the behavior, mood and judgment of persons is a legitimate area of concern over which the legislature has the power to regulate.[5] State statutes have been upheld which impose criminal sanctions on one who is unlawfully under the influence of narcotic drugs, for inhaling glue with the intent to be-

---

[3]   Robinson v. California, 370 U.S. 660, 8 L.Ed.2d 758, 82 S. Ct. 1417 (1962); State v. Martin, 192 La. 704, 189 So. 109 (1939).

[4]   Manson v. State, 166 Tex Crim. 514, 316 S.W.2d 414 (1958); People v. Sinclair, 387 Mich. 91, 194 N.W.2d 878 (1972).

[5]   People v. Fillhart, 403 N.Y.S.2d 642 (1978).

come intoxicated, and outlawing the use of marijuana in a private place and elsewhere.[6]

§ 11.3 Uniform Controlled Substances Act

The Uniform Controlled Substances Act was promulgated by the National Conference of Commissioners on Uniform State Laws to create a coordinated and codified system of drug control, similar to that utilized at the federal level. The Act sets out prohibited activities in detail but vests the authority to administer the Act in an agency to be established by the state legislature. As the Act authorizes the agency or person who administers it to implement, enforce and regulate the provisions of the act, this authority is often vested in a high-ranking state official or a committee. For example, the authority could be vested in the Office of the Attorney General, a department of health, a division of public safety or other agency within the state responsible for regulating and enforcing the drug laws.

To make the Uniform Act consistent with the federal act, the Uniform Act follows the federal Controlled Substances law and lists all of the controlled substances in five schedules which are identical with the federal law. However, the Uniform Act does not prevent a state from adding or removing substances from the schedule or from reclassifying substances from one schedule to another.

In categorizing the substances, eight criteria were followed:

(1) its actual or relative potential for abuse,
(2) scientific evidence of pharmacological effects,
(3) the state of current scientific knowledge regarding the substance,
(4) its history and pattern of abuse,
(5) the scope, duration and significance of abuse,
(6) what, if any, risks there are to the public health,
(7) its psychic or psychological dependence liability and
(8) whether the substance is an immediate precursor of a substance already controlled.

The intent is to create reasonable flexibility within the Uniform Act so that, as new substances are discovered or found to have an abuse potential,

---

[6] State v. Brown, 103 Ariz. 289, 440 P.2d 909 (1968); People v. Orozco, 266 Cal. App. 507, 72 Cal. Rptr. 452 (1968); Borras v. State, 229 So. 2d 244 (Fla. 1970), *cert. denied,* 400 U.S. 808, 27 L.Ed.2d 37, 91 S. Ct. 70 (1970).

they can speedily be brought under control without constant resort to the legislature.

§ 11.4 Definitions

Much of the Uniform Controlled Substances Act deals with the manufacture and distribution of controlled substances within the state and the registration of such persons or agencies. Many definitions in the Act relate to this activity. However, there are some definitions in the Act which are of particular interest to criminal justice personnel.[7]

"Controlled substance" means a drug, substance or immediate precursor in Schedules 1-5 of Article II of the Act.

"Narcotic Drug" means any of the following, either produced directly or indirectly by extraction from substances of vegetable origin, or independently by means of chemical synthesis or by a combination of extraction and chemical synthesis:

(i)   opium and opiate and any salt, compound, derivative or preparation of opium or opiate;

(ii) any salt, compound, isomer, derivative or preparation thereof which is chemically equivalent or identical with any of the substances referred to in clause 2, but not including the isoquinoline alkaloids of opium;

(iii) opium poppy and poppy straw;

(iv) coca leaves and any salt, compound, derivative or preparation of coca leaves and any salt, compound, isomer, derivative or preparation thereof which is chemically equivalent or identical with any of these substances, but not including decocanized coca leaves or extractions of coca leaves which do not contain cocaine or ecgonine.[8]

"Deliver" means the actual, constructive or attempted transfer from one person to another of a controlled substance, whether or not there is an agency relationship.

---

[7] For the text of the Uniform Act and variation notes and annotation materials, *see* Uniform Laws Annotated, Master Edition, Volume 9.

[8] The definitions vary from state to state. Even though the laws are generally uniform, the state statutes must be consulted for specific laws, definitions and categories of substances that are declared to be controlled substances.

"Person" means individual, corporation, government or governmental subdivision or agency, business, trust, estate, partnership or association or any other legal entity.

§ 11.5 Standards and Schedules

All controlled substances are categorized in either Schedules I, II, III, IV or V. Under the Uniform Controlled Substances Act, the schedules are identical with the federal law; however, this does not prevent a state from adding or removing substances from the Schedule or from reclassifying the substances from one schedule to another.

The purpose of the classification is to create a coordinated codified system of drug control regulation and to establish some criteria for prescribing specific fines or sentences. The Controlled Substances Act does not itself designate specific fines or sentences but leaves this up to the discretion of the individual states.[9]

In the Uniform Controlled Substances Act and in the states that have adopted this as part of the statute or code of that state, all controlled substances are categorized into five schedules. However, the intent of the writers of the Act is to create reasonable flexibility in the Uniform Act so that as new substances are discovered or found to have abuse potential, they can speedily be brought under control without constant resort to the legislature. The Act includes these guidelines for determining the category into which the controlled substances generally will be included.

Schedule I   The Uniform Controlled Substances Act recommends that the appropriate person or agency place a substance in Schedule I if it is found that the substance:

(1) has a high potential for abuse; and
(2) has no accepted medical use or treatment in the United States or lacks accepted safety for use in treatment under medical supervision.[10]

---

[9] *See* Part II of the book for the Florida statute on Drug Abuse, Prevention and Control (Chapter 893 Fla. Stat. Ann., Vol. 22B, 1988, Cumulative Pocket Part). The Florida statute follows generally the Uniform Code but includes some additional definitions, specific violations and penalties.

[10] *See* the Uniform Controlled Substances Act for a list of substances included on Schedule I. *See also* the Florida statute in Part II for a list of substances included in Schedule I in that

Schedule II	The recommended test for determining which substances are to be included in Schedule II are:

(1) the substance has high potential for abuse;

(2) the substance has currently accepted medical use in treatment in the United States, or currently accepted medical use with severe restrictions; and

(3) the abuse of the substance may lead to severe psychic or physical dependence.

Schedule III	The Uniform Controlled Substances Act recommends that the test to be applied in determining whether a controlled substance will be included in Schedule III is:

(1) the substance has a potential for abuse less than the substances listed in Schedules I and II;

(2) the substance has currently accepted medical use in treatment in the United States; and

(3) abuse of the substance may lead to moderate or low physical dependence or high psychological dependence.

Schedule IV	It is recommended that a substance be included in Schedule IV if:

(1) the substance has a low potential for abuse relative to substances in Schedule III;

(2) the substance has currently accepted medical use and treatment in the United States; and

(3) abuse of the substance may lead to limited physical dependence or

---

statute. Reference is made to this Florida statute for substances included in the other four schedules that are discussed.

psychological dependence relative
to the substances in Schedule III.

Schedule V　　It is recommended that the appropriate agency place a substance in Schedule V if it finds that:

(1) the substance has low potential for abuse relative to the controlled substances listed in Schedule IV;

(2) the substance has currently accepted medical use in treatment in the United States; and

(3) the substance has limited physical dependence or psychological dependence liability relative to the controlled substances listed in Schedule IV.

§ 11.6 Regulating the Manufacture, Distribution and Dispensing of Controlled Substances

The Uniform Controlled Substances Act and state statutes require persons who engage in, or intend to engage in, the manufacture, distribution or dispensing of controlled substances to be registered by the state. The purpose of this part of the Act or statute is to allow the state to know who is responsible for a substance and who is dealing in the substances. This also gives those investigating violations specific authority to prosecute when the controlled substance laws have been violated.

Statutes requiring pharmacists and practitioners to register, maintain records, and only prescribe, administer and dispense of controlled substances as provided in the Act have generally been held to be constitutional and are not so vague as to deny due process.[11]

The Act and statutes give detailed instructions as to who may distribute the controlled substances enumerated and provide for suspension and revocation of licenses for failure to comply with the law. Also, the Act and the state statutes make it unlawful for any person to manufacture, deliver or possess with intent to manufacture or deliver a controlled substance, and the

---

[11] Cohn v. Dept. of Professional Regulations, 477 So. 2d 1039 (1985).

state statutes provide penalties determined by the classification of the substance.[12]

§ 11.7 Prohibited Acts Relating to Controlled Substances

State statutes are generally uniform and specific in designating what conduct is unlawful. The state laws must be consulted to determine the definitions, the elements of each offense and the penalties affixed.[13] However, statutes of most states prohibit:

(1) trafficking in a controlled substance except as authorized,
(2) possession of a controlled substance except as authorized,
(3) dispensing, prescribing, distributing or administering a controlled substance except as authorized,
(4) obtaining or attempting to obtain a controlled substance by fraud, deceit, misrepresentation or subterfuge,
(5) possession, manufacture, sale, dispensing, prescribing, distributing or administering any counterfeit substance and
(6) certain advertising of controlled substances.

The penalties vary but are generally levied according to the category of substance involved.

As one might expect, the provisions of the acts prohibiting activities related to controlled substances have been challenged many times in both federal and state courts. Due to careful preparation, the laws have been upheld as not in violation of the due process clauses of the Constitution; nor do the acts generally violate the right of privacy. For example, in *Maisler v. State*, a Florida court held that legislation proscribing private possession of cannabis is not violative of the Constitution.[14] Nor was the inclusion of cannabis as a part of the Comprehensive Drug Abuse and Prevention and Control Act, which makes it unlawful to possess counterfeits in an amount greater than 100 pounds, unreasonable or in violation of the equal protection provisions of the Constitution.[15]

---

[12] *See* Article IV of the Uniform Controlled Substances Act and § 893.13 of the Florida statute in Part II.

[13] *See* § 893.13 of the Florida statute in Part II and Chapter 218A of the Kentucky Revised Statutes.

[14] Maisler v. State, 425 So. 2d 107 (Fla. 1982).

[15] Albo v. State, 379 So. 2d 648 (Fla. 1980).

The "possession" violations also have generally withstood constitutional challenge. However, the definition of what constitutes possession is still somewhat in doubt. For example, in one case the court held that there need not be actual handling of an article, nor is it necessary that it be actually upon a person of the accused to constitute possession.[16] In the *Brider* case, the court agreed there must only be conscious and substantial possession by an accused; it is not necessary that it be actually upon the person of the accused. In another case the court determined that "possession" or "control" within the meaning of the drug statutes means either actual physical possession with knowledge of the same or constructive possession where the accused knows of the presence of the item on or about his premises and has ability to maintain control over it.[17] However, it has been held that if the premises containing a controlled substance is not in the exclusive but in joint possession of the accused, knowledge of the substance and ability to maintain control over it will not be inferred, but must be established by proof consisting of either evidence establishing accused's actual knowledge or evidence of circumstances from which knowledge can be inferred.[18]

Other cases have noted that a narcotics defendant's presence as a passenger in a bed of a pick-up truck in which other persons were transporting cocaine was insufficient to show that the defendant actually or constructively possessed cocaine, for purposes of trafficking.[19] And a defendant who was found sitting on a bedroom floor, talking on the telephone, in front of a closet containing cocaine, did not have constructive possession of cocaine absent a showing that the defendant was more than a mere visitor in the house or that she could otherwise exercise dominion or control over the drug.[20]

All state statutes prohibit the unlawful possession of designated controlled substances with intent to sell, purchase, manufacture or deliver. In proving the possession element of the offense, the prosecutor must introduce evidence to show either actual or constructive possession. This has been the subject of many challenges in both federal and state courts. Generally the courts have found the necessary element of possession if there is some clear evidence connecting the suspect to the drugs. Some examples will make this more clear.

In a case decided in 1988, the Richmond, Virginia police in executing a search warrant at the home of a person named Minor, found the plaintiff, Brown and two others sitting in the master bedroom of a home. On the bed,

---

[16]   State v. Brider, 386 So. 2d 818 (Fla. 1980).

[17]   Ellis v. State, 346 So. 2d 1044 (Fla. 1977).

[18]   Giddens v. State, 443 So. 2d 1087 (Fla. 1984).

[19]   Harris v. State, 501 So. 2d 735 (Fla. 1987).

[20]   Brooks v. State, 501 So. 2d 176 (1987).

the police found a mirror with cocaine on it, two pounds of cocaine, a strainer with cocaine residue and plastic bags containing cocaine. All of the men were seated within arm's reach of each other and the cocaine. Other drug-related accessories were found throughout the room. Brown was convicted of possession and on appeal claimed that he had no actual constructive possession. The reviewing court affirmed the conviction finding that the evidence established Brown's constructive possession of the cocaine found in the home. The court reasoned that as Brown had admitted to having used cocaine in the past, and he was within arm's length of two pounds of cocaine and packaging paraphernalia, he was aware of the presence of the cocaine and it was subject to his control.[21]

In another case the suspect was stopped for speeding. The trooper searched the car which the suspect was driving and found a bag under the seat which contained 53 grams of pure cocaine. The suspect denied ownership of both the car and the cocaine and denied having knowledge of the cocaine. The car had, in fact, been borrowed from a friend. In approving a guilty finding, the reviewing court noted that possession does not require that the defendant be found with the cocaine in his hand, or otherwise on his person. Where an individual knowingly has physical control over something and it is in possession, it is for the jury to decide the credibility of the testimony that he was unaware of the presence of the cocaine. In this case the evidence was sufficient for the defendant to be found guilty beyond a reasonable doubt.[22]

On the other hand, if the prosecution does not show dominion and control beyond a reasonable doubt, a conviction cannot stand. For example, where the police, pursuant to a search warrant, searched an apartment and found the suspect who was a visitor in the apartment and who admitted that he occasionally spent the night there, this was not sufficient to establish constructive possession. According to that court, to support a conviction based on constructive possession the state must produce evidence of statements or conduct of the accused, or other facts or circumstances, which tend to show that the accused was aware of both the presence and of the character of the drugs.[23] Here the evidence failed to establish that the suspect was aware of the presence and character of the drugs or that they were subject to his dominion and control. Therefore, the conviction was reversed.

In order to find one guilty of possession with intent to distribute both elements, possession and intent to distribute, must be proved. In finding that both elements were present, a reviewing court acknowledged that the state

---

[21] Brown v. Commonwealth, 364 S.E.2d 773 (Va. 1988). *See* case in Part II.

[22] Reed v. State, 367 S.E.2d 809 (Ga. 1988).

[23] Wynn v. Commonwealth of Virginia, 362 S.E.2d 193 (Va. 1987).

has the burden of establishing both that the defendant knew of the presence of the narcotics and that such narcotics were immediately and exclusively in his control. The court found, however, that proof of knowledge may be shown by evidence of facts, statements or conduct, tending to show that the defendant was aware of the narcotics' existence where such were found. Proof of the defendant's control of the premises where the narcotics were found provides an inference of knowledge and possession which may sustain a verdict of guilty. As to the question of intent to deliver, this may be inferred from the amount of narcotics seized when such amount greatly exceeds that reasonably intended for the defendant's own use.[24]

As the quantity or type of substance will determine the penalty, it is important that the investigator carefully document pertinent information. For example, an information which charged delivery of cannabis without specifying the amount or alleging that the delivery was for some consideration resulted in only a misdemeanor conviction rather than a felony.[25] And when the information charging the defendant with possession did not allege that the possession was with intent to sell, manufacture or deliver, the defendant only could be charged with a third rather than a second degree felony.[26]

§ 11.8   Seizure and Confiscation of Controlled Substances, Vehicles and Drug Paraphernalia

To further discourage manufacture, possession or traffic in controlled substances, many states have enacted statutes which authorize seizure and forfeiture of the substance as well as the forfeiture of any vessel, vehicle, aircraft or drug paraphernalia which has been used or is being used in violation of any provisions of the act. A good example of such a statute is that of Florida, which declares controlled substances handled, delivered, possessed or distributed contrary to provisions of the act to be contraband and subject to seizure and confiscation.[27] In addition, the Florida statute, as well as other state statutes, authorize the seizure and forfeiture as authorized by the contraband forfeiture act of any vessel, vehicle, aircraft or drug paraphernalia which has been or is being used in violation of the provisions of the law, or in, upon, or by means of which any violation of the chapter has taken or is taking place.

---

[24]   People v. Carrasquilla, 522 N.E.2d (1988).

[25]   Young v. State, 439 So. 2d 306 (Fla. 1983).

[26]   Chestnut v. State, 404 So. 2d 1064 (Fla. 1981).

[27]   See § 893.12 of the Florida statute in Part II.

This Section also makes it the duty of any officer or agent to seize the vessel, vehicle or aircraft and place it in the custody of such person as may be authorized or designated for that purpose by the respective law enforcement agency pursuant to those provisions.

§ 11.9 Powers of Enforcement Personnel

To ensure that individuals charged with the enforcement of the provisions of the Act have the necessary police power, the Uniform Controlled Substances Act includes a provision which would give full enforcement authority to enforcement personnel within the state. Although this would seem not to be necessary in most instances, it does make clear that officers enforcing the provision of the act have the authority to:

(1) carry firearms in the performance of their duties,
(2) execute and serve search warrants,
(3) make arrests without a warrant for any offense under this act committed in the officer's presence if he has probable cause to believe that the person to be arrested has committed or is committing a violation of the Act which may constitute a felony,
(4) seize property pursuant to the Act and
(5) perform other enforcement duties as designated.[28]

The Uniform Controlled Substances Act specifically states that one of the purposes is to make uniform the laws with respect to the subject of this Act among those states which enact it. To a great extent this purpose has been achieved. The Act, as modified and included in the state statutes, has withstood many challenges and has resulted in not only uniform enforcement in the states but has made the state laws compatible with federal statutes. Nevertheless, it is important that those who are enforcing the respective state or federal laws consult the respective state statutes and the decisions which have been rendered to interpret those statutes.[29]

---

[28] Section 501, Uniform Controlled Substances Act.

[29] *See* Klotter and Kanovitz, CONSTITUTIONAL LAW (5th ed. 1985) with 1987 Supplement for cases relating to detention of a suspect thought to be harboring contraband while a search warrant is executed, aerial observation of a fenced-in backyard where narcotics were being cultivated, search of luggage at airports, use of a dog to detect narcotics, plain view seizure of narcotics after an arrest of a student's roommate, discovery of narcotics by

§ 11.10　Authority of the U.S. Congress to Regulate and Control Use of Narcotic Drugs

Prior to 1970 there were numerous separate federal drug control statutes on the books, each of which was aimed at a particular set of drug problems. Some of these acts relied upon the taxing power of Congress, others relied upon the authority granted to Congress under the Interstate Commerce Clause of the Constitution. The Narcotics Manufacturing Act of 1960, which set up a licensing system for narcotic drug manufacturers, relied upon the commerce power rather than the power to tax. In 1965 amendments to the Food, Drug and Cosmetic Act, dealing with dangerous drugs, were found to be within the power of Congress to regulate interstate commerce.[30]

The Comprehensive Drug Abuse Prevention and Control Act of 1970 for the first time created an all-encompassing scheme covering both narcotics and dangerous drugs. The provisions of this Section, authorizing the Secretary of HEW to make scientific evaluations and recommendations regarding the classification of a drug, were challenged but held to be constitutional.[31] The constitutional authorization for the 1970 Act was entirely based on the commerce clause, the taxing power no longer being relied upon. In the case of *Perez v. United States*, the Supreme Court found that as jurisdiction is based upon the general finding by Congress, there is no requirement that the particular interstate activity against which a sanction was laid had no effect on commerce.[32]

§ 11.11　Role of the Federal Government in Drug Abuse Prevention and Control

As the illegal manufacture, distribution and use of narcotics became recognized as a national problem, the President of the United States and Congress became aware of the necessity to assist in their control. After many attempts to draft and enforce legislation relating to drug control, a strategy council on drug abuse and drug traffic prevention was appointed. In the 1979 Federal

---

agents of a common carrier and seizure of narcotics from closed containers found in motor vehicles.

[30] United States v. Walsh, 331 U.S. 432, 91 L.Ed. 1585, 67 S. Ct. 1283 (1947).

[31] United States v. Pastor, 557 F.2d 930 (2d Cir. 1977); United States v. Davis, 564 F.2d 840 (9th Cir. 1977).

[32] Perez v. United States, 402 U.S. 146, 28 L.Ed.2d 686, 91 S. Ct. 1357 (1971).

strategy prepared for the President by the Strategy Council on Drug Abuse pursuant to the Drug Abuse Office and Treatment Act of 1972, the Council recommended some strategies and guidelines, first pointing out that cooperative efforts which capitalize on the full capabilities of the federal, state and local law enforcement authorities were necessary to curtail illegal drug trafficking.[33] Among other things the Strategy Council recommended that teams of attorneys and support staff be appointed to coordinate investigations and prosecution of major drug violators, inspect drug manufacturers and distribution facilities and prosecute violators, use the statutory authority to reschedule drugs which have abuse potential by placing them in the appropriate drug schedule, and to improve investigative skills and coordination.

Despite the efforts of the state and federal law enforcement agencies, the use of illegal drugs continued. As a result more recently in 1984, 1986, and again in 1988, federal legislation was drafted to make it less difficult to prosecute violators and to increase the penalties. In 1986, Congress enacted a very comprehensive law entitled the Anti-Drug Abuse Act of 1986. In addition to creating new offenses, the main thrust of the act was to increase the penalties for drug offenders. Also, legislation was enacted which authorized the Department of Defense to assist in enforcing the drug laws. Over the objections raised by the Secretary of Defense and military officials, both houses of Congress passed bills broadening the role of the military in the drug war.

§ 11.12   Schedules of Controlled Substances – Federal

Section 812 of Title 21 of the U.S. Code provides:

> (a)   There are established five schedules of controlled substances, to be known as Schedules I, II, II, IV and V. Such schedules shall initially consist of the substances listed in this Section. The schedules established by this Section shall be updated and republished on a semi-annual basis during the two- year period beginning one year after October 27, 1970 and shall be updated and republished on an annual basis thereafter.[34]

The criteria for determining which drug was to be placed in each schedule is set out in the statute and is similar to those criteria used in establishing the schedule for the respective states. In 1982 a federal court of appeals agreed

---

[33]   Abrams, Federal Criminal Law and Its Enforcement (West 1986).

[34]   *See* 21 U.S.C. § 812 as amended for a list of the drugs in each of the five schedules.

with the lower court that Congress does have authority to provide a comprehensive classification scheme authorizing the attorney general to reclassify marijuana in view of the scientific evidence presented.[35]   In this case the court found that the defendant did not meet his heavy burden of proving the irrationality of a Schedule I classification of marijuana in light of the ongoing dispute as to physical and psychological effects of marijuana, its potential for abuse and whether it had any medical value.

§ 11.13   Regulating the Manufacture, Distribution and Dispensing of Controlled Substances – Federal

Title 21, § 841 of the U.S.C. provides that:

(a)   Except as authorized by this subchapter, it shall be unlawful for any person knowingly or intentionally --

(1)   to manufacture, distribute, dispense or possess with intent to manufacture, distribute or dispense a controlled substance; or

(2)   to create, distribute, dispense or possess with intent to distribute or dispense, a counterfeit substance.[36]

In investigating and prosecuting violations of this Section, each element must be proved beyond a reasonable doubt. In one case the court enumerated three elements which must be proven by the government in order to sustain conviction for possession of heroin with intent to distribute:

(1)   knowing,
(2)   possession of heroin,
(3)   with intent to distribute it.

In the *Vergara* case the court added that the elements may be proved by circumstantial as well as direct evidence and possession may be shown if the heroin was possessed jointly among several defendants.[37]

---

[35]   United States v. Fogarty, 692 F.2d 542 (8th Cir. 1982) *cert. denied,* 460 U.S. 1040, 75 L.Ed.2d 792, 103 S. Ct. 1434 (1982). *See* case in Part II.

[36]   U.S.C., Title 21, § 841, reference is made to the 1988 Cumulative Annual Pocket Part and 40 Crim. Law Rptr. 3120 for provision added by the Anti-Drug Abuse Act of 1986.

[37]   United States v. Vergara, 687 F.2d 57 (5th Cir. 1981).

While the offense of possession with intent to distribute requires the government to prove beyond a reasonable doubt that the defendant knowingly possessed a controlled substance with intent to distribute it, a person can be convicted of importation of heroin and possession with intent to distribute even though he believed he was carrying cocaine rather than heroin.[38]

In proving the possession element, a Federal Court decided that the prosecution must show that the defendant had ultimate control over the drugs; it need not have been literally in hand or on the premises that he occupied but he must have a right to possess them. But mere association with those who possess drugs is not good enough to justify a conviction.[39]

§ 11.14 Possession of Controlled Substances – Federal

Section 844 of Title 21 of the U.S.C. as amended in 1986 provides that:

(a) it shall be unlawful for any person knowingly or intentionally to possess a controlled substance unless such substance was obtained directly, or pursuant to a valid prescription order, from a practitioner while acting in the course of his professional practice, or except as otherwise authorized by this subchapter or subchapter II of this chapter.

Any person who violates this law may be sentenced to a term of imprisonment of not more than one year and shall be fined a minimum of $1,000 but not more than $5,000 or both. The sentencing provision continues with a very elaborate scheme for sentencing those who have had two or more prior convictions for any drug offense chargeable under the laws of the State, or a combination of two or more such offenses have become final.

Subsection (c) of this provision includes a definition of drug or narcotic offense:

As used in this Section, the term "drug or narcotic offense" means any offense which proscribes the possession, distribution, manufacture, cultivation, sale, transfer or the attempt or conspiracy to possess, distribute, manufacture, cultivate, sell or transfer any sub-

---

[38] United States v. Samad, 754 F.2d 1091 (4th Cir. 1984); United States v. Kairouz, 751 F.2d 467 (1st Cir. 1985).

[39] United States v. Manzella, 791 F.2d 1263 (7th Cir. 1986).

stance on the possession of which is prohibited under this sub-chapter.[40]

To convict one under the provision of this act, the investigator must obtain information to show that the suspect:

(1) knowingly or intentionally,
(2) possessed,
(3) a controlled substance.

In considering the knowledge or intent element, a Federal court held that "irrespective of what the defendant's intentions were regarding the ultimate disposition of heroin he claimed to have found while performing his duties as a janitor in prison, the defendant's knowledge of the illicit nature of the substance and purposeful possession of the substance was in violation of the heroin possession statute."[41]

One does not have to have actual possession of the controlled substance to be in violation of this Section. A person having an association with those having physical control of the drug so as to enable him to assure their production, without difficulty, to a customer as a matter of course, may be held to have constructive possession.[42]

§ 11.15 Other Federal Drug-Related Offenses

Chapter 13 of Title 21 of the U.S. Code, as amended by legislation in 1984, 1986 and 1988, comprehensively regulates and controls the manufacture, distribution, dispensing and possession of controlled substances as enumerated in the acts. In addition to the Sections discussed in previous paragraphs, those involved in enforcing this act or who are working with others who are enforcing the act should be aware of other provisions that are available to control the unlawful use of drugs. Some of the other Federal statutes are noted.

Section 845, as amended, includes a separate provision prohibiting distribution of a controlled substance to a person under 21 years of age. This Section mandates a greater penalty for those who violate this Section, with a

---

[40] 18 U.S.C. § 844 as amended by the Drug Possession Penalty Act of 1986. The Anti-Drug Abuse Act of 1988 authorizes fines up to $10,000 for having "personal use" of drugs such as marijuana and cocaine.

[41] United States v. Halloway, 744 F.2d 527 (6th Cir. 1984).

[42] United States v. White, 660 F.2d 1178 (7th Cir. 1981).

provision that a term of imprisonment under this Subsection shall not be less than one year.

Section 845 (A) makes it a separate violation for one to distribute or manufacture a controlled substance in, on or within 1,000 feet of the real property comprising a public or private elementary, vocational or secondary school or a public or private college, junior college or university.

Section 845 (B), which is part of the juvenile drug trafficking act of 1986, makes it unlawful for any person at least 18 years of age to knowingly and intentionally:

(1) employ, hire, use, persuade, induce, entice or coerce, a person under the age of 18 to violate the provisions of the subchapter and provides a penalty for violation.

In 1986 the Congress of the United States added subtitle H, "Money Laundering Control Act of 1986." This created a new offense for laundering the monetary instruments with a separate penalty if one is convicted of laundering money knowing that the property involved in the financial transaction represents the proceeds of some form of unlawful activity.[43]

The Anti-Drug Abuse Act of 1988 further strengthens the authority of enforcement agents to continue the war on drugs. The 1988 Act focuses on curbing the demand for drugs at home as well as stopping the supply from abroad. In addition to increasing penalties for personal use of drugs, the Act includes the death penalty for those convicted of drug-related killings. A new provision adds a federal penalty for endangering human life while illegally manufacturing drugs and provides a mandatory life term for three-time felony drug offenders.[44]

In addition to the criminal penalties, a drug conviction could result in loss of federal benefits. To develop a national strategy to control drugs, the 1988 Act creates a cabinet post to be filled by a "drug czar."

Although there is some renewed focus on the need to cut demand for drugs in the United States, the principle thrust of the federal strategy is to interdict the supply of drugs through criminal enforcement. To more successfully reach these goals, the Anti-Drug Abuse Act of 1986 made provision for 1.7 billion dollars to be devoted to the drug war, in addition to increasing the fines and prison sentences for federal drug offenses. As discussed, $223 million was allocated to assistance to state and local law enforcement agencies.

While the federal government is assuming more responsibility for the control of illegal drug-related matters, the cooperation of the federal and

---

[43] Subtitle H, § 1351, Anti-Drug Abuse Act of 1986, Public Law 99-570.

[44] Anti-Drug Abuse Act of 1988, §§ 6301 and 6452, 134 Cong. Rec. H 11155, Oct. 21, 1988.

state agents is necessary if illegal use of drugs is to be curtailed. Those investigators who are involved in the enforcement of the drug laws must be familiar with the laws of the state in which they have authority and the federal laws in order to make the cooperative effort effective.

§ 11.16 Summary

As the use of illicit drugs in this country has risen, state and federal legislation has been enacted to identify and control substances which are extremely harmful when improperly utilized. In an effort to obtain some uniformity in the enforcement of state laws, most states have adopted the provisions of the Uniform Controlled Substances Act.

The Uniform Controlled Substances Act sets out prohibited activities in detail and vests the authority to administer the act in an agency to be established by the state legislature. To make the Act consistent with the federal laws, the Uniform Act follows the Federal Controlled Substances Law and lists all of the controlled substances in five schedules which are identical with the federal law. The act includes guidelines for determining the category into which the controlled substance generally will be included.

The Uniform Controlled Substances Act and state statutes require persons who engage in, or intend to engage in, the manufacture, distribution or dispensing of controlled substances to be registered by the state. These acts make it unlawful for any person to manufacture, deliver or possess, with intent to manufacture or deliver, a controlled substance and provide penalties determined by the classification of the substance.

In addition, all state statutes prohibit:

(1) trafficking in a controlled substance except as authorized,
(2) possession of a controlled substance except as authorized,
(3) dispensing, prescribing, distributing or administering a controlled substance except as authorized,
(4) obtaining or attempting to obtain a controlled substance by fraud, deceit, misrepresentation or subterfuge,
(5) possession, manufacture, sale, dispensing, prescribing, distributing or administering any counterfeit substance and
(6) certain advertising of a controlled substance.

Penalties vary but are generally levied according to the category of substance involved. Although the uniform laws have been challenged on many occasions, they have generally withstood constitutional challenge.

In addition to criminal penalties, most states authorize confiscation of controlled substances as well as vehicles used in the transportation of such substances and drug paraphernalia.

As the illegal manufacture, distribution and use of narcotics became recognized as a national problem, federal legislation was enacted to control the use of drugs. Legislation in 1984, 1986 and 1988 further increased the authority of federal officials and made it less difficult to prosecute violators. The criteria for determining which drug is to be placed in each schedule is set out in the statute and is similar to those criteria used in establishing the schedule for the respective states.

Under the federal law, as under the state law, possession of a controlled substance is prohibited. Persons who violate this may be prosecuted in federal as well as in state court.

In addition to the possession statutes, federal laws regulate the manufacture, distribution and dispensing of controlled substances. Under the 1988 Act, conviction for violation of a federal law could result in loss of federal benefits in addition to the criminal penalties.

While the federal government has assumed more responsibility for the control of illegal drugs and related matters, the cooperation of the federal and state agencies is necessary if illegal use of drugs is to be curtailed.

Chapter 12
PREPARATORY ACTIVITY CRIMES

...However, it is quite clear that under California law an overt act, which, when added to the requisite intent, is sufficient to bring about a criminal attempt, need not be the last proximate or ultimate step towards commission of the substantive crime....Police officers need not wait until a suspect, who aims a gun at his intended victim, actually pulls the trigger before they arrest him; nor do these officers need to wait until a suspect, who is forcing the lock of a bank door, actually breaks in before they arrest him for attempted burglary.

People v. Staples,
6 Cal. App. 3d 61,
85 Cal. Rptr 589 (1970).

§ 12.1 Introduction

A person or persons may be guilty of an offense if the acts or conduct is part of the preparation for the commission of another offense. These usually consist of "attempt," "conspiracy," and "solicitation" and are categorized under various headings.[1] To reach those who have not actually perpetrated one of the traditional substantive crimes but have been involved in preparing to commit crimes, legislative bodies have provided penalties for these preparatory acts.

The term "preparatory activity crimes" has been chosen for this chapter as the terms "incompleted criminal conduct" or "inchoate crimes" do not accurately convey the rationale for the criminal liability imposed. In fact, a crime such as conspiracy is completed even though the offense ultimately intended is never committed. Conspiracy then is not an uncompleted offense but a completed offense if all of the elements are present. "Inchoate" is defined as "in an initial or early stage." While it is true that attempt, conspiracy and solicitation occur at an early stage of the process, the offense is often complete without reference to the fact that the traditional substantive crime has not been perpetrated. In this chapter, the three most often charged preparatory activity crimes (attempt, solicitation and conspiracy) are defined and explained.

§ 12.2 Attempt

An attempt to commit a crime has been defined as an act done with intent to commit a crime, beyond mere preparation, but falling short of its actual commission.[2] It is also defined as "any overt act done with intent to commit the crime which and except for the interference of some cause preventing the carrying out of the intent, would have resulted in the commission of the crime."[3]

The distinction between an "intent" and an "attempt" to do a thing is that the former implies the purpose only while the latter implies both the purpose and an actual effort to carry that purpose into execution. As the purpose of the law concerning criminal intent is to permit the courts to adjudge a penalty in cases where conduct falls short of a completed substantive crime, an at-

---

[1] LaFave & Scott, CRIMINAL LAW (1972).

[2] State v. Reis, 230 N.C. 272, 52 S.E.2d 880 (1949).

[3] State v. Leach, 36 Wash. 2d 641, 219 P.2d 972 (1950).

tempt to commit a crime is, as a general rule, an indictable offense which is separate and distinct from the substantive crime.[4]

As the elements of the offense of attempt are often not too clear and difficult to prove, many courts have framed their own definitions. Some of these will indicate the requirements that are necessary to prove this offense.

> To constitute "attempt" it is essential that the defendant, with the intent of committing the particular crime, should have done some overt act adapted to, approximating and which in ordinary and likely course of things would result in the commission thereof; the act must reach far enough toward the accomplishment of the desired result to amount to consummation and must not be merely preparatory; it need not be the last proximate act to consummation of the offense attempted but must approach sufficiently near it to stand either as the first or some subsequent step in the direct movement towards the commission of the offense after preparations are made.[5]

Another court coined a shorter definition:

> An "attempt" to commit a crime is an act done with intent to commit that crime, carried beyond mere preparation to commit it, but falling short of its actual commission.[6]

While mere preparation to commit an offense does not constitute an attempt, preparation plus an overt act going beyond mere preparation toward commission of the crime does constitute the offense.[7]

But the criminal law is not designed to impose liability for bad thoughts alone. While one might consider committing a specific crime, such thoughts are not sufficient unless there is an overt act to go along with the intent. The overt act must be sufficiently proximate to the intended crime to form one of the natural series of acts which the intent requires for its full execution. There must be an act done which more or less directly tends to the commission of the crime.[8]

Unless the essential elements are established by statute, the requisite elements of an "attempt" to commit a crime are:

---

[4]   People v. Crane, 302 Ill. 217, 134 N.E. 99 (1922).

[5]   State v. Dowd, 220 S.E.2d 393 (N.C. 1975).

[6]   State v. Goodman, 322 S.E.2d 408 (N.C. 1984).

[7]   Fleming v. State, 374 So. 2d 954 (Fla. 1979).

[8]   Gilley v. Commonwealth, 280 Ky. 306, 133 S.W.2d 67 (1939).

(1) an intent to commit it,
(2) an overt act toward its commission,
(3) failure of consummation and
(4) the apparent possibility of commission.[9]

§ 12.3 Impossibility as a Defense

Can a person be guilty of attempt if it is impossible to succeed in the attempt? For example, can a man commit the crime of attempted rape when he has the intent to commit the rape, enters a home where he thinks a woman is in bed and pulls the covers back, before being interrupted, when in fact there is no woman in the bed, but instead a dummy?

The courts have differed on the effect of showing that the defendant could not have succeeded in the attempt. There is agreement that in order to constitute an indictable attempt to commit crime, its consummation must be apparently possible and there must be at least an apparent ability to commit it. The general rule is that factual impossibility does not constitute a defense. For example, where a defendant attempted to steal money from the victim's pocket and did everything he could to effect the theft, but the crime failed only because the pocket was empty, impossibility was not a defense.[10]

Also the courts have held that it is not necessary that there be a present ability to complete the crime. Therefore, "if there is an apparent ability to commit the crime in the way attempted, the attempt is indictable, although, unknown to the person making the attempt, the crime cannot be committed, because the means employed are in fact unsuitable, or because of extrinsic facts, such as the non-existence of some essential object or an obstruction by the intended victim or by a third person.[11]

However, if it is *legally* impossible to do that which is attempted to be done, the attempt is not indictable. For example, if the defendant attempts to bribe a juror by offering money to a person he mistakenly believes to be a juror, according to at least one court, this would not constitute a crime as it is legally impossible to commit the crime.[12]

---

[9] State v. Stewart, 537 S.W.2d 579 (Mo. 1976). *See* case in Part II; Clemons v. State, 39 Ala. App. 386, 101 S.W.2d 640 (1958).

[10] People v. Fiegelman, 33 Cal. App. 2d 100, 91 P.2d 156 (1933).

[11] 22 C.J.S. *Criminal Law* § 77 (1961).

[12] State v. Taylor, 345 Mo. 325, 133 S.W.2d 336 (1939).

§ 12.4 Abandonment as a Defense

Abandonment or withdrawal is a defense if the attempt to commit a crime is freely and voluntarily abandoned before the act is put in progress for final execution, if there is no outside cause prompting the abandonment. To state this differently, if a person voluntarily abandoned his proposed plan of crime before actual commission of the crime and he does so voluntarily, he cannot be held guilty of an attempt.[13]

Abandonment is no defense and should not be a defense if failure to complete the crime is due to extraneous intervening circumstances. For example, failure to complete the crime because of a threatened arrest or appearance of the police is not the free and voluntary abandonment necessary to constitute a defense.[14]

§ 12.5 Contemporary Statutory Modifications

1. Model Penal Code[15]

§ 5.01 Criminal Attempt

(1) *Definition of Attempt.* A person is guilty of an attempt to commit a crime if, acting with the kind of culpability otherwise required for commission of the crime, he:

  (a) purposely engages in conduct which would constitute the crime if the attendant circumstances were as he believes them to be; or

  (b) when causing a particular result is an element of the crime, does or omits to do anything with the purpose of causing or with the belief that it will cause such result without further conduct on his part; or

  (c) purposely does or omits to do anything which, under the circumstances as he believes them to be, is an act or omission constituting a substantial step in a course of conduct planned to culminate in his commission of the crime.

---

[13] People v. Montgomery, 47 Cal. App. 2d 1, 117 P.2d 437 (1941).

[14] People v. Walker, 33 Cal. 2d 250, 201 P.2d 6 (1948), *cert. denied,* 336 U.S. 940, 69 S. Ct. 744, 93 L.Ed. 1098 (1949).

[15] Model Penal Code § 5.01 (Proposed Official Draft 1980).

(2) *Conduct Which May Be Held Substantial Step Under Subsection (1)(c).* Conduct shall not be held to constitute a substantial step under Subsection (1)(c) of this Section unless it is strongly corroborative of the actor's criminal purpose. Without negating the sufficiency of other conduct, the following, if strongly corroborative of the actor's criminal purpose, shall not be held insufficient as a matter of law:

  (a) lying in wait, searching for or following the contemplated victim of the crime;

  (b) enticing or seeking to entice the contemplated victim of the crime to go to the place contemplated for its commission;

  (c) reconnoitering the place contemplated for the commission of the crime;

  (d) unlawful entry of a structure, vehicle or enclosure in which it is contemplated that the crime will be committed;

  (e) possession of materials to be employed in the commission of the crime, which are specially designed for such unlawful use or which can serve no lawful purpose of the actor under the circumstances;

  (f) possession, collection or fabrication of materials to be employed in the commission of the crime, at or near the place contemplated for its commission, where such possession, collection or fabrication serves no lawful purpose of the actor under the circumstances;

  (g) soliciting an innocent agent to engage in conduct constituting an element of the crime.

(3) *Conduct Designed to Aid Another in Commission of a Crime.* A person who engages in conduct designed to aid another to commit a crime which would establish his complicity under § 2.06 if the crime were committed by such other person, is guilty of an attempt to commit the crime, although the crime is not committed or attempted by such other person.

(4) *Renunciation of Criminal Purpose.* When the actor's conduct would otherwise constitute an attempt under Subsection (1)(b) or (1)(c) of this Section, it is an affirmative defense that he abandoned his effort to commit the crime or otherwise prevented its commission, under circumstances manifesting a complete and voluntary renunciation of his criminal purpose. The establishment of such defense does not, however, affect

the liability of an accomplice who did not join in such abandonment or prevention.

Within the meaning of this Article, renunciation of criminal purpose is not voluntary if it is motivated, in whole or in part, by circumstances, not present or apparent at the inception of the actor's course of conduct, which increase the probability of detection or apprehension or which make more difficult the accomplishment of the criminal purpose. Renunciation is not complete if it is motivated by a decision to postpone the criminal conduct until a more advantageous time or to transfer the criminal effort to another but similar objective or victim.

The Model Penal Code deviates from the traditional approach as it does not recognize the defense of legal impossibility. The attempt is defined in terms of conduct which would constitute the crime if circumstances were as the defendant believed them to be. The Section relating to defenses carries out the rationale that a person should be held criminally liable if he has clearly demonstrated intent to commit a crime and has gone as far as he could in implementing that purpose.

2. Federal Code

In addition to the general state laws relating to attempt, the U.S. Code makes it a federal offense to attempt to commit specific acts.

Under § 351, Title 18 of the U.S. Code it is a federal offense to kill or attempt to kill any individual who is a member of Congress, a member of the Supreme Court, a member of the President's Cabinet or other designated ranking official. This Section also provides a penalty up to life imprisonment or death when one of the designated persons is kidnapped. The attempt provision states:

Whoever attempts to kill or kidnap any individual designated in Subsection (a) of this Section shall be punished by imprisonment for any term of years or for life.[16]

Title 18, § 1751 makes it a crime punishable by imprisonment for any term of years or by life if one is convicted of attempting to kill or kidnap the President of the United States, President Elect, Vice-President, Vice-President Elect or members of the President's staff.

---

[16]   18 U.S.C. § 351(c).

Other federal attempt provisions include penalties for attempt to commit murder or manslaughter,[17] attempt to kill foreign officials,[18] or attempt to escape.[19]

3. Other statutes and codes

Many of the states that have recently enacted new codes or statutes have created general attempt offenses which replace scores of statutes creating special attempt crimes. Some state statutes still include provisions for punishment for "attempted rape," "attempted arson" and "attempted burglary," but the more recent approach is to consolidate all of the statutes into a single attempt provision uniformly relating the penalty for criminal attempt to the penalty for the crime attempted. An example of such a statute is that of Kentucky which provides:

§ 506.010 -- Criminal attempt[20]
(1) A person is guilty of criminal attempt to commit a crime when, acting with the kind of culpability otherwise required for commission of the crime, he:

    (a) intentionally engages in conduct which would constitute the crime if the attendant circumstances were as he believes them to be; or

    (b) intentionally does or omits to do anything which, under the circumstances as he believes them to be, is a substantial step in a course of conduct planned to culminate in his commission of the crime.

(2) Conduct shall not be held to constitute a substantial step under Subsection (1)(b) unless it is an act or omission which leaves no reasonable doubt as to the defendant's intention to commit the crime which he is charged with attempting.

(3) A person is guilty of criminal attempt to commit a crime when he engages in conduct intended to aid another person to commit that crime, although the crime is not committed or attempted by the other person, provided that his conduct would

---

[17]   18 U.S.C. § 113.

[18]   18 U.S.C. § 1116.

[19]   18 U.S.C. § 751.

[20]   Ky. Rev. Stat. § 506.010 (1975).

establish complicity under § 21 of this Act if the crime were committed by the other person.

(4) A criminal attempt is a:

    (a) Class B felony when the crime attempted is a Class A felony or capital offense;

    (b) Class C felony when the crime attempted is a Class B felony;

    (c) Class A misdemeanor when the crime attempted is a Class C or D felony;

    (d) Class B misdemeanor when the crime attempted is a misdemeanor.

Under this Section, a criminal attempt may be committed in three different ways. A person may be guilty of an attempt where he intentionally engages in conduct which would constitute an offense if the circumstances were in fact as he perceived them to be. The impossibility of completing the offense is no defense to the charge of criminal attempt. Secondly, a person is guilty of an attempt if:

(1) an intention by the defendant to commit an offense is indicated and

(2) an act or a motion to act "constitutes a substantial step in a course of conduct planned to culminate in this commission of the crime.

Thirdly, a person may be guilty of attempt if he intentionally engages in conduct which aids another to commit or attempt to commit a crime but the other person never attempts to commit the crime. The rationale here is that such conduct is criminal attempt because it clearly indicates the dangerousness of the defendant and his disposition toward criminality.

Section 506.020 of the Kentucky Penal Code deals with the defense of renunciation. As with most modern codes, this makes voluntary renunciation a defense to criminal attempt. It provides that renunciation is not voluntary within the meaning of this provision if motivated by a "belief that circumstances exist which pose a particular threat of apprehension or detection." This is interpreted to mean that if an offense is not completed due to the interference by a police officer, the defense of renunciation would not be available.[21]

---

[21]   Luttrell v. Commonwealth, 554 S.W.2d 75 (Ky. 1977).

While the general criminal attempt statutes are most often used as a vehicle for prosecuting those who attempt to commit crimes, many state laws include wording which makes an attempt to commit a specific crime punishable. This is especially true where the offense involves narcotics. For example, a Florida statute makes it "unlawful for any person to acquire or obtain, or attempt to acquire or obtain, possession of a controlled substance by misrepresentation, fraud, forgery, deception or subterfuge."[22] Under this statute attempted possession of heroin, cocaine or marijuana is a crime.[23] In interpreting this provision of the statute, a Florida court agreed that admission by the defendant that he came to the motel room where cocaine was found to buy cocaine was sufficient to sustain a conviction for attempted possession of cocaine.[24]

The offense of criminal attempt is especially important to enforcement officials. Often it is overlooked and no action is taken when the intended offense is not consummated. However, the legislatures in all jurisdictions have recognized that a person who goes as far as possible in implementing a criminal purpose manifests a dangerousness sufficient to warrant some sanctions. The rationale for including attempt as an offense is that other crimes might be prevented by taking action against the person who has indicated this criminal purpose.

§ 12.6 Criminal Solicitation

The offense of solicitation was punishable at common law without regard to the nature of substantive crime solicited; that is, criminal solicitation of murder had the same potential sanction as criminal solicitation of larceny.[25]

The common law crime of solicitation is defined as "to solicit another to commit a felony." The rationale for making solicitation of another to commit an offense a separate offense is similar to the rationale for making attempt a crime: the criminal culpability of the solicitor is as great as it would be if the proposal were accepted and the underlying offense completed.

The elements of solicitation are:

   (a)   an intent to promote or facilitate the commission of a particular criminal offense and

[22] Fla. Stat. Ann., § 893.13.
[23] Walker v. State, 389 So. 2d 312 (Fla. 1980).
[24] Morton v. State, 496 So. 2d 999 (Fla. 1986).
[25] Commonwealth v. Randolph, 146 Pa. 83, 23 A. 388 (1882).

(b)　some overt act such as the initiatory act of solicitation, request, command or encouragement.

The offense is complete even though the person solicited refuses to commit the crime.[26]

§ 12.7 Contemporary Statutory Modifications

Although solicitation was recognized as an offense at common law, it was not made a statutory offense in all states. The offense of solicitation was punishable at common law as a misdemeanor without regard to the nature of the substantive crime solicited; however, recently enacted statutes provide a penalty structure that gears the penalty to the crime solicited.

1. Model Penal Code[27]

§ 5.02 Criminal Solicitation
(1)　Definition of Solicitation. A person is guilty of solicitation to commit a crime if with purpose of promoting or facilitating its commission he commands, encourages or requests another person to engage in specific conduct which would constitute such crime or an attempt to commit such crime or which would establish his complicity in its commission or attempted commission.
(2)　Uncommunicated Solicitation. It is immaterial under Subsection (1) of this Section that the actor fails to communicate with the person he solicits to commit a crime if his conduct was designed to effect such communication.
(3)　Renunciation of Criminal Purpose. It is an affirmative defense that the actor, after soliciting another person to commit a crime, persuaded him not to do so or otherwise prevented the commission of the crime, under circumstances manifesting a complete and voluntary renunciation of his criminal purpose.

Under the Model Penal Code it is necessary to show "purpose" (the mental element) plus requesting another to engage in specific conduct. The

---

[26]　People v. Burt, 45 Cal. 2d 311, 288 P.2d 503 (1955).
[27]　Model Penal Code, § 502 (Proposed Official Draft 1980).

Code includes a specific defense of renunciation provided the renunciation is complete and voluntary.

2. Other statutes and codes

Some states follow the Model Penal Code while others take a different approach. In Illinois the statute provides:

A person commits solicitation when, with intent that an offense be committed, he commands, encourages or requests another to commit the offense.[28]

Under the Illinois code specific intent is required for a conviction of the crime of solicitation but the intent may be inferred from surrounding circumstances and acts of the defendant.[29] In addition to the element of specific intent the prosecution must show that the defendant commanded, encouraged or requested another to commit a specific crime. The offense is complete when the principal offense is commanded, requested or encouraged with the specific intent that the principal offense be committed.[30]

Many of the recently enacted statutes include specific provisions regarding the defense of renunciation or incapacity. The wording of the renunciation provision is usually similar to the wording of Subsection 3 of the Model Code. Generally the incapacity provision of the statutes provides for a defense if the accused would not be guilty of the principal offense committed because of some individual incapacity the accused might have, such as under age; but it would not be a defense for the accused that the *person solicited* would not be guilty of the principal offense, because of some legal incapacity or immunity.

§ 12.8 Conspiracy

Conspiracy was an offense known to the English common law and is an offense under all state statutes. The rationale for making conspiracy a crime is that society, having power to punish for dangerous behavior, cannot be powerless against those who work to bring about that behavior.[31] As one court

---

[28] Ill. Rev. Stat. ch. 38, § 8-1 (1961).

[29] People v. Lewis, 84 Ill. App. 3d 556, 406 N.E.2d 11 (1980).

[30] People v. McCommon, 79 Ill. App. 3d, 399 N.E.2d 224 (1979).

[31] Scales v. United States, 367 U.S. 203, 6 L.Ed.2d 782, 81 S. Ct. 1469 (1961).

indicated, the law punishes for conspiracy because it does not deem it prudent to wait until the criminal plan has reached fruition.[32]

Conspiracy has been defined as a combination between two or more persons to accomplish a criminal or unlawful purpose, or some purpose, not in itself criminal or unlawful, by criminal or unlawful means.[33] It has also been defined as "an agreement among conspirators, an act of conspiring together; and it necessarily implies acting in concert, undertaking some joint action."[34]

As in the crime of attempt, it must be shown that one of the conspirators committed an overt act in furtherance of the conspiracy. One court defined conspiracy as:

"Conspiracy" consists in a corrupt agreement between two or more persons to do an unlawful act, existence of which agreement may be established by direct proof, or by inference, as deduction from acts and conduct, which discloses the common design on their part to act together for accomplishment of an unlawful purpose.[35]

As these cases indicate, there must be at least two persons agreeing to do an act; that is, the conspiracy is a joint undertaking or a combination, agreement or understanding, tacit or otherwise, between two or more persons for the purpose of committing the unlawful act. Secondly, there must be an overt act committed by one or more parties to the agreement in furtherance of the object of the conspiracy. The overt act must at least start to carry the conspiracy into effect or must reach far enough toward the accomplishment of the desired result to amount to the commencement of the consummation.[36]

Although the specific elements of a conspiracy depend to a great extent upon the wording of the state statute, generally the elements are:

(a)   an object to be accomplished,
(b)   a plan or scheme embodying means to accomplish that object,
(c)   an agreement or understanding between two or more of the defendants whereby they become definitely committed to co-

---

[32]   United States v. Cryan, 490 F.Supp. 1234 (D.N.J. 1980).

[33]   Miller v. United States, 382 F.2d 583 (9th Cir. 1967); United States v. Heck, 449 F.2d 778 (9th Cir. 1974).

[34]   People v. Blinkley, 25 Ill. App. 3d 27, 322 N.E.2d 514 (1975).

[35]   Kennemore v. State, 149 S.E.2d 791 (Ga. 1966).

[36]   Hall v. United States, 109 F.2d 976 (10th Cir. 1940); State v. Porro, 377 A.2d 909 (N.J. 1977).

operate for the accomplishment of the object by the means embodied in the agreement and

(d) an overt act.[37]

As the essence of the crime of "conspiracy" is the agreement rather than the commission of the objective substantive crime; conspiring to commit a crime is an offense separate and distinct from the crime which may be the objective of the "conspiracy."[38] It is not double jeopardy to bring criminal action against a defendant under the conspiracy statute as well as the substantive crime statute.

§ 12.9 Withdrawal as a Defense

Traditionally withdrawal from the criminal conspiracy did not constitute a defense to the crime,[39] but most courts now recognize that if a defendant effectively withdraws from the criminal conspiracy, it is a defense. The majority of federal courts confronted with the issue have held that it is the defendant who bears the burden of proving withdrawal.[40] However, in a 1981 case, the U.S. Court of Appeals for the 7th Circuit concluded that due process requires the government to disprove withdrawal beyond a reasonable doubt once the defendant has met the burden of going forward with evidence of withdrawal.[41]

In order to constitute withdrawal, evidence must be introduced to show that the defendant disavowed or defeated the purpose of the conspiracy.

§ 12.10 Contemporary Statutory Modifications

1. Model Penal Code[42]

§ 5.03 Criminal Conspiracy

(1) Definition of Conspiracy. A person is guilty of conspiracy with another person or persons to commit a crime if with the purpose of promoting or facilitating its commission he:

---

[37] Commonwealth v. Hayes, 205 Pa. Super. 338, 209 A.2d 38 (1965).

[38] United States v. Cantu, 557 F.2d 1173 (5th Cir. 1977).

[39] Orear v. United States, 261 F. 257 (5th Cir. 1919).

[40] United States v. Bradsby, 628 F.2d 901 (5th Cir. 1980); Krasn v. United States, 614 F.2d 1229 (9th Cir. 1980).

[41] United States v. Read, 658 F.2d 1225 (7th Cir. 1981).

[42] Model Penal Code § 5.03 (Proposed Official Draft 1980).

    (a)   agrees with such other person or persons that they or one or more of them will engage in conduct which constitutes such crime or an attempt or solicitation to commit such crime; or

    (b)   agrees to aid such other person or persons in the planning or commission of such crime or of an attempt of solicitation to commit such crime.

(2)   Scope of Conspiratorial Relationship. If a person guilty of conspiracy, as defined by Subsection (1) of this Section, knows that a person with whom he conspires to commit a crime has conspired with another person or persons to commit the same crime, he is guilty of conspiring with such other person or persons, whether or not he knows their identity, to commit such crime.

(3)   Conspiracy With Multiple Criminal Objectives. If a person conspires to commit a number of crimes, he is guilty of only one conspiracy so long as such multiple crimes are the object of the same agreement or continuous conspiratorial relationship.

(4)   Joinder and Venue in Conspiracy Prosecutions.

    (a)   Subject to the provisions of paragraph (b) of this Subsection, two or more persons charged with criminal conspiracy may be prosecuted jointly if:

        (i)   they are charged with conspiring with one another; or

        (ii)   the conspiracies alleged, whether they have the same or different parties, are so related that they constitute different aspects of a scheme of organized criminal conduct.

    (b)   In any joint prosecution under paragraph (a) of this Subsection:

        (i)   no defendant shall be charged with a conspiracy in any county [parish or district] other than one in which he entered into such conspiracy or in which an overt act pursuant to such conspiracy was done by him or by a person with whom he conspired; and

      (ii) neither the liability of any defendant nor the admissibility against him of evidence of acts or declarations of another shall be enlarged by such joinder; and

      (iii) the Court shall order a severance or take a special verdict as to any defendant who so requests, if it deems it necessary or appropriate to promote the fair determination of his guilt or innocence and shall take any other proper measures to protect the fairness of the trial.

(5) Overt Act. No person may be convicted of conspiracy to commit a crime, other than a felony of the first or second degree, unless an overt act in pursuance of such conspiracy is alleged and proved to have been done by him or by a person with whom he conspired.

(6) Renunciation of Criminal Purpose. It is an affirmative defense that the actor, after conspiring to commit a crime, thwarted the success of the conspiracy, under circumstances manifesting a complete and voluntary renunciation of his criminal purpose.

(7) Duration of Conspiracy. For purposes of § 1.04(4):

    (a) conspiracy is a continuing course of conduct which terminates when the crime or crimes which are its object are committed or the agreement that they be committed is abandoned by the defendant and by those with whom he conspired; and

    (b) such abandonment is presumed if neither the defendant nor anyone with whom he conspired does any overt act in pursuance of the conspiracy during the applicable period of limitation; and

    (c) if an individual abandons the agreement, the conspiracy is terminated as to him only if and when he advises those with whom he conspired of his abandonment or he informs the law enforcement authorities of the existence of the conspiracy and of his participation therein.

Under the Model Penal Code the offense is committed if there is an agreement with another person or persons to engage in such conduct which constitutes a crime or an attempt or solicitation to commit such crime; or where the agreement is to aid such other person or persons in the planning or commission of such crime or of an attempt or solicitation to commit such crime.

The Code handles the overt act element by providing that an overt act is a requirement in cases other than a felony of the first or second degree. It is an affirmative defense that the actor, after conspiring to commit a crime, thwarted the success of the conspiracy, under circumstances manifesting a complete and voluntary renunciation of criminal purpose. It is interesting to note that the Model Penal Code also only requires an agreement "by" the defendant rather than between the parties. This makes it possible to convict a person of conspiracy with a person who has been acquitted or a police officer who has pretended to be a conspirator.

2. Federal Code

The U.S. Code includes a separate chapter relating to the offense of conspiracy.[43] Section 371 of Title 18 defines the offense of conspiracy and establishes the penalty for violation.

> If two or more persons conspire either to commit any offense against the United States, or to defraud the United States or any agency thereof in any manner or for any purpose and one or more such persons do any act to effect the object of the conspiracy, each shall be fined not more than $10,000 or imprisoned not more than 5 years or both.

> If, however, the offense, the commission of which is the object of the conspiracy, is a misdemeanor only, the punishment for such conspiracy shall not exceed the maximum punishment provided for each misdemeanor.

One of the purposes of this statute is to punish for a concerted action involving a plurality of actors which makes the crime easier to perpetrate and harder to detect. The protection of society from the dangers of concerted criminal activity of more than one person justifies making criminal conspiracy a federal violation.[44]

---

[43] 18 U.S.C. ch. 1900.01 *et seq.*

[44] United States v. Kohne, 347 F.Supp. 1178 (D. Pa. 1972); United States v. Feola, 420 U.S. 671, 43 L.Ed.2d 541, 95 S. Ct. 1255 (1975).

The thousands of cases cited in Title 18, § 371 of the U.S. Code Annotated are evidence of the extent this statute has been utilized in prosecuting federal crimes.

In order to convict one for a violation of the conspiracy statute the prosecution must establish that,

(1) two or more persons,
(2) conspired or combined together,
(3) to accomplish an unlawful purpose and
(4) the identity of the offense which the defendants allegedly conspired to commit.

In addition to the general conspiracy statute, conspiracy provisions are included in other federal statutes. For example, the Racketeer Influence and Corrupt Organization statute (RICO) makes it a federal offense to use or invest income derived from a pattern of racketeering activity to acquire an enterprise engaged in or affecting interstate commerce, to acquire an interest in such enterprise through a pattern of racketeering activity, to conduct the affairs of an enterprise through a pattern of racketeering activity or to conspire to commit any of these violations.[45]

This statute, with the conspiracy clause, has resulted in the conviction of those engaged in well organized racketeering activities which involve kidnapping, gambling, robbery, bribery and extortion as well as authorizing prosecution of officials who operate on a local level. As an example, the sheriff of Bryan County, Oklahoma was convicted of violation of this federal statute when it was found that he used his position as sheriff to extort payoffs from club operators and others in return for selective enforcement of the liquor, gambling and other laws. Evidence introduced at the trial indicated that the sheriff and a "bag man" conspired to collect payoffs after agreeing not to harass a club operator for failure to close at the required time and for directing a deputy to terminate his investigation of gambling conducted at the club.[46] The court in approving the conviction stated:

> The object of a RICO conspiracy must be to violate a substantive RICO provision....In this instance the substantive RICO offense was conducting or participating in the operation of the Bryan County Sheriff's Office through a pattern of racketeering activity.

---

[45] Racketeering Influenced and Corrupt Organization Act, 18 U.S.C. § 1961.
[46] United States v. Hampton, 786 F.2d 977 (10th Cir. 1986).

3. Other statutes and codes

Many of the more recently revised codes follow at least in part the Model Penal Code. An example of a state statute that takes a somewhat different approach is that of Indiana. That statute provides that:[47]

§ 35-41-5-2. Conspiracy.

(a) A person conspires to commit a felony when, with intent to commit the felony, he agrees with another person to commit the felony. However, a conspiracy to commit murder is a Class A felony.

(b) The state must allege and prove that either the person or the person with whom he agreed performed an overt act in furtherance of the agreement.

(c) It is no defense that the person with whom the accused person is alleged to have conspired:

    (1) Has not been prosecuted;
    (2) Has not been convicted;
    (3) Has been acquitted;
    (4) Has been convicted of a different crime;
    (5) Cannot be prosecuted for any reason; or
    (6) Lacked the capacity to commit the crime. [IC 35-41-5-2, as added by Acts 1976, P.L. 148, § 1, p. 718; 1977, P.L. 340, § 23, p. 1533.]

The Indiana statute specifically provides that the prosecution must present evidence to prove an overt act in furtherance of the agreement and states that it shall be no defense that the person who performed the act has not been prosecuted, has not been convicted, has not been acquitted, has been convicted of a different crime, or cannot be prosecuted for any reason or lacked the capacity to commit the crime. This takes away some of the indefiniteness that sometimes makes it difficult to prosecute for a conspiracy.

Because of the wording of the statute, the Indiana courts have found that it is no defense to the charge of conspiracy that one of the conspirators was an undercover police agent.[48] The Indiana Court of Appeals also made it clear that in proving a conspiracy it is not necessary to prove that the object of the conspiracy has been carried out.[49]

---

[47] Ind. Code Ann. § 35-41-52 (Burns 1977).

[48] Williams v. State, 274 Ind. 578, 412 N.E.2d 1211 (1980). *See* case in Part II.

[49] Lee v. State, 397 N.E.2d 1047 (Ind. Ct. App. 1979), *cert. denied,* 449 U.S. 983, 101 S. Ct. 399, 66 L.Ed.2d 245 (1980).

In some states the statute includes a provision regarding the defense of renunciation.[50] Under the provisions of these statutes it is a defense if the facts manifest a voluntary and complete renunciation of the criminal purpose and the defendant. However, renunciation is not voluntary if motivated by the belief that circumstances exist which pose a particular threat of apprehension or detection.

§ 12.11 Summary

Persons may be guilty of an offense if their acts or conduct are part of the preparation for the commission of substantive crimes even though those crimes are not consummated. The rationale of the lawmakers is that conduct which clearly indicates the dangerousness of a defendant or a predisposition toward criminality should not go unpunished even though the intended criminal act is not completed. These preparatory activity crimes usually consist of "attempt," "conspiracy," and "solicitation."

One may be punished for attempt if the prosecution can show intent to commit a crime plus performance of some overt act, toward the commission of the crime. To constitute attempt the defendant's conduct must be more than mere preparatory but it is not necessary to show that the ultimate step toward commission of the substantive crime occurred. The fact that it is impossible to commit the crime is not necessarily a defense; however, its consummation must be at least apparently possible. Also, abandonment or withdrawal is a defense if the intent to commit the crime is freely and voluntarily abandoned before the act was put in progress for final execution and if no outside cause prompted the abandonment.

The crime of solicitation consists of:

(a) an intent to promote or facilitate the commission of a particular criminal offense and

(b) some overt act such as the initiatory act of solicitation, request, command or encouragement.

At common law the offense of solicitation was punishable as a misdemeanor without regard to the nature of the substantive crime solicited. However, some recently enacted statutes provide a penalty structure that is geared to the penalty for the crime solicited.

---

[50] Ky. Rev. Stat. § 506.060 (1975).

The crime of conspiracy was an offense under the English common law and is an offense in all states. The rationale for making conspiracy a crime is that society, having power to punish for dangerous behavior, cannot be powerless against those who work to bring about that behavior.

Conspiracy has been defined as an agreement or combination of two or more persons to do a criminal or unlawful act or to accomplish a criminal or unlawful purpose, followed by an overt act. The essential elements are:

(a) an object to be accomplished,

(b) a plan or scheme embodying means to accomplish that object,

(c) an agreement or understanding between two or more of the defendants whereby they become definitely committed to co-operate for the accomplishment of the object by the means embodied in the agreement or by any effectual means,

(d) an overt act.

Withdrawal from a conspiracy may be a defense; that is the defendant may introduce evidence to show that he disavowed or defeated the purpose of the conspiracy before the agreement was carried out. While the majority rule seems to be that the defendant bears the burden of proving withdrawal from a conspiracy, at least one court has held that due process requires the government to disprove withdrawal beyond a reasonable doubt once the defendant has met the burden of going forward with evidence of withdrawal.

Chapter 13
CAPACITY AND DEFENSES

The right-wrong test has its roots in England. There, by the first quarter of the eighteenth century, an accused escaped punishment if he could not distinguish "good and evil," i.e. if he "doth not know what he is doing, no more than a...wild beast."

Durham v. United States,
214 F.2d 862,
94 U.S. App. D.C. 228 (1954).

§ 13.1 Introduction

One purpose of criminal law is to establish and define standards of human conduct. Members of society are generally expected to conform to those standards and the law assumes capacity upon the part of all persons, except those in certain exemptive classes, to comply with the standards of conduct. A general legal principle is that all persons have the power to choose between right and wrong and to do or refrain from doing that which the law commands.

Notwithstanding this general principle the courts in England and other countries early recognized that there are situations where persons, for one reason or another, do not have the capacity to distinguish between right and wrong or do not have the capacity to form the mental intent required as an element of some crimes. Also, the law recognized that, although the person who commits an act which would ordinarily be a crime knows the difference between right and wrong, he has the right to avail himself of defenses that the law recognizes and permits.

While the courts have maintained that exceptions should be strictly interpreted and that the law does not seek technical excuses to enable criminals to escape the consequences of their crimes, it is common practice for defendants to avoid conviction by claiming incapacity or one of the recognized defenses.[1]

In this chapter most of the common defenses claimed by defendants who are accused of crime are considered. They include incapacity to commit crimes due to infancy or mental impairment and other defenses such as entrapment, alibi, duress or compulsion, necessity, ignorance or mistake or acting under authority or direction of others and self-defense and statute of limitation defenses.

§ 13.2 Infancy or Immaturity

A crime is not committed if the mind of the person doing the act is innocent; therefore, an infant is exempt from criminal responsibility for his acts if sufficient mental capacity to entertain the criminal intent is wanting. At common law a child, under the age of seven, was conclusively presumed incapable of having the necessary criminal intent and could not commit a crime. Even if the child confessed to the act, and even if the state introduced evidence to in-

---

[1]   Ford v. Commonwealth, 177 Va. 889, 15 S.E.2d 50 (1941).

dicate the child knew the difference between right and wrong, there could be no conviction for that crime.[2]

At common law a child between the ages of seven and fourteen was presumed not to have the capacity to commit the crime, however, the presumption was rebuttable; that is, the prosecution could introduce evidence to show that, in fact, the child did possess the necessary mental capacity to entertain the criminal intent.

While the common law definitions and distinctions are followed in a few states and have had a significant bearing on statutory laws in other states, most state statutes now allocate jurisdiction between the criminal and juvenile courts. At the present time, all states have by statute established juvenile court systems which deal with those juveniles who have been charged with criminal violations. However, even in those states that have enacted juvenile justice laws, the question of capacity often still enters into the picture. For example, in the case of *State v. Q.D.*, the Supreme Court of Washington was called upon to determine if the state statutory presumption of infant incapacity applied in juvenile proceedings. A Washington state statute provides, in part, that:

> Children under the age of 8 are incapable of committing crime. Children of 8 and under 12 years of age are presumed to be incapable of committing crime, but this presumption may be removed by proof that they have sufficient capacity to understand the act or neglect and to know that it was wrong.[3]

In this case, evidence indicated that an 11 1/2-year-old juvenile was found on the school grounds at 2:00 p.m. with keys belonging to the night custodian and with the burglar alarm key. Evidence was also introduced to show that the suspect juvenile had the capacity to understand the charges against him and that he appeared to know his rights. The trial judge found that the evidence was sufficient to show that the 11-year-old juvenile had committed trespass in the first degree. On appeal, the questions were whether the statutory presumption of incapacity applies to juvenile jurisdictions, and if it does, what standard of proof is required to rebut the presumption of incapacity.

The Supreme Court of the State of Washington traced the common law and recent developments in the juvenile justice system. The summary of that court is that:

---

[2]   Angelo v. People, 96 Ill. 209 (1880).

[3]   State v. Q.D., 685 P.2d 557 (Wash. 1984). *See* case in Part II.

At common law, children below the age of 7 were conclusively presumed to be incapable of committing crime, and children over the age of 14 were presumed capable and treated as adults. Children between these ages were rebuttably presumed incapable of committing crime. Washington codified these presumptions amending the age of conclusive incapacity to 7, and presumed capacity to 12 years of age. As recently as 1975, the legislature again included the infancy defense in the criminal code. The purpose of the presumption is to protect from the criminal justice system those individuals of tender years who are less capable than adults of appreciating the wrongfulness of their behavior.

The infancy defense fell into disuse during the early part of the century with the advent of reforms intended to substitute treatment and rehabilitation for punishment of juvenile offenders. This *parens patriae* system, believed not to be a criminal one, had no need of the infancy defense.

The juvenile justice system, in recent years, has evolved from a *parens patriae* scheme to one more akin to adult criminal proceedings. The U.S. Supreme Court has been critical of the *parens patriae* scheme as failing to provide safeguards due an adult criminal defendant, while subjecting the juvenile defendant to similar stigma and possible loss of liberty. See *In re Gault*, 387 U.S. 1, 87 S. Ct. 1428, 18 L.E.2d 527 (1966); and *In re Winship*, 397 U.S. 358, 90 S. Ct. 1068, 25 L.Ed.2d 368 (1977). This court has acknowledged Washington's departure from a strictly *parens patriae* scheme to a more criminal one, involving both rehabilitation and punishment. *In re Smiley*, 96 Wash. 2d 950, 640 P.2d 7 (1981). Being a criminal defense, RCW 9A.04.050 should be available to juvenile proceedings that are criminal in nature.

The principles of construction of criminal statutes, made necessary by our recognition of the criminal nature of juvenile court proceedings also compel us to conclude that RCW 9A.04.050 applies to proceedings in juvenile courts.

A finding that RCW 9A.04.050 does not apply to juvenile courts would render that statute meaningless or superfluous contrary to rules of construction. Juvenile courts have exclusive jurisdiction over all individuals under the chronological age of 18 who have committed acts designated criminal if committed by an adult. Declination of jurisdiction and transfer to adult court is limited to instances where it is in the best interest of the juvenile or the public. Thus, all juveniles who can avail themselves of the infancy defense will come under the jurisdiction of the juvenile court, and most will remain there. Goals of the Juvenile Justice Act of 1977 include accountability for criminal behavior and punishment commensurate with age and crime. A goal of the criminal code is to safeguard conduct that is not culpable. The infancy defense which excludes from criminal condemnation persons not capable of culpable, criminal acts, is consistent with the overlapping goals of the Juvenile Justice Act of 1977 and the Washington Criminal Code.

In the majority of the states, criminal acts committed by juveniles are generally considered in juvenile court. Exceptions, however, are made when certain more serious crimes are committed, in which case the juvenile court may waive jurisdiction. While the juvenile court must afford a hearing before a case can be transferred from juvenile court to criminal court, there is some indication that more juveniles, especially those who have reached the chronological age of 16 or above, will be processed through the adult criminal procedure channels where the crimes are of a serious nature.

1. Model Penal Code

The Model Penal Code establishes the age at which the juvenile court shall have exclusive jurisdiction and briefly states the procedure to be followed in transferring a case from the juvenile court to the criminal court. Section 4.10 of the Model Penal Code provides:

Immaturity Excluding Criminal Conviction;
Transfer of Proceedings to Juvenile Court
(1) A person shall not be tried for or convicted of an offense if:

    (a) at the time of the conduct charged to constitute the offense he was less than sixteen years of age, in which case the juvenile court shall have exclusive jurisdiction; or

    (b) at the time of the conduct charged to constitute the offense he was sixteen or seventeen years of age, unless:

        (i) the Juvenile Court has no jurisdiction over him or

        (ii) the Juvenile Court has entered an order waiving jurisdiction and consenting to the institution of criminal proceedings against him.

(2) No court shall have jurisdiction to try or convict a person of an offense if criminal proceedings against him are barred by Subsection (1) of this Section. When it appears that a person charged with the commission of an offense may be of such an age that criminal proceedings may be barred under Subsection

(1) of this Section, the Court shall hold a hearing thereon, and the burden shall be on the prosecution to establish to the satisfaction of the Court that the criminal proceeding is not barred upon such grounds. If the Court determines that the proceeding is barred, custody of the person charged shall be surrendered to the Juvenile Court, and the case, including all papers and processes relating thereto, shall be transferred.

This Section proposes that no one less than 16 years old at the time of the alleged offense may be tried for or convicted of the offense in criminal court. However, if the juvenile was 16 or over, but under 18 at the time of the offense, the juvenile court, after a hearing, may enter an order waiving jurisdiction and consenting to the criminal proceedings.

2. Federal Code

Chapter 403 of Title 18, U.S.C. entitled "Juvenile Delinquency" defines the procedure for disposing of juvenile cases in federal courts. For the purpose of this chapter, a juvenile is a person who has not attained his eighteenth birthday. It is a policy of the federal government to surrender jurisdiction in juvenile cases to the appropriate legal authorities of the state. In fact, Title 18, § 5032 specifically provides that the proceedings shall not be in a U.S. Court unless the attorney general certifies through the appropriate district court of the United States that:

(1) the juvenile court or other appropriate court of the state does not have jurisdiction or refuses to assume jurisdiction over said juvenile with respect to such alleged act of juvenile delinquency,
(2) the state does not have available programs and services adequate for the needs of the juveniles or
(3) the offense charged is a crime of violence that is a felony or offense described in specific Sections of the federal law under Title 21, and there is a substantial federal interest in the case or the offense to warrant the exercise of Federal jurisdiction.

If the juvenile delinquent is not surrendered to state authorities, the case is processed as provided in Chapter 403 of Title 18 of the U.S. Code. If the juvenile is alleged to have committed an act after his sixteenth birthday which if committed by an adult would be a felony offense that has an element thereof the use, attempted use or threatened use of physical force against the person of another, or that, by its very nature, involves a substantial risk of physical force against the person of another may be used in committing the offense or would be an offense described in specific Sections of the Code, then the case may be transferred to the appropriate district court of the United States for criminal prosecution.

The purpose of this chapter of the Federal Code is to enhance the juvenile system by removing juveniles from the ordinary criminal justice system and by providing a separate system of treatment for them; to be helpful and rehabilitative, rather than punitive and to reduce to some extent the stigma of criminal conviction.[4]

In determining that the court did not abuse its discretion in ordering a 17-year-old defendant to be prosecuted under the criminal laws as an adult, one court commented that "considering the heinous nature of the offense, the defendant's history of resistance to counseling efforts and defiance of authority and the slight prospects of rehabilitation before age 21, when, if proceeded against as a juvenile, defendant would be released, rehabilitated or not,"[5] there was no abuse of discretion.

§ 13.3 Mental Impairment

Often in a criminal case the defendant claims that he is entitled to an acquittal because at the time of the crime he was so impaired by mental illness or retardation as to be "insane" within the meaning of the criminal law definition. Mental incapacity or insanity may be availed of by one accused of crimes at several points in criminal procedure and for several different purposes. In some instances, the term "insanity" is distinguished from "incompetency to stand trial"; "insanity" referring to the defendant's state at the time of the crime and "incompetency to stand trial" referring to the mental condition of the accused at the time of the trial. Most often, however, the issue to be determined relates to the mental condition of the defendant at the time of the commission of the act which is alleged to constitute the crime for which he is on trial.

If the issue is raised by the defendant, the court must determine whether or not the defendant was possessed of sufficient mental capacity to have the necessary criminal intent. The absence of a mental capacity to form the criminal intent in many instances is sufficient to establish the innocence of the defendant. In order to raise the issue a defendant need only present evidence that is sufficient to raise a reasonable doubt as to his sanity before the

---

[4] United States v. Frasquillo-Zomosa, 626 F.2d 99 (9th Cir. 1980), *cert. denied*, 449 U.S. 987, 66 L.Ed.2d 249, 101 S. Ct. 405 (1980); United States v. Hill, 538 F.2d 1072 (4th Cir. 1976).

[5] United States v. A.W.J., 804 F.2d 492 (8th Cir. 1986).

burden of proof shifts to the state. When the burden shifts to the state, then the prosecution must introduce evidence to prove sanity beyond a reasonable doubt.[6] In the *Doyle* case, the reviewing court indicated that as the state introduced no evidence at all on the issue of sanity it failed to meet this burden.

What is the test for "insanity"? There is considerable disagreement as to what standard should be used to determine if a mental disorder or impairment is sufficient to render the defendant legally not guilty because of insanity. Some of the tests have been developed over a period of many years and the courts and legislatures are still in the process of developing more appropriate tests. The more common tests are discussed here.

1. M'Naghten Rule

The traditional standard is one that was developed in 1843 and is still applied in most American jurisdictions today.[7]

In the *M'Naghten* case, Daniel M'Naghten was charged with murder. At the trial, the medical evidence showed he was in a seriously disordered mental condition at the time of the incident. The jury returned a verdict of not guilty after being instructed to convict if the defendant was in a sound state of mind at the time, but he would be entitled to a verdict in his favor if he "had not the use of his understanding so as to know he was doing a wrong or wicked act."

After the defendant in the *M'Naghten* case had been acquitted on the grounds of insanity, the English judges determined that jurors should be told in all cases that every man is presumed to be sane, and to possess a sufficient degree of reason to be responsible for his crimes, until the contrary be proven to their satisfaction, and that, to establish a defense on the ground of insanity, it must be clearly proven that, at the time the act was committed, the accused was laboring under such a defect of reason, from disease of the mind, as not to know the nature and quality of the act he was doing, or, if he did know it, that he did not know he was doing what was wrong.

This test has been and is still followed in most jurisdictions. Briefly stated, the test is "was the defendant at the time of committing the act laboring under such a defect of reason, from disease of the mind, as not to know the nature and quality of the act he was doing; or, if he did know it, he did not know he was doing what was wrong?"

This test is often referred to as the right-wrong test. To establish criminal incapacity under this test, a defendant must introduce at least some evidence to show that, as a result of his mental condition, he:

---

6   State v. Doyle, 117 Ariz. 349, 572 P.2d 1187 (1977).

7   M'Naghten Rule, 8 Eng.Rep. 718 (1843).

(1) did not know the nature and quality of his act; or

(2) did not know that the act was wrong.

Some difficulty has been encountered in applying the more than 100-year-old M'Naghten Rule in modern times where trained psychiatrists and psychologists have difficulty in defining terms. For example, in Tennessee where the M'Naghten Rule is still followed, the defendant was charged with and convicted of rape. At the trial he entered a plea of not guilty by reason of insanity.[8] Evidence was introduced by way of expert testimony indicating that the defendant suffered from non-remissive paranoid schizophrenia when he committed the crime. The state conceded that the defendant suffered from paranoid schizophrenia, but introduced expert testimony that the defendant was in a period of remission when he committed the crime, a condition the state alleged did not satisfy the M'Naghten Rule.

The court held that paranoid schizophrenia does not constitute legal insanity under the M'Naghten Rule when the defendant is at a period of remission, and that a *prima facie* case of legal insanity in such a case may only be established by the accused offering proof that at the time of the crime he was not in remission. In this case the court found that the defendant failed to meet his burden of proof of non-remission; therefore, he failed to establish a *prima facie* case of insanity.

Because of the difficulty in applying the M'Naghten Rule other rules have developed in the United States.[9]

2. Irresistible Impulse Rule

The Irresistible Impulse Rule has been added to the right-wrong test in some states but has been rejected in most others and in England and Canada. In the states where the Irresistible Impulse Rule is followed, the third element to the right-wrong test, namely that of "irresistible impulse," has been added. The theory is that if a person acts under an insane, irresistible impulse, from disease of the mind, he is incapable of restraining himself, though he may know that he is doing wrong.[10] To state this differently a person may know at the time the act was committed the nature and quality of the act he was doing, and (or) that what he was doing was wrong, but still by reason of a

---

[8] Farber v. State, 559 S.W.2d 318 (Tenn. 1977).

[9] Graham v. State, 547 S.W.2d 531 (Tenn. 1977). *See* case in Part II.

[10] People v. Lowhone, 292 Ill. 32, 126 N.E. 620 (1920).

mental disease, he may have lost power to choose between right and wrong and to avoid doing the act, his free agency being at the time destroyed.[11]

In another case, the court made this point about the Irresistible Impulse Rule:

> The jury must be satisfied that at the time of committing the act, the accused, as a result of disease of the mind:
>
>   (a)   did not know the nature and quality of the act or
>   (b)   did not know that it was wrong or
>   (c)   was incapable of preventing himself from doing it.[12]

3. Durham Rule

In 1954, the District of Columbia court concluded that the proper solution was to discard all tests of insanity and have the jury determine

   (1)   whether the defendant was sane or insane at the time of the alleged crime and if he was insane
   (2)   whether the harmful act was the product of his insanity.[13]

Apparently the D.C. court took the position that the right-wrong test and the irresistible impulse test had not been displaced but were merely supplemented by the "product" test and that it was proper for the jury to be instructed as to all three.[14]

The objective of the court was to simplify the test and to make it possible to use more modern methods of determining mental impairment or disease. This rule has been criticized in that it provides no criteria for the guidance of the jury but hands the case to them for verdict to be returned on the basis of intuition or conjecture rather than law.[15] Many of the critics also feel that the test is too broad and leaves too much to the jury with inadequate guidance. Today the rule has only a limited following and has in fact been abandoned by the District of Columbia in the case of *U.S. v. Brawner*.[16]

---

[11]   Parsons v. State, 81 Ala. 577, 2 So. 854 (1887).

[12]   State v. White, 58 N.M. 324, 270 P.2d 727 (1954).

[13]   Durham v. United States, 214 F.2d 862 (D.C. Cir. 1954).

[14]   Douglas v. United States, 239 F.2d 52 (D.C. Cir. 1956).

[15]   United States v. Smith, 5 C.M.A. 314, 17 C.M.R. 3 (1954).

[16]   United States v. Brawner, 471 F.2d 969 (D.C. Cir. 1972).

4. Model Penal Code Test

In an effort to establish a standard that can be applied in the various states, the drafters of the Model Penal Code prepared this provision:[17]

   (1) A person is not responsible for criminal conduct if at the time of such conduct as a result of mental disease or defect he lacks substantial capacity either to appreciate the criminality of his conduct or to conform his conduct to the requirements of the law.

   (2) The terms "mental disease or defect" do not include an abnormality manifested only by repeated criminal or otherwise anti-social conduct.

Under the provisions of the Code, a defendant is entitled to acquittal by reason of insanity if the evidence shows that because of a mental disease or defect he:

   (a) lacked substantial capacity to appreciate the criminality of his conduct; or

   (b) lacked substantial capacity to conform his conduct to the requirement of the law.

Although the Model Code approach has been looked upon favorably by many jurisdictions, most states have not yet adopted the formula presented.

From the foregoing it is obvious that the questions relating to mental impairment as a defense to crime have not been solved. At the present time it is safe to say that the majority of the states still follow the M'Naghten Rule with possibly some modifications.

The issue of insanity also may arise when determining if the defendant is capable of making a proper defense or aiding his attorney or securing evidence at the time of the trial. The test for competency to stand trial was set forth in the case of *Dusky v. U.S.* as follows:

Whether he (accused) has sufficient present ability to consult with his lawyer with a reasonable degree of rational understanding and whether he has a rational as well as factual understanding of the proceedings against him.[18]

---

[17] Model Penal Code § 4.01 (Proposed Official Draft 1955).

[18] Dusky v. United States, 362 U.S. 402, 80 S. Ct. 788, 4 L.Ed.2d 824 (1960).

In the case of *Dunn v. Commonwealth*, the Kentucky court approved the test as follows:

> The test is whether he has substantial capacity to comprehend the nature and consequences of the proceeding pending against him and to participate rationally in his defense. It is not necessary that this determination be made by a jury.[19]

Although these standards are worded differently, the Federal and State requirements are basically the same.

A third point at which the issue of insanity may arise is after conviction and before judgment. The policy of the law is that insane persons should not be punished even though they may be convicted criminals. Therefore, if it is determined that one who has been accused of crime is insane, then the law provides that he shall not go to prison.[20]

5. Federal Code

Following the jury's verdict of "not guilty by reason of insanity" in the John Hinckley, Jr. case, both the House and Senate received proposals to modify or completely abolish the insanity defense. In July, 1982 the full Senate Judiciary Committee conducted hearings on proposed legislation. During the hearings, U.S. Attorney General William French Smith and Associate Attorney General Rudolph W. Giuliani testified that modification of the insanity defense is a major element in the program to restore effective law enforcement. They criticized the insanity test modeled after the Model Penal Code suggesting that mental disease or defects, like any other motivation, should be taken into account only at the time of sentencing.

In 1986 Congress passed the "Insanity Reform Act of 1986."[21] The federal law now provides that:

    (a) Affirmative Defense. It is an affirmative defense to a prosecution under any Federal statute that, at the time of the commission of the acts constituting the offense, the defendant, as result of a severe mental disease or defect, was unable to appreciate the nature and quality or the wrongfulness of his acts. Mental disease or defect does not otherwise constitute defense.

---

[19] Dunn v. Commonwealth, 573 S.W.2d 651 (Ky. 1978).

[20] State v. Pritchett, 106 N.C. 667, 11 S.E. 357 (1890); Laros v. Commonwealth, 84 Pa. 200 (1877).

[21] 18 U.S.C. § 4241 *et. seq.*.

(b) Burden of Proof. The defendant has the burden of proving the defense of insanity by clear and convincing evidence.

One of the key factors in this federal law is that it shifts the burden of the insanity defense to defendant. The defendant must demonstrate by *clear and convincing* evidence that his "severe mental disease or defect" caused him not to appreciate the nature and quality of his wrongful acts. The provisions of the Insanity Reform Act, requiring a defendant to prove insanity by clear and convincing evidence, were challenged as being unconstitutional. However, in two 1986 Federal cases the courts considering the questions agreed that the provisions of the act shifting the affirmative defense of insanity to the defendant does not violate the due process clauses.[22]

Title 18, § 4241 of the U.S. Code sets forth the procedures for establishing the mental capacity of the defendant to stand trial.

As state and federal legislative bodies and the courts reevaluate the tests for insanity, it can be anticipated that more state and federal statutes will be modified. There is some indication that committee hearings conducted by the Senate Judiciary Committee in 1982 will shed some light on the insanity defense problem and will result in more uniform laws that will withstand constitutional challenges.

§ 13.4 Entrapment

When members of Congress claimed the government had created rather than uncovered criminal conduct, the term "entrapment" became a household word. In referring to the investigative tactics used in the "ABSCAM" cases, the U.S. District Court for the Eastern District of New York summed up its appraisal of the investigation tactics with this paragraph:

> While the government's conduct of the investigation was not flawless, the overall work of the FBI...reflects a moderate, fair, careful approach to an undercover investigation which suddenly and unexpectedly proved effective in uncovering corruption in Congress.[23]

In the case before that court, seven defendants, including four former members of the House of Representatives, failed to convince the court they

---

[22] United States v. Freeman, 804 F.2d 1574 (11th Cir. 1986); United States v. Amos, 803 F.2d 419 (8th Cir. 1986).

[23] United States v. Myers, 527 F.Supp. 1206 (E.D.N.Y. 1981).

were victims of entrapment or that the agents responsible for ABSCAM acted "outrageously."

The U.S. Court of Appeals for the Third District agreed that the action by the U.S. Government agents did not amount to entrapment. In the case before that court, the facts were as follows. The investigators, posing as representatives of an Arab sheik, told the defendants that the sheik was interested in building a hotel in Philadelphia, but that he wanted to make sure of having friends in high places to take care of any problems that might crop up. A defendant, Schwartz, accepted a $30,000 payment from the agents and Congressman Jannotti received $10,000. The court found that the evidence presented at the trial, particularly the video tapes showing the defendant taking the payments, supported a jury's finding of predisposition.[24]

The entrapment claim is not new. Not only has the defense been claimed in courts, it has often been advanced by those who are charged with the crime when challenging the legality of an arrest by police officers. Too often criminal justice personnel are not familiar with the scope of the term and are hesitant to use techniques that are, in fact, legally valid. In the *Jannotti* case, the reviewing court stated that "the Supreme Court's entrapment cases teach that entrapment occurs when a defendant who is not predisposed to commit a crime does so as a result of the government's inducement." In that case the entrapment issue was submitted to the jury, which found that there was no entrapment.

The defense of entrapment was first recognized by the Supreme Court in *Sorrells v. United States*.[25] In the *Sorrells* case, Chief Justice Hughes noted that merely to afford an opportunity or facilities for the commission of the offense does not defeat the prosecution. In the case the majority continued with this:

> However, a different question is presented when the criminal design originates with the officials of the government and they implant in the mind of an innocent person the disposition to commit the alleged offense and induce its commission in order that they may prosecute.

The views of the Supreme Court were solidified in *Sherman v. United States* in 1958.[26] In this case the persistent solicitation by an informer in the fact of obvious reluctance, resulted in not only procurement of the source of

---

[24]   United States v. Janotti, 673 F.2d 578 (3d Cir. 1982).

[25]   287 U.S. 435, 77 L.Ed. 413, 53 S. Ct. 210 (1932).

[26]   356 U.S. 369, 2 L.Ed.2d 848, 78 S. Ct. 819 (1958).

narcotics, but also in inducing the defendant to return to the use of narcotics after he had "shook" the habit. In stating the rule, the court commented:

> The function of law enforcement is the prevention of crime and the apprehension of criminals. Manifestly, the function does not include the manufacturing of crime. Criminal activity is such that stealth and strategy are necessary weapons in the arsenal of the police officer. However, a different question is presented when the criminal design originates with the officials of the government, and may implant in the mind of the innocent person the disposition to commit the alleged offense and induce its commission in order that they may prosecute.

The distinction between what is or is not entrapment has been articulated in many cases. Some examples are:

> Government conduct which originates criminal design and implants it in the mind of innocent or unwilling defendants is "entrapment."[27]

> In order to have a valid claim of "entrapment," there must exist activity by the state in the nature of an inducement to commit a crime which the accused would not have otherwise committed, though providing the mere opportunity to commit the crime is not sufficient.[28]

> The defense of "entrapment" exists when the criminal design originates with government officials or agents and they implant in the mind of an innocent person the disposition to commit the crime and induce its commission....The defense is destroyed by defendant's predisposition to commit the crime, regardless of the nature and extent of the government's involvement.[29]

> Where the person has readiness and willingness to break the law, the mere fact that government agents provide what appears to be favorable opportunity is not "entrapment."[30]

From these cases a reasonable test in determining what is entrapment can be formulated. In the *Sherman* case which was decided by the Supreme

---

[27]   United States v. Tavelman, 650 F.2d 1133 (9th Cir. 1981).

[28]   State v. Montano, 571 P.2d 291 (Ariz. 1977).

[29]   United States v. Navar, 611 F.2d 1156 (5th Cir. 1980).

[30]   United States v. Punch, 722 F.2d 146 (5th Cir. 1983).

Court, the court emphasized that merely affording an opportunity for the commission of the crime does not constitute entrapment. On the other hand, where the criminal conduct was the product of the creative activity of law enforcement officials, then this is entrapment and a conviction under these circumstances will not stand.

At the present time the great majority of cases in which entrapment defense is interposed involve a charge of some drug offense. According to a study of 405 federal entrapment opinions, rendered between 1970 and 1975, 65 of the cases fell into the category of drug offenses.[31] However, the defense of entrapment has been asserted in the context of a wide variety of criminal activities including prostitution, alcohol offenses, counterfeiting and bribery of public officials.[32]

There is some question as to whether the defense of entrapment can be asserted in the very serious crimes such as murder. For example, the Model Penal Code does not authorize the defense when causing or threatening bodily injury is an element of the offense.

1. Model Penal Code

The Model Penal Code provides:[33]

Section 2.13. Entrapment

(1) A public law enforcement official or a person acting in cooperation with such an official perpetrates an entrapment if for the purpose of obtaining evidence of the commission of an offense, he induces or encourages another person to engage in conduct constituting such offense by either:

(a) making knowingly false representations designed to induce the belief that such conduct is not prohibited; or

(b) employing methods of persuasion or inducement that create a substantial risk that such an offense will be committed by persons other than those who are ready to commit it.

---

[31]   Park, *The Entrapment Controversy*, 60 MINN. L. REV. 163 (1976); Ridling v. State, 719 S.W.2d 1 (Ark. 1986). *See* case in Part II.

[32]   Abrams, FEDERAL CRIMINAL LAW AND ITS ENFORCEMENT 421 (West 1986).

[33]   Model Penal Code, § 2.13.

(2) Except as provided in Subsection (3) of this Section, a person prosecuted for an offense shall be acquitted if he proves by the preponderance of evidence that his conduct occurred in response to an entrapment. The issue of entrapment shall be tried by the Court in the absence of the jury.

(3) The defense afforded by this Section is unavailable when causing or threatening bodily injury is an element of the offense charged and the prosecution is based on conduct causing or threatening such injury to a person other than the person perpetrating the entrapment.

The Model Penal Code designates two ways in which a public law enforcement official or person acting in cooperation with such an official can perpetrate an entrapment. The first is by making representations known to be false for the purpose of inducing a belief that the conduct is not prohibited by law. The second is by employing methods of persuasion that create a substantial risk that such offense would be committed by persons other than those who are ready to commit it. However, the Model Penal Code has an exception which denies the defense in situations where the defendant causes or threatens bodily injury to someone other than the person perpetrating the entrapment.

2. Other statutes and codes

While many states choose to rely upon the entrapment defense as defined by the respective courts, some states have enacted statutes which codify the defense. One such statute is that of Colorado. It provides:

The commission of acts which would otherwise constitute an offense is not criminal if the defendant engaged in the proscribed conduct because he was induced to do so by a law enforcement official or other person acting under his direction, seeking to obtain that evidence for the purpose of prosecution, and the methods used to obtain that evidence were such as to create a substantial risk that the acts would be committed by a person who, but for such inducement, would not have conceived or engaged in conduct of the sort induced. Merely affording a person an opportunity to commit an offense is not entrapment even though representations or inducements calculated to overcome the offender's fear of detection are used.[34]

---

[34] Col. Rev. Stat. § 18-1-709.

This statute and other state statutes contain provisions that provide that merely affording the person an opportunity to commit an offense is not entrapment.

In a Colorado case in which the statute quoted was cited, the court held that the entrapment is an affirmative defense which is to be submitted to the trier of fact; that is, the defendant has the responsibility of introducing evidence which would indicate entrapment. However, once the defendant has presented credible evidence on the issue, the prosecution must prove beyond a reasonable doubt no entrapment has occurred.[35]

The line between police conduct which amounts to entrapment and merely affording an opportunity for the defendant to commit the offense is often a fine one. In showing the willingness of the defendant to engage in criminal conduct, especially in conduct involving illegal drugs, the question arises as to whether evidence of prior use of illegal drugs is admissible. The general rule is that a defendant's unlawful involvement with a controlled substance can be given consideration when evaluating his previous commission to commit other narcotic offenses.[36]

In the *Eib* case, evidence was introduced to show that the appellant sold cocaine on two different occasions to a Kansas City police officer after the transactions were negotiated by a police informant. After arrangements were made by the informant, the appellant handed the officer cocaine which was contained in clear plastic bags, and received $300 for the cocaine. On appeal, the defendant claimed that the sale was the result of entrapment by the officer and the informant. The reviewing court, however, noted that "to show entrapment, the defendant must show both unlawful mental inducement to engage in unlawful conduct and his lack of predisposition." The reviewing court in determining what evidence is admissible to show predisposition, held that a "defendant's unlawful involvement with a controlled substance can be given consideration when evaluating his previous position to commit other narcotics offenses." The court continued by stating that "more specifically the defendant's prior use of other illegal drugs constitutes substantial evidence of predisposition in cases involving the sale of narcotics."

As the entrapment issue is one of the defendants' most often-used challenges, especially in narcotics cases, the guidelines established in the cases and statutes should be carefully considered by enforcement officers. Also, it is a good idea for departments to establish policies after reviewing cases and seeking advice from attorneys general and prosecutors.

---

[35] Bailey v. People, 630 P.2d 1062 (Col. 1987).

[36] State v. Eib, 716 S.W.2d 304 (Mo. 1986) and cases cited therein.

§ 13.5   Alibi

The law sanctions defenses including the defense of alibi to prevent a person from being unjustly convicted. But while safeguards are thrown around the accused, the law does not seek technical excuses to enable criminals to escape the consequences of their acts.

The defense of alibi is universally recognized but safeguards have been established to avoid the abuse of this defense. For example, it is not enough for the accused to say that he was not at the scene of the crime; he must show that he was at another specified place at the time the crime was committed.[37]

The term "alibi" in Latin means elsewhere. It is a defense that places the defendant at the relevant time in a different place than the scene involved and so removed therefrom as to render it impossible for him to be the guilty party.[38] In the context of a criminal prosecution, "alibi" denotes an attempt by the defendant to demonstrate he did not commit the crime because, at the time, he was in another place or so far away or in a situation preventing his doing the act charged against him.[39]

While some courts indicate that alibi is an affirmative offense that seeks to negate elements of the crime charged, others insist that alibi is not an affirmative defense but that the fact of the defendant's presence elsewhere is an affirmative fact logically operative to negate his presence at the time and place of the crime.[40]

In the case of *State v. El-Tabech*, the defendant, after being convicted of first degree murder, claimed on appeal that between 7:00 p.m. and 7:30 p.m. at the time the crime was committed, he was out of the house purchasing ice cream and therefore could not have committed the murder. The state, however, produced evidence that the murder occurred some time between 6:15 p.m. and 7:30 p.m. and, therefore, it was possible for the jury to find the defendant had committed the murder before he left home to purchase the ice cream. In explaining the alibi defense, the court, in quoting other cases, commented:

> In the context of a criminal prosecution, "alibi" denotes an attempt by the defendant to demonstrate he "did not commit the crime because at the time he was in another place so far away, or in a situation preventing his doing the thing charged against him. . . ."

---

[37]   Commonwealth v. McQueen, 178 Pa. Super. 38, 112 A.2d 820 (1955).

[38]   Commonwealth v. Warrington, 326 A.2d 427 (Pa. 1974).

[39]   State v. El-Tabech, 405 N.W.2d 585 (Neb. 1987). *See* case in Part II.

[40]   State v. Armstad, 283 S.W.2d 577 (Mo. 1955).

"Strictly speaking, *alibi evidence* is merely rebuttal evidence directed to that part of the state's evidence which tends to identity the defendant as the person who committed the alleged crime."

In acknowledging that the alibi defense is not truly an independent affirmative defense, the court noted that it is simply evidence in support of the defendant's plea of not guilty and should not be treated merely as evidence tending to disprove one of the essential factors in the case of the prosecution. In this case the reviewing court affirmed the conviction of the defendant.

If the defendant is successful in convincing the jury, or the judge in a case where there is no jury, that he was at another place and that he therefore could not have committed the crime, this "alibi" defense is a complete defense and precludes the possibility of guilt.[41]

The defendant may claim the defense of alibi at the trial even though he did not tell the police or district attorney that he had an alibi defense. In one case the defendant was convicted of robbery, attempted robbery, assault and criminal possession of a weapon. At the trial, the defendant presented an alibi defense. The district attorney encouraged the jury to infer that the alibi defense was a recent fabrication since the defendant was silent about the alibi from the time of his arrest until trial. The Appellate Division reversed the defendant's conviction pointing out that a defendant has no obligation, when in custody, to tell either the police or the district attorney that he has an alibi defense.[42]

§ 13.6 Duress or Compulsion

What would ordinarily be a criminal act may be excused at law if the act is committed under duress or compulsion. Except in the case of homicide, an act which would otherwise constitute a crime may be excused when committed under duress or compulsion which is present, imminent and impending and which produces a well grounded apprehension of death or serious bodily harm if the act is not done.[43]

There are conditions to the application of this defense in criminal cases. The coercion must be of such a nature as to induce a well-grounded apprehension of death or serious bodily harm and there must be no reasonable op-

---

[41] People v. Woodson, 41 Cal. Rptr. 487 (1964); State v. Martin, 2 Ariz. App. 510, 410 P.2d 132 (1966).

[42] People v. Smoot, 59 A.D.2d 898, 399 N.Y.S.2d 133 (N.Y. App. Div. 1977).

[43] United States v. Anthony, 145 F.Supp. 323 (M.D. Pa. 1956); Jackson v. State, 558 S.W.2d 816 (Mo. Ct. App. 1977).

portunity to escape the compulsion without committing the crime.[44] Also a threat of future injury is not enough to justify committing a crime. If there is a possibility of seeking help and avoiding the necessity of taking action, this avenue must be pursued. However, the theory that there must be a "gun to the head" is not a required condition to the application of this defense.[45]

In order for duress or compulsion to be recognized as a defense to criminal charges, the compulsion must come from an outside source and be such as to remove the will of the actor. Applying this rationale, a North Dakota court affirmed a lower court's decision that the defendant's claim that he was compelled to commit robberies in order to provide money for his family for food and shelter did not constitute "duress" as a defense to robbery charges.[46]

It is again emphasized that the common law does not recognize any compulsion, even the threat of instant death, as sufficient to excuse the intentional killing of an innocent person.[47] The common law rule is still recognized and has been incorporated in some of the statutes. For example, this common law rule was applied in the case of *Harris v. State* in 1977.[48] Here the court refused an instruction submitted by the defense that "if defendant was not intending any wrong, was swept along by a party of persons whom he did not resist, he would not be responsible for any wrong done if he was compelled to do the said wrong." The reviewing court stated that the instruction was properly refused when the defendant was indicted for murdering a prison guard during a riot. The court explained that the instruction was an incorrect statement of law for two reasons:

(1) the common law rule that compulsion does not justify the taking of a life of an innocent person, and

(2) the fact that the defendant knew that the riot was about to occur and could have escaped from the cell block before it took place.

Under some statutes, a threat against property or reputation is not sufficient to excuse criminal conduct.[49] Some state statutes also deny the defense of duress to an individual who intentionally or wantonly places himself in a situation in which coercion is likely to be applied. For example, if one joins

---

[44] State v. St. Clair, 262 S.W.2d 25 (1953); Jackson v. State, 504 S.W.2d 488 (Tex. Crim. App. 1974).

[45] People v. Unger, 33 Ill. App. 3d 770, 338 N.E.2d 442 (Ill. App. Ct. 1975).

[46] State v. Gann, 244 N.W.2d 746 (N.D. 1976).

[47] Arp v. State, 97 Ala. 5, 12 So. 301 (1893).

[48] 352 So. 2d 460 (Ala. Crim. App. 1977).

[49] Ky. Rev. Stat. § 501.090 (1974).

criminal activity voluntarily and seeks exoneration for some act committed by him in the course of the activity by asserting that a companion threatened him with death, the defense of duress is not available.

1. Model Penal Code

Section 2.09 of the Model Penal Code contains this recommended statute relating to duress.[50]

(1) It is an affirmative defense that the actor engaged in the conduct charged to constitute an offense because he was coerced to do so by the use of, or a threat to use, unlawful force against his person or the person of another, that a person of reasonable firmness in his situation would have been unable to resist.

(2) The defense provided by this Section is unavailable if the actor recklessly placed himself in a situation in which it was probable that he would be subjected to duress. The defense is also unavailable if he was negligent in placing himself in such a situation whenever negligence suffices to establish culpability for the offense charged.

(3) It is not a defense that a woman acted on the command of her husband, unless she acted under such coercion as would establish a defense under this Section. (The presumption that a woman acting in the presence of her husband is coerced is abolished.)

(4) When the conduct of the actor would otherwise be justifiable under § 3.02, this Section does not preclude such defense.

According to the comments following the Model Penal Code, at the time the Code was considered 20 states had legislation dealing with the defense of duress in criminal cases. The Model Code recognizes some of the provisions of the state statutes in existence and also some of the common law exceptions.

Under the Code the defense of duress is not established simply by the fact the defendant was coerced; he must have been coerced in circumstances under which a person of reasonable firmness in his situation would likewise have been unable to resist. Subsection (2) of the Code deprives the actor of the duress defense if he recklessly places himself in a situation in which it was probable that he would be subject to duress.

---

[50] Model Penal Code, § 2.09.

§ 13.7 Necessity

For reasons of policy, if the harm which will result from compliance with the law is greater than that which will result from violation of it, one who is accused of violating the law may advance the defense of necessity. The traditional view is that the pressure or the factors that made the violation necessary must come from the physical forces of nature rather than from human beings. As discussed in the previous Section, if the pressure is from others, the defense, if applicable, is duress rather than necessity.

The defense of necessity is and should be very strictly applied. Under this theory, one may be justified by necessity in violating the law and causing harm in order to avoid a greater harm by complying with the law. However, the defense will not be recognized unless the defendant acted with the intention of avoiding the greater harm, and it is for the court, not the defendant, to weigh the relative harmfulness of the two alternatives.

1. Model Penal Code

Section 302 of the Model Penal Code includes the recommended Model statute relating to necessity under the Title "Choice of Evils."[51]

(1) Conduct that the actor believes to be necessary to avoid a harm or evil to himself or to another is justified, provided that:

(a) the harm or evil sought to be avoided by such conduct is greater than that sought to be prevented by the law defining the offense charged; and

(b) neither the Code nor other law defining the offense provides exceptions or defenses dealing with specific situations involved; and

(c) a legislative purpose to exclude the justification claim does not otherwise plainly appear.

Under this provision of the Code, as in the common law and other statutes, the evil sought to be avoided must be greater than that sought to be prevented by the law defining the offense. Also, the legislature must not have previously foreclosed the choice that was made by resolving the conflict of values at stake. According to the comments following this Section, the Sec-

---

[51] Model Penal Code, § 302.

tion accepts the view that the principle of necessity, properly conceived, affords a general justification for conduct that would otherwise constitute an offense. In giving some examples in the commentary it is noted that under this Section property may be destroyed to prevent the threat of fire, a speed limit may be violated in pursuing a suspected criminal and an ambulance may pass a traffic light.[52]

§ 13.8 Ignorance or Mistake

One rule which is settled in our legal system is that ignorance of the law or mistake of the law is no excuse. Mistake about the law is disallowed as a defense because of practical considerations. It would be very difficult to prove in every situation that the person charged with a violation of the law knew the law. However, where a specific intent is essential to constitute the crime charged, then ignorance of the law negates the existence of such intent.[53]

If there is an honest and reasonable mistake of fact, such ignorance or mistake of fact will sometimes exempt one from criminal liability unless the mistake arises from want of proper care on the part of the accused. The question as to whether one acts in good faith, honestly and without fault or negligence is determined by the circumstances as they appear to the person when the mistake is made and the effect which the surrounding circumstances might reasonably be expected to have on his mind in forming the intent, criminal or otherwise, upon which he acted.[54]

If there is a mistake of fact, one will be relieved of criminal liability only if his belief is of such a nature that the conduct would have been lawful had the facts been as he reasonably supposed them to be.

§ 13.9 Acting Under Authority or Direction of Others

Those who are charged with crime often seek to justify their actions by explaining that they acted because they were ordered to do so. This defense is very difficult to demonstrate, especially where one acts under the authority of a military or quasi-military commanding officer. However, the general law is that, except insofar as the element of duress or compulsion may be present,

---

[52] *See* the Model Penal Code for a discussion of the rationale for this defense and a list of the states that have adopted all or parts of the Model Penal Code.

[53] United States v. Ehrlichman, 376 F.Supp. 29 (D.D.C. 1974).

[54] United States v. Squires, 440 F.2d 859 (2d Cir. 1971); United States v. Jewell, 532 F.2d 697 (9th Cir. 1976), *cert. denied,* 426 U.S. 951, 96 S. Ct. 3173, 49 L.Ed.2d 1188 (1976).

the fact that one undertakes a crime or performs a criminal act under the authority or direction of a supervisor, one nevertheless is responsible for that act.[55]

An exception to the general law is recognized where a statute provides a lay person acting on the orders of a peace officer is immune from prosecution for violations so committed.[56] This defense applies only if the person accused is acting directly under the order of the police officer who is at that time carrying out his assigned responsibilities.

§ 13.10   Self-Defense

An act which might otherwise be a crime is not punishable if the act was committed in self-defense. The general rule is that a person is privileged to use force as reasonably appears necessary to defend himself against an apparent threat or unlawful and immediate violence from another. Availability of this privilege as a defense to a criminal charge is dependent under prevailing law upon a showing that:

(1) the defendant believed physical force to be necessary for self-protection,
(2) his belief was based upon reasonable ground, and
(3) the force used was believed necessary to avoid imminent danger and
(4) the force used was not in excess of that believed necessary to repel the unlawful attack.

As indicated in the above statement, the amount of force which may be justifiable must be reasonably related to the threatened harm which the user seeks to avoid. He may justifiably use deadly force against another in self-defense only if he reasonably believes that the other is about to inflict unlawful death or serious bodily harm upon him and that it is necessary to use the deadly force to prevent it.[57]

While most self-defense cases involve the use of firearms or other weapons where the force would be considered deadly force, it can be logically argued that one may commit assault or battery with one's fist without in-

---

[55] Canalas v. State, 496 S.W.2d 614 (Tex. Crim. App. 1973).

[56] People v. Benford, 53 Cal. 2d 1, 345 P.2d 928 (1959).

[57] State v. Philbrick, 402 A.2d 59 (Me. 1979).

tending death or serious bodily harm.[58] It follows that necessary force may be used to protect one from such an assault.

In reference to the reasonable belief of imminent danger, apparently it is only necessary that the person who claims self-defense honestly and actually believe that the force used was necessary.[59] Under the statutes and under the case law, the person claiming self-defense must show evidence that he reasonably perceived an "imminent" danger. If the danger is to take place some time in the future and can be avoided, then the defense will not prevail.

Where self-defense is pleaded as a defense to a charge, a defendant must be allowed to introduce evidence to show that his belief that he was in danger was reasonable. For example, in an aggravated assault case the court found it was reversible error to refuse to allow the defendant to show that there had been a longstanding dispute with the victim and the victim's brother over a $400 debt.[60] In this case the victim was outside in a car while his brother went to the defendant's door to collect a debt. The defendant came outside and fired three shots at the victim. Days before the accident the victim had broken the defendant's nose. The trial court had refused to admit evidence that the victim's brother had waved a gun at the defendant and threatened to shoot him nine months before the incident. This refusal, according to the court, was error and the conviction was reversed. The court pointed out that the testimony bore on the issue of self-defense; and although the victim himself had not communicated the threat, it was relevant to prove the hostility of both the brothers. Further, the evidence would have been admissible to demonstrate bias and hostility against the defendant.

1. Model Penal Code

The Model Penal Code includes a very comprehensive Section relating to the use of force and self-protection.[61] Under this Section the use of force upon or toward another person is justifiable when the actor believes that such force is immediately necessary for the purpose of protecting himself against the use of unlawful force by such other person on the present occasion. Under this Section, the actor's actual belief is sufficient to support the defense.

The Model Code contains limitations on justifying necessity for the use of force. Specifically the use of force is not justified to resist an arrest that the actor knows is being made by a police officer although the arrest is un-

---

[58] State v. Clay, 297 N.C. 555, 256 S.E.2d 176 (1979). *See* case in Part II.

[59] State v. Kelley, 97 N.J. 178, 478 A.2d 364 (1984).

[60] Manofsky v. State, 354 So. 2d 1249 (1978).

[61] Model Penal Code, § 3.04.

lawful. Also, the use of deadly force is not justified if the actor can avoid the necessity of using such force with complete safety by taking certain alternative steps such as retreating, surrendering possession of the thing to a person asserting the claim of a right thereto or complying with the demand that he abstain from action that he has no duty to take.[62]

§ 13.11 Time Limitations (Statute of Limitations)

A defendant charged with a crime may claim that he should not be tried for that offense as the time limitation for prosecution has expired. This is often referred to as the statute of limitations defense. In the absence of statutes specifically applicable to criminal cases the prosecution may be instituted at any time however long after the commission of the criminal act, however, most jurisdictions have enacted statutes to limit the time for the commencement of some criminal proceedings. These statutes vary in their terms and almost always provide that a prosecution for murder may be commenced at any time.

The rationale for the time limitations is that the defendant should have some substantial safeguards against an erroneous conviction because of the staleness of the evidence and that the defendant is entitled to a reasonably speedy trial. Therefore, when the defendant claims that the statutory time has expired, the guilt or innocence of the defendant is not an issue. If the statutory time has expired, the defendant is entitled to an acquittal as a matter of right, not of grace.

Criminal justice personnel are especially concerned with the commencement of the running of the statutory period. Generally speaking, a statute of limitations begins to run as soon as the offense is completed. While ordinarily determining the date of the crime is not difficult, in some instances this can cause a problem, especially in drug-related cases where several offenses are committed over a period of time.

As a general rule, the time begins to run when the crime is committed and runs until the prosecution is commenced. Depending upon the provisions of the statute, the running of the time is stopped by the filing of an indictment or information or at the time a complaint is laid before a magistrate and a warrant of arrest issued.[63]

It is obvious that justice would not be served if the defendant conceals himself or otherwise makes it impossible for an investigation to take place or

---

[62] *See* Article III, § 7 of the Model Penal Code for comments explaining provisions of the Code.

[63] Jarrett v. State, 49 Okla. Crim. Rep. 162, 292 P. 888 (1930).

for the prosecution to commence. To overcome this possibility of defeating justice, statutes have been enacted which provide that if the person who has committed the offense is absent from the state, or so conceals himself that process cannot be served upon him, or conceals the fact of the crime, the time of the absence or concealment is not to be included in computing the period of limitations. This is often referred to as "tolling" the statute of limitations.

As state statutes differ in establishing the specific time limitations, it is necessary to consult the respective statutes. However, there are some provisions that are common to most statutes. For example, all statutes provide that a prosecution for murder may be commenced at any time.

Some statutes provide that the prosecution for any felony is not subject to a period of limitations and may be commenced at any time. An example of the latter provision is that of Kentucky. The Kentucky statute provides:

K.R.S. 505.050 Time Limitations

Except as otherwise expressly provided, the prosecution of a felony is not subject to a period of limitation and may be commenced at any time.

(2) Except as otherwise expressly provided, the prosecution of an offense other than felony must be commenced within one year after it is committed.

(3) For the purpose of this Section, an offense is committed either when every element occurs, or if a legislative purpose to prohibit a continuing course of conduct plainly appears, at the time in the course of conduct of the defendant's complicity therein is terminated.[64]

1. Model Penal Code

The Model Penal Code includes a time limitation for all offenses including felonies and misdemeanors except murder. In the case of murder, the prosecution may be commenced at any time. This recommended statute specifies four periods of limitation: six years for felonies of the first degree; three years for less serious felonies; two years for misdemeanors; and six months for petty misdemeanors and violations.

The Penal Code also includes a Subsection defining when an offense is commenced for statute of limitations purposes and indicates specifically when the time of limitations does not run.[65]

---

[64]   Ky. Rev. Stat., § 505.050.

[65]   Model Penal Code, § 1.06.

§ 13.12   Other Defenses

One can expect that the defendant will seek to avoid conviction by claiming that statutes were unconstitutional as being vague or overbroad, or that evidence is inadmissible due to an illegal search and seizure, improper techniques in obtaining a confession or violation of the right to counsel.[66]

§ 13.13   Summary

The courts have recognized that there are situations where persons who commit acts which would ordinarily be crimes may introduce evidence to show they do not have the capacity to form the criminal intent required as an element of some crimes or to demonstrate other legitimate defenses.

An infant is exempt from criminal responsibility for his act if sufficient mental capacity to entertain the criminal act is wanting. Also most states provide a method of treating juvenile offenders which is distinct from that of treating adult offenders.

Under the common law, and by statutes and court decisions in all states, mental incapacity or insanity may be availed of by one accused of crimes at several points in the criminal procedure. Several tests have been used by the courts over the years to determine if the mental disorder or impairment is sufficient to render the defendant legally not guilty because of insanity. These include the M'Naghten Rule, the Irresistible Impulse Rule, the Durham Rule and more recently the Model Penal Code test. The law in this area is still developing. The issue of insanity or mental impairment may arise also when determining if the defendant is capable of making a proper defense or aiding his attorney or securing evidence at the time of the trial.

"Entrapment" is a defense in a criminal case. Entrapment occurs when the criminal conduct is a product of the "creative activity" of law enforcement officials. That is, if the criminal design originates in the mind of the police and not with the accused then entrapment is a proper defense. The rationale for entrapment defense is that no person should be convicted for a crime that he was induced to commit by the very government who is prosecuting him for committing the crime.

The defense of alibi is universally recognized. Safeguards have been established to avoid the abuse of this defense. The defense of alibi is that the

---

[66] *See* Klotter & Kanovitz, CONSTITUTIONAL LAW (5th ed. 1985).

accused was at another place than that at which the alleged crime was committed at the time it was committed.

What would ordinarily be a criminal act may be excused at law if the act is committed under duress or compulsion. In order to excuse an act which would ordinarily be a crime, the compulsion or coercion must be present, imminent and impending.

Closely related to duress and compulsion is the defense of necessity. The general rule is that "a criminal offense may be justified or excused if done under necessity." As in the case of other defenses, this defense is not available unless specific conditions exist.

Although ignorance of the law or mistake of the law is no excuse, if there is an honest and reasonable mistake of fact, such ignorance or mistake of fact will sometimes exempt one from criminal liability unless the mistake arises from a want of proper care on the part of the accused.

Self-defense is a defense in a criminal case if the force used by the defendant reasonably appears necessary to defend him against an apparent threat of lawful and immediate violence from another. In order to successfully claim this defense the defendant must show that he believed physical force to be necessary for self protection against an unlawful attack, his belief was based upon reasonable grounds, the force used was believed necessary to avoid imminent danger, and the force used was not in excess of that believed necessary to repel the unlawful attack. The statutes differ as to what force is justified and under what circumstances.

A defendant may avoid prosecution if he can show that the time limitation as stated by statute has expired. If the time between the offense and the beginning of the prosecution is longer than that enumerated in the statute, the defendant has an absolute right to an acquittal even though he may be obviously guilty of the offense.

Criminal justice personnel, in carrying out their responsibilities, should be aware that defendants are entitled to presenting evidence which will convince the jury or other fact finder that they should be found not guilty due to incapacity or one of the other defenses. Recognizing that these defenses will be brought forward, evidence should be collected which will counter the defenses.

PART II
JUDICIAL DECISIONS

PART II: TABLE OF CASES

Cases relating to Chapter 1

SOURCES, DISTINCTIONS
AND LIMITATIONS

UNITED STATES, Petitioner,

v.

Josephine M. POWELL

423 U.S. 87, 46 L.Ed.2d 228, 96 S.Ct. 316 (1975).

Decided Dec. 2, 1975.

Mr. Justice REHNQUIST delivered the opinion for the Court.

The Court of Appeals in a brief *per curiam* opinion held that portion of an Act of Congress prohibiting the mailing of firearms "capable of being concealed on the person," 18 U.S.C. § 1715, to be unconstitutionally vague, and we granted certiorari to review this determination. 420 U.S. 971, 95 S.Ct. 1390, 43 L.Ed.2d 651 (1975). Respondent was found guilty of having violated the statute by a jury in the United States District Court for the Eastern District of Washington, and was sentenced by that court to a term of two years' imprisonment. The testimony adduced at trial showed that a Mrs. Theresa Bailey received by mail an unsolicited package from Spokane, Wash., addressed to her at her home in Tacoma, Wash. The package contained two shotguns, shotgun shells and 20 or 30 hacksaw blades.

While the source of this package was unknown to Mrs. Bailey, its receipt by her not unnaturally turned her thoughts to her husband George, an inmate at nearby McNeil Island Federal Penitentiary. Her husband, however, disclaimed any knowledge of the package or its contents. Mrs. Bailey turned the package over to federal officials, and subsequent investigation disclosed that both of the shotguns had been purchased on the same date. One had been purchased by respondent, and another by an unidentified woman.

Ten days after having received the first package, Mrs. Bailey received a telephone call from an unknown woman who advised her that a second package was coming but that "it was a mistake." The caller advised her to give the package to "Sally." When Mrs. Bailey replied that she "did not have the address or any way of giving it to Sally," the caller said she would call back.

Several days later, the second package arrived, and Mrs. Bailey gave it unopened to the investigating agents. The return address was that of

485

respondent, and it was later determined that the package bore respondent's handwriting. This package contained a sawed-off shotgun with a barrel length of 10 inches and an overall length of 22⅛ inches, together with two boxes of shotgun shells.

Respondent was indicted on a single count of mailing a firearm capable of being concealed on the person (the sawed-off shotgun contained in the second package), in violation of 18 U.S.C. § 1715. At trial there was evidence that the weapon could be concealed on an average person. Respondent was convicted by a jury which was instructed that in order to return a guilty verdict it must find that she "knowingly caused to be delivered by mail a firearm capable of being concealed on the person."

She appealed her judgment of conviction to the Court of Appeals, and that court held that the portion of § 1715 proscribing the mailing of "other firearms capable of being concealed on the person" was so vague that it violated the Due Process Clause of the Fifth Amendment to the United States Constitution. 501 F.2d 1136 (1974). Citing *Lanzetta v. New Jersey,* 306 U.S. 451, 59 S.Ct. 618, 83 L.Ed. 888 (1939), the court held that, although it was clear that a pistol could be concealed on the person, "the statutory prohibition as it might relate to sawed-off shotguns is not so readily recognizable to persons of common experience and intelligence." 501 F.2d, at 1137.

While the Court of Appeals considered only the constitutional claim, respondent in this Court makes a statutory argument which may fairly be described as an alternative basis for affirming the judgment of that court. She contends that as a matter of statutory construction, particularly in light of the doctrine of *ejusdem generis,* the

language "other firearms capable of being concealed on the person" simply does not extend to sawed-off shotguns. We must decide this threshold question of statutory interpretation first, since if we find the statute inapplicable to respondent, it will be unnecessary to reach the constitutional question, *Dandridge v. Williams* 397 U.S. 471, 475-476, 90 S.Ct. 1153, 1156, 25 L.Ed.2d 491 (1970).

The thrust of respondent's argument is that the more general language of the statute ("fire-arms") should be limited by the more specific language ("pistols and revolvers") so that the phrase "other firearms capable of being concealed on the person" would be limited to "concealable weapons such as pistols and revolvers."

We reject this contention. The statute by its terms bans the mailing of "firearms capable of being concealed on the person," and we would be justified in narrowing the statute only if such a narrow reading was supported by evidence of congressional intent over and above the language of the statute.

In *Gooch v. United States,* 297 U.S. 124, 128, 56 S.Ct. 395, 397, 80 L.Ed. 522 (1936), the Court said:

> "The rule of *ejusdem generis,* while firmly established, is only an instrumentality for ascertaining the correct meaning of words when there is uncertainty. Ordinarily, it limits general terms which follow specific ones to matters similar to those specified; but it may not be used to defeat the obvious purpose of legislation. And, while penal statutes are narrowly construed, this does not require rejection of that sense of the words which best harmonizes with the context and the end in view."

The legislative history of this particular provision is sparse, but the

House report indicates that the purpose of the bill upon which § 1715 is based was to avoid having the Post Office serve as an instrumentality for the violation of local laws which prohibited the purchase and possession of weapons. H.R. Rep. No. 610, 69th Cong., 1st Sess. (1926). It would seem that sawed-off shotguns would be even more likely to be prohibited by local laws than would pistols and revolvers. A statement by the author of the bill, Representative Miller of Washington, on the floor of the House indicates that the purpose of the bill was to make it more difficult for criminals to obtain concealable weapons. 66 Cong.Rec. 726 (1924). To narrow the meaning of the language Congress used so as to limit it to only those weapons which could be concealed as readily as pistols or revolvers would not comport with that purpose. Cf. *United States v. Alpers*, 338 U.S. 680, 682, 70 S.Ct. 352, 354, 94 L.Ed. 457 (1950).

We therefore hold that a properly instructed jury could have found the 22-inch sawed-off shotgun mailed by respondent to have been a "[firearm] capable of being concealed on the person" within the meaning of 18 U.S.C. § 1715. Having done so, we turn to the Court of Appeals' holding that this portion of the statute was unconstitutionally vague.

We said last Term that "[i]t is well established that vagueness challenges to statutes which do not involved First Amendment freedoms must be examined in the light of the facts of the case at hand." *United States v. Mazurie*, 419 U.S. 544, 550, 95 S.Ct. 710, 714, 42 L.Ed.2d 706 (1975). The Court of Appeals dealt with the statute generally, rather than as applied to respondent in this case. It must necessarily have concluded, therefore, that the prohibition against mailing "firearms

capable of being concealed on the person" proscribed no comprehensible course of conduct at all. It is well settled, of course, that such a statute may not constitutionally be applied to any set of facts. *Lanzetta v. New Jersey*, 306 U.S. at 453, 59 S.Ct. at 619; *Connally v. General Const. Co.*, 269 U.S. 385, 391, 46 S.Ct. 126, 127, 70 L.Ed. 322 (1926).

An example of such a vague statute is found in *United States v. Cohen Grocery Co.*, 255 U.S. 81, 89, 41 S.Ct. 298, 300, 65 L.Ed. 516 (1921). The statute there prohibited any person from "willfully...mak[ing] any unjust or unreasonable rate or charge in...dealing in or with any necessaries...." So worded it "forbids no specific or definite act" and "leaves open...the widest conceivable inquiry, the scope of which no one can foresee and the result of which no one can foreshadow or adequately guard against." *Ibid.*

On the other hand, a statute which provides that certain oversized or heavy loads must be transported by the "shortest practicable route" is not unconstitutionally vague. *Sproles v. Binford*, 286 U.S. 374, 393, 52 S.Ct. 581, 587, 76 L.Ed. 1167 (1932). The carrier has been given clear notice that a reasonably ascertainable standard of conduct is mandated; it is for him to insure that his actions do not fall outside the legal limits. The sugar dealer in Cohen, to the contrary, could have had no idea in advance what an "unreasonable rate" would be because that would have been determined by the vagaries of supply and demand, factors over which he had no control. Engaged in a lawful business which Congress had in no way sought to proscribe, he could not have charged *any* price with the confidence that it would not be later found unreasonable.

But the challenged language of 18 U.S.C. § 1715 is quite different from that of the statute involved in *Cohen*. It intelligibly forbids a definite course of conduct: the mailing of concealable firearms. While doubts as to the applicability of the language in marginal fact situations may be conceived, we think that the statute gave respondent adequate warning that her mailing of a 22-inch-long sawed-off shotgun was a criminal offense. Even as to more doubtful cases than that of respondent, we have said that "the law is full of instances where a man's fate depends on his estimating rightly, that is, as the jury subsequently estimates it, some matter of degree." *Nash v. United States* 229 U.S. 373, 377, 33 S.Ct. 780, 781, 57 L.Ed. 1232 (1913).

The Court of Appeals questioned whether the "person" referred to in the statute to measure capability of concealment was to be "the person mailing the firearm, the person receiving the firearm, or, perhaps, an average person, male or female, wearing whatever garb might be reasonably appropriate, wherever the place and whatever the season." 501 F.2d, at 1137. But we think it fair to attribute to Congress the common sense meaning that such a person would be an average person garbed in a manner to aid, rather than hinder, concealment of the weapons. Such straining to inject doubt as to the meaning of words where no doubt would be felt by the normal reader is not required by the "void for vagueness" doctrine, and we will not indulge in it.

The Court of Appeals also observed that "[t]o require Congress to delimit the size of the firearms (other than pistols and revolvers) that it intends to declare unmailable is certainly to impose no insurmountable burden upon it...." *Ibid.* Had Congress chosen to delimit the size of the firearms intended to be declared unmailable, it would have written a different statute and in some respects a narrower one than it actually wrote. To the extent that it was intended to proscribe the mailing of all weapons capable of being concealed on the person, a statute so limited would have been less inclusive than the one Congress actually wrote.

But the more important disagreement we have with this observation of the Court of Appeals is that it seriously misconceives the "void for vagueness" doctrine. The fact that Congress might, without difficulty, have chosen "[c]learer and more precise language" equally capable of achieving the end which it sought does not mean that the statute which it in fact drafted is unconstitutionally vague. *United States v. Petrillo,* 332 U.S. 1, 7, 67 S.Ct. 1538, 1541, 91 L.Ed. 1877 (1947).

The judgment of the Court of Appeals is reversed.

Mr. Justice STEWART, concurring in part and dissenting in part.

I agree with the Court that the statutory provision before us is not unconstitutionally vague, because I think the provision has an objectively measurable meaning under established principles of statutory construction. Specifically, I think the rule of *ejusdem generis* is applicable here, and that 18 U.S.C. § 1715 must thus be read specifically to make criminal the mailing of a pistol or revolver, or of any firearm *as* "capable of being concealed on the person" as a pistol or revolver.

The rule of *ejusdem generis* is applicable in a setting such as this unless its application would defeat the intention of Congress or render the general statutory language meaningless. See *United States v. Alpers*, 338 U.S. 680, 682, 70 S.Ct. 352, 354, 94 L.Ed. 457; *United States v. Salen*, 235 U.S. 237, 249-251, 35 S.Ct. 51, 53, 59 L.Ed. 210; *United States v. Stever*, 222 U.S. 167, 174-175, 32 S.Ct. 51, 53, 56 L.Ed. 145. Application of the rule in the present situation entails neither of those results. Instead of draining meaning from the general language of the statute, an *ejusdem generis* construction gives to that language an ascertainable and intelligible content. And, instead of defeating the intention of Congress, an *ejusdem generis* construction coincides with the legislative intent.

The legislative history of the bill on which § 1715 was based contains persuasive indications that it was not intended to apply to firearms larger than the largest pistols or revolvers. Representative Miller, the bill's author, made it clear that the legislative concern was not with the "shotgun, the rifle, or any firearm used in hunting or by the sportsman." 66 Cong.Rec. 727. As a supporter of the legislation stated: "The purpose...is to prevent the shipment of pistols and revolvers through the mails." 67 Cong. Rec. 12041. The only reference to sawed-off shotguns came in a question posed by Representative McKeown: "Is there anything in this bill that will prevent the citizens of Oklahoma from buying sawed-off shotguns to defend themselves against these bank-robbing bandits?" Representative Blanton, an opponent of the bill, responded: "That may come next. Sometimes a revolver is more necessary than a sawed-off shotgun." 66 Cong. Rec. 729. In the absence of more concrete indicia of legislative intent, the pregnant silence that followed Representative Blanton's response can surely be taken as an indication that Congress intended the law to reach only weapons of the same general size as pistols and revolvers.

I would vacate the judgment of the Court of Appeals and remand the case to that court for further proceedings consistent with these views.

In the Matter of Samuel WINSHIP, Appellant.
397 U.S. 358, 90 S.Ct. 1068 (1970)
Decided March 31, 1970.

Mr. Justice BRENNAN delivered the opinion of the Court.

Constitutional questions decided by this Court concerning the juvenile process have centered on the adjudicatory stage at "which a determination is made as to whether a juvenile is a delinquent' as a result of alleged misconduct on his part, with the consequence that he may be committed to a state institution." *In re Gault*, 387 U.S. 1, 13, 87 S.Ct. 1428, 1436, 18 L.Ed.2d 527 (1967). Gault decided that, although the Fourteenth Amendment does not require that the hearing at this stage conform with all the requirements of a criminal trial or even of the usual administrative proceeding, the Due Process Clause does require application during the adjudicatory hearing of " 'the essentials of due process and fair treatment.' " This case presents the single, narrow question whether proof beyond a reasonable doubt is among the "essentials of due process and fair treatment" required during the adjudicatory stage when a juvenile is charged with an act which would constitute a crime if committed by an adult.

Section 712 of the New York Family Court Act defines a juvenile delinquent as "a person over seven and less than sixteen years of age who does any act which, if done by an adult, would constitute a crime." During a 1967 adjudicatory hearing, conducted pursuant to § 742 of the Act, a judge in New York Family Court found that appellant, then a 12-year-old boy, had entered a locker and stolen $112 from a woman's pocketbook. The petition which charged appellant with delinquency alleged that his act, "if done by an adult, would constitute the crime or crimes of Larceny." The judge acknowledged that the proof might not establish guilt beyond a reasonable doubt, but rejected appellant's contention that such proof was required by the Fourteenth Amendment. The judge relied instead on § 744(b) of the New York Family Court Act which provides that "[a]ny determination at the conclusion of [an adjudicatory] hearing that a [juvenile] did an act or acts must be based on a preponderance of the evidence." During a subsequent dispositional hearing, appellant was ordered placed in a training school for an initial period of 18 months, subject to annual extension of his commitment until his 18th birthday—six years in appellant's case. The Appellate Division of the New York Supreme Court, First Judicial Department, affirmed without opinion, 30 A.D.2d 781, 291 N.Y.S.2d 1005 (1968). The New York Court of Appeals then affirmed by a four-to-three vote, expressly sustaining the constitutionality of § 744(b), 24 N.Y.2d 196, 299 N.Y.S.2d 414, 247

N.E.2d 253 (1969). We noted probable jurisdiction, 396 U.S. 885, 90 S. Ct. 179, 24 L.Ed.2d 160 (1969). We reverse.

The requirement that guilt of a criminal charge be established by proof beyond a reasonable doubt dates at least from our early years as a Nation. The "demand for a higher degree of persuasion in criminal cases was recurrently expressed from ancient times, [though] its crystallization into the formula beyond a reasonable doubt' seems to have occurred as late as 1798. It is now accepted in common law jurisdictions as the measure of persuasion by which the prosecution must convince the trier of all the essential elements of guilt." C. McCormick, Evidence § 321, pp. 681-682 (1954); see also 9 J. Wigmore, Evidence, § 2497 (3d ed. 1940). Although virtually unanimous adherence to the reasonable-doubt standard in common-law jurisdictions may not conclusively establish it as a requirement of due process, such adherence does "reflect a profound judgment about the way in which law should be enforced and justice administered." *Duncan v. Louisiana* 391 U.S. 145, 155, 88 S. Ct. 1444, 1451, 20 L.Ed.2d 491 (1968).

Expressions in many opinions of this Court indicate that it has long been assumed that proof of a criminal charge beyond a reasonable doubt is constitutionally required. Mr. Justice Frankfurter stated that "[i]t is the duty of the Government to establish * * * guilt beyond a reasonable doubt. This notion—basic in our law and rightly one of the boasts of a free society—is a requirement and a safeguard of due process of law in the historic, procedural content of 'due process.' " *Leland v. Oregon,* 343 U.S., at 802-803, 72 S. Ct., at 1009 (dissenting opinion). In a similar vein, the Court said in *Brinegar v. United States*, 338 U.S., at 174, 69 S. Ct., at 1310, that "[g]uilt in a criminal case must be proved beyond a reasonable doubt and by evidence confined to that which long experience in the common-law tradition, to some extent embodied in the Constitution, has crystallized into rules of evidence consistent with that standard. These rules are historically grounded rights of our system, developed to safeguard men from dubious and unjust convictions, with resulting forfeitures of life, liberty and property." *Davis v. United States*, 160 U.S., at 488, 16 S. Ct., at 358 stated that the requirement is implicit in "constitutions * * * [which] recognize the fundamental principles that are deemed essential for the protection of life and liberty." In *Davis* a murder conviction was reversed because the trial judge instructed the jury that it was their duty to convict when the evidence was equally balanced regarding the sanity of the accused. This Court said: "On the contrary, he is entitled to an acquittal of the specific crime charged, if upon all the evidence, there is reasonable doubt whether he was capable in law of committing crime. * * * No man should be deprived of his life under the forms of law unless the jurors who try him are able, upon their consciences, to say that the evidence before them * * * is sufficient to show beyond a reasonable doubt the existence of every fact necessary to constitute the crime charged."

The reasonable-doubt standard plays a vital role in the American scheme of criminal procedure. It is a prime instrument for reducing the risk of convictions resting on factual error. The standard provides concrete substance for the presumption of innocence— that bedrock "axiomatic and elementary" principle whose "enforcement

lies at the foundation of the administration of our criminal law." *Coffin v. United States*, 156 U.S., at 453, 15 S. Ct., at 403. As the dissenters in the New York Court of Appeals observed, and we agree, "a person accused of a crime * * * would be at a severe disadvantage, a disadvantage amounting to a lack of fundamental fairness, if he could be adjudged guilty and imprisoned for years on the strength of the same evidence as would suffice in a civil case."

The requirement of proof beyond a reasonable doubt has this vital role in our criminal procedure for cogent reasons. The accused during a criminal prosecution has at stake interest of immense importance, both because of the possibility that he may lose his liberty upon conviction and because of the certainty that he would be stigmatized by the conviction. Accordingly, a society that values the good name and freedom of every individual should not condemn a man for commission of a crime when there is reasonable doubt about his guilt. As we said in *Speiser v. Randall*, 357 U.S., at 525-526, 78 S. Ct., at 1342: "There is always in litigation a margin of error, representing error in factfinding, which both parties must take into account. Where one party has at stake an interest of transcending value—as a criminal defendant his liberty—this margin of error is reduced as to him by the process of placing on the other party the burden of * * * persuading the factfinder at the conclusion of the trial of his guilt beyond a reasonable doubt. Due process commands that no man shall lose his liberty unless the Government has borne the burden of * * * convincing the factfinder of his guilt." To this end, the reasonable-doubt standard is indispensable, for it "impresses on the trier of fact the necessity of reaching a subjective state of certitude of the facts in issue." Dorsen & Rezneck, In Re Gault and the Future of Juvenile Law, 1 Family Law Quarterly, No. 4, pp. 1, 26 (1967).

Moreover, use of the reasonable-doubt standard is indispensable to command the respect and confidence of the community in applications of the criminal law. It is critical that the moral force of the criminal law not be diluted by a standard of proof that leaves people in doubt whether innocent men are being condemned. It is also important in our free society that every individual going about his ordinary affairs have confidence that his government cannot adjudge him guilty of a criminal offense without convincing a proper factfinder of his guilt with utmost certainty.

Lest there remain any doubt about the constitutional stature of the reasonable-doubt standard, we explicitly hold that the Due Process Clause protects the accused against conviction except upon proof beyond a reasonable doubt of every fact necessary to constitute the crime with which he is charged.

We turn to the question whether juveniles, like adults, are constitutionally entitled to proof beyond a reasonable doubt when they are charged with violation of a criminal law. The same considerations that demand extreme caution in factfinding to protect the innocent adult apply as well to the innocent child. We do not find convincing the contrary arguments of the New York Court of Appeals. *Gault* rendered untenable much of the reasoning relied upon by that court to sustain the constitutionality of § 744(b). The Court of Appeals indicated that a delinquency adjudication "is not a conviction' (§ 781); that it affects no right or privilege, including the right to hold public office or to obtain a license

(§ 782); and a cloak of protective confidentiality is thrown around all the proceedings (§§ 783-784)." 24 N.Y.2d, at 200, 299 N.Y.2d, at 417-418, 247 N.E.2d, at 255-256. The court said further: "The delinquency status is not made a crime; and the proceedings are not criminal. There is, hence, no deprivation of due process in the statutory provision [challenged by appellant] * * *." 24 N.Y.2d, at 203, 299 N.Y.S.2d, at 420, 247 N.E.2d, at 257. In effect the Court of Appeals distinguished the proceedings in question here from a criminal prosecution by use of what *Gault* called the "civil' label-of-convenience which has been attached to juvenile proceedings." 387 U.S., at 50, 87 S. Ct., at 1455. But *Gault* expressly rejected that distinction as a reason for holding the Due Process Clause inapplicable to a juvenile proceeding. The Court of Appeals also attempted to justify the preponderance standard on the related ground that juvenile proceedings are designed "not to punish, but to save the child." Again, however, *Gault* expressly rejected this justification. We made clear in that decision that civil labels and good intentions do not themselves obviate the need for criminal due process safeguards in juvenile courts, for "[a] proceeding where the issue is whether the child will be found to be delinquent' and subjected to the loss of his liberty for years is comparable in seriousness to a felony prosecution."

Nor do we perceive any merit in the argument that to afford juveniles the protection of proof beyond a reasonable doubt would risk destruction of beneficial aspects of the juvenile process. Use of the reasonable-doubt standard during the adjudicatory hearing will not disturb New York's policies that a finding that a child has violated a criminal law does not constitute a criminal conviction, that such a finding does not deprive the child of his civil rights, and that juvenile proceedings are confidential. Nor will there be any effect on the informality, flexibility, or speed of the hearing at which the factfinding takes place. And the opportunity during the post-adjudicatory or dispositional hearing for a wide-ranging review of the child's social history and for his individualized treatment will remain unimpaired. Similarly, there will be no effect on the procedures distinctive to juvenile proceedings that are employed prior to the adjudicatory hearing.

The Court of Appeals observed that "a child's best interest is not necessarily, or even probably, promoted if he wins in the particular inquiry which may bring him to the juvenile court." It is true, of course, that the juvenile may be engaging in a general course of conduct inimical to his welfare that calls for judicial intervention. But that intervention cannot take the form of subjecting the child to the stigma of a finding that he violated a criminal law and to the possibility of institutional confinement on proof insufficient to convict him were he an adult.

We conclude, as we concluded regarding the essential due process safeguards applied in *Gault,* that the observance of the standard of proof beyond a reasonable doubt "will not compel the States to abandon or displace any of the substantive benefits of the juvenile process."

Finally, we reject the Court of Appeals' suggestion that there is, in any even, only a "tenuous difference" between the reasonable-doubt and preponderance standards. The suggestion is singularly unpersuasive. In this very case, the trial judge's ability to distinguish between the two standards enabled him to make a finding of guilt

that he conceded he might not have made under the standard of proof beyond a reasonable doubt. Indeed, the trial judge's action evidences the accuracy of the observation of commentators that "the preponderance test is susceptible to the misinterpretation that it calls on the trier of fact merely to perform an abstract weighing of the evidence in order to determine which side has produced the greater quantum, without regard to its effect in convincing his mind of the truth of the proposition asserted."

In sum, the constitutional safeguard of proof beyond a reasonable doubt is as much required during the adjudicatory stage of a delinquency proceeding as are those constitutional safeguards applied in *Gault*—notice of charges, right to counsel, the rights of confrontation and examination and the privilege against self-incrimination. We therefore hold, in agreement with Chief Judge Fuld in dissent in the Court of Appeals, "that, where a 12-year-old child is charged with an act of stealing which renders him liable to confinement for as long as six years, then, as a matter of due process * * * the case against him must be proved beyond a reasonable doubt."

Reversed.

Concurring and dissenting opinions not included.

Cases relating to Chapter 2
PRINCIPLES OF CRIMINAL LIABILITY

Raymond Lee SUTTON

v.

COMMONWEALTH of Virginia.

Virginia Gray SUTTON

v.

COMMONWEALTH of Virginia.

Supreme Court of Virginia.
Jan. 18, 1985.
324 S.E.2d 665

COCHRAN, Justice.

In a joint trial, the trial court, sitting without a jury, convicted Raymond Lee Sutton and Virginia Gray Sutton, his wife, of the rape of Virginia's 15-year-old niece on July 23, 1982. Virginia was convicted as a principal in the second degree. The court sentenced each to confinement in the penitentiary for 30 years. In separate appeals, consolidated for argument, each contends that the evidence is not sufficient to sustain the conviction.

The prosecutrix, Beverly ____, complained to the authorities in February of 1983. Raymond gave a signed statement admitting that he and Beverly had a sexual relationship after she came to live with him and his wife in 1982 and that he had sexual intercourse with Beverly more than once. The statement was introduced in evidence as an exhibit at trial. We will review the evidence, of course, in the light most favorable to the Commonwealth.

Beverly lived with her parents in North Carolina until they were divorced when she was seven. For the next five years she lived with her mother in Fayetteville. When she was ten, she was raped by a male friend of her mother. She began to drink alcoholic beverages and use drugs. Her mother, no longer able to control her, sent Beverly to live with her father in another location in North Carolina when she was 12. Describing life with her father as "horrible," Beverly said that he beat her "all the time." Beverly, who has had a hearing problem throughout her life, wears a hearing aid and reads lips.

While she was growing up, Beverly often saw her mother's sister, Virginia, and Virginia's husband, Raymond. Beverly corresponded with Virginia during the period 1979-1981 when the Suttons were living in Germany. Raymond, age 44, was an Army sergeant with 12 years of service at the time of trial. The Suttons were aware of Beverly's use of alcohol and drugs; they knew that her father beat her. Beverly testified that she had not used drugs for four years before the trial, except for the use of marijuana on one occasion.

Beverly visited the Suttons for two weeks in December of 1981. During this visit, Virginia told her that before the Suttons went to Germany, Raymond had sexual intercourse with Beverly's sister who was then living with them. Virginia further stated that it would be good for Beverly to have sexual intercourse with Raymond. Virginia, believing that Beverly thought that all men would beat her because her father did so, suggested that she could overcome her fear by going to bed with Raymond. On each of the two occasions that Virginia brought up the subject, Beverly rejected the suggestion.

About two or three in the morning on Christmas Day, 1981, Raymond and Beverly returned home in his van from his landlady's residence. Parking in the driveway, Raymond began kissing and fondling Beverly and even "got [her] down" on the floor of the vehicle. Beverly begged Raymond to leave her alone, and he finally released her. Beverly said she was scared at the time and was also afraid to tell her father what had happened. The next day Raymond informed Virginia of the incident; Virginia advised Beverly that she should have submitted to Raymond, that it would have helped her.

During the December visit, the Suttons talked to Beverly about getting her away from her father because of his mistreatment of her. In May, after her father had administered another beating, Beverly called the Suttons to report the intolerable situation. In July, after the school session was over, the Suttons brought Beverly from her father's home in North Carolina to their home in Newport News. For a week, her older sister also stayed with the Suttons. After her sister left, Ray-

mond tried to get Beverly to go to bed with him. When she refused, he became angry. Subsequently, Raymond and Beverly agreed that, in order to get school clothes and anything she needed, she would have sexual intercourse with him. Her choice was to agree or to return to her father, who would beat her. She did not know where her mother was at that time.

The Suttons and Beverly spent a July weekend in North Carolina. Upon their return on July 18, Raymond again attempted to have sexual intercourse with Beverly; she "begged and begged" until he abandoned the effort. Raymond again became angry. The next day, Virginia charged Beverly with thinking she was "too good to go to bed with" her uncle and warned that if she were not "any better than that," Virginia would take her back to North Carolina. Virginia said that it was Beverly's fault that Raymond was "hurting."

Beverly had observed violence in the Suttons' home. She saw Virginia and Raymond hit each other during arguments. She once saw Raymond strike his stepson in the face, causing him to bleed. Beverly believed the Suttons when they said that since they had custody of her, they could punish her for anything she did of which they disapproved.

On July 22, the Suttons took Beverly to get birth control pills for which the Suttons paid. The next night, Beverly went to bed early. Raymond came into her bedroom, waked her, began to talk, and fondled her breasts and vaginal area. She repeatedly begged him to leave her alone, but he would not do so. His voice rose as he became angry. She was frightened when he began to fondle her again. She testified, "I was so scared, I didn't push him away, and I didn't say anything except to please stop." She was afraid that either the Suttons would send her back to North Carolina or Raymond might become so angry that he would beat her. She could not fight him off, she was too scared to move. Raymond forced himself on her. She thought he was "mad" at her and was afraid that he would hit her, so they had sexual intercourse. Their earlier agreement to have sexual relations "never crossed" her mind. She recorded in her diary that she and Raymond "made love" on July 23.

After this first incident, Raymond and Beverly had sexual intercourse a number of times. Beverly said she was afraid not to comply. Virginia expressed the desire to see her husband have intercourse with her niece; accordingly, on two occasions, all three were in the same bed when the act occurred.

Several months later, Raymond asked Beverly to try to get her friend Teresa to go to bed with him. Beverly then revealed to Teresa and Beth, another friend, what had transpired between Raymond and herself. Teresa testified that Beverly was upset, that she said she had been abused but was afraid to tell anyone about it. With the encouragement of Teresa, Teresa's mother, and Beth, Beverly went to the school guidance counselor and to the police and made a full report.

Raymond, testifying in his own behalf, acknowledged that he and his wife believed Beverly when she told them that her father beat her and she was afraid of him. When Raymond first asked Beverly to have sexual relations with him in July she refused. He asked her again "to see whether she had changed her mind." Raymond, conceding that he wanted to have sex with her, said he agreed that he would make sure she would not have to return to her father if she submitted. He admitted that he first had sexual intercourse with her on July 23. Raymond denied ever threatening, assaulting, coercing, or intimidating Beverly. He admitted that he gave her the money to buy birth control pills. He also admitted that he had discussed with Virginia more than once his desire to have sex with Beverly and that on two occasions Virginia was on the bed with him when he was having sexual intercourse with Beverly.

1. Raymond Lee Sutton

Prior to its amendment in 1981, Code § 18.2-61 (Repl.Vol. 1975) provided punishment for any person who shall "carnally know a female of 13 years of age or more against her will, by force."

Code § 18.2-61 (Repl.Vol. 1982), as amended (Acts 1981, c. 397), provides in pertinent part as follows:

If any person has sexual intercourse with a female or causes a female to engage in sexual intercourse with any person and such act is accomplished (i) against her will, by force, threat, or intimidation..., he or she shall, in the discretion of the court or jury, be punished with confinement in the penitentiary for life or for any term not less than five years.

In substituting the words "sexual intercourse" for "carnally know" the General Assembly made no change in meaning. But the definition of rape was significantly enlarged. Under the statute prior to amendment, it was necessary to prove sexual intercourse against the victim's will "by force." Under the amended statute it is sufficient to prove sexual intercourse against the victim's will "by force, threat or intimidation."...

The evidence shows that an atmosphere of fear was developed and maintained by the Suttons to intimidate this 15-year-old physically handicapped girl and that her fear of bodily harm was reasonable. We hold that the evidence is sufficient to affirm Raymond's conviction of rape.

2. Virginia Gray Sutton

Virginia Sutton was convicted of rape as a principal in the second degree. Principals in the second degree and accessories before the fact may be indicted, tried, convicted, and punished as principals in the first degree. Code § 18.2-18; *Riddick v. Commonwealth*, 226 Va. 244, 248, 308 S.E.2d 117, 119 (1983). To sustain Virginia's conviction as a principal in the second degree, it must be established that the offense was committed by Raymond as principal in the first degree. *See Sult v. Commonwealth*, 221 Va. 915, 918, 275 S.E.2d 608, 609 (1981). But the fact that she is incapable of committing the offense as a principal in the first degree does not absolve her of criminal liability for aiding and abetting Raymond in commission of the offense. *See Adkins v. Commonwealth*, 175 Va. 590, 600-01, 9 S.E.2d 349, 353 (1940).

To establish Virginia as a principal in the second degree, the Commonwealth was required to prove that she was present, either actually or constructively, when the rape was committed. *See Spradlin v. Commonwealth*, 195 Va. 523, 526, 79 S.E.2d 443, 445 (1954); *Foster v. Commonwealth*, 179 Va. 96, 99, 18 S.E.2d 314, 315 (1942). Presence alone, however, is not sufficient to make Virginia a principal in the second degree. It must also be established that she procured, encouraged, countenanced, or approved Raymond's commission of the crime; she must have shared his criminal intent or have committed some overt act in furtherance of the offense. *See Augustine v. Commonwealth*, 226 Va. 120, 124, 306 S.E.2d 886, 888-89 (1983); *Hall v. Commonwealth*, 225 Va. 533, 536, 303 S.E.2d 903, 904 (1983). Virginia Sutton's actions meet these requirements for a principal in the second degree to rape as that crime is now defined by Code § 18.2-61.

The trial judge found, from undisputed evidence, that Virginia solicited Beverly to have sexual intercourse with Raymond. The judge also found that both Virginia and Raymond knew that Beverly was afraid to go back to her father. By preying on that fear, Virginia applied relentless pressure on Beverly to submit to Raymond. Shortly before July 23, Virginia reproached Beverly for refusing to submit to Raymond and threatened to return her to her father if she maintained the attitude that she was "too good to go to bed with [her] uncle." On July 22, Virginia and Raymond took Beverly to get birth control pills and paid for the purchase. When Raymond and Beverly had intercourse the following night, Beverly testified, she was afraid that Virginia would send her back to North Carolina.

During the rape, Virginia was not physically present but was in bed in another room. Nevertheless, her malevolent, intimidating influence on her niece was present and continued unabated. This evidence is sufficient to establish Virginia's constructive presence during the commission of the crime. Long ago, this Court said in *Dull's Case*, 66 Va. (25 Gratt.) 965, 977, (1875), of constructive presence:

the presence need not be a strict, actual, immediate presence, such a presence as would make [the defendant] an eye or ear witness of what passes, but may be a constructive presence. So that if several persons set out together... upon one common design, be it murder or other felony, or for any other purpose unlawful in itself, and each takes the part assigned him;... they are all, provided the fact be committed, in the eyes of the law, present at it. ... (quoting 1 Russell on Crimes 27 (3d ed. 1845)).

In this case, Virginia and Raymond discussed Raymond's desire to have intercourse with Beverly and Beverly's resistance. They embarked on a common purpose of inducing Beverly by intimidation to submit to Raymond's advances. Virginia's part in the scheme was to so overcome Beverly with the prospect of returning to North Carolina and a life of physical abuse that she would no longer refuse Raymond's demands. By her reprimands of Beverly and her warning about the consequences of continued resistance, Virginia executed her part in the crime and helped ensure the success of their common enterprise.

The evidence also adequately establishes that Virginia shared Raymond's criminal intent and committed overt acts in furtherance of the crime. She and Raymond were determined to have Beverly submit. They knew her fear of her father and could have intended no less than to coerce her submission by their threat to return her to him. Virginia contends that she did no more than encourage Beverly to consent, but the very nature of the inducements she used contradicts this argument. She did more than urge consent when, by stating the alternative, she placed Bev-

erly in the untenable position of submitting against her will or risking physical injury at her father's hand. Coerced submission is not consent, and Virginia's purpose was to achieve such submission. Her motive, showing the depths of her depravity, is revealed in her determination to see her husband and her niece engage in sexual intercourse so that she could help Beverly improve her technique.

Nor can Virginia argue that statements she made several days prior to the rape incident were too removed to constitute intimidation during the crime. The threat of being sent home was an ongoing force in a series of repeated confrontations with Raymond. The warning was not limited to one specific encounter but was intended to, and in fact did, induce submission to a continuing sexual relationship. As such it was sufficiently close to the events of July 23 to instill fear in Beverly and induce her submission. Because she procured, encouraged, countenanced, and approved Raymond's having sexual intercourse with Beverly against her will by intimidation, the trial court properly found her guilty of rape as a principal in the second degree.

Accordingly, we will affirm both convictions.

Affirmed as to Record No. 831787.

Affirmed as to Record No. 831788.

POFF, J., concurring.
STEPHENSON, J., dissenting in Record No. 831788.
COMPTON, J., joins in dissent.
Dissenting opinions not included.

Lawrence ROBINSON, Appellant,
v.
State of CALIFORNIA
370 U.S. 660, 8 L.Ed.2d 758, 82 S.Ct. 1417
Decided June 25, 1962.

Mr. Justice STEWART delivered the opinion of the Court.

A California statute makes it a criminal offense for a person to "be addicted to the use of narcotics." This appeal draws into question the constitutionality of that provision of the state law, as construed by the California courts in the present case.

The appellant was convicted after a jury trial in the Municipal Court of Los Angeles. The evidence against him was given by two Los Angeles police officers. Officer Brown testified that he had had occasion to examine the appellant's arms one evening on a street in Los Angeles some four months before the trial. The officer testified that at that time he had observed "scar tissue and discoloration on the inside" of the appellant's right arm, and "what appeared to be numerous needle marks and a scab which was approximately three inches below the crook of the elbow" on the appellant's left arm. The officer also testified that the appellant under questioning had admitted to the occasional use of narcotics.

Officer Lindquist testified that he had examined the appellant the following morning in the Central Jail in Los Angeles. The officer stated that at the time he had observed discolorations and scabs on the appellant's arms, and he identified photographs which had been taken of the appellant's arms shortly after his arrest the night before. Based upon more than ten years of experience as a member of the Narcotic Division of the Los Angeles Police Department, the witness gave his opinion that "these marks and the discoloration were the result of the injection of hypodermic needles into the tissue into the vein that was not sterile." He stated that the scabs were several days old at the time of his examination, and that the appellant was neither under the influence of narcotics nor suffering withdrawal symptoms at the time he saw him. This witness also testified that the appellant had admitted using narcotics in the past.

The appellant testified in his own behalf, denying the alleged conversations with the police officers and denying that he had ever used narcotics or been addicted to their use. He explained the marks on his arm as resulting from an allergic condition contracted during his military service. His testimony was corroborated by two witnesses.

The trial judge instructed the jury that the statute made it a misdemeanor for a person "either to use narcotics, or to be addicted to the use of narcotics * * *. That portion of the statute referring to the 'use' of narcotics is based upon the 'act' of using. That portion of the statute referring to 'addicted to the use' of narcotics is based upon a condition or status. They are not identical. * * * To be addicted to the use of narcotics is said to be a status or condition and not an act. It is a continuing offense and differs from most other offenses in the fact that [it] is chronic rather than acute; that it continues after it is complete and subjects the offender to arrest at any time before he reforms. The existence of such a chronic condition may be ascertained from a single examination, if the characteristic reactions of that condition be found present."

The judge further instructed the jury that the appellant could be convicted under a general verdict if the jury agreed *either* that he was of the "status" *or* had committed the "act" denounced by the statute. "All that the People must show is either that the defendant did use a narcotic in Los Angeles County, or that while in the City of Los Angeles he was addicted to the use of narcotics * * *."

Under these instructions the jury returned a verdict finding the appellant "guilty of the offense charged." An appeal was taken to the Appellate Department of the Los Angeles County Superior Court, "the highest court of a State in which a decision could be had" in this case. Although expressing some doubt as to the constitutionality of "the crime of being a narcotic addict," the reviewing court in an unreported opinion affirmed the judgment of conviction, citing two of its own previous unreported decisions which had upheld the constitutionality of the statute. We noted probable jurisdiction of this appeal, 368 U.S. 918, 82 S.Ct. 244, 7 L.Ed.2d 133, because it squarely presents the issue whether the statute as construed by the California courts in this case is repugnant to the Fourteenth Amendment of the Constitution.

The broad power of a State to regulate the narcotic drugs traffic within its borders is not here in issue. More than 40 years ago, in *Whipple v. Martinson,* this Court explicitly recognized the validity of that power: "There can be no question of the authority of the state in the exercise of its police power to regulate the administration, sale, pre-

scription and use of dangerous and habit-forming drugs * * *. The right to exercise this power is so manifest in the interest of the public health and welfare, that it is unnecessary to enter upon a discussion of it beyond saying that it is too firmly established to be successfully called in question." 256 U.S. at 45, 41 S.Ct. at 426.

Such regulation, it can be assumed, could take a variety of valid forms. A State might impose criminal sanctions, for example, against the unauthorized manufacture, prescription, sale, purchase, or possession of narcotics within its borders. In the interest of discouraging the violation of such laws, or in the interest of the general health or welfare of its inhabitants, a State might establish a program of compulsory treatment for those addicted to narcotics. Such a program of treatment might require periods of involuntary confinement. And penal sanctions might be imposed for failure to comply with established compulsory treatment procedures. Or a State might choose to attack the evils of narcotics traffic on broader fronts also—through public health education, for example, or by efforts to ameliorate the economic and social conditions under which those evils might be thought to flourish. In short, the range of valid choice which a State might make in this area is undoubtedly a wide one, and the wisdom of any particular choice within the allowable spectrum is not for us to decide. Upon that premise we turn to the California law in issue here.

It would be possible to construe the statute under which the appellant was convicted as one which is operative only upon proof of the actual use of narcotics within the State's jurisdiction. But the California courts have not so construed this law. Although there was evidence in the present case that the appellant had used narcotics in Los Angeles, the jury was instructed that they could convict him even if they disbelieved that evidence. The appellant could be convicted, they were told, if they found simply that the appellant's "status" or "chronic condition" was that of being "addicted to the use of narcotics." And it is impossible to know from the jury's verdict that the defendant was not convicted upon precisely such a finding.

The instructions of the trial court, implicitly approved on appeal, amounted to "a ruling on a question of state law that is as binding on us as though the precise words had been written" into the statute. *Terminiello v. Chicago* 337 U.S. 1, 4, 69 S.Ct. 894, 895, 93 L.Ed. 1131. "We can only take the statute as the state courts read it." *Id.*, at 6, 69 S.Ct. at 896. Indeed, in their brief in this Court counsel for the State have emphasized that it is "the proof of addiction by circumstantial evidence * * * by the tell-tale track of needle marks and scabs over the veins of his arms, that remains the gist of the section."

This statute, therefore, is not one which punishes a person for the use of narcotics, for their purchase, sale or possession, or for antisocial or disorderly behavior resulting from their administration. It is not a law which even purports to provide or require medical treatment. Rather, we deal with a statute which makes the "status" of narcotic addiction a criminal offense, for which the offender may be prosecuted "at any time before he reforms." California has said that a person can be continuously guilty of this offense, whether or not he has ever used or possessed any narcotics within the State, and whether or not he has been guilty of any antisocial behavior there.

It is unlikely that any State at this moment in history would attempt to make it a criminal offense for a person to be mentally ill, or a leper, or to be afflicted with a venereal disease. A State might determine that the general health and welfare require that the victims of these and other human afflictions be dealt with by compulsory treatment, involving quarantine, confinement, or sequestration. But, in the light of contemporary human knowledge, a law which made a criminal offense of such a disease would doubtless be universally thought to be an infliction of cruel and unusual punishment in violation of the Eighth and Fourteenth Amendments.

We cannot but consider the statute before us as of the same category. In this Court counsel for the State recognized that narcotic addiction is an illness. Indeed, it is apparently an illness which may be contracted innocently or involuntarily. We hold that a state law which imprisons a person thus afflicted as a criminal, even though he has never touched any narcotic drug within the State or been guilty of any irregular behavior there, inflicts a cruel and unusual punishment in violation of the Fourteenth Amendment. To be sure, imprisonment for 90 days is not, in the abstract, a punishment which is either cruel or unusual. But the question cannot be considered in the abstract. Even one day in prison would be a cruel and unusual punishment for the "crime" of having a common cold.

We are not unmindful that the vicious evils of the narcotics traffic have occasioned the grave concern of government. There are, as we have said, countless fronts on which those evils may be legitimately attacked. We deal in this case only with an individual provision of a particularized local law as it has so far been interpreted by the California courts.

Reversed.

Concurring and dissenting opinions not included.

UNITED STATES of America, Appellee,
v.
David GUILLETTE and Robert Joost, Appellants
United States Court of Appeals, Second Circuit
547 F.2d 743
Decided Dec. 20, 1976.

KELLEHER, District Judge.

Following a jury trial in the District Court of Connecticut, appellants David Guillette and Robert Joost were convicted of conspiracy to deprive a citizen of his civil rights in violation of 18 U.S.C. § 241 (1970). The jury also found Guillette guilty of using force to influence a federal witness in violation of 18 U.S.C. § 1503 (1970). The convictions result from a concerted government effort, spanning several years and involving numerous trials, to prosecute those persons responsible for the death of Daniel LaPolla, who was scheduled to be a key prosecution witness in a federal firearms case.

The events leading to appellants' conviction began in November 1971 with the burglary of a National Guard Armory in Westerly, Rhode Island, in which 30 automatic rifles were stolen. Two months later LaPolla approached federal agents who had been investigating the burglary and offered information on those responsible for the theft and the whereabouts of the rifles. Based on this and additional information obtained with the help of LaPolla, a Hartford federal grand jury indicted Guillette and Joost, together with William Marrapese and Nicholas Zinni, for interstate transportation of stolen firearms. LaPolla, named as an unin-

dicted co-conspirator by the grand jury, was expected to offer vital testimony incriminating the four defendants in the break-in and subsequent efforts to find a buyer for the rifles. However, on September 29, 1972, just weeks before the firearms trial was to begin, the government lost its key witness when LaPolla was killed as a bomb exploded in his home in Oneco, Connecticut. Following an investigation of the bombing, a federal grand jury in Connecticut returned a three count indictment against Guillette, Joost, Marrapese and Zinni, charging them with conspiracy to deprive LaPolla of his civil rights, viz. the right to testify in a federal prosecution (18 U.S.C. § 241), obstruction of justice by force and violence (18 U.S.C. § 1503), and use of an explosive device in the commission of a felony (18 U.S.C. § 844(h)(1)). Thereafter the prosecution effort went through a series of trials and mistrials, eventually culminating in the verdicts of guilty obtained against appellants in their third trial. Appellants' initial trial, which had been severed from that of the other defendants, resulted in guilty verdicts against both defendants on all counts, but the convictions were reversed and a new trial ordered after a key government witness, John Housand, recanted admittedly perjurious testimony he gave during the trial.

Prior to commencement of appellants' second trial, Marrapese, who had been convicted of all three counts in a separate trial, agreed to cooperate with the government and testify against his co-conspirators. The second trial, however, resulted in no convictions; the jury acquitted Joost of counts 2 and 3 of the indictment and was unable to reach a verdict on the first count against him and on all three counts against Guillette. At the third trial, with the aid of Marrapese's testimony, the government was successful in obtaining guilty verdicts against Guillette for conspiracy and obstruction of justice through use of force and a guilty verdict against Joost for conspiracy. Both defendants timely prosecuted this appeal of their respective convictions.

The evidence offered by Housand in the first trial and Marrapese in the second and third trials principally established the prosecution's version of the alleged conspiracy to silence LaPolla as a witness in the firearms prosecution. According to their testimony, the conspiracy commenced with Guillette and Joost, together with Marrapese, Bucci and Housand, met following their arrests for the theft of the automatic rifles to consider the upcoming prosecution (May 8 meeting). During the course of this meeting, Housand was offered $5,000 to kill LaPolla, who by this time had been earmarked by the group as an informant. Upon further reflection, however, the group thought it ill-advised to carry through with these plans until an assessment of the strengths of the government's case and defendants' chances for acquittal could be made. Thereafter the conspiracy evolved into a plan to find LaPolla and use bribery and physical coercion to dissuade him from testifying. Because LaPolla was being held in protective custody, however, Marrapese was unable to locate him for the purpose of effectuating the revised scheme.

After several months of futile searching had passed, according to Marrapese's testimony, Guillette informed him that unless LaPolla were found soon and persuaded to cooperate, they would have to "dump" him. Marrapese, Joost and Guillette subsequently intensified their search. They conducted continuous surveillance of LaPolla's home in Oneco, Connecticut, even to the point of hiring a pilot to fly aerial photo-reconnaissance over the house and surrounding area. To disguise the purpose of the flights, Guillette told the pilot that he was searching for a man in order to serve a summons on him. Later on Guillette and Joost, together with other members of the group, attended funeral services for LaPolla's brother in hopes of finding LaPolla present, but were turned away by federal agents. Finally, on September 29, the day of LaPolla's death, Guillette confided in Marrapese that he had "just left a package for your buddy up there." That afternoon LaPolla, ignoring instructions to stay away from his residence, drove home and leaving the car running in the driveway opened the front door of his house, touching off a massive explosion which killed LaPolla instantly.

Appellants set forth numerous grounds for reversal of their convictions, but we find it necessary to address in detail only the more substantial questions. Initially, we note that appellants' contention that the trial court did not have jurisdiction to entertain the prosecution under 18 U.S.C. § 241 is without merit. Section 241 makes it a crime for two or more persons to conspire to "injure, oppress, threaten, or intimidate any citizen in the free exercise or enjoyment of any right or privilege secured to him by the Constitution...." This Court in *United States v. Pacelli,* 491 F.2d 1108, 1113-15 (2d Cir. 1974), *cert. denied,* 419 U.S. 826, 95 S.Ct. 43, 42 L.Ed.2d. 49 (1974) held unequivocally that the right to be a witness in a federal trial is a civil right secured by the Constitution and protected from infringement or deprivation by § 241. Since appellants have presented nothing to this Court to indicate that *Pacelli* does not control the facts of the case at bar, we adhere to our holding in that decision and proceed to consider their other contentions.

Jury Instructions

Appellants interpose three grounds of error with respect to jury instructions which were and were not given during trial: (1) the trial court erred in refusing to instruct the jury that if it found that LaPolla's death resulted from his accidental detonation of a bomb that he himself planted, it could not find the defendants guilty of a § 241 conspiracy with death resulting; (2) supplemental instructions did not properly advise the jury of the requisite elements of culpable participation in a conspiracy; and (3) the trial court erred in failing to give defendants' requested alibi instruction.

At all three trials appellants argued that LaPolla was killed when he accidentally detonated a bomb which he himself installed as a booby trap aimed at defendants and others who were searching for him. Relying upon this theory, appellants requested a jury instruction that if the jury were to find that the death was accidental or if the jury was not persuaded beyond a reasonable doubt that death was deliberate, defendants could not be found guilty of conspiracy with death resulting. Section 241 provides that a sentence of life imprisonment may be imposed "if death results" from a prohibited conspiracy, whereas a simple conspiracy not resulting in death is punishable by a maximum term of ten years. Because both appellants received sentences of 25 years on their conspiracy convictions, the denial of the requested jury charge on accidental death played a significant role in the determination of their punishment and raises a substantial question concerning the scope of criminal culpability imposed by § 241.

The trial judge instructed the jury that even if LaPolla died accidentally through his own actions, the defendants would nonetheless be guilty of conspiracy with death resulting if LaPolla's death was "induced or brought about by some act of a conspiracy in furtherance of the purposes of a conspiracy." The crucial portion of the Court's instruction on the effect of accidental death follows:

Death results from the conspiracy charged in the indictment if it was caused by an act of one or more of the conspirators in furtherance of the purpose of the conspiracy.

Death, whether accidental or intentional, does not result from the conspiracy if caused by LaPolla's own act, unrelated to the conspiracy or its purposes provided the death was not induced or brought about by some act of a conspirator in furtherance of the purposes of the conspiracy. Likewise, death, whether accidental or intentional, does not result from the conspiracy if caused by the acts of any person who was not a member of the conspiracy or even if it were caused by a member of the conspiracy but not in furtherance of its purpose or within the scope of the conspiracy.

A fundamental principle of criminal law is that a person is held responsible for all consequences proximately caused by his criminal conduct. The concept of proximate cause incorporates the notion that an accused may be charged with a criminal offense even though his acts were not the immediate cause of the victim's death or injury. *See generally* 40 C.J.S. Homicide § 11, at 854. In many situations giving rise to criminal liability, the death or injury is not directly caused by the acts of the defendant but rather results from intervening forces or events, such as negligent medical treatment, escape attempts, or the negligent or intentional acts of a third party. Where such intervening events are foreseeable and naturally result from a perpetrator's criminal conduct, the law considers the chain of legal causation unbroken and holds the perpetrator criminally responsible for the resulting harm. *See, e.g., State v. Schaub,* 231 Minn. 512, 44 N.W.2d 61, 63-64 (1950) (intervening act of third party); *People v. McGee,* 31 Cal.2d 229, 187 P.2d 706, 712-13 (1947) negligent medical treatment); *Whiteside v. State,* 115 Tex.Cr. 274, 29 S.W.2d 399, 401-02 (Crim.App. 1930) (escape attempt). This principle applies even where the direct cause of death is a force set in motion by the victim himself. For example, if a person acting on a well grounded and reasonable fear of death or bodily injury induced by an accused's threats or actual assaults, dies in an attempt to extricate himself from the danger, the accused bears criminal liability for the death. See *People v. Smith,* 56 Ill.2d 328, 307 N.E.2d 353, 355 (1974); *State v. Myers,* 7 N.J. 465, 81 A.2d 710, 715 (1951); *Whaley v. State,* 157 Fla. 593, 26 So.2d 656, 658 (1946). Thus under the common law even if LaPolla died

from an explosion that he himself had accidentally caused, appellants would still be considered in the chain of legal causation if the immediate cause of death—setting a bomb as a booby trap—was a foreseeable protective reaction to their criminal efforts to locate and dissuade him from testifying.

We find the principle of proximate cause embodied in § 241 through the phrase "if death results." Section 241 derives from one of the earliest pieces of civil rights legislation enacted by the Congress and was designed to protect persons in the free and uninhibited exercise of their individual liberties. Throughout its long history it has been invoked to redress infringements of such important constitutional rights as the right to vote, *Anderson v. United States,* 417 U.S. 211, 94 S.Ct. 2253, 41 L.Ed.2d 20 (1974), the right to equality in public accommodations, *United States v. Johnson,* 390 U.S. 563, 88 S.Ct. 1231, 20 L.Ed.2d 132 (1968), the right to travel interstate, *United States v. Guest,* 383 U.S. 745, 86 S.Ct. 1170, 16 L.Ed.2d 239 (1966), the rights secured by the Fourteenth Amendment, *United States v. Guest, supra; United States v. Price,* 383 U.S. 787, 86 S.Ct. 1152, 16 L.Ed.2d 267 (1966). Enacted as a purely criminal statutory provision, its purpose would be frustrated by any artificial restrictions placed on its scope. When the Congress provided that a conspiracy to violate a citizen's civil rights may be punished by life imprisonment if death results, we must consider it to have been fully cognizant of the principles of legal causation discussed above. The accepted practice among federal courts in construing a federal criminal statute which uses a common law term without defining it is to give the term its common law meaning. *See United States v. Turley,* 352 U.S. 407,

77 S.Ct. 397, 1 L.Ed.2d 430 (1957); *United States v. Bell,* 505 F.2d 539 (7th Cir. 1974), *cert. denied,* 420 U.S. 964, 95 S.Ct. 1357, 43 L.Ed.2d 442 (1975). To confine the meaning of "result" to direct causation not only would be at odds with common law principles of legal causation but also would seriously impair the effectiveness of § 241. The more severe punishment prescribed for those conspiracies resulting in death was designed to deter the type of conduct that creates a risk of loss of life or serious bodily injury. Construing the statute as requiring only direct causation would merely encourage those bent on depriving others of their constitutional rights to devise round-about but potentially dangerous means of achieving their ends. Consequently, appellants were not entitled to their requested jury charges, and the one given by the trial judge, considered in its entirety, was sufficient to convey to the jury the legal principles governing the offense charged.

With respect to the trial court's supplemental instruction to the jury on the requisite elements of culpable participation in a conspiracy, appellants complain that the instruction failed properly to advise the jury that mere knowledge of or acquiescence in the conspiracy is not a sufficient basis for a finding of guilt. In considering objections of this sort, appellate courts must view the contested jury instructions in the context of the total charge; isolated improper comments by the trial judge do not compel reversal if the instruction is otherwise correct and nonprejudicial. *See Cupp v. Naughten,* 414 U.S. 141, 146-47, 94 S.Ct. 396, 38 L.Ed.2d 368 (1973); *United States v. Malizia,* 503 F.2d 578, 583 (2d Cir. 1974), *cert. denied,* 420 U.S. 912, 95 S.Ct. 834, 42 L.Ed.2d 843 (1975).

Having reviewed the supplemental instruction as well as the main charge on participation in a conspiracy, we are convinced the jury was properly informed that it could not consider appellants members of the conspiracy unless it found that they affirmatively joined it and promoted its objectives. In response to the jury's request for a clarification of the elements of culpable participation in a conspiracy, the trial court noted a co-conspirator "must in some way indicate or show that he is going along with this (conspiracy), that he is in on it, that he is a part of this arrangement, that he adopts this plan as his own and that he is going to promote it...as his own, and that he has a stake in its outcome." This charge more than adequately conveyed to the jury that mere knowledge is not sufficient, that before it could find either of the appellants a member of the conspiracy it must be convinced of his affirmative embracing of the unlawful objectives and his intent to achieve those objectives.

At trial both Guillette and Joost specifically denied that they were present at the crucial May 8 meeting at which the plan to kill LaPolla purportedly was devised and introduced testimony of a number of alibi witnesses to corroborate their stories. Based on this evidence, they jointly requested that the jury be instructed to return a verdict of not guilty on the conspiracy count if the jurors had a reasonable doubt as to whether appellants did attend the meeting. Appellants now contend the trial court's failure to so instruct was reversible error.

The May 8 meeting unquestionably was an important element in the prosecution's case, and the alibi testimony offered by Joost and Guillette cast genuine doubt on the credibility of Marrapese, who was the sole witness testifying to appellants' presence at the meeting. However, appellants were convicted of a conspiracy which encompassed several months and numerous acts undertaken to further its unlawful end, of which the May 8 meeting was only one. The gist of a conspiracy is an agreement among conspirators to commit an offense accompanied by an overt act in furtherance of its purpose. *United States v. Falcone*, 311 U.S. 205, 61 S.Ct. 204, 85 L.Ed. 128 (1940). A defendant need not be a member of the conspiracy from its inception but may join later and incur liability for the conspiracy's unlawful acts committed both before and after his adoption of the conspiracy. *See United States v. Dardi*, 330 F.2d 316 (2d Cir.), *cert. denied*, 379 U.S. 845, 85 S.Ct. 50, 13 L.Ed.2d 50 (1964). Thus even if the jury did not believe Marrapese's testimony that Guillette and Joost were present at the May 8 meeting, there was other evidence sufficient to support a finding of appellants' membership in the conspiracy.

Appellants place great reliance on this Court's recent decision in *United States v. Burse*, 531 F.2d 1151 (2d Cir. 1976), which considered the proper instruction to a jury on an alibi defense in a conspiracy prosecution, but a close reading of that opinion reveals that the reliance is misplaced. In that decision we held that failure to caution a jury against considering disbelieved alibi testimony as evidence of a defendant's guilt constituted reversible error where such an instruction was requested, and the evidence against the defendant was not overwhelming, and the prosecution's conspiracy theory rested heavily on defendant's presence at the scene of the substantive crime. In so holding the Court sought to safeguard defendants from a danger likely to arise when

jurors, untrained in the law, disbelieve alibi testimony and are inclined to view the failure of the defense as a sign of the defendant's guilt.

The instruction requested by appellants in the case at bar, however, differs in a significant respect from the one we thought appropriate in *Burse*. The charge sought by appellants, while reminding the jury of the government's burden in light of the alibi defense, principally advanced the proposition that the jury must return a verdict of not guilty on the conspiracy charge if it was not convinced beyond a reasonable doubt that Guillette and Joost attended the May 8 meeting. As noted earlier, since the offense charged was conspiracy, the government was not required to prove appellants' attendance at the May 8 meeting beyond a reasonable doubt and thus the trial court did not err in refusing to so instruct the jury. The alibi, if believed by the jury, established no more than that appellants did not participate in one of numerous overt acts of the conspiracy.

In light of the misleading alibi instruction proposed by appellants and the other evidence on the record indicating their participation in the conspiracy, we view the trial court's failure to caution the jury on the government's unchanging burden of proof as harmless error. The requested instruction was neither in writing nor a proper statement of the controlling law. *See United States v. Coughlin*, 514 F.2d 904, 907 (2d Cir. 1975). The alibi testimony itself, the reliability of which was subject to some doubt, was less than overwhelming in comparison to Marrapese's account, and the jury was thoroughly instructed that the government must establish every element of the crime beyond a reasonable doubt. *See United States v. Cole*, 453 F.2d 902, 906 (8th Cir. 1972); *United*

States v. Erlenbaugh, 452 F.2d 967, 975 (7th Cir. 1971), aff'd on other grounds, 409 U.S. 239, 93 S.Ct. 477, 34 L.Ed.2d 446 (1972). Moreover, attendance at the May 8 meeting was not an essential element of the crime, and thus an alibi would not have been a total defense. See United States v. Lee, 483 F.2d 968, 970 (5th Cir. 1973).

Validity of Indictment

* * *

Exclusion of Souca Confession

The trial court refused to admit testimony of a government informant that he had been told by one Anthony Souca that he was the one who killed LaPolla. Despite considerable efforts, the government was not able to locate Souca in order to verify the informant's account. Appellants argue that the trial court committed prejudicial error in refusing to order the prosecution to produce the informant for the purpose of offering trial testimony on Souca's alleged confession or at least to admit into evidence the transcript of an earlier in camera examination of the informant in which details of the confession were given.

The admissibility into evidence of hearsay statements against penal interest is controlled by Federal Rule of Evidence 804(b)(3) which was in effect at the time of trial. Rule 804(b)(3), in providing that "a statement tending to expose the declarant to criminal liability and offering to exculpate the accused is not admissible unless corroborating circumstances clearly indicate the trustworthiness of the statement," significantly departs from a prior rule in the federal system barring the use of such hearsay declarations that had stood since its inception in Donnelly v. United States, 228 U.S. 243, 33 S.Ct. 449, 57 L.Ed. 820

(1913). The significant change, of course, is that now declarations against penal interest are deemed an exception to the hearsay rule and subject to admission as such if there is sufficient corroborating evidence to indicate their trustworthiness. The requirement of corroboration was written into the Rule to guard against the inherent danger that third party confessions tending to exculpate a defendant are the result of fabrication. See Advisory Comm. Notes, Fed.R.Evid. 804(b)(3). And the possibility of fabrication, of course, is only enhanced when the hearsay declarant is not available for examination at the trial.

The determination whether corroborating circumstances clearly indicate the trustworthiness of a third party confession lies within the sound discretion of the trial court, which is aptly situated to weigh the reliability of the circumstances surrounding the declaration, and this Court will review the exclusion of the Souca confession only for an abuse of discretion. To guide our review we turn to the Supreme Court's decision in Chambers v. Mississippi 410 U.S. 284, 93 S.Ct. 1038, 35 L.Ed.2d 297 (1975), which sets forth four general considerations relevant to an investigation of the trustworthiness of third party confessions. 410 U.S. at 300-01, 93 S.Ct. 1038.

(1) the time of the declaration and the party to whom the declaration was made.

(2) the existence of corroborating evidence in the case.

(3) the extent to which the declaration is really against the declarant's penal interest.

(4) the availability of the declarant as a witness.

See also United States v. Wingate, 520 F.2d 309, 316 (2d Cir. 1975), cert.

denied, 423 U.S. 1074, 96 S.Ct. 858, 47 L.Ed.2d 84 (1976). While these considerations are not exhaustive and absolute, they do suggest the nature of an appropriate inquiry by a district court faced with the proffer of a third party confession. Considering the circumstances of Souca's declaration, we are of the view that the trial court did not abuse its discretion in refusing to admit any evidence of the confession. Souca made his incriminating statement some four months after LaPolla's death and to a police informant whom he had just met. By contrast, the declarant in *Chambers* confided in several friends shortly after the murder for which he claimed responsibility. Moreover, Souca made his confession while drinking with the informant, and evidence that Souca had had a number of drinks casts additional doubt on the reliability of his declaration. *See United States v. Sheard,* 154 U.S. App.D.C. 9, 473 F.2d 139, 149 (D.C.Cir.1972), *cert. denied,* 412 U.S. 943, 93 S.Ct. 2784, 37 L.Ed.2d 404 (1973). Souca's account also lacks any significant corroborating evidence. Although there apparently exists in the general vicinity of the alleged meeting a bar fitting the description given by the informant, the record in the case at bar reveals no independent evidence tying Souca to LaPolla's murder, such as reports of eye witnesses placing him in the vicinity of LaPolla's home at the time of the bombing or evidence of efforts to locate LaPolla while he was being held in protective custody. Finally, we note that the government was unable to find Souca and bring him to trial to testify concerning his alleged confession, thus depriving the prosecution of an opportunity to cross-examine him and depriving the jury of the opportunity to view his demeanor and weigh his responses. *See Chambers v. Mississippi,* 410 U.S. at 301, 93 S.Ct. at 1048. Under these circumstances, it was within the trial court's discretion to exclude the informant's testimony.

* * *

...Finally, having reviewed the record in its entirety and considering the evidence in the light most favorable to the government, *Glasser v. United States,* 315 U.S. 60, 80, 62 S.Ct. 457, 86 L.Ed. 680 (1942), we find that it is sufficient to sustain the jury's determination of guilt with respect to both appellants.

Affirmed.

Cases relating to Chapter 3

OFFENSES AGAINST PERSONS (EXCLUDING SEX OFFENSES)

UNITED STATES of America,
Plaintiff-Appellee,

v.

Ronald Glen SHAW,
Defendant-Appellant.

United States Court of Appeals,
Fifth Circuit.
March 15, 1983.
701 F.2d 367 (1983)

Facts

Late Christmas night, 1980, Kenneth Brinkley was driving his automobile down a secluded two-lane highway in the sparsely populated area of Mississippi known as the Natchez Trace Parkway.[1] With him in the car were his son, his fiance, Linda Johnson, and her children, 12-year-old Lachelle and nine-year-old Terrell Johnson. The three children were sleeping in the back seat. While passing the Ballard Creek rest area, Brinkley noticed a parked pickup truck, which appeared to be a dark-colored, red and white late model Ford with chrome trim on the side. Brinkley had seen no other vehicles on the road. Immediately after Brinkley passed the rest area, a rifle shot ripped through the car's back seat. The bullet struck the young Johnson

1. The Natchez Trace Parkway is a federal highway reservation in the Northern District of Mississippi, under the concurrent jurisdiction of Mississippi and the United States.

boy in the legs and hit his sister in the hip.

Brinkley quickly sought help in the nearby town of Mathiston, telling the local police where the shooting had taken place and describing the pickup he had seen in the Ballard Creek rest area immediately prior to the shooting. Relying on this information, three officers proceeded to the Trace Highway about a half mile north of the rest area. After waiting approximately ten or fifteen minutes they saw a late model, two-tone pickup approaching from the south at 35 to 40 miles per hour. Shaw was apprehended in the truck after a chase in which speeds exceeded 110 miles per hour. Shaw was frisked and told his vehicle fit the description of one at the scene of the shooting. He was arrested for speeding and driving while intoxicated, handcuffed, and placed in a patrol car.

After Shaw got out of the truck, one of the officers shined a light through its open door and saw four bullets on the floor on the driver's side. Another officer then released the seat latch and folded back the driver's seat. Behind the seat, fully cocked, was a .35 caliber rifle. Shaw was read his *Miranda* rights and told of the traffic charges. He made no statement to police. Shaw was then driven to the sheriff's office in Ackerman, Mississippi. After he was again read his *Miranda* rights, he indicated that he wished to answer questions. Shaw told the sheriff that he had been "driving around" on the Natchez Trace Highway and stopped at "a pull-off place" because he was sick. He emphatically denied that he had fired his gun since deer hunting that afternoon.

Later that same night young Terrell Johnson died of his wounds. The next day, Friday, December 26, Shaw was questioned by FBI agents. He repeated his story that he did not load or fire his rifle after dark on Christmas Day. That night, a janitor at the hospital discovered in the hospital treatment room the bullet which had struck the two children. Saturday afternoon, December 27, FBI agents interviewed Shaw again. The agents showed Shaw the battered slug, and told him that ballistic tests were going to be performed on the bullet. Shaw then stated that he would answer no more questions without having an attorney present, and the interview was terminated. Shaw's parents were told that a ballistic report would be received by Monday morning, the 29th.

Around 10:30 a.m. Monday, Shaw's parents called one of the agents and said that their son wanted to talk to him. The agent responded that he could not speak to Shaw because Shaw had requested an attorney. The parents insisted, and the FBI agent went to see Shaw in person, accompanied by another agent. At this point, the ballistic report had been received. It indicated conclusively that Shaw's rifle

had been the one to fire the shot. The agents readvised Shaw of his rights. Shaw explained that he, not his parents, wanted the agents to hear the story. The agents had Shaw carefully study a written *Miranda* waiver, which he signed. The agents then agreed to listen to Shaw's story. Shaw said that his earlier statement was false, that on Christmas night he had been "head-lighting deer" from the Pigeon Roost rest stop, and while walking into the woods north of the area he had slipped and fallen, causing his gun to go off as it hit the ground. He saw the car pass, and worried that he had hit it, but because the car seemed to be proceeding normally, he assumed that it had not been hit. He then went back to his truck, waited a few minutes, and began driving on the Trace Highway where he was stopped by the police.

On December 30, the sheriff filed a state complaint for first degree murder of Terrell Johnson. Following appointment of counsel and a preliminary hearing on January 12, 1981, Shaw was bound over to the federal grand jury, and on January 29, indicted.

At the conclusion of trial, the jury found Shaw guilty on all counts. His motions for judgments of acquittal and for a new trial were denied, and he was sentenced to imprisonment for life, plus twenty-one total years for the other offenses. This appeal follows.

I. SEARCH OF VEHICLE

A. *At Time of Apprehension*

Shaw's first contention is that the district court erred in not suppressing as evidence the rifle and shells seized by the officers from his pickup during the initial stop on the night of December 25, 1980.

[1] It is a cardinal principle of Fourth Amendment jurisprudence that searches conducted outside the judicial

process of obtaining a warrant are *per se* unreasonable, except those conducted in a few narrowly defined situations. The exceptional situations are those in which "the societal costs of obtaining a warrant, such as danger to law officers or risk of loss or destruction of evidence, outweigh the interest of recourse to a neutral magistrate." *Arkansas v. Sanders,* 442 U.S. 753, 759, 99 S.Ct. 2586, 2590, 61 L.Ed.2d 235 (1979); *Coolidge v. New Hampshire,* 403 U.S. 443, 455, 91 S.Ct. 2022, 2032, 29 L.Ed.2d 564 (1971). Predicated on this "exigent circumstances" rationale is the so-called "automobile exception," first articulated by the Supreme Court in *Carroll v. United States,* 267 U.S. 132, 45 S.Ct. 280, 69 L.Ed. 543 (1925). In *Carroll,* the Supreme Court held that a warrantless search of an automobile on a highway is not unreasonable within the meaning of the Fourth Amendment so long as the police have probable cause to believe that the "contents of the automobile offend against the law." *Id.* at 159, 45 S.Ct. at 287.

* * *

IV. SUFFICIENCY OF THE EVIDENCE

Shaw next challenges the sufficiency of the evidence to support the jury's verdict of guilty of first degree murder under 18 U.S.C. § 1111. He does not assert that the government failed to prove that he killed Terrell Johnson. The evidence clearly established that he fired the fatal shot. He does argue, however, that the government's evidence is insufficient to support the first degree murder conviction because it failed to establish that he committed the homicide with premeditation.

In determining the sufficiency of the evidence, a court of appeals must view the evidence and all reasonable inferences which may be drawn therefrom, in the light most favorable to the government. *Glasser v. United States,* 315 U.S. 60, 80, 62 S.Ct. 457, 469, 86 L.Ed. 680 (1942). We will affirm if "any rational trier of fact could have found the essential elements of the crime beyond a reasonable doubt."

Section 1111 retains a common law distinction between second degree murder, which requires a killing with malice aforethought, and first degree murder, which in addition to malice aforethought requires a killing with premeditation and deliberation. Although it is clear that deliberation and premeditation under § 1111 involve a prior design to commit murder, no particular period of time is necessary for such deliberation and premeditation. *See United States v. Blue Thunder,* 604 F.2d 550, 553 (8th Cir.) *cert. denied,* 444 U.S. 902, 100 S.Ct. 215, 62 L.Ed.2d 139 (1979)....There must be some appreciable time for reflection and consideration before execution of the act, although the period of time "does not require the lapse of days or hours or even minutes." *Bostic v. United States,* 94 F.2d 636, 638 (D.C.Cir. 1937), *cert. denied,* 303 U.S. 635, 58 S.Ct. 523, 82 L.Ed. 1095 (1938).

The distinction which marks the line between "deliberation" sufficient to support a conviction of first degree murder and the lesser killing with malice which supports conviction of second degree murder is less than clear. Commentators agree that the difference between the two standards is vague and obscure. Perhaps the best that can be said of deliberation is that it requires a "cool mind" that is capable of reflection, and of premeditation that it requires that the one with the "cool mind" did, in fact, reflect, at least for a short period of time before his act of killing. We are aided in our analysis of this element by the specific wording of the federal statute. If the evidence supports a finding that Shaw was "lying in wait," he shall be guilty of murder in the first degree. With these standards in mind, we turn to our consideration of the evidence offered at Shaw's trial.

Brinkley, the driver of the car in which the children were riding, and Mrs. Johnson, the children's mother, both testified that they were certain that the shooting had occurred almost immediately after their car had passed the Ballard Creek rest stop. Both explained that their certainty was due to the fact that Brinkley, a long distance truck driver, had previously had an accident on the Natchez Trace Highway and that he was looking for his "special tree" a mile and a half north of the Ballard Creek rest stop in order to show Mrs. Johnson where the accident had taken place. Three police officers and one FBI agent testified that there was a "mashed down area" behind two large oak trees on the east side of the highway at the Ballard Creek rest stop. The indentation was described as three or four inches deep and approximately six feet long, including an area where it appeared the leaves had been kicked aside to accommodate a person's elbows. According to the local sheriff, the appearance of the leaves left the "impression there that appeared that someone had been lying behind these trees, concealing himself from the Natchez Trace."

Two witnesses, Ann and Lee Avery, driving together on the Natchez Trace Highway approximately an hour before the shooting occurred, testified that they had come across a "pretty late model" two-tone Ford pickup of a "light and dark" color, pulled off the side of the road. The truck's lights were off, and a man was leaning out of the driver's window, pointing a rifle down the highway in the direction the two were heading. Lee Avery testified that the truck looked silver or gray and blue or maroon. He also identified the rifle as a "lever-action" type with a curved lever as was the rifle belonging to Shaw. Avery was sure of this identification of the gun because he owned an identical rifle of a different caliber. On cross-examination Shaw admitted being in the same area with his truck at the time described by the Averys. A park officer testified that on the evenings of December 22 and 23, he had seen a pickup "just like" Shaw's with its lights off parked near Ballard Creek. The truck was the same color and model as Shaw's, but had no license plates on the rear and did not have a dog pen in the back as did Shaw's the night he was arrested.

Although Shaw had originally denied that he had fired his gun on the night of the 25th, his story at trial was basically that he had been drinking and "riding around" on Christmas night and decided to go to the Natchez Trace in order to "headlight some deer." He pulled over near the Old Trace rest stop, saw a deer crossing the highway in front of him, and shot at it. Believing he had hit the deer, he turned off the truck lights and left the truck to go after the animal. At that time, he heard a car approaching from the south. Aware that his possession of a rifle was illegal, he attempted to conceal himself behind a pine tree on the side of the road. Simultaneously, he slipped and fell, and as he hit the ground, the rifle discharged and the Brinkley car passed in front of him.

None of the evidence corroborated Shaw's story. Brinkley and Mrs. Johnson testified that the truck's grill was facing them as they approached, not parked heading up the highway as Shaw claimed. Both were certain the shooting had taken at the Ballard Creek, not the Old Trace rest stop, as claimed by Shaw. Although Shaw explained that he was on the deserted highway after midnight with a loaded high powered rifle because he was pursuing a shot deer, the evidence strongly suggested that no shot had been fired prior to the one that killed the Johnson child. Despite an exhaustive search, no spent shell was ever located, at either Ballard Creek or the Old Trace. In addition, police discovered five live rounds in the cab of the truck, four on the floor, and one jammed in the gun's magazine. If one adds the shell that killed the child, the total number of bullets retrieved was seven—the maximum capacity of the rifle. If Shaw's story about having shot the deer were truthful, there would have been eight shells—one over the maximum capacity of the rifle.

It is uncontroverted that Shaw was on the Natchez Trace Highway after midnight with a fully loaded rifle, and that he fired the shot which killed the child. There is scant explanation for the shooting, save his unsupported story that he was attempting to pursue a wounded deer. Testimony by the Averys and the park ranger support an inference that Shaw had been parked on the highway, once with his lights off and his rifle aimed down the road, on an earlier occasion. Shaw evaded apprehension when first confronted by police. The fact of the hollowed-out area of leaves at Ballard Creek contra-dicts his version of the facts and bolsters that he was lying in wait to take aim at a passing car. And most important, Shaw repeatedly changed his story, and admitted that his statements to the police and FBI on December 26 and December 27 were a lie.

The government's case was largely circumstantial. But, whether the evidence is direct or circumstantial, the scope of the review of the evidence is the same. *See United States v. Bell,* 678 F.2d 547, 549 n. 3 (5th Cir.) (en banc), *cert. granted,* _____ U.S. _____, 103 S.Ct. 444, 74 L.Ed.2d 600 (1982). Accepting all reasonable inferences and credibility choices gathered from the evidence in the light most favorable to the government, we must decide if the jury's verdict was supportable. It is not necessary that the evidence exclude every reasonable hypothesis of innocence or be totally inconsistent with every conclusion except that of guilt. We will reverse only if a reasonably minded jury must necessarily have entertained a reasonable doubt of the defendant's guilt. *United States v. Alonzo,* 681 F.2d 997, 1000 (5th Cir. 1982); *United States v. Herman,* 576 F.2d 1139, 1144 (5th Cir. 1978). We are convinced that the evidence presented in this case permitted a reasonable jury to conclude that Shaw's story was false, that he was lying in wait behind the trees at Ballard Creek, and that he formed a conscious choice to shoot at the Brinkley's passing car. The totality of the evidence supports the jury's finding of premeditation and guilt as charged.

Ricky Wayne TISON and
Raymond Curtis Tison, Petitioners
v.
ARIZONA
Argued November 3, 1986.
Decided April 21, 1987.
107 S.Ct. 1676

Syllabus

Petitioner brothers, along with other members of their family, planned and effected the escape of their father from prison where he was serving a life sentence for having killed a guard during a previous escape. Petitioners entered the prison with a chest filled with guns, armed their father and another convicted murderer, later helped to abduct, detain, and rob a family of four, and watched their father and the other convict murder the members of that family with shotguns. Although they both later stated that they were surprised by the shooting, neither petitioner made any effort to help the victims, but drove away in the victims' car with the rest of the escape party. After the Arizona Supreme Court affirmed petitioners' individual convictions for capital murder under that State's felony-murder and accomplice-liability statutes, petitioners collaterally attacked their death sentences in state postconviction proceedings, alleging that *Enmund v. Florida,* 458 U.S. 782, 102 S.Ct. 3368, 73 L.Ed.2d 1140, which had been decided in the interim, required reversal. However, the State Supreme Court determined that they should be executed, holding that *Enmund* requires a finding of "intent to kill," and interpreting that phrase to include situations in which the defendant intended, contemplated, or anticipated that lethal force would or might be used, or that life would or might be taken in accomplishing the underlying felony. Despite finding that petitioners did not specifically intend that the victims die, plan the homicides in advance, or actually fire the shots, the court ruled that the requisite intent was established by evidence that petitioners played an active part in planning and executing the break-out and in the events that led to the murders, and that they did nothing to interfere with the killings nor to disassociate themselves from the killers afterward. Although only one of the petitioners testified that he would have been willing to kill, the court found that both of them could have anticipated the use of lethal force.

Held: Although petitioners neither intended to kill the victims nor inflicted the fatal wounds, the record might support a finding that they had the culpable mental state of reckless indifference to human life. The Eighth Amendment does not prohibit the death penalty as disproportionate in the case of a defendant whose participation in a felony that results in murder is major and whose mental state is one of reckless indifference. A survey of state felony murder laws and judicial decisions after *Enmund* indicates a societal consensus that that combination of factors may justify the death penalty even without a specific "intent to kill." Reckless disregard for human life also represents a highly culpable mental state that may support a capital sentencing judgment in combination with major participation in the felony resulting in death. Because the Arizona Supreme Court affirmed these death sentences upon a finding that the defendants "intended, contemplated, or anticipated that lethal force would or might be used or that life would or might be taken," the case must be remanded.

142 Ariz. 446, 690 P.2d 747, and 142 Ariz. 454, 690 P.2d 755, vacated and remanded.

O'CONNOR, J., delivered the opinion of the Court, in which REHNQUIST, C.J., and WHITE, POWELL, and SCALIA, JJ., joined. BRENNAN, J., filed a dissenting opinion, in which MARSHALL, J., joined, and in Parts I, II, III, and IV-A of which BLACKMUN and STEVENS, JJ., joined.

See full case for felony-murder rationale.

STATE of Tennessee, Appellee,

v.

James Clark THORNTON, III, Appellant.

Supreme Court of Tennessee,
at Jackson.
May 4, 1987.
703 S.W.2d 309 (Tenn. 1987)

Opinion

HARBISON, Justice.

Appellant was convicted of murder in the first degree as a result of shooting his wife's paramour in the home of appellant and his wife on May 3, 1983. Appellant found his wife and the victim, Mark McConkey, engaged in sexual relations in the front bedroom of appellant's home. He fired a single shot which struck McConkey in the left hip. The victim died 16 days later as a result of a massive infection resulting from the bullet wound. Before the night in question appellant had never been acquainted with McConkey or had any previous contact with him.

Appellant and his wife had been married just under four years; and their three-year-old son was in the home in an upstairs bedroom when the shooting occurred in a downstairs bedroom. Appellant and his wife had been separated for about six weeks, but no divorce action had been filed and appellant had been making a serious effort toward reconciliation with his wife.

Under these undisputed facts, in our opinion, the case does not warrant a conviction of homicide greater than that of voluntary manslaughter. The charges accordingly will be reduced to that offense, and the cause will be remanded to the trial court for sentencing and disposition on that basis.

In several previous decisions from this Court and in the almost unanimous course of judicial authority from other states, the encountering by a spouse of the situation which occurred here has been held, as a matter of law, to constitute sufficient provocation to reduce a charge of homicide from one of the degrees of murder to manslaughter absent actual malice, such as a previous grudge, revenge, or the like. Every case, of course, must be decided upon its own facts, but the facts in the present case were entirely undisputed. Appellant's wife testified at the trial and admitted her unfaithfulness to her husband and simply sought to excuse it upon the view that she was separated from him, and that she had told him earlier on the evening of the homicide that she had met someone else and planned to "date" him. In fact she had met McConkey on the evening of Saturday, April 30, 1983, and had had intimate sexual relations with him on that night and on each of the succeeding three nights, including the night of May 3 just before appellant burst into the bedroom and found both of them nude and in bed together.

The previous Tennessee cases, in chronological order, are *Toler v. State,* 152 Tenn. 1, 260 S.W. 134 (1924); *Davis v. State,* 161 Tenn. 23, 28 S.W.2d 993 (1930); *Drye v. State,* 181 Tenn. 637, 184 S.W.2d 10 (1944); *Whitsett v. State,* 201 Tenn. 317, 299 S.W.2d 2 (1957). *See generally Temples v. State,* 183 Tenn. 531, 194 S.W.2d 332 (1946); 2 Wharton's Criminal Law § 163 (14th ed., C.E. Torcia, 1979); 40 Am.Jur.2d *Homicide* § 65 (1968); 20 C.J.S. *Homicide* § 49 (1944).

A. *The Factual Background*

As previously stated, there is almost no dispute as to the material facts in this case. Appellant, James Clark Thornton, III, was 31 years of age at the time of the trial of this case in June 1984. His wife, Lavinia, was 27 years of age; they had been married on May 19, 1979, and at the time of the homicide had one child, a son about three years of age. Appellant was a second-year law student at Memphis State University, having previously received his undergraduate degree from the University of Tennessee at Chattanooga. His wife had not completed her undergraduate work when the parties married, but at the time of the homicide she was taking some additional class work toward her undergraduate degree. The victim, Mark McConkey, was 25 years of age, single, and a third-year student at the University of Tennessee Medical School in Memphis.

As stated, appellant had never met McConkey and did not even know his name. Mrs. Thornton had met him four days before the homicide and had engaged in sexual relations with him in the home belonging to her and appellant every night since that time, including the night of the homicide. She testified that she thought that when she told her husband that she might want to "date" someone else, that this, in modern society, indicated that she intended to have sexual relations. In that manner she sought to mitigate her infidelity and misconduct toward a husband who had never been unfaithful to her insofar as disclosed by the record.

The marriage of the parties was in some difficulty, apparently as a result of dissatisfaction of Mrs. Thornton. She had advised her husband in March 1983 that she wanted to be separated from him for a time, and he had voluntarily taken an apartment about two miles away from their home. He visited the home almost daily, however, and there has been no suggestion that he was ever guilty of violence, physical misconduct or mistreatment toward his wife or son. He was particularly devoted to the child, and frequently kept the child with him at his apartment on weekends or in the evenings.

Appellant had graduated from a public high school in Chattanooga, after having taken his first three years of high school at a private institution, Baylor. During his junior year at Baylor it was discovered that he had developed a severe case of scoliosis, or curvature of the spine, and he had undergone surgery to correct that condition. He was disabled to the point that he received a vocational rehabilitation grant which enabled him to attend undergraduate school at the University of Tennessee at Chattanooga. He was slightly built, being only five feet six inches in height and weighing about 125 to 130 pounds. McConkey was an athlete, a former basketball and football player in high school. He was five feet nine inches in height and weighed about 183 pounds.

Mrs. Thornton testified that she told McConkey when she first met him that she was married but separated from her husband. She had consulted an attorney and had signed a divorce petition, but the same apparently had not been filed on the date of the homicide.

Appellant, according to uncontradicted testimony, was deeply disturbed over the separation of the parties. He had sought assistance from a marriage counselor, and had persuaded his wife to go with him to the marriage counselor on several occasions. They had a joint meeting scheduled with the counselor on May 4, the day after the homicide. Appellant testified that the parties had agreed to a separation of six months, and both he and the marriage counselor testified that the parties had agreed that they would not have sexual relations with each other or with anyone else during that period. Mrs. Thornton denied making that agreement, but she did admit meeting with the marriage counselor on several occasions.

Mrs. Thornton was from a very wealthy family and had a generous trust fund which enabled the parties to live on a much more elaborate scale than most graduate students. Appellant, however, had also inherited some property through his family. This had been sold at a profit, and all of his assets had been invested in the home which the parties had purchased in Memphis, together with substantial additions from Mrs. Thornton. It was suggested by the State throughout the trial that appellant was insincere in his concern for the marriage, and that his principal concern was for his financial security.

The record indicates that as early as May 1, two days before the homicide, Mrs. Thornton had stated to her husband that she did not think that the parties would ever be reconciled. On the evening of May 3, appellant picked her and their child up at their home, and the three went to dinner. Again on that occasion Mrs. Thornton reiterated that she thought that the marriage was over, and on this occasion she told appellant that she planned to date someone else whom she had met. Appellant was concerned over the situation, but on a previous occasion his wife had told him that she had had sexual relations with another student, and this had proved to be false.

He returned his wife and child to their home at about 7:30 p.m. and then went to his apartment to study for a final examination in the law school.

He called two close friends of the parties, however, and discussed his marital situation with them. Both of them verified that he was very concerned about the situation, but both told him that they believed that his wife was serious about going through with a divorce. One of them advised him that his wife apparently did not believe his feelings about a reconciliation were sincere.

Acting on that suggestion, appellant returned to the home of the parties in his automobile, stating that he wanted to try once more to convince his wife that he was indeed sincere. When he arrived at the home he saw an automobile parked in the driveway. He did not recognize the car as being one belonging to any of his wife's friends. Accordingly he parked around the corner and walked back to the house. Observing from the rear of the house, he saw his wife and McConkey in the kitchen with the child. He observed as Mrs. Thornton washed some laundry for McConkey and as they were eating dinner. Thereafter they sat and read. They drank wine and smoked some marijuana, and appellant saw them kissing.

He decided to go home to get his camera, but before doing so he let the air out of one of the tires on McConkey's car. He went to his apartment, and obtained his camera and an old pistol which had belonged to his father. He visited a convenience store in an attempt to find film for the camera, and finally obtained some at a drugstore. He then returned to the marital residence, arriving at about 9:30 p.m. He testified that he intended to take pictures for the purpose of showing them to the marriage counselor on the next day and possibly also for use in evidence if divorce proceedings did ensue.

Appellant spent more than an hour in the back yard of his home observing his wife and McConkey in the den and kitchen. Thereafter they left the den area, but appellant remained behind the house, thinking that McConkey was about to leave. When he went around the house, however, he found that McConkey's car was still in the driveway and saw the drapes in the front guest bedroom downstairs had been closed. He listened near the window and heard unmistakeable sounds of sexual intercourse. He then burst through the front door and into the bedroom where he found the nude couple and attempted to take some pictures. At that point he testified that he thought McConkey was attempting to attack him. In all events he drew his pistol and fired a single shot, striking McConkey in the left hip. Appellant did not harm either his wife or child, although Mrs. Thornton said that he did make some threats against her. He went upstairs and brought down the little boy, who had been awakened and who was crying. He assisted in giving directions to enable an ambulance to bring aid to McConkey, and he remained at the house until the police arrived.

Appellant testified that he simply lost control and "exploded" when he found his wife in bed with the victim. He testified that he had armed himself because McConkey was much larger than he, and he felt that he needed protection if there was trouble when he returned to the residence with the camera.

Appellant testified that he did not intend to kill McConkey, but simply to shoot him in order to disable him and also because of his outrage at the situation which he had found. The single shot was not aimed at a vital organ, but the victim ultimately died because of the spread of a massive infection from the wound.

The marriage counselor who had been seeing appellant and his wife examined appellant on a number of occasions after the shooting. When McConkey died 16 days later, appellant attempted to take his own life. The psychologist, Dr. Hunsacker, testified that appellant was under severe emotional pressure at the time of shooting to the point that he believed appellant had a brief period of temporary insanity and was not legally responsible for his actions. An expert on behalf of the State testified to the contrary with respect to the issue of temporary insanity, but she testified that appellant was undoubtedly under severe emotional stress on the evening in question both before and at the time of the shooting.

Appellant attempted to interpose alternative defenses of self-defense and insanity. The jury rejected both of these defenses, and we agree with the Court of Criminal Appeals that this was entirely within their province. We further agree with the Court of Criminal Appeals that the State is entitled to the strongest legitimate view of the evidence on appeal. *See State v. Cabbage*, 571 S.W.2d 832 (Tenn. 1978).

There are, however, legal principles with respect to the sufficiency of provocation to reduce charges of homicide from murder to manslaughter, and, in our opinion, these principles are controlling here.

B. *The Legal Issues*

The attorneys who represented appellant at trial and in the Court of Criminal Appeals, as well as in the original application for review in this Court, assigned twelve issues as error. The lead attorney for appellant, however, died after review was granted

in this Court, and counsel arguing the case orally conceded that only one real issue was presented in this case; that is, whether the homicide was a degree of murder or voluntary manslaughter. With the issue of insanity, or legal responsibility, having been resolved against appellant, we agree with that assertion. The record does not support a finding of justifiable homicide from self defense, and there was ample testimony from which the jury could reject a defense of insanity or lack of mental capacity.

Nevertheless, as previously stated, it has long been a well-settled legal principle that the commission of unlawful sexual intercourse with a female relative is an act obviously calculated to arouse ungovernable passion, and that the killing of the seducer or adulterer under the influence or in the heat of passion constitutes voluntary manslaughter, and not murder, in the absence of evidence of actual malice. The Court further stated:

"It is necessary to reduce killing to manslaughter that the passion should be so great as to render the defendant incapable of deliberation or premeditation. If the circumstances be such as are calculated to produce such excitement and passion as would obscure the reason of an ordinary man and induce him, under such excitement and passion, to strike the blow that causes the death of the deceased, this will reduce the killing to manslaughter. *Seals v. State*, 3 Baxt., 459.

"We think the facts of the instant case meet this test, and that defendant was improperly convicted of murder in the second degree." 152 Tenn. at 13, 260 S.W. at 137.

The Court pointed out that if there had been sufficient time for the passion or emotion of the defendant to cool before the shooting, then a verdict of murder might be sustained. It found no such time in that case, nor, in our opinion, was there any such showing in the present case. ...

The facts of the present case are far stronger than any of the foregoing. Appellant actually discovered his wife *in flagrante delicto* with a man who was a total stranger to him, and at a time when appellant was trying to save his marriage and was deeply concerned about both his wife and his young child. He did not fire a shot or in any way harm the victim until he actually discovered the victim and his wife engaged in sexual intercourse in appellant's own home. In our opinion the passions of any reasonable person would have been inflamed and intensely aroused by this sort of discovery, given the factual background of this case. Even though he was not legally insane so as to relieve him of all criminal responsibility for the tragic

death which occurred, in our opinion this was a classic case of voluntary manslaughter and no more.

We are of the opinion that the necessary elements of malice and premeditation were not demonstrated in this case and that the appellant acted under legally sufficient provocation. The conviction of murder in the first degree is set aside, and the cause will be remanded to the trial court for sentencing of the defendant for voluntary manslaughter and for such other disposition as may be appropriate in view of the time already served by the appellant. Costs of the appeal are taxed to the State. All other costs will be fixed by the trial court.

BROCK, C.J., FONES, J., and GREER, Special Justice, concur.

DROWOTA, J., files separate Opinion, concurring in part and dissenting in part.

Concurring opinions not included.

Danny S. RIDDLE
v.
The STATE

Court of Appeals of Georgia, Division No. 2
145 Ga.App. 328, 243 S.E.2d 607
Feb. 24, 1978
Rehearing Denied March 16, 1978

WEBB, Judge.

A person commits aggravated assault when he attempts to commit a violent injury to the person of another with a deadly weapon. Criminal Code §§ 26-1301(a), 1302(b). Danny Riddle, having been so convicted, contends

that the evidence was insufficient to show that he had intended to commit a violent injury upon English, the purported victim, or that the weapon used was a deadly weapon, or that he had performed any act constituting a substantial step toward commission of the battery as required by Criminal Code

§ 26-1001. We disagree and affirm the conviction.

There is evidence in the record which, if believed by the jury, shows an attempted work-related shooting. As his shift was nearing an end at 7:00 a.m. Riddle became involved in an altercation about overtime pay with English, his superior, growing more and more hostile and threatening to "beat his ass." As the conflict escalated English informed him that he had nothing more to say and that he would recommend to "Personnel" that he be fired for insubordination, profanity and refusing to work. English then worked in his office until about 7:30 a.m. when he went to his car in the parking lot and found Riddle waiting for him. Riddle asked for an apology, English refused, and Riddle replied that he would "get" him "because I have something for you."

Later that night as English's shift started Riddle drove up and parked two or three feet from the "big door" at the plant and had English paged to that area. English went there in company with others, whereupon Riddle got out of his car and approached the group just inside the plant. Riddle stated that he wanted to talk to English, that he had just been fired, to which English replied that he had nothing more to say. According to English, Riddle said, " Well, goddamn-it, I have something to say to you.' [Or I've got something for you,' according to another witness]. And he proceeded to go back to his car and he stuck the top part of his body into the passenger's side of his car."

English, fearing that Riddle might be pulling a gun out of the car, ran "as fast as he could" down through the plant into the "blowing wool room." According to the eyewitnesses English's fears were well-founded because Riddle got a pump-type, 12-gauge, sawed-off shotgun from the car and "brought the weapon in. It was about hip-high. He brought the weapon up to about shoulder-high, pumped the gun, started lifting it up toward his shoulder as he was coming into the plant." An employee between Riddle and English raised his hands and said "Don't shoot that thing," and another witness went to call the sheriff.

According to an eyewitness who hunted a lot and was familiar with guns, the pumping action would "load" the gun or throw a shell into the firing chamber. This witness stated: "*A.* He came back in. *Q.* Was he walking slow? *A.* He came in at a medium speed. He wasn't really running and he wasn't walking either. *Q.* Okay. What action did he take when he first came in? This is just inside the doors. What did Mr. Riddle do? *A.* He came in and looked down through the plant, and as he did he pumped the gun. [English] had already went inside the blowing wool room. *Q.* Okay. Did he turn at all or did he just come in a look around? *A.* He came in and looked toward the way [English] had went. *Q.* Okay. After he came in and looked where [English] had gone, what did he do then? *A.* He saw [English] had already went inside the blowing room. He went back outside the plant, almost to the end of the blowing room, and then he turned around and came back and got in his car, and left."

1. " 'In every assault there must be an intent to injure. The test is, was there a present purpose of doing bodily injury?' " *Godboult v. State,* 38 Ga.App. 137, 138, 142 S.E. 704 (1928).

" 'A person will not be presumed to act with criminal intention, but the trier of facts may find such intention upon consideration of the words, conduct, demeanor, motive, and all other circumstances connected with the act for which the accused is prosecuted.' Code Ann. § 26-605. Whether the requisite intent is manifested by the circumstances is a question for the trier of fact, and, on review, this court will not disturb the factual determination unless it is contrary to the evidence and clearly erroneous. (Citations omitted.)" *J.A.T. v. State,* 136 Ga.App. 540, 541, 221 S.E.2d 702, 703 (1975).

We cannot say that the jury's determination here was contrary to the evidence or clearly erroneous. *Burton v. State,* 109 Ga. 134, 34 S.E. 286 (1899), relied upon by Riddle, does not require a different result since the crime charged there was assault with intent to murder which requires a specific intent to kill (*Wright v. State,* 168 Ga. 690, 691(1), 148 S.E. 731 (1929)), whereas "[a]n intent to kill is not an element of aggravated assault with a deadly weapon." *Emmons v. State,* 142 Ga.App. 553, 554, 236 S.E.2d 536, 537 (1977).

In any event that case is factually distinguishable since the pistol was caught in the lining of defendant's coat as he attempted to draw it and there was no pumping, no pointing, and no threat. But even were the instant case controlled by standards relating to assault with intent to murder we would think it more like *Williams v. State,* 125 Ga. 235, 54 S.E. 186 (1906) than *Burton, supra.* While we cannot say that the evidence demanded a finding that Riddle intended to shoot English, nevertheless virtually everything in the case points to that conclusion except Riddle's testimony that he had no gun at all but merely picked up a metal skid and threw it into the trash on the way to his car.

2. "[B]y definition an assault is nothing more than an attempted battery," *Scott v. State,* 141 Ga.App. 848, 849, 234 S.E.2d 685, 687 (1977), and an attempt is complete "when, with intent to commit a specific crime [here a battery], he performs any act which constitutes a substantial step toward the commission of that crime." Criminal Code § 26-1001.

Riddle contends that he had not performed a "substantial step" toward committing a battery upon English, but we disagree. "[Criminal Code § 26-1001] requires that the act be a substantial step toward the commission of the crime. This is about as specific as this sort of definition can be. This language makes it clear that something more than the minimal act sometimes found to suffice for the overt act of conspiracy is required. Essentially the question is whether the accused has gone past preparation and has begun perpetration..." Criminal Code Ch. 26-10, p. 130, Committee Notes.

Thus a mere threat is insufficient, *Hudson v. State,* 135 Ga.App. 739, 741, 218 S.E.2d 905 (1975), and even the case law prior to the new Criminal Code likewise drew distinctions between mere preparation, on the one hand, and "physical effort" to commit the battery, on the other. *Brown v. State,* 95 Ga. 481, 20 S.E. 495 (1894). The principle was stated in *Leverett v. State,* 20 Ga.App. 748(1), 93 S.E. 232 (1917), as follows: "Acts merely preparatory for the commission of a crime, and not proximately leading to its consummation, do not constitute an attempt to commit the crime. *Groves v. State,* 116 Ga. 516, 42 S.E. 755, 59 L.R.A. 598. 'Attempt' is more comprehensive than 'intent,' and implies both the purpose and an actual effort to carry the purpose into execution (*Smith v. State,* 126 Ga. 544, 546, 55

S.E. 475) and, in general, to constitute an attempt, there must be an act done in pursuance of the intent, and more or less directly tending to the commission of the crime. *Groves v. State, supra.*" *See also Bell v. State,* 118 Ga.App. 291, 292, 163 S.E.2d 323 (1968).

Hence if the defendant makes threats and picks up rocks in his hands, but makes no attempt to throw them, assault is not shown. *Penny v. State,* 114 Ga. 77, 39 S.E. 871 (1901). But if the defendant goes further and draws back as if to throw them "violence has commenced and the assault is complete"; and this result obtains even if the actual throwing of the rocks is prevented by counter-menace of the victim or the interference of a third party. *Rutherford v. State,* 5 Ga.App. 482, 63 S.E. 570 (1908).

In the instant case the jury was authorized to find that Riddle had gone past preparation and begun perpetration when, having the motivation to injure English and having made threats to do so, he procured his gun and set off on a course intended to intercept his victim, pumping or "loading" the gun for firing, and bringing it up to his shoulder and leveling it off for firing as he advanced, only to find that his wary victim was disappearing behind another door with a lead-time of two seconds, in the estimation of one witness. In these circumstances we believe that Riddle has "drawn back" to launch the projectile, that the violence has commenced, and that he must answer for it.

Although it is contended that there could be no assault as a matter of law because no shot was fired and the victim did, in fact, foil the plot by escaping, this was no defense prior to the new Criminal Code (*Rutherford v. State,* 5 Ga.App. 482, 63 S.E. 570, *supra*), and it is without significance now. "It is no defense to a charge of criminal attempt that the crime the accused is charged with attempting was, under the attendant circumstances, factually or legally impossible of commission if such crime could have been committed had the attendant circumstances been as the accused believed them to be." Criminal Code § 26-1002. Thus it is no defense here that the battery which the jury could find was attempted to be committed by Riddle was rendered factually impossible by English's escape.

3. Finally it is contended that there was no evidence that the shotgun was loaded and capable of being fired; but we think that the jury could legitimately infer that these matters were so because the defendant acted as if they were so. "[W]hether the instrument used constitutes a deadly weapon is properly for the jury's determination." *Quarles v. State,* 130 Ga.App. 756, 757, 204 S.E.2d 467, 469 (1974). *See also Watts v. State,* 142 Ga.App. 857, 859, 237 S.E.2d 231 (1977), the broad implication being that a firearm is a deadly weapon per se.

Judgment affirmed.

QUILLIAN, P.J., and McMURRAY, J., concur.

Cases Relating to Chapter 4

OFFENSES AGAINST THE PERSON—SEX RELATED

The PEOPLE, Plaintiff and Respondent,

v.

David Herberto VELA, Defendant and Appellant.

Cr. F002772.
Court of Appeal, Fifth District.
Sept. 17, 1985.
Review Denied Dec. 31, 1985.*
218 Cal. Rptr. 161

Opinion

BEST, Associate Justice.

"Once penetration has occurred with the female's consent, if the female changes her mind does force from that point (where she changes her mind) constitute rape?"

On this appeal we must determine the answer to the above question and the effect of the trial court's failure to provide the jury with the correct answer.

Defendant, then 19 years of age, was charged with the forcible rape of Miss M., then 14 years of age, the alleged rape occurring during the evening hours of November 20, 1982, near Bakersfield, California. The testimony of Miss M., together with other prosecution evidence, was more than sufficient to support a finding by the jury that defendant was guilty of rape by force of Miss M. However, during its case-in-chief, the prosecution presented evidence of a statement given by defendant to Deputy Eddy of the

Kern County Sheriff's Department. Defendant's statement to Deputy Eddy, if believed to be true, together with all the other evidence, would have supported findings by the jury that Miss M. initially consented to an act of sexual intercourse with defendant; that during the act she changed her mind and made defendant aware that she had withdrawn her consent; and that defendant, without interruption of penetration, continued the act of sexual intercourse against the will of Miss M. by means of force.

During deliberations, the jury sent a note to the trial court that read, "Once penetration has occurred with the female's consent, if the female changes her mind does force from that point (where she changes her mind) constitute rape?"

Pursuant to agreement of counsel, the court answered the question in the affirmative. The trial court and attorneys then did further research on the matter and concluded that an affirmative answer to the jury's question may have been incorrect. In the meantime, the jury returned a verdict finding defendant guilty of rape and personal infliction of great bodily injury. The trial court then polled the jury on the question of whether its verdict was based on the circumstances described in the note. Two jurors answered "Yes" and ten jurors answered "No." The trial court then advised the jury:

"The note that you gave us yesterday, quite frankly, is something that took us a while to check on. And to be candid with you, we do not have a definitive answer to that question, okay? The attorneys and I have discussed it, and, quite frankly, we are not sure that I gave you the correct answer or not.

"What I would like you to do is to go back in and deliberate further with the understanding that the question I answered yesterday I now must tell you I do not have an answer for you. You will then have to decide it as if I had not answered that particular question in that particular fashion."

The trial court then reinstructed the jury on the crime of rape. After further deliberations, the jury returned a unanimous verdict of guilty. No inquiry was made on this verdict as to the theory upon which the jurors based their finding that defendant was guilty of rape.

Discussion

In withdrawing its answer to the jury's question and telling the jury that there was no definitive answer, the trial court left the jury uninstructed on the point of law raised by the question. [1] It is settled that in criminal cases the court must *sua sponte* instruct on the general principles of law which are *raised by the evidence* and which are necessary for the people's understanding of the case. (*People v. Hood* (1969)

1 Cal.3d 444, 449, 82 Cal.Rptr. 618, 462 P.2d 370; *People v. Wilson* (1967) 66 Cal.2d 749, 759, 59 Cal.Rptr. 156, 427 P.2d 820.) "Just as the law imposes a *sua sponte* obligation to instruct on certain principles of law in the first place (those rules openly and closely connected with the case) so does it impose on the judge a duty to reinstruct on the point if it becomes apparent to him that the jury may be confused on the law." (*People v. Valenzuela* (1977) 76 Cal.App.3d 218, 221, 142 Cal.Rptr. 655.) Moreover, as stated in *People v. Stewart* (1976) 16 Cal.3d 133, 140, 127 Cal.Rptr. 117, 544 P.2d 1317, the court is under an " '...obligation to instruct on defenses,...and on the relationship of these defenses to the elements of the charged offense...' where '...it appears that the defendant is relying on such a defense, or if there is substantial evidence supportive of such a defense....' "

It was, therefore, incumbent on the trial court, in the instant case, to answer correctly the question posed by the jury, and the failure to do so constituted error. Whether such error was prejudicial to defendant and requires reversal of the judgment depends upon whether the answer to the jury's question is "Yes" or "No." We are in sympathy with the trial court because this question is one of first impression in California. For guidance, we turn to the scant authority from other jurisdictions.

In a trial for rape in Maryland, the jury, during deliberations, addressed the following question to the trial judge: "When a possible consensual sexual relationship becomes non-consensual for some reason, during the course of the action—can the act then be considered rape?" (*Battle v. State* (1980) 287 Md. 675, 414 A.2d 1266,

1268). The appellate court in *Battle v. State* held the act could not be a rape and that the trial court erred in answering the question in the affirmative. The appellate court first noted that case law is unanimous in holding consent given at any time subsequent to the act of intercourse will not prevent the act from being a rape. It also noted that authorities have established that consent at any time prior to penetration will prevent the act from being a rape. The court also discussed cases that hold a victim may give consent throughout the preparatory acts, but if the victim withdraws consent before penetration and if the act is thereafter accomplished by force, there is a rape. (*Id.,* 414 A.2d at pp. 1269-1270.) After reviewing these cases and finding no discussion of withdrawal of consent in midact, the court concluded: "Given the fact that consent must precede penetration, it follows in our view that although a woman may have consented to a sexual encounter, even to intercourse, if that consent is withdrawn prior to the act of penetration, then it cannot be said that she has consented to sexual intercourse. On the other hand, ordinarily if she consents prior to penetration and withdraws the consent following penetration, there is no rape." (*Id.* at p. 1270.)

The same conclusion was reached in a North Carolina case. In *State v. Way* (1979) 297 N.C. 293, 254 S.E.2d 760, the jury also asked during deliberations if consent could be withdrawn and a rape conviction found. The trial and appellate courts said yes, but the Supreme Court said no. This court noted that the normal situation in which consent was withdrawn was that in which more than one act of intercourse occurred. In such case, consent to one act did not mean all acts of intercourse were consented to by the victim. The court then noted, without citing authority, that when only one act of intercourse is accomplished, if the victim consents initially and withdraws that consent in midact no rape occurred. The court stated, "If the actual penetration is accomplished with the woman's consent, the accused is not guilty of rape, although he may be guilty of another crime because of his subsequent actions." (*Id.,* 254 S.E.2d at p. 762.)

These cases point out that the presence or absence of consent at the moment of initial penetration appears to be the crucial point in the crime of rape. For example, if at the moment of penetration the victim has not consented, no amount of consent given thereafter will prevent the act from being a rape. Also, a victim may give consent during preparatory acts all the way up to the moment of penetration, but the victim may withdraw that consent immediately before penetration and if communicated to the perpetrator, the act of intercourse that follows will be a rape no matter how much consent was given prior to penetration. It follows that if consent is given at the moment of penetration, that act of intercourse will be shielded from being a rape even if consent is later withdrawn during the act.

California case law and statutory law also seem to focus on the moment of penetration as the crucial moment of the crime of rape.

Penal Code § 261 provides in relevant part the following definition of rape: "Rape is an act of sexual intercourse accomplished with a person not the spouse of the perpetrator, under any of the following circumstances:... (2) Where it is accomplished against a person's will by means of force or fear of immediate and unlawful bodily injury on the person or another." To be convicted of rape the defendant must engage in an act of sexual intercourse of the person, the person must not be the spouse of the defendant, the act of intercourse must be against the will of the person, and the act must be accomplished by force. (See CALJIC No. 10 (rev. 1982).) In essence, then, rape may be defined as nonconsensual sexual intercourse. (*People v. Key* (1984) 153 Cal.App.3d 888, 895, 203 Cal.Rptr. 144.)

It is well settled that "Any sexual penetration, however slight, is sufficient to complete the crime." (Pen. Code § 263.) The California Supreme Court also has noted that in order for a conviction of rape to stand, the victim must be alive at the moment of penetration. (*People v. Stanworth* (1974) 11 Cal.3d 588, 604-605, fn. 15, 114 Cal.Rptr. 250, 522 P.2d 1058.) The Supreme Court noted that Penal Code § 263 provides in part, " '[t]he essential guilt of rape consists in the outrage to the person and feelings of the female.' " The court then reasoned there can be no rape of a dead person because at the moment of sexual penetration there is no outrage to the feelings of the dead victim.

As noted above, the essence of the crime of rape is the outrage to the person and feelings of the female resulting from the nonconsensual violation of her womanhood. When a female willingly consents to an act of sexual intercourse, the penetration by the male cannot constitute a violation of her womanhood nor cause outrage to her person and feelings. If she withdraws consent during the act of sexual intercourse and the male forcibly continues the act without interruption, the female may certainly feel outrage because of the force applied or because the male ignores her wishes, but the sense of outrage to her person and feel-

ings could hardly be of the same magnitude as that resulting from an initial nonconsensual violation of her womanhood. It would seem, therefore, that the essential guilt of rape as stated in Penal Code § 263 is lacking in the withdrawn consent scenario.

Our conclusion that no rape occurs under these circumstances does not preclude the perpetrator from being found guilty of another crime or crimes warranted by the evidence. Consent at the moment of penetration does not give the male a license to commit any act of force upon the female. It has been held that while withdrawn consent after penetration or during the act of sexual intercourse negates a rape, the male may be guilty of another crime, such as assault or battery. (*State v. Way, supra,* 254 S.E.2d at p. 762; *see* Annot. (1963) 91 A.L.R.2d 591, 597-598; *see* Comment (1954) 6 Stan.L.Rev. 719, 726, fn. 36.) It is also settled that each act of nonconsensual sexual penetration of a victim constitutes a separate rape offense. If a female initially consents to an act of sexual intercourse but thereafter withdraws her consent, each subsequent act of sexual penetration accomplished by force or fear will constitute a separate and distinct act of rape.

We hold that, under the circumstances of this case, the trial court's error in failing to answer the jury's question in the negative was prejudicial to defendant and reversal of the judgment is required. After the initial verdict was announced, two jurors advised the trial court that their finding that defendant was guilty of rape was based upon a state of the evidence as described in the jury's question. When the trial court withdrew its previous answer and left the jury uninstructed on the point, it is entirely possible, if not probable, that one or more of the jurors based their final verdict on such a state of the evidence.

A remand for retrial being required, we find it neither necessary nor appropriate to address defendant's remaining claims of error.

The judgment is reversed.

The PEOPLE of the State of New York, Respondent,
v.
Mario LIBERTA, Appellant.
Court of Appeals of New York.
Dec. 20, 1984.
474 N.E.2d 567

Opinion of the Court

WACHTLER, Judge.

The defendant, while living apart from his wife pursuant to a Family Court order, forcibly raped and sodomized her in the presence of their 2½-year-old son. Under the New York Penal Law a married man ordinarily cannot be prosecuted for raping or sodomizing his wife. The defendant, however, though married at the time of the incident, is treated as an unmarried man under the Penal Law because of the Family Court order. On this appeal, he contends that because of the exemption for married men, the statutes for rape in the first degree (Penal Law, § 130.35) and sodomy in the first degree (Penal Law, § 130.50), violate the equal protection clause of the Federal Constitution (U.S. Const., 14th Amdt.). The defendant also contends that the rape statute violates equal protection because only men, and not women, can be prosecuted under it.

I

Defendant Mario Liberta and Denise Liberta were married in 1978. Shortly after the birth of their son, in October of that year, Mario began to beat Denise. In early 1980 Denise brought a proceeding in the Family Court in Erie County seeking protection from the defendant. On April 30, 1980, a temporary order of protection was issued to her by the Family Court. Under this order, the defendant was to move out and remain away from the family home, and stay away from Denise. The order provided that the defendant could visit with his son once each weekend.

On the weekend of March 21, 1981, Mario, who was then living in a motel, did not visit his son. On Tuesday, March 24, 1981 he called Denise to ask if he could visit his son that day. Denise would not allow the defendant to come to her house, but she did agree to allow him to pick up their son and her and take them both back to his motel after being assured that a friend of his would be with them at all times.

The defendant and his friend picked up Denise and their son and the four of them drove to defendant's motel.

When they arrived at the motel the friend left. As soon as only Mario, Denise, and their son were alone in the motel room, Mario attacked Denise, threatened to kill her, and forced her to perform fellatio on him and to engage in sexual intercourse with him. The son was in the room during the entire episode, and the defendant forced Denise to tell their son to watch what the defendant was doing to her.

The defendant allowed Denise and their son to leave shortly after the incident. Denise, after going to her parents' home, went to a hospital to be treated for scratches on her neck and bruises on her head and back, all inflicted by her husband. She also went to the police station, and on the next day she swore out a felony complaint against the defendant. On July 15, 1981, the defendant was indicted for rape in the first degree and sodomy in the first degree.

II

Section 130.35 of the Penal Law provides in relevant part that "A male is guilty of rape in the first degree when he engages in sexual intercourse with a female * * * by forcible compulsion." "Female", for purposes of the rape statute, is defined as "any female person who is not married to the actor" (Penal Law, § 130.00, subd. 4). Section 130.50 of the Penal Law provides in relevant part that "a person is guilty of sodomy in the first degree when he engages in deviate sexual intercourse with another person * * * by forcible compulsion." "Deviate sexual intercourse" is defined as "sexual conduct between persons not married to each other consisting of contact between the penis and the anus, the

mouth and penis, or the mouth and the vulva" (Penal Law, § 130.00, subd. 2). Thus, due to the "not married" language in the definitions of "female" and "deviate sexual intercourse," there is a "marital exemption" for both forcible rape and forcible sodomy. The marital exemption itself, however, has certain exceptions. For purposes of the rape and sodomy statutes, a husband and wife are considered to be "not married" if at the time of the sexual assault they "are living apart * * * pursuant to a valid and effective: (i) order issued by a court of competent jurisdiction which by its terms or in its effect requires such living apart, or (ii) decree or judgment of separation, or (iii) written agreement of separation" (Penal Law, § 130.00, subd. 4).

Defendant moved to dismiss the indictment, asserting that because he and Denise were still married at the time of the incident he came within the "marital exemption" to both rape and sodomy. The People opposed the motion, contending that the temporary order of protection required Mario and Denise to live apart, and they in fact were living apart, and thus were "not married" for purposes of the statutes. The trial court granted the defendant's motion and dismissed the indictment, concluding that the temporary order of protection did not require Mario and Denise to live apart from each other, but instead required only that he remain away from her, and that therefore the "marital exemption" applied.

On appeal by the People, the Appellate Division, 90 A.D.2d 681, 455 N.Y.S.2d 882, reversed the trial court, reinstated the indictment, and remanded the case for trial. The Appellate Division held that a Family Court order of protection is within the scope of "[an] order * * * which by its terms or in its effect requires such living apart" even though it is directed only at a husband, and thus found that Mario and Denise were "not married" for purposes of the statute at the time of the incident.

The defendant was then convicted of rape in the first degree and sodomy in the first degree and the conviction was affirmed by the Appellate Division, 100 A.D.2d 741, 473 N.Y.S.2d 636. Defendant asserts on this appeal that the temporary order of protection is not the type of order which enables a court to treat him and Denise as "not married" and that thus he is within the marital exemption. Defendant next asserts, assuming that because of the Family Court order he is treated just as any unmarried male would be, that he cannot be convicted of either rape in the first degree or sodomy in the first degree because both statutes are unconstitutional. Specifically, he contends that both statutes violate equal protection because they burden some, but not all males (all but those within the "marital exemption"), and that the rape statute also violates equal protection for burdening only men, and not women. The lower courts rejected the defendant's constitutional arguments, finding that neither statute violated the equal protection clause in the Fourteenth Amendment. Although we affirm the conviction of the defendant, we do not agree with the constitutional analysis of the lower courts and instead conclude that the marital and gender exemptions must be read out of the statutes prohibiting forcible rape and sodomy.

III

We first address the defendant's argument that, despite the order of protection, he was within the "marital exemption" to rape and sodomy and thus could not be prosecuted for either crime. Until 1978, the marital exemption applied as long as the marriage still legally existed. In 1978, the Legislature expanded the definition of "not married" to include those cases where the husband and wife were living apart pursuant to either a court order "which by its terms or in its effect requires such living apart" or a decree, judgment, or written agreement of separation (L.1978, ch. 735; see Penal Law, § 130.00, subd. 4). We agree with the Appellate Division that the order of protection in the present case falls squarely within the first of these situations.

The legislative memorandum submitted with the original version of the 1978 amendment, after referring to the situations brought within the scope of "not married," stated: "In each of the alternatives set forth in this bill, there must be documentary evidence of a settled and mutual intention to dissolve the marital relationship, or a court determination that the spouses should, for the well-being of one or both, live apart" (N.Y.Legis.Ann., 1978, pp. 403-404). Although the language of the amendment was subsequently changed to the form in which it was enacted, this legislative memorandum was submitted with the final version of the bill. In addition to this clear statement of legislative intent, the plain language of the statute indicates that an order of protection is within the meaning of an order "which by its terms or in its effect requires [the spouses to live] apart". This language would be virtually meaningless if it did not encompass an order of protection, as the statute separately provides for the other obvious situation where a court order would require spouses to live apart, i.e., where there is a decree or judgment of separation.

Accordingly, the defendant was properly found to have been statutorily "not married" to Denise at the time of the rape.

IV

The defendant's constitutional challenges to the rape and sodomy statutes are premised on his being considered "not married" to Denise and are the same challenges as could be made by any unmarried male convicted under these statutes. The defendant's claim is that both statutes violate equal protection because they are underinclusive classifications which burden him, but not others similarly situated (see Tribe, American Constitutional Law, p. 997). A litigant has standing to raise this claim even though he does not contend that under no circumstances could the burden of the statute be imposed upon him. This rule of standing applies as well to a defendant in a criminal prosecution who, while conceding that it is within the power of a State to make criminal the behavior covered by a statute, asserts that the statute he is prosecuted under violates equal protection because it burdens him but not others. Thus, defendant's constitutional claims are properly before this court.

A. The Marital Exemption

As noted above, under the Penal Law a married man ordinarily cannot be convicted of forcibly raping or sodomizing his wife. This is the so-called marital exemption for rape (see 1881 Penal Code, tit. X, ch. II, § 278). Although a marital exemption was not explicit in earlier rape statutes (see 1863 Rev.Stats. part 4, ch. I, tit. 2, art. 2, § 22), an 1852 treatise stated that a man could not be guilty of raping his wife (Barbour, Criminal Law of State of New York [2d ed.], p. 69). The

assumption, even before the marital exemption was codified, that a man could not be guilty of raping his wife, is traceable to a statement made by the 17th century English jurist Lord Hale, who wrote: "[T]he husband cannot be guilty of a rape committed by himself upon his lawful wife, for by their mutual matrimonial consent and contract the wife hath given up herself in this kind unto her husband, which she cannot retract" (1 Hale, History of Pleas of the Crown, p. 629). Although Hale cited no authority for his statement it was relied on by State Legislatures which enacted rape statutes with a marital exemption and by courts which established a common-law exemption for husbands.

The first American case to recognize the marital exemption was decided in 1857 by the Supreme Judicial Court of Massachusetts, which stated in dictum that it would always be a defense to rape to show marriage to the victim (*Commonwealth v. Fogerty,* 74 Mass. 489). Decisions to the same effect by other courts followed, usually with no rationale or authority cited other than Hale's implied consent view. In New York, a 1922 decision noted the marital exemption in the Penal Law and stated that it existed "on account of the matrimonial consent which [the wife] has given, and which she cannot retract" (*People v. Meli,* 193 N.Y.S. 365, 366 [Sup.Ct.]).

Presently, over 40 States still retain some form of marital exemption for rape. While the marital exemption is subject to an equal protection challenge, because it classifies unmarried men differently than married men, the equal protection clause does not prohibit a State from making classifications, provided the statute does not arbitrarily burden a particular group of individuals (*Reed v. Reed,* 404 U.S.

71, 75-76, 92 S.Ct. 251, 253-254, 30 L.Ed.2d 225). Where a statute draws a distinction based upon marital status, the classification must be reasonable and must be based upon "some ground of difference that rationally explains the different treatment."

We find that there is no rational basis for distinguishing between marital rape and nonmarital rape. The various rationales which have been asserted in defense of the exemption are either based upon archaic notions about the consent and property rights incident to marriage or are simply unable to withstand even the slightest scrutiny. We therefore declare the marital exemption for rape in the New York statute to be unconstitutional.

Lord Hale's notion of an irrevocable implied consent by a married woman to sexual intercourse has been cited most frequently in support of the marital exemption ("Equal Protection Considerations," *supra*, n. 6, 16 N.Eng.L.Rev., at p. 21). Any argument based on a supposed consent, however, is untenable. Rape is not simply a sexual act to which one party does not consent. Rather, it is a degrading, violent act which violates the bodily integrity of the victim and frequently causes severe, long-lasting physical and psychic harm (*see Coker v. Georgia*, 433 U.S. 584, 597-598, 97 S.Ct. 2861, 2868-2869, 53 L.Ed.2d 982; Note, Rape Reform and a Statutory Consent Defense, 74 J. of Crim. L. & Criminology 1518, 1519, 1527-1528). To ever imply consent to such an act is irrational and absurd. Other than in the context of rape statutes, marriage has never been viewed as giving a husband the right to coerced intercourse on demand (*see De Angelis v. De Angelis*, 54 A.D.2d 1088, 388 N.Y.S.2d 744; "Abolishing The Marital Exemption," *supra*, at n.

4, 1983 U. of Ill.L.Rev., at p. 207; "Marital Rape Exemption," *supra* at n. 5, 52 N.Y.U.L.Rev., at pp. 311-312). Certainly, then, a marriage license should not be viewed as a license for a husband to forcibly rape his wife with impunity. A married woman has the same right to control her own body as does an unmarried woman. If a husband feels "aggrieved" by his wife's refusal to engage in sexual intercourse, he should seek relief in the courts governing domestic relations, not in "violent or forceful self-help" (*State v. Smith*, 85 N.J. 193, 206, 426 A.2d 38).

The other traditional justifications for the marital exemption were the common-law doctrines that a woman was the property of her husband and that the legal existence of the woman was "incorporated and consolidated into that of the husband" (1 Blackstone's Commentaries [1966 ed.], p. 430; *see State v. Smith, supra*, at pp. 204-205, 426 A.2d 38; "Marital Rape Exemption," *supra*, n. 5, 52 N.Y.U.L.Rev., at pp. 309-310). Both these doctrines, of course, have long been rejected in this State. Indeed, "[n]owhere in the common-law world—[or] in any modern society— is a woman regarded as chattel or demeaned by denial of a separate legal identity and the dignity associated with recognition as a whole human being."

Because the traditional justifications for the marital exemption no longer have any validity, other arguments have been advanced in its defense. The first of these recent rationales, which is stressed by the People in this case, is that the marital exemption protects against governmental intrusion into marital privacy and promotes reconciliation of the spouses, and thus that elimination of the exemption would be disruptive to marriages. While protecting marital privacy and encouraging reconciliation are legitimate State interests, there is no rational relation between allowing a husband to forcibly rape his wife and these interests. The marital exemption simply does not further marital privacy because this right of privacy protects consensual acts, not violent sexual assaults. Just as a husband cannot invoke a right of marital privacy to escape liability for beating his wife, he cannot justifiably rape his wife under the guise of a right to privacy.

Similarly, it is not tenable to argue that elimination of the marital exemption would disrupt marriages because it would discourage reconciliation. Clearly, it is the violent act of rape and not the subsequent attempt of the wife to seek protection through the criminal justice system which "disrupts" a marriage (*Weishaupt v. Commonwealth*, 227 Va. 389, 315 S.E.2d 847, at p. 855). Moreover, if the marriage has already reached the point where intercourse is accomplished by violent assault it is doubtful that there is anything left to reconcile (see *Trammel v. United States*, 445 U.S. 40, 52, 100 S.Ct. 906, 913, 63 L.Ed.2d 186). This, of course, is particularly true if the wife is willing to bring criminal charges against her husband which could result in a lengthy jail sentence.

Another rationale sometimes advanced in support of the marital exemption is that marital rape would be a difficult crime to prove. A related argument is that allowing such prosecutions could lead to fabricated complaints by "vindictive" wives. The difficulty of proof argument is based on the problem of showing lack of consent. Proving lack of consent, however, is often the most difficult part of any rape prosecution, particularly where the rapist and the victim had a prior relationship (see "Spousal Exemption to Rape," *supra*, at n. 4, 65 Marq.L.Rev., at p. 125; "Marital Rape Exemption," *supra*, n. 5, 52 N.Y.U.L.Rev., at p. 314). Similarly, the possibility that married women will fabricate complaints would seem to be no greater than the possibility of unmarried women doing so. The criminal justice system, with all of its built-in safeguards, is presumed to be capable of handling any false complaints. Indeed, if the possibility of fabricated complaints were a basis for not criminalizing behavior which would otherwise be sanctioned, virtually all crimes other than homicides would go unpunished.

The final argument in defense of the marital exemption is that marital rape is not as serious an offense as other rape and is thus adequately dealt with by the possibility of prosecution under criminal statutes, such as assault statutes, which provide for less severe punishment. The fact that rape statutes exist, however, is a recognition that the harm caused by a forcible rape is different, and more severe, than the harm caused by an ordinary assault. Under the Penal Law, assault is generally a misdemeanor unless either the victim suffers "serious physical injury" or a deadly weapon or dangerous instrument is used (Penal Law, §§ 120.00, 120.05, 120.10). Thus, if the defendant had been living with Denise at the time he forcibly raped and sodomized her he probably could not have been charged with a felony, let alone a felony with punishment equal to that for rape in the first degree.

Moreover, there is no evidence to support the argument that marital rape has less severe consequences than other rape. On the contrary, numerous studies have shown that marital rape is frequently quite violent and generally has *more* severe, traumatic effects on the victim than other rape.

Among the recent decisions in this country addressing the marital exemption, only one court has concluded that there is a rational basis for it (*see People v. Brown*, 632 P.2d 1025 [Col.]). We agree with the other courts which have analyzed the exemption, which have been unable to find any present justification for it (*see People v. De Stefano*, 121 Misc.2d 113, 467 N.Y. S.2d 506; *Commonwealth v. Chretien*, 383 Mass. 123, 417 N.E.2d 1203; *State v. Smith*, 85 N.J. 193, 426 A.2d 38, *supra; Weishaupt v. Commonwealth*, 227 Va. 389, 315 S.E.2d 847, *supra; State v. Rider*, 449 So.2d 903 [Fla.App.]; *State v. Smith*, 401 So.2d 1126 [Fla.App.]). Justice Holmes wrote: "It is revolting to have no better reason for a rule of law than that so it was laid down in the time of Henry IV. It is still more revolting if the grounds upon which it was laid down have vanished long since, and the rule simply persists from blind imitation of the past." This statement is an apt characterization of the marital exemption; it lacks a rational basis, and therefore violates the equal protection clauses of both the Federal and State Constitutions (U.S. Const., 14th Amdt., § 1; N.Y. Const., art. I, § 11).

B. *The Exemption for Females*

Under the Penal Law only males can be convicted of rape in the first degree. Insofar as the rape statute applies to acts of "sexual intercourse," which, as defined in the Penal Law (*see* Penal Law, § 130.00) can only occur between a male and a female, it is true that a female cannot physically rape a female and that therefore there is no denial of equal protection when punishing only males for forcibly engaging in sexual intercourse with females. The equal protection issue, however, stems from the fact that the statute applies to males who forcibly rape females but does not apply to females who forcibly rape males.

Rape statutes historically applied only to conduct by males against females, largely because the purpose behind the proscription was to protect the chastity of women and thus their property value to their fathers or husbands (*see State v. Smith*, 85 N.J. at p. 204, 426 A.2d 38, *supra;* 2 Burdick, Law of Crime, pp. 218-225; Comment, Rape Laws, Equal Protection, and Privacy Rights, 54 Tulane L.Rev. 456, 457 [hereafter cited as "Rape Laws"]). New York's rape statute has always protected only females, and has thus applied only to males (*see* Penal Law, § 130.35; 1909 Penal Law, § 2010; 1881 Penal Code, tit. X, ch. II, § 278). Presently New York is one of only 10 jurisdictions that does not have a gender-neutral statute for forcible rape.

A statute which treats males and females differently violates equal protection unless the classification is substantially related to the achievement of an important governmental objective. This test applies whether the statute discriminates against males or against females. The People bear the burden of showing both the existence of an important objective and the substantial relationship between the discrimination in the statute and that objective. This burden is not met in the present case, and therefore the gender exemption also renders the statute unconstitutional.

The first argument advanced by the People in support of the exemption for females is that because only females can become pregnant the State may constitutionally differentiate between forcible rapes of females and forcible rapes of males. This court and the United States Supreme Court have upheld statutes which subject males to criminal liability for engaging in sexual intercourse with underage females without the converse being true (*People v. Whidden, supra; Michael M. v. Sonoma County Superior Ct.,* 450 U.S. 464, 101 S.Ct. 1200, 67 L.Ed.2d 437, *supra*). The rationale behind these decisions was that the primary purpose of such "statutory rape" laws is to protect against the harm caused by teenage pregnancies, there being no need to provide the same protection to young males.

There is no evidence, however, that preventing pregnancies is a primary purpose of the statute prohibiting forcible rape, nor does such a purpose seem likely (*see* "Rape Laws," *op. cit.,* 54 Tulane L.Rev., at p. 467). Rather, the very fact that the statute proscribes "forcible compulsion" shows that its overriding purpose is to protect a woman from an unwanted, forcible, and often violent sexual intrusion into her body. Thus, due to the different purposes behind forcible rape laws and "statutory" (consensual) rape laws, the cases upholding the gender discrimination in the latter are not decisive with respect to the former, and the People cannot meet their burden here by simply stating that only females can become pregnant.

The People also claim that the discrimination is justified because a female rape victim "faces the probability of medical, sociological, and psychological problems unique to her gender." This same argument, when advanced in support of the discrimination in the statutory rape laws, was rejected by this court in *People v. Whidden* (51 N.Y.2d at p. 461, 434 N.Y.S.2d 937, 415 N.E.2d 927, *supra*), and it is no more convincing in the present case. "[A]n ' "archaic and overbroad" ' generalization' * * *

which is evidently grounded in long-standing stereotypical notions of the differences between the sexes, simply cannot serve as a legitimate rationale for a penal provision that is addressed only to adult males" (*id., quoting Craig v. Boren,* 429 U.S. at p. 198, 97 S.Ct. at p. 457, *supra*; cf. *Orr v. Orr,* 440 U.S. at p. 283, 99 S.Ct. at p. 1114, *supra*; Tribe, Constitutional Law, p. 1066).

Finally, the People suggest that a gender-neutral law for forcible rape is unnecessary, and that therefore the present law is constitutional, because a woman either cannot actually rape a man or such attacks, if possible, are extremely rare. Although the "physiologically impossible" argument has been accepted by several courts, it is simply wrong. The argument is premised on the notion that a man cannot engage in sexual intercourse unless he is sexually aroused, and if he is aroused then he is consenting to intercourse. "Sexual intercourse" however, "occurs upon any penetration, however slight" (Penal Law, § 130.00); this degree of contact can be achieved without a male being aroused and thus without his consent.

As to the "infrequency" argument, while forcible sexual assaults by females upon males are undoubtedly less common than those by males upon females this numerical disparity cannot by itself make the gender discrimination constitutional. Women may well be responsible for a far lower number of all serious crimes than are men, but such a disparity would not make it permissible for the State to punish only men who commit, for example, robbery (cf. *Craig v. Boren,* 429 U.S. at pp. 200-204, 97 S.Ct. at pp. 458-461, *supra*).

To meet their burden of showing that a gender-based law is substantially related to an important governmental objective the People must set forth an " 'exceedingly persuasive justification' " for the classification, which requires, among other things, a showing that the gender-based law serves the governmental objective better than would a gender-neutral law. The fact that the act of a female forcibly raping a male may be a difficult or rare occurrence does not mean that the gender exemption satisfies the constitutional test. A gender-neutral law would indisputably better serve, even if only marginally, the objective of deterring and punishing forcible sexual assaults. The only persons "benefitted" by the gender exemption are females who forcibly rape males. As the Supreme Court has stated, "[a] gender-based classification which, as compared to a gender-neutral one, generates additional benefits only for those it has no reason to prefer cannot survive equal protection scrutiny" (*Orr v. Orr*, 440 U.S. at pp. 282-283, 99 S.Ct. at pp. 1113-1114).

Accordingly, we find that § 130.35 of the Penal Law violates equal protection because it exempts females from criminal liability for forcible rape.

V

Having found that the statutes for rape in the first degree and sodomy in the first degree are unconstitutionally underinclusive, the remaining issue is the appropriate remedy for these equal protection violations. When a statute is constitutionally defective because of underinclusion, a court may either strike the statute, and thus make it applicable to nobody, or extend the coverage of the statute to those formerly excluded. Accordingly, the unconstitutionality of one part of a criminal statute does not necessarily render the entire statute void.

This court's task is to discern what course the Legislature would have chosen to follow if it had foreseen our conclusions as to underinclusiveness. As Judge Cardozo wrote over 50 years ago, " 'The question is in every case whether the Legislature, if partial invalidity had been foreseen, would have wished the statute to be enforced with the invalid part exscinded, or rejected altogether' " ([" '(u)nless it is evident that the legislature would not have enacted those provisions which are within its power, independently of that which is not, the invalid part may be dropped if what is left is fully operative as a law' "]). These principles of severance apply as well where elimination of an invalid exemption will impose burdens on those not formerly burdened by the statute, and where the exemption is part of a criminal statute.

The question then is whether the Legislature would prefer to have statutes which cover forcible rape and sodomy, with no exemption for married men who rape or sodomize their wives and no exception made for females who rape males, or instead to have no statutes proscribing forcible rape and sodomy. In any case where a court must decide whether to sever an exemption or instead declare an entire statute a nullity it must look at the importance of the statute, the significance of the exemption within the over-all statutory scheme, and the effects of striking down the statute. Forcible sexual assaults have historically been treated as serious crimes and certainly remain so today (*see, generally, Coker v. Georgia*, 433 U.S. 584, 97 S.Ct. 2861, 53 L.Ed.2d 982, *supra*. Statutes prohibiting such behavior are of the utmost importance, and to declare such statutes a nullity would have a disastrous effect on the public interest and safety. The inevitable conclusion is that the Legislature would prefer to eliminate the exemptions and thereby preserve the statutes. Accordingly we choose the remedy of striking the marital exemption from §§ 130.35 and 130.50 of the Penal Law and the gender exemption from § 130.35 of the Penal Law, so that it is now the law of this State that any person who engages in sexual intercourse or deviate sexual intercourse with any other person by forcible compulsion is guilty of either rape in the first degree or sodomy in the first degree. Because the statutes under which the defendant was convicted are not being struck down, his conviction is affirmed.

Though our decision does not "create a crime," it does, of course, enlarge the scope of two criminal statutes. We recognize that a court should be reluctant to expand criminal statutes, due to the danger of usurping the role of the Legislature, but in this case overriding policy concerns dictate our following such a course in light of the catastrophic effect that striking down the statutes and thus creating a hiatus would have. Courts in other States have in numerous cases applied these same principles in eliminating an unconstitutional exception from a criminal statute and thereby enlarging the scope of the statute. The decision most similar factually to the present one comes from the Alaska Supreme Court in *Plas v. State,* 598 P.2d 966 (Alaska). That court addressed an equal protection challenge by a female prostitute to a statute which criminalized prostitution, and defined it as a female offering her body for sexual intercourse for hire. The court agreed with the defendant that the statute violated equal protection because it covered only females, but chose to remedy this underinclusion by striking the definition, thereby expanding the statute to cover any person who

engaged in prostitution, and affirmed her conviction.

The defendant cannot claim that our decision to retain the rape and sodomy statutes, and thereby affirm his conviction, denies him due process of the law. The due process clause of the Fourteenth Amendment requires that an accused have had fair warning at the time of his conduct that such conduct was made criminal by the State (*see Bouie v. City of Columbia,* 378 U.S. 347, 84 S.Ct. 1697, 12 L.Ed.2d 894). Defendant did not come within any of the exemptions which we have stricken, and thus his conduct was covered by the statutes as they existed at the time of his attack on Denise.

Neither can it be said that by the affirmance of his conviction the defendant is deprived of a constitutionally protected right to equal protection. The remedy chosen by our opinion is to extend the coverage of the provisions for forcible rape and sodomy to all those to whom these provisions can constitutionally be applied. While this remedy does treat the defendant differently than, for example, a married man who, while living with his wife, raped her prior to this decision, the distinction is rational inasmuch as it is justified by the limitations imposed on our remedy by the notice requirements of the due process clause (U.S. Const., 14th Amdt.), and the prohibition against ex post facto laws (U.S. Const., art. I, § 10). Thus, for purposes of choosing the proper remedy, the defendant is simply not similarly situated to those persons who were not within the scope of the statutes as they existed prior to our decision.

To reverse the defendant's conviction would mean that all those persons now awaiting trial for forcible rape or sodomy would be entitled to dismissal of the indictment. Indeed if we were to reverse no person arrested for forcible rape or sodomy prior to the date of this decision could be prosecuted for that offense, and every person already convicted of forcible rape or sodomy who raised the equal protection challenge would be entitled to have the conviction vacated. As the equal protection clause does not require us to reach such a result, we decline to do so.

Accordingly, the order of the Appellate Division should be affirmed.

COOKE, C., and JASEN, JONES, MEYER and KAYE, JJ., concur. SIMONS, J., taking no part.

Order affirmed.

Charles Gregory DONOHO, Appellant,

v.

The STATE of Texas, Appellee

Court of Appeals of Texas,
628 S.W.2d 483. Jan. 12, 1982.
Rehearing Denied Feb. 9, 1982.

BLEIL, Justice.

Charles Donoho appeals his conviction of committing deviate sexual intercourse in a public place. After a jury trial, the court set punishment at a $250.00 fine and confinement for ninety days, probated for one year. The three grounds of error challenge the sufficiency of the evidence to support the verdict.

In reviewing sufficiency of the evidence questions we do not determine the credibility of the witnesses. We look at the evidence in the light most favorable to the verdict and determine whether there is evidence which the jury could have believed in arriving at their verdict. *Rogers v. State,* 550 S.W.2d 78 (Tex.Crim.App. 1977). We find the evidence sufficient and affirm the judgment.

Officer Charles Roberts, a Dallas police officer, was the only witness in this case. He indicated that on May 4, 1979, he was assigned to the vice-con-trol division of the police department. On that date, he, together with Officer Cox of the police department, went to "The Locker," a gay bar located in Dallas. He went inside and sat on a stool in front of the well lighted dance area. Donoho and two other persons were on the dance floor. While dancing with another man, James Roberson, Donoho got down on his knees and placed his mouth against the genital area of Roberson who stood there moving back and forth. Donoho placed his mouth on Roberson's genital area and made kissing motions while actually rubbing the area. This continued about thirty seconds and the officer stated that Roberson just moved back and forth forcing his pelvic area, "It appeared to me, even closer into the— into the defendant's mouth."

Critical to the case is the following exchange which occurred during the prosecution's direct examination of Roberts: "*Q.* And did this defendant, Charles Gregory Donoho, place his mouth in contact with the genitals of James Ronald Roberson? *A.* Yes, sir, he did. *Mr. Aranson:* Your Honor, repetitive. *The Court:* Sustained. *Mr. Aranson:* And I'd ask that the answer be stricken. *The Court:* The jury will disregard the last question and answer and consider it for no purpose."

By his objection to the testimony on the basis of its being repetitious, the appellant is estopped to assert that matters objected to and excluded were not sufficiently established at trial.

Officer Roberts' answer established that James Roberson had genitals and that there was contact between Donoho's mouth and Roberson's genitals. Appellant's objection and motion to strike that testimony on the basis that it was repetitious estops him from now assuming a contrary position. *Texas Department of Public Safety v. Cannon,* 547 S.W.2d 302 (Tex.Civ.App.—Dallas 1976, writ ref'd n.r.e.); *Yarber v. Pennell,* 443 S.W.2d 382 (Tex.Civ.App.—Dallas 1969, writ ref'd n.r.e.); *Lobit v. Crouch,* 323 S.W.2d 618 (Tex.Civ.App.—Austin 1959, writ ref'd n.r.e.). Thus, sufficient evidence exists to establish that Roberson, a man, had genitals and that there was contact between his genitals and Donoho's mouth.

Donoho also argues that there was insufficient evidence of contact between his mouth and Roberson's genitals because there was no testimony that flesh-to-flesh contact occurred. This contention requires a close look at the statute under which Donoho was charged. Section 21.07, Tex. Penal Code Ann., entitled "Public Lewdness" provides in part:

"(a) A person commits an offense if he knowingly engages in any of the following acts in a public place...,

* * *

"(2) an act of deviate sexual intercourse;"

* * *

The Penal Code, § 21.01 defines "deviate sexual intercourse" as any contact between any part of the genitals of one person and the mouth or anus of another person. This term, as defined in § 21.01, requires only *any contact,* not penetration, and is consistent with prior law. *Sinclair v. State,* 166 Tex.Cr.R. 167, 311 S.W.2d 824 (1958).

Donoho contends that contact must require "flesh being placed upon flesh." He recognizes that the case of *Resnick v. State,* 574 S.W.2d 558 (Tex.Crim.App.1978), rejected a similar claim in dealing with a prosecution under § 21.07(a)(3), Texas Penal Code Ann., which prohibits public acts of "sexual contact." "Sexual contact" means any touching of the anus or any part of the genitals of another person or the breast of a female, ten years or older, with intent to gratify sexual desire.

In *Resnick,* the defendant and a police officer went into an adult movie house in Dallas. The officer put coins in the movie unit and while he and the defendant watched the movie, the defendant placed his hand on the genitals of the officer, even though the officer wore pants which were zipped. In rejecting Resnick's argument that the sexual contact required flesh-to-flesh contact, the court concluded that to touch or to contact does not require a flesh-to-flesh meeting. The court further explained that if flesh-to-flesh contact were required, a defendant who thrust his hand under a person's underwear and fondled his or her genitals publicly could not be prosecuted for public lewdness if he were wearing a glove. Employing such an analysis dealing with deviate sexual intercourse, a court-imposed flesh-to-flesh requirement might arguably preclude prosecution for public lewdness by one committing deviate sexual intercourse while using a prophylactic device.

In any instance, if the legislature intended to require that there be flesh-to-flesh contact or penetration for the offense of deviate sexual intercourse to be committed, it could have so provided. We hold that the evidence is sufficient to support the verdict under the facts of this case and the applicable Penal Code provisions.

We affirm.

Cases relating to Chapter 5
OFFENSES AGAINST PROPERTY— DESTRUCTION AND INTRUSION OFFENSES

STATE of North Carolina
v.
Sherrill WYATT
Court of Appeals of North Carolina.
269 S.E.2d 717 (1980).

Defendant was charged with arson. He was convicted as charged and appeals from the judgment imposing a prison term of not less than fifteen nor more than fifty years.

The State's evidence tends to show the following: On the evening of 11 March 1979, a fire occurred in Building 9, Pisgah View Apartments in Asheville. The fire was confined to Apartment 9F. There was extensive incidental damage to Apartment 9E which was occupied by Brenda Dockery (or Brockley). Harold Ray, a codefendant, testified that defendant Wyatt set two fires in Apartment. He also testified that no one lived in 9F on the night of the fire. Defendant's stepmother, Vina Mae Wyatt, testified that she moved out of Apartment 9F about a week before the fire; that there were bad feelings between her and the defendant, such that the defendant had threatened to destroy her apartment; and that she now lives in 21A Pisgah View Apartments. Two residents of the Apartments testified that on the night of the fire they saw defendant running out of Apartment 9F, and soon thereafter they observed the fire.

Defendant alleged that his codefendant Ray set the fires. He also introduced evidence of his work as a buyer for the Interagency Narcotics Squad. Other facts will be stated in the opinion.

Atty. Gen. Rufus L. Edmisten by Associate Atty. Gen. Fred R. Gamin, Raleigh, for the State.

Gray, Kimel & Connolly by David G. Gray, Asheville, for defendant-appellant.

CLARK, Judge.

Defendant's primary assignment of error is that he was not arraigned and tried on a proper bill of indictment. That indictment charges as follows:

[T]hat on or about the 11th day of March, 1979, in Buncombe County Sherrill Wyatt, aka Sherrill David Wheeler unlawfully and willfully did feloniously and maliciously burn the dwelling house inhabited by Vina Mae Wyatt and located at 9F Pisgah View Apartments, Asheville, North Carolina. At the time of the burning Brenda Dockery was in the adjoining apartment located at 9E Pisgah View

545

Apartments in violation of the following law: G.S. 14-58.

Defendant suggests that the indictment is fatally defective in that it fails to describe a dwelling house, so inhabited, which would charge the defendant with common law arson. The purpose of the indictment is to inform the defendant of the charge against him with sufficient certainty to enable him to prepare his defense. *State v. Gates*, 107 N.C. 832, 12 S.E. 319 (1890). To this end, a valid indictment must allege all the essential elements of the offense charged. *State v. Greer*, 238 N.C. 325, 77 S.E.2d 917 (1953). Necessary elements of common law arson include that the place burned be "the dwelling house of another" and that the house be occupied at the time of the burning. *State v. Long*, 243 N.C. 393, 90 S.E.2d 739 (1956). Although we see no problem with the occupancy requirement since Brenda Dockery was alleged to have been "in" 9E at the time of the burning, we believe the requirement of a "dwelling house of another" deserves some discussion.

The defendant argues on the authority of 6A C.J.S., Arson § 32 (1979) and one very old case, *State v. Sandy*, 25 N.C. (3 Ired.) 570 (1843), that each separate apartment within Building 9 constitutes a separate and distinct dwelling house. He notes that since Mrs. Wyatt no longer dwelt in 9F there could be no common law arson of that apartment; and that since Brenda Dockery's apartment was apparently not actually charred, there can be no common law arson of that apartment. The State's contention is that Building 9 of Pisgah View Apartments (comprised of Apartments A, B, C, D, E & F) constituted one dwelling house such that the requirements of a

burning could be satisfied by the charring in 9F while the requirement of occupancy could be satisfied by Dockery's presence in 9E. The State relies upon the recent case of *State v. Jones*, 296 N.C. 75, 248 S.E.2d 858 (1978). We agree with the State that the rationale of *State v. Jones, supra*, is controlling in this case. We note that C.J.S. is no more than persuasive authority and that other persuasive authority opposes the view expressed therein. *See, e.g.*, R. Perkins Criminal Law 183 (1957). *State v. Sandy, supra*, is not controlling because it dealt with the statutory offense of burning a storehouse. As noted by our Supreme Court, per Exum, Justice, "[T]he main purpose of common law arson is to protect against danger to those persons who might be in the dwelling house which is burned. Where there are several apartments in a single building, this purpose can be served only by subjecting to punishment for arson any person who sets fire to any part of the building." *Jones, supra*, at 77-78, 248 S.E.2d at 860. We note that unlike *State v. Sandy, supra*, the Jones case dealt directly with common law arson. We hold, therefore, that reference in the indictment to Apartments 9F and 9E was sufficient to put the defendant on notice that he was charged with a burning at Building 9 of Pisgah View Apartments and that the recitation of one of the true occupants of the building, Dockery, together with the designation of "dwelling house" in the indictment was sufficient to put the defendant on notice of that element of the crime charged. We note further that the traditional recitation of whose dwelling house was burned is intended simply to put the defendant on notice of the place he is charged with burning so that he can defend his case. We hold that the indictment here sufficiently alleges all of the essential elements of the crime charged.

Defendant also assigns as error that portion of the judge's charge which states:

> "So I charge you if you find from the evidence beyond a reasonable doubt that on or about March 11, 1979, the Defendant Sherrill Wyatt, maliciously burned Apartment 9F, Pisgah View Apartments, which was inhabited by Miss Vina Mae Wyatt, or Mr. Wethers or Mrs. Parson [sic], by setting the living room and bedroom closets on fire it would be your duty to return a verdict of guilty of arson."

We agree with the defendant that there was no evidence to support a finding that either Mr. Wethers or Mrs. Parton were in Apartment 9F. However, the judge followed that instruction with instructions as follows:

> "I further charge if you find from the evidence beyond a reasonable doubt that on or about March 11, 1979, Sherrill Wyatt maliciously burned an apartment in building 9 of the Pisgah View Apartments, which was inhabited by either Mrs. Vina Mae Wyatt or Mr. Wethers or Mrs. Parton, by setting fire to the living room and bedroom closets of Apartment 9F it would be your duty to return a verdict of guilty of arson."

This instruction, combined with his painstaking and accurate review of the evidence would make clear to the jury that Wethers and Parton were not in 9F but in 9E and 9A respectively. The evidence reveals that at the time of the fire Wethers was occupying Apartment 9E with Brenda Dockery (Brockley), who in the indictment was allegedly "in the adjoining apartment." In view of our ruling that Building 9 of Pisgah View Apartments constituted a single dwelling house, it is immaterial which person occupied which apartment. And for the same reason there was not material variance between the indictment and the proof. It was material and essential that the state both allege and prove that the defendant did maliciously burn an inhabited dwelling house. The State did both. We find no prejudicial error.

No error.

MORRIS, C. J., and HARRY C. MARTIN, J., concur.

STATE of Louisiana
v.
Thomas ROBINSON.

Court of Appeal of Louisiana, Fifth Circuit.

Nov. 9, 1983.

441 So.2d 364

GRISBAUM, Judge.

Thomas Robinson was charged with simple burglary of an inhabited dwelling in violation of La.R.S. 14:62.2. After a trial by jury, he was found guilty. On October 6, 1982 he was sentenced to four years at hard labor. From this conviction and sentence, defendant appeals. We affirm.

Assignments of Error

1) The trial court committed reversible error [under *State v. Johnson,* 389 So.2d 372 (La. 1980)] when it failed to instruct the jury as to the purpose of the State's cross-examination of defendant's character witness regarding defendant's prior criminal record. 2) The trial court committed reversible error by denying defendant's Motion for a New Trial, which was based upon the absence of any evidence showing an intent to permanently deprive the victim of his television set.

Facts

On April 20, 1982, at about 12 noon, Leon Duville was driving down the street on which he lives when he observed Willie Thomas in his friend's (Lester Mitchell's) front yard. The defendant, Thomas Robinson, was standing in his own yard near the fence that divides his property from that of Mitchell's. Mr. Duville observed the two subjects standing in close proximity to one another, divided only by the fence. Upon returning from a convenience store, Mr. Duville observed Willie Thomas pass a small portable television set over the fence and hand it to the defendant, Robinson. Mr. Duville immediately recognized the set as belonging to his friend, Mitchell. Mr. Duville further noticed that a window on the side of Mitchell's house was broken.

Mr. Duville then stopped his truck and approached Willie Thomas, who was now in defendant Robinson's yard and was standing in the doorway of the garage. Duville testified that "I told Willie Thomas that he was wrong for what they was doing...."

Mr. Duville returned to his job and later that afternoon advised Mitchell of what had transpired. Mitchell returned home, checked his residence, and found the window in his son's bedroom had been broken. The television was in the room, but it had been moved from its original location and was unplugged. The police were summoned to Mitchell's house and that afternoon, upon the complaint of the victim and the statement given by Duville, both Thomas Robinson and Willie Thomas were arrested.

* * *

Assignment of Error No. 2

The issue presented by this assignment of error is whether the evidence presented is sufficient to support the jury's finding of the essential elements of the crime of simple burglary of an inhabited dwelling, La.R.S. 14:62.2. A defendant has not been afforded due process unless, viewing the evidence in the light most favorable to the prosecution, any rational trier of fact could conclude that the State proved the essential elements of the crime beyond a reasonable doubt. *Jackson v. Virginia,* 443 U.S. 307, 319, 99 S.Ct. 2781, 2789, 61 L.Ed.2d 560, 573 (1979); *State v. Foy,* 439 So.2d 433 (1983); *State v. Johnson,* 438 So.2d 1091 at 1102; *State v. Graham,* 422 So.2d 123, 129 (La. 1982). In cases where an essential element of the crime is not proven by direct evidence, La.R.S. 15:438 provides a methodology for review of this evidence. This rule restrains the finder of fact in the first instance, as well as the reviewer on appeal, to accept as proven all that the evidence tends to prove and then to convict only if every reasonable hypothesis of innocence is excluded.

upheld statutes which subject males to criminal liability for engaging in sexual intercourse with underage females without the converse being true *(People v. Whidden, supra; Michael M. v. Sonoma County Superior Ct.*, 450 U.S. 464, 101 S.Ct. 1200, 67 L.Ed.2d 437, *supra).* The rationale behind these decisions was that the primary purpose of such "statutory rape" laws is to protect against the harm caused by teenage pregnancies, there being no need to provide the same protection to young males.

There is no evidence, however, that preventing pregnancies is a primary purpose of the statute prohibiting forcible rape, nor does such a purpose seem likely *(see* "Rape Laws," *op. cit.*, 54 Tulane L.Rev., at p. 467). Rather, the very fact that the statute proscribes "forcible compulsion" shows that its overriding purpose is to protect a woman from an unwanted, forcible, and often violent sexual intrusion into her body. Thus, due to the different purposes behind forcible rape laws and "statutory" (consensual) rape laws, the cases upholding the gender discrimination in the latter are not decisive with respect to the former, and the People cannot meet their burden here by simply stating that only females can become pregnant.

The People also claim that the discrimination is justified because a female rape victim "faces the probability of medical, sociological, and psychological problems unique to her gender." This same argument, when advanced in support of the discrimination in the statutory rape laws, was rejected by this court in *People v. Whidden* (51 N.Y.2d at p. 461, 434 N.Y.S.2d 937, 415 N.E.2d 927, *supra*), and it is no more convincing in the present case. "[A]n ' "archaic and overbroad" generalization' * * *

which is evidently grounded in long-standing stereotypical notions of the differences between the sexes, simply cannot serve as a legitimate rationale for a penal provision that is addressed only to adult males" *(id., quoting Craig v. Boren,* 429 U.S. at p. 198, 97 S.Ct. at p. 457, *supra*; cf. *Orr v. Orr,* 440 U.S. at p. 283, 99 S.Ct. at p. 1114, *supra*; Tribe, Constitutional Law, p. 1066).

Finally, the People suggest that a gender-neutral law for forcible rape is unnecessary, and that therefore the present law is constitutional, because a woman either cannot actually rape a man or such attacks, if possible, are extremely rare. Although the "physiologically impossible" argument has been accepted by several courts, it is simply wrong. The argument is premised on the notion that a man cannot engage in sexual intercourse unless he is sexually aroused, and if he is aroused then he is consenting to intercourse. "Sexual intercourse" however, "occurs upon any penetration, however slight" (Penal Law, § 130.00); this degree of contact can be achieved without a male being aroused and thus without his consent.

As to the "infrequency" argument, while forcible sexual assaults by females upon males are undoubtedly less common than those by males upon females this numerical disparity cannot by itself make the gender discrimination constitutional. Women may well be responsible for a far lower number of all serious crimes than are men, but such a disparity would not make it permissible for the State to punish only men who commit, for example, robbery (cf. *Craig v. Boren,* 429 U.S. at pp. 200-204, 97 S.Ct. at pp. 458-461, *supra*).

To meet their burden of showing that a gender-based law is substantially bility of being called in to account for his actions and that he specifically intended to permanently deprive the victim of his television set. The contrary inference (drawn from the television being found in the bedroom) that the defendant only "borrowed" the television without an intent to permanently deprive the victim of the television, is contradicted by the broken bedroom window. Moreover, this inference is also contradicted by the eyewitness's admonishing the third party. This admonishment was not met with any reassurance that the television set was only being "borrowed" at that time.

We conclude the evidence is sufficient to support an ultimate finding that the reasonable findings and inferences permitted by the evidence exclude every reasonable hypothesis of innocence. The State has proven every element of the offense of simple burglary of an inhabited dwelling beyond a reasonable doubt. Therefore, this court finds the trial court did not commit reversible error by denying defendant's motion for a new trial.

For the reasons assigned, the defendant's conviction and sentence are affirmed.

Affirmed.

**The PEOPLE of the State of Illinois,
Plaintiff-Appellee,
v.
Ora THOMPSON et al.,
Defendants-Appellants.**

**56 Ill.App.3d 557
14 Ill.Dec. 312**

**Appellate Court of Illinois,
Third District.**

Jan. 9, 1978.

Rehearing Denied Feb. 22, 1978.

372 N.E.2d 117

STENGEL, Presiding Justice.

This was a joint misdemeanor prosecution of ten persons for criminal trespass to land (Ill.Rev.Stat. 1975, ch. 38, par. 21-3(a), (b)). After a jury trial in the Peoria County Circuit Court, all ten defendants were found guilty, and each was sentenced to a six-month term of conditional discharge and

ordered to pay a $50 fine.

On April 26, 1976, the Board of Education of School District No. 150 held a public meeting at the Diagnostic Learning Center Administration Building in Peoria. The meeting commenced at 6:30 p.m. and was attended by numerous people, including the ten defendants in this case, who did not attend the meeting as a group. Most of them came to the meeting to speak on a variety of issues of individual concern, and some of them had received prior permission from the Board to do so. However, only one defendant, McFarland Bragg, actually spoke at the meeting. After defendant Bragg had been at the podium for a short time, he was interrupted by Board President Vilberg, who advised the speaker that his time was up. Bragg's microphone was turned off, but he continued to stand at the podium throughout the meeting. A second defendant, Alvin Richards, was recognized and afforded an opportunity to speak, but refused to do so, stating that the person at the podium (Bragg) had gone unrecognized. None of the other defendants were given an opportunity to speak at the meeting.

The Board meeting ended at approximately 8:45 p.m., but testimony differed as to whether a motion to adjourn was made. Defendants testified they heard no such motion. In any event, the Board members and the majority of the audience left the room at that time. The ten defendants remained. Defendant John Gwynn allegedly stated that "they would stay until they were heard." Sergeant Mildred Adderholtz, the officer in charge of security for the Board meeting, left the room to converse with District No. 150 Superintendent Harry Whitaker and to telephone the head of security for District No. 150, Chief Robert Beecraft. Adderholtz returned to the room and, acting on Superintendent Whitaker's instructions, asked defendants to leave. She advised defendants that the building would be secured in one hour and anyone remaining would be arrested. Chief Beecraft arrived at the building shortly thereafter and reiterated Sergeant Adderholtz' request and warning. Beecraft was also acting on directions from Superintendent Whitaker. At approximately 10 p.m. officers of the Peoria Police Department arrived on the scene and further advised defendants that if they did not leave immediately, District No. 150 personnel would sign warrants for their arrest. Defendants refused to leave and were arrested. Defendants did not resist arrest, and they engaged in no violent or disruptive conduct throughout the incident. Defendants appeal their convictions.

Defendant's primary contention on appeal is that application of the criminal trespass statute to their conduct in this case deprived them of their rights under the First Amendment to the U.S. Constitution. Defendants argue that they had a right to attend the school board meeting of April 26, 1976, and further that they had a right to hear others who came to speak under the Open Meetings Act (Ill. Rev. Stat. 1975, ch. 102, par. 41, et seq.), which requires school boards to hold open meetings, and also under the Board's policy of allowing interested persons to speak at Board meetings if they secured prior permission to do so. According to defendants' theory, the Board ended its meeting without a motion to adjourn solely because the Board members did not want to hear the ideas defendants intended to express. Defendants claim this informal adjournment of the meeting denied them their right to speak and to hear others speak. Most importantly, defendants argue that their continued presence in the building after being requested to depart was a protest against the Board's denial of their rights and thus was a constitutionally protected exercise of free speech. Defendants conclude that the State is unconstitutionally punishing them for exercising their First Amendment rights of free speech and free association.

First Amendment guarantees are not confined to verbal expressions, but also extend to "symbolic speech," non-verbal means of communicating ideas. (*Brown v. State of Louisiana* (1966), 383 U.S. 131, 86 S.Ct. 719, 15 L.Ed.2d 637.) Defendants' conduct in this case might well be considered "symbolic speech" as defendants' refusal to leave the building was based upon their desire to communicate their protest against what they believed to be a denial of their rights. Clearly defendants had the right to associate together to protest the school board's action. (*NAACP v. Alabama* (1958), 357 U.S. 449, 78 S.Ct. 1163, 2 L.Ed.2d 1488.) However, the issue in the case is not the right to protest, but the place, time, and manner of protest. The courts have rejected the contention that people who want to propagandize protests or views have a constitutional right to do so whenever and wherever and however they please. (*Cox v. Louisiana* (1965), 379 U.S. 536, 85 S.Ct. 453, 13 L.Ed.2d 471; *Adderly v. Florida* (1966), 385 U.S. 39, 87 S.Ct. 242, 17 L.Ed.2d 149.) "[R]easonable 'time, place and manner' regulations may be necessary to further significant governmental interests and are permitted." (*Grayned v. City of Rockford* (1972), 408 U.S. 104, 115, 92 S.Ct. 2294, 2303, 33 L.Ed.2d 222.)

The court said in *Food Employees v. Logan Plaza*, 391 U.S. 308, 320, 88 S.Ct. 1601, 1609, 20 L.Ed.2d 603 (1968):

"Even where municipal or State property is open to the public generally, the exercise of First Amendment rights may be regulated so as to prevent interference with the use to which the property is ordinarily put by the State."

Although ideas may not be regulated, conduct, even conduct expressly engaged in to convey an idea, may be.

In the present case defendants are not being punished for the ideas they sought to express but rather for the conduct which they chose as a medium to express those ideas. The criminal trespass statute applies to anyone who "remains upon the land of another after receiving notice from the owner * * * to depart." (Ill. Rev. Stat. 1975, ch. 38, par. 21-3(a).) Defendants in this case refused to leave one of District 150's educational buildings after being requested to do so by personnel acting under instructions from the District Superintendent. School District 150, the owner of the building in question, clearly had a right to ask defendants to leave. "The State, no less than a private owner of property, has power to preserve the property under its control for the use to which it is lawfully dedicated." Moreover, the request that defendants leave the premises was reasonable since the normal activity of the building in question was educational and it was not a public meeting place. Although defendants certainly had a right to attend the public meeting earlier held in the building, that meeting had been over for more than an hour when defendants were arrested. The Board members and most of the audience had departed by 10 p.m., which was the normal time to close and secure the building. There was no evidence that defendants were singled out for exclusion from the building solely because of their purpose of protest. In essence, School District 150 made a reasonable request that defendants depart the building they were occupying, and defendants are being punished in this case for disobeying that rightful and reasonable request. We find that the provisions of Illinois Revised Statutes 1975, ch. 38, par. 21-3, and the use to which the statute has been put are reasonable and nondiscriminatory. We hold that the provisions here considered do not violate First Amendment guarantees of free speech and assembly.

Defendants cite statutory provisions which require governmental entities such as a school board to hold open meetings (Ill. Rev. Stat. 1975, ch. 102, par. 41, et seq.) and the Board's policy of allowing interested persons to speak at Board meetings. These points raised by defendants do not affect our decision. Although the legislative provisions cited by defendants do require a school board to open its meetings to the public, they do not require the Board to allow all members of the public to speak at those meetings. Furthermore, whether or not School District 150 violated its own policy is irrelevant since such a violation by the Board could not confer upon defendants the right to trespass on District 150 property. Equally irrelevant to the case is defendants' failure to hear a motion to adjourn the meeting. Motions to adjourn may be customary at such meetings, but they are not required by law. The important facts are that defendants must have known the meeting had ended when the Board members and audience left the room, and that all of the defendants heard the security officer's request that they depart. Similarly the lack of disruption or interference during the incident is also of no consequence since the statute under which defendants were convicted simply does not require any disruption or interference. Remaining upon the land of another after being requested to leave is sufficient to complete the offense. Ill. Rev. Stat. 1975, ch. 38, par. 21-3(a).

Defendants place heavy reliance on *Brown v. Louisiana* (1966), 383 U.S. 131, 86 S.Ct. 719, 15 L.Ed.2d 637. In that case the U.S. Supreme Court reversed the convictions of five black defendants who were charged under a disturbing the peace statute for disobeying a request to leave the reading room of a racially segregated public library. The crucial distinction between *Brown* and the case at hand is that the defendants in *Brown* were "in a place where the protestant had every right to be." The defendants in *Brown* were in a public library reading room during regular library hours. The only reason they were requested to leave was their race. That is clearly an unreasonable request under the First and Fourteenth Amendments. In the present case, on the contrary, the request that defendants depart was reasonable because, as discussed above, defendants had no right to be in the school building at 10 p.m., more than an hour after the school board meeting ended. The defendants' presence, whether for the purpose of protest or not, was basically incompatible with the normal activity of that place at that time, and it is not unconstitutional for the State to punish defendants for refusing to leave when receiving a reasonable request to do so.

Next, defendants advance three contentions which relate to the concept of ownership as embodied in the criminal trespass statute. That statute provides that a defendant is guilty of criminal trespass to land if he "remains upon the land of another after receiving notice from the owner * * * to depart." (Ill. Rev. Stat. 1975, ch. 38, par. 21-3(a).)

Defendants first contend that the complaint in this case insufficiently stated the offense of criminal trespass in failing to allege that the owner of the building in question had given defendants the required notice to depart.

Although defendants did successfully challenge two initial complaints, they stipulated prior to trial that School District 150 was the owner of the Diagnostic Learning Center Administrative Building. Having proceeded to trial on the basis of that stipulation, defendants' contention must be judged as though raised for the first time on appeal. (*People v. Gilmore* (1976), 63 Ill.2d 23, 344 N.E.2d 456.) The test to be applied is whether the complaint set forth the elements of the offense with sufficient specificity to permit defendants to prepare a proper defense and to permit a conviction or acquittal to be pleaded in bar of future prosecutions. (*People v. Mahle* (1974), 57 Ill.2d 279, 312 N.E.2d 267.) We are convinced that the charge in this case meets this test. The complaint specified that defendants "did knowingly remain *upon the land* of Peoria Public School District 150" and that the security officers were "acting at the direction of said owner" in asking defendants to depart. (Emphasis added.) These allegations were sufficiently specific to inform defendants that School District 150 was the alleged owner of the building and that the security officers were acting at the request of the owner. Thus, the essential elements of the offense were contained in the charge, and the complaint was sufficient.

Defendants also contend that there was insufficient evidence presented to prove that the "owner" of the building in question gave them notice to depart. Evidence adduced at trial did establish that officers Adderholtz and Beecraft were acting on instructions from Superintendent Whitaker in asking defendants to depart, but defendants deny that Whitaker had authority from the owner, School District 150, to give those instructions. We believe Super-

intendent Whitaker had such authority.

A District Superintendent is an agent of the District School Board, and his authority is delineated by statute. (*Classroom Teachers Ass'n v. Board of Ed. of United Twp. High School Dist. No. 30, East Moline* (3d Dist. 1973), 15 Ill.App.3d 224, 304 N.E.2d 516.) Section 10-21.4 of the School Code (Ill.Rev.Stat. 1975, ch. 122, par. 10-21.4) provides that school district superintendents "shall have charge of the administration of the schools under the direction of the board of education." This broad grant of administrative authority to the superintendent includes the authority to notify trespassers to depart from school buildings. (See *People v. Spencer* (1st Dist. 1971), 131 Ill.App.2d 551, 268 N.E.2d 192, where it was held that a high school principal had authority under the criminal trespass statute to give defendant the required notice to depart.)

Finally, defendants contend that the trial court erred in refusing to give the following non-I.P.I instruction:

"When I say 'owner,' I mean a person or organization who has legal or rightful title to the land and buildings."

Defendants claim that the concept of ownership was central to the case and that they were prejudiced by the trial court's refusal to inform the jury of the preceding definition of owner. We disagree.

A non-I.P.I. instruction is required to be simple, brief, impartial, and free from argument. (Ill.Rev.Stat. 1975, ch. 110A, par. 451(a); *People v. Poe* (1971), 48 Ill.2d 506, 272 N.E.2d 28.) Defendants' instruction does not meet those requirements. The proposed definition of owner includes only a person or organization who has legal title.

Such a narrow definition would fail to advise the jury of the myriad of other senses in which the word "owner" may be used. (*Robinson v. Walker* (1st Dist. 1965), 63 Ill.App.2d 204, 211 N.E.2d 488.) Of particular importance in this case is the instruction's failure to advise that an "owner" may act through an agent. Since the agency relationship between Superintendent Whitaker and the school board was crucial to the State's theory of the case, the instruction cannot be considered impartial or free from argument. The decision whether to give a tendered non-I.P.I. instruction is within the discretion of the trial court. (*People v. Hines* (5th Dist. 1975), 28 Ill.App.3d 976, 329 N.E.2d 903.) The trial court in this case gave two instructions (I.P.I. Instruction Nos. 9 and 10) which adequately set forth the elements of criminal trespass to land. Hence, we do not believe the trial court erred in refusing to give the instruction tendered by defendants.

In the light of the view which we take of this case, the only remaining issue is the sufficiency of the evidence. We find that the evidence was sufficient in law to show that the defendants refused to leave after being requested to do so by an authorized agent of the school district. This court cannot hold that the defendants were constitutionally free to ignore the numerous warnings to leave and to ignore all the procedures of the statute involved. Respect for judicial process cannot be turned off and on as though it were a hot water faucet. The civilizing hand of law alone can give durable and lasting meaning to constitutional freedom.

For the foregoing reasons, the judgment of the Circuit Court of Peoria County is affirmed.

Affirmed.

STOUDER and SCOTT, JJ., concur.

Cases relating to Chapter 6

OFFENSES INVOLVING THEFT

The PEOPLE of the State of California,
Plaintiff and Respondent,

v.

Curtis Dale ESTES,
Defendant and Appellant.

Court of Appeal, First District,
Sept. 15, 1983.

Hearing Denied Nov. 9, 1983.

194 Cal.Rptr. 909

LOW, Presiding Justice.

In this case we affirm a robbery conviction for the taking of personal property owned by Sears, Roebuck & Company in the immediate presence of a security guard, using force and fear to complete the taking. Defendant Curtis Estes appeals from a judgment entered after a jury found him guilty of robbery (Pen.Code, § 211) by personal use of a deadly weapon (Pen.Code, § 12022, subd. (b)) and petty theft (Pen.Code, § 484) arising out of the theft of merchandise from a Sears department store. Defendant entered the Sears store in Larwin Plaza, Vallejo, wearing only jeans and a t-shirt and was observed by Carl Tatem, a security guard employed by Sears. Tatem next saw defendant wearing a corduroy coat of the type sold by Sears, and watched him removed a down-filled vest from a rack, take off the coat, put on the vest, then the coat, and leave the store without paying for the items. Tatem followed defendant outside the store, identified himself, and confronted him about the coat and vest in the parking lot about five feet

from the store. Defendant refused to accompany Tatem to the store and began to walk away. As Tatem attempted to detain him, defendant pulled out a knife, swung it at Tatem, and threatened to kill Tatem. Tatem, who was unarmed, returned to the store for help.

Shortly thereafter, Tatem returned to the parking lot with Mel Roberts, the Sears' security manager. Tatem and Roberts confronted defendant and again asked him to accompany them back to the store. Defendant still clutched the knife in his hand. After some time, defendant returned to the store with Tatem and Roberts, but denied using the knife and denied stealing the coat and vest. At the trial, defendant admitted stealing the coat and vest from the store, but again denied using force or fear against the security guard, or any other person.

Defendant argues that the property was not taken from a person since the security guard did not have the authority or control over the property. "Robbery is the felonious taking of personal property in the possession of another, from his person or immediate

557

presence, and against his will, accomplished by force or fear." (Pen.Code, § 211.)

It is not necessary that the victim of the robbery also be the owner of the goods taken. Robbery is an offense against the person who has either actual or constructive possession over the goods. Thus, a store employee may be a victim of robbery even though he does not own the property taken and is not in charge or in immediate control of the property at the time of the crime. Nor is it a defense that the victim was a visitor to a store and was not the true owner of money or property taken. Furthermore, a person may be convicted of robbing a janitor or night watchman by taking the employer's property.

Defendant attempts to distinguish these cases on the grounds that these victims were the only persons present at the times of robbery and accordingly were the only persons who had constructive possession from which the personal property could be taken. Defendant reasons that in this case the store manager and sales clerks were the only ones with responsibility over the goods and thus they and not the guard, Tatem, could be the only victims.

The victim was employed by Sears to prevent thefts of merchandise. As the agent of the owner and a person directly responsible for the security of the items, Tatem was in constructive possession of the merchandise to the same degree as a salesperson. Simply because there were other people present in the store who also had constructive possession of the personal property is not relevant, since more than one person may constructively possess personal property at the same time and be a victim of the same offender.

Defendant further alleges that the merchandise was not taken from the "immediate presence" of the security guard. The evidence establishes that appellant forcibly resisted the security guard's efforts to retake the property and used that force to remove the items from the guard's immediate presence. By preventing the guard from regaining control over the merchandise, defendant is held to have taken the property as if the guard had actual possession of the goods in the first instance.

In *Anderson,* defendant entered a pawn shop and posing as a customer asked the salesman to show him a shotgun and shells. The salesman complied. No force was used at this point. Defendant took the shotgun, loaded it, and robbed the salesman at gunpoint. The court rejected the contention that there was no robbery since defendant obtained possession of the merchandise without force or fear. A robbery is not completed at the moment the robber obtains possession of the stolen property. The crime of robbery includes the element of asportation, the robber's escape with the loot being considered as important in the commission of the crime as gaining possession of the property. Here, as in *Anderson,* a robbery occurs when defendant uses force or fear in resisting attempts to regain the property or in attempting to remove the property from the owner's immediate presence regardless of the means by which defendant originally acquired the property.

Defendant further claims that the robbery verdict cannot stand since his assaultive behavior was not contemporaneous with the taking of the merchandise from the store. Defendant maintains that he was, at most, guilty of petty theft and a subsequent assault. Appellant's theory is contrary to the law. The crime of robbery is a continuing offense that begins from the time of the original taking until the robber reaches a place of relative safety. It is sufficient to support the conviction that appellant used force to prevent the guard from retaking the property and to facilitate his escape. The crime is not divisible into a series of separate acts. Defendant's guilt is not to be weighed at each step of the robbery as it unfolds. The events constituting the crime of robbery, although they may extend over large distances and take some time to complete, are linked by a single-mindedness of purpose. (*See People v. Laursen* (1972) 8 Cal.3d 192, 199-200, 104 Cal.Rptr. 425, 501 P.2d 1145.) Whether defendant used force to gain original possession of the property or to resist attempts to retake the stolen property, force was applied against the guard in furtherance of the robbery and can properly be used to sustain the conviction.

A similar result was reached in *People v. Kent* (1981) 125 Cal.App.3d 207, 178 Cal.Rptr. 28. There defendant used a ruse to enter the victim's house. While defendant was alone in the kitchen he took cash from the victim's purse. A short time later the victim discovered the money was missing and confronted defendant. At that point defendant struck the victim, brandished a knife and demanded more money. Defendant left the premises without obtaining additional cash. His conviction of robbery was affirmed. The court rejected defendant's contention "that the jury could have reasonably concluded that the taking of the money constituted a mere larceny and that the application of force or fear occurred after the larceny was completed."

Finally, theft is a lesser included offense within robbery, and defendant could not be convicted of both petty theft and robbery. A defendant cannot be convicted both of the greater offense and the lesser included offense. Where there is sufficient evidence to sustain the conviction of the greater offense, the conviction of the lesser offense must be reversed.

Here, the jury convicted defendant of both the robbery of the security guard, Tatem, and the petty theft from the Sears store. The theft of the property from Tatem was also a theft from the Sears store since Tatem, as Sears' agent, was in constructive possession of the merchandise. Therefore, the theft from the store was a lesser included offense to the robbery of Tatem. Since there is substantial evidence to support the conviction of robbery, we must reverse the conviction for petty theft.

Lastly, appellant argues that the trial court improperly instructed the jury. We have examined this contention and find neither error nor reversible error.

The conviction of petty theft (Pen.Code, § 484) is reversed. In all other respects, the judgment is affirmed.

KING and HANING, JJ., concur.

UNITED STATES of America, Appellee,

v.

Lohman Ray MAYS, Jr., Appellant.

United States Court of Appeals, Eighth Circuit.

Submitted Nov. 13, 1986.

Decided July 2, 1987.

822 F.2d 793

WOLLMAN, Circuit Judge.

Lohman Ray Mays, Jr., appeals his conviction for armed bank robbery in violation of 18 U.S.C. § 2113(a) and (d). We affirm.

On May 28, 1985, the Eagle Rock, Missouri, branch of the Commerce Bank (Commerce Bank) was robbed by a man wearing a face mask made of mesh material and armed with a .45 caliber automatic pistol. Included in the $28,000 taken in the robbery were bait bills with serial numbers that had been previously recorded and dye pack devices containing red dye that were activated by a radio transmitter when carried through the front door of the bank. Employees of the bank heard the dye packs explode when the robber left the bank and saw the robber drive away from the bank in a dark green four-wheel drive vehicle.

Gary Dunnam, a bank manager at the Commerce Bank, identified Mays as the robber from a photographic lineup. At trial, Dunnam again identified Mays as the robber. He testified that he saw Mays come through the front door of the bank, turn his cap around so that the mesh material covered his face, and pull out a .45 caliber automatic handgun. Dunnam testified that he had a clear view of Mays during the robbery and that based upon that perception he was able to iden-

tify Mays in the photo spread shown to him.

Patricia Ann Barrett testified as a government witness under a grant of immunity from prosecution for the Commerce Bank robbery. She was currently serving an eight-year federal sentence for the armed bank robbery of the Bellows Falls Trust Company in Londonderry, Vermont.

Ms. Barrett (no Bonnie Parker she) testified that she had participated in the Commerce Bank robbery with Mays. She stated that during the robbery she had remained in a stolen Bronco truck in front of the bank while Mays went into the bank. Following the robbery, she and Mays drove to a wooded area, where they abandoned the Bronco under a parachute and then left on foot with the money to where they had previously hidden their motorcycles, on which they then departed the state.

The government introduced dye-stained money found in a room in the Days Inn Motel in Northglenn, Colorado. Ms. Barrett testified that she and Mays had stayed with another friend in the Days Inn Motel and that they had forgotten some of the dye-stained money in a closet. She stated that the dye-stained money introduced at trial looked similar to the money stolen from the Commerce Bank.

Ms. Barrett also testified regarding the robbery that she and Mays had committed at the Bellows Falls Trust Company. She testified that before that robbery she and Mays stole a four-wheel-drive Toyota to drive to the bank. They carried out the robbery armed with .45 caliber automatics. They then drove away in the stolen Toyota, abandoned it for a previously hidden vehicle, and left for an isolated wooded area, where they first broke into a travel trailer, remaining there for a short time, and then broke into a hunting lodge, where they remained for two days.

I.

The federally insured status of a bank is an essential element that must be proved to sustain a conviction under 18 U.S.C. § 2113(a) and (d). *United States v. Glidden,* 688 F.2d 58 (8th Cir. 1982); *Scruggs v. United States,* 450 F.2d 359 (8th Cir. 1971), *cert. denied,* 405 U.S. 1071, 92 S.Ct. 1521, 31 L.Ed.2d 804 (1972). Mays argues that the government failed to prove this element beyond a reasonable doubt. We do not agree.

Dunnam testified that the bank was insured with the Federal Deposit Insurance Corporation (FDIC). He also identified both the FDIC certificate and the check that was used to pay for the FDIC coverage for the period during which the robbery occurred. Such evidence alone has been held to be sufficient to support the finding that the institution was federally insured.

We have held that a bank officer's testimony is sufficient to support a finding that a financial institution was federally insured. *United States v. Glidden,* 688 F.2d at 59. We think that the same evidentiary weight should be accorded the testimony of a bank manager. Accordingly, we conclude there was sufficient evidence to support a finding that the bank was federally insured on the date of the robbery.

II.

Mays contends that the district court erred in admitting the dye-stained money into evidence. He argues that although the chain of custody is not relevant when a witness positively identifies an object as the actual object about which he testifies, *United States v. Derring,* 592 F.2d 1003 (8th Cir. 1979), such was not the case in the present action. None of the essential witnesses in the chain of custody could testify that those bills were identical to the dye-stained bills they received.

The government's evidence showed that a motel employee discovered the money while cleaning a room. She took the money to the motel's restaurant manager, who counted the money and called the police. The police took the money to their property room and later sent it to the FBI for chemical analysis. It was determined by the FBI that the money was dyed with the same chemical substance used by the company which supplied the dye packs to the Commerce Bank. The FBI also determined that certain bills were a part of the Commerce Bank's bait list. These bills were introduced separately at trial. Ms. Barrett also testified that the bag and the money found at the motel appeared similar to the bag and the money left by them in the Days Inn Motel.

Also introduced by the government at trial was dye-stained currency recovered from the deposits of Quiznos Restaurant in Denver, Colorado. An employee of the restaurant testified that a man paid for a drink with a ten-dollar bill and asked her to change ten ten-dollar bills for five twenty-dollar bills. She stated that all the bills had red dye on them. The FBI determined that this money was dyed with the same chemical substance used by the company which supplied dye packs to the Commerce Bank. An FBI agent also testified that when he interviewed Mays following his arrest, Mays told him that he had left some of his money in the Days Inn Motel, and that he had also exchanged some money at Quiznos Restaurant.

A trial court's ruling concerning the admissibility of evidence can be reversed only upon a showing that a clear abuse of discretion has occurred. *United States v. Jones,* 687 F.2d 1265 (8th Cir. 1982). Factors to be considered in making a determination of the admissibility of a physical exhibit include the nature of the article, the circumstances surrounding its preservation and custody, and the likelihood of others tampering with it. *United States v. Brown,* 482 F.2d 1226, 1278 (8th Cir. 1973). If upon consideration of such factors the trial judge is satisfied that in reasonable probability the article has not been changed in any respect, it is admissible. d. Furthermore, the integrity of evidence is presumed to be preserved unless there is a showing of bad faith, ill will, or proof that the evidence has been tampered with. *United States v. Gatewood,* 786 F.2d 821 (8th Cir. 1986).

Given Ms. Barrett's testimony, Mays' admissions, and the other testimony on point, we conclude that Mays' challenge to the admission of the dye-stained bills must fail. The trial court did not abuse its discretion in admitting this evidence.

III.

Mays argues that the district court abused its discretion under Fed.R.Evid. 404(b) in allowing Ms. Barrett to testify to the Bellows Falls Trust Company robbery and the subsequent breaking and entering of the travel trailer and the hunting lodge.

Fed.R.Evid. 404(b) states:

(b) * * * Evidence of other crimes, wrongs, or acts is not admissible to prove the character of a person in order to show that he acted in conformity therewith. It may, however, be admissible for other purposes, such as proof of motive, opportunity, intent, preparation, plan, knowledge, identity, or absence of mistake or accident.

Mays contends that the government introduced the evidence of other crimes to show that Mays had a propensity towards criminal behavior, not to show proof of motive, identity or plan as required under Rule 404(b).

The standard for the admission of evidence of other crimes is well established. *United States v. Gustafson,* 728 F.2d 1078, 1082-83 (8th Cir.), *cert. denied,* 469 U.S. 979, 105 S.Ct. 380, 83 L.Ed.2d 315 (1984).

Our cases reveal certain requirements which must be met for other crimes evidence to be admissible under the rule: (1) a material issue on which other crimes evidence may be admissible has been raised * * *; (2) the proffered evidence is relevant to that issue * * *; (3) the evidence of the other crimes is clear and convincing * * *. In addition, to be admissible on such issues as intent, knowledge, or plan, the other crimes evidence must relate to wrongdoing "similar in kind and reasonably close in time to the charge at trial." * * * Finally, evidence otherwise admissible under Rule 404(b) may be excluded under Fed. R.Evid. 403, "if its probative value is substantially outweighed by the danger of unfair prejudice...." (citations omitted) Gustafson, 728 F.2d at 1082-83.

The trial court is vested with broad discretion in deciding whether to admit other crimes evidence. Our role on appeal is to determine whether the district court abused its discretion in admitting such evidence. *United States v. Evans,* 697 F.2d 240, 248 (8th Cir.), *cert. denied,* 460 U.S. 1086, 103 S.Ct. 1779, 76 L.Ed.2d 350 (1983); *United States v. Hall,* 565 F.2d 1052 (8th Cir. 1977).

The material issues on which evidence of other criminal acts was admissible were the motive and identity of those who committed the Commerce Bank Robbery. Ms. Barrett's testimony regarding the theft of the Toyota four-wheel-drive truck and the Bellows Falls robbery was relevant to these issues and was therefore admissible. Ms. Barrett acknowledged on direct examination that the motive she and Mays had to commit the robberies was to secure enough funds to start a new life together. Moreover, both the Bellows Falls and the Commerce Bank robberies were similar enough to establish some identity between the robberies. Both banks were located in an isolated rural area; before both robberies a four-wheel drive vehicle was stolen and later abandoned; and in both robberies a .45 caliber automatic pistol was used.

The evidence of the Bellows Falls robbery and the theft of the Toyota was clear and convincing: Ms. Barrett had been convicted and sentenced for her participation in that robbery.

The task of balancing the probative value of this evidence against its prejudicial value is primarily for the trial court, and we normally defer to its judgment. *United States v. Bass,* 794 F.2d 1305 (8th Cir.), *cert. denied,* _____U.S._____, 107 S.Ct. 233, 93 L.Ed.2d 159 (1986). The trial court gave a limiting instruction that told the jury that this evidence could not be used to decide whether Mays carried out the Commerce Bank robbery. Such an instruction diminishes the danger of any unfair prejudice arising from the admission of other acts. *Gustafson, supra* at 1084. The admission of the challenged testimony, therefore, was not an abuse of the district court's discretion.

We do hold, however, that the admission of Ms. Barrett's testimony regarding the breaking and entering subsequent to the Bellows Falls Trust Company robbery was an abuse of discretion under Rule 404(b). This evidence was not relevant to any material issue in this case, and it did not aid in establishing identity or motive. Furthermore, the evidence did not fall within the very limited category of other crimes evidence that is so integral to the crime charged as to not be extrinsic and therefore not governed by Rule 404(b).

In light of the other substantial evidence of Mays' guilt, however, we hold that the admission of the breaking and entering evidence was harmless error. *United States v. McCrady,* 774 F.2d 868 (8th Cir. 1985).

IV.

Mays asserts that Dunnam's in-court identification should not have been allowed because it was the product of an impermissibly suggestive photo spread.

A two-step inquiry is employed in reviewing a photographic display. The first step is to determine whether the photographic display was impermissibly suggestive. If found impermissibly suggestive, the second inquiry is whether under the totality of the circumstances the display created a substantial risk of misidentification at trial.

Mays argues that the photo spread was unnecessarily suggestive because only two of the photos portrayed persons with facial hair. In *United States v. Wilson,* 787 F.2d 375 (8th Cir.), *cert. denied,* ____U.S.____, 107 S.Ct. 197, 93 L.Ed.2d 129 (1986), this court held that a photo spread was not unnecessarily suggestive where the suspect was the only Hispanic included in the display. The court stated that in the absence of differences in appearance tending to isolate the accused photograph, the identification procedure is not unnecessarily suggestive. *Id.* at 385. Because all of the persons in the photo spread had general physical characteristics compatible with Mays', the display was not unduly suggestive. Accordingly, the district court did not abuse its discretion in allowing Dunnam's in-court identification of Mays.

V.

Mays also argues that the district court's failure to give a specific jury instruction on the reliability of eyewitness testimony denied him a fair trial. We have approved a specific jury instruction on the reliability of eyewitness testimony in cases in which the reliability of eyewitness identification of a defendant presents a serious question. *United States v. Cain,* 616 F.2d 1056 (8th Cir. 1980). It is reversible error for a trial court to refuse this specific jury instruction where the government's case rests solely on questionable eyewitness identification. *United States v. Greene,* 591 F.2d 471 (8th Cir. 1979). Although the district judge might well have given such an instruction, in view of the other corroborating evidence of Mays' guilt, specifically the testimony of Ms. Barrett, the district court did not commit prejudicial error in refusing to do so.

The judgment of conviction is affirmed.

COMMONWEALTH of Pennsylvania
v.
Carol Gwendolyn COWARD, a/k/a
Carol Gwendolyn Gantz, Appellant.

Superior Court of Pennsylvania.
Submitted April 2, 1984.
Filed July 27, 1984.
478 A.2d 1384.

WIEAND, Judge:

If a woman is the recipient of a food voucher issued for the sole purpose of enabling her to obtain supplemental foods for her children, does she commit theft by failure to make required disposition when she sells the food voucher to a stranger for cash? We conclude that proof of these facts was sufficient to sustain a conviction and affirm the judgment of sentence.

Carol Gwendolyn Coward, a/k/a Carol Gwendolyn Gantz, was a participant in the federally funded WIC program designed to provide dietary supplements for needy children and pregnant women. The program was funded by the U.S. Department of Agriculture and administered by the Pennsylvania Department of Health. Ms. Coward applied for benefits in late 1979; in order to qualify, she was required to sign a participation agreement by the terms of which she promised to use coupons issued to her in accordance with the department's rules and regulations. These rules provided, inter alia, that food vouchers could not be sold for cash. Thereafter, Ms. Coward received monthly vouchers, issued by the Department of Health in Lancaster, which listed the foods for which she could negotiate them. At the time of issuance, she was required to affix her signature; when she purchased food, she was required to again endorse the voucher, this time in the presence of the merchant. The vouchers were thus negotiated in a manner similar to that in which traveler's checks are negotiated. By surrendering the properly endorsed voucher, the merchant was then able to obtain reimbursement from WIC funds. On May 9, 1981, Ms. Coward sold a voucher, worth thirty dollars, for the sum of twenty dollars. The purchaser was an informant, and the sale was observed by the police. Following jury trial she was found guilty of theft by failing to make required disposition in violation of 18 Pa.C.S. § 3927. A motion in arrest of judgment was denied, and appellant was directed to pay a fine of $25.00 and make restitution; she was placed on probation for a period of one year.

The provisions of 18 Pa.C.S. § 3927(a) are as follows:

§ 3927. Theft by failure to make required disposition of funds received

(a) Offense defined.—A person who obtains property on agreement, or subject to a known legal obligation, to make specified payments or other disposition, whether from such property or its proceeds or from his own property to be reserved in equivalent amount, is guilty of theft if he intentionally deals with the property obtained as his own and fails to make the required payment or disposition. The foregoing applies notwithstanding that it may be impossible to identify particular property as belonging to the victim at the time of the failure of the actor to make the required payment or disposition.

This section is based upon section 223.8 of the Model Penal Code and replaces the fraudulent conversion and embezzlement sections of the Penal Code of June 24, 1939, P.L. 872 (repealed and replaced effective June 6, 1973). The Commonwealth, in order to prove a violation of this section, must prove the existence of four elements as follows: (1) obtaining the property of another; (2) subject to an agreement or known legal obligation to make specified payments or other disposition thereof; (3) intentional dealing with the property so received as the defendant's own; and (4) failure to make the required disposition.

Appellant contends that the evidence failed to establish that she disposed of the voucher in violation of a known obligation to make some other disposition thereof. There is no merit in this contention. The agreement signed by appellant contained a provision which required her to use vouchers solely for the purchase of WIC approved foods

566 CRIMINAL LAW

and another which warned against the sale of vouchers. Willful misuse of food vouchers, it provided, could lead to removal from the program and criminal prosecution. Because appellant signed the agreement, a jury could infer that she had knowledge of the uses which she was required to make of WIC food vouchers.

A more difficult issue is whether appellant, in failing to use the food voucher for its required purpose, was disposing of the "property of another." Despite a contrary suggestion by the drafters of the Model Penal Code, the traditional rule in Pennsylvania that a person cannot be guilty of converting his or her own property has continued. *See: Commonwealth v. Austin, supra* 258 Pa.Super. at 466-467, 393 A.2d at 39; W. LaFave & A. Scott, Handbook on Criminal Law 648 (1972); 3 Wharton's Criminal Law § 419 at 439 (14th ed. 1980).

Thus, in *Austin,* the Court reversed a section 3927 conviction where a home improvement contractor had received advance money on a contract and had ceased to perform his contract, having spent less than half of the advance money for materials. We held that although defendant's acts of failing to perform and keeping the advance money may have constituted a breach of contract, the defendant did not "fraudulently take the money of another." *Id.* 258 Pa.Super. at 468, 393 A.2d at 39. *Austin* continued the rule which had been established in cases decided under the Penal Code that a defendant could not properly be convicted of an embezzlement-type crime where both possession *and* title of property had passed to the defendant prior to the alleged conversion.

In the instant case, however, appellant had received an equivalent of money which was to be used for the sole purpose of purchasing specific food supplements for other persons, i.e., her children. Because the food vouchers were not intended to be used for her own benefit, appellant occupied a position comparable to that of a guardian or trustee. Such a person can be convicted of an embezzlement-type offense if he or she misappropriates funds for a use inconsistent with the purpose for which the funds are held. *See: Commonwealth v. Levi,* 44 Pa.Super. 253 (1910) (trustee); *Commonwealth v. Kaufman,* 9 Pa.Super. 310 (1899) (guardian); 5 P.L.E. Embezzlement and Related Offenses § 5. *See also: State v. Magee,* 201 Kan. 566, 441 P.2d 863 (1968); 3 Wharton's Criminal Law § 412, *supra.* Because appellant held the vouchers for the use and benefit of others, she could be convicted of a violation of 18 Pa.C.S. § 3927 if she failed to use the vouchers for their intended purpose, i.e., to purchase specific foods for her children. *Commonwealth v. Bhojwani,* 242 Pa.Super. 406, 364 A.2d 335 (1976) (defendant accepted orders and advance payments for clothing to be purchased from "partner" in Hong Kong and failed to use money for that purpose).

In view of appellant's agreement, both her ownership and use of the food vouchers were restricted. She could not properly negotiate the voucher for her own benefit. Negotiation was proper only when done in accordance with and for the purposes recited in her WIC agreement. Evidence that she sold the voucher for cash to a stranger was sufficient to sustain a conviction for theft by failing to make proper disposition thereof.

The judgment of sentence is affirmed.

Cases relating to Chapter 7

FORGERY AND OTHER FRAUD OFFENSES

STATE of North Carolina

v.

Pierce Oliver Kidd BREWER, Robert A. Burch, Robert M. Burch,
George Masefield, Martin J. Hamilton, Walter Schoenfeldt,
Pfaff & Kendall, a corporation,
Traffic and Street Sign Company, a corporation

Supreme Court of North Carolina
Feb. 1, 1963
258 N.C. 533
129 S.E.2d 262

NOTE: Defendants were charged with conspiracy to violate and with violating G.S. Sec. 14-153 of the North Carolina statute which prohibits influencing agents and servants from violating duties owed employees. They were found guilty and appealed. Only the part of the case which pertains to the Bribery statute is included here.

In the two briefs of appellants the second question presented for decision is: Did the trial court err in refusing to quash the indictment on the ground that G.S. § 14-355 upon which the indictment is based, is unconstitutional and repugnant to the "due process of law" clause of section one of the 14th Amendment to the United States Constitution, and to "the law of the land" clause of Article I, section 17, of the North Carolina Constitution, in that the statute is so vague and indefinite, it is void for uncertainty, and on the further ground that the statute constitutes an arbitrary, capricious and unreasonable exercise of the police power of the State?

The General Assembly at its 1913 Session enacted Chapter 190 of the Public Laws of North Carolina, which is entitled "An act to prohibit influencing agents, employees and servants." Section one of this act is codified as G.S. § 14-353, and section two of this act is codified as G.S. § 14-354.

G.S. § 14-353 reads:

"Influencing agents and servants in violating duties owed employers.—Any person who gives, offers or promises to an agent, employee or servant any gift or gratuity whatever with intent to influence his action in relation to his principal's, employer's or master's business; any agent, employee or servant who requests or accepts a gift or gratuity or a promise to make a gift or to do an act beneficial to himself, under an

567

agreement or with an understanding that he shall act in any particular manner in relation to his principal's, employer's or master's business; any agent, employee or servant who, being authorized to procure materials, supplies or other articles either by purchase or contract for his principal, employer or master, or to employ service or labor for his principal, employer or master, receives, directly or indirectly, for himself or for another, a commission, discount or bonus from the person who makes such sale or contract, or furnishes such materials, supplies or other articles, or from a person who renders such service or labor; and any person who gives or offers such an agent, employee or servant such commission, discount or bonus, shall be guilty of a misdemeanor and shall be punished in the discretion of the court."

G.S. § 14-354 provides that a witness may be required to give self-criminating evidence in respect to the crime denounced in G.S. § 14-353, but, if he does, no suit or prosecution can be based thereon, except for perjury committed in so testifying.

Appellants may challenge the constitutionality of G.S. § 14-353 by a motion to quash the indictment, which charges a violation of this statute. *State v. Glidden Co.,* 228 N.C. 664, 46 S.E.2d 860; 16 C.J.S. Constitutional Law § 96, pp. 343-344.

The General Assembly of North Carolina, unless it is limited by constitutional provisions imposed by the State or Federal Constitution, has the inherent power to define and punish any act as a crime, because it is indisputably a part of the police power of the State. The expediency of making any such enactment is a matter of which the General Assembly is the proper judge. The remedy for unjust or unwise legislation, not obnoxious to constitutional objections, if such be enacted, is to be found in a change by the people of their representatives, according to the methods provided by the Constitution and the laws of the State. However, the act of the General Assembly declaring what shall constitute a crime must have some substantial relation to the ends sought to be accomplished. *State v. Yarboro,* 194 N.C. 498, 140 S.E. 216; *People v. Belcastro,* 356 Ill. 144, 190 N.E. 301, 92 A.L.R. 1223; 22 C.J.S. Criminal Law § 13; 14 Am.Jur., Criminal Law, secs. 16 and 22; Wharton's Criminal Law and Procedure, 1957, Vol. I, Sec. 16.

In passing upon the constitutionality of G.S. § 14-353, we start with the presumption that it is constitutional, and it must be so held by this Court, unless it is in conflict with some constitutional provision of the State or Federal Constitution. *State v. Warren,* 252 N.C. 690, 114 S.E.2d 660; *State v. Lueders,* 214 N.C. 558, 200 S.E. 22. "We cannot overturn a statute because we do not like it; for our likes and dislikes affect us as citizens, not as judges." *Wright v. Hart,* 182 N.Y. 330, 353, 75 N.E. 404, 412, 2 L.R.A., N.S., 338, 350, 3 Ann.Cas. 263, 271.

The books are filled with statements by the Courts of the rule that a crime must be defined in a penal statute with appropriate certainty and definiteness. In *Connally v. General Construction Co.,* 269 U.S. 385, 46 S.Ct. 126, 70 L.Ed. 322, the Court said:

"That the terms of a penal statute creating a new offense must be sufficiently explicit to inform those who are subject to it what conduct on their part will render them liable to its penalties is a well-recognized requirement, consonant alike with ordinary notions of fair play and the settled rules of law; and a statute which either forbids or requires the doing of an act in terms so vague that men of common intelligence must necessarily guess at its meaning and differ as to its application violates the first essential of due process of law." ...

Twelve states have statutes prohibiting the general practice of bribery in commercial relationships or influencing agents, employees and servants in commercial relationships, analogous to our statute codified as G.S. §§ 14-353 and 14-354: Connecticut, Louisiana, Massachusetts, Michigan, Nebraska, New York, Pennsylvania, Rhode Island, South Carolina, Virginia, Washington and Wisconsin. In addition to statutes of this general type, there are seventeen states which have statutes making it a crime to bribe a particular type of employee, notable agents or employees in charge of purchasing or hiring: Arizona, California, Connecticut, Indiana, Kentucky, Maine, Michigan, Montana, Nevada, New Jersey, New York, Oregon, Tennessee, Texas, Utah, Washington and Wisconsin. CONTROL OF NON-GOVERNMENTAL CORRUPTION BY CRIMINAL LEGISLATION, University of Pennsylvania Law Review, Vol. 108, p. 848 (1960), where on pp. 864 and 866 a chart gives the names of the states and sets forth the specific statutes. Incidentally, North Carolina has statutes making athletic corruption a crime. G.S. §§ 14-373, 14-374, 14-375, 14-376, and 14-377.

The New York statute outlaws the corruption of employees, agents and servants and of purchasing and hiring agents in particular. The University of Pennsylvania Law Review, Vol. 108, p. 852, states: "Since this statute [New York] is broadest in scope, has been more widely enforced than any other, and has served as a prototype for the legislation of several other states, it will be dealt with in some detail." In note 29 to this sentence it states that Connecticut, Massachusetts, Michigan, Nebraska, North Carolina, South Carolina, Virginia, and Wisconsin, all have statutes similar to New York's. The note specifies the statute of each state, and gives G.S. § 14-353 for North Carolina....

G.S. § 14-353 is divisible into four parts. First, it provides that "[a]ny person who gives, offers or promises to an agent, employee or servant any gift or gratuity whatever *with intent to influence his action in relation to his principal's, employer's or master's business*" shall be guilty of a misdemeanor. (Emphasis supplied.) The intent specified is an essential element of the offense. The acts prohibited are stated in words sufficiently explicit, clear and definite to inform any man of ordinary intelligence what conduct on his part will render him liable to its penalties. If a person does the prohibited act or acts specified in this part of the statute with the intent explicitly stated therein, he is guilty of what is commonly called "commercial bribery." In *American Distilling Co. v. Wisconsin Liquor Co.*, 7 Cir., 104 F.2d 582, 123 A.L.R. 739, the Court said:

"The vice of conduct labeled 'commercial bribery,' as related to unfair trade practices, is the advantage which one competitor secures over his fellow competitors by his secret and corrupt dealing with employees or agents of prospective purchasers." Surely a violation of this part of G.S. § 14-353 is related to unfair trade practices, and is an unfair method of competition. The contention of defendants that the language of this part of the statute is so broad as to prohibit the customary habit of tipping is untenable. Customary tipping is in obedience to custom or in appreciation of service, and is done with no intent to influence the action of the person receiving the tip in relation to his or her employer's business, and as to tipping done in such a manner the statute is not applicable. However, it is possible that a person by tipping an agent, servant or employee with the intent specified in this part of the statute could bring himself within its penalties: e.g., by giving substantial amounts or considerations and calling them tips.

The second part of the statute provides that "any agent, employee or servant who requests or accepts a gift or gratuity or a promise to make a gift or to do an act beneficial to himself *under an agreement or with an understanding that he shall act in any particular manner in relation to his principal's, employer's or master's business*" shall be guilty of a misdemeanor. (Emphasis supplied.) The agreement or understanding in the words emphasized is an essential element of the offense. Although this part of the statute employs general terms, the words used are sufficiently explicit and definite to convey to any man of ordinary intelligence and understanding an adequate description of the prohibited act or acts, and to inform him of what conduct on his part will render him liable to its penalties. The plain intent and purpose of this part of G.S. § 14-353 is to prohibit any agent, employee or servant from being disloyal and unfaithful to his principal, employer or master. The Holy Bible in the New Testament, St. Matthew, chapter 6, verse 24 (King James Version) says: "No man can serve two masters: for either he will hate the one, and love the other; or else he will hold to the one, and despise the other." A statement of an eternal truth.

The third and fourth parts of G.S. § 14-353 refer to a commission, discount or bonus received by any agent, employee or servant under the circumstances therein specified and to any person who gives or offers such an agent, employee, or servant such commission, discount or bonus.

The indictment charges the defendants with a violation of the first two parts of G.S. § 14-353. It is so stated in defendants' briefs.

We are here concerned with the first two parts of G.S. § 14-353, which are divisible and separable from the remainder of the statute.

In our opinion, and we so hold, the first two parts of G.S. § 14-353, which the indictment charges the defendant violated, are not repugnant to the "due process of law" clause of section one of the 14th Amendment to the United States Constitution, and to "the law of the land" clause of Article I, section 17, of the North Carolina Constitution, and are a reasonable and proper exercise of the police power of the State.

The activities necessary to accomplish the offenses prohibited by G.S. § 14-353, and similar statutes, require no violence, embody no traces in lasting form, and frequently, if not almost entirely, have no witnesses other than persons implicated or potentially implicated. Once completed, they leave few persons, if any, aware of being damaged. The enforcement problems, which arise from the very nature of the offenses, are extremely difficult, because of lack of evidence. This is probably the prime reason why so few persons have been prosecuted for violating these statutes.

In view of the structure of modern business organizations and the demands made upon the individual by present-day business, both the opportunities, and the practice of bribing or unlawfully influencing the agents and employees of others seem to be increasing. There is general agreement that where an agent or employee receives money or other consideration from a person in return for the agent's or employee's efforts to further that person's interests in business dealings between him and the principal or employer, such an act or acts on the part of the agent or employee and on the part of the person who gives the money or other consideration to the agent or employee should be prohibited. For articles in respect to the acts prohibited by G.S. § 14-353, and similar statutes, and "commercial bribery" and influencing of employees, see: Minnesota Law Review, Vol. 46, p. 599 (1961-2), "Commercial Bribery: The Need for Legislation in Minnesota"; University of Pennsylvania Law Review, Vol. 108, p. 848 (1960), "Control of Nongovernmental Corruption by Criminal Legislation"; Harvard Law Review, Vol. 45, p. 1248 (1931-2), "Bribery in Commercial Relationships"; Columbia Law Review, Vol. 28, p. 799 (1928), "Commercial Bribery." In the Minnesota Law Review Article, p. 630, there is set forth a Proposed Commercial Bribery Statute....

We have written at length, because, so far as we know, the constitutionality of statutes substantially similar to G.S. § 14-353 has not been challenged, except in the New York case of People v. Davis. In 57 C.J.S. Master and Servant, § 639, entitled "Bribing Servant with Intent to Influence His Relation with Master," it is said: "The validity of such statutes has been upheld * * *." In support of the text it cites one case, the New York case of *People v. Davis,* Sp.Sess., 160 N.Y.S. 769.

Incidentally, the statutes of the following States somewhat similar to our G.S. § 14-353 do not contain language like the New York statute, "without the knowledge and consent of the principal, employer or master of such agent, employee or servant": Connecticut, Conn.Gen.Rev.Stat. § 53-266; Massachusetts, Mass.Ann.Laws, ch. 271, § 39; Michigan, Comp.Laws 1948, Sec. 750.125; Rhode Island, R.I.Gen. Laws Ann., secs. 11-7-3 and 11-7-4; South Carolina, S.C.Code, Sec. 16-570; Washington, Wash.Rev.Code, secs. 49.44.060 and 49.44.070; and Wisconsin, Wis.Stat.Ann., Sec. 134.05.

All the assignments of error by defendant Brewer, all the assignments of error by defendant Robert A. Burch, and all the assignments of error by defendant Robert M. Burch have been considered, and all and every one of them are overruled. All the judgments entered against defendant Brewer, all the judgements entered against defendant Robert A. Burch, and all the judgments entered against defendant Robert M. Burch are Affirmed.

HIGGINS, J., took no part in the consideration or decision of this case.

STATE of Louisiana
v.
Alvin J. FRALEY
Court of Appeal of Louisiana, Fourth Circuit.
Dec. 9, 1986.
499 So.2d 1304

(Parts of case omitted.)
ARMSTRONG, Judge.

The defendant, Alvin Fraley, was charged with and convicted of one count of illegal possession of stolen property valued at $500.00 or more, a violation of LSA-R.S. 14:69, three counts of forgery, violations of LSA-R.S. 14:72, and one count of injuring public documents, a violation of LSA-R.S. 14:132. On January 16, 1985 defendant's motion for a new trial was denied, and he was sentenced to serve four ten-year sentences at hard labor as to counts one through four and one five-year sentence at hard labor as to count five. Sentences were to run concurrently. The defendant filed a motion for appeal which was granted by the trial court. On February 14, 1985 the state filed a multiple bill of information against the defendant. On April 16, 1985 the trial court set aside defendant's original sentence and sentenced him as a fourth offender to serve twenty years at hard labor. On April 24, 1985 defendant filed a motion for appeal. The trial court granted the motion, consolidating it with the previous appeal filed on January 16, 1985. Defense counsel asserts eight assignments of error. Additionally, the defendant has filed a pro se brief in which he assigns three errors....

Viewing the evidence in the light most favorable to the prosecution, these are salient facts:

Sometime in May of 1984, a brown 1984 Thunderbird automobile was stolen from the lot of Interstate Ford. Mr. Ritter, assistant manager of Interstate Ford, testified that the value of the Thunderbird was $10,800.00 and that Interstate Ford did not consent to the taking of the car from the dealership lot.

On June 10, 1984, Lieutenant John Ruth was driving in his patrol car on Downman Road. He stopped at a red light at the intersection of Downman Road and Chef Menteur Highway. The defendant, driving a 1984 brown Thunderbird, stopped in the lane next to him. Ruth looked over and noticed that the defendant was wearing a wig. The defendant saw Ruth looking at him. The defendant jerked his head and stared straight ahead. When Ruth saw that the defendant's car did not have a brake tag, he started to follow the defendant. Ruth noticed that although the car was a brand new Thunderbird, the license plate was from Arizona and was several years old. He then stopped the defendant and requested identification. The defendant produced a driver's license which had been issued three days prior to this stop. The name on the driver's license was James Wallace Simpson. The defendant's picture was on the license. Ruth was unable to see the vehicle identification number (VIN) on the dash board of the car. Ruth asked the defendant who owned the car, the defendant replied that it was his. When defendant could not find the registration papers to the car, he told Ruth they were at his home. Ruth asked the defendant what the address on the driver's license was but the defendant was unable to tell him. The defendant then told Ruth that the car belonged to another person. When the defendant opened the trunk of the car to search for the registration papers, Ruth saw two license plates in the trunk.

While the defendant was stopped, Ruth radioed for reinforcements. Officer Blanque responded to the call. When he looked at the dashboard of the car, he discovered that paper had been taped over the VIN. Blanque called in the VIN and discovered that the car had been stolen from Interstate Ford. Blanque also saw the license plates in the trunk. In addition he saw a tablet of blank baptismal certificates. Blanque told the defendant that he did not believe the defendant was James Wallace Simpson. The defendant took out of his wallet a birth certificate and a baptismal certificate in the name of James Wallace Simpson. Blanque stated that when the birth certificate was set on the dash board of the car, he could see writing underneath a blacked-out portion of the certificate. The writing indicated that James Wallace Simpson had died in 1959.

The defendant was arrested and brought to Central Lockup where he was fingerprinted. The defendant was informed that if he signed the fingerprint card with a name that was not his, he would also be charged with injuring public documents, a violation of LSA-R.S. 14:132. The defendant signed the fingerprint card as James Wallace Simpson. His prints were sent through the NCIC computer. It was discovered that the defendant was Alvin Fraley.

At trial, it was stipulated that D.A. Investigator Harry Nelson took a handwriting sample from the defendant and forwarded it to Officer James Dupre of the Crime Lab.

Officer James Dupre qualified as an expert in handwriting identification and comparison. He compared the handwriting sample taken from the defendant with the baptismal certificate of "James Wallace Simpson." He testified that they were probably written by the same person.

Officer Glynn Burmaster was stipulated an expert in fingerprint identification. He compared a fingerprint card signed by Alvin Fraley with the fingerprint card signed by James Wallace Simpson and concluded that they were the same person.

The defendant was charged with and convicted of one count of illegal possession of stolen things, a violation of La. R.S. 14:69. That statute provides in pertinent part:

Illegal possession of stolen things is the intentional possessing, procuring, receiving, or concealing of anything of value which has been the subject of any robbery or theft, under circumstances which indicate that the offender knew or had good reason to believe that the thing was the subject of one of these offenses.

The four essential elements that must be proven to sustain a conviction of this crime are: (1) that the item was stolen; (2) that the item was of value; (3) that the defendant knew or should have known the property was stolen; and (4) that the defendant intentionally procured, received, or concealed the property. *State v. Walker*, 350 So.2d 176 (La. 1977); *State v. Moore* 439 So.2d 1178 (La.App. 4th Cir. 1983) *writ den.* 443 So.2d 587 (La. 1983). The court has also held that the mere possession of stolen property does not create a presumption that the possessor knew or had good reason to believe it was stolen. *State v. Ennis,* 414 So.2d 661 (La. 1982).

The testimony in the present case shows that the defendant was stopped while driving a stolen 1984 Ford Thunderbird worth almost $11,000.00. The VIN on the dashboard had been taped over. The license plate was much older than the car and was from the state of Arizona. The defendant first told the officers that the car was his. It was only when he was unable to produce the registration that he told the police officers that the car belonged to someone else. Given these facts, a rational trier of fact could have found the defendant guilty of receiving stolen property beyond a reasonable doubt.

The defendant was charged with and convicted of three counts of forgery, a violation of R.S. 14:72. That statute provides in pertinent part:

Forgery is the false making or altering, with intent to defraud, of any signature to, or any part of, any writing purporting to have legal efficacy.

Issuing or transferring, with intent to defraud, a forged writing, known by the offender to be a forged writing, shall also constitute forgery.

In *State v. Tomlinson,* 457 So.2d 651 (La. 1984) the court stated:

Thus, forgery may be committed by acting with an intent to defraud to either (1) make or alter a signature or another part of an instrument, or (2) issue or transfer an instrument known to be forged. *Id.* at 652.

In *State v. Thomas,* 454 So.2d 833, 834 (La.App. 4th Cir. 1984) this court set forth the elements of the crime of forgery: 1) issuing or transferring,

2) with intent to defraud, 3) a forged writing, 4) known by the defendant to be forged. See also *State v. Francis,* 482 So.2d 154 (La.App. 4th Cir. 1986).

In *State v. Marler,* 428 So.2d 954 (La. App. 1st Cir. 1983) *writ den.* 433 So.2d 151 (La. 1983) the court noted that:

It is the essence of forgery that the writing purports to be the act of another person. *State v. Melson,* 161 La. 423, 108 So. 794 (1926). It is unnecessary to prove that the offender intended to defraud any particular person. *State v. Laborde,* 120 La. 136, 45 So. 38 (1907). The criminal intent required for forgery is to defraud any person, and it suffices if the forged instrument has prejudiced or might prejudice the rights of another. An intent to profit by the act is not a necessary element of the offense. *State v. Jacobs,* 195 La. 281, 196 So. 347 (1940); *State v. Laborde, supra.* Moreover, specific intent is a state of mind and need not be proved as a fact but may be inferred from the circumstances and transactions of the case. *State v. Williams,* 383 So.2d 369 (La. 1980), *writ denied,* 449 U.S. 1103, 101 S.Ct. 899, 66 L.Ed.2d 828 (1981).

In addition to an intent to defraud, forgery requires that the falsification be made upon a "writing purporting to have legal efficacy." La.R.S. 14:72.

In count one of the bill of information, the defendant was charged with the forgery of a baptismal certificate. At trial, the State produced evidence to show that the handwriting on the baptismal certificate and the defendant's handwriting sample were probably written by the same person, that the defendant had a stack of blank baptismal certificates and that the name on the certificate was the alias the defendant was using. Any rational trier of fact could have found the defendant guilty of forgery of the baptismal certificate.

In count three the defendant was charged with forgery of a Louisiana driver's license. At trial the State introduced the license which had been issued several days prior to the defendant's arrest. The driver's license was issued to James Wallace Simpson, the alias the defendant was using. Although the State did not compare the defendant's signature on the handwriting exemplar and the signature on the driver's license, the jury viewed both documents and could have compared them. Any rational trier of fact could have found the defendant guilty of forgery of a driver's license beyond a reasonable doubt.

On count four, the defendant was charged and convicted of forging a birth certificate. We find the evidence sufficient to support this conviction. The evidence shows that the defendant was in the sole possession of, and was using, the birth certificate of the individual whose identity he had assumed as an alias and that the date of death on the certificate had been obliterated. We believe this strong circumstantial evidence supports the conclusion that a rational juror, viewing the evidence in the light most favorable to the State, could have found the elements of the crime of forging the birth certificate.

The defendant was charged with and convicted of count five of the bill of information with injuring a public rec-

ord, a violation of R.S. 14:132. That statute provides in pertinent part:

Injuring public records is the intentional removal, mutilation, destruction, alteration, falsification, or concealment of any record, document, or other thing, filed or deposited by authority of law, in any public office or with any public officer.

Thus, in this case, to support a conviction for injuring public records the State must prove that the defendant 1) intentionally falsified 2) a document 3) filed or deposited 4) by authority of law 5) in any public office. At trial, the State proved that the police officer informed the defendant that if he did not sign his own name he would be committing a crime, that the defendant signed a false name and that an NCIC check revealed that the name was false. The card was then filed with the police department and made a permanent record of NCIC. Any rational trier of fact could have found the defendant guilty beyond a reasonable doubt of injuring public records....

For the foregoing reasons defendant's convictions are affirmed. The trial court's finding and sentencing of defendant as a fourth offender is set aside as the trial court was without jurisdiction to conduct the multiple offender proceedings, and defendant's original sentences for convictions on counts one, two, three, for and five are reinstated.

Convictions affirmed; sentence vacated; original sentences reinstated.

Cases relating to Chapter 8
OFFENSES INVOLVING MORALITY AND DECENCY

STATE of Connecticut
v.
Barbara ALLEN
Superior Court of Connecticut, Appellate Session
Decided June 6, 1980
37 Conn.Sup. 506, 424 A.2d 651

DALY, Judge.

After a trial to the jury the defendant was convicted of prostitution in violation of General Statutes § 53a-82. The defendant appeals from the judgment rendered on the verdict and from the denial of her motion to set aside the verdict.

The jury reasonably could have found the following facts: At approximately 1:40 a.m. on March 25, 1976, a New Haven undercover officer was stopped at a traffic light at the intersection of Park and Chapel streets. He observed the defendant approach a car stopped in front of him and open and close the passenger door. The defendant then approached the officer's car, opened the passenger door and inquired if the officer had twenty dollars. Upon hearing an affirmative response, the defendant got into the car. A conversation ensued during which the defendant offered to have sex for twenty dollars. Shortly thereafter, both noticed a marked police cruiser in the area. The defendant urged the undercover officer to say, in the event that they were stopped, that he was taking her home or something

to that effect. The officer drove to a prearranged location near a school where the defendant was arrested by other officers. No sexual activity was ever engaged in nor was there any transfer of money.

The defendant has assigned five counts of error in the conduct of the trial proceedings. Because our disposition of this case requires a remand for a new trial, we will first consider the defendant's challenge to the constitutionality of the prostitution statute under which she was convicted.

The defendant claims that General Statutes §53a-82 suffers from the constitutional infirmities of vagueness and overbreadth, and that it infringes on her fundamental right of privacy. The defendant assumes a heavy burden in making this constitutional attack. In passing on the constitutionality of a legislative act, we will make every presumption and intendment in favor of its validity, and sustain the statute unless its unconstitutionality is established beyond a reasonable doubt. *New Milford v. SCA Services of Connecticut, Inc.*, 174 Conn. 146, 148, 384 A.2d 337 (1977); *Horton v. Meskill*, 172 Conn. 615, 650, 376 A.2d 359 (1977).

Laws must give a person of ordinary intelligence a reasonable opportunity to know what is prohibited so that he may act accordingly. *Stolberg v. Caldwell,* 175 Conn. 586, 610, 402 A.2d 763 (1978). "A statute...which forbids or requires conduct in terms so vague that persons of common intelligence must necessarily guess at its meaning and differ as to its application violates the first essential of due process.["] The constitution, however, requires no more than a reasonable degree of certainty. "The test is whether the language conveys sufficiently definite warning as to the proscribed conduct when measured by common understanding and practices." *Jordan v. De George,* 341 U.S. 223, 231-32, 71 S.Ct. 703, 708, 95 L.Ed. 886 (1951); *State v. Chetcuti, supra,* 173 Conn. 167-68, 377 A.2d 263.

General Statutes § 53a-82 provides as follows: "A person is guilty of prostitution when such person engages or agrees or offers to engage in sexual conduct with another person in return for a fee." The defendant contends that the statutory terms "sexual conduct" and "fee" are so inherently uncertain in their meaning that they failed to apprise her that her conduct was proscribed. She claims that the statute is unconstitutionally vague and that her conviction thereunder violated her right to due process of law under the fifth and fourteenth amendments to the United States constitution and article first, § 8 of the Connecticut constitution.

Due process requires only that the law give sufficient warning to enable individuals to conduct themselves so as to avoid that which is forbidden. *Rose v. Locke,* 423 U.S. 48, 50, 96 S.Ct. 243, 244, 46 L.Ed.2d 185 (1975); *State v. Pickering,* Conn. (41 Conn. L.J., No. 36, pp. 1, 4) (1980). It is recognized that many statutes will have some inherent vagueness, for "[i]n most English words and phrases there lurk uncertainties." *Robinson v. United States,* 324 U.S. 282, 286, 65 S.Ct. 666, 668, 89 L.Ed. 944 (1945); *Rose v. Locke, supra.* In order to ascertain a statute's meaning it is often necessary to refer to judicial opinions involving the statute, to the common law, or to legal treatises or dictionaries. *State v. Pickering, supra.* The defendant correctly notes that the terms "sexual conduct" and "fee" are not further defined by the penal code in the context of prostitution. It also appears that no Connecticut judicial opinion has ever interpreted the specific language of this statute. Nonetheless, the meaning of the statutory language is clear and is sufficient to warn the ordinary person of the prohibited conduct.

While the language of this statute has not been previously construed by Connecticut courts, the identical language which appears in the New York penal code has withstood several constitutional vagueness challenges. *United States v. Herrera,* 584 F.2d 1137 (2d Cir. 1978); *People v. Costello,* 90 Misc.2d 431, 395 N.Y.S.2d 139 (1977); *People v. Block,* 71 Misc.2d 714, 337 N.Y.S.2d 153 (1972). We agree with the rationale propounded in those decisions that the terms "sexual conduct" and "fee," when appearing in the context of a statute prohibiting prostitution, have a commonly understood meaning. General Statutes §1-1(a) provides that "[i]n the construction of the statutes, words and phrases shall be construed according to the commonly approved usage of the language; and technical words and phrases, and such as have acquired a peculiar and appropriate meaning in the law, shall be construed and understood accordingly."

Dictionary definitions provide a fair explanation of the meaning of these terms. "Conduct" is defined as "[b]ehavior as portrayed by that which one does or omits to do." Ballentine's Law Dictionary (3d Ed.). "Sexual" conduct would thus be defined as conduct "of, characteristic of, or involving sex, the sexes, the organs of sex and their functions, or the instincts, drives, behavior, etc. associated with sex." Webster, Second New World Dictionary. The term "fee" is generally defined to be a remuneration charged for the rendering of professional services—"Compensation often in the form of a fixed charge for professional service or for special and requested exercise of talent or of skill"; Webster, Third New International Dictionary; "[p]ayment asked or given for professional services, admissions, licenses, tuition, etc.; charge." Webster, Second New World Dictionary.

Further clarity is given to the meaning of the terms "sexual conduct" and "fee" by the fact that they appear in the context of a statute prohibiting prostitution. While certain words may appear unconstitutionally vague when viewed in a vacuum, when viewed in the next context of a statute they can provide fair notice of the conduct sought to be prohibited. *State v. Carter,* 89 Wash.2d 236, 239, 570 P.2d 1218 (1977). The statute under attack is entitled "Prostitution: Class A misdemeanor." The term "prostitution" is defined as "the act or practice of indulging in promiscuous sexual relations esp. for payment." Webster, Third New International Dictionary. "Prostitution" has a commonly understood meaning which has often been commented on by courts, including our own. "'Prostitution...normally suggests sexual relations for hire.'" *Cleveland v. United States,* 329 U.S.

14, 17, [67 S.Ct. 13, 14, 91 L.Ed. 12]." *State v. Allen,* 2 Conn. Cir. 594, 597, 203 A.2d 248 (1964). See 77 A.L.R.3d 519.

The language of § 53a-82 is sufficiently precise to give the defendant fair notice that her conduct was prohibited. "The definition of prostitution as being a person who engages or agrees or offers to engage in sexual conduct with another person in return for a fee is not so vague as to make persons of common intelligence guess at its meaning. Although the prohibitions may not satisfy those intent on finding fault at any cost, they are set out in terms that can be sufficiently understood and complied with by the ordinary person exercising ordinary common sense." *United States v. Herrera, supra,* 1149.

The defendant also claims that § 53a-82 is unconstitutionally vague on its face. Although the general rule is that the constitutionality of a statutory provision being attacked as void for vagueness is determined by the statute's applicability to the particular facts at issue, a statute may be challenged for vagueness on its face where it has the potential to inhibit the exercise of the first amendment freedoms of free speech and assembly. *Smith v. Goguen,* 415 U.S. 566, 573, 94 S.Ct. 1242, 1247, 39 L.Ed.2d 605 (1974); *State v. Pickering, supra,* 2, n. 3. The defendant claims that the prostitution statute infringes upon protected first amendment freedoms, and that she therefore may challenge the validity of its application to marginal situations even though her own conduct may clearly fall within the statute's proscriptions. This aspect of the defendant's constitutional vagueness challenge is essentially identical to her claim of overbreadth. While the vices of statutory vagueness and overbreadth are distinct; *Mitchell v. King, supra,* 169 Conn. 143, 363 A.2d 68; they are often congruent and are functionally indistinguishable when applied in the area of the first amendment. See note, "The First Amendment Overbreadth Doctrine," 83 Harv.L.Rev. 844, 845 (1970). Statutory language that is overbroad may also inhibit the exercise of first amendment freedoms.

Statutes regulating public morals, including the regulation and punishment of prostitution and related offenses, fall within the exercise of the state's police power. 63 Am.Jur.2d, Prostitution § 2. The state clearly has a legitimate interest in regulating the commercialization of sex. *People v. Costello, supra.* While § 53a-82 may arguably have some impact on freedom of association, any such impact is minimal and is clearly permissible as incidental to the furtherance of a substantial government interest. *United States v. O'Brien,* 391 U.S. 367, 377, 88 S.Ct. 1673, 1679, 20 L.Ed.2d 672 (1968). Because the statute prohibits offering or agreeing to engage in sexual conduct for a fee, it also has some impact on speech. This category of speech, however, is not within the protective embrace of the first amendment. Speech incident to solicitation for prostitution advances no social value; it is essentially commercial in nature and is doubtlessly intended to sell a product. As such it is within the reach of state regulation. "[W]hile freedom of communicating information and disseminating opinion enjoys the fullest protection of the first amendment, the constitution imposes no such restraint on government as respects purely commercial advertising."

Because we hold that this statute has no real and substantial impact on first amendment freedoms, the defendant's vagueness and overbreadth challenges to the facial validity of the statute must fail.

The final theory upon which the defendant assails the statute is her fundamental right to privacy under the federal and state constitutions. It appears that the constitutional right to privacy under the federal and state constitutions has never been extended to encompass prostitutes plying their trade on the street, and the defendant has cited no authority which persuades us so to extend it. See, e.g., contra, *Morgan v. Detroit, supra; United States v. Moses, supra; District of Columbia v. Garcia, supra.*

The defendant has also assigned error to the court's instructions to the jury with respect to intent. Because our ruling on this issue is dispositive of the case, we need not address the other claims of error.

Although General Statutes § 53a-82 does not expressly define a mental element, a *general intent* to do the proscribed act of one's own volition is an element of the crime of prostitution. See *State v. Husser,* 161 Conn. 513, 516, 290 A.2d 336 (1971). The trial court charged, in part, on the element of intent as follows: "Now, in any crime, of course, we have the element of intent, and ordinarily, the state has no obligation to prove intent, and that is because a person is presumed to have intended to do the act which he did do. Accordingly, until some evidence enters into the case that indicates that the intent to commit the crime alleged was not present, or could not be present because of some condition, up until that point the state has the right to rely on the presumption that the accused intended to commit the acts which he did commit."

The defendant claims that this charge impermissibly shifted the burden of proof on the element of intent from the prosecution to her. Although the defendant took no exception to this portion of the charge, we consider the question as one involving exceptional circumstances because it involves the defendant's constitutional right to a fair trial. *State v. Moye,* 177 Conn. 487, 490, 418 A.2d 870 (1979); *State v. Evans,* 165 Conn. 61, 70, 327 A.2d 576 (1973).

In *Sandstrom v. Montana,* 442 U.S. 510, 513, 99 S.Ct. 2450, 2453, 61 L.Ed.2d 39 (1979), the United States Supreme Court held unconstitutional the jury instruction that " '[t]he law presumes that a person intends the ordinary consequences of his voluntary acts.' " The vice of such an instruction is that the jury may reasonably interpret it to establish the defendant's intent as a conclusion, or to shift the burden of proof on the element of intent to the accused. Because the jury instruction given in the present case could have precisely the same effect, it is unconstitutionally impermissible. *Sandstrom v. Montana, supra; State v. Harrison,* _____ Conn. _____, pp. _____, _____, 425 A.2d 111 (1979). The other instructions given were inadequate to cure the harmful potential of that portion of the charge.

There is error, the judgement is set aside, and a new trial is ordered.

In this opinion PARSKEY and O'BRIEN, JJ., concurred.

The PEOPLE of the State of Illinois, Plaintiff-Appellee
v.
Robert RODE, James F. Speer, Victoria Stone, Isadore Goldberg, Michael Sybole, Alfred Mears, Eric B. Laclair, Paul R. Valhon, Edward Skrocki, Robert Calfee, William Weiser, William G. Dehn, Defendants-Appellants
Appellate Court of Illinois, First District, First Division
Feb. 14, 1978
57 Ill.App.3d 645, 373 N.E.2d 605

GOLDBERG, Presiding Justice.

This record brings before us for review 15 convictions for sale of magazines in violation of the obscenity statute. (Ill.Rev.Stat. 1975, ch. 38, par. 11-20.) Since 3 of the defendants are involved in 2 separate cases, there are a total of 12 individuals who have appealed. All of the cases were consolidated in the trial court.

The brief filed in behalf of all defendants raises two issues. First, the trial court erred in finding the defendant Mears guilty of obscenity because the evidence is insufficient to establish that this defendant sold the publication with knowledge of the nature and contents thereof or recklessly failed to exercise reasonable inspection thereof. The second point urged by defendants is that books and magazines "which are the subject matter of these proceedings" are not obscene in the constitutional sense and are protected expressions under the first and fourteenth amendments to the United States Constitution.

We will first consider the issue of obscenity. As shown, this has been raised in defendants' brief in a general manner as to each and all of the defendants. It is first necessary to refer to the absence of all of the publications, except one, from this record. Each of the reports of proceedings show that the prosecution offered in evidence and the trial court received in evidence all of the allegedly obscene publications. The complete record was filed in this court on February 24, 1977, but none of the exhibits were provided in the usual manner by any of the appellants. On November 7, 1977, we allowed a motion by the State to supplement the record by filing the exhibit received in evidence in one of the cases; the proceedings involving defendant Alfred Mears (*nisi prius* No. 75-MCI E701258).

This situation raises the same point which was considered by this court in *People v. Speer* (1977), 52 Ill.App.3d 203, 211, 367 N.E.2d 372. This court pointed out, with the citation of ample authority, that in the ordinary case where the record on appeal is incomplete, it is the duty of a reviewing court to based its decision on every reasonable presumption favorable to the judgment appealed from and all doubts arising from the lack of a complete record should be resolved in favor of that judgment. As a matter of general practice this court has affirmed judgments where the failure of an appellant to discharge his responsibility under the rules of the Supreme Court of Illinois has made proper review impossible. However, as stated in *Speer*, in obscenity cases, "we are required to make an independent judgment of whether this material is constitutionally protected." (*Speer*, 52 Ill.App.3d 203, 209, 9 Ill.Dec. 938, 942, 367 N.E.2d 372, 376.) In *Speer*,

which also involved multiple defendants, one of the publications was not available "for our review, though it was submitted as part of the record on appeal to this court." (52 Ill.App.3d 203, 211, 9 Ill.Dec. 938, 367 N.E.2d 372, 377.) The court accordingly reversed the conviction of the single defendant as to which the publication was not available for examination by the court.

In our opinion, the record before us presents a different situation. The various reports of proceedings show that the allegedly obscene publications were offered and received in evidence in each of the cases. None of these exhibits was filed in this court with the sole exception of the one filed by the State to supplement the record with leave of this court. Thus, we are obliged to classify this case as one in which the defendants have failed to provide us with necessary parts of the record. We are therefore obliged to affirm the decision reached by the trial court and the resulting convictions in all of the cases in which defendants have failed to make the publication in issue available for our inspection. We are able to make an independent evaluation and judgment only in the case involving the defendant Alfred Mears.

The obscenity guidelines now in effect in Illinois are found in *People v. Ward* (1976), 63 Ill.2d 437, 349 N.E.2d 47, *aff'd.*, 431 U.S. 767, 97 S.Ct. 2085, 52 L.Ed.2d 738. All of the necessary material is set out with careful accuracy in the opinion of this court in *Speer*, 52 Ill.App.3d 203, 209-11, 9 Ill.Dec. 938, 367 N.E.2d 372. A repetition of these guidelines in this opinion is unnecessary.

The publication before us is entitled "Sex Styles Today, Vol. I, No. 1." It also has a notation on the front "Photo-Illustrations and Case Histories.'' The cover and some of the photographs are reproduced in color. We need not describe the various photographs beyond stating that, in our opinion, any reasonable person would immediately classify the entire publication as obscene in accordance with the guidelines set out in *Speer.*

Turning next to the issue of scienter, we find that the brief for all defendants raises this issue only as to the defendant Alfred Mears. In our opinion, the lack of argument in defendants' brief regarding the evidence as concerns knowledge of the remaining defendants is a waiver of this point as to all of the defendants except Alfred Mears. (Ill.Rev.Stat. 1975, ch. 110A, par. 341(e)(7); *People ex rel. Rappaport v. Drazek* (1975), 30 Ill.App.3d 310, 317, 332 N.E.2d 532 and cases there cited. Compare *Collins v. Westlake Comm. Hospital* (1974), 57 Ill.2d 388, 391-93, 312 N.E.2d 614.) Accordingly we reject this contention as to each and all of the defendants other than Alfred Mears.

As regards the Mears conviction, the publication in question has already been described, However, defendants urge a lack of scienter in that when defendant Mears sold the publication he had no knowledge of its type or contents. The evidence was produced in part by a stipulation of the parties which brought out that a police officer paid 50 cents as an admission fee to enter the store in which Mears was employed. The officer picked up a copy of the publication and brought it to Mears at the checkout counter. The officer placed the publication face up on the counter in front of Mears. Mears looked at the magazine and requested an additional $9.50. The price of the publication was $10 and Mears gave the officer a credit in the amount of the admission fee. The officer paid $9.50 and then completed the arrest. The officer asked Mears if he would sell that type of publication to a minor and Mears responded that he would not. The record also shows that Mears had been employed by the book store for two months prior to this sale. His duties were that of clerk and cashier and he did nothing concerning selection of the merchandise.

It is correct, as defendant Mears urges, that knowledge of the seller is an essential element of a conviction for obscenity. However, it is equally correct that scienter, like any other legally material fact, may be proved by circumstantial evidence. (See *People v. Williams* (1977), 66 Ill.2d 478, 484-85, 6 Ill.Dec. 854, 363 N.E.2d 801.) The authorities on this point, with particular reference to the situation before us, are collected and the arguments brought out in detail in *Speer* (52 Ill.App.3d 203, 212-13, 9 Ill.Dec. 938, 367 N.E.2d 372.) In our opinion, the circumstances in the case before us leave no doubt as to full knowledge by defendant Mears concerning his activities. As above pointed out, one glance at the cover of the publication is sufficient to establish its complete obscenity. It is difficult to conceive that a clerk-cashier who has worked in a book store for two months would not be fully apprised of the type and character of this publication simply by looking at it. The statement of defendant Mears that he would not sell the publication to a minor is another circumstance showing scienter. The inordinately high price charged for this publication and the fact that a book store and magazine purveyor charges an admission fee of 50 cents are additional circumstances which prove scienter beyond reasonable doubt.

Accordingly, the judgment appealed from in the case regarding Alfred

Mears is affirmed. All remaining judgments and convictions involved in this appeal are also affirmed.

Judgments affirmed.

McGLOON and O'CONNOR, JJ., concur.

The STATE of Montana, Plaintiff and Respondent
v.
Roy George CROSBY, Jr., alias Gary Bernard Wilkinson, Defendant and Appellant

Supreme Court of Montana
Decided Nov. 14, 1966
Rehearing Denied Dec. 15, 1966
420 P.2d 431

JAMES T. HARRISON, Chief Justice.

This is an appeal by the defendant from a judgment entered on a jury verdict finding him guilty of the commission of the crime of bigamy on two counts. The defendant was sentenced to two years in the state prison on each count, the terms to run consecutively.

The defendant and the State have agreed to let this appeal be determined on the merits of Instructions 2, 4A and 7.

The issue presented then is whether these instructions are a correct statement of the law.

The record before this court reveals the following sequence of marriages and divorces by the defendant:

1. Married Dorothy Fortney on May 27, 1948;
2. Married Lily Shaw on March 1, 1955, under an alias of Gary Bernard Wilkinson;
3. Divorced Dorothy Fortney Crosby on June 17, 1955;
4. Married Bonita Jarvi on October 27, 1956;
5. Divorced Bonita Jarvi Crosby on January 7, 1958;
6. Married May Lou Daniels on May 14, 1958;
7. Married Bonita Jarvi Crosby on August 19, 1958;
8. Divorced Bonita Jarvi Crosby on February 11, 1960;
9. Married Judy Lohrer on February 11, 1960.

At the trial, the defendant did not introduce any evidence which would prove a divorce between him and Mary Lou Daniels Crosby prior to his marriage to Bonita Crosby or Judy Lohrer.

Section 94-701, R.C.M. 1947, defines bigamy in this manner: "Every person having a husband or wife living who marries any other person, except in the cases specified in the next section, is guilty of bigamy."

Section 94-702, R.C.M. 1947, sets forth the following exceptions:

"The last section does not extend:

"1. To any person by reason of any former marriage, whose husband or wife by such marriage has been absent for five successive years, without being known to such person within that time to be living; nor,

"2. To any person by reason of any former marriage which has been pronounced void, annulled or dissolved by the judgment of a competent court."

From the facts which have been previously set forth it is apparent that the State proved the elements of the crime of bigamy. The State showed a marriage to Mary Lou Daniels and subsequent marriage to Bonita Crosby and Judy Lohrer without the benefit of a divorce.

We look then to Instructions 2, 4A and 7 to determine if they are reversible error.

Instruction 7 reads in the matter:

"You are instructed that it is the law of the State of Montana that every person having a husband or wife living who marries any other person, is guilty of bigamy."

We find no error in this Instruction as this is simply a statement of what is stated in section 94-701 with the reference to the exceptions left out. In this case defendant does not claim the benefit of the exceptions.

Instruction 2 reads in this manner:

"The State has the burden to prove beyond a reasonable doubt the material elements of the offense charged, this means that the State must establish that the defendant entered into a marriage and that thereafter while that wife was still living the defendant entered into another marriage with another woman in the County of Missoula, State of Montana, or in some other State or County and that thereafter they lived together as husband and wife in the County of Missoula, State of Montana.

"If the State proves these material allegations then the defendant before he can be found not guilty has the burden to prove that the prior marriage has been lawfully terminated by some competent tribunal which in the State of Montana can only be a District Court."

Again we find that this instruction is a correct recital of the law of this state.

Instruction 4A does present somewhat of a problem, but we do not feel that it is reversible error in light of Instructions 2 and 7 which were correct statements of the law.

Instruction 4A attempts to explain the three types of marriages that can be contracted. It says there are (1) absolute marriages; (2) voidable marriages; and (3) void marriages. This instruction may confuse the distinction between void marriages and voidable marriages, but this error is harmless in this case in light of the facts presented at the trial and the correct statement of the law in the other instructions.

In this connection, the entire thrust of the defense at the trial and here on appeal is that even though the marriage to Mary Lou Daniels was proven and tacitly admitted (defendant conducted his own defense and cross-examination), that the Daniels marriage was absolutely void because the defendant had still another wife under the alias name Wilkinson. Under the civil statute, section 48-111, R.C.M. 1947, such a marriage is void from the beginning.

However, as we have seen before from our quotation of the criminal statute, section 94-702, *supra,* such voidness must have been declared by a court of competent jurisdiction; such a determination of voidness cannot be made by the person involved to avoid being charged with a criminal act.

Defendant's position comes down to this: Once one marriage is consummated, thereafter all other marriages are void and such subsequent marriages cannot be bigamous. Our criminal statutory law is to the contrary.

No reversible error appearing, the judgment is affirmed.

JOHN CONWAY HARRISON, ADAIR and CASTLES, JJ., concur.

DOYLE, Justice (concurring in part; dissenting in part):

I concur in the majority opinion that the defendant was legally convicted of the crime alleged in the second count of the Information, but I vigorously dissent to the sustaining of the conviction on the first count of the Information, being the alleged bigamous marriage to Mary Lou Daniels on May 14, 1958.

The quantity and quality of the affirmative evidence is totally inadequate to sustain the conviction on the first count of the Information in my opinion.

William L. WEBSTER, Attorney General of Missouri, et al., Appellant

v.

REPRODUCTIVE HEALTH SERVICES et al.

Argued April 26, 1989
Decided July 3, 1989
—— U.S. ——, —— L.Ed.2d ——, 109 S.Ct. 3040

Syllabus

Appellees, state-employed health professionals and private nonprofit corporations providing abortion services, brought suit in the District Court for declaratory and injunctive relief challenging the constitutionality of a Missouri Statute regulating the performance of abortions. The statute, inter alia: (1) sets forth "findings" in its preamble that "[t]he life of each human being begins at conception," and that "unborn children have protectable interests in life, health, and well-being," §§ 1.205.1(1), 1.205.1(2), and requires that all state laws be interpreted to provide unborn children with the same rights enjoyed by other persons, subject to the Federal Constitution and this Court's precedents,

§ 1.205.2; (2) specifies that a physician, prior to performing an abortion on any woman whom he has reason to believe is 20 or more weeks pregnant, must ascertain whether the fetus is "viable" by performing "such medical examinations and tests as are necessary to make a finding of [the fetus'] gestational age, weight, and lung maturity," § 188.029; (3) prohibits the use of public employees and facilities to perform or assist abortions not necessary not necessary to save the mother's life, §§ 188.210, 188.215; and (4) makes it unlawful to use public funds, employees, or facilities for the purpose of "encouraging or counseling" a woman to have an abortion not necessary to save her life, §§ 188.205, 188.210, 188.215. The District Court struck down each of the above provisions, among others, and enjoined their enforcement. The Court of Appeals affirmed, ruling that the provisions in question violated this Court's decision in *Roe v. Wade,* 410 U.S. 113, 93 S.Ct. 705, 35 L. Ed. 2d 147 and subsequent cases.

Held: The judgment is reversed.

851 F.2d 1071 (CA8), reversed.

THE CHIEF JUSTICE delivered the opinion of the Court with respect to parts I, II-A, II-B, II-C, concluding that:

1. This Court need not pass on the constitutionality of the Missouri statute's preamble. In invalidating the preamble, the Court of Appeals misconceived the meaning of the dictum in *Akron v. Akron Center for Reproductive Health, Inc.,* 462 U.S. 416, 444, 103 S.Ct. 2481, 2500, 76 L. Ed. 2d 687, that "a State may not adopt one theory of when life begins to justify its regulation of abortions." That statement means only that a State could not "justify" any abortion regulation otherwise invalid under *Roe v. Wade* on the ground that it embodied the State's view about when life begins. The preamble does not by its terms regulate abortions or any other aspect of appellee's medical practice, and § 1.205.2 can be interpreted to do no more than offer protections to unborn children in tort and probate law, which is permissible under *Roe v. Wade, supra,* 410 U.S., at 161-162, 93 S.Ct., at 730-731. This Court has emphasized that *Roe* implies no limitation on a State's authority to make a value judgment favoring childbirth over abortion, *Maher v. Roe,* 432 U.S. 464, 474, 97 S.Ct. 2376, 2382-83, 53 L. Ed. 2d 484, and the preamble can be read simply to express that sort of value judgment.

The extent to which the preamble's language might be used to interpret other state statutes or regulations is something that only the state courts can definitively decide, and, until those courts have applied the preamble to restrict appellees' activities in some concrete way, it is inappropriate for federal courts to address its meaning. *Alabama State Federation of Labor v. McAdory,* 325 U.S. 450, 460, 65 S.Ct. 1384, 1389, 89 L. Ed 1725. Pp. 3049-3051.

2. The restrictions in §§ 188.210 and 188.215 of the Missouri statute on the use of public employees and facilities for the performance or assistance of nontherapeutic abortions do not contravene this Court's abortion decisions. The Due Process Clauses generally confer no affirmative right to governmental aid, even where such aid may be necessary to secure life, liberty, or property interests of which the government may not deprive the individual. *DeShaney v. Winnebago County Dept. of Social Services,* 489 U.S. ____, ____, 109 S.Ct. 998, ____, 103 L. Ed. 2d 249. Thus, in *Maher v. Roe, supra; Poelker v. Doe,* 432 U.S. 519, 97 S.Ct. 2391, 53 L. Ed. 2d 528; and *Harris v. McRae,* 448 U.S. 297, 100 S.Ct. 2671, 65 L. Ed. 2d 784, this Court upheld governmental regulations withholding public funds for nontherapeutic abortions but allowing payments for medical services related to childbirth, recognizing that a government's decision to favor childbirth over abortion through the allocation of public funds does not violate *Roe v. Wade.* A State may implement that same value judgment through the allocation of other public resources, such

as hospitals and medical staff. There is no merit to the claim that *Maher, Poelker* and *McRae* must be distinguished on the grounds that preventing access to a public facility narrows or forecloses the availability of abortion. Just as in those cases, Missouri's decision to use public facilities and employees to encourage childbirth over abortion places no governmental obstacle in the path of the woman who chooses to terminate her pregnancy, but leaves her with the same choices as if the State had decided not to operate any hospitals at all. The challenged provisions restrict her ability to obtain an abortion only to the extent that she chooses to use a physician affiliated with a public hospital. Also without merit is the assertion that *Maher, Poelker,* and *McRae,* must be distinguished on the ground that, since the evidence shows that all of a public facility's costs in providing abortion services are recouped when the patient pays such that no public funds are expended, the Missouri statute goes beyond expressing a preference for childbirth over abortion by creating an obstacle to the right to choose abortion that cannot stand absent a compelling state interest. Nothing in the Constitution requires States to enter or remain in the abortion business or entitles private physicians and their patients to access to public facilities for the performance of abortions. Indeed, if the State does recoup all of its costs in performing abortions and no state subsidy, direct or indirect, is available, it is difficult to see how any procreational choice is burdened by the State's ban on the use of its facilities or employees for performing abortions. The cases in question all support the view that the State need

not commit any resources to performing abortions, even if it can turn a profit by doing so. Pp. 3050-3053.

3. The controversy over § 188.205's prohibition on the use of public funds to encourage or counsel a woman to have a nontherapeutic abortion is moot. The Court of Appeals did not consider § 188.205 separately from §§ 188.210 and 188.215—which respectively prohibit the use of public employees and facilities for such counseling— in holding all three sections unconstitutionally vague and violative of a woman's right to choose an abortion. Missouri has appealed only the invalidation of § 188.205. In light of the State's claim, which this Court accepts for purposes of decision, that § 188.205 is not directed at the primary conduct of physicians or health care providers, but is simply an instruction to the State's fiscal officers not to allocate public funds for abortion counseling, appellees contend that they are not "adversely" affected by the section and therefore that there is no longer a case or controversy before the Court on this question. Since plaintiffs are masters of their complaints even at the appellate stage and since appellees no longer seek equitable relief on their § 188.205 claim, the Court of Appeals is directed to vacate the District Court's judgment with instructions to dismiss the relevant part of the complain with prejudice. *Deakins v. Monaghan,* 484 U.S. 193, 200, 108 S.Ct. 523, ____, 98 L. Ed. 2d 529. P. 3053.

The Chief Justice, joined by Justice WHITE and Justice KENNEDY, concluded in Parts II-D and III that:

1. Section 188.029 of the Missouri statute—which specifies, in its first

sentence, that a physician, before performing an abortion on a woman he has reason to believe is carrying an unborn child of 20 or more weeks gestational age, shall first determine if the unborn child is viable by using that degree of care, skill, and proficiency that is commonly exercised by practitioners in the field; but which then provides, in its second sentence, that, in making the viability determination, the physician shall perform such medical examinations and tests as are necessary to make a finding of the unborn child's gestational age, weight, and lung maturity—is constitutional, since it permissibly furthers the State's interest in protecting potential human life. Pp. 3054-3058.

(a) The Court of Appeals committed plain error in reading § 188.029 as requiring that after 20 weeks the specified tests must be performed. That section makes sense only if its second sentence is read to require only those tests that are useful in making subsidiary viability findings. Reading the sentence to require the tests *in all circumstances,* including when the physician's reasonable professional judgment indicates that they would be irrelevant to determining viability or even dangerous to the mother and the fetus, would conflict with the first sentence's *requirement* that the physician apply his reasonable professional skill and judgment. It would also be incongruous to read the provision, especially the word "necessary," to require tests irrelevant to the expressed statutory purpose of determining viability. Pp. 3054-3055.

(b) Section 188.029 is reasonably designed to ensure that abortions are not performed where the fetus is viable. The section's tests are intended to determine viability, the State having chosen viability as the point at which its interest in potential human life must be safeguarded. The section creates what is essentially a presumption of viability at 20 weeks, which the physician, prior to performing an abortion, must rebut with tests—including, if feasible, those for gestational age, fetal weight, and lung capacity—indicating that the fetus is not viable. While the District Court found that uncontradicted medical evidence established that a 20-week fetus is *not* viable, and that 23 to 24 weeks' gestation is the earliest point at which a reasonable possibility of viability exists, it also found that there may be a 4-week error in estimating gestational age, which supports testing at 20 weeks. Pp. 3055-3056.

(c) Section 188.029 conflicts with *Roe v. Wade* and cases following it. Since the section's tests will undoubtedly show in many cases that the fetus is not viable, the tests will have been performed for what were in fact second-trimester abortions. While *Roe,* 410 U.S., at 162, 93 S.Ct., at 731, recognized the State's interest in protecting potential human life as "important and legitimate," it also limited state involvement in second-trimester abortions to protect maternal health, id., at 164, 93 S.Ct. at 732, and allowed States to regulate or proscribe abortions to protect the unborn child only after viability, id., at 165, 93 S.Ct., at 732-33. Since the tests in question regulate the physician's discretion in determining the viability of the fetus, § 188.029 conflicts with language in *Colautti v. Franklin,* 439 U.S. 379, 388-389, 99 S.Ct. 675, 681-683, 58 L. Ed. 2d 596, stating that the viability determination is, and must be, a matter for the responsible attending physician's judgment. And, in light of District Court findings that the tests increase the expenses of abortion, their validity may also be questioned under *Akron, supra,* 462 U.S., at 434-435, 103 S.Ct., at 2494-2495, which held that a requirement that second-trimester abortions be performed in hospitals was invalid because it substantially increased the expenses of those procedures. Pp. 3055-3056.

(d) The doubt cast on the Missouri statute by these cases is not so much a flaw in the statute as it is a reflection of the fact that Roe's rigid trimester analysis has proved to be unsound in principle and unworkable in practice. In such circumstances, this Court does not refrain from reconsidering prior constitutional rulings, notwithstanding *stare decisis. E.g., Garcia v. San Antonio Metropolitan Transit Authority,* 469 U.S. 528, 105 S.Ct. 1005, 83 L. Ed. 2d 1016. The *Roe* framework is hardly consistent with the notion of a Constitution like ours that is cast in general terms and usually speaks in general principles. The framework's key elements—trimesters and viabi-

lity—are not found in the Constitution's text, and, since the bounds of the inquiry are essentially indeterminate, the result has been a web of legal rules that have become increasingly intricate, resembling a code of regulations rather than a body of constitutional doctrine. There is also no reason why the State's compelling interest in protecting potential human life should not extend throughout pregnancy rather than coming into existence only at the point of viability. Thus, the *Roe* trimester framework should be abandoned. Pp. 3056-3057.

(e) There is no merit to the dissent's contention that the Court should join in a "great issues" debate as to whether the Constitution includes and "unenumerated" general right to privacy as recognized in cases such as *Griswold v. Connecticut,* 381 U.S. 479, 85 S.Ct. 1678, 14 L. Ed. 2d 510. Unlike *Roe, Griswold* did not purport to adopt a whole framework, complete with detailed rules and distinctions, to govern the cases in which the asserted liberty interest would apply. The *Roe* framework sought to deal with areas of medical practice traditionally left to the States, and to balance once and for all, by reference only to the calendar, the State's interest in protecting potential human life against the claims of a pregnant woman to decide whether or not to abort. The Court's experience in applying *Roe* in later cases suggests that there is wisdom in not necessarily attempting to elaborate the differences between a "fundamental right" to an abortion, *Akron, supra,* 462 U.S., at 420, n. 1, 103 S.Ct., at 2487, n. 1, a "limited fundamental constitutional right," post, at 3055, or a liberty interest protected by the Due Process Clause. Moreover, although this decision will undoubtedly allow more governmental regulation of abortion than was permissible before, the goal of constitutional adjudication is not to remove inexorably "politically divisive" issues from the ambit of the legislative process, but is, rather, to hold true the balance between that which the Constitution puts beyond the reach of the democratic process and that which it does not. Furthermore, the suggestion that legislative bodies, in a Nation where more than half the population is female, will treat this decision as an invitation to enact abortion laws reminiscent of the dark ages misreads the decision and does scant justice to those who serve in such bodies and the people who elect them. Pp. 3057-3058.

2. This case affords no occasion to disturb *Roe's* holding that a Texas statute which criminalized *all* nontherapeutic abortions unconstitutionally infringed the right to an abortion derived from the Due Process Clause. *Roe* is distinguishable on its facts, since Missouri has determined that viability is the point at which its interest in potential human life must be safeguarded. P. 3058.

Justice O'CONNOR, agreeing that it was plain error for the Court of Appeals to interpret the second sentence of § 188.029 as meaning that doctors must perform tests to find gestational age, fetal weight, and lung maturity, concluded that the section was constitutional as properly interpreted by the plurality, and that the plurality should therefore not have proceeded to reconsider *Roe v. Wade.* This Court refrains from deciding constitutional questions where there is no need to do so, and generally does not formulate a constitutional rule broader than the precise facts to which it is to be applied. *Ashwander v. TVA,* 297 U.S. 288, 346, 347, 56 S.Ct. 466, 482-483, 483, 80 L. Ed. 688. Since appellees did not appeal the District Court's ruling that the first sentence of § 188.029 is constitutional, there is no dispute between the parties over the presumption of viability at 20 weeks created by that first sentence. Moreover, as properly interpreted by the plurality, the section's second sentence does nothing more than delineate means by which the unchallenged 20-week presumption may be overcome if those means are useful in determining viability and can be prudently employed. As so interpreted, the viability testing requirements do not conflict with any of the Court's abortion decisions. As the plurality recognizes, under its interpretation of § 188.029's second sentence, the viability testing requirements promote the State's interest in potential life. This Court has recognized that a State may promote that interest when viability is possible. *Thornburgh v. American College of Obstetricians and Gynecologists,* 476 U.S. 747, 770-771, 106 S.Ct. 2169, 2183-2184, 90 L. Ed. 2d 779. Similarly, the basis for reliance by the lower courts on *Colautti v. Franklin,* 439 U.S. 379, 388-389, 99 S.Ct. 675, 681-683, 58 L. Ed. 2d 596, disappears when § 188.029 is properly interpreted to require only *subsidiary* viability findings, since the State has not attempted to substitute its judgment for the physician's ascertainment of viability, which therefore remains "the critical point." Nor does the marginal increase in the cost of an abortion created by § 188.029's viability testing provision, as interpreted, conflict with *Akron v. Akron Center for Reproductive Health,* 462 U.S. 416, 434-439, 103 S.Ct. 2481, 2494-2497, 76 L. Ed. 2d 687, since, here, such costs do not place a "heavy, and unnecessary burden" on a woman's abortion decision, whereas the statutory requirement in Akron, which related to previability abortions, more than doubled a woman's costs. Moreover, the statutory requirement in Akron involved second-trimester abortions generally; § 188.029 concerns only tests and examinations to determine viability when viability is possible. The State's compelling interest in potential life postviability renders its interest in determining the critical point of viability equally compelling. *Thornburgh, supra,* 476 U.S., at 770-771, 106 S.Ct., at 2183-2184. When the constitutional invalidity of a State's abortion statute actually turns upon the constitutional validity of *Roe,* there will be time enough to reexamine *Roe,* and to do so carefully. Pp. 3060-3064.

Justice SCALIA would reconsider and explicitly overrule *Roe v. Wade.* Avoiding the *Roe* question by deciding this case in as narrow a manner as possible is not required by precedent and not justified by policy. To do so is needlessly to prolong this Court's involvement in a field where the answers to the central questions are political rather than juridical, and thus to make the Court the object of the sort of organized pressure that political institutions in a democracy ought to receive. It is particularly perverse to decide this case as narrowly as possible in order to avoid reading the inexpressibly "broader-than-was-required-by-the-precise-facts" structure established by *Roe v. Wade.* The question of *Roe's* validity is presented here, inasmuch as § 188.029 constitutes a legislative imposition on the judgment of the physician concerning the point of viability, and increases the cost of an abortion. It does palpable harm, if the states can and would eliminate largely unrestricted abortion, skillfully to refrain from telling them so. Pp. 3064-3067.

REHNQUIST, C.J., announced the judgment of the Court and delivered the opinion for a unanimous Court with respect to Part II-C, the opinion of the Court with respect to Parts I, II-A, and II-B, in which WHITE, O'CONNOR, SCALIA, and KENNEDY, J.J., joined, and an opinion with respect to Parts II-D and III, in which WHITE and KENNEDY, J.J., joined. O'CONNOR, J. and SCALIA, J., filed opinions concurring in part and concurring in the judgment. BLACKMUN, J. filed an opinion concurring in part and dissenting in part, in which BRENNAN and MARSHALL, J.J., joined. STEVENS, J., filed an opinion concurring in part and dissenting in part.

Cases relating to Chapter 9

OFFENSES AGAINST THE PUBLIC PEACE

John KASPER, Plaintiff In Error,

v.

STATE of Tennessee, Defendant In Error

Supreme Court of Tennessee
July 27, 1959
On Petition for Rehearing Sept. 3, 1959
326 S.W.2d 664

SWEPSTON, Justice.

Plaintiff in error, John Kasper, hereinafter called defendant, was convicted for inciting a riot and sentenced to serve for a period of six months in the Davidson County Workhouse and pay a fine of $500.

There have been filed in behalf of defendant 20 assignments of error, some of which overlap, but counsel has not seen fit to file any written brief or argument in support of said assignments of error.

Under assignments 1, 3, 4 and 8 it is insisted that the court erred in not sustaining the motion to quash the array of jurors upon the alleged grounds that they did not comprise a cross Section of the County either geographically or economically; that they were a biased and prejudiced panel of jurors holding strong opinions in opposition to defendant; in refusing to grant the motion for change of venue.

We have examined the record thoroughly in this regard and we find absolutely no merit whatever in these insistences. The trial judge heard ample evidence in regard thereto and

gave the same most careful attention. Hence we overrule those assignments.

The second assignment of error is that there is no common law offense of inciting to riot because it is alleged that the indictment or presentment is based on the common law and that the same has been expressly repealed by the adoption of the State and Federal Constitutions on those subjects and that no legislation covering the subject has been enacted.

There is no merit in this insistence because Art. XI, Sec. 1 of the Constitution of this State expressly provides otherwise and it has been so held in *Henley v. State,* 98 Tenn. 665, 41 S.W. 352, 1104, 39 L.R.A. 126.

Assignments 5, 6 and 7 are that the evidence preponderates against the verdict and in favor of his innocence; the proof fails to show that as many as 3 people were assembled at any time as would be necessary to establish the existence of a riot; that the proof fails to show that a riot ever occurred, and if so, in the presence of the defendant.

It thus becomes necessary to refer to the evidence. The State offered the following evidence:

The defendant, a native of New Jersey, and a graduate of Columbia University, Class of 1951, came to Nashville, Tennessee, about the end of July, 1957. At that time there was considerable feeling and unrest among a substantial number of residents of Nashville because of a Federal District Court order requiring the first grades in all City schools to be integrated upon the opening of the September 1957 term of school.

The defendant had appeared before the City School Board in an attempt to prevent integrating the first grade in the public schools. He began making speeches sometime in the early part of August around in various places. It was shown by the testimony of a Mr. Fullerton, a newspaper reporter for the Nashville Tennesseean, that at a meeting on the first Sunday in August, 1957, the defendant said in substance "Well, he said that people were getting pretty excited about it (the school opening) and he said, we don't want any trouble here but people are getting pretty excited. I remember he said, I had a fellow come up to me and say, 'John, why don't you hang the School Board.' He said, 'I don't say we should do that,' and he said 'another fellow came up to me, John, I have got a shot gun, we might have to use it to defend myself and my family and I can do it.' He said, another fellow came up to me and said, 'John, I don't want to have any trouble here but my kids aren't going to school with Negroes, and if I have some dynamite, I know how to use it.' "

This witness stated that the defendant kept repeating the above statement in substance and that in all these references that he made to violence he purported to be quoting somebody else and not saying these things himself.

This witness attended another meet-ing the latter part of the month of the same nature. The defendant continued speaking around in various places before the opening of schools on August 27 for enrollment of pupils. On one of those occasions he spoke in front of the Davidson County Court-house and on that occasion he made extremely derogatory remarks about Governor Clement, Mayor West and other officials, including the School Board. He said the School Board had a Jew and Negroes on it and they were nothing but pushbuttons for the Mayor. He referred to Negro people generally as "niggers" and said the Jews were agitating and promoting this trouble with the Negroes to the point where the Negroes thought they were better than the people he was speaking to. He said the Negro is better than the Jew and that the Jews were Christ killers. Again he said he was not advocating any violence but there would be bomb-ings, dynamiting, bloodshed and prob-ably killings but regardless, they were not going to put Negroes in our schools. That statement brought on some loud talking and clapping of hands. On this occasion the defen-dant's hat was passed around among the crowd to take up a collection which defendant said was to defray the expense of printing literature and the money was turned over to him. The only literature passed out at the first meeting was announcement of the schedule of future meetings. At a sub-sequent meeting in the same spot, other literature to be referred to here-inafter was passed out.

An [sic] August 27, the enrollment date for the schools, the defendant appeared at at least five of the schools and made inquiry about the number of Negro children registered, if any, and created a disturbance by urging the people not to let their children go into the schools or urging them to withdraw them as a result of which a very substantial number of children were withdrawn from each of the schools.

Then on September 9, the day the schools were to begin classes, the defendant engaged in the same performance. For instance, at the Caldwell School there were some people there before the defendant arrived and they were quiet. After he arrived and began speaking, the crowd increased and became loud and traffic was blocked so that the police officer made him move on. Defendant in departing told the crowd to follow him to the Buena Vista School. Then at Fehr's School where defendant appeared on September 9, there were 156 pupils there before he came and only 40 afterwards. The mob yelled for the lady principal to come out and they threatened to get her. During the disturbance the colored janitor's automobile was burned. After the crowd had dispersed, the school-yard was filled with sticks, stones and broken bottles.

This principal definitely testified that part of the threats made against her were made while the defendant was talking to the crowd asking them to boycott and picket the schools. She named more than 4 people in the crowd.

Then that night of September 9, the big show came off. The meeting started out in front of the War Memorial Building in Nashville but as the crowd grew in size and were blocking traffic on Capitol Boulevard, the meeting was moved to the steps of the Capitol Building. The crowd was estimated to be in the beginning a little more than 100 but increased to the maximum estimate by some witnesses of 700. At this meeting the defendant spoke his usual line of stating what would happen if the integration was

proceeded with but was careful of course, not to make any statements or threats as to what he would do himself personally. He designated pickets to go to some of the schools; he held up a rope with a noose in the end of it and suggested that a lot of people would like to see Z. Alexander Looby hanged (this latter person being a Negro lawyer and a member of the City Government of the City of Nashville). The defendant posed for a picture holding some wooden mallets crossed in his hands, these mallets being the type used by stonemasons.

At this meeting there was passed out with the name of the defendant on the reverse side of some printed material that stated that these were the last days of peace between the white and Negro races and tended to question the motive and sincerity of national, state and county officials and urged that the white people stiffen their backs and prevent the integration of schools with their shotguns. There was also passed out by the defendant or those aiding him in the conduct of his meetings and speeches a picture of a Negro boy kissing a white girl.

The evidence shows that the crowd reacted to these things as one would expect. Immediately thereafter, according to one witness, at least 150 people who had attended the meeting in front of the Capitol repaired to Fehr [sic] School where a riot occurred. The crowd was breaking glass and running all over everything.

About 2:00 a.m. that same night, the Hattie Cotton School was dynamited and partly demolished.

We deem it unnecessary to go into further details as we are of opinion that there is ample evidence both direct and circumstantial, to fully support the verdict of the jury. We would like, however, to make this comment. The defendant's insistence is that he does not believe in violence and has never at any time advocated violence; that he came here for the purpose of promoting friendly race relations. He admits the general tenor of statements attributed to him by numerous witnesses, but insists that he was simply quoting predictions by others.

As for his alleged non-violence attitude, it seems to be a case of the voice of Jacob and the hand of Esau. As for race relations, his every move was consistent with and conducive to nothing but disruptive race relations.

Evidently we must overrule these assignments.

Assignments 10 and 14 relate to the refusal of the trial judge to permit counsel for defendant to cross-examine two witnesses relative to their being beaten by police officers and causing them to make statements. The State concedes that this was error but we do not think so under the circumstances of this case. These men did testify that they were beaten by the police and that they were afraid of the police but under questioning by the trial judge, they testified in the absence of the jury that regardless of their claim of having been beaten that what they had said in their statements and in their testimony was the truth. The trial judge was satisfied with their statements that they were telling the truth and he was very careful all through the trial not to get into side issues but to stick strictly to the charge in the indictment. We do not think that this was error but even so, in view of all the mass of evidence otherwise, we agree with the State that it is harmless error.

The same thing may be said of assignment 19 with reference to Constable Peek. That is, the trial judge was not interested in Peek's conversation with the defendant when he arrested

him and sought to elicit from defendant a history of his views and theories about Communism, race relations, etc.

Assignments 9, 11 and 12 relate to matters introduced in evidence consisting of a baseball bat, a mallet, etc., found in the car of witness Crimmons after he had been attending the defendant's meetings and about a piece of wire; also a sound film taken of the meeting on the night of September 9 showing the crowd in front of the Capitol.

Crimmons had been associating with the defendant, driving him around and also taking orders from him about picketing. It was proper to put these items found in his car before the jury to let them decide whether they were relevant to the charge in the indictment. The film was also properly authenticated and introduced for whatever it was worth and that also was for the jury. There is some question about the type of wire, whether it was suitable for discharging dynamite, but that is likewise a matter that was for the jury so that we can see no merit in these assignments.

We have examined the other assignments and find no merit in them. There is no doubt in anybody's mind that any citizen has a right to express his opinion about the opinion of the Supreme Court of the United States in the integration cases but the right of free speech is limited just as are all other so-called rights and when one goes beyond a proper expression of opinion and incites to riot, he has gone beyond the area of freedom of speech. The great Justice Oliver Wendell Holmes said that no one has a right to yell "Fire" in a crowded theater when there is no fire.

Before closing we wish to make the following comment. The trial judge made a preliminary statement to counsel that he would confine the evidence strictly to the charge in the indictment and there would not be tolerated any side issues. He enforced this ruling strictly and impartially as well as humanly possible. It is well that he did for many reasons including the fact that approximately fifty witnesses testified.

The judge commended counsel for the efficiency and propriety of their efforts. We most heartily commend the judge for his fairness and efficiency.

All assignments are overruled and the judgment below is affirmed.

Opinion on Petition to Rehear

SWEPSTON, Justice.

John Kasper has filed a petition to rehear in the above styled case. The same was filed by Kasper *pro se* on August 27, 1959, which is more than 10 days allowed for the filing of petitions to rehear and accordingly does not comply with Rule 32 of this Court.

In view of the statement in said petition that the petitioner is incarcerated and that it is "practically impossible" to employ new counsel on short notice, we have examined the petition.

The result of our examination is that no new argument appears therein, no new authority is adduced, and no material fact is pointed out as overlooked. Therefore, in accordance with said Rule 32 *supra* said petition is overruled.

The Clerk of this Court will notify said John Kasper by sending him a copy hereof addressed to him at P.M.B. 16391, Tallahassee, Florida.

Sam THOMPSON, Petitioner,
v.
CITY OF LOUISVILLE et al.
362 U.S. 199, 80 S.Ct. 624
Decided March 21, 1960

Mr. Justice BLACK delivered the opinion of the Court.

Petitioner was found guilty in the Police Court of Louisville, Kentucky, of two offenses—loitering and disorderly conduct. The ultimate question presented to us is whether the charges against petitioner were so totally devoid of evidentiary support as to render his conviction unconstitutional under the Due Process Clause of the Fourteenth Amendment. Decision of this question turns not on the sufficiency of the evidence, but on whether this conviction rests upon any evidence at all.

The facts as shown by the record are short and simple. Petitioner, a long-time resident of the Louisville area, went into the Liberty End Cafe about 6:20 p.m. Saturday, January 24, 1959. In addition to selling food the cafe was licensed to sell beer to the public and some 12 to 30 patrons were present during the time petitioner was there. When petitioner had been in the cafe about half an hour, two Louisville police officers came in on a "routine check." Upon seeing petitioner "out there on the floor dancing by himself," one of the officers, according to his testimony, went up to the manager who was sitting on a stool nearby and asked him how long petitioner had been in there and if he had bought anything. The officer testified that upon being told by the manager that petitioner had been there "a little over a half-hour and that he had not bought anything," he accosted Thompson and "asked him what was his reason for being in there and he said he was waiting on a bus." The officer then informed petitioner that he was under arrest and took him outside. This was the arrest for loitering. After going outside, the officer testified, petitioner "was very argumentative—he argued with us back and forth and so then we placed a disorderly conduct charge on him." Admittedly the disorderly conduct conviction rests solely on this one sentence description of petitioner's conduct after he left the cafe.

The foregoing evidence includes all that the city offered against him, except a record purportedly showing a total of 54 previous arrests of petitioner. Before putting on his defense, petitioner moved for a dismissal of the charges against him on the ground that a judgment of conviction on this record would deprive him of property and liberty[1] without due process of law under the Fourteenth Amendment in that (1) there was no evidence to support findings of guilt and (2) the two arrests and prosecutions were reprisals against him because petitioner had employed counsel and demanded a judicial hearing to defend himself against prior and

1. Upon conviction and sentence under §§ 85-8, 85-12 and 85-13 of the ordinances of the City of Louisville, petitioner would be subject to imprisonement, fine or confinement in the workhouse upon default of payment of a fine.

allegedly baseless charges by the police.[2] This motion was denied.

Petitioner then put in evidence on his own behalf, none of which in any way strengthened the city's case. He testified that he bought, and one of the cafe employees served him, a dish of macaroni and a glass of beer and that he remained in the cafe waiting for a bus to go home.[3] Further evidence showed without dispute that at the time of his arrest petitioner gave the officers his home address; that he had money with him, and a bus schedule showing that a bus to his home would stop within half a block of the cafe at about 7:30 p.m.; that he owned two unimproved lots of land; that in addition to work he had done for others, he had regularly worked one day or more a week for the same family for 30 years; that he paid no rent in the home where he lived and that his meager income was sufficient to meet his needs. The cafe manager testified that petitioner had frequently

2. Petitioner added that the effect of convictions here would be to deny him redress for the prior alleged arbitrary and unlawful arrests. This was based on the fact that, under Kentucky law, conviction bars suits for malicious prosecution and even for false imprisonment. Thus, petitioner says, he is subject to arbitrary and continued arrests neither reviewable by regular appellate procedures nor subject to challenge in independent civil actions.

3. The officer's previous testimony that petitioner had bought no food or drink is seriously undermined, if not contradicted, by the manager's testimony at trial. There the manager stated that the officer "asked me I had [sic] sold him any thing to eat and I said no and he said any beer and I said no * * *." (Emphasis supplied.) And the manager acknowledged that petitioner might have bought something and been served by a waiter or waitress without the manager noticing it. Whether there was a purchase or not, however, is of no significance to the issue.

patronized the cafe, and that he had never told petitioner that he was unwelcome there. The manager further testified that on this very occasion he saw petitioner "standing there in the middle of the floor and patting his foot," and that he did not at any time during the petitioner's stay there object to anything he was doing. There is no evidence that anyone else in the cafe objected to petitioner's shuffling his feet in rhythm with the music of the jukebox or that his conduct was boisterous or offensive to anyone present. At the close of his evidence, petitioner repeated his motion for dismissal of the charges on the ground that a conviction on the foregoing evidence would deprive him of liberty and property without due process under the Fourteenth Amendment. The court denied the motion, convicted him of both offenses, and fined him $10 on each charge. A motion for new trial, on the same grounds, also was denied, which exhausted petitioner's remedies in the police court.

Since police court fines of less than $20 on a single charge are not appealable or otherwise reviewable in any other Kentucky court, petitioner asked the police court to stay the judgments so that he might have an opportunity to apply for certiorari to this Court (before his case became moot) to review the due process contentions he raised. The police court suspended judgment for 24 hours during which time petitioner sought a longer stay from the Kentucky Circuit Court. That court, after examining the police court's judgments and transcript, granted a stay concluding that "there appears to be merit" in the contention that "there is no evidence upon which conviction and sentence by the Police Court could be based" and that petitioner's "Federal Constitutional claims

are substantial and not frivolous." On appeal by the city, the Kentucky Court of Appeals held that the Circuit Court lacked the power to grant the stay it did, but nevertheless went on to take the extraordinary step of granting its own stay, even though petitioner had made no original application to that court for such a stay. Explaining its reason, the Court of Appeals took occasion to agree with the Circuit Court that petitioner's "federal constitutional claims are substantial and not frivolous." The Court of Appeals then went on to say that petitioner

"appears to have a real question as to whether he has been denied due process under the Fourteenth Amendment of the Federal Constitution, yet this substantive right cannot be tested unless we grant him a stay of execution because his fines are not appealable and will be satisfied by being served in jail before he can prepare and file his petition for certiorari. Appellee's substantive right of due process is of no avail to him unless this court grants him the ancillary right whereby he may test same in the Supreme Court."

Our examination of the record presented in the petition for certiorari convinced us that although the fines here are small, the due process questions presented are substantial and we therefore granted certiorari to review the police court's judgments. 360 U.S. 916, 79 S.Ct. 1433, 3 L.Ed.2d 1532. Compare *Yick Wo v. Hopkins,* 118 U.S. 356, 6 S.Ct. 1064, 30 L.Ed. 220 (San Francisco Police Judges Court judgment imposing a $10 fine, upheld by state appellate court, held invalid as in contravention of the Fourteenth Amendment).

The city correctly assumes here that if there is no support for these convictions in the record they are void as denials of due process. The pertinent portion of the city ordinance under which petitioner was convicted of loitering reads as follows:

"It shall be unlawful for any person * * *, without visible means of support, or who cannot give a satisfactory account of himself, * * * to sleep, lie, loaf, or trespass in or about any premises, building, or other structure in the City of Louisville, without first having obtained the consent of the owner or controller of said premises, structure, or building; * * *" § 85-12, Ordinances of the City of Louisville.

In addition to the fact that petitioner proved he had "visible means of support," the prosecutor at trial said "This is a loitering charge here. There is no charge of no visible means of support." Moreover, there is no suggesting that petitioner was sleeping, lying or trespassing in or about this cafe. Accordingly he could only have been convicted for being unable to give a satisfactory account of himself while loitering in the cafe, without the consent of the manager. Under the words of the ordinance itself, if the evidence fails to prove all three elements of this loitering charge, the conviction is not supported by evidence, in which event it does not comport with due process of law. The record is entirely lacking in evidence to support any of the charges.

Here, petitioner spent about half an hour on a Saturday evening in January in a public cafe which sold food and beer to the public. When asked to account for his presence there, he said he was waiting for a bus. The city concedes that there is no law making it an offense for a person in such a cafe to "dance," "shuffle" or "pat" his feet in time to music. The undisputed testimony of the manager, who did not know whether petitioner had bought macaroni and beer or not but who did see the petitioner, shuffling or dancing, was that petitioner was welcome there. The manager testified that he did not at any time during petitioner's stay in the cafe object to anything petitioner was doing and that he never saw petitioner do anything that would cause any objection. Surely this is implied consent, which the city admitted in oral argument satisfies the ordinance. The arresting officer admitted that there was nothing in any way "vulgar" about what he called petitioner's "ordinary dance," whatever relevance, if any, vulgarity might have to a charge of loitering. There simply is no semblance of evidence from which any person could reasonably infer that petitioner could not give a satisfactory account of himself or that he was loitering or loafing there (in the ordinary sense of the words) without "the consent of the owner or controller" of the cafe.

Petitioner's conviction for disorderly conduct was under § 85-8 of the city ordinance which, without definition, provides that "[w]hoever shall be found guilty of disorderly conduct in the City of Louisville shall be fined * * *." etc. The only evidence of "disorderly conduct" was the single statement of the policeman that after petitioner was arrested and taken out of the cafe he was very argumentative. There is no testimony that petitioner raised his voice, used offensive language, resisted the officers or engaged in any conduct of any kind likely in any way to adversely affect the good order and tranquillity of the City of Louisville. The only information the record contains on what the petitioner was "argumentative" about is his statement that he asked the officers "what they arrested me for." We assume, for we are justified in assuming, that merely "arguing" with a policeman is not, because it could not be, "disorderly conduct" as a matter of the substantive law of Kentucky. *See Lanzetta v. State of New Jersey,* 306 U.S. 451, 59 S.Ct. 618, 83 L.Ed. 888. Moreover, Kentucky law itself seems to provide that if a man wrongfully arrested fails to object to the arresting officer, he waives any right to complain later that the arrest was unlawful. *Nickell v. Commonwealth, Ky.,* 285 S.W.2d 495, 496.

Thus we find no evidence whatever in the record to support these convictions. Just as "Conviction upon a charge not made would be sheer denial of due process," so is it a violation of due process to convict and punish a man without evidence of his guilt.

The judgments are reversed and the cause is remanded to the Police Court of the City of Louisville for proceedings not inconsistent with this opinion.

Reversed and remanded.

UNITED STATES of America, Appellee

v.

Frederick Lyle McINTYRE, Appellant

UNITED STATES of America, Appellee

v.

Dale Irwin VanBUSKIRK, Appellant

U.S. Court of Appeals, Ninth Circuit
Sept. 25, 1978
Rehearings Denied Nov. 13, 1978
582 F.2d 1221

GOODWIN, Circuit Judge:

McIntyre and VanBuskirk appeal their convictions for violating and conspiring to violate 18 U.S.C. § 2511(1)(a) and (b) (Title III of the Omnibus Crime Control and Safe Streets Act of 1968).[1]

VanBuskirk was Chief of Police of Globe, Arizona, and McIntyre was a Lieutenant in that department. The Assistant Chief of Police was Robert McGann. VanBuskirk and McIntyre suspected McGann of leaking damaging information to political enemies of VanBuskirk. McIntyre also suspected

1. (1) Except as otherwise specifically provided in this chapter any person who—
   (a) willfully intercepts, endeavors to intercept, or procures any other person to intercept or endeavor to intercept, any wire or oral communication;

   (b) willfully uses, endeavors to use, or procures any other person to use or endeavor to use any electronic, mechanical, or other device to intercept any oral communication...shall be fined not more than $10,000 or imprisoned not more than five years, or both.

McGann of narcotics trafficking.

On several occasions, McIntyre met with Officers Johnson and Ambos to discuss ways of confirming his suspicions concerning McGann. The three agreed that electronic surveillance of McGann's office would best serve that purpose. McIntyre and Johnson also met with VanBuskirk in a city park near the police station. During this meeting VanBuskirk approved of the plan to "bug" McGann's office if it "could be done legally."

Several days after the meeting in the park, Officer Johnson placed a microphone and transmitter in a briefcase in McGann's office. Johnson and Ambos attempted to monitor McGann's conversations. They were able to overhear only a brief exchange between McGann and Sergeant Gary Stucker. Johnson returned to McGann's office after 45 minutes and removed the briefcase, ending the surveillance. At no time did any of the participants seek a court order or McGann's consent for the surveillance.

The defendants raise four issues on appeal: (1) McGann's reasonable expectation of privacy in his office; (2) the "willfulness" of defendants' conduct within the meaning of Title III; (3) the sufficiency of the evidence; and (4) the exclusion of VanBuskirk's exculpatory polygraph.

Reasonable Expectation of Privacy

Title III prohibits the interception of "wire" and "oral communications." For purposes of §§ 2511 et seq., § 2510(2) defines "oral communication" as "any oral communication uttered by a person exhibiting an expectation that such communication is not subject to interception under circumstances justifying such expectation."

The legislative history behind § 2510(2) reflects Congress's intent that *Katz v. United States,* 389 U.S. 347, 88 S.Ct. 507, 19 L.Ed.2d 576 (1967), serve as a guide to define communications that are uttered under circumstances justifying an expectation of privacy. S.Rep.No. 1097, 90th Cong., 2d Sess., reprinted in [1968] U.S. Code Cong. & Admin. News pp. 2112, 2178. Guided by Katz, our inquiry is whether the communications overhead by Johnson and Ambos were uttered by a person (1) who has a subjective expectation of privacy, and (2) whose expectation was objectively reasonable. *United States v. Freie,* 545 F.2d 1217, 1223 (9th Cir. 1976).

There is no question that McGann had a subjective expectation of privacy. At trial McGann testified that he believed that normal conversations in his office could not be overheard, even when the doors to his office were open.

Defendants contend, however, that McGann's expectation of privacy was objectively unreasonable. First, they say that McGann could not reasonably expect to be free from "administrative internal affairs investigations." Second, they say that the architecture of McGann's office made his expectation of privacy unreasonable. Both contentions must fail.

A police officer is not, by virtue of his profession, deprived of the protection of the Constitution. *Garrity v. New Jersey,* 385 U.S. 493, 87 S.Ct. 616, 17 L.Ed.2d 562 (1967). This protection extends to warrantless eavesdropping to overhear conversations from an official's desk and office. *Berger v. New York,* 388 U.S. 41, 87 S.Ct. 1873, 18 L.Ed. 2d 1040 (1967); *United States v. Kahan,* 350 F.Supp. 784 (S.D.N.Y. 1972), *rev'd on other grounds,* 479 F.2d 290 (2d Cir. 1973), *rev'd* 415 U.S. 239, 94 S.Ct. 1179, 39 L.Ed.2d 297 (1974).

An established regulatory scheme or specific office practice may, under some circumstances, diminish an employee's reasonable expectation of privacy. *United States v. Davis*, 482 F.2d 893 (9th Cir. 1973); *United States v. Speights*, 557 F.2d 362 (3d Cir. 1977). But defendants here have failed to show a regulatory scheme or specific office practice which would have alerted McGann to expect random monitoring of his conversations. Evidence that other, unconsented, "bugging" may have occurred within the Globe Police Department does not alter our conclusion. Sporadic illegal eavesdropping does not create a regulatory scheme or a specific office practice. In an event, the "bugging" here cannot be termed an "administrative" search.

Neither can the "bugging" be justified as an "internal affairs investigation." An employer may search the work area of an employee for misplaced property or, in some circumstances, to supervise work performance. *United States v. Bunkers*, 521 F.2d 1217 (9th Cir.), *cert. denied*, 423 U.S. 989, 96 S.Ct. 400, 46 L.Ed.2d 307 (1975); *United States v. Blok*, 88 U.S.App.D.C. 326, 328, 188 F.2d 1019, 1021 (1951). But defendants' purpose in "bugging" McGann was, at least in part, to confirm their suspicion that he was involved in external crime (narcotics). Therefore, the "bugging" was not an "internal affairs investigation," but part of a criminal investigation, the area of activity for which Title III was written.

Defendants next argue that the physical characteristics of McGann's office made his expectation of privacy unreasonable. At trial defendants introduced evidence to show that at the time of the "bugging" McGann's office doors were open, and that a records clerk worked fifteen feet away in an adjacent room.

We cannot accept the argument that an open door made McGann's expectation of privacy unreasonable. Johnson testified that conversations in McGann's office were difficult to overhear even with the office doors open. As noted previously, McGann believed his office conversations to be private. A business office need not be sealed to offer its occupant a reasonable degree of privacy. The evidence supported a finding that McGann had a reasonable expectation of privacy in his office. It follows that the conversation attempted to be overhead by Johnson and Ambos between McGann and Sergeant Stucker was an "oral communication" within the meaning of 18 U.S.C. § 2510(2).

"Willfulness" Under § 2511(1)(a) and (b)

Title III prohibits only the "willful" interception of communications. Defendants contend that their action was not "willful" because they believed in good faith that their conduct was legitimate.

Defendants testified that they had sought and followed the advice of a communications technician for the Department of Public Safety. There was no testimony that the communications technician told them that the use of a hidden microphone was proper in an "internal investigation" of the police department. This defense, however, amounts only to a defense of "ignorance of the law," which this and other courts have pointed out from time to time is no defense. *See, e.g., United States v. Mathews*, 518 F.2d 1296 (9th Cir. 1975).

In *United States v. Schilleci*, 545 F.2d 519 (5th Cir. 1977), the court held in reversing a conviction for violating the same statute that a mistaken belief that the eavesdropping was legal was no defense. The question for the trier of fact is not whether the defendant thought his conduct was legal, but whether the defendant's state of mind was "willful." Ignorance of the law in some cases may convince a jury that the prosecution did not prove willfulness, but such ignorance is relevant only because the issue of willfulness may open up the question of motive.

The meaning of "willful" has not been uniformly applied in federal criminal statutes. It has become necessary to examine each statute to determine legislative intent in using the word "willfully."

A Senate Report cites *United States v. Murdock*, 290 U.S. 389, 54 S.Ct. 223, 78 L.Ed. 381 (1933), as a guide to interpreting "willfulness" within the meaning of Title III. S.Rep.No. 1097, 90th Cong., 2d Sess., *reprinted in* [1968] U.S. Code Cong. & Admin. News, pp. 2112, 2181. In *Murdock*, the Court held that a "willful" violation of a revenue act requires more than a mere misunderstanding as to tax liability. A "willful" act is one done with a "bad purpose" or "evil motive." 290 U.S. at 394-95, 54 S.Ct. 223.

The "bad purpose" requirement implicit in Title III indicates that Congress did not intend to subject police officers to criminal sanctions merely because they fail to comply with some of the statute's technical requirements. But Congress did not intend to immunize police officers from Title III penalties simply because they are police officers. The statute is full of references to law enforcement officers as targets of the legislation.

A police officer acts outside the scope of his duties with "bad purpose," and hence "willfully" within the meaning of Title III, when he or she engages in electronic surveillance (1) without a court order, and (2) in the absence of the kind of emergency described in 18 U.S.C. § 2518(7). Unless the proscribed conduct is otherwise excused, it can result in both civil and criminal liability.

VanBuskirk's approval of the "bugging" only if it "could be done legally" does not automatically excuse him from criminal liability. VanBuskirk's good faith was a question of fact. McIntyre informed VanBuskirk that he suspected that McGann was trafficking in narcotics. Thus, VanBuskirk knew, or should have known, that the surveillance to discover evidence of crime would require a court order. It is interesting that McIntyre and VanBuskirk felt it necessary to hold this conversation "in the park." The trier of fact could find from all the evidence that VanBuskirk "willfully" participated in the endeavor to "bug" McGann's office. *Cf. United States v. Barker*, 178 U.S.App.D.C. 174, 182-83, 546 F.2d 940, 948-49 (1976).

Sufficiency of Proof

Defendants contend that the government failed to prove the allegations in the indictment. The indictment reads, in pertinent part:

> "***FREDERICK LYLE McINTYRE and DALE IRWIN VanBUSKIRK, willfully did intercept, endeavor to intercept, and procure other persons to intercept and endeavor to intercept oral communications***, all the aforesaid oral communications being between individuals then present in the office of Robert M. McGann in the Globe, Arizona, Police Department and made and sent by and between persons over a telephone located in the office of Robert M. McGann.***"

Defendants claim a fatal variance between the indictment and the government's proof because no evidence was offered at trial to prove that there were any communications by and between persons over McGann's telephone during the "bugging." This claim also must fail.

The indictment, following the statutory language, charges the defendants with *procuring others to endeavor to intercept* oral communications. Whether, in fact, McGann made or received any telephone calls during the life of the "bug" is immaterial. The evidence at trial proved that defendants did cause (procure) Johnson and Ambos to try (endeavor) to intercept McGann's conversations.

Admission of VanBuskirk's Polygraph

Prior to trial VanBuskirk participated in a polygraph test administered by the F.B.I. The trial judge refused to admit the results for any purpose. VanBuskirk asserts that this refusal was an abuse of discretion.

This court has recognized the wide discretion district judges have in admitting or excluding polygraphs. In *United States v. Marshall,* 526 F.2d 1349 (9th Cir. 1975), we said, "[A] trial court will rarely abuse its discretion by refusing to admit the evidence, even for a limited purpose and under limited conditions." 526 F.2d at 1360. No facts in the instant case suggest that the trial judge abused her discretion. The administration of the test by a government agent does not establish its reliability or require its receipt in evidence.

Affirmed.

Cases relating to Chapter 10
OFFENSES AGAINST PUBLIC JUSTICE AND ADMINISTRATION

The PEOPLE of the State of New York, Respondent

v.

Robert STANARD, Appellant

Court of Appeals of New York

June 9, 1977

42 N.Y.2d 74, 365 N.E.2d 857

GABRIELLI, Judge.

The defendant stands convicted of the crime of perjury in the first degree (Penal Law, § 210.15) following his retrial on an indictment which arose from testimony which he gave to a Grand Jury of Bronx County investigating police corruption in the Seventh Division. The conviction upon his first trial was reversed because prejudicial and excessive background testimony on police corruption generally was improperly received in evidence (32 N.Y.2d 143, 344 N.Y.S.2d 331, 297 N.E.2d 77).

The Appellate Division has unanimously affirmed this second conviction (52 A.D.2d 1098, 384 N.Y.S.2d 713) and defendant advances several claims of error, but we are not persuaded that any of these claims warrant reversal, and we therefore affirm.

In June, 1968, the Grand Jury began an investigation of police corruption involving payments to police officials made by persons engaged in illegal policy and gambling activities, for the purpose of obtaining protection from arrest and prosecution. The investigation stemmed in part from information furnished by Patrolman Frank Serpico. The defendant, a New York City police officer at the time, was called as a witness and gave sworn testimony, under a grant of immunity, on two occasions in November, 1968. Among other matters, the defendant was queried about his attendance at a meeting with Patrolmen Andrew Taylor, James Paretti, William McAuliffe, and a known "policy" operator, Juan Carreras, at the Carreras residence, 1761 Lacombe Ave., Bronx, New York, on January 8, 1968. The People charge, inter alia, that the meeting was arranged by these officers for the purpose of assuring the continued collection of protection payments from Carreras. Defendant denied ever attending such a meeting and this denial was the basis for the first count of the indictment upon which he was convicted.

The first count of the indictment charged defendant with falsely denying that he attended the meeting at the home of Carreras for the purpose of collecting protection money, and he asserts that a crucial element of the charge is the illegal purpose of the meeting. The thrust of his argument is twofold. First, he contends that there is insufficient proof of the charge in the indictment to sustain his conviction and, secondly, he urges that the illegal purpose element is necessary to show that the false swearing was material to the Grand Jury proceeding. Since materiality is a necessary element of first degree perjury (Penal Law, § 210.15) he thus maintains that the absence of an illegal purpose, as claimed by him, renders the false swearing harmless. We reject these arguments.

The indictment charged the defendant with denying under oath that he entered the Carreras home to collect protection money "or for any purpose whatsoever."[1] Contrary to appellant's assertion, the indictment also charges defendant with denying being on the specified premises for any purpose. During the Grand Jury investigation the following colloquy occurred:

"*Q*. * * * Were you ever present in any location but more specifically in a location at 1761 Lacombe Avenue, County of the Bronx, in a basement at that address present at that address aside from yourself in that basement were Ptl. McAuliffe, Paretti, Taylor and Juan Carreras?

"*A*. I was never present with Mr. Carreras and the patrolmen that you named.

1. The indictment charged that: "The defendant did then and there testify before said Grand Jury under oath * * * that he, the said defendant, did not enter and remain at 1761 Lacombe Ave., Bronx, New York, the home of Juan Carreras and Dolores Carreras, with Patrolman Andrew Taylor, Patrolman James Paretti, and Patrolman William P. McAuliffe, on or about January 8, 1968, or at any other time for the purpose of collecting money due defendant and his fellow patromen for protecting Juan Carreras' Mutuel Race Horse Policy Business, or for any purpose whatsoever."

"*Q*. Therefore you deny being present at that location with those people?

"*A*. No; I don't.

"*Q*. At that location with those people?

"*A*. I deny ever being with those people, but it's possible that I was at the location.

"*Q*. Well, if you were never with those people how could you have been at that location with those people? The question is twofold.

"*A*. Well, it's a twofold answer. I would say I was never at that location with those people."

This and other Grand Jury testimony clearly demonstrates that defendant repeatedly denied being at the Carreras home with his fellow patrolmen, whether or not the purpose of the meeting was specified in the question. Juan Carreras testified that appellant attended the meeting and that protection payments were discussed along with certain operational problems of the "policy" business. Dolores Carreras corroborated the appellant's identity, his presence at her home, the date, the place of the meeting, and the presence of the other three officers. Thus, there was sufficient evidence to find defendant guilty.

Section 210.50 of the Penal Law requires that proof of falsity in a perjury prosecution "may not be established by the uncorroborated testimony of a single witness." The falsity of the statement made by appellant that he did not attend the meeting with his fellow officers was, as indicated, proven by the direct testimony of two witnesses and is thus sufficiently corroborated. Corroboration need not necessarily consist of direct evidence, however, but may be based on circumstantial evidence which furnishes partial proof of the falsity (*People v. Sabella,* 35 N.Y.2d 158, 168, 359 N.Y.S.2d 100, 108, 316 N.E.2d 569, 575). Thus assuming *arguendo* that corroborative proof of the illegal nature of the meeting is necessary in this case, as defendant unsuccessfully insists, we believe it has nonetheless been established by adequate circumstantial evidence. Dolores Carreras testified that she had personally made protection payments to Officers McAuliffe and Paretti. These payments were usually made on the first day of each month but the Carrerases were unable to make the regular payment in January, 1968. On January 8 Officer McAuliffe telephoned the Carreras residence and Dolores told him that she and her husband had lost all their money in the policy business and would be unable to make any payment or continue their operations. The meeting at the Carreras home, attended by McAuliffe, Paretti and appellant, followed shortly after the officer's telephone call on that same day. These facts, coupled with her identity testimony, permit the compelling inference and serve as sufficient proof that the purpose of the meeting was to discuss illegal payments. This independent evidence offered by Dolores Carreras fairly "tends to connect the defendant with the commission of the crime in such a way as may reasonably satisfy the jury that the [witness] is telling the truth" (*People v. Sabella, supra,* p. 169, 359 N.Y.S.2d p. 109, 316 N.E.2d p. 575, quoting *People v. Dixon,* 231 N.Y. 111, 116, 131 N.E. 752, 753) and is, therefore, sufficient circumstantial evidence to satisfy the corroboration requirement as to the illegal nature of the meeting (*People v. Sabella, supra; People v. Doody,* 172 N.Y. 165, 172, 64 N.E. 807, 808), and the conviction will not be overturned.

Perjury in the first degree also requires a false swearing which is "material to the action, proceeding or matter in which it is made" (Penal Law, § 210.15). The appellant, as noted, may not prevail on his claim that there was an absence of proof of an illegal purpose for the meeting, and that his false denial of ever attending the meeting is thus immaterial to a Grand Jury investigation of police corruption. Materiality is an essential element of the crime of perjury in the first degree (*see People v. Teal,* 196 N.Y. 372, 376, 89 N.E. 1086, 1087; *People ex rel. Hageman v. Corrigan,* 195 N.Y. 1, 9, 87 N.E. 792, 794; *People v. Courtney,* 94 N.Y. 490, 494; *Wood v. People,* 59 N.Y. 117, 121-122; cf. *People v. Ianniello,* 36 N.Y.2d 137, 143, 365 N.Y.S.2d 821, 825, 325 N.E.2d 146, 148); false swearing, to be material, must reflect on the matter under consideration during the action or proceeding in which it is made. As stated in *Wood v. People* (*supra,* p. 123): "It is not necessary that the false statement should tend directly to prove the issue in order to sustain an indictment. If the matter falsely sworn to is circumstantially material or tends to support and give credit to the witness in respect to the main fact, it is perjury." Under the facts in this case the appellant falsely denied, during a Grand Jury investigation into police corruption, that he met surreptitiously with three other police officers and a known gambler in the basement of the home of the gambler. Although evidence of the meeting would not by itself prove police corruption, the occurrence of the meeting, along with the other evidence in the case tends to support the existence of the corrupt nature and purpose of the meeting. Under these circumstances the false swearing must be deemed material, whether or not the illegal purpose is included as part of the charge.

* * *

During the course of the trial defendant sought his personnel file from the police department. Although his demands were initially thwarted, the court eventually ordered release of the file. After perusing the file defendant's counsel claimed that the prosecution had suppressed evidence by removing all relevant information prior to release. There can be no doubt that the People have a duty to disclose exculpatory information under their control (*Giglio v. United States*, 405 U.S. 150, 153-154, 92 S.Ct. 763, 31 L.Ed.2d 104; *Brady v. Maryland*, 373 U.S. 83, 87, 83 S.Ct. 1194, 10 L.Ed.2d 215; *People v. Simmons*, 36 N.Y.2d 126, 131, 365 N.Y.S.2d 812, 815, 325 N.E.2d 139, 142) whether the nondisclosure is intentional or negligent (*People v. Simmons, supra*). No facts were presented, however, to advise or inform the court what was missing from the file and how it might be exculpatory or to support in any way the charge of suppressing evidence. Under these circumstances the defendant has shown insufficient facts to raise any issue whether the prosecutor or the police suppressed portions of the file.

The appellant's other allegations of error have been duly considered by the court and found to be without merit.

Accordingly, the order of the Appellate Division should be affirmed.

Dissenting opinions not included.

Ottie Bernard POLK
v.
COMMONWEALTH of Virginia.
Court of Appeals of Virginia.
Aug. 4, 1987.
358 S.E.2d 770

KEENAN, Judge.

Ottie B. Polk was convicted in a bench trial of obstructing justice by threats or force in violation of Code § 18.2-460(A).[1] He was sentenced to six months in jail, with five months suspended, and fined $100. On appeal, Polk argues that: (1) the evidence was insufficient to support his conviction because words alone will not support a conviction under Code § 18.2-460(A), and because there was no evidence of his criminal intent; and (2) he was entitled to use reasonable force to resist arrest, under the authority of *United States v. Moore*, 332 F.Supp. 919 (E.D.Va.1971). We affirm Polk's conviction, finding that his verbal threat to kill was sufficient to constitute an obstruction of justice under

1. *Code § 18.2-460(A) provides: If any person, by threats, or force, knowingly attempts to intimidate or impede a judge, magistrate, justice, juror, witness, or any law-enforcement officer, lawfully engaged in his duties as such, or to obstruct or impede the administration of justice in any court, he shall be deemed to be guilty of a Class 1 misdemeanor.

Code § 18.2-460(A), that there was sufficient evidence of his criminal intent, and that *Moore* is inapplicable because it did not interpret Code § 18.2-460(A), and unlike the facts presented here, it dealt with an apparently illegal arrest.

I.

At trial, the evidence showed that Polk was stopped pursuant to a license "checking detail" operated by the Lancaster County Sheriff's Department and the Virginia State Police. Deputy Sheriff Martin Shirilla effected the stop. Upon realizing that he had stopped Polk about one year earlier concerning "some discrepancy about his driving status," Shirilla radioed to his dispatcher to confirm the status of Polk's license. The dispatcher informed Shirilla that Polk's license was suspended, and that there was an outstanding bench warrant for Polk's arrest on a charge of failing to appear in court. Based on this information, Shirilla arrested Polk.

Shirilla testified that, at the time of the arrest, Polk threatened to sue him for false arrest and further stated: "If I lose, I'll get you some other way." Polk was handcuffed, placed in Shirilla's vehicle, and transported to the Lancaster County Sheriff's office where Shirilla served him with the failure to appear warrant. Shirilla testified that while they were awaiting the arrival of a magistrate, Polk continually repeated statements such as "I'm going to get you," and "I'm going to get even." Shirilla testified that he then read Polk his *Miranda* warnings and asked him:

"Are you talking civil suit or are you looking for a piece of my ass?" According to Shirilla, Polk responded: "I'm going to get you."

When the magistrate arrived, Shirilla left the booking room to talk to him. Deputy Casto, who had assisted Shirilla in Polk's arrest, remained with Polk in the booking room. Casto testified that after Shirilla left the room, Polk stated that he was going to kill him. Casto concluded that Polk was referring to Shirilla. When Shirilla returned, Casto apparently related this threat to Shirilla. Shirilla testified that based on his conversation with Casto, he obtained a warrant charging Polk with obstruction of justice.

According to Shirilla, a final threat occurred after Polk had been charged with the obstruction offense. The threat occurred when Polk was issued jail clothing and was being taken to the shower. Shirilla testified that at that time he heard Polk say: "I've got five friends to help me take care of him."

During the entire sequence of these events, neither Shirilla nor Casto observed Polk make any physically threatening gestures or possess any weapons. On cross-examination, Shirilla acknowledged that, except for the verbal exchanges, the arrest proceeded in a normal fashion.

It was later learned that Polk's license was not, in fact, suspended at the time of his arrest, and the failure to appear charge had already been disposed of. Polk testified in his own behalf. He denied having threatened to kill Shirilla, although he admitted saying that he would sue him. Polk specifically denied making a comment about having five friends who would "get" Shirilla. Polk testified that he did not even have five friends. No other witnesses were called by the defense.

In finding the defendant guilty, the court stated:

There's no question in the mind of this court about the extent of his threats and the language that he used and I feel that he is guilty in violating the law, in violating the statute of obstructing an officer in the discharge of his duties, and...so find him guilty.

II.

Polk first challenges the sufficiency of the evidence. He contends that the Commonwealth failed to prove: (1) that his words alone constituted an attempt to intimidate or impede within the meaning of Code § 18.2-460(A); and (2) that he actually intended to intimidate or impede Shirilla.

Initially, we reject Polk's argument that words alone cannot constitute a violation under Code § 18.2-460(A) without evidence that they caused fear or apprehension in the recipient, or delay in the legal process. The plain language of Code § 18.2-460(A) provides that *threats* constitute a violation of the statute when they are knowingly made in an attempt to intimidate or impede law enforcement officers who are performing their duties. Thus, it is the threats made by the offender, coupled with his intent, that constitute the offense. The resulting effect of the offender's threats, such as fear, apprehension, or delay, is not an element of the crime defined in Code § 18.2-460. By the express terms of the statute, it is immaterial whether the officer is placed in fear or apprehension. The offense is complete when the attempt to intimidate is made. Where a statute contains language which has a definite and precise meaning, and is expressed in clear and concise terms which manifest the intent, courts must adopt that plain meaning. *Miller v. Commonwealth,* 172 Va. 639, 648, 2 S.E.2d 343, 347 (1939). We, therefore, conclude that Polk's statement that he would kill Shirilla was a threat as contemplated by the statute.

We disagree with Polk's contention that the Supreme Court's decision in *Jones v. Commonwealth,* 141 Va. 471, 126 S.E. 74 (1925), cited with approval in *Love v. Commonwealth,* 212 Va. 492, 184 S.E.2d 769 (1971), is contrary to our interpretation of Code § 18.2-460(A). Polk directs our attention to the following language in *Jones:*

To constitute obstruction of an officer in the performance of his duty, it is not necessary that there be an actual or technical assault upon the officer, but there must be acts clearly indicating an intention on the part of the accused to prevent the officer from performing his duty, as to "obstruct" ordinarily implies opposition or resistance by direct action and forcible or threatened means. It means to obstruct the officer himself not merely to oppose or impede the process with which the officer is armed.

In *Jones,* the accused was charged with violating former Code § 55-C, what was known as the Mapp Prohibition Law (1918 Va. Acts, Chapter 388). That statute provided:

Any person who shall hinder or obstruct any officer of this state charged with the duty of inspecting baggage for ardent spirits...shall be deemed guilty of a misdemeanor.

This statute required actual hindrance or obstruction of the officer. The definition of "obstruction" cited above included the requirement of opposition or resistance by direct action. In contrast, Code § 18.2-460(A) provides that an attempt to intimidate or impede by threats, in itself, constitutes a substantive offense. Since *Jones* involved a statute requiring actual "obstruction," it is not applicable here. Code § 18.2-460(A), in contrast, is violated when, by threats or force, one *attempts* to intimidate or impede a law enforcement officer.

We also disagree with Polk's contention that the Supreme Court's holding in *Love* is contrary to our interpretation of Code § 18.2-460(A). In *Love,* the Supreme Court did not address whether words alone could constitute an attempt to intimidate or impede. In that case, the accused confronted police officers with a shotgun when they attempted to serve an arrest warrant on him. In finding that the accused had clearly attempted to impede and obstruct an orderly arrest, the court was not required to resolve whether words alone can constitute a violation of the statute.

Polk also argues that since he was under arrest and in custody when he made his threat to kill Shirilla, he could not have performed a direct ineffectual act toward the commission of the offense, and therefore, no attempted crime was completed. This argument, however, confuses an attempt to commit a substantive offense with the substantive offense defined in Code § 18.2-460(A). As defined in that Section, threats knowingly made in an attempt to intimidate or impede constitute the offense. There is no overt act requirement, as such, contained in the statute.

We turn now to consider Polk's claim that there was insufficient evidence of his criminal intent. Specifically, he argues that the evidence does not show that he actually intended to intimidate or impede Deputy Shirilla. In reviewing this claim, we examine the evidence presented in the light most favorable to the Commonwealth, and accord to the evidence all reasonable inferences fairly deducible therefrom. *Crumble v. Commonwealth,* 2 Va. App. 231, 233, 343 S.E.2d 359, 361 (1986).

Intent is the purpose formed in a person's mind which may be shown by his statements or conduct. *Johnson v. Commonwealth,* 209 Va. 291, 295, 163 S.E.2d 570, 574 (1968). We find that the trier of fact was entitled to conclude that Polk threatened to kill Shirilla, and that this threat made by Polk to Shirilla demonstrated his intent to intimidate Shirilla from completion of the post-arrest processing. For this reason, we hold that the evidence presented was sufficient to establish Polk's criminal intent.

III.

Finally, Polk argues that he was entitled to use reasonable force to resist arrest. In support of his argument, he relies exclusively on *United States v. Moore,* 332 F.Supp. 919 (E.D.Va.1971). In *Moore,* the accused grabbed the arm of an officer who was in the process of arresting her husband for simple assault. The court held that she was not criminally liable for this conduct, and emphasized that the arrest appeared unlawful to the wife because she did not know the difference between an ''arrest'' and an ''apprehension'' under the Uniform Code of Military Justice. *Id.* at 921. In *Moore,* the court also emphasized the fact that unnecessary force was used in effecting the husband's arrest. *Id.* at 920.

We believe that the *Moore* decision is inapplicable to the case at bar. First, although Polk argues that he was entitled to use reasonable force to resist arrest, he does not contest that he was lawfully arrested based upon the information given Shirilla by his dispatcher. Instead, he contends that since, contrary to the information received by Shirilla, his license was not suspended and there was no pending failure to appear charge, he was entitled to offer reasonable resistance. We disagree. An individual is not entitled to resist a lawful arrest. *West Virginia v. Jarvis,* 310 S.E.2d 467, 470 (W.Va. 1983); *see Wright v. Bailey,* 544 F.2d 737, 739-40 (4th Cir. 1976). Further, Polk does not argue, and the record does not show, any use of unnecessary or unreasonable force by the officers making the arrest. Therefore, we reject Polk's argument that he was entitled to use reasonable able force under the authority of *Moore.*

In summary, we find that words alone may constitute an offense under Code § 18.2-460(A) when the words are threats knowingly made in an attempt to intimidate or impede law enforcement officers who are performing their duties; that the evidence was sufficient to demonstrate Polk's criminal intent; and that Polk cannot avoid criminal liability for his actions under the authority of *Moore.* Accordingly, we affirm his conviction.

Affirmed.

Rita L. SNABB, Appellant,

v.

STATE of Texas, Appellee.

Court of Appeals of Texas, Corpus Christi.

Dec. 20, 1984.

683 S.W.2d 850

Before the Court en banc.

OPINION

PER CURIAM.

Appellant was convicted by the court of the misdemeanor offense of escape. Punishment was assessed by the court at a fine of $100.00, and thirty days in jail. The jail term was probated for one year.

Appellant's keys were found in the restaurant at the Corpus Christi International Airport. She was paged on the public address system, and when she claimed her keys from Officer Mitchell he determined that appellant was intoxicated. The officer returned her keys on the condition that someone else would drive her, otherwise she would be arrested if he caught her driving in her inebriated state.

Appellant agreed to the officer's condition, but then disregarded his warning. When appellant attempted to leave the airport parking lot in her vehicle, Officer Mitchell and his partner pursued appellant on foot and eventually stopped appellant, but not without considerable difficulty.

Officer Mitchell advised appellant she was under arrest, then ordered her to gather her possessions, lock her vehicle, and come with him. Appellant became abusive, refused to cooperate, and then began to run from the officer. She disregarded his command to stop, and did not stop until Officer Mitchell chased her down and grabbed her by the arm.

In a single ground of error, appellant alleges the evidence is insufficient to show that she was under arrest or that she actually escaped from the custody of the officers.

TEX. PENAL CODE ANN. § 38.07(a) (Vernon 1974) provides as follows:

"A person arrested for, charged with, or convicted of an offense commits an offense if he escapes from custody."

"The elements of escape are that a person (1) escape (2) from custody (3) after having been arrested for, charged with or convicted of an offense." *Henderson v. State,* 600 S.W.2d 788, 789 (Tex.Crim.App. 1979).

Officer Mitchell testified that when he advised appellant she was under arrest and to gather he possessions, the window of the car was rolled down and he was talking with her face to face. He also testified that when so advised, appellant became irate and began to use profanity. Mitchell's partner, Officer Bates, testified that appellant stated to the officers that they were security guards and could not arrest her.

Obviously, the officers intended to arrest appellant, and they were ultimately successful. However, the offense of escape occurs *after having been arrested,* not before the arrest is complete.

TEX. CODE CRIM. PROC. ANN. Art. 15-22 (Vernon 1977) provides that:

"A person is arrested when he has been actually placed under restraint or taken into custody by an officer or person executing a warrant of arrest, or by an officer or person arresting without a warrant."

In *Smith v. State,* 219 S.W.2d 454 (Tex.Crim.App. 1949), the court set out the following facts:

He [defendant] was then approached by an officer who grabbed him from behind, disarmed him and told him to come and go to jail, at which time he refused to go, and the difficulty then ensued as the two officers attempted to detain him. He escaped and left the officers who were unable to detain him. Subsequently...they peacefully took appellant into custody.

219 S.W.2d at 456.

The issue in *Smith* was whether the defendant's resistance was admissible as *res gestae* of the offense or inadmissible as proof of an extraneous offense. In holding that the proceedings relative to defendant's arrest were properly admitted, the Court of Criminal Appeals wrote:

An arrest of a person carries with it an element of detention, custody or control of the accused. The mere fact that an officer makes the statement to an accused that he is under arrest does not complete the arrest. There must be custody or detention and submission to such arrest.

219 S.W.2d at 456. Also:

He was either under arrest or not under arrest; and it is the writer's opinion that the arrest had not been completed. He had to be taken into custody and detained. While he may have been told that he was under arrest, still when the officer attempted to complete the arrest, appellant refused to submit thereto, and his arrest and detention were not completed. It had to again take place, all the proceedings consuming about five minutes.

Id. at 457.

In light of *Smith,* we are constrained to hold that appellant's arrest was not complete when she fled from Officer Mitchell. The elements of detention and control were lacking, and appellant refused to submit to the officer's authority. This is demonstrated by Officer Mitchell's own testimony:

Q. She ran about 20 feet, and you grabbed her. You had to physically restrain her. Is that correct?

A. Yes, sir.

Q. Okay. At that time, when you physically restrained her, that was really the first time that her movement was actually totally restrained. Is that correct?

A. Yes, sir, that's correct.

Q. All right. And, from that point on, you had hold of her?

A. Yes, sir.

Q. And she wasn't getting away from you at that point.

A. Well, she tried to get away. We had—Like I said, it was beginning to look like we was going to drag her.

Q. You had to fight with her and drag her?

A. All the way to the terminal.

Q. All the way to the terminal. And when did you put handcuffs on her?

A. We put the handcuffs on her once we got her inside at the checkpoint. We had one of the female attendants officers search her for us, and then we handcuffed her and sat her down on the chair.

In *McCrory v. State,* 643 S.W.2d 725 (Tex.Crim.App. 1982), the court wrote:

It is doubtful that Texas law recognizes such a thing as being placed under "formal" arrest. "A person is arrested when he has been placed under restraint or taken into custody...." Article 15.22, V.A.C.C.P. No form of words is required, *White v. State,* 601 S.W.2d 364 (Tex. Crim. App. 1980).

643 S.W.2d at 726 n. 3. Cases determining the "point of arrest" under TEX. CODE CRIM. PROC. ANN. Art. 15.22 (Vernon 1977) have concluded that an arrest occurs at the moment that a person's freedom of movement is restricted or restrained. *White,* at 601 S.W.2d 365-66.

In *White,* the defendant was arrested when held at gunpoint in a spread-eagled position. In *Harding v. State,* 500 S.W.2d 870 (Tex.Crim.App. 1973), the officer testified that he "held" the defendant. The court wrote:

"It is not the actual physical taking into custody that will constitute an arrest. An arrest is complete whenever a person's liberty of movement is restricted or restrained. In the situation at bar, the arrest took place when Gonzales held' appellant for the San Antonio Police."

500 S.W.2d at 873. However, the opinion in *Harding* is silent as to what actions constituted "held." In *Maldonado v. State,* 528 S.W.2d 234 (Tex.Crim.App. 1975), the defendant had paid his fines and was walking out of the courthouse when "stopped" by a DPS investigator. 528 S.W.2d at 237. The court held that the defendant was "under arrest," writing:

For the next three hours, or between 9:00 a.m. and noon, Prince continued to talk to appellant in a room in the Sheriff's office at the courthouse. Although appellant was apparently left unattended at times for this three hour period, he was nevertheless restrained of his liberty.

Prince had already once restrained appellant from leaving the courthouse. If Prince had observed him trying to leave again, it is reasonable to infer that he would have stopped him again.

Id.

We conclude that in the instant case appellant's liberty of movement was not restricted or restrained until she was chased and grabbed by Officer Mitchell. In the State's brief, seven events are set out to show that "dominion and control were being exercised over her." We note that all of these occurred while appellant was in her car being chased by the officers who were on foot.

We disagree with the State that verbal commands were sufficient to effect an arrest when appellant refused to submit to those commands. In *Wyatt v. State,* 120 Tex.Cr.R. 3, 47 S.W.2d 827 (1932), the offense was aiding a prisoner to escape. The "prisoner" was one Hines, about whom the court stated, "it seems apparent that the officer did not at any time have Hines in custody or under his control...." *Id.* at 829. Essential to the conviction of the defendant was that the prisoner be under arrest. The court reversed, notwithstanding that Hines had been ordered out of the field a half-dozen times by the constable, was told the

constable had two warrants for his arrest, was kicked, and then did get through the fence when the constable pulled his pistol. *Id.* 47 S.W.2d at 828.

In *Wyatt,* the court set out the following quotation:

To constitute an arrest it is necessary that the officer should assume custody and control over the party, either by force or with his consent, and it has been held that neither the utterance of words indicating an intention to arrest on the part of the person uttering them, nor the reading of the warrant is of itself sufficient.

Id. 47 S.W.2d at 829.

[4] It would appear that appellant violated TEX. PENAL CODE Ann. § 38.04 (Vernon 1974) which makes it an offense to intentionally flee from a peace officer *attempting* to arrest him. However, the State sought to impose the harsher penalty provided for in the escape statute. By so choosing, the State assumed the burden to prove a completed arrest and custody. The State showed that the officers had a difficult time apprehending appellant as she did not want to be detained; this is not enough. We hold the evidence is insufficient to show that appellant escaped from an arrest or from custody. The judgment of the trial court is reversed and a judgment of acquittal entered.

Cases relating to Chapter 11

DRUG-RELATED OFFENSES

James Randolph BROWN

v.

COMMONWEALTH of Virginia.

Court of Appeals of Virginia.

Feb. 2, 1988.

364 S.E.2d 773 (1988)

HODGES, Judge.

James Randolph Brown was convicted at a bench trial of possession of cocaine with intent to distribute in violation of Code § 18.2-248. The court sentenced Brown to twenty years in the penitentiary with five years suspended. In this appeal, Brown argues that the Commonwealth's evidence was insufficient to sustain his conviction. We disagree and affirm.

At approximately 9:30 p.m. on November 19, 1985, the Richmond police executed a search warrant at the residence of Sylvester and Michael Minor. The appellant, the two Minors, and two other men were present at the time. As one of the men was about to exit the residence, Detective Fleming entered and chased him down a hallway. Detective Fleming paused at the door of the master bedroom and observed the appellant seated on a stool next to the bed. He was between the Minor brothers who were sitting on the bed, one at the head and one at the foot.

Detective Clavert followed Fleming into the residence. When he reached the master bedroom, the appellant was exiting it. He detained him there. No drugs or drug paraphernalia were found on his person.

On the bed, the police found a mirror with cocaine on it, two pounds of cocaine, a strainer with cocaine residue on it, and plastic bags containing cocaine. All three men were seated within arm's reach of each other and the cocaine on the bed. The value of the uncut cocaine was approximately $45,000. A triple-beam scale was on a speaker next to where the appellant was seated. A bag of cocaine and $60 were on the nightstand. On the floor next to the bed, the police also found some bottles of commonly used cutting agents, five spoons with cocaine residue on them, plastic tooters, a pair of scissors, blue twisties, and two boxes of baggies. The police found cocaine packaged for street distribution in the den.

After waiving his rights, the appellant admitted using cocaine in the past but denied that he presently used it. He stated that he came to the house to get some albums and make some tapes. At trial, the appellant explained that he went into the bedroom to watch a game on television. He saw Calvin Brake bending over and snorting something. Brake offered him some, but he refused. He, however, remained in the room.

Where the sufficiency of the evidence is challenged on appeal, the court must consider the evidence in the light most favorable to the Commonwealth, giving to it all reasonable inferences fairly deducible therefrom. *Higginbotham v. Commonwealth,* 216 Va. 349, 352, 218 S.E.2d 534, 537 (1975); *Hambury v. Commonwealth,* 3 Va.App. 435, 437, 350 S.E.2d 524, 524 (1986). Furthermore, the "judgment of a trial court sitting without a jury is entitled to the same weight as a jury verdict and will not be disturbed on appeal unless plainly wrong or without evidence to support it." *Hambury,* 3 Va.App. at 437, 350 S.E.2d at 524 (citing Code § 8.01-680; *Evans v. Commonwealth,* 215 Va. 609, 613, 212 S.E.2d 268, 271 (1975).

To support a conviction based upon constructive possession, the Commonwealth "must point to evidence of acts, statements, or conduct of the accused or other facts or circumstances which tend to show that the defendant was aware of both the presence and character of the substance and that it was subject to his dominion and control." *Powers v. Commonwealth,* 227 Va. 474, 476, 316 S.E.2d 739, 740 (1984) (citing *Eckhart v. Commonwealth* 222 Va. 447, 450, 281 S.E.2d 853, 855 (1981)). Possession does not have to be exclusive. *Ritter v. Commonwealth,* 210 Va. 732, 741, 173 S.E.2d 799, 806 (1970).

Based upon the appellant's admitted prior cocaine use and the location and visibility of the cocaine, the trial court could reasonably infer that the appellant was aware of the presence and character of the cocaine. Indeed, appellant's counsel conceded during the oral argument that Brown had the requisite knowledge of the cocaine. He rests his appeal on his contention that the Commonwealth failed to prove that the cocaine was subject to his dominion and control. Appellant argues that

his proximity to the drugs was all that was shown and that is insufficient to establish possession. We disagree.

While mere proximity to a controlled substance is insufficient to establish possession, it is a factor to consider when determining whether the accused constructively possessed drugs. *Lane v. Commonwealth,* 223 Va. 713, 716, 292 S.E.2d 358, 360 (1982); *Gillis v. Commonwealth,* 215 Va. 298, 301, 208 S.E.2d 768, 770-771 (1974); *Hambury,* 3 Va.App. at 438, 350 S.E.2d at 525. Like Brown, the defendant in *Eckhart* alleged that her conviction of possession of marijuana with intent to distribute was based solely on her proximity to the drugs. The Supreme Court of Virginia, however, found that the evidence was sufficient to sustain the defendant's conviction based upon constructive possession where the defendant, who was holding a baby, was seated outside the open door to a baby's room which contained marijuana and drug paraphernalia that was visible from the defendant's position. The court found that the trial court "could reasonably conclude that she was aware of the contents of the room and stationed herself where she could exercise dominion and control over the marijuana." *Eckhart,* 222 Va. at 451, 281 S.E.2d at 855.

Likewise, the evidence establishes more than mere proximity in this case. Brown was in a far better position to exercise dominion and control over the drugs than the defendant in *Eckhart.* Appellant and the two Minors were seated around a substantial amount of cocaine and drug paraphernalia. Brown was *within arm's reach* of the cocaine and he was beside the scales and other drug paraphernalia. This fact clearly distinguishes the case at bar from *Huvar v. Commonwealth,* 212 Va. 667, 187 S.E.2d 177 (1972), which the appellant relies upon, where the defendant's conviction of drug possession was reversed because there was no evidence that he owned, possessed, or exercised any control over the drugs found. In *Huvar,* a large quantity of drugs was found in plain view throughout the apartment in which 11 people were present, but the defendant, who did not reside there, was discovered in the bathroom where no drugs were found. *Id.* at 668, 187 S.E.2d at 178.

Although the appellant explained his presence in the house, the court did not have to accept his testimony as true. When the court sits as fact-finder, it has the same authority as the jury to reject the defendant's testimony as incredible. *Crumble v. Commonwealth,* 2 Va.App. 231, 236, 343 S.E.2d 359, 362 (1986).

If from the improbability of his story and his manner of relating it, or from its contradictions within itself, or by the attending facts and circumstances, the jury is convinced that he is not speaking the truth, it may reject his testimony, even though his reputation for truth is not attacked and he is not contradicted by other witnesses. *Id.* (quoting *Randolph v. Commonwealth,* 190 Va. 256, 263, 56 S.E.2d 226, 229 (1949)).

When considering the totality of the circumstances, the appellant's proximity to the drugs, combined with his knowledge of their presence and the fact that he was in the house about an hour is sufficient to show that the cocaine was subject to his dominion and control. Furthermore, the quantity of drugs, their packaging, and the presence of drug and packaging paraphernalia were factors which established an intent to distribute. *See Eckhart,* 222 Va. at 451, 281 S.E.2d at 855 (citations omitted).

Therefore, we hold that the evidence was sufficient to support the appellant's conviction.

Accordingly, we affirm.

Affirmed.

Florida Statutes Annotated

Chapter 893
Drug Abuse Prevention and Control

§ 893.02 Definitions.—The following words and phrases as used in this chapter have the following meanings, unless the context otherwise requires:

(1) "Administer" means the direct application of a controlled substance, whether by injection, inhalation, ingestion, or any other means, to the body of a person or animal.

(2) "Analog" or "chemical analog" means a structural derivative of a parent compound that is a controlled substance.

(3) "Cannabis" means all parts of any plant of the genus Cannabis, whether growing or not; the seeds thereof; the resin extracted from any part of the plant; and every compound, manufacture, salt, derivative, mixture, or preparation of the plant or its seeds or resin.

(4) "Controlled substance" means any substance named or described in Schedules I through V of § 893.03. Laws controlling the manufacture,

distribution, preparation, dispensing, or administration of such substances are drug abuse laws.

(5) "Deliver" or "delivery" means the actual, constructive, or attempted transfer from one person to another of a controlled substance, whether or not there is an agency relationship.

(6) "Dispense" means the transfer of possession of one or more doses of a medicinal drug by a pharmacist or other licensed practitioner to the ultimate consumer thereof or to one who represents that it is his intention not to consume or use the same but to transfer the same to the ultimate consumer or user for consumption by the ultimate consumer or user.

(7) "Distribute" means to deliver other than by administering or dispensing, a controlled substance.

(8) "Distributor" means a person who distributes.

(9) "Department" means the Department of Health and Rehabilitative Services.

(10) "Hospital" means an institution for the care and treatment of the sick and injured, licensed pursuant to the provisions of chapter 395 or owned or operated by the state or federal government.

(11) "Laboratory" means a laboratory approved by the Drug Enforcement Administration as proper to be entrusted with the custody of controlled substances for scientific, medical, or instructional purposes or to aid law enforcement officers and prosecuting attorneys in the enforcement of this chapter.

(12)(a) "Manufacture" means the production, preparation, propagation, compounding, cultivating, growing, conversion, or processing of a controlled substance either directly or indirectly, by extraction from substances of natural origin, or independently by means of chemical synthesis, or by a combination of extraction and chemical synthesis, and includes any packaging of the substance or labeling or relabeling of its container, except that this term does not include the preparation, compounding, packaging, or labeling of a controlled substance by:

1. A practitioner or pharmacist as an incident to his administering or delivering of a controlled substance in the course of his professional practice.

2. A practitioner, or by his authorized agent under his supervision, or the purpose of, or as an incident to, research, teaching, or chemical analysis, and not for sale.

(b) "Manufacturer" means and includes every person who prepares, derives, produces, compounds, or repackages any drug as defined by the Florida Drug and Cosmetic Act. However, this definition does not apply to manufacturers of patent or proprietary preparations as defined in the Florida Pharmacy Act. Pharmacies, and pharmacists employed thereby, are specifically excluded from this definition.

(13) "Patient" means an individual to whom a controlled substance is lawfully dispensed or administered pursuant to the provisions of this chapter.

(14) "Pharmacist" means a person who is licensed pursuant to chapter 465 to practice the profession of pharmacy in this state.

(15) "Potential for abuse" means that a substance has properties of a central nervous system stimulant or depressant or an hallucinogen, that creates a substantial likelihood of its being any of the following:

(a) Used in amounts that create a hazard to the user's health or the safety of the community; or

(b) Diverted from legal channels and distributed through illegal channels; or

(c) Taken on the user's own initiative rather than on the basis of professional medical advice.

Proof of potential for abuse can be based upon a showing that these activities are already taking place, or upon a showing that the nature and properties of the substance make it reasonable to assume that there is a substantial likelihood that such activities will take place, in other than isolated or occasional instances.

(16) "Practitioner" means a physician licensed pursuant to chapter 458, a dentist licensed pursuant to chapter 466, a veterinarian licensed pursuant to chapter 474, an osteopathic physician licensed pursuant to chapter 459, a naturopath licensed pursuant to chapter 462, or a podiatrist licensed pursuant to chapter 461, provided such practitioner holds a valid federal controlled substance registry number.

(17) "Prescription" means and includes an order for drugs or medicinal supplies written, signed, or transmitted by word of mouth, telephone, telegram, or other means of communication by a duly licensed practitioner licensed by the laws of the state to prescribe such drugs or medicinal supplies, issued in good faith and in the course of professional practice, intended to be filled, compounded, or dispensed by another person licensed by the laws of the state to do so, and meeting the requirements of § 893.04. The term shall also include an order for drugs or medicinal supplies so transmitted or written by a physician, dentist, veterinarian, or other practitioner licensed to practice in a state other than Florida, but only if the pharmacist called upon to fill such an order determines, in the exercise of his professional judgment, that the order was issued pursuant to a valid patient-physician relationship, that it

is authentic, and that the drugs or medicinal supplies so ordered are considered necessary for the continuation of treatment of a chronic or recurrent illness. However, if the physician writing the prescription is not known to the pharmacist, the pharmacist shall obtain proof to a reasonable certainty of the validity of said prescription. A prescription order for a controlled substance shall not be issued on the same prescription blank with another prescription order for a controlled substance which is named or described in a different schedule, nor shall any prescription order for a controlled substance be issued on the same prescription blank as a prescription order for a medicinal drug as defined in § 465.031(5), which does not fall within the definition of a controlled substance as defined in this act.

(18) "Wholesaler" means any person who acts as a jobber, wholesale merchant, or broker, or an agent thereof, who sells or distributes for resale any drug as defined by the Florida Drug and Cosmetic Act. However, this definition does not apply to persons who sell only patent or proprietary preparations as defined in the Florida Pharmacy Act. Pharmacies, and pharmacists employed thereby, are specifically excluded from this definition.

§ 893.03 Standards and schedules.—The substances enumerated herein are controlled by this chapter. The controlled substances listed or to be listed in Schedules I, II, III, IV, and V are included by whatever official, common, usual, chemical, or trade name designated. The provisions of this act shall not be construed to include within any of the schedules herein contained any excluded nonprescription Drugs listed within the purview of 21, C.F.R. § 1308.22, styled "Excluded Substances."

(1) SCHEDULE I.—A substance in Schedule I has a high potential for abuse and has no currently accepted medical use in treatment in the United States, and in its use under medical supervision does not meet accepted safety standards except for such uses provided for in § 402.36. The following substances are controlled in Schedule I:

(a) Unless specifically excepted or unless listed in another schedule, any of the following substances, including their isomers, esters, ethers, salts, and salts of isomers, esters, and ethers, whenever the existence of such isomers, esters, ethers, and salts is possible within the specific chemical designation:

1. Acetylmethadol.
2. Alfentanil.
3. Allylprodine.
4. Alphacetylmathadol.
5. Alphamethadol.
6. Alpha-methylfentanyl (N-[1-(alpha-methyl-betaphenyl) ethyl-4-piperidyl] propionanilide; 1-(1-methyl-2-phenylethyl)-4-(N-propanilido) piperidine).
7. Alphaprodine.
8. Benzethidine.
9. Betacetylmethadol.
10. Betameprodine.
11. Bethamethadol.
12. Betaprodine.
13. Clonitazene.
14. Dextromoramide.
15. Diampromide.
16. Diethylthiambutene.
17. Difenoxin.
18. Dimenoxadol.
19. Dimepheptanol.
20. Dimethylthiambutene.
21. Dioxaphetyl butyrate.
22. Dipipanone.
23. Ethylmethylthiambutene.
24. Etonitazene.
25. Extoxeridine.
26. Furethidine.
27. Hydroxypethidine.
28. Ketobemidone.
29. Levomoramide.
30. Levophenacylmorphan.
31. 3-Methylfentanyl (N-[3-methyl-1-(2-phenylethyl)-4-piperidyl]-N-phenylpropanamide).
32. Morpheridine.
33. Noracymethadol.
34. Norlevorphanol.
35. Normethadone.
36. Norpipanone.
37. Phenadoxone.
38. Phenampromide.
39. Phenomorphan.
40. Phenoperidine.
41. Piritramide.
42. Proheptazine.
43. Properidine.
44. Propiram.
45. Racemoramide.
46. Tilidine.
47. Trimeperidine.

(b) Unless specifically excepted or unless listed in another schedule, any of the following substances, their salts, isomers, and salts of isomers, whenever the existence of such salts, isomers, and salts of isomers is possible within the specific chemical designation:

1. Acetorphine.
2. Acetyldihydrocodeine.
3. Benzylmorphine.
4. Codeine methylbromide.
5. Codeine-N-Oxide.
6. Cyprenorphine.
7. Desomorphine.
8. Dihydromorphine.
9. Drotebanol.
10. Etorphine (except hydrochloride salt).
11. Heroin.
12. Hydromorphinol.
13. Methyldesorphine.

14. Methyldihydromorphine.
15. Monacetylmorphine.
16. Morphine methylbromide.
17. Morphine methylsulfonate.
18. Morphine-N-Oxide.
19. Myrophine.
20. Nicocodine.
21. Nicomorphine.
22. Normorphine.
23. Pholocodine.
24. Thebacon.

(c) Unless specifically excepted or unless listed in another schedule, any material, compound, mixture, or preparation which contains any quantity of the following hallucinogenic substances, or which contains any of their salts, isomers, and salts of isomers, whenever the existence of such salts, isomers, and salts of isomers is possible within the specific chemical designation:

1. 4-Bromo-2,5-dimethoxy-amphetamine.
2. Bufotenine.
3. Cannabis.
4. Diethyltryptamine.
5. 2,5-Dimethoxyamphetamine.
6. Dimethyltryptamine.
7. N-Ethyl-1-phenylcyclohexyl-amine.
8. N-Ethyl-3-piperidyl benzilate.
9. N-ethylamphetamine.
10. Fenethylline.
11. Ibogaine.
12. Lysergic acid diethylamide.
13. Mecloqualone.
14. Mescaline.
15. 5-Methoxy-3,4-methylene-dioxyamphetamine.
16. 4-methoxyamphetamine.
17. 4-Methyl-2,5-dimethoxy-amphetamine.
18. 3,4-Methylenedioxy-amphetamine.
19. N-Methyl-3-piperidyl benzilate.
20. Parahexyl.
21. Peyote.

22. N-(1-Phenylcyclohexyl)-pyrrolidine.
23. Psilocybin.
24. Psilocyn.
25. Tetrahydrocannabinols.
26. 1-[1-(2-Thienyl)-cyclohexyl]-piperidine.
27. 3,4,5-Trimethoxy-amphetamine.

(d) Notwithstanding the aforementioned fact that Schedule I substances have no currently accepted medical use, the legislature recognizes certain substances which are currently accepted for certain limited medical uses in treatment in the United States but have a high potential for abuse. Accordingly, unless specifically excepted or unless listed in another schedule, any material, compound, mixture, or preparation which contains any quantity of methaqualone, including its salts, isomers, optical isomers, salts of their isomers, and salts of these optical isomers, is controlled in Schedule I.

(2) SCHEDULE II.—A substance in Schedule II has a high potential for abuse and has a currently accepted but severely restricted medical use in treatment in the United States, and abuse of the substance may lead to severe psychological or physical dependence. The following substances are controlled in Schedule II:

(a) Unless specifically excepted or unless listed in another schedule, any of the following substances, whether produced directly or indirectly by extraction from substances of vegetable origin or independently by means of chemical synthesis:

1. Opium and any salt, compound, derivative or preparation of opium except isoquinoline alkaloids of opium; including but not limited to the following:
a. Raw opium.

b. Opium extracts.
c. Opium fluid extracts.
d. Powdered opium.
e. Granulated opium.
f. Tincture of opium.
g. Codeine.
h. Ethylmorphine.
i. Ethophine hydrochloride.
j. Hydrocodone.
k. Hydromorphone.
l. Metopon.
m. Morphine.
n. Oxycodone.
o. Oxymorphone.
p. Thebaine.

2. Any salt, compound, derivative or preparation of a substance which is chemically equivalent to or identical with any of the substances referred to in subparagraph 1, except that these substances shall not include the isoquinoline alkaloids of opium.

3. Any part of the plant of the species Papaver somniferum, L.

4. Cocaine or ecgonine, including any of their steroisomers, and any salt, compound, derivative, or preparation of cocaine or ecgonine.

(b) Unless specifically excepted or unless listed in another schedule, any of the following substances, including their isomers, esters, ethers, salts and salts of isomers, esters, ethers, whenever the existence of such isomers, esters, ethers, and salts is possible within the specific chemical designation:

1. Alphaprodine.
2. Anileridine.
3. Bezitramide.
4. Bulk dextropropoxyphene (non-dosage forms).
5. Dihydrocodeine.
6. Diphenoxylate.
7. Fentanyl.
8. Isomethadone.
9. Levomethorphan.
10. Levorphanol.

11. Metazocine.
12. Methadone.
13. Methadone-Intermediate, 4-cyano-2-dimethylamino-4,4-diphenylbutane.
14. Moramide-Intermediate, 2-methyl-3-orpholoino-1,1-diphenyl-propane-carboxylic acid.
15. Pethidine (meperidine).
16. Pethidine-Intermediate-A, 4-cyano-1-methyl-4-phenylpiperidine.
17. Pethidine-Intermediate-B, ethyl-4-phenylpiperidine-4-carboxylate.
18. Pethidine-Intermediate-C, 1-methyl-4-phenylpiperidine-4-carboxylic acid.
19. Phenazocine.
20. Phencyclidine.
21. 1-Phenylcyclohexylamine.
22. Piminodine.
23. 1-Piperidinocyclohexane-carbonitrile.
24. Racemethorphan.
25. Racemorphan.
26. Sufentanil.

(c) Unless specifically excepted or unless listed in another schedule, any material, compound, mixture, or preparation which contains any quantity of the following substances, including their salts, isomers, optical isomers, salts of their isomers, and salts of their optical isomers having a stimulant effect on the central nervous system:

1. Amobarbital.
2. Amphetamine.
3. Methamphetamine.
4. Methylphenidate.
5. Pentobarbital.
6. Phenmetrazine.
7. Phenylacetone.
8. Secobarbital.

(3) SCHEDULE III.—A substance in Schedule III has a potential for abuse less than the substances contained in Schedules I and II and has a

currently accepted medical use in treatment in the United States, and abuse of the substance may lead to moderate or low physical dependency or high psychological dependence. The following substances are controlled in Schedule III:

(a) Unless specifically excepted or unless listed in another schedule, any material, compound, mixture, or preparation which contains any quantity of the following substances having a depressant or stimulant effect on the nervous system:

1. Any substance which contains any quantity of a derivative of barbituric acid, including thiobarbituric acid, or any salt of a derivative of barbituric acid or thiobarbituric acid.

2. Benzphetamine.
3. Chlorhexadol.
4. Chlorphentermine.
5. Clortermine.
6. Gluthethimide.
7. Lysergic acid.
8. Lysergic acid amide.
9. Methyprylon.
10. Phendimetrazine.
11. Sulfondiethylmethane.
12. Sulfonethylemthane.
13. Sulfonmethane.

(b) Nalorphine.

(c) Unless specifically excepted or unless listed in another schedule, any material, compound, mixture, or preparation containing limited quantities of any of the following controlled substances or any sales thereof:

1. Not more than 1.8 grams of codeine per 100 milliliters or not more than 90 milligrams per dosage unit, with an equal or greater quantity of an isoquinoline alkaloid of opium.

2. Not more than 1.8 grams of codeine per 100 milliliters or not more than 90 milligrams per dosage unit, with recognized therapeutic amounts of one or more active ingredients which are not controlled substances.

3. Not more than 300 milligrams of dihydrocodeinone per 100 milliliters or not more than 15 milligrams per dosage unit, with a fourfold or greater quantity of an isoquinoline alkaloid of opium.

4. Not more than 300 milligrams of dihydrocodeinone per 100 milliliters or not more than 15 milligrams per dosage unit, with recognized therapeutic amounts of one or more active ingredients which are not controlled substances.

5. Not more than 1.8 grams of dihydrocodeine per 100 milliliters or not more than 90 milligrams per dosage unit, with recognized therapeutic amounts of one or more active ingredients which are not controlled substances.

6. Not more than 300 milligrams of ethylmorphine per 100 milliliters or not more than 15 milligrams per dosage unit, with one or more active, non-narcotic ingredients in recognized therapeutic amounts.

7. Not more than 50 milligrams of morphine per 100 milliliters or per 100 grams, with recognized therapeutic amounts of one or more active ingredients which are not controlled substances.

(4) SCHEDULE IV.—A substance in Schedule IV has a low potential for abuse relative to the substances in Schedule III and has a currently accepted medical use in treatment in the United States, and abuse of the substance may lead to limited physical or psychological dependence relative to the substances in Schedule III. Unless specifically excepted or unless listed in another schedule, any material, compound, mixture, or preparation which contains any quantity of the following substances, including its salts, isomers, and salts of isomers

whenever the existence of such salts, isomers, and salts of isomers is possible within the specific chemical designation are controlled in Schedule IV:

(a) Alprazolam.
(b) Barbital.
(c) Bromazepam.
(d) Camazepam.
(e) Chloralbetaine.
(f) Chloralhydrate.
(g) Chlordiazepoxide.
(h) Clobazam.
(i) Clonazepam.
(j) Clorazepate.
(k) Clotiazepam.
(l) Cloxazolam.
(m) Delorazepam.
(n) Dextropropoxyphene (dosageforms).
(o) Diazepam.
(p) Diethylpropion.
(q) Estazolam.
(r) Ethchlorvynol.
(s) Ethinamate.
(t) Ethylloflazepate.
(u) Fenfluramine.
(v) Fludiazepam.
(w) Flunitrazepam.
(x) Flurazepam.
(y) Halazepam.
(z) Haloxazolam.
(aa) Ketazolam.
(bb) Loprazolam.
(cc) Lorazepam.
(dd) Lormetazepam.
(ee) Mazindol.
(ff) Mebutamate.
(gg) Medazepam.
(hh) Meprobamate.
(ii) Methohexital.
(jj) Methylphenobarbital.
(kk) Nimetazepam.
(ll) Nitrazepam.
(mm) Nordiazepam.
(nn) Oxazepam.
(oo) Oxazolam.
(pp) Paraldehyde.
(qq) Pemoline.
(rr) Pentazocine.
(ss) Petrichloral.
(tt) Phenobarbital.
(uu) Phentermine.
(vv) Pinazepam.
(ww) Pipradrol.
(xx) Prazepam.
(yy) Tetrazepam.
(zz) SPA[(-)-1dimethylamino-1,2 diphenylethane].
(aaa) Temazepam.
(bbb) Triazolam.

(5) SCHEDULE V.—A substance, compound, mixture, or preparation of a substance in Schedule V has a low potential for abuse relative to the substances in Schedule IV and has a currently accepted medical use in treatment in the United States, and abuse of such compound, mixture, or preparation may lead to limited physical or psychological dependence relative to the substances in Schedule IV.

(a) Substances controlled in Schedule V include any compound, mixture, or preparation containing any of the following limited quantities of controlled substances, which shall include one or more active medicinal ingredients which are not controlled substances in sufficient proportion to confer upon the compound, mixture, or preparation valuable medicinal qualities other than those possessed by the controlled substance alone:

1. Not more than 200 milligrams of codeine per 100 milliliters or per 100 grams.

2. Not more than 100 milligrams of dihydrocodeine per 100 milliliters or per 100 grams.

3. Not more than 100 milligrams of ethylmorphine per 100 milliliters or per 100 grams.

4. Not more than 2.5 milligrams of diphenoxylate and not less than 25 micrograms of atropine sulfate per dosage unit.

5. Not more than 100 milligrams of opium per 100 milliliters or per 100 grams.

(b) Narcotic drugs. Unless specifically excepted or unless listed in another schedule, any material, compound, mixture, or preparation containing any of the following narcotic drugs and their salts, as set forth below:

1. Buprenorphine.

§ 893.04 Pharmacist and practitioner.—

(1) A pharmacist, in good faith and in the course of professional practice only, may dispense controlled substances upon a written or oral prescription of a practitioner, under the following conditions:

(a) Oral prescriptions must be promptly reduced to writing by the pharmacist.

(b) The written prescription must be dated and signed by the prescribing practitioner on the day when issued.

(c) There shall appear on the face of the prescription or written record thereof for the controlled substance the following information:

1. The full name and address of the person for whom, or the owner of the animal for which, the controlled substance is dispensed.

2. The full name and address of the prescribing practitioner and his federal controlled substance registry number shall be printed thereon.

3. If the prescription is for an animal, the species of animal for which the controlled substance is prescribed.

4. The name of the controlled substance prescribed and the strength, quantity, and directions for use thereof.

5. The number of the prescription, as recorded in the prescription files of the pharmacy in which it is filled.

6. The initials of the pharmacist filling the prescription and the date filled.

(d) The prescription shall be retained on file by the proprietor of the pharmacy in which it is filled for a period of two years.

(e) Affixed to the original container in which a controlled substance is delivered upon a prescription or authorized refill thereof, as hereinafter provided, there shall be a label bearing the following information:

1. The name and address of the pharmacy from which such controlled substance was dispensed.

2. The date on which the prescription for such controlled substance was filled.

3. The number of such prescription, as recorded in the prescription files of the pharmacy in which it is filled.

4. The name of the prescribing practitioner.

5. The name of the patient for whom, or the owner and species of the animal for which, the controlled substance is prescribed.

6. The directions for the use of the controlled substance prescribed in the prescription.

7. A clear, concise warning that it is a crime to transfer the controlled substance to any person other than the patient for whom prescribed.

(f) A prescription for a controlled substance listed in Schedule II may be dispensed only upon a written prescription of a practitioner, except that in an emergency situation, as defined by regulation of the Department of Health and Rehabilitative Services, such controlled substance may be dispensed upon oral prescription. No prescription for a controlled substance listed in Schedule II may be refilled.

(g) No prescription for a controlled substance listed in Schedules III, IV, or V may be filled or refilled more than five times within a period of six months after the date on which the prescription was written unless the prescription is renewed by a practitioner.

(2) The legal owner of any stock of controlled substances in a pharmacy, upon discontinuance of dealing in controlled substances, may sell said stock to a manufacturer, wholesaler, or pharmacy. Such controlled substances may be sold only upon an order form, when such an order form is required for sale by the drug abuse laws of the United States or this state, or regulations pursuant thereto.

§ 893.05 Practitioners and persons administering controlled substances in their absence.—

(1) A practitioner, in good faith and in the course of his professional practice only, may prescribe, administer, dispense, mix, or otherwise prepare a controlled substance, or he may cause the same to be administered by a licensed nurse or an intern practitioner under his direction and supervision only. A veterinarian may so prescribe, administer, dispense, mix or prepare a controlled substance for use on animals only, and may cause it to be administered by an assistant or orderly under his direction and supervision only.

(2) When any controlled substance is dispensed by a practitioner there shall be affixed to the original container in which the controlled substance is delivered a label on which appears:

(a) The date of delivery.

(b) The directions for use of such controlled substance.

(c) The name and address of such practitioner.

(d) The name of the patient and, if such controlled substance is prescribed for an animal, a statement describing the species of the animal.

(e) A clear, concise warning that it is a crime to transfer the controlled substance to any person other than the patient for whom prescribed.

(3) Any person who obtains from a practitioner or his agent, or pursuant to prescription, any controlled substance for administration to a patient during the absence of such practitioner shall return to such practitioner any unused portion of such controlled substance when it is no longer required by the patient.

§ 893.06 Distribution of controlled substances; order forms; labeling and packaging requirements.—

(1) Controlled substances in Schedules I and II shall be distributed by a duly licensed manufacturer, distributor, or wholesaler to a duly licensed manufacturer, wholesaler, distributor, practitioner, pharmacy, as defined in chapter 465, hospital, or laboratory only pursuant to an order form. It shall be deemed a compliance with this subsection if the parties to the transaction have complied with federal law respecting the use of order forms.

(2) Possession or control of controlled substances obtained as authorized by this section shall be lawful if in the regular course of business, occupation, profession, employment, or duty.

(3) A person in charge of a hospital or laboratory or in the employ of this state or of any other state, or of any political subdivision thereof, and a master or other proper officer of a ship or aircraft, who obtains controlled substances under the provisions of this section or otherwise, shall not administer, dispense, or otherwise use such controlled substances within this state, except within the scope of his employment or official duty, and then only for scientific or medicinal purposes and subject to the provisions of this chapter.

(4) It shall be unlawful to distribute a controlled substance in a commercial

container unless such container bears a label showing the name and address of the manufacturer, the quantity, kind, and form of controlled substance contained therein, and the identifying symbol for such substance, as required by federal law. No person except a pharmacist, for the purpose of dispensing a prescription, or a practitioner, for the purpose of dispensing a controlled substance to a patient, shall alter, deface, or remove any labels so affixed.

§ 893.07 Records.—

(1) Every person who engages in the manufacture, compounding, mixing, cultivating, growing, or by any other process producing or preparing, or in the dispensing, importation, or, as a wholesaler, distribution of controlled substances shall:

(a) On January 1, 1974, or as soon thereafter as any person first engages in such activity, and every second year thereafter, make a complete and accurate record of all stocks of controlled substances on hand. The inventory may be prepared on the regular physical inventory date which is nearest to, and does not vary by more than six months from, the biennial date that would otherwise apply. As additional substances are designated for control under this chapter they shall be inventoried as provided for in the subsection.

(b) On and after January 1, 1974, maintain, on a current basis, a complete and accurate record of each substance manufactured, received, sold, delivered, or otherwise disposed of by him, except that this subsection shall not require the maintenance of a perpetual inventory.

Compliance with the provisions of federal law pertaining to the keeping of records of controlled substances shall be deemed a compliance with the requirements of this subsection.

(2) The record of controlled substances received shall in every case show:

(a) The date of receipt.

(b) The name and address of the person from whom received.

(c) The kind and quantity of controlled substances received.

(3) The record of all controlled substances sold, administered, dispensed, or otherwise disposed of shall show:

(a) The date of selling, administering, or dispensing.

(b) The correct name and address of the person to whom or for whose use, or the owner and species of animal for which, sold, administered, or dispensed.

(c) The kind and quantity of controlled substances sold, administered, or dispensed.

(4) Every inventory or record required by this chapter, including prescription records, shall be maintained:

(a) Separately from all other records of the registrant, or

(b) Alternatively, in the case of Schedule III, IV, or V controlled substances, in such form that information required by this chapter is readily retrievable from the ordinary business records of the registrant.

In either case, records shall be kept and made available for a period of at least two years for inspection and copying by law enforcement officers whose duty it is to enforce the laws of this state relating to controlled substances.

(5) Each person shall maintain a record which shall contain a detailed list of controlled substances lost, destroyed, or stolen, if any; the kind and quantity of such controlled substances; and the date of the discovering of such loss, destruction, or theft.

§ 893.08 Exceptions.—

(1) The following may be distributed at retail without a prescription, but only by a registered pharmacist:

(a) Any compound, mixture, or preparation described in Schedule V.

(b) Any compound, mixture, or preparation containing any depressant or stimulant substance described in § 893.03(2)(a) or (c) except any amphetamine drug or sympathomimetic amine drug or compound designated as a Schedule II controlled substance pursuant to the chapter; in § 893.03(3)(a); or in Schedule IV, if:

1. The compound, mixture, or preparation contains one or more active medicinal ingredients not having depressant or stimulant effect on the central nervous system, and

2. Such ingredients are included therein in such combinations, quantity, proportion or concentration as to vitiate the potential for abuse of the controlled substances which do have a depressant or stimulant effect on the central nervous system.

(2) No compound, mixture, or preparation may be dispensed under subsection (1) unless such substance may, under the Federal Food, Drug, and Cosmetic Act, be lawfully sold at retail without a prescription.

(3) The exemptions authorized by this section shall be subject to the following conditions:

(a) The compounds, mixtures, and preparations referred to in subsection (1) may be dispensed to persons under age eighteen only on prescription. A bound volume must be maintained as a record of sale at retail of excepted compounds, mixtures, and preparations, and the pharmacist must require suitable identification from every unknown purchaser.

(b) Such compounds, mixtures, and preparations shall be sold by the pharmacist in good faith as a medicine and not for the purpose of evading the provisions of this chapter. The pharmacist may, in his discretion, withhold sale to any person whom he reasonably believes is attempting to purchase excepted compounds, mixtures, or preparations for the purpose of abuse.

(c) The total quantity of controlled substance listed in Schedule V which may be sold to any one purchaser within a given 48-hour period shall not exceed 120 milligrams of codeine, 60 milligrams dihydrocodeine, 30 milligrams of ethyl morphine, or 240 milligrams of opium.

(d) Nothing in this section shall be construed to limit the kind and quantity of any controlled substance that may be prescribed, administered, or dispensed to any person, or for the use of any person or animal, when it is prescribed, administered, or dispensed in compliance with the general provisions of this chapter.

(4) The dextrorotatory isomer of 3-meth-oxy-n-methylmorphinan and its salts (dextromethorphan) shall not be deemed to be included in any schedule by reasons of enactment of this chapter.

§ 893.09 Enforcement.—

(1) The Department of Law Enforcement, all state agencies which regulate professions of institutions affected by the provisions of this chapter, and all peace officers of the state shall enforce all provisions of this chapter except those specifically delegated, and shall cooperate with all agencies charged with the enforcement of the laws of the United States, this state, and all other states relating to controlled substances.

(2) Any agency authorized to enforce this chapter shall have the right to institute an action in its own name to enjoin the violation of any of the provisions of this chapter. Said action for an injunction shall be in addition to any other action, proceeding, or remedy authorized by law.

(3) All law enforcement officers whose duty it is to enforce this chapter shall have authority to administer oaths in connection with their official duties, and any person making a material false statement under oath before such law enforcement officers shall be deemed guilty of perjury and subject to the same punishment as prescribed for perjury.

(4) It shall be unlawful and punishable as provided in chapter 843 for any person to interfere with any such law enforcement officer in the performance of his official duties. It shall also be unlawful for any person falsely to represent himself to be authorized to enforce the drug abuse laws of this state, the United States, or any other state.

(5) No civil or criminal liability shall be imposed by virtue of this chapter upon any person whose duty it is to enforce the provisions of this chapter by reason of his being lawfully engaged in the enforcement of any law or municipal ordinance relating to controlled substances.

§ 893.10 Burden of proof.—

(1) It shall not be necessary for the state to negative any exemption or exception set forth in this chapter in any indictment, information, or other pleading or in any trial, hearing, or other proceeding under this chapter, and the burden of going forward with the evidence with respect to any such exemption or exception shall be upon the person claiming its benefit.

(2) In the case of a person charged under §§ 893.14(1) with the possession of a controlled substance, the label required under § 893.04(1) or § 893.05(2) shall be admissible in evidence and shall be prima facie evidence that such substance was obtained pursuant to a valid prescription form or dispensed by a practitioner while acting in the course of his professional practice.

§ 893.105 Testing and destruction of seized substances.—

(1) Any controlled substance seized as evidence may be sample tested and weighed by the seizing agency after the seizure. Any such samples and the analysis thereof shall be admissible into evidence in any civil or criminal action for the purpose of proving the nature, composition, and weight of the substance seized. In addition, the seizing agency may photograph or videotape, for use at trial, the controlled substance seized.

(2) Controlled substances that are not retained for sample testing as provided in subsection (1) may be destroyed pursuant to a court order issued in accordance with § 893.12.

§ 893.12 Contraband; seizure, forfeiture, sale.—

(1) All substances controlled by this chapter which may be handled, delivered, possessed, or distributed contrary to any provisions of this chapter and all such controlled substances the lawful possession of which is not established or the title to which cannot be ascertained are declared to be contraband, shall be subject to seizure and confiscation by any person whose duty it is to enforce the provisions of the chapter, and shall be disposed of as follows:

(a) Except as in this section otherwise provided, the court having jurisdiction shall order such controlled substances forfeited and destroyed. A record of the place where said controlled substances were seized, of the kinds and quantities of controlled substances destroyed, and of the time, place, and manner of destruction shall be kept, and a return under oath reporting said destruction shall be made to the court or magistrate and to the U.S. Drug Enforcement Administration by the officer who destroys them.

(b) Upon written application by the Department of Health and Rehabilitative Services, the court by whom the forfeiture of such controlled substances has been decreed may order the delivery of any of them to said department for distribution or destruction as hereinafter provided.

(c) Upon application by any hospital or laboratory within the state not operated for private gain, the department may, in its discretion, deliver any controlled substances that have come into its custody by authority of this section to the applicant for medical use. The department may from time to time deliver excess stocks of such controlled substances to the U.S. Drug Enforcement Administration or destroy same.

(d) The department shall keep a full and complete record of all controlled substances received and of all controlled substances disposed of, showing:

1. The exact kinds, quantities, and forms of such controlled substances;
2. The persons from whom received and to whom delivered;
3. By whose authority received, delivered, and destroyed; and
4. The dates of the receipt, disposal, or destruction,

which bid shall be open to inspection by all persons charged with the enforcement of federal and state drug abuse laws.

(2) Any vessel, vehicle, aircraft or drug paraphernalia, as defined in § 893.145, which has been or is being used in violation of any provision of this chapter, or in, upon, or by means of which any violation of this chapter has taken or is taking place may be seized and forfeited as provided by the Florida Contraband Forfeiture Act.

(3) Any law enforcement agency is empowered to authorize or designate offices, agents, or other persons to carry out the seizure provisions of this section. It shall be the duty of any officer, agent, or other person so authorized or designated, or authorized by law, whenever he shall discover any vessel, vehicle, or aircraft which has been or is being used in violation of any of the provisions of this chapter, or in, upon or by means of which any violation of this chapter has taken or is taking place, to seize such vessel, vehicle, or aircraft and place it in the custody of such person as may be authorized or designated for that purpose by the respective law enforcement agency pursuant to these provisions.

(4) The rights of any bona fide holder of a duly recorded mortgage or duly recorded vendor's privilege on the property seized under this chapter shall not be affected by the seizure.

§ 893.13 Prohibited acts; penalties.—

(1)(a) Except as authorized by this chapter and chapter 499, it is unlawful for any person to sell, manufacture, or deliver, a controlled substance. Any person who violates this provision with respect to:

1. A controlled substance named or described in § 893.03(1)(a), (1)(b), (1)(d), (2)(a), or (2)(b) is guilty of a felony of the second degree, punishable as provided in § 775.082, § 775.083 and § 775.084.

2. A controlled substance named or described in § 893.03(1)(c), (2)(c), (3), or (4) is guilty of a felony of the third degree, punishable as provided in § 775.082, § 775.083, or § 775.084.

3. A controlled substance named or described in § 893.03(5) is guilty of a misdemeanor of the first degree, punishable as provided in § 775.082 or § 775.083.

(b) Except as provided in this chapter, it is unlawful to sell, deliver, or possess in excess of ten grams of any substance named or described in § 893.03(1)(a) or (1)(b), or any combination thereof. Any person who violates this paragraph is guilty of a felony of the first degree, punishable as provided in § 775.082, § 775.083, or § 775.084.

(c) Except as authorized by this chapter, it is unlawful for any person over the age of eighteen years to deliver any controlled substance to a person under the age of eighteen years. Any person who violates this provision with respect to:

1. A controlled substance named or described in § 893.03(1)(a), (1)(b), (2)(a), or (2)(b) is guilty of a felony of the first degree, punishable as provided in § 775.082, § 775.083, or § 775.084.

2. A controlled substance named or described in § 893.03(1)(c), (1)(d), (2)(c), (3), or (4) is guilty of a felony of the second degree, punishable as provided in § 775.082, § 775.083, or § 775.084. Imposition of sentence shall not be suspended or deferred nor shall the person so convicted be placed on probation.

(d) It is unlawful for any person to bring into this state any controlled substance unless the possession of such controlled substance is authorized by this chapter or unless said person is licensed to do so by the appropriate federal agency. Any person who violates this provision with respect to:

1. A controlled substance named or described in § 893.03(1)(a), (1)(b), (2)(a), or (2)(b) is guilty of a felony of the second degree, punishable as provided in § 775.082, § 775.083, or § 775.084.

2. A controlled substance named or described in § 893.03(1)(c), (1)(d), (2)(c), (3), or (4) is guilty of a felony of the third degree, punishable as

provided in § 775.082, § 775.083, or § 775.084.

3. A controlled substance named or described in § 893.03(5) is guilty of a misdemeanor of the first degree, punishable as provided in § 775.082 or § 775.083.

(e) It is unlawful for any person to be in actual or constructive possession of a controlled substance unless such controlled substance was lawfully obtained from a practitioner or pursuant to a valid prescription or order of a practitioner while acting in the course of his professional practice or to be in actual or constructive possession of a controlled substance except as otherwise authorized by this chapter. Any person who violates this provision is guilty of a felony of the third degree, punishable as provided in § 775.082, § 775.083, or § 775.084.

(f) If the offense is the possession or delivery without consideration of not more than twenty grams of cannabis, as defined in this chapter, that person shall be guilty of a misdemeanor of the first degree, punishable as provided in § 775.082 and § 775.083. For purposes of this subsection, "cannabis" does not include resin extracted from plants of the genus Cannabis, or any compound manufacture, salt, derivative, mixture, or preparation of such resin.

(g) Notwithstanding any provision to the contrary of the laws of this state relating to arrest, a law enforcement officer may arrest without warrant any person who he has probable cause to believe is violating the provisions of this chapter relating to possession of cannabis.

(2)(a) It is unlawful for any person:

1. To distribute or dispense a controlled substance in violation of the provisions of this chapter relating thereto;

2. To refuse or fail to make, keep, or furnish any record, notification, order form, statement, invoice, or information required under this chapter;

3. To refuse an entry into any premises for any inspection or to refuse to allow any inspection authorized by this chapter;

4. To distribute a controlled substance named or described in § 893.03-(1) or (2) except pursuant to an order form as required by § 893.06;

5. To keep or maintain any store, shop, warehouse, dwelling, building, vehicle, boat, aircraft, or other structure or place which is resorted to by persons using controlled substances in violation of this chapter for the purpose of using these substances, or which is used for keeping or selling them in violation of this chapter;

6. To use to his own personal advantage, or to reveal, any information obtained in enforcement of this chapter except in a prosecution of administrative hearing for a violation of this chapter;

7. To withhold information from a practitioner from whom he seeks to obtain a controlled substance or a prescription for a controlled substance that such person has received a controlled substance or a prescription for a controlled substance of like therapeutic use from another practitioner within the last 30 days.

8. To possess a prescription form which has not been completed and signed by the practitioner whose name appears printed thereon, unless the person is such practitioner is an agent or employee of such practitioner, is a pharmacist, or is a supplier of prescription forms authorized by the practitioner to possess such forms.

(b) Any person who violates the provisions of paragraph (a) above shall be guilty of a misdemeanor of the first degree, punishable as provided in § 775.082, § 775.083, or § 775.084; except that upon a second or subsequent violation such person is guilty of a felony of the third degree, punishable as provided in § 775.082, § 775.083, or § 775.084.

(3)(a) It is unlawful for any person:

1. To acquire or obtain, or attempt to acquire or obtain, possession of a controlled substance by misrepresentation, fraud, forgery, deception or subterfuge;

2. To affix any false or forged label to a package or receptacle containing a controlled substance;

3. To furnish false or fraudulent material information in, or omit any material information from, any report or other document required to be kept or filed under this chapter or any record required to be kept by this chapter.

(b) Any person who violates the provisions of paragraph (a) is guilty of a felony of the third degree, punishable as provided in § 775.082, § 775.083, or § 775.084.

(4) The provisions of subsections (1), (2), and (3) of this section are not applicable to:

(a) The delivery for medical or scientific purpose only of controlled substances to persons included in any of the classes hereinafter named, or to the agents or employees of such persons, for use in the usual course of their business or profession or in the performance of their official duties.

(b) The actual or constructive possession of controlled substances for such use by such persons or their agents or employees, to wit:

1. Pharmacists.

2. Practitioners.

3. Persons who procure controlled substances in good faith and in the course of professional practice only, by or under the supervision of

pharmacists or practitioners employed by them, or for the purpose of lawful research, teaching, or testing, and not for resale.

4. Hospitals which procure controlled substances for lawful administration by practitioners, but only for use by or in the particular hospital.

5. Officers or employees of state, federal, or local governments acting in their official capacity only, or informers acting under their jurisdiction.

6. Common carriers.

7. Manufacturers, wholesalers, and distributors.

(c) The delivery of controlled substances by a law enforcement officer for bona fide law enforcement purposes in the course of an active criminal investigation.

§ 893.135 Trafficking; mandatory sentences; suspension or reduction of sentences; conspiracy to engage in trafficking.—

(1) Except as authorized in this chapter or in chapter 499 and notwithstanding the provisions of § 893.13:

(a) Any person who knowingly sells, manufactures, delivers, or brings into this state, or who is knowingly in actual or constructive possession of, in excess of 100 pounds of cannabis is guilty of a felony of the first degree, which felony shall be known as "Trafficking in cannabis." If the quantity of cannabis involved:

1. Is in excess of 100 pounds, but less than 2,000 pounds, such persons hall be sentenced to a mandatory minimum term of imprisonment of 3 calendar years and to pay a fine of $25,000.

2. Is 2,000 pounds or more, but less than 10,000 pounds, such person shall be sentenced to a mandatory minimum term of imprisonment of 5 calendar years and to pay a fine of $50,000.

3. Is 10,000 pounds or more, such

person shall be sentenced to a mandatory minimum term of imprisonment of 15 calendar years and to pay a fine of $200,000.

(b) Any person who knowingly sells, manufactures, delivers, or brings into this state, or who is knowingly in actual or constructive possession of, 28 grams or more of cocaine as described in § 893.03(2)(a)4. or of any mixture containing cocaine, is guilty of a felony of the first degree, which felony shall be known as "trafficking in cocaine." If the quantity involved:

1. Is 28 grams or more, but less than 200 grams, such person shall be sentenced to a mandatory minimum term of imprisonment of 3 calendar years and to pay a fine of $50,000.

2. Is 200 grams or more, but less than 400 grams, such person shall be sentenced to a mandatory minimum term of imprisonment of 5 calendar years and to pay a fine of $100,000.

3. Is 400 grams or more, such person shall be sentenced to a mandatory minimum term of imprisonment of 15 calendar years and to pay a fine of $250,000.

(c) Any person who knowingly sells, manufactures, delivers, or brings into this state, or who is knowingly in actual or constructive possession of, 4 grams or more of any morphine, opium, or any salt, isomer, or salt of an isomer thereof, including heroin, as described in § 893.03(1)(b) or § 893.03(2)(a), or 4 grams or more of any mixture containing any such substance, is guilty of a felony of the first degree, which felony shall be known as "Trafficking in Illegal Drugs." If the quantity involved:

1. Is 4 grams or more, but less than 14 grams, such person shall be sentenced to a mandatory minimum term of imprisonment of 3 calendar years and to pay a fine of $50,000.

2. Is 14 grams or more, but less than 28 grams, such person shall be sentenced to a mandatory minimum term of imprisonment of 10 calendar years and to pay a fine of $100,000.

3. Is 28 grams or more, such person shall be sentenced to a mandatory minimum term of imprisonment of 25 calendar years and to pay a fine of $500,000.

(d) Any person who knowingly sells, manufactures, delivers, or brings into this state, or who is knowingly in actual or constructive possession of, 28 grams or more of phencyclidine or of any mixture containing phencyclidine, as described in § 893.03(2)(b), is guilty of a felony of the first degree, which felony shall be known as "trafficking in phencyclidine." If the quantity involved:

1. Is 28 grams or more, but less than 200 grams, such person shall be sentenced to a mandatory minimum term of imprisonment of 3 calendar years and to pay a fine of $50,000.

2. Is 200 grams or more, but less than 400 grams, such person shall be sentenced to a mandatory minimum term of imprisonment of 5 calendar years and to pay a fine of $100,000.

3. Is 400 grams or more, such person shall be sentenced to a mandatory minimum term of imprisonment of 15 calendar years and to pay a fine of $250,000.

(e) Any person who knowingly sells, manufactures, delivers, or brings into this state, or who is knowingly in actual or constructive possession of, 200 grams or more of methaqualone or of any mixture containing methaqualone, as described in § 893.03(1)(d), is guilty of a felony of the first degree, which felony shall be known as "trafficking in methaqualone." If the quantity involved:

1. Is 200 grams or more, but less than 5 kilograms, such person shall be sentenced to a mandatory minimum term of imprisonment of 3 calendar years and to pay a fine of $50,000.

2. Is 5 kilograms or more, but less than 25 kilograms, such person shall be sentenced to a mandatory minimum term of imprisonment of 5 calendar years and to pay a fine of $100,000.

3. Is 25 kilograms or more, such person shall be sentenced to a mandatory minimum term of imprisonment of 15 calendar years and to pay a fine of $250,000.

(2) Notwithstanding the provisions of § 948.01, with respect to any person who is found to have violated this section, adjudication of guilt or imposition of sentence shall not be suspended, deferred, or withheld, nor shall such person be eligible for parole prior to serving the mandatory minimum term of imprisonment prescribed by this section.

(3) The state attorney may move the sentencing court to reduce or suspend the sentence of any person who is convicted of a violation of this section and who provides substantial assistance in the identification, arrest, or conviction of any of his accomplices, accessories, co-conspirators, or principals. The arresting agency shall be given an opportunity to be heard in aggravation or mitigation in reference to any such motion. Upon good cause shown, the motion may be filed and heard in camera. The judge hearing the motion may reduce or suspend the sentence if he finds that the defendant rendered such substantial assistance.

(4) Any person who agrees, conspires, combines, or confederates with another person to commit any act prohibited by subsection (1) is guilty of a felony of the first degree, and is punishable as if he had actually committed such prohibited act. Nothing in this subsection shall be construed to

prohibit a separate conviction and sentence for a violation of this subsection and any violation of subsection (1).

§ 893.145 "Drug paraphernalia" defined.—

The term "drug paraphernalia" means all equipment, products, and materials of any kind which are used, intended for use, or designed for use in planting, propagating, cultivating, growing, harvesting, manufacturing, compounding, converting, producing, processing, preparing, testing, analyzing, packaging, repackaging, storing, containing, concealing, injecting, ingesting, inhaling, or otherwise introducing into the human body a controlled substance in violation of this chapter. Drug paraphernalia is deemed to be contraband which shall be subject to civil forfeiture. It includes, but is not limited to:

(1) Kits used, intended for use, or designed for use in planting, propagating, cultivating, growing, or harvesting of any species of plant which is a controlled substance or from which a controlled substance can be derived.

(2) Kits used, intended for use, or designed for use in manufacturing, compounding, converting, producing, processing, or preparing controlled substances.

(3) Isomerization devices used, intended for use, or designed for use in increasing the potency of any species of plant which is a controlled substance.

(4) Testing equipment used, intended for use, or designed for use in identifying, or in analyzing the strength, effectiveness, or purity of, controlled substances.

(5) Scales and balances used, intended for use, or designed for use in weighing or measuring controlled substances.

(6) Diluents and adulterants, such as quinine hydrochloride, mannitol, mannite, dextrose, and lactose used, intended for use, or designed for use in cutting controlled substances.

(7) Separation gins and sifters used, intended for use, or designed for use in removing twigs and seeds from, or in otherwise cleaning or refining, cannabis.

(8) Blenders, bowls, containers, spoons, and mixing devices used, intended for use, or designed for use in compounding controlled substances.

(9) Capsules, balloons, envelopes, and other containers used, intended for use, or designed for use in packaging small quantities of controlled substances.

(10) Containers and other objects used, intended for use, or designed for use in storing or concealing controlled substances.

(11) Hypodermic syringes, needles, and other objects used, intended for use, or designed for use in parenterally injecting controlled substances into the human body.

(12) Objects used, intended for use, or designed for use in ingesting, inhaling, or otherwise introducing cannabis, cocaine, hashish, or hashish oil into the human body, such as:

(a) Metal, wooden, acrylic, glass, stone, plastic, or ceramic pipes with or without screens, permanent screens, hashish heads, or punctured metal bowls.

(b) Water pipes

(c) Carburetion tubes and devices.

(d) Smoking and carburetion masks.

(e) Roach clips: meaning objects used to hold burning material, such as a cannabis cigarette, that has become too small or too short to be held in the hand.

(f) Miniature cocaine spoons, and cocaine vials.

(g) Chamber pipes.

(h) Carburetor pipes.
(i) Electric pipes.
(j) Air-driven pipes.
(k) Chillums.
(l) Bongs.
(m) Ice pipes or chillers.

§ 893.146 Determination of paraphernalia.—In determining whether an object is drug paraphernalia, a court or other authority or jury shall consider, in addition to all other logically relevant factors, the following:

(1) Statements by an owner or by anyone in control of the object concerning its use.

(2) The proximity of the object, in time and space, to a direct violation of this act.

(3) The proximity of the object to controlled substances.

(4) The existence of any residue of controlled substances on the object.

(5) Direct or circumstantial evidence of the intent of an owner, or of anyone in control of the object, to deliver it to persons who he knows, or should reasonably know, intend to use the object to facilitate a violation of this act. The innocence of an owner, or of anyone in control of the object, as to a direct violation of this act shall not prevent a finding that the object is intended for use, or designed for use, as drug paraphernalia.

(6) Instructions, oral or written, provided with the object concerning its use.

(7) Descriptive materials accompanying the object which explain or depict its use.

(8) Any advertising concerning its use.

(9) The manner in which the object is displayed for sale.

(10) Whether the owner, or anyone in control of the object, is a legitimate supplier of like or related items to the community, such as a licensed distributor of or dealer in tobacco products.

(11) Direct or circumstantial evidence of the ratio of sales of the object or objects to the total sales of the business enterprise.

(12) The existence and scope of legitimate uses for the object in the community.

(13) Expert testimony concerning its use.

§ 893.147 Use, possession, manufacture, delivery, or advertisement of drug paraphernalia.—

(1) USE OR POSSESSION OF DRUG PARAPHERNALIA.—It is unlawful for any person to use, or to possess with intent to use, drug paraphernalia:

(a) To plant, propagate, cultivate, grow, harvest, manufacture, compound, convert, produce, process, prepare, test, analyze, pack, repack, store, contain, or conceal a controlled substance in violation of this chapter; or

(b) To inject, ingest, inhale, or otherwise introduce into the human body a controlled substance in violation of this chapter.

Any person who violates this subsection is guilty of a misdemeanor of the first degree, punishable as provided in § 775.082, § 775.083, or § 775.084.

(2) MANUFACTURE OR DELIVERY OF DRUG PARAPHERNALIA.—It is unlawful for any person to deliver, possess with intent to deliver, or manufacture with intent to deliver drug paraphernalia, knowing, or under circumstances where one reasonable should know, that it will be used:

(a) To plant, propagate, cultivate, grow, harvest, manufacture, compound, convert, produce, process, prepare, test, analyze, pack, repack, store, contain, or conceal a controlled substance in violation of this act; or

(b) To inject, ingest, inhale, or otherwise introduce into the human body a controlled substance in violation of this act.

Any person who violates this subsection is guilty of a felony of the third degree, punishable as provided in § 775.082, § 775.083, or § 775.084.

(3) DELIVERY OF DRUG PARAPHERNALIA TO A MINOR.—

(a) Any person 18 years of age or over who violates subsection (2) by delivering drug paraphernalia to a person under 18 years of age is guilty of a felony of the second degree, punishable as provided in § 775.082, § 775.083, or § 775.084.

(b) It is unlawful for any person to sell or otherwise deliver hypodermic syringes, needles, or other objects which may be used, are intended for use, or are designed for use in parenterally injecting substances into the human body to any person under 18 years of age, except that hypodermic syringes, needles, or other such objects may be lawfully dispensed to a person under 18 years of age by a licensed practitioner, parent or legal guardian or by a pharmacist pursuant to a valid prescription for same. Any person who violates the provisions of this paragraph is guilty of a misdemeanor of the first degree, punishable as provided in § 775.082, § 775.083, or § 775.084.

(4) ADVERTISEMENT OF DRUG PARAPHERNALIA.—It is unlawful for any person to place in any newspaper, magazine, handbill, or other publication any advertisement, knowing, or under circumstances where one reasonably should know, that the purpose of the advertisement, in whole or in part, is to promote the sale of objects designed or intended for use as drug paraphernalia. Any person who violates this subsection is guilty of a misdemeanor of the first degree, punishable as provided in § 775.082, § 775.083, or § 775.084.

UNITED STATES of America, Appellee,

v.

Gregory Richard FOGARTY, Appellant.

United States Court of Appeals,
Eighth Circuit.

Submitted Sept. 16, 1982.

Decided Nov. 10, 1982.

692 F.2d 542

Rehearing Denied Dec. 9, 1982.

Certiorari Denied March 21, 1983.

See 103 S.Ct. 1434.

FLOYD R. GIBSON, Senior Circuit Judge.

Gregory Richard Fogarty was convicted at a bench trial on stipulated facts of one count of conspiracy to import marijuana in violation of 21 U.S.C. §§ 952(a) and 963 (1976), and one count of conspiracy to possess marijuana with the intent to distribute in violation of 21 U.S.C. §§ 841(a)(1) and 846. Fogarty appeals his conviction, claiming (1) that the district court should have granted his motion to dismiss the indictment under the Speedy Trial Act of 1974 and (2) that the classification of marijuana in the Federal Controlled Substances Act is arbitrary and capricious, violating the due process and equal protection mandates of the Fifth Amendment to the U.S. Constitution. We reject Fogarty's claims and affirm his conviction.

I. Factual Background

A federal grand jury indictment was handed down on August 19, 1981, charging Fogarty and six others with conspiracy to import and distribute marijuana. The indictment, which was made public on October 23, 1981, culminated a lengthy and complicated Federal Drug Enforcement Administration investigation beginning January 20, 1980, when a DC-7 aircraft containing 26,000 pounds of marijuana (with an estimated street value of approximately $18 million) landed in north central South Dakota and was seized by local law enforcement officers. The indictment named ten unindicted coconspirators and alleged 45 overt acts occurring at various places in eight states and three foreign countries.

Fogarty was arraigned on September 8, 1981, and was joined for trial with four other indicted coconspirators (codefendants). Beginning in mid-October, 1981, Fogarty's codefendants filed numerous pretrial motions. The district court issued an order on October 23, 1981 requiring all pretrial motions to be submitted by November 13, 1981, with the United States having until November 27, 1981 to respond and the defendants having an addi-

tional five days to file their replies. On November 2, 1981, the district court scheduled the defendants' trial for December 7, 1981.

Among the pretrial motions were the continuance motions filed by three of Fogarty's codefendants on October 15, 1981. While Fogarty did not join in these motions, he did file eight pretrial motions of his own on November 16, 1981, including a motion to sever his trial from the other defendants and a motion to dismiss the indictment for failure to comply with the Speedy Trial Act.

On November 24, 1981, the district court issued an order granting the three codefendants' motions to continue and moving the trial date from December 7, 1981 to January 6, 1982. On December 10, 1981, the court denied Fogarty's motions to dismiss and to sever and, accordingly, determined that Fogarty would be tried along with his four coconspirator/codefendants on January 6, 1982. The remaining pretrial motions were disposed of on December 22, 1981.

Before January 6, 1982, Fogarty's four codefendants pled guilty under plea bargaining agreements. Fogarty was tried pursuant to stipulated facts on January 6, 1982. His right to raise the issues in the instant appeal were expressly preserved at trial.

* * *

The Controlled Substances Act

Fogarty also contends that his conviction should be reversed because of the alleged unconstitutionality of the Federal Controlled Substances Act. 21 U.S.C. §§ 801-904 (1976) (CSA or Act). Specifically, Fogarty claims that the classification of marijuana as a

Schedule I controlled substance,[1] *Id.* at § 812(b), Schedule I(c)(10), is irrational and arbitrary, violating the due process and equal protection mandates of the Fifth Amendment to the U.S. Constitution. The gist of this claim is that the weight of current medical knowledge purportedly shows that marijuana does not satisfy the three statutory criteria necessary for inclusion in Schedule I—(A) high potential for abuse, (B) no currently accepted medical use, and (C) lack of accepted safety for use of the drug under medical supervision. 21 U.S.C. § 812(b)(1). Fogarty places particular emphasis on the number of currently accepted medical uses for marijuana, including therapeutic uses in the treatment of glaucoma and cancer.

In addressing this argument, we first note the highly deferential standard of review applicable here. Because there is no fundamental constitutional right to import, sell, or possess marijuana, the legislative classification complained of here must be upheld unless it bears no rational relationship to a legitimate government purpose. *United States v. Kiffer,* 477 F.2d 349, 352 (2nd Cir. 1972), *cert. denied,* 414 U.S. 831, 94 S.Ct. 165, 38 L.Ed.2d 65 (1973). Accordingly, "the judiciary may not sit as a superlegislature to

judge the wisdom or desirability of legislative policy determinations made in areas that neither affect fundamental rights nor proceed along suspect lines...." *New Orleans v. Dukes,* 427 U.S. 297, 303, 96 S.Ct. 2513, 2516, 49 L.Ed.2d 511 (1976). Furthermore, judicial self-restraint is especially appropriate where as here the challenged classification entails legislative judgments on a whole host of controversial medical, scientific, and social issues. *Marshall v. United States,* 414 U.S. 417, 427, 94 S.Ct. 700, 706, 38 L.Ed.2d 618 (1974); *also see Kiffer,* 477 F.2d at 352. As noted in *Williamson v. Lee Optical, Inc.,* 348 U.S. 483, 488, 75 S.Ct. 461, 464, 99 L.Ed. 563 (1954): "It is enough that there is an evil at hand for correction, and that it might be thought that the particular legislative measure was a rational way to correct it."

With this in mind, we conclude that Fogarty has not met his heavy burden of proving the irrationality of the Schedule I classification of marijuana.[2] First, the ongoing vigorous

---

1. The severity of statutory sanctions for drug distribution and related offenses depends on the schedule in which the drug is classified, with the most severe penalties typically attached to Schedule I substances and the least severe penalties attaching to Schedule IV and V substances. 21 U.S.C. § 841(b). Congress made the initial classifications of controlled substances. However, recognizing that scientific information concerning controlled substances could change, Congress empowered the Attorney General to hear petitions for the reclassification or removal of drugs from the schedules. *Id.* at § 811.

2. In so holding we are in accordance with the heretofore uniformly held view among federal courts that the Schedule I classification of marijuana is rational and, therefore, not violative of equal protection or due process. *See United States v. Kiffer,* 477 F.2d 349, 356-57 (2d Cir. 1972), *cert. denied,* 414 U.S. 831, 94 S. Ct. 165, 38 L.Ed.2d 65 (1973); *United States v. Erwin,* 602 F.2d 1183, 1185 (5th Cir. 1979) (Attorney General's failure to reclassify marijuana did not violate defendant's equal protection or due process rights); *United States v. Maiden,* 355 F.Supp. 743, 749 (D.Conn.1973); *Nat. Org. for Reform of Marijuana Laws v. Bell,* 488 F.Supp. 123, 140 (D.D.C.1980) (Three Judge Court); *Wolkind v. Selph,* 495 F.Supp. 507, 513 (D.Va.1980), *aff'd,* 649 F.2d 865 (4th Cir. 1981) (Virginia's Controlled Substances Act, which classified marijuana as a Schedule I substance,

dispute as to the physical and psychological effects of marijuana, its potential for abuse, and whether it has any medical value, supports the rationality of the continued Schedule I classification. *See National Organization for Reform of Marijuana Laws v. Bell,* 488 F.Supp. 123, 128-30, 136, 139-40 (D.D.C. 1980) (Three Judge Court) for Judge Tamm's excellent discussion of the current state of medical and scientific knowledge concerning the uses and effects of marijuana. Furthermore, the three statutory criteria for Schedule I classification set out in § 812(b)(1)—high potential for abuse, no medically accepted use, and no safe use even under medical supervision—should

complied with equal protection and due process mandates); *United States v. Creswell,* 515 F.Supp. 1268, 1271 (E.D.N.Y.1981) (DEA's decision not to reclassify marijuana was not arbitrary nor an abuse of discretion in view of the continued controversial effects of marijuana).

not be read as being either cumulative or exclusive. Thus, even assuming, arguendo, that marijuana has some currently accepted medical uses, the Schedule I classification may nevertheless be rational in view of countervailing factors such as the current pattern, scope, and significance of marijuana abuse and the risk it poses to public health. *See* 21 U.S.C. § 811 (c)(1)-(8). Finally, it should be noted that under Section 811 Congress has provided a comprehensive reclassification scheme, authorizing the Attorney General to reclassify marijuana in view of new scientific evidence. In establishing this scheme, Congress provided an efficient and flexible means of assuring the continued rationality of the classification of controlled substances, such as marijuana. *See, Kiffer,* 477 F.2d at 357.

Judgment affirmed. Costs assessed against Appellant.

Cases relating to Chapter 12
PREPARATORY ACTIVITY CRIMES

STATE of Missouri, Respondent,
v.
Donald STEWART, Appellant.
Missouri Court of Appeals,
St. Louis District,
Division Two.
537 S.W.2d 579
April 13, 1976.

CLEMENS, Presiding Judge.

This case stems from a planned payroll robbery that didn't quite happen. A jury found defendant guilty of attempted first-degree robbery and carrying a concealed weapon. Pursuant to the verdicts the court sentenced defendant to eight years' imprisonment on the attempted robbery charge and two years' imprisonment on the concealed weapons charge, to run consecutively. Defendant appeals.

We first take up defendant's contention that despite evidence of prolonged planning and *preparation* to rob, there was no *overt act* sufficient to constitute an *attempt* to rob. The gist of the State's case was that defendant and three accomplices planned to rob a courier as he left a bank with payroll money, armed themselves, took their assigned positions outside the bank and as the courier left the bank the police intervened and arrested the four men.

Two basic principles apply. The first is unchallenged: Where two or more persons knowingly act together unlawfully, the act of each is the act of all in the eyes of the law. Second, the four requisite elements of an attempt to

commit a crime are an intent to commit it, an overt act toward its commission, failure of consummation and the apparent possibility of commission. The challenged element here is the "overt act." *State v. Thomas, infra,* that is, did the acts go beyond mere preparation and become perpetration? We take a closer look at the evidence.

The State's principal testimony came from Raymond Jones, whom defendant had recruited as one of the robbers, and from Paul Bosch whom Jones in turn had recruited. We summarize their testimony.

Some two months before the final act, defendant Donald Stewart, a sometime bondsman and security officer, had learned that every other Thursday morning a police officer-courier left the Jefferson Bank carrying money for a police department payroll. Stewart solicited Raymond Jones to aid in robbing the courier as he left the bank. More men would be needed, so Jones recruited Paul Bosch and Guy Burroughs. The four men met often and various plans were discussed, agreed upon, and modified. Defendant Stewart supplied Bosch and Burroughs with pistols and ammunition. By one of the plans Burroughs, the look-out man, was to be armed with Stewart's carbine rifle and cover the robbery from a nearby rooftop to prevent interference. The final plan was for Jones and Bosch, with drawn pistols, to intercept the courier as he moved from the bank toward his car in an adjoining parking lot, then to rob and disable him. Burroughs was to protect Jones and Bosch from action by the bank's guard stationed in a building on the parking lot and was to take whatever action necessary to prevent the guard from interfering or pursuing. Meanwhile, defendant was to wait a block away in his parked car with motor running, in full view of the robbery, drive up, get Jones and Bosch, and escape.

From time to time the four men "cased the joint" and made "dry runs." (On one occasion they headed for the bank intending to carry out the robbery but their plans aborted when the car ran out of gas.)

The final plan was to rob the courier on February 21, 1974. Meanwhile, treachery had crept in. Paul Bosch decided to drop out and for reasons of his own told St. Louis police in detail of the plot and its planning. In turn, police put Stewart, Jones and Burroughs under surveillance and got regular telephone reports from Bosch about preparations for the robbery. The police made detailed plans to thwart the robbery. On the morning of February 21, 16 policemen were stationed in, around and atop the bank, most in civilian clothes. They had alerted the courier to the plot.

At the appointed hour, defendants Stewart, Jones, Bosch and Burroughs drove to the bank and saw the courier's car in the parking lot. Each took his planned position, Jones and Bosch some 60 feet from the bank door, ready to intercept and rob the courier

as he headed for his parked car with the payroll money. The courier left the bank door toward his parked car, but had walked only 15 feet when, on signal from the police officer in charge, the police arrested all four "suspects." None had yet drawn a weapon nor threatened the courier.

We revert to the four requisite elements of an attempted crime. Here, there was clear evidence of intent to rob, of the possibility of robbing and of failure of consummation. The challenged element is the overt act. In 21 Am.Jur.2d, Criminal Law, at § 111, it is pointed out that "no definite line can be drawn" between preparation and the overt act necessary to constitute criminal attempt, but "it may be said that preparation consists in devising or arranging the means or measures necessary for commission of the offense and that the attempt is the direct movement toward the commission after the preparations are made." Cases cited *infra* support this.

Although Missouri cases state principles governing attempts, none is so factually similar to precisely solve the issue here. We adopt the general principles of *State v. Thomas*, 438 S.W.2d 441[5-11] (Mo. 1969): "An 'attempt' is an intent to do a particular thing which the law has declared to be a crime, 'coupled with an act towards the doing, sufficient, both in magnitude and in proximity to the fact intended, to be taken cognizance of by the law, that does not concern itself with things trivial and small. Or, more briefly, an attempt is an intent to do a particular criminal thing, with an act towards it falling short of the thing intended.' ...To be found guilty of an attempt to commit a crime there must be some overt act in part execution of the intent to commit the crime, which falls short of the completion of the crime, which overt act must move directly toward the consummation of the crime.... Mere preparation is not sufficient to constitute an attempt to commit a crime. The defendant must have taken steps going beyond mere preparation, by doing something bringing him nearer the crime he intends to commit. 22 C.J.S. Criminal Law § 75(2), p. 231. The act need not, however, be the ultimate step toward, or the last proximate, or the last possible, act to the consummation of the crime attempted to be perpetrated."

These principles in *Thomas* were applied where the State charged defendant with attempting to cash a bogus check. Defendant gave a storekeeper a false name, falsely claimed he was an employee of the maker, identified himself by a forged driver's license, and presented the check for cashing. He was arrested and contended on appeal he was not guilty of an attempt to pass the check since he had not committed an overt act by endorsing the check. Denying this contention, the court said: "It is reasonable to conclude that but for the alertness of the store's representatives the crime would have been consummated; that there was no inherent impossibility but rather an apparent possibility of committing the crime; that the intervening circumstances which thwarted the consummation of the crime occurred as a result of the actions of third parties, acting apart from and independent of appellant's will and control. Appellant's acts went beyond mere preparation; they went far enough toward the eventuality of obtaining the cash so as to cross the line which divides criminal intention from criminal attempt." See also Comments on MAI-CR, Attempts, pp. 2-5.

We also look beyond Missouri decisions for answers to the question: What

acts constitute an attempt? A logical factor is the proximity to the crime's completion. The Model Penal Code is enlightening. At §§ 5.01 and 5.02 it declares one guilty of attempt who purposely does an act constituting a substantial step planned to culminate in committing the crime.

Each case must be considered in the light of its own facts, and the problem is to determine at what point a defendant's acts go beyond preparation and are in the nature of perpetration.

Other courts have considered cases factually similar to our problem and determined what acts have gone beyond preparation and become criminal perpetration.

In *People v. Stites*, 75 Cal. 570, 17 P. 693 (1888), the defendant and an accomplice intended to place a homemade bomb on a streetcar track. Defendant made the bomb and started with it to meet his accomplice at the planned place but was arrested in route. Upholding conviction for attempted bombing, the court reasoned: "Before he left house he was already fully prepared, and carried with him the instrument he was to use in effecting the crime he intended; nothing, in fact, remained for him to do but deposit it on the railway, at the time easily within his reach."

In *Stokes v. State*, 92 Miss. 415, 46 So. 627 (1908), the defendant paid a gunman to kill his victim. The defendant procured a loaded pistol and after dark went with the gunman to the intended place of ambush, where they expected the victim to appear. Police arrested defendant as he handed the pistol to the gunman. Although the victim had not yet appeared, the court upheld defendant's conviction for attempted murder.

In *Bell v. State*, 118 Ga.App. 291, 163 S.E.2d 323 (1968), the court upheld the sufficiency of an indictment charging that defendant intended to destroy a place of business and entered thereon with dynamite in his possession. Without specifically distinguishing between preparation and perpetration, the court viewed the indictment in the light of Georgia's statutory definition of attempt as "*any* act toward the commission of such crime." The court held that "it is sufficient if there is an act done in pursuance of the intent, and *more or less* directly tending to but falling short of, the commission of the crime."

In *People v. Gibson,* 94 Cal. App. 2d 468, 210 P.2d 747 (1949), the defendant intended to burglarize a store. Late at night when walking down an alley carrying a ladder and a sack of burglar tools he was arrested near the store. On appeal for attempted burglary, the court illustrated the principle of attempted crime: "When a man threatens to kill his neighbor then (1) buys a gun and (2) conceals himself on the neighbor's premises, his two acts are clearly done in furtherance of his declared purpose." Having thus distinguished the elements of preparations and perpetration, the court upheld defendant's conviction for attempted burglary, saying: "Slight acts in furtherance of a criminal purpose...are sufficient [to constitute an attempt] when they constitute a direct movement towards the consummation which was prevented by an agency inhibitive of the offense."

In *People v. Gormley,* 222 App.Div. 256, 225 N.Y.S. 653 (1927), the court upheld an attempted robbery conviction where defendants were found armed and lurking near a bank, intending to rob a messenger, but before the messenger appeared police arrested them. The court upheld defendants' conviction for attempted robbery.

These out-of-state cases upheld convictions based on an overt act, that is, an act going beyond preparation and constituting perpetration. Better to view the case before us, we contrast these out-of-state convictions with hypothetical cases that do *not* constitute attempts because they do not go beyond preparation. We quote Perkins Criminal Law, Second Edition, page 560: "A, intending to murder X, conceals a long dagger in his clothing and goes out to discover where X may be found. A is arrested on a charge of attempting to murder X before receiving a lead as to X's whereabouts....B also intends to murder X but has a different plan. He has prepared some poisoned candy, knowing X is very fond of that kind, and intends to send it to X. B is arrested on a charge of attempted murder while the poisoned candy is still in his possession.... C has placed combustibles in X's dwelling house intending to return and set the fire at a later time. He is arrested on a charge of attempted arson while at his own home waiting for the appropriate moment....D intends to break into X's house at midnight and steal certain valuable goods kept there. With this in mind he has procured an effective set of burglar's tools, but is arrested in his own home about noon on a charge of attempted burglary....E has obtained some counterfeit foreign treasury notes which he intends to pass as genuine. He received them late at night with no thought of using them until the following day. He is arrested that night on a charge of attempting to utter counterfeit foreign securities."

These examples of no attempt each show a negative factor precluding conviction. We find no such negative factor in our case.

We must now evaluate our case, applying the general principles recited

above in *State v. Thomas,* 438 S.W.2d
441[5-11] (Mo. 1969), and considering
the applications of those principles in
the out-of-state cases cited above. So
considered, we hold that when defendant Stewart and his three accomplices
conspired to rob the courier, agreed
upon detailed plans as to where, when
and how each man was to do his part
and escape, then armed themselves
with deadly weapons—all this might
be considered mere preparation. But
when the four men drove to the bank,
alit and took up their assigned positions, then being armed, ready, willing
and able to intercept, assault and rob
the courier, they had then gone beyond
mere preparation. This conduct, under
the principles announced in *Thomas,
supra,* was "an act towards the doing,
sufficient, both in magnitude and in
proximity to the fact intended, to be
taken cognizance of by the law...."

We hold the evidence supported the
charge of attempted robbery.

Having denied defendant's challenge
to the sufficiency of the evidence, we
look to his contention the trial court
erred in admitting into evidence a carbine rifle discovered by a warrantless
search of his getaway car some hours
after defendant's arrest when police
had towed the car to a garage.

The State admits the carbine rifle
was not seized as an incident to defendant's arrest, but contends the police
had reasonable cause to believe defendant's car contained material evidence
of the attempted robbery. Defendant
had supplied his accomplices with
pistols and shotguns and at one point
Guy Burroughs had defendant's carbine rifle. Police knew that at one of
the early planning sessions defendant
had planned that at the robbery Guy
Burroughs would be on a rooftop with
the carbine to prevent interference with
the robbery. Since defendant's automobile was an instrumentality of the
attempted crime, its search was a valid
step in investigating the robbery and
preserving evidence pertinent to it.
State v. Barngrover, 513 S.W.2d
751[1,2] (Mo.App.1974), and *see
Texas v. White,* 423 U.S. 67, 96 S. Ct.
304, 46 L.Ed.2d 209 (1975). We find
no prejudicial error concerning the
carbine rifle.

Concerning the charge of carrying a
concealed weapon, defendant contends
the court erred in admitting into evidence the pistol police took from him
as he sat in his getaway car. Defendant
concedes the taking was incidental to
his arrest but contends the arrest was
improper since an attempted robbery
was not proven. We have ruled against
defendant on his premise, so his conclusion falls.

Judgment affirmed.

McMILLIAN and RENDLEN, JJ.,
concur.

Carl Nathaniel WILLIAMS, Appellant
v.
STATE of Indiana, Appellee
412 N.E.2d 1211
Supreme Court of Indiana
Dec. 8, 1980

DeBRULER, Justice.

Appellant and his wife, Diane Williams, were indicted by the Grand Jury of Lake County for conspiracy to commit murder, a Class A felony, Ind.Code § 35-41- 5-2 (Burns 1979). Both were convicted in a trial by jury, and appellant received a sentence of 25 years. On appeal he raises two issues:

(1) whether the evidence is sufficient to support his conviction; and

(2) whether entrapment was present as a matter of law.

The evidence when viewed most favorably to the verdict discloses the following:

Appellant, his wife, and an undercover policeman posing as an illegal drug dealer were together in the dining room of appellant's house, when the wife discovered an article on the front page of a local newspaper written by one Alan Doyle which described her arrest and that of appellant on charges of being in possession of two stolen cars. She became angry and showed the article to appellant.

Appellant read the article for himself. His wife asked what he was going to do about the article. Appellant then said that he wanted something done about it and said very loudly, "those lousy bastards. They've done it to me again." The policeman interjected that he ought to see a lawyer. The wife said lawyers would not do any good. Appellant agreed. He said that he was tired of dealing with lawyers.

The wife, wringing her hands, again asked appellant what he was going to do about the article. Appellant replied that he wanted the man shut up, and asked the undercover policeman whether he would undertake an extra service, and the policeman asked what he meant by that. Appellant replied that he wanted to stop this kind of malicious slander. The policeman said that just breaking their legs and arms would not shut them up. The wife agreed.

Appellant again asked the policeman if he would like to perform an extra service, and added, "I want Alan Doyle killed. I never want to see or hear of him again." Ms. Williams was standing at the time with her hand on her husband's shoulder.

The policeman said that he did not do such things himself but could put appellant in contact with somebody who would. He said further that such people require specific knowledge about the intended victim.

The wife stated that she knew someone down at the newspaper and gave the name. Appellant offered to go down to the newspaper himself. His wife discouraged him in that.

Appellant then got up and went to another part of the house and returned with a two-way radio which he gave to the policeman saying that it was a Gary police radio and would help him out. As the policeman prepared to leave he told them again that he needed to know specifics about the reporter.

Ms. Williams said she could handle that and agreed to supply such information to him. The policeman then left with the radio, promising to contact them the next day.

Appellant was visited the following day by the undercover policeman who was accompanied by another policeman posing as a contract killer. The second officer had a body transmitter secreted on his person. It was agreed in a conversation that appellant would pay a total of $1,000 for killing Alan Doyle and actually paid $500 at the time to the second officer and agreed to pay an additional $500 after the task was completed.

Several days later the policeman telephoned appellant and his wife. In this conversation which was also recorded the wife made a veiled and general statement in which she revealed that she knew the reporter was to be "taken care" of, and appellant made a statement which confirmed his obligation to get specific information about the reporter's habits.

Several days thereafter, appellant and the two undercover policemen drove through the city and appellant pointed out the building in which the reporter worked.

(1) In challenging the sufficiency of the evidence appellant writes that the State's burden to show an agreement has not been met and that if an agreement is present, it is between appellant and a police officer, and that the law will not permit a conviction under such circumstances. In resolving this issue, we do not resolve questions of credibility but look to the evidence and reasonable inferences therefrom which support the verdict. *Smith v. State* (1970) 254 Ind. 401, 260 N.E.2d 558. The conviction will be affirmed if from that viewpoint there is evidence of probative value from which a reasonable

trier of fact could infer that appellant was guilty beyond a reasonable doubt. *Taylor v. State* (1973) 260 Ind. 64, 291 N.E.2d 890; *Glover v. State* (1970) 253 Ind. 536, 255 N.E.2d 657. The statute defining the crime of conspiracy reads as follows:

"(a) A person conspires to commit a felony when, with intent to commit the felony, he agrees with another person to commit the felony. A conspiracy to commit a felony is a felony of the same class as the underlying felony. However, a conspiracy to commit murder is a Class A felony.

"(b) The state must allege and prove that either the person or the person with whom he agreed performed an overt act in furtherance of the agreement.

"(c) It is no defense that the person with whom the accused person is alleged to have conspired:
(1) has not been prosecuted;
(2) has not been convicted;
(3) has been acquitted;
(4) has been convicted of a different crime;
(5) cannot be prosecuted for any reason; and
(6) lacked the capacity to commit the crime." Ind. Code § 35-41-5-2 (Burns 1979)

The question here is whether the evidence warranted the jury in concluding that appellant, with the intent to commit a homicide, agreed with another person to commit that offense. From the evidence recited above, the trier of fact could have concluded that a scheme to kill Alan Doyle was formed around the dining room table in appellant's house when the article was first under discussion. Appellant, his wife, and the undercover officer were each participants in it. Appellant called for the killing of Doyle. Appellant's wife agreed to cooperate to accomplish that object by her assent and her offer to procure specific information regarding Doyle's habits. In so doing she clearly associated herself with the illegal plan. Appellant completed the offense, for both himself and his wife, when, on the day following the initial conversation, he delivered $500 to the undercover officer to perform the killing. This was an overt act in furtherance of the agreement. There was additional purposeful behavior in furtherance of the scheme, when appellant pointed out Doyle's work place to the police officer posing as the actual assassin. The evidence is sufficient to warrant the verdict of guilty.

Appellant appears to argue that the fact that one of the conspirators was a police officer should demonstrate conclusively the insufficiency of evidence or the inapplicability of the statute. This argument was rejected in *Garcia v. State* (1979) Ind., 394 N.E.2d 106. There we held that it was no defense to a conspiracy charge under our present statute that the person with whom the accused person is alleged to have conspired is an undercover police agent feigning cooperation and agreement.

(2) Appellant next contends that the defense of entrapment was established as a matter of law. This defense is governed by statute which provides:

"Entrapment.—(a) It is a defense that:
(1) The prohibited conduct of the person was the product of a law-enforcement officer, or his agent, using persuasion or other means likely to cause the person to engage in the conduct; and
(2) The person was not predisposed to commit the offense.

"(b) Conduct merely affording a person an opportunity to commit the offense does not constitute entrapment." Ind. Code § 35-41-3-9 (Burns 1979)

When the defense of entrapment has been raised, as it was in this case by the testimony of the undercover police officer, the successful prosecution of the case becomes dependent upon whether the State can prove that the prohibited conduct of the accused was not the product of the efforts of the law enforcement official involved or that the accused was predisposed to engage in such conduct anyway. *Hardin v. State* (1976), 265 Ind. 635, 358 N.E.2d 134.

But for the fact, unknown to appellant at the time, that the man posing as an illegal drug dealer was an undercover policeman, the evidence presented at the trial, when taken as a whole, would have warranted a verdict of guilty against that man as a co-conspirator. However, the jury could also have consistently inferred that the conversation supplied by him in the dining room of appellant's house did not produce the plan or purpose to kill Doyle. The trier of fact could reasonably have concluded that the plan was formulated and joined in by appellant because of his personal anger and frustration at the injury he felt from the newspaper article, made more violent and bitter by his wife's insistence and enthusiasm for some form of revenge. Appellant rejected the idea of seeing a lawyer, and requested instead that the undercover policeman undertake an "extra service," and angrily said that he wanted Doyle "shut up." The officer asked then what he meant by shutting somebody up. Appellant responded that "he wanted to stop this kind of malicious slander." The officer then flatly stated, "just by breaking their legs and arms necessarily wouldn't shut them up." Appellant's wife agreed and said "that's right." Appellant then asked the undercover officer again if he would like to perform an "extra service." The officer asked him what he meant by that. It was then that appellant said he wanted Doyle killed.

Appellant argues that the statement of the officer regarding the breaking of arms and legs implanted the idea of killing into his mind and in so doing produced the plan to kill Doyle. Two reasons demonstrate the invalidity of this position. First, appellant used the phrase "extra service" both before and after the officer's suggestive comment. It served to convey his meaning on both occasions, and it is reasonable to infer that it carried the same meaning on both occasions, i.e., to kill.

Second, in order for the suggestive comment of the officer to have produced prohibited conduct, it must have had a persuasive or other force causing that conduct. The comment had no such force. It was not a question calling for an answer, but a flat logical assertion, and appellant's wife immediately agreed to it. When appellant thereafter asked the officer again whether he would do an "extra service," and upon inquiry translated that request into his desire to have Doyle killed, that which was activating him was his own thoughtful consideration and his desire to achieve revenge, and not the comment of the officer. We are satisfied that evidence was sufficient to show that appellant was not "innocently lured and enticed to commit the illegal act." *Gray v. State* (1967), 249 Ind. 629, 231 N.E.2d 793.

Appellant also isolates two points in the record which he contends show that he tried to disassociate himself from the idea of killing Doyle, but was persuaded by the undercover officers from doing so. At one point appellant told the agents in the course of a telephone conversation to hold off. In context this request was made to give appellant time to gather the specific information regarding the victim. It was therefore in furtherance of the scheme and not contrary to it. At the other point in the record indicated by appellant we find no inference relative to this contention.

The evidence was sufficient to negate the defense of entrapment. The defense was, therefore, not established as a matter of law.

The conviction is affirmed.

GIVAN, C.J., and HUNTER, PRENTICE and PIVARNIK, JJ., concur.

Cases relating to Chapter 13
CAPACITY AND DEFENSES

102 Wash.2d 19
STATE of Washington, Respondent
v.
Q.D. and M.S., b.d. 11/4/70, Appellants.
Supreme Court of Washington, En Banc.
685 P.2d 557
June 14, 1984.

DIMMICK, Justice.

Two juveniles appeal from separate adjudications which found that they had committed offenses which if committed by an adult would be crimes. The Court of Appeals, in these consolidated appeals, certified to this court the questions whether the statutory presumption of infant incapacity, RCW 9A.04.050,1 applies to juvenile adjudications, and if it does, what standard of proof is required to rebut the presumption. Each defendant argues that the trial court's determinations of capacity were erroneous under any standard. Appellant Q.D. additionally argues that there was insufficient evidence to convict him of trespass in the first degree. Appellant M.S. contends that the imposition of a penalty under the crime victims' compensation act is either inapplicable or discretionary in juvenile court dispositions.

We hold that (1) RCW 9A.04.050 applies to juvenile adjudications, (2) the standard of proof necessary to rebut the presumption of incapacity is clear and convincing proof, (3) the State proved that M.S. possessed requisite capacity, but we do not reach the issue in Q.D.'s case because (4) there

was insufficient evidence of entry to convict Q.D. of trespass, and (5) the imposition of a crime victims' compensation act penalty applies to juvenile court dispositions. Accordingly, Q.D.'s conviction is reversed, and M.S.'s conviction and disposition are affirmed.

Appellant Q.D. was found to have capacity per RCW 9A.04.050 in a pretrial hearing. He was 11½ years old at the time of the alleged offense. At trial a different judge determined he had committed trespass in the first degree. The evidence introduced to show capacity consisted of testimony from a caseworker and a detective who had worked with him in connection with this plea of guilty to a burglary committed at age 10 years. The caseworker testified that Q.D. was familiar with the justice system, was street wise, and that he used his age as a shield. The detective told the court that Q.D. was cooperative in the burglary investigation, and he appeared to know his rights. The evidence in the guilt phase consisted of testimony from the principal and a custodial engineer of the school in which Q.D. was charged with trespass. The engineer testified that he saw Q.D. sitting on the school

655

grounds about 2 p.m. playing with some keys that looked like the set belonging to the night custodian. When the engineer checked his desk which was in an unlocked office, he found that the keys were missing, as was the burglar alarm key. The engineer could not be certain that he had seen the keys since the morning. He called the principal and they brought Q.D. into the office. When Q.D. arose from the chair he had been sitting on in the office, the burglar alarm key was discovered on a radiator behind the chair.

Appellant M.S., in a single proceeding, was found to have capacity and to have committed indecent liberties on a 4½-year-old child for whom she was babysitting. Evidence included the testimony of the victim, the victim's mother, a physician who had examined the victim, and a social worker who had interviewed the victim. M.S. was less than 3 months away from being 12 years old at the time of the offense. The issue of capacity was first raised by the defendant in a motion to dismiss at the close of the State's evidence. The State argued that defendant's proximity to the age when capacity is assumed, the defendant's threats to the victim not to tell what had happened, and her secrecy in carrying out the act were ample proof of capacity. The trial judge, in his oral ruling finding capacity, stated that the responsibility entrusted to the defendant by the victim's mother and her own parents in permitting her to babysit showed a recognition of the defendant's maturity.

I
APPLICABILITY OF RCW 9A.04.050 TO JUVENILE COURTS

Counsel for both the State and the defendants urge us to hold that the infant incapacity defense in RCW 9A.04.050 applies to juvenile proceedings. We so hold.

At common law, children below the age of 7 were conclusively presumed to be incapable of committing crime, and children over the age of 14 were presumed capable and treated as adults. Children between these ages were rebuttably presumed incapable of committing crime. Washington codified these presumptions amending the age of conclusive incapacity to 7, and presumed capacity to 12 years of age. As recently as 1975, the Legislature again included the infancy defense in the criminal code. The purpose of the presumption is to protect from the criminal justice system those individuals of tender years who are less capable than adults of appreciating the wrongfulness of their behavior.

The infancy defense fell into disuse during the early part of the century with the advent of reforms intended to substitute treatment and rehabilitation for punishment of juvenile offenders. This *parens patriae* system, believed not to be a criminal one, had no need for the infancy defense.

The juvenile justice system in recent years has evolved from *parens patriae* scheme to one more akin to adult criminal proceedings. The United States Supreme Court has been critical of the *parens patriae* scheme as failing to provide safeguards due an adult criminal defendant, while subjecting the juvenile defendant to similar stigma, and possible loss of liberty. *See In re Gault*, 387 U.S. 1, 87 S.Ct. 1428, 18 L.Ed.2d 527 (1966); and *In re Winship*, 397 U.S. 358, 90 S.Ct. 1068, 25 L.Ed.2d 368 (1977). This court has acknowledged Washington's departure from a strictly *parens patriae* scheme to a more criminal one, involving both rehabilitation and punishment. *In re*

Smiley, 96 Wash.2d 650, 640 P.2d 7 (1982). Being a criminal defense, RCW 9A.04.050 should be available to juvenile proceedings that are criminal in nature.

The principles of construction of criminal statutes, made necessary by our recognition of the criminal nature of juvenile court proceedings, also compel us to conclude that RCW 9A.04.050 applies to proceedings in juvenile courts.

A finding that RCW 9A.04.050 does not apply to juvenile courts would render that statute meaningless or superfluous contrary to rules of construction. *See Avlonitis v. Seattle Dist Ct.,* 97 Wash.2d 131, 641 P.2d 169, 646 P.2d 128 (1982). Juvenile courts have exclusive jurisdiction over all individuals under the chronological age of 18 who have committed acts designated criminal if committed by an adult. RCW 13.04.011(1), .030(6); RCW 13.40.020(15). Declination of jurisdiction and transfer to adult court is limited to instances where it is in the best interest of the juvenile or the public. *State v. Holland,* 98 Wash.2d 507, 656 P.2d 1056 (1983). Thus, all juveniles who can avail themselves of the infancy defense will come under the jurisdiction of the juvenile court, and most will remain there. Implied statutory repeals are found not to exist where the two statutes can be reconciled and given effect. Goals of the Juvenile Justice Act of 1977 include accountability for criminal behavior and punishment commensurate with age and crime. RCW 13.40.010. A goal of the criminal code is to safeguard conduct that is not culpable. RCW 9A.04.020. The infancy defense which excludes from criminal condemnation persons not capable of culpable, criminal acts, is consistent with the overlapping goals of the Juvenile Justice Act of 1977 and the Washington Criminal Code.

II
STANDARD OF PROOF UNDER RCW 9A.04.050

The State has the burden of rebutting the statutory presumption of incapacity of juveniles age 8 and less than 12 years. Capacity must be found to exist separate from the specific mental element of the crime charged. While capacity is similar to the mental element of a specific crime or offense, it is not an element of the offense, but is rather a general determination that the individual understood the act and its wrongfulness. Both defendants liken the incapacity presumption to a jurisdictional presumption. Were capacity an element of the crime, proof beyond a reasonable doubt would be required. *In re Winship, supra; State v. Roberts,* 88 Wash.2d 337, 562 P.2d 1259 (1977). But capacity, not being an element of the crime, does not require as stringent a standard of proof.

Few jurisdictions have ruled on the appropriate standard of proof necessary to rebut the presumption of incapacity, and fewer still have discussed their reasoning for preferring one standard over another. It appears that other states have split between requiring proof beyond a reasonable doubt, and clear and convincing proof.

Our recent discussion of the standard of proof to be applied in involuntary commitment proceedings offers guidance. In *Dunner v. McLaughlin,* 100 Wash.2d 832, 676 P.2d 444 (1984), we held that the burden of proof should be by clear, cogent and convincing evidence. In so holding, we recognized that the preponderance of the evidence standard was inadequate, but the proof beyond a reasonable doubt standard imposed a burden which, as a practical matter, was unreasonably difficult, thus undercutting the State's legitimate interests.

The Legislature, by requiring the State to rebut the presumption of incapacity, has assumed a greater burden than the minimal proof imposed by the preponderance of the evidence standard. On the other hand, to require the State to prove capacity beyond a reasonable doubt when the State must also prove the specific mental element of the charged offense by the same standard, is unnecessarily duplicative. Frequently, the same facts required to prove mens rea will be probative of capacity, yet the overlap is not complete. Capacity to be culpable must exist in order to maintain the specific mental element of the charged offense. Once the generalized determination of capacity is found, the State must prove beyond a reasonable doubt that the juvenile defendant possessed the specific mental element. The clear and convincing standard reflects the State's assumption of a greater burden than does the preponderance of the evidence standard. At the same time, the liberty interest of the juvenile is fully protected by the requirement of proof beyond a reasonable doubt of the specific mental element. We therefore require the State to rebut the presumption of incapacity by clear and convincing evidence.

III
EVIDENCE OF CAPACITY

We do not need to reach the question of whether there was substantial evidence to show that Q.D. understood the act of trespass or understood it to be wrong, as we reverse on other grounds. (See part IV of this opinion.) Nevertheless, a discussion of capacity in this case may prove instructive to trial courts. Q.D. argues that the evidence showed only that he was familiar with the juvenile system through his previous plea of guilty to a burglary charge, but did not show he understood the act and wrongfulness of trespass. The language of RCW 9A.04.050 clearly indicates that a capacity determination must be made in reference to the specific act charged: "understand *the act*...and to know that *it* was wrong." (Italics ours.) If Q.D. is correct that the evidence showed no more than a general understanding of the justice system, he would be correct in concluding that the State did not show an understanding and knowing wrongfulness of trespass. In addition, an understanding of the wrongfulness of burglary does not alone establish capacity in regard to trespass. While both offenses include entry or unlawfully remaining in a building, burglary also requires an intent to commit a crime against a person or property therein. *Compare* RCW 9A.52.030 *with* RCW 9A.52.070. Defendant may well understand that it is wrong to enter a locked building with the intention of committing a crime, but not know that entering an unlocked school building was wrong.

The issue of capacity was first raised on M.S.'s motion to dismiss at the end of the trial. The judge stated in response to arguments of counsel that he was persuaded by the confidence in defendant's maturity held by the mother of the victim and her own parents in permitting her to assume the responsibility for babysitting. Contrary to defendant's arguments that the trial judge created a *prima facie* proof of capacity based solely on babysitting, there was other evidence to support his finding of capacity. The defendant waited until she and the victim were alone evidencing a desire for secrecy. The defendant later admonished the victim not to tell what happened, further supporting the finding that the defendant knew the act was wrong. Lastly, the defendant was less than 3 months from the age at which capacity is presumed to exist. There was clear and convincing circumstantial evidence that M.S. understood the act of indecent liberties and knew it to be wrong.

Finally, in response to the parties' requests for guidelines concerning the forum of the capacity hearing, we find the separate hearing in Q.D.'s case, and the single hearing of capacity and the substantive charge in M.S.'s case to be appropriate under the different circumstances in each. In Q.D.'s case, prior criminal history was the basis for attempting to prove capacity, and thus a separate hearing avoided prejudice. In M.S.'s case, the facts of the offense were offered to show capacity, and a separate hearing would be unduly repetitive. Rather than delineating a rigid rule, the circumstances should dictate whether a separate hearing is appropriate. *See State v. Koloske,* 100 Wash.2d 889, 676 P.2d 456 (1984), where we declined endorsement of a fixed forum for ruling on admissibility of impeachment evidence. In the event that it is necessary to show capacity by proof of both criminal history and the particular facts of the offense charged, caution should be employed to prevent the introduction of evidence of prior history from prejudicing the determination on the merits.

IV

SUFFICIENCY OF EVIDENCE
OF TRESPASS

Q.D. contends that the evidence introduced to show trespass in the first degree was insufficient to show he entered or remained unlawfully in the building, and, at most, showed possession of recently stolen goods. He argues that possession of recently stolen goods, without other evidence of guilt, is insufficient to show entry in a trespass charge just as it is in burglary. We agree.

Recently, in *State v. Mace,* 97 Wash.2d 840, 650 P.2d 217 (1982), we reiterated the long-standing law in Washington that proof of possession of recently stolen property is not *prima facie* evidence of burglary unless accompanied by other evidence of guilt. *See State v. Garske,* 74 Wash.2d 901, 447 P.2d 167 (1968); *State v. Portee,* 25 Wash.2d 246, 170 P.2d 326 (1946). Other evidence of guilt may include a false or improbable explanation of possession, flight, use of a fictitious name, or the presence of the accused near the scene of the crime. *State v. Mace, supra.* While Q.D. was on the school grounds with the keys, the keys were not known to be missing until he was seen with them, and they had last been seen several hours before in a desk in an unlocked office. Thus, both the absence of evidence that he was near the scene at a time proximate to the disappearance of the keys, and the absence of other evidence corroborative of guilt require us to conclude that there was insufficient evidence of trespass in the first degree. We therefore reverse Q.D.'s conviction.

V

APPLICABILITY OF RCW 7.68.035
TO JUVENILE PROCEEDINGS

After M.S. was found guilty, in addition to community supervision and community service, the court imposed a $50 assessment pursuant to RCW 7.68.035. Contrary to appellant's assertions, RCW 7.68, Victims of Crimes—Compensation, Assistance, applies to juvenile proceedings. At the time of M.S.'s disposition, the pertinent portions of the act read:

(1) Whenever any person is found guilty in any court of competent jurisdiction of having committed a crime,...there shall be imposed by the court upon such convicted person a penalty assessment of fifty dollars for a felony or gross misdemeanor and twenty-five dollars for a misdemeanor. The assessment shall be in addition to any other penalty or fine imposed by law.

...

(7) Penalty assessments under this Section shall also be imposed in juvenile offense dispositions under Title 13 RCW.

The Legislature later amended subdivision 7 by adding the sentence, "Upon motion of a party and a showing of good cause, the court may modify the penalty assessment in the disposition of juvenile offenses under Title 13 RCW." Laws of 1983, ch. 239, § 1.

The juvenile justice act provides:

The provisions of chapters 13.04 and 13.40 RCW, as now or hereafter amended, shall be the exclusive authority for the adjudication and disposition of juvenile offenders except where otherwise expressly provided. RCW 13.04.450.

The crime victims compensation act expressly and unambiguously provides for the application of the penalty in juvenile dispositions. Being clear on its face, and unambiguous, we need not interpret the language. *State v. McIntyre,* 92 Wash.2d 620, 600 P.2d 1009 (1979). While a general statute is usually subjugated to a specific stat-

ute, here the crime victims compensation act specifically and expressly addresses itself to the juvenile justice act thus prevailing over rules of statutory construction. *See State v. Sargent,* 36 Wash. App. 463, 674 P.2d 1268 (1984).

We are likewise not persuaded that the Legislature intended a discretionary application. The use of the word "shall" creates an imperative obligation unless a different legislative intent can be discerned. *State v. Bryan,* 93 Wash.2d 177, 606 P.2d 1228 (1980). The subsequent amendment to subdivision 7 permits the court, on a showing of good cause, to modify the assessment. Significantly, the Legislature did not substitute "may" for "shall," and in addition, impliedly required the imposition of the assessment preliminary to the permissive modification upon the party's motion and showing of good cause. *State v. Sargent, supra.*

CONCLUSION

The infancy defense, codified in RCW 9A.04.050 applies to juvenile proceedings. The proof that a juvenile of 8 years and less than 12 years understood the charged act and knew it to be wrong is by clear and convincing evidence. Because the State met this burden in M.S.'s case, the finding that she committed indecent liberties is affirmed. M.S.'s disposition, which included a $50 penalty assessment under RCW 7.68.035, applicable in a juvenile proceeding, is likewise affirmed. Because the State failed to prove Q.D.'s entry into the school building, his conviction is reversed.

WILLIAMS, C.J., and DOLLIVER, ROSELLINI, DORE, UTTER, PEARSON, and BRACHTENBACH, JJ., and CUNNINGHAM, J., Pro Tem., concur.

Larry Gene GRAHAM, Petitioner
v.
STATE of Tennessee, Respondent
Supreme Court of Tennessee
Jan. 31, 1977
Rehearing Denied Feb. 28, 1977
547 S.W.2d 531

OPINION

HENRY, Justice.

We granted certiorari in this criminal action to consider four significant questions, viz:

a. The right of an indigent criminal defendant, pleading not guilty by reason of insanity, to a psychiatric examination at state expense.

b. The admissibility of hospital records under the Uniform Business Records as Evidence Act (Sections 24-712, 24-715, T.C.A.) in a criminal action.

c. The correct test for determining the question of criminal responsibility.

d. The correct jury instruction with respect to the burden of proof in criminal prosecutions wherein insanity is pleaded as a defense.

I.
Factual Background

Petitioner was convicted of bank robbery, grand larceny and assault with intent to commit murder. All convictions grew out of a bizarre series of events that occurred in the Chattanooga vicinity on 14 October 1974.

Petitioner, a twenty-eight (28) year old man, with a history of mental disorders, marital difficulties and occupa-tional problems, was residing in Chattanooga with his parents. He had been married and was the father of five (5) children. The record suggests his wife's infidelity; and that she lost her life in an automobile wreck while out with other men. The children ulti-mately were placed in a foster home by the Tennessee Department of Public Welfare (now Department of Human Services).

He had been treated in the psychi-atric ward of Baroness Erlanger Hospi-tal from May 19, 1973, to June 19, 1973, with diagnosis of "paranoid state," followed by treatment at Cen-tral State Psychiatric Hospital. He was again treated at Baroness Erlanger from February 15, 1974 to February 19, 1974, for the same malady, fol-lowed by treatment at Moccasin Bend Psychiatric Hospital.

On 14 October 1974, he went to the office of Dr. J.S. Cheatham, who had treated him while a patient at Baroness Erlanger, but the doctor was out. After leaving the doctor's office, he pur-chased and consumed a half pint of whiskey. It should be noted that peti-tioner was a problem drinker, if not an alcoholic.

Thus fortified he began his foray. First he went to a hardware store located in the vicinity of his home, where his father formerly worked, where he normally traded, and whose owner had known him for many years.

There, in plain view, after pricing a shotgun, he took the gun and two boxes of shells and openly and slowly walked out of the store with them.

Next he went to a service station where he was known by one of the attendants and, after being refused credit, brandished the stolen shotgun and ordered the attendant to fill up his automobile. After the attendant complied, he sped off before the cap could be replaced on the gasoline tank. But, as he left he "throwed out a billfold" containing full identification.

He then drove out the Red Bank branch of Hamilton Bank where he entered the banking room and, without mask or other disguise, robbed a teller of approximately $2400, sauntered out and drove off at a normal rate of speed.

By this time the police had been alerted and ultimately he was pursued by a policeman. He stopped his car and the police car stopped behind him. As the policeman got out of his car petitioner shot and wounded him, rolled him over to the side of the road, and kicked him a few times. He then took charge of the police car and drove it around for a short time with the blue light flashing and rotating. He returned, got back in his own car, and started toward Dayton. He surrendered to the Rhea County Sheriff in the vicinity of Graysville. Subsequently, he made a full confession.

Petitioner's sole defense was "not guilty by reason of insanity."

After his conviction he appealed to the Court of Criminal Appeals and that Court affirmed the verdict of the jury and the judgment of the trial court thereon.

No assignment challenges the sufficiency of the evidence. Indeed, the petitioner, testifying in his own behalf, admitted each offense. The sole issues before the Court are those hereinabove set forth.

II.
Right to Psychiatric Examination

Prior to the trial petitioner's court appointed counsel moved the Court for an examination by a private psychiatrist, at State expense. The trial judge's denial of this motion forms the basis of petitioner's first assignment in this Court.

There is no statutory predicate for the appointment of a private psychiatrist. Section 33-708(a), T.C.A., provides as follows:

> When a person charged with a criminal offense is believed to be incompetent to stand trial, or there is a question as to his mental capacity at the time of the commission of the crime, the criminal or circuit court judge before whom the case is to be tried may, upon his own motion or upon petition by the district attorney general or by the attorney for the defendant and after hearing, order the defendant to be evaluated on an outpatient basis by the *community mental health center* designated by the commissioner to serve the court or, if the evaluation cannot be made by the center, on an outpatient basis by the *state hospital* or the state supported hospital designated by the commissioner to serve the court. If in the opinion of those performing the mental health evaluation, further evaluation is needed, the court may order the defendant hospitalized, and if in a *state hospital or state supported hospital*, in the custody of the commissioner for not more than thirty (30) days for the sole purpose of further evaluation. (Emphasis supplied.)

It will be noted that the statute is discretionary, since it in no sense requires such an examination, nor does it specify that the examination be conducted by a psychiatrist as opposed to a psychologist, nor does it contemplate the employment of a private practitioner.

Since there is no statutory sanction for the employment of a private psychiatrist at state expense, we look to case law for precedent. Our investigation into the law leads us to the conclusion that this is an area wherein the law has not been fully and finally settled. There is an apparent cleavage, with no qualitative or quantitative preponderance. See annotation, *Right of Indigent Defendant in Criminal Case to Aid of State by Appointment of Investigator or Expert,* 34 A.L.R.3d 1256, and more particularly, Sections 6(c) and (d).

Pertinent to the issue is the rationale of *Ross v. Moffitt,* 417 U.S. 600, 94 S.Ct. 2437, 41 L.Ed.2d 341 (1974), wherein the Court was dealing with the due process right of an indigent defendant to a second tier appellate review. There the Court said:

> The Fourteenth Amendment "does not require absolute equality or precisely equal advantages" (citations omitted), nor does it require the State to "equalize economic conditions." 417 U.S. at 612, 94 S.Ct. at 2444.

In *Collins v. State,* 506 S.W.2d 179 (Tenn.Cr.App.1973), the defendant, prior to preliminary hearing, was committed to Central State Psychiatric Hospital for observation and a report thereof was submitted to the Court. Subsequently, both at a hearing to determine competency to stand trial and at the main trial, the reporting psychiatrist testified for the defendant, although "some of his testimony was damaging." 506 S.W.2d at 187. The trial judge rejected a motion to appoint a private psychiatrist, at state expense, and the Court affirmed, holding that the defendant had no right to a "psychiatric advocate."

The *Collins* court relied in part on *United States ex rel. Smith v. Baldi,* 344 U.S. 561, 73 S.Ct. 391, 97 L.Ed. 549 (1953), which held that the state was not required to appoint a psychiatrist to make a pre-trial examination of an indigent patient.

See also Crum v. State, 530 S.W.2d 103 (Tenn.Cr.App. 1975).

Essentially this is a matter that addresses itself to the judgment and discretion of the legislature. Thus far it has not seen fit to provide such services to indigent defendants.

In this particular case the defendant called as a witness a highly qualified psychiatrist whose testimony fully supported his plea of insanity. We cannot see that he was prejudiced by the action of the trial judge, in law or in fact.

We hold that an indigent defendant does not have a right under the federal or state constitution, to the services of a private psychiatrist, at state expense.

* * *

We hold that the trial court committed prejudicial and reversible error in declining to admit the Erlanger Hospital records for general evidentiary purposes.

IV.
Tests of Criminal Responsibility

The issue of the defendant's criminal responsibility is fairly raised by the pleadings and proof. We discuss the various tests.

A. *M'Naghten Rules*

M'Naghten's Case, 1 C. & K. 130, 10 CL. & F. 200, 8 Eng.Rep. 718, was decided by the House of Lords in 1843.

Daniel M'Naghten had murdered Edward Drummond, the secretary to Sir Robert Peel, the then Prime Minister of England. In the ensuing trial the jury found him to be "not guilty by reason of insanity." History records that the Queen and her subjects were incensed, and a great hue and cry resounded throughout the realm. The matter was debated in the House of Lords and it was determined that they should "take the opinion of the Judges on the law governing such cases." Five questions were put to the 15 judges of England and the rules that emerged, since known as the *M'Naghten* rules, were as follows:

[T]o establish a defence on the ground of insanity, it must be clearly proved that, at the time of the committing of the act, the party accused was labouring under such a defect of reason, from disease of the mind, as *not to know the nature and quality of the act* he was doing; or, if he did know it, that he did not know he was doing what was wrong. (Emphasis supplied.) 8 Eng.Rep. at 722.

It will be noted that we refer to the *M'Naghten* rules. We do this because scholarly texts and the more precise judicial opinions use this terminology, and correctly so because there are *two* rules. The failure of the courts of some jurisdictions, including Tennessee, to recognize this has caused the rules to become called the *M'Naghten* rules, with a resulting confusing and narrowing of the original rules.

There are two *M'Naghten* tests: (1) knowledge of the nature and quality of the act and (2) knowledge of its wrongfulness. These criteria are expressed in the conjunctive in that it must be shown that the defendant knew right from wrong and knew the nature and quality of the act, in order to convict of a crime while laboring under a defect of reason or disease of the mind. If a defendant does not know the nature and quality of the act he is insane; if he knows this but does not know right from wrong, he is insane.

The failure to recognize and apply both prongs of this two-prong test operates to narrow the rules.

In Guttmacher & Weihofen, Psychiatry and the Law, Norton & Co. (1952) at page 404, the effect of applying only the right and wrong dichotomy, is expressed thusly:

A defendant may remember many details of his act. The prosecutor may emphasize this fact, may bring out all the little details that the defendant can recall, and may argue from this that the accused has been shown to know what he was doing. But memory of details is not knowledge of the *nature and quality of the act. That calls for something deeper and more vital.* (Emphasis supplied.)

Brakel and Rock, in an American Bar Foundation study, captioned The Mentally Disabled and the Law, Revised Edition (2nd) 1971, at pages 379-80, pose the problem thusly:

Despite the inclusion of alternative tests in the original *M'Naghten* case, the most common form in which the *M'Naghten* test now appears is *"whether the defendant had the capacity to know right from wrong in respect to the particular act charged."* Most jurisdictions which apply *M'Naghten* seem to assume that the requirement of "knowing the nature and quality of the act" adds nothing to the right-wrong test. A cogent argument might be made that a person may be able to retain intellectual knowledge of right and wrong and yet not understand the *"nature and quality"* of his act (i.e., its social significance). (Emphasis supplied.)

It is of interest to note that Tennessee has adhered consistently to so much of *M'Naghten* as relates to "right and wrong." No reported decision of this Court, in any criminal case, has discussed the "nature and quality" portion of the rules.

In their 1971 study Brakel & Rock, at page 380, state that "[t]oday *M'Naghten* is the sole test of criminal responsibility in fewer than half of the states. Reference to 21 Am.Jur.2d, Criminal Law, Sec. 33 and an annotation appearing in 45 A.L.R.2d at 1447, will indicate that *possibly* as many as twenty-seven (27)[1] American jurisdictions basically apply *M'Naghten*.

Numerous criticisms of *M'Naghten* have surfaced in recent years. After pointing out that "[t]he most cogent criticism of the rules is that they fail to aid in the identification of many persons accused of crime who suffer from serious mental disorders," the Tennessee Law Revision Commission, in its Proposed Final Draft, Tennessee Code of Criminal Procedure, 1973, on page 38 lists other "valid criticisms":

(1) the concept of "right and wrong" is essentially an ethical or moral concept which forces the witnesses and decisionmaker to make moral, rather than medical, social, and legal judgments;

---

1. Arizona, Arkansas, California, Delaware, Florida, Georgia, Hawaii, Iowa, Kansas, Louisiana, Minnesota, Mississippi, Nebraska, Nevada, New Jersey, New Mexico, New York, North Carolina, North Dakota, Oklahoma, Oregon, Rhode Island, South Carolina, South Dakota, Tennessee, Washington and Wyoming.

(2) the rules evolved at a time when "faculty psychology" held sway, and today the mind is known not to be neatly compartmentalized; and

(3) the rules may well have been intended to apply only to one type of illness, that characterized by delusions.

We think that unquestionably the rules tend to enforce outmoded and erroneous psychological theories, tend to limit or distort psychiatric testimony, focus on the ability to distinguish between right and wrong, ignoring the individual's ability to exercise self-control; focus on cognition and ignore the volitional aspects of personality; and punish persons for conduct beyond their capacity of control.

In a word, its application is an impediment to the fair trial that is a part of the birthright of every American citizen.

We hold with Justice Cardozo:

If insanity is not to be a defense, let us say so frankly and even brutally, but let us not mock ourselves with a definition that palters with reality. Such a method is neither good morals nor good science nor good law.

B. *The Irresistible Impulse Test*

Under this test a criminal defendant is said to be relieved of criminal responsibility when his mental condition is such as to deprive him of his willpower to resist the impulse to commit the crime, despite his knowledge of whether the act is right or wrong. This test does not stand alone as a test for insanity in any jurisdiction, and we reject it, believing that it is not sufficiently comprehensive.

C. *The Product Rule (Durham)*

Under this rule a defendant is excused from criminal responsibility when his act was "the product of mental disease or mental defect." This test was announced in *Durham v. United States,* 94 U.S.App.D.C. 228, 214 F.2d 862 (1954); however, it was subsequently obliterated by the same Circuit in *United States v. Brawner,* 153 U.S.App.D.C. 1, 471 F.2d 969 (1972). We do not feel that this test is sufficiently complete or comprehensive to justify its adoption.

D. *Model Penal Code*

The American Law Institute in its Model Penal Code, Proposed Official Draft, Section 4.02(1) proposes the following standard:

(1) A person is not responsible for criminal conduct if at the time of such conduct as a result of mental disease or defect he lacks substantial capacity either to appreciate the criminality [wrongfulness] of his conduct or to conform his conduct to the requirements of law.

(2) As used in this Article, the terms 'mental disease or defect' do not include an abnormality manifested only by repeated criminal or otherwise antisocial conduct.

Reference to Section 39-601 of the Proposed Final Draft of the Tennessee Criminal Code and Code of Criminal Procedure will reveal substantially the same provision.[2] The Comment to the Model Penal Code accepts the theory of the combined *M'Naghten* and irresistible impulse tests that take "account of the impairment of volitional capacity no less than impairment of cognition," but it rejects both of these tests as being too narrow.

2. Model Penal Code, Section 4.01, Comments, at 156-59.

It is obvious that the phrase "to appreciate the criminality of his conduct" in the Model Penal Code is a substitute for the *M'Naghten* clause "to know the nature and quality of the act he was doing."

While we recognize that this test, like any other test of insanity, is not perfect and will itself produce problems, we are persuaded that it is the best test of insanity in existence today, combining as it does, the essential elements of cognition, volition and capacity to control behavior. In actuality it is essentially a refinement and restatement of the full *M'Naghten* rules.

E. *The M'Naghten Rule in Tennessee*

Tennessee case law, pertinent to the issue of criminal responsibility, began with *Dove v. State,* 50 Tenn. 348 (1871) and evolved in consistent fashion, with emphasis being placed upon the "right from wrong" aspects of the *M'Naghten* rules.

The often-cited case of *Spurlock v. State,* 212 Tenn. 132, 368 S.W.2d 299 (1963) marks the last time this rule came under careful scrutiny in this Court. The Court correctly noted that the *M'Naghten* Rule "is followed by every State except one (*State v. Pike,* 49 N.H. 399), and every Federal Circuit except two (Durham and Currens [*United States v. Currens,* 290 F.2d 751, 3rd Cir.])...." 212 Tenn. at 140, 368 S.W.2d at 303.

In the intervening thirteen (13) years, the rule of *M'Naghten* has been substantially eroded. As heretofore pointed out, as a maximum, it is followed only by twenty-seven (27) state jurisdictions. Further reference to the same A.L.R. and American Jurisprudence citations as those contained in Subsection A of this Section of this opinion, will reveal that the ALI Penal Code test has been adopted in at least seventeen (17) state jurisdictions[3] and in all the federal circuits except the First.

F. Federal Cases

We look briefly at the federal jurisdictions.

Since *Spurlock, supra,* the District of Columbia departed from the *Durham* Rule and adopted a variation of the tests proposed by the American Law Institute in its Model Penal Code. *United States v. Brawner,* 153 U.S.App.D.C. 1, 471 F.2d 969 (1972). *See also Bethea v. U.S.,* 365 A.2d 64 (D.C.App. 1976). The rule announced in *United States v. Currens,* 290 F.2d 751 (1961), a modified version of the Model Penal Code, continues in effect in the Third Circuit.

Six months after *Spurlock* the 10th Circuit handed down its decision in *Wion v. United States,* 325 F.2d 420 (10th Cir. 1963). Judge Murrah, writing for the Court in adopting Section 4.01(1) of the ALI Model Penal Code, stated:

We think this simple test of criminal responsibility allows the behavioral scientists "full freedom to put their professional findings and conclusions before the court and jury * * *." (Citations omitted.) "[e]ven under the right-wrong test, no evidence should be excluded which reasonably tends to show the mental condition of the defendant at the time of the offense." (Citation omitted.) This should go far toward bridging the gulf between psychiatry and the law, if indeed there is

3. Alaska, Connecticut, Idaho, Illinois, Indiana, Kentucky, Maine, Maryland, Massachusetts, Missouri, Montana, Ohio, Texas, Vermont, West Virginia, Wisconsin and District of Columbia.

one, and it will also give the trial judge a definition which he can articulate to the lay jury. 325 F.2d at 430.

In 1966 the Second Circuit joined the parade of jurisdictions moving toward the ALI Model Penal Code. In *United States v. Freeman,* 357 F.2d 606 (2nd Cir. 1966), Judge Kaufman set the moral tone and the underlying philosophy of the opinion as follows:

The criminal law it has been said, is an expression of the moral sense of the community. The fact that the law has, for centuries, regarded certain wrongdoers as improper subjects for punishment is a testament to the extent to which that moral sense has developed. Thus, society has recognized over the years that none of the three asserted purposes of the criminal law—rehabilitation, deterrence and retribution—is satisfied when the truly irresponsible, those who lack substantial capacity to control their actions, are punished. 357 F.2d at 615.

The court, after a scholarly and elaborate discussion of the *M'Naghten* Rules, the history of their adoption, the numerous vices inherent in them, and after discussing other rules, traced the history of the formulation of the ALI Model Penal Code and concluded that Section 4.01 was "the soundest [test] yet formulated" and adopted it as the standard of criminal responsibility in the Second Circuit. 357 F.2d at 622.

In 1972, the Eighth Circuit, in *United States v. Frazier,* 458 F.2d 911, 915 (8th Cir. 1972), adopted the full ALI Model Penal Code rule holding:

[W]e simply find that the substance of the ALI rule invites a broader medical-legal investigation, provides improved means for communication by medical specialists, offers a better basis for understanding of complex issues by triers of fact and overall serves the desired end in the administration of our criminal laws. 458 F.2d at 917.

The Seventh Circuit, in 1967, in *United States v. Shapiro,* 383 F.2d 680, 685 (7th Cir. 1967) (en banc), adopting the full ALI rule, but substituting the word "wrongfulness" in the place of "criminality" so that the rule requires an appreciation of the wrongfulness of conduct as opposed to its criminality.

The following year (1968), the Fourth Circuit in *United States v. Chandler,* 393 F.2d 920 (4th Cir. 1968), in an opinion by Chief Judge Haynsworth, rejected the *M'Naghten* test and adopted the full Model Penal Code Rule, observing that:

The American Law Institute's formulation has achieved wide acceptance....It substantially meets all of the criticism of the old rules and remedies their presently apparent deficiencies. It avoids the misunderstandings inherent in an undiscriminating use of the Durham prescription. For the present, for indiscriminate application, it is, in our opinion, the preferred formulation. With appropriate balance between cognition and volition, it demands an unrestricted inquiry into the whole personality of a defendant who surmounts the threshold question of doubt of his responsibility. Its verbiage is understandable by psychiatrists; it imposes no limitation upon their testimony, and yet, to a substantial extent, it avoids a diagnostic approach and leaves the jury free to make its findings in terms of a standard which society prescribes and juries may apply. 393 F.2d at 926.

The Fifth Circuit in *Blake v. United States,* 407 F.2d 908 (5th Cir. 1969), in a most excellent opinion by Judge Griffin Bell, recognizing the number of federal jurisdictions that had adopted the Model Penal Code, and stressing the value of uniformity, adopted the full Code, or both paragraphs of Section 4.01 (*See supra,* and Sec. V, *infra.*)

The opinion of the Sixth Circuit in *United States v. Smith,* 404 F.2d 720 (6th Cir. 1968) has come under our particular scrutiny. There the Court, in a most excellent opinion by Judge Edwards, made the following apt observation:

The primary distinction between the Currens test as formulated by Judge Biggs and the ALI formulation is that the ALI retains specific reference to the *M'Naghten* test of knowledge of the wrongfulness of the act committed. Of course, the problem with *M'Naghten* as a test of insanity was that it defined a very limited class of the insane. *M'Naghten* was certainly deficient as an exclusive test. But the ALI test eliminates the exclusive character of *M'Naghten* while retaining its substance as one of the tests of criminal responsibility. We do not regard this difference as a critical one. 404 F.2d at 726.

The Court adopted the first paragraph of the Model Penal Code, classifying it as "a test which a jury will readily comprehend; one which comports with and makes available modern scientific knowledge and one which may serve to aid the continuing development of the federal law," 404 F.2d at 727, and outlined questions for jury consideration relating to the criminal responsibility of a defendant pleading insanity as follows:

(1) Was he suffering from a mental illness at the time of the commission of the crime?

(2) Was that illness such as to prevent his knowing the wrongfulness of his act?

(3) Was the mental illness such as to render him substantially incapable of conforming his conduct to the requirements of the law he is charged with violating? *Ibid.*

Then the Court observes that "[a] negative finding as to the first question or negative findings as to both the second and third questions would require rejection of the insanity defense. An affirmative finding as to the first question, plus an affirmative finding as to either the second or third question, would require a jury verdict of not guilty' because of defendant's lack of criminal responsibility." *Ibid.*

We approve these questions since they succinctly state the precise issues that would be raised under the application of the Model Penal Code.

In *Spurlock, supra,* the Court followed *Andersen v. United States,* 237 F.2d 118, decided by the Ninth Circuit in 1956.

In *Wade v. United States,* 426 F.2d 64 (9th Cir. 1970) (en banc), adopted § 4.01(1) of the Model Penal Code.

V.
Adoption of ALI Rule

We adopt the American Law Institute Model Penal Code, Section 4.01 (1962), reading as follows:

(1) A person is not responsible for criminal conduct if at the time of such conduct as a result of mental disease or defect he lacks substantial capacity either to appreciate the wrongfulness of his conduct or to conform his conduct to the requirements of law.

(2) As used in this Article, the terms "mental disease or defect" do not include any abnormality manifested only by repeated criminal or otherwise antisocial conduct.

It will be noted that we have used the word "wrongfulness" in the place of "criminality" so that the rule requires an appreciation of the wrongfulness of conduct as opposed to its criminality. Trial judges will formulate charges which will accurately reflect this standard. In this connection, we expressly approve the questions set forth in *United States v. Smith,* 404 F.2d 720, at page 727 (6th Cir. 1968). We also invite attention to suggested charges in *United States v. Brawner,* 153 U.S.App.D.C. 1, 471 F.2d 969, at page 1008 (1972), and in *Wion v. United States,* 325 F.2d 420, at 430 (10th Cir. 1963). While we do not approve these referenced charges in their verbatim form, we do commend them as sources for the consideration of trial judges, along with existing Tennessee law. The so-called *M'Naghten* Rules will not be charged.

We adopt the Model Penal Code primarily because it is simpler to adopt a new rule in harmony with the all but universal federal rule and with the rule being adopted by a significant number of state jurisdictions, and emerge with a better based standard of criminal responsibility. We recognize that there is not a vast difference between the rule we adopt and the *M'Naghten* Rules as they should be applied. The new rule, however, does spell out the specifics of volition and the individual capacity to control his conduct. These elements inhered in the *M'Naghten* Rules, but it is evident that they were not applied. In the last analysis the determination of insanity is for the jury and when it has had the advantage of competent testimony—medical and lay—we are persuaded that under any rule, correct conclusions will be reached. We feel that the formulation of the Model Penal Code will be easier for juries to understand and will provide a simpler basis for jury instruction.

We feel that it is appropriate that we call attention to a deficiency in Tennessee law relating to the disposition of a criminal defendant found not guilty by reason of insanity. Sec. 33-709, T.C.A. provides that under these circumstances "the district attorney-general *may* seek hospitalization...if he determines hospitalization to be justified." (Emphasis supplied.)

We feel compelled to recommend to the Legislature that this particular provision of the law be changed so as to clothe the trial judge with the authority to cause the defendant to be committed to the custody of the Commissioner of Mental Health to be placed in an appropriate institution for custody, care and treatment. See Sec. 40-2321, Proposed Penal Code, Tennessee Law Revision Commission. We do not think the disposition of such a defendant should be left to the discretion of the district attorney-general.

The Model Penal Code standards will be applied (1) in all criminal trials or retrials beginning on or after the date of the release of this opinion and (2) in all cases wherein appropriate special requests were submitted during the trial of the action, or the issue otherwise was fairly raised in the trial court and supported by competent and credible testimony, and the conviction has not become final. Under no set of circumstances will the rule be applied to the advantage of any defendant whose conviction has already become final, i.e., where appellate review through the courts of this state has been completed.

VI.
Standard of Proof

The remaining assignment of error addresses itself to the burden of proof in those cases where the defendant enters a plea of "not guilty" by reason of insanity.

The rules are well established in this jurisdiction. If the evidence adduced either by the defendant or the State raises a reasonable doubt as to the defendant's sanity, the burden of proof on that issue shifts to the State. The State must then establish the defendant's sanity to the satisfaction of the jury and beyond a reasonable doubt. *Collins v. State,* 506 S.W.2d 179 (Tenn.Cr.App. 1973); *Covey v. State,* 504 S.W.2d 387 (Tenn.Cr.App. 1973). The jury should be instructed to that effect.

In the instant case the jury instruction was not as specific on this point as it should have been; however, the trial judge repeatedly charged the jury that it was the duty of the State to establish its case beyond a reasonable doubt. When consideration is given to the charge in its entirety, we are unable to say that it was prejudicially erroneous.

The judgments of the Court of Criminal Appeals and the Trial Court are reversed on the basis of the error in excluding medical records under the Uniform Business Records as Evidence Act, and this cause is remanded for retrial under the standards delineated in this opinion. We expressly do not reverse this particular case on the basis of the use of the M'Naghten Rules since the trial judge and the Court of Criminal Appeals correctly applied Tennessee Law. In this case, we have adopted a new standard of criminal responsibility considered by us to be more in keeping with the demand of contemporary American jurisprudence and more consonant with considerations of justice.

COOPER, C.J., and FONES, BROCK and HARBISON, JJ., concur.

OPINION ON PETITION TO REHEAR

HENRY, Justice.

The petition of the State of Tennessee for a rehearing is respectfully denied. Nothing in this opinion is subject to the construction that all cases wherein an insanity defense was interposed will *ipso facto* be subject to retrial.

James K. RIDLING, Appellant,

v.

STATE of Arkansas, Appellee.

Court of Appeals of Arkansas,
En Banc.

719 S.W.2d 1

Nov. 12, 1986.

MAYFIELD, Judge.

The appellant was convicted of selling a controlled substance, cocaine, and sentenced to ten years in the Arkansas Department of Correction. The case was tried twice, with the first trial resulting in a hung jury. We set out the following factual summary taken from the combined evidence of both trials.

During the summer and fall of 1983, undercover operations were conducted by the Arkansas State Police with regard to narcotic traffic in Crittenden County, Arkansas. The investigation was made in cooperation with the West Memphis Police Department. During the investigation, an individual was arrested who provided information and assisted in the investigation of another individual named Troy Powers. As a result, Powers and his girlfriend, who later became his wife, were arrested and charged with the sale of marijuana.

Powers agreed to become a confidential informer and there is testimony that he was "developed" by Officer Carter of the West Memphis Police Department and later "passed" to John Brackin, who was a criminal investigator with the Arkansas State Police. In August of 1983, at Brackin's direction, Powers purchased cocaine from an individual named Gene Guin. The following day, Powers had a conversation with the appellant in the Crittenden County Courthouse and was told that appellant knew he had purchased the cocaine from Guin. Powers told Trooper Brackin about this conversation and there is evidence that about this point in time the investigation of the officers had begun to focus on one Larry Rogers.

After the conversation between appellant and Troy Powers, whom appellant had known for many years, Powers began to build upon his relationship with appellant. Powers told appellant that he was being pursued by the internal revenue department and his ex-wife for money, that he was in bad financial shape, had a heart condition, and was trying to get a construction contract that could literally make or break him. He told the appellant that in order to cinch the construction contract he had to get some cocaine to give to the person in charge of approving the contract. Eventually, the appellant agreed to provide cocaine for Powers and his business associate, who was, in fact, Sergeant Larry Gleghorn of the Arkansas State Police, and the exchange of cocaine was made on September 2, 1983.

On October 5, 1983, the appellant received a telephone call from Lt. Jim Presley of the West Memphis Police Department requesting that he come to the police department to look at some property. This was admittedly a ruse and when the appellant arrived he was greeted by Lt. Presley, Trooper Brackin, and Officer Stevens of the Crittenden County Sheriff's Office and appellant was requested to sit down and view a video tape of the transaction of September 2, 1983.

Following the playing of the tape, appellant was informed that if he cooperated he (according to his version) would not be prosecuted but otherwise he would get 40 years to life. Appellant testified that he inquired about an attorney but was dissuaded from seeking legal advice and that he cooperated at that time with the police to the extent that he made a telephone call to Larry Rogers and arranged a narcotic purchase from him. The appellant also testified that he was allowed to leave with instructions to come back the next day to follow up on the transaction and that night he talked to an attorney and was told that immunity could not be arranged by the

police officers but would have to be arranged by the prosecuting attorney. So, the next day, according to appellant, he notified Sergeant Presley that he wanted an attorney to discuss with the police officers the offer of immunity and to advise him of his rights in that regard. The appellant testified that Presley advised him that a certain West Memphis attorney could be arranged for him if he would come to the police headquarters but, since this attorney was not familiar to the appellant, this offer was declined. Appellant said that he suggested another attorney but Presley said he would be arrested if he did not come to the police headquarters immediately. Appellant did not go to the police headquarters and he was subsequently arrested, tried, and convicted.

Appellant's main defense was entrapment. However, during the second trial the court would not allow appellant to introduce evidence of events that occurred after the transaction on September 2, 1983, when he sold the cocaine to the undercover agent, Sergeant Gleghorn. It was the appellant's contention that events after the September 2 transaction were admissible to show the entire scheme of things. He contended that this evidence would help establish his defense of entrapment by showing that the law enforcement officers desired to have him help them catch "bigger fish," to wit, Larry Rogers, and when he refused to help them in this regard, he was prosecuted for the September 2 transaction. The trial court explained that he had admitted the evidence in the first trial but was now convinced that it was not proper. As a result of the court's ruling, it was agreed that the evidence of the first trial relating to the events that occurred after September 2, 1983, which the appellant desired to proffer as proof on the issue of entrapment, could be made a part of the record.

We think this evidence was admissible and that the trial court erred in refusing to allow it to be introduced at the second trial. Ark.Stat.Ann. § 41-209 (Repl. 1977) provides as follows:

(1) It is an affirmative defense that the defendant was entrapped into committing an offense.

(2) Entrapment occurs when a law enforcement officer or any person acting in cooperation with him, induces the commission of an offense by using persuasion or other means likely to cause normallylaw-abiding persons to commit the offense. Conduct merely affording a person an opportunity to commit an offense does not constitute an entrapment.

In *Spears v. State,* 264 Ark. 83, 568 S.W.2d 492 (1978), the court said that under the provisions of the above statute:

Primary importance is accorded to the conduct of a law enforcement officer, or the person acting in cooperation with him....Any evidence having any tendency to make the existence of entrapment more probable is admissible....The accused should be allowed a reasonable latitude in presenting whatever facts and circumstances he claims constitute an entrapment, subject to ordinary rules of admissibility. 264 Ark. at 92, 568 S.W.2d 492.

In the instant case, although the court did admit testimony by Officer Carter and Trooper Brackin that the decision to "induce" appellant to provide cocaine for the undercover man was the product of a joint discussion between them and Powers, the court's ruling excluded evidence from which the jury could find that after the police officers video taped the September 2, 1983 sale they called the appellant to come view that taped occurrence and that they then suggested that he cooperate with them to help them catch "bigger fish" and that his failure to so cooperate would get him 40 years, but if he did cooperate, he would not be prosecuted. The court's ruling also eliminated the testimony, given in the first trial by Trooper John Brackin, that on October 5, 1983, when the appellant was called to view the taped occurrence of September 2, Brackin wanted the appellant to arrange a purchase from Rogers because Gene Guin had left the jurisdiction, and that a case was not made against Rogers until after the arrangements with the appellant fell through on October 5, 1983, and they finally found Guin and got him to make a purchase from Rogers. All of the above evidence, we believe, was admissible on the appellant's defense of entrapment.

The trial court was very generous in allowing the appellant to make a proffer of proof of all the testimony in the first trial that appellant thought was admissible on his defense of entrapment, and we do not hold that all of the evidence of events that occurred after September 2, 1983, are necessarily admissible on retrial. We do hold, however, that the trial court unduly limited the appellant's evidence on his entrapment defense by refusing to let him show *any* evidence of events that occurred after September 2, 1983. In this connection, we call attention to the commentary to Ark.Stat.Ann. § 41-209, *supra,* which states that the statute attributes more importance to the conduct of the law enforcement officer than to any predisposition of the defendant and that the obvious purpose is to discourage governmental activity that might induce innocent persons to engage in criminal conduct. Here, the thrust of the appellant's defense of entrapment is that the police have selected him, and caused an informant of theirs to persuade him to sell the informant cocaine in violation of the law, so that he can be used by the police, under threat of prosecution, to make purchases from "bigger fish" that the police are after. The jury is entitled to hear this evidence in considering the issue of whether appellant has been entrapped.

The appellant also contends that the trial court should have granted his motion for directed verdict made at the conclusion of the State's evidence in the first trial. Apparently, he would have us reverse and dismiss the charges against him, even after the second trial, because he was entitled to that relief in the first trial. Suffice it to say, we are cited no authority for this novel contention and, in addition, we do not agree that he was entitled to that relief in the first trial. Appellant's argument is based upon the contention that his defense of entrapment was established as a matter of law. Entrapment, however, is ordinarily a fact question, *Walls v. State,* 280 Ark. 291, 658 S.W.2d 362 (1983), and we think the evidence in the first trial presented a factual question on that issue.

It is also argued that members of the city police department, the county sheriff's office, and the state police department promised that the charges against appellant would be dismissed if he cooperated in helping them to catch "bigger fish" who were engaged in narcotic traffic in Crittenden County and that it would be unconscionable not to enforce the agreement made. *Cooper v. U.S.,* 594 F.2d 12 (4th Cir. 1979), and cases from the states of Iowa, Washington and Maryland are cited in support of this proposition. In *Hammers v. State,* 263 Ark. 378, 565 S.W.2d 406 (1978), the Arkansas Supreme Court reversed a conviction and dismissed the charge when it held the *record established* that the defendant in the case had an agreement with the State for immunity from prosecution. But, in the instant case, the record does not *establish* that the appellant had an agreement that he would not be prosecuted if he cooperated with the police. To the contrary, the law enforcement officers testified that they made no such promise. There is authority that "the police in their own right do not have authority to commit the state to anything by way of declining to prosecute," *Butler v. State,* 462 A.2d 1230, 1233 (Md.Ct.Spec.App.1983), but in any event, whether such an agreement has been made is a question of fact. We cannot say the trial court's decision on that point was "clearly against the preponderance of the evidence." See *Hammers v. State,* 261 Ark. 585, 603, 550 S.W.2d 432 (1977) (the remand which gave rise to the second opinion in *Hammers v. State,* 263 Ark. 378, 565 S.W.2d 406, *supra*).

Another contention is that the prosecutor made improper and prejudicial remarks to the jury during closing argument; however, there was no objection to these remarks at the time and the point cannot be raised for the first time on appeal. *Wicks v. State,* 270 Ark. 781, 606 S.W.2d 366 (1980).

The appellant also argues that a video tape of a meeting between Powers and appellant on August 24, 1983, was inadmissible in the State's case in chief because its only relevance was to show predisposition to sell a controlled substance and this evidence would only be admissible in rebuttal to appellant's defense of entrapment. We do not agree. Unlike the case of *Spears v. State, supra,* relied upon by appellant for this point, in the instant case, there was evidence of entrapment in the State's evidence in chief, therefore, evidence of predisposition was also admissible during the presentation of the State's case in chief.

Appellant's last two points for reversal deal with the trial court's refusal to grant him a continuance of the second trial, and the refusal to grant his motion for mistrial because a potential juror indicated during *voir dire* that he had a preconceived opinion about the case. Since neither matter is likely to arise again on retrial, we see no reason to discuss these points. For the error in refusing to admit the evidence which we have discussed, this case is reversed and remanded for a new trial.

WRIGHT, Special Judge, agrees.
GLAZE, J., not participating.

STATE of Nebraska, Appellee,
v.
Mohamed EL-TABECH, Appellant.

405 N.W.2d 585
Supreme Court of Nebraska.
May 15, 1987.

PER CURIAM.

The appellant, Mohamed El-Tabech, was found guilty of murder in the first degree, in violation of Neb.Rev.Stat. § 28-303(1) (Reissued 1985), and use of a deadly weapon to commit a felony, in violation of Neb.Rev.Stat. § 28-1205(1) (Reissue 1985). He was sentenced to life imprisonment for the first degree murder conviction and 20 years' imprisonment for use of a deadly weapon conviction, the sentence on the second conviction to run consecutively to the first conviction. He has now appealed to this court, specifically assigning as error the following:

I.

Whether a defendant is entitled to an untrammeled attorney/client relationship.

II.

Whether the defendant is entitled to some additional community input into the life-death decision beyond a petit jury verdict on the issues of guilt-innocence.

III.

Whether the evidence was sufficient to support a conviction for murder in the first degree.

IV.

Whether the defendant is entitled to have his jury correctly instructed, pursuant to a Nebraska Jury Instruction, on his theory of the defense, if that defense is supported by evidence in the record.

V.

Whether the trial court violated the Fifth, Sixth, and Fourteenth Amendments to the U.S. Constitution by death qualifying a jury in a capital case where the jury has absolutely nothing to do with punishment.

VI.

Whether the trial court violated Article I, Section 6 of the Constitution of the State of Nebraska by death qualifying the jury in a capital case when the jury has absolutely nothing to do with punishment.

VII.

Whether the trial court abused its discretion in death qualifying the jury.

We believe that none of the assignments of error entitle El-Tabech to a new trial, and, for that reason, we affirm the convictions and sentences.

On June 24, 1984, in response to a 911 emergency call, police and emergency personnel were dispatched to a home in Lincoln, Nebraska. Linda Woodruff, a paramedic employed by Eastern Ambulance Service, was the first to arrive at the scene. Upon entering the house, she observed El-Tabech seated on the floor, rocking back and forth and pointing to the back of the house.

El-Tabech's wife, Lynn El-Tabech, was found lying on a bed with a white terry cloth bathrobe belt tied tightly around her neck. Both the condition and temperature of her body indicated that she had not been dead for very long. Woodruff unsuccessfully attempted to untie the belt and then obtained scissors from the ambulance and cut the belt from around the decedent's neck. Shortly thereafter other emergency personnel and the police arrived.

There was testimony from various witnesses regarding alleged remarks made by El-Tabech at that time. Woodruff recalled that she heard El-Tabech say, "Don't take me to jail" as he was being taken to a police car. Lieutenant Soukup of the Lincoln Police Department heard El-Tabech say, "Who will take care of me now?" while he was on the porch of the residence. Sharon Hebbard, a neighbor who was 150 feet away from the El-Tabech porch, testified she heard El-Tabech say, "I didn't mean to" or "I didn't mean to do it." Officer Sims of the Lincoln Police Department, who transported El-Tabech to the police station and observed him, heard him say, "Do you got whoever did that?" and "I swear I'll kill them."

In investigating the crime the State produced the following evidence. The neighbor, Sharon Hebbard, claimed to have overheard an argument at the El-Tabech residence around 11 a.m. or noon on the day that Ms. El-Tabech was murdered. Hebbard testified that, while seated on the porch with her husband, she heard a 30-minute argument going on at the El-Tabech residence. Hebbard remembered hearing a woman's voice say, "Leave me alone" and "Don't touch me." Hebbard's testimony was corroborated by her husband, who had also overheard the arguing.

David James, a member of the Mormon church that El-Tabech attended, testified that he spoke with El-Tabech at about 3 p.m. on the day of the murder. El-Tabech called the church where James was in meetings. According to James, El-Tabech was quite upset and asked James if James would come right over and talk with him and the decedent. When James told him that he could not make it until later, El-Tabech advised James that he and the decedent were having troubles. Specifically, James said he heard the decedent in the background say something to the effect of "I'm leaving. I'm going for a walk." El-Tabech then said, "Well, when will you be back?" and the decedent said, "I don't know." Then, El-Tabech said to James, "Well, she's leaving me."

A waitress at a Village Inn Restaurant in Lincoln testified that she arrived at work at 4 p.m. on the day of the murder. She recalled that she waited on El-Tabech, who was dining with a woman, at about 5:30 p.m. She was able to ascertain this by reason of the computer at the restaurant, which prints the date and time an order is presented to the kitchen cooks. The waitress testified that the time printed on the ticket reflecting El-Tabech's order was 5:36 p.m. She testified she heard the couple arguing when she took their food to their table. Specifically, she testified, "He said, 'You never tell me where you're going. I have a right to know where you are.' " She further testified that the statements were made in an angry, loud voice. When she returned to the table at approximately 6 p.m. to pick up their meal plates, El-Tabech apologized to the waitress for his loud voice, saying "Excuse me for my voice. Married life is not easy." According to the waitress, when she clocked out on break at 6:07 p.m., El-Tabech and the woman were still in the restaurant. When she returned from break at 6:41 p.m., El-Tabech and his companion were no longer in the restaurant.

The State also called Gertrude Makovicka, a neighbor of El-Tabech's. Makovicka and her husband returned home from an afternoon of visiting at approximately 5:30 p.m. on the day of the murder. At 6 p.m. she and her husband started watching "60 Minutes." She testified that they watched the show until its completion at 7 p.m. During part of the time, she was work-

ing in the kitchen, washing strawberries. She could both see the TV set and observe the El-Tabech residence from the kitchen. She testified that she saw the El-Tabechs arrive home at about 6:15 p.m. She further testified that shortly after 7 p.m. she went out on her porch. After she had been sitting outside for 5 to 10 minutes, she observed El-Tabech come out of his house. He got into his car, drove up to Vine Street, and then turned onto Vine, heading west. She remained on her porch and approximately 10 minutes later observed El-Tabech return with a small package. During the time that he was gone, Makovicka testified she did not see anybody go into or come out of the El-Tabech residence. About 5 minutes after El-Tabech arrived back at his residence, Makovicka saw the first emergency vehicle arrive.

Rhonda James, wife of David James, testified that she spoke to El-Tabech on the phone just before 6:30 p.m. She took the phone call at the church. She testified that El-Tabech "sounded upset, and he wanted to visit with [her husband]." El-Tabech asked that her husband come right by on his way home. She said she would relay the message to her husband but, in fact, did not tell him until after the family had gotten home from church.

James attempted to call El-Tabech around 7 p.m., but no one answered the phone.

An employee at the Save-Mart grocery, located at 45th and Vine Streets, testified that on June 24, 1984, she was working on cash register No. 5. When a person makes a purchase, the cash register prints on the receipt what was purchased, the amount, the date, the time, and the check stand number. While she did not remember a particular purchase of ice cream bars at

7:23 p.m. on the evening of the murder, the receipt in evidence indicates that such a purchase did take place at that time.

The decedent's father, Elmer Prusia, testified that he started trying to call his daughter on the telephone shortly after 5:30 p.m. on June 24, 1984. He had received a call for her on his own phone at about 5:25 p.m. The caller had left a message which Prusia was attempting to relay to his daughter. When he did not get an answer initially, he intermittently redialed his daughter's number while watching television. Finally, at about 7:35 p.m., he got a busy signal. When he called again at 7:50 or 7:55 p.m., the phone was answered by emergency personnel.

The decedent's mother described El-Tabech as very attentive for the affection of her daughter. She further testified to an incident which had occurred on Memorial Day, when El-Tabech had been particularly upset that the decedent was not wearing her wedding ring. The decedent's mother also testified that on Father's Day preceding the day of the killing, her daughter and El-Tabech had advised them that they were expecting a child. The mother further corroborated the testimony of the decedent's father with regard to his attempts to reach his daughter by phone.

The decedent's sister was also called and testified. Specifically, she testified with regard to the announcement of her sister's pregnancy. El-Tabech insisted that no one was to know about the pregnancy and was quoted as saying, "Who knows what may happen in the next few months." The decedent's sister also testified with regard to her observations concerning El-Tabech's demeanor and her concerns over his view of women generally. The sister testified that El-Tabech was against his wife's wearing makeup and that he tended to have aggressive behavior toward her. She also testified that over the course of the 6 months of the marriage, the decedent had, on a number of occasions, indicated that she did not favor the attention that was being bestowed upon her and, in fact, had specifically informed El-Tabech to "[l]eave me alone." The decedent's sister further testified that it was her observation that the decedent had become more and more concerned with the attention from her husband and that she had in some ways "withdrawn." This testimony was corroborated by the sister's husband.

El-Tabech called Khalil Chehab as a witness for the defense. Chehab testified that he had known El-Tabech since high school in Lebanon. At the time of the trial he had not seen El-Tabech in 8 or 9 years. However, during the summer of 1983, while on a visit to Lebanon, he had learned that El-Tabech was in the United States. He obtained El-Tabech's phone number and address. Upon his return from Lebanon to California, he made a phone call and spoke with the decedent. In March or April of 1984, he received a letter from El-Tabech in which he was informed of the new telephone number for the El-Tabechs.

He then testified that on June 24, 1984, he was working at a Taco Bell restaurant in California. He was scheduled to work from 11 a.m. until 5 p.m., but was told by the manager to take off work at 4 p.m. He testified that after he got off work at 4 p.m., he called his wife from a pay telephone inside the Taco Bell, but she was not at home. He stayed in the restaurant, had something to eat, and then decided to call his parents in Lebanon. The reasons he gave for calling Lebanon from a pay phone were that he did not want his wife to know about it and he wanted to be able to prevent his mother from talking too long.

He testified that he made this overseas call to his mother at about 5 p.m. California time, or 7 p.m. local time. During this phone call he received a message for El-Tabech. When he got off the phone, he again tried to call his wife but still received no answer. According to Chehab this was a little after 5 p.m. California time. He then decided to call El-Tabech and give him the message. He claims that he called the El-Tabech number and a woman who identified herself as the decedent answered. He asked for El-Tabech but was unable to speak with him. He then testified that he asked to and did leave a message for El-Tabech with the woman who answered the phone. After this phone call, he again called his wife and she answered. Within a few minutes she picked him up, and the couple went shopping.

On cross-examination, Chehab stated that he remembered the events of that day because of his call to Lebanon and an argument he had with his wife. He did admit, however, that he was not wearing a wristwatch on the day in question and that he was estimating the times. With these facts in mind, we now review El-Tabech's assignments of error.

* * *

IV.

Whether the defendant is entitled to have his jury correctly instructed, pursuant to a Nebraska Jury Instruction, on his theory of the defense, if that defense is supported by evidence in the record.

In essence what this assignment of error addresses is the question of whether prejudicial error was committed by the court when it refused to instruct the jury on the question of alibi. At the close of all of the evidence, El-Tabech submitted a proposed instruction providing as follows:

The defendant contends that at or about the time the crimes with which the defendant stands charged were allegedly being committed the defendant was at such a distant and different place that he could not have committed said crimes.

The defendant is not required to prove such defense. It is sufficient if the evidence raises a reasonable doubt in your minds as to his presence at the time and place the crimes are alleged to have been committed; and if from all the evidence in the case you are not satisfied beyond a reasonable doubt of defendant's presence at the commission of the crimes charged against him, then you should find him not guilty.

We believe that there are at least two reasons why the district court's refusal to give the requested instruction was not error. In the first instance, alibi in Nebraska is not an affirmative defense. In the case of *Hall v. State,* 135 Neb. 188, 191, 280 N.W. 847, 848 (1938), this court said:

While the holdings in all of the courts cannot be reconciled, yet the majority of the courts hold that alibi evidence is not to be considered by itself, but in connection with all the other evidence, and that alibi is not an independent affirmative defense in the same sense that insanity is regarded as an affirmative defense. Annotation, 67 A.L.R. 138. Therefore, it was not error for the court to fail to give the jury an instruction on alibi.

Recent court decisions elsewhere have also determined that alibi is not an affirmative defense. The U.S. Court of Appeals for the Fourth Circuit, in *Adkins v. Bordenkircher*, 674 F.2d 279, 282 (4th Cir. 1982), observed:

> An alibi, however, negates *every* fact necessary to prove a breaking and entering; the defendant could not commit the offense if he was elsewhere at the time. When viewed under the *Patterson* standard, the West Virginia court's characterization of the alibi as an affirmative defense must be rejected. (Emphasis in original.)

Likewise, the Supreme Court of Hawaii, in the case of *State v. Cordeira*, ____ Haw. ____, ____, 707 P.2d 373, 376 (1985), said:

> In the context of a criminal prosecution, "alibi" denotes an attempt by the defendant to demonstrate he "did not commit the crime because, at the time, he was in another place so far away, or in a situation preventing his doing the thing charged against him." [Citation omitted.] "Strictly speaking, *alibi evidence* is merely rebuttal evidence directed to that part of the state's evidence which tends to identify the defendant as the person who committed the alleged crime." *Witt v. State*, 205 Ind. 499, 503, 185 N.E. 645, 647 (1933). (Emphasis added.) Though Rule 12.1 of the Hawaii Rules of Penal Procedure requires the defendant to give notice of an intention to rely upon the defense of alibi, it is not an affirmative defense.

And, in *Wright v. State*, 169 Ga.App. 693, 697, 314 S.E.2d 709, 712 (1984), the court said:

> Although alibi has often been treated as an affirmative defense, it "is not truly an independent affir-

mative defense. It is simply evidence in support of a defendant's plea of not guilty, and should be treated merely as 'evidence tending to disprove one of the essential factors in the case of the prosecution, that is, presence of the defendant at the time and place of the alleged crime.' " *Parham v. State*, 120 Ga.App. 723, 727, 171 S.E.2d 911 (1969); accord, *Rivers v. State*, 250 Ga. 288, 298 S.E.2d 10 (1982).

In the instant case the jury was instructed that the State had the burden of proving each and every element of the crime, including the fact that the accused committed the act as charged. The failure to instruct the jury on the alibi did not relieve the State of its full burden of proof.

Secondly, the evidence in the instant case was not sufficient to justify the giving of an instruction on alibi. In the early case of *Mays v. State*, 72 Neb. 723, 725, 101 N.W. 979, 980 (1904), this court said:

> "A defendant, to establish an *alibi*, must not only show he was present at some other place about the time of the alleged crime, but also that he was at such other place such a length of time that it was impossible for him to have been at the place where the crime was committed, either before or after the time he was at such other place." [Citation omitted.] (Emphasis in original.) *See State v. Sutton*, 220 Neb. 128, 368 N.W.2d 492 (1985).

Other courts which have reviewed this issue have reached the same conclusion. *See Greenhow v. United States*, 490 A.2d 1130 (D.C.1985); *People v. Fritz*, 84 Ill.2d 72, 48 Ill.Dec. 880, 417 N.E.2d 612 (1981); *State v. Gillespie*, 163 N.W.2d 922 (Iowa 1969).

El-Tabech's defense or alibi was that between 7 p.m. and 7:30 p.m. he was out of the house purchasing ice cream and therefore could not have committed the murder. The State, however, produced evidence that the murder occurred sometime between 6:15 p.m. and 7:30 p.m., and, therefore, it was possible for the jury to find that El-Tabech had committed the murder before he left the home to purchase the ice cream. It was therefore not error for the court to refuse to give the instruction on alibi.

V.

Whether the trial court violated the Fifth, Sixth, and Fourteenth Amendments to the U.S. Constitution by death qualifying a jury in a capital case where the jury has absolutely nothing to do with punishment.

VI.

Whether the trial court violated Article I, Section 6 of the Constitution of the State of Nebraska by death qualifying the jury in a capital case when the jury has absolutely nothing to do with punishment.

VII.

Whether the trial court abused its discretion in death qualifying the jury.

The last three assignments of error can be discussed together. Each of the above assignments of error was recently considered by this court in *State v. Burchett*, 224 Neb. 444, 399

N.W.2d 258 (1986), and rejected. In *State v. Burchett, supra* at 452, 399 N.W.2d at 264, we held that any argument that a "death-qualified" jury is partial or biased must fail because " 'an impartial *jury* consists of nothing more than *"jurors"* who will conscientiously apply the law and find the facts.' " (Emphasis in original.) *Citing Lockhart v. McCree, ____ U.S. ____, 106 S.Ct. 1758, 90 L.Ed.2d 137 (1986).*

We further said in *Burchett, supra* at 224 Neb. 450-51, 399 N.W.2d at 263:

While a prospective juror's attitudes about capital punishment are irrelevant to sentencing in Nebraska, they may be relevant to his ability to fairly determine the defendant's guilt or innocence. Prospective jurors who are excused because they are unable either to fairly determine guilt or to fairly impose a sentence because of their opposition to capital punishment are both subsets of the group of death penalty opponents which the defendant maintains is a cognizable group. The U.S. Supreme Court rejected the cognizable group claim in *McCree, supra,* and we do the same.

Having thus examined and rejected each of appellant's assignments of error, the judgment and sentences of the district court are affirmed.

AFFIRMED.

297 N.C. 555
STATE of North Carolina
v.
Maude Mae CLAY.
Supreme Court of North Carolina.
256 S.E.2d 176
July 12, 1979.

Appeal by the State from the decision of the Court of Appeals, reported in 39 N.C. App. 150, 249 S.E.2d 843 (1978), granting defendant a new trial based on Judge John C. Martin's denial of defendant's motion to suppress confession evidence at the 13 February 1978 Criminal Session of Alamance Superior Court.

Defendant was charged in a bill of indictment, proper in form, with assault with a deadly weapon with intent to kill inflicting serious bodily injury.

The State presented evidence which tended to show that on the afternoon or early evening of 3 September 1977, Nathaniel Evans went to defendant's house to buy a drink of liquor and while there became engaged in a scuffle with defendant because of her refusal to sell him a bowl of cooked okra. Evans went home but returned to defendant's house around 11:00 p.m. and was invited into the house by Verla Turner. Evans testified that after he entered the house, Turner pulled a knife on him, and he started backing towards the door. Defendant then told Turner to get the shotgun so she could shoot Evans. When Turner returned with the gun, Evans turned and started out the door and was shot in the leg. He fell to the floor, and when he looked up, defendant was trying to take the gun from Turner to shoot him again. Evans further testified that he did not see who shot him.

Burlington police officers Barrow and Perry testified that they went to defendant's residence at approximately 1:05 a.m. in response to a call reporting a domestic problem. The officers did not realize until they arrived at the residence that there had been a shooting. At that time, they gave defendant the *Miranda* warnings and in response to their questions were told by defendant that Turner had shot Evans. The two officers then accompanied Evans to the hospital while other policemen remained at defendant's house. Barrow and Perry returned to defendant's residence at about 3:10 a.m. and once again asked her who shot Evans. At this time, she stated that she had shot him. At trial, defendant moved to suppress this statement. The trial judge conducted a *voir dire* hearing as a result of which he concluded that defendant's statement was "the result of an on-the-scene investigation rather than custodial interrogation" and denied the motion to suppress.

Defendant presented evidence which tended to show that Evans had threatened to kill her and had pulled a knife on Turner earlier that evening. There was also evidence that Evans was drunk at the time of the shooting and that he had a reputation for being a violent and fighting man.

The trial judge submitted to the jury the possible verdicts of assault with a deadly weapon with intent to kill inflicting serious injury, assault with a deadly weapon inflicting serious injury, assault with a deadly weapon, and not guilty. The jury found defendant guilty of assault with a deadly weapon inflicting serious injury. From judgment imposing a sentence of four to five years, defendant appealed.

The Court of Appeals, in an opinion written by Judge Hedrick, Judge Morris concurring, granted defendant a new trial on the grounds that defendant's inculpatory statement was the result of custodial interrogation and should not have been admitted into evidence. Judge Harry Martin dissented on the grounds that the evidence presented on *voir dire* supported the trial judge's conclusion that defendant's inculpatory statement was voluntary and did not stem from a custodial interrogation. The State appealed.

* * *

Defendant argues that the trial judge erred in instructing the jury in that he failed to distinguish between the elements of self-defense when there is an intent to kill and the elements of self-defense where that intent is absent. Defendant's contention seems to be that if she did not act with intent to kill, her assault would be excused by the law of self-defense if it reasonably appeared to be necessary to protect herself from bodily injury or offensive physical contact. However, we think the inquiry relative to self-defense in such cases should focus not on the presence or absence of defendant's intent to kill, but on the amount of force used by the defendant in repelling the attack and the nature of the attack with which the defendant was faced.

It is clear that where one has inflicted serious injury upon another with intent to kill, such assault would

be justified as being in self-defense only if the defendant was in actual or apparent danger of death or great bodily harm at the hands of the other. *State v. Anderson,* 230 N.C. 54, 51 S.E.2d 895 (1949). Our cases also provide that a defendant can use force in self-defense even though the threat he attempts to repel is less than death or great bodily harm. *State v. Fletcher,* 268 N.C. 140, 150 S.E.2d 54 (1966); *State v. Anderson, supra.* However, some confusion arises with regard to the amount of force which may be used in self-defense to protect against bodily injury or offensive physical contact.

In *State v. Anderson, supra,* the defendant was charged with assault with a deadly weapon with intent to kill inflicting serious injuries. Defendant offered evidence tending to show self-defense, and the trial judge submitted to the jury the possible verdicts of guilty of felonious assault, the lesser included offense of nonfelonious assault with a deadly weapon, and not guilty. In its charge to the jury, the court, without qualification, instructed:

One is permitted to fight in self-defense or kill in self-defense when it is necessary for him to do so in order to avoid death or great bodily harm.

Finding this instruction to be erroneous, this Court, speaking through Justice Ervin, stated:

...In final result, it charged the jury that one is never privileged by law to employ force in self protection unless he is threatened with death or great bodily harm.

* * *

The law does not compel any man to submit in meekness to indignities or violence to his person merely because such indignities or violence stop short of threatening him with death or great bodily harm. If one is without fault in provoking, or engaging in, or continuing a difficulty with another, he is privileged by the law of self-defense to use such force against the other as is actually or reasonably necessary under the circumstances to protect himself from bodily injury or offensive physical contact at the hands of the other, even though he is not thereby put in actual or apparent danger of death or great bodily harm.

In *State v. Fletcher, supra,* defendant was also charged with assault with a deadly weapon with intent to kill inflicting serious injury. The trial judge instructed the jury that in order to have the benefit of the principle of self-defense, the defendant must show that he used a deadly weapon only to protect himself from death or great bodily harm. This Court held that the instruction was erroneous because it improperly placed on the defendant the burden of satisfying the jury that he acted in self-defense. Relying on *State v. Anderson, supra,* the Court found the instruction objectionable in another respect:

> Moreover, the court's instructions imply defendant could not lawfully use force in self-defense unless he was threatened with death or great bodily harm. We find no instruction with reference to the right of defendant to defend himself against a non-felonious assault. Failure to instruct the jury with reference to defendant's right of self-defense in respect of repelling a nonfelonious assault is prejudicial error.

Even though the weapons used in those cases were not deadly weapons per se, both *Anderson* and *Fletcher* may leave the impression that a defendant may assault another with a deadly weapon if it reasonably appears that such assault is necessary to protect the defendant from bodily injury or offensive physical contact. Notwithstanding the language in *Anderson* and *Fletcher,* we hold that a defendant may employ deadly force in self-defense only if it reasonably appears to be necessary to protect against death or great bodily harm. We define deadly force as force likely to cause death or great bodily harm. *See Commonwealth v. Klein,* 363 N.E.2d 1313 (Mass.1977). This follows from our definition of deadly weapon, to wit, an instrument which is likely to produce death or great bodily harm, under the circumstances of its use. *State v. Cauley,* 244 N.C. 701, 94 S.E.2d 915 (1956); *State v. Perry,* 226 N.C. 530, 39 S.E.2d 460 (1946). In so holding, we expressly reject defendant's contention, and any implication in our cases in support thereof, that a defendant would be justified by the principles of self-defense in employing deadly force to protect against bodily injury or offensive physical contact. Our decision says, in effect, that where the assault being made upon defendant is insufficient to give rise to a reasonable apprehension of death or great bodily harm, then the use of deadly force by defendant to protect himself from bodily injury or offensive physical contact is excessive force as a matter of law. Although we may hear protestations to the contrary, this decision will not compel anyone "to submit in meekness to indignities or violence to his person merely because such indignities or violence stop short of threatening him with death or great bodily harm." In such cases, a person so accosted may use such force, short of deadly force, as reasonably appears to him to be necessary under the circumstances to prevent bodily injury of offensive physical contact. This decision precludes the use of deadly force to prevent bodily injury or offensive physical contact and in so doing recognizes the premium we place on human life. However, it does not preclude the use of deadly force where such force reasonably appears to be necessary to prevent death or great bodily harm. The reasonableness of defendant's apprehension of death or great bodily harm must be determined by the jury on the basis of all the facts and circumstances as they appeared to defendant at the time. *State v. Ellerbe,* 223 N.C. 770, 28 S.E.2d 519 (1944). Among the circumstances to be considered by the jury are the size, age and strength of defendant's assailant in relation to that of defendant; the fierceness or persistence of the assault upon defendant; whether the assailant had or appeared to have a weapon in his possession; and the reputation of the assailant for danger and violence.

In instant case, after instructing the jury on the elements of the offenses submitted, the trial judge instructed on self-defense, in part, as follows:

Now, members of the jury, if the defendant acted in self defense, her actions are excused and she is not guilty. The State has the burden of proving from the evidence beyond a reasonable doubt that the defendant did not act in self defense.

Now if you find from the evidence beyond a reasonable doubt that the defendant assaulted Nate Evans with a deadly weapon with intent to kill inflicting serious injury or assaulted him with a deadly weapon inflicting serious injury or assaulted him with a deadly weapon, that offense, or assault, would be excused as being in self defense only if the circum-

stances at the time that she acted were such as would create in the mind of a person of ordinary firmness a reasonable belief that such action was necessary to protect herself from death or great bodily harm or to protect her home from attack and the circumstances did create such a belief in her mind.

* * *

However, the force used cannot have been excessive. This means that the defendant has the right to use only such force as reasonably appeared to her to be necessary under the circumstances to protect herself from *bodily injury or offensive physical contact.* In making the determination, you should consider the circumstances as you find them to have existed from the evidence, including the size, age, and strength of the defendant as compared to that of Cleo Evans, the fierceness of the assault, if any, upon the defendant, whether or not Cleo Evans had a weapon in his possession, and the reputation if any of Cleo Evans for danger and violence. [Emphasis added.]

* * *

Now, if you find from the evidence beyond a reasonable doubt that the defendant did assault Nate Evans, but do not find that she had an intent to kill, that assault would be excused as being in self defense if the circumstances at the time she acted were such as would create in the mind of a person of ordinary firmness a reasonable belief that such action was necessary to protect herself from *bodily injury or offensive physical contact* or to protect her home from attack and the circumstances did create such a belief in her mind even though she was not thereby put in actual danger of death or great bodily harm. [Emphasis added.]

* * *

If, members of the jury, however, although you are satisfied beyond a reasonable doubt that Maude May Clay committed an assault upon Cleo Nate Evans with a deadly weapon inflicting serious bodily injury with intent to kill or that she committed an assault upon him inflicting serious injury with a deadly weapon or that she committed an assault upon him with a deadly weapon, you may return a verdict of guilty only if the State has satisfied you beyond a reasonable doubt that Maude May Clay did not act in self defense—that is, that Maude May Clay did not reasonably believe that the assault was necessary to protect herself from death or serious bodily injury or her home from attack or that she, Maude May Clay, used excessive force or was the aggressor. If you do not so find or have a reasonable doubt, then Maude May Clay would be justified by self defense and it would be your duty to return a verdict of not guilty.

We note that in instructing on self-defense, the trial judge adhered, virtually verbatim, to the pattern jury instruction applicable to the case. However, we believe that in light of our holding in this case, that instruction is defective in part. The references to "bodily injury or offensive physical contact" in the two paragraphs dealing with excessive force and absence of an intent to kill are not warranted in instant case because defendant employed a deadly weapon or deadly force. Such error does not require a new trial, however, because the instruction was more favorable than that to which defendant was entitled.

In cases involving assault with a deadly weapon, trial judges should, in the charge, instruct that the assault would be excused as being in self-defense only if the circumstances at the time the defendant acted were such as would create in the mind of a person of ordinary firmness a reasonable belief that such action was necessary to protect himself from death or great bodily harm. If the weapon used is a deadly weapon per se, no reference should be made at any point in the charge to "bodily injury or offensive physical contact." If the weapon used is not a deadly weapon per se, the trial judge should instruct the jury that if they find that defendant assaulted the victim *but do not find that he used a deadly weapon,* that assault would be excused as being in self-defense if the circumstances at the time he acted were such as would create in the mind of a person of ordinary firmness a reasonable belief that such action was necessary to protect himself from "bodily injury or offensive physical contact." In determining whether the weapon used was a deadly weapon, the jury should consider the nature of the weapon, the manner in which it was used, and the size and strength of the defendant as compared to the victim.

In summary, we hold that the trial judge correctly denied defendant's motion to suppress and that the instructions on self-defense were not prejudicial to defendant. The decision of the Court of Appeals granting defendant a new trial is

REVERSED.
SHARP, C.J., concurs in result.

APPENDICES

Appendix 1

THE CODE OF THE LAWS
OF THE
UNITED STATES OF AMERICA

TITLE 18

CRIMES AND CRIMINAL PROCEDURE

PART I – CRIMES

Appendix 2

Special maritime and territorial jurisdiction of the United States defined*

The term "special maritime and territorial jurisdiction of the United States", as used in this title, includes:

(1) The high seas, any other waters within the admiralty and maritime jurisdiction of the United States and out of the jurisdiction of any particular State, and any vessel belonging in whole or in part to the United States or any citizen thereof, or to any corporation created by or under the laws of the United States, or of any State, Territory, District, or possession thereof, when such vessel is within the admiralty and maritime jurisdiction of the United States and out of the jurisdiction of any particular state.

(2) Any vessel registered, licensed, or enrolled under the laws of the United States, and being on a voyage upon the waters of any of the Great Lakes, or any of the waters connecting them, or upon the Saint Lawrence River where the same constitutes the International Boundary Line.

(3) Any lands reserved or acquired for the use of the United States, and under the exclusive or concurrent jurisdiction thereof, or any place purchased or otherwise acquired by the United States by consent of the legislature of the State in

---

*Title 18, Sec. 7, United States Code.
Vessels have the nationality of the nation whose flag they are entitled to fly and are subject to that nation's jurisdiction when on the high seas. U.S. v. Arra, C.A. Puerto Rico 1980, 630 F.2d 836.

which the same shall be, for the erection of a fort, magazine, arsenal, dockyard, or other needful building.

(4) Any island, rock, or key containing deposits of guano, which may, at the discretion of the President, be considered as appertaining to the United States.

(5) Any aircraft belonging in whole or in part to the United States, or any citizen thereof, or to any corporation created by or under the laws of the United States, or any State, Territory, District, or possession thereof, while such aircraft is in flight over the high seas, or over any other waters within the admiralty and maritime jurisdiction of the United States and out of the jurisdiction of any particular state.

(6) Any vehicle used or designed for flight or navigation in space and on the registry of the United States pursuant to the Treaty on Principles Governing the Activities of States in the Exploration and Use of Outer Space, Including the Moon and Other Celestial Bodies and the Convention on Registration of Objects Launched into Outer Space, while that vehicle is in flight, which is from the moment when all external doors are closed on Earth following embarkation until the moment when one such door is opened on Earth for disembarkation or in the case of a forced landing, until the competent authorities take over the responsibility for the vehicle and for persons and property aboard.

(7) Any place outside the jurisdiction of any nation with respect to an offense by or against a national of the United States.

Appendix 3

Uniform Controlled Substances Act

Table of Jurisdictions
Wherein Either the Uniform Controlled Substances Act
or the Uniform Narcotic Drug Act has been Adopted

Jurisdiction	Statutory Citation
Alabama	Code 1975, §§ 20-2-1 to 20-2-93
Alaska	AS 11.71.010 to 11.71.900, 17.30.010 to 17.30.900
Arizona	Code 1987, §§ 5-64-101 to 5-64-608
Arkansas	Ark.Stats. §§ 82-2601 to 82-2643
California	West's Ann.Cal. Health & Safety Code, §§ 11000 to 11651
Colorado	C.R.S. 12-22-301 to 12-22-322
Connecticut	C.G.S.A. §§ 21a-240 to 21a-308
Delaware	16 Del.C. §§ 4701 to 4796
District of Columbia	D.C. Code 1981, §§ 33-501 to 33-567
Florida	West's F.S.A. §§ 893.01 to 893.15
Georgia	O.C.G.A. §§ 16-13-20 to 16-13-56
Guam	9 G.C.A. §§ 67.10 to 67.98
Hawaii	HRS §§ 329-1 to 329-58
Idaho	I.C. §§ 37-2701 to 37-2751

Illinois	S.H.A. ch. 56½, 1100 to 1603
Indiana	West's A.I.C. 35-48-1-1 to 35-48-1-14
Iowa	I.C.A. §§ 204.101 to 204.602
Kansas	K.S.A. 65-4101 to 65-4140
Kentucky	KRS 218A.010 to 218A.991
Louisiana	LSA-R.S. 40:961 to 40:995
Maine	17-A M.R.S.A. §§ 1101 to 1116; 22 M.R.S.A. §§ 2361 to 2383A
Maryland	Code 1957, art. 27, §§ 276 to 302
Massachusetts	M.G.L.A. c. 94C, §§ 1 to 48
Michigan	M.C.L.A. §§ 333.7101 to 333.7545
Minnesota	M.S.A. §§ 152.01 to 152.20
Mississippi	Code 1972, §§ 41-29-101 to 41-29-175
Missouri	V.A.M.S. §§ 195.010 to 195.320
Montana	MCA 50-32-101 to 50-32-405
Nebraska	R.R.S.1943, § 28-401 et seq.
Nevada	N.R.S. 453.011 to 453.361
New Jersey	N.J.S.A. 24:21-1 to 24:21-53
New Mexico	NMSA 1978, §§ 30-31-1 to 30-31-41
New York	McKinney's Public Health Law §§ 3300 to 3396
North Carolina	G.S. §§ 90-86 to 90-113.8
North Dakota	NDCC 19-03.1-01 to 19-03.1-43
Ohio	R.C. §§ 3719.01 to 3719.99
Oklahoma	63 Okl. St. Ann. §§ 2-101 to 2-610
Oregon	ORS 475.005 to 475.285, 475.992 to 475.995
Pennsylvania	35 P.S. §§ 780-101 to 780-144
Puerto Rico	24 L.P.R.A. §§ 2101 to 2607
Rhode Island	Gen. Laws 1956, §§ 21-28-1.01 to 21-28-6.02
South Carolina	Code 1976, §§ 44-53-110 to 44-53-590
South Dakota	SDCL 34-20B-1 to 34-20B-114
Tennessee	T.C.A. §§ 39-6-401 to 39-6-419, 53-11-301 to 53-11-414

Texas	Vernon's Ann.Texas Civ.St. art. 4476-15
Utah	U.C.A.1953, 58-37-1 to 58-37-19
Virgin Islands	19 V.I.C. §§ 591 to 630a
Virginia	Code 1950, § 54-524.1 et seq.
Washington	West's RCWA 69.50.101 to 69.50.607
West Virginia	Code, 60A-1-101 to 60A-6-605
Wisconsin	W.S.A. 161.001 to 161.62
Wyoming	W.S. 1977, §§ 35-7-1001 to 35-7-1057

Appendix 4

Electronic Communications Act of 1986
Public Law 99-508 amending Title 18, U.S.C. 2510-2520

§ 2511   Interception and disclosure of wire, oral, or electronic communications prohibited

(1) Except as otherwise specifically provided in this chapter any person who –
   (a) intentionally intercepts, endeavors to intercept, or procures any other person to intercept or endeavor to intercept, any wire, oral, or electronic communications;
   (b) intentionally uses, endeavors to use, or procures any other person to use or endeavor to use any electronic, mechanical, or other device to intercept any oral communication when –

     (i) such device is affixed to, or otherwise transmits a signal through a wire, cable, or other like connection used in wire communications; or

     (ii) such device transmits communications by radio, or interferes with the transmission of such communication; or

     (iii) such person knows, or has reason to know, that such device or any component thereof has been sent through the mail or transported in interstate or foreign commerce; or

     (iv) such use or endeavor to use (A) takes place on the premises of any business or other commercial establishment the operations of which affect interstate or foreign commerce; or (B) obtains or is for the purpose of obtaining information relating to the operations of any business or other commercial establishment the operations of which affect interstate or foreign commerce; or

699

    (v) such person acts in the District of Columbia, the Commonwealth of Puerto Rico, or any territory or possession of the United States:

(c) intentionally discloses, or endeavors to disclose, to any other person the contents of any wire, oral, or electronic communication, knowing or having reason to know that the information was obtained through the interception of a wire, oral, or electronic communication in violation of this subsection; or

(d) intentionally uses, or endeavors to use, the contents of any wire, oral or electronic communication, knowing or having reason to know that the information was obtained through the interception of a wire, oral, or electronic communication in violation of this subsection; shall be punished as provided in subsection (4) or shall be subject to suit as provided in subsection (5).

(2)(a)(i) It shall not be unlawful under this chapter for an operator of a switchboard, or an officer, employee, or agent of a provider of wire or electronic communication service, whose facilities are used in the transmission of a wire communication, to intercept, disclose, or use that communication in the normal course of his employment while engaged in any activity which is a necessary incident to the rendition of his service or to the protection of the rights or property of the provider of that service, except that a provider of wire communication service to the public shall not utilize service observing or random monitoring except for mechanical or service quality control checks.

    (ii) Notwithstanding any other law, providers of wire or electronic communication service, their officers, employees, and agents, landlords, custodians, or other persons, are authorized to provide information, facilities, or technical assistance to persons authorized by law to intercept wire, oral, or electronic communications or to conduct electronic surveillance, as defined in section 101 of the Foreign Intelligence Surveillance Act of 1978, if such provider, its officers, employees, or agents, landlord, custodian, or other specified person, has been provided with —

        (A) a court order directing such assistance signed by the authorizing judge, or

        (B) a certification in writing by a person specified in section 2518(7) of this title or the Attorney General of the United States that no warrant or court order is required by law, that all statutory requirements have been met, and that the specified assistance is required,

setting forth the period of time during which the provision of the information, facilities, or technical assistance is authorized and specifying the information, facilities or technical assistance required. No provider of wire or electronic communication service, officer, employee, or agent thereof, or landlord, or custodian, or other specified person shall disclose the existence of any interception or surveillance or the device used to accomplish the interception or surveillance with respect to which the person has been furnished a court order or certification under this chapter, except as may otherwise be required by legal process and then only after prior notification to the Attorney General or to the principal prosecuting attorney of a State or any political subdivision of a State, as may be appropriate. Any such disclosure, shall render such person liable for the civil damages provided for in section 2520. No cause of action shall lie in any court against any provider of wire or electronic communication service, its officers, employees, or agents, landlord, custodian, or other specified person for providing information, facilities, or assistance in accordance with the terms of a court order or certification under this chapter.

(b) It shall not be lawful under this chapter for an officer, employee, or agent of the Federal Communications Commission, in the normal course of his employment and in discharge of the monitoring responsibilities exercised by the Commission in the enforcement of chapter 5 of Title 47 of the United States Code, to intercept a wire or electronic communication, or oral communication transmitted by radio, or to disclose or use the information thereby obtained.

(c) It shall not be unlawful under this chapter for a person acting under color of law to intercept a wire, oral, or electronic communication, where such person is a party to the communication or one of the parties to the communication has given prior consent to such interception.

(d) It shall not be unlawful under this chapter for a person not acting under color of law to intercept a wire, oral, or electronic communication where such person is a party to the communication or where one of the parties to the communication has given prior consent to such interception unless such communication is intercepted for the purpose of committing any criminal or tortious act in violation of the Constitution or laws of the United States or of any State.

(e) Notwithstanding any other provision of this title or section 705 or 706 of the Communications Act of 1934, it shall not be lawful for an officer, employee, or agent of the United States in the normal course of his official duty to conduct electronic surveillance, as defined in section 101 of the Foreign Intelligence Surveillance Act of 1978, as authorized by that Act.

(f) Nothing contained in this chapter or chapter 121, or section 705 of the Communications Act of 1934, shall be deemed to affect the acquisition by the United States Government of foreign intelligence information from international or foreign communications, or foreign intelligence activities conducted in accordance with otherwise applicable Federal law involving a foreign electronic communications system, utilizing a means other than electronic surveillance as defined in section 101 of the Foreign Intelligence Surveillance Act of 1978, and procedures in this chapter nad the Foreign Intelligence Surveillance Act of 1978 shall be the exclusive means by which electronic surveillance, as defined in section 101 of such Act, and the interception of domestic wire and oral communications may be conducted.

(g) It shall not be unlawful under this chapter or chapter 121 of this title for any person –

(i) to intercept or access an electronic communication made through an electronic communication system that is configured so that such electronic communication is readily accessible to the general public;

(ii) to intercept any radio communication which is transmitted –

(I) by any station for the use of the general public, or that relates to ships, aircraft, vehicles, or persons in distress;

(II) by any governmental, law enforcement, civil defense, private land mobile, or public safety communications system, including police and fire, readily accessible to the general public;

(III) by a station operating on an authorized frequency within the bands allocated to the amateur, citizens band, or general mobile radio services; or

(IV) by any marine or aeronautical communications system;

(iii) to engage in any conduct which –

   (I) is prohibited by section 633 of the Communications Act of 1934; or

   (II) is excepted from the application of section 705(a) of the Communications Act of 1934 by section 705(b) of that Act;

(iv) to intercept any wire or electronic communication the transmission of which is causing harmful interference to any lawfully operating station or consumer electronic equipment, to the extent necessary to identify the source of such interference; or

(v) for other users of the same frequency to intercept any radio communication made through a system that utilizes frequencies monitored by individuals engaged in the provision or the use of such system, if such communication is not scrambled or encrypted.

(h) It shall not be unlawful under this chapter –

(i) to use a pen register or a trap and trace device (as those terms are defined for the purposes of chapter 206 (relating to pen registers and trap and trace devices) of this title); or

(ii) for a provider of electronic communication service to record the fact that a wire or electronic communication was initiated or completed in order to protect such provider, another provider furnishing service toward the completion of the wire or electronic communication, or a user of that service, from fraudulent, unlawful or abusive use of such service.

(3)(a) Except as provided in paragraph (b) of this subsection, a person or entity providing an electronic communication service to the public shall not intentionally divulge the contents of any communication (other than one to such person or entity, or an agent thereof) while in transmission on that service to any person or entity other than an addressee or intended recipient of such communication or an agent of such addressee or intended recipient.

(b) A person or entity providing electronic communication service to the public may divulge the contents of any such communication –

(i) as otherwise authorized in section 2511(2)(a) or 2517 of this title;

(ii) with the lawful consent of the originator or any addressee or intended recipient of such communication;

(iii) to a person employed or authorized, or whose facilities are used, to forward such communication to its destination; or

(iv) which were inadvertently obtained by the service provider and which appear to pertain to the commission of a crime, if such divulgence is made to a law enforcement agency.

(4)(a) Except as provided in paragraph (b) of this subsection or in subsection (5), whoever violates subsection (1) of this section shall be fined under this title or imprisoned not more than five years, or both.

(b) If this offense is a first offense under paragraph (a) of this subsection and is not for a tortious or illegal purpose or for purposes of direct or indirect commercial advantage or private commercial gain, and the wire or electronic communication with respect to which the offense under paragraph (a) is a radio communication that is not scrambled or encrypted, then –

(i) if the communication is not the radio portion of a cellular telephone communication, a public land mobile radio service communication or a paging service communication, and the conduct is not that described in subsection (5), the offender shall be fined under this title or imprisoned not more than one year, or both; and

(ii) if the communication is the radio portion of a cellular telephone communication, a public land mobile radio service communication, or a paging service communication, the offender shall be fined not more than $500.

(c) Conduct otherwise an offense under this subsection that consists of or relates to the interception of a satellite transmission that is not encrypted or scrambled and that is transmitted –

(i) to a broadcasting station for purposes of retransmission to the general public; or

(ii) as an audio subcarrier intended for redistribution to facilities open to the public, but not including data transmissions or telephone calls, is not an offense under this subsection unless the conduct is for the purposes of direct or indirect commercial advantage or private financial gain.

(5)(a)(1) If the communication is –

(A) a private satellite video communication that is not scrambled or encrypted and the conduct in violation of this chapter is the private viewing of that communication and is not for a tortious or illegal purpose or for purposes of direct or indirect commercial advantage or private commercial gain; or

(B) a radio communication that is transmitted on frequencies allocated under subpart D of part 74 of the rules of the Federal Communications Commission that is not scrambled or encrypted and the conduct in violation of this chapter is not for a tortious or illegal purpose or for purposes of direct or indirect commercial advantage or private commercial gain,

then the person who engages in such conduct shall be subject to suit by the Federal Government in a court of competent jurisdiction.

(ii) In an action under this subsection –

(A) if the violation of this chapter is a first offense for the person under paragraph (a) of subsection (4) and such person has not been found liable in a civil action under section 2520 of this title, the Federal Government shall be entitled to appropriate injunctive relief; and

(B) if the violation of this chapter is a second or subsequent offense under paragraph (a) of subsection (4) or such person has been found liable in any prior civil action under section 2520, the person shall be subject to a mandatory $500 civil fine.

(b) The court may use any means within its authority to enforce an injunction issued under paragraph (ii)(A), and shall impose a civil fine of not less than $500 for each violation of such an injunction.

INDEX

TABLE OF CASES

This list includes all cases cited in the text. Page numbers are in boldface type. Cases in boldface type are printed in Part II of the text.

TABLE OF CASES

719

Coates v. City of Cincinnati, 402 U.S. 611, 91 S. Ct. 1686,
79 L. Ed. 2d 214 (1971) 8
Cohn v. Dept. of Professional Regulations, 477 So. 2d 1039 (Fla. 1985) 414
Colbert v. State, 125 Wis. 423, 104 N.W. 61 (1905) 161
Coleman v. Commonwealth, 280 Ky. 410, 133 S.W. 555 (1939) 108
Commonwealth v. A Juvenile, 6 Mass. App. 194,
374 N.E.2d 335 (1978) 293
Commonwealth v. Apriceno, 131 Pa. Super. 158, 198 A. 515 (1938) 339
Commonwealth v. Ashley, 248 Mass. 259, 142 N.E. 788 (1924) 318
Commonwealth v. Austin, 393 A.2d 36 (Pa. Super. 1978) 221
Commonwealth v. Benoit, 347 Mass. 1, 196 N.E.2d 228 (1964) 279
Commonwealth v. Breth, 44 Pa. 56 (1915) 35
Commonwealth v. Burke, 105 Mass. 376, 7 Am. Rep. 531 (1870) 118
Commonwealth v. Coward, 478 A.2d 1384 (Pa. Super. Ct. 1984) 221, 222
Commonwealth v. Davis, 28 Mass. (11 Pick. 432) (1831) 368
Commonwealth v. Day, 599 S.W.2d 166 (Ky. 1980) 216
Commonwealth v. Fogarty, 74 Mass. 489 (1857) 128
Commonwealth v. Goldston, 366 N.E.2d 744 (Mass. 1987) 54
Commonwealth v. Hayes, 205 Pa. Super. 338, 209 A.2d 38 (1965) 440
Commonwealth v. Hill, 237 Pa. Super., 353 A.2d 870 (1975) 87
Commonwealth v. Hussey, 157 Mass. 415, 32 N.E. 362 (1892) 288
Commonwealth v. Johnson, 615 S.W.2d 1 (Ky. 1981) 395
Commonwealth v. Libby, 358 Mass. 617, 26 N.E.2d 641 (1971) 290
Commonwealth v. McQueen, 178 Pa. Super. 38, 112 A.2d 820 (1955) 469
Commonwealth v. Medeiros, 479 N.E.2d 1371 (Mass. 1985) 71, 80
Comm. v. Mink, 123 Mass. 422 (1877) 84
Commonwealth v. Myers, 223 Pa. Super. 75, 297 A.2d 151 (1972) 175
Commonwealth v. Noxon, 319 Mass. 495, 66 N.E.2d 814 (1946) 58
Commonwealth v. Paese, 220 Pa. 371, 69 A. 891 (1908) 70
Commonwealth v. Potts, 314 Pa. Super. 256, 460 A.2d 1127 (1983) 293
Commonwealth v. Randolph, 146 Pa. 83, 23 A. 388 (1882) 436
Commonwealth v. Richardson, 313 Mass. 632, 48 N.E.2d 678 (1943) 184
Commonwealth v. 707 Main Corporation, 371 Mass. 374,
357 N.E.2d 753 (1976) 303
Commonwealth v. Stephens, 143 Pa. Super. 394, 17 A.2d 919 (1941) 116
Commonwealth v. Stingel, 146 Pa. 359, 40 A.2d 140 (1944) 294
Commonwealth v. Van Schaack, 16 Mass. 104 (1819) 160